de Havilland Biplane Transports

Paul Hayes & Bernard King

Gatwick Aviation Society
in association with Aviation Classics
Coulsdon, April 2003

ISBN 0-9530413-2-8
A catalogue record for this book is available from the British Library

First edition published April 2003

Editorial and distribution address:

Gatwick Aviation Society
c/o Aviation Classics
P. O. Box 2004
Coulsdon
Surrey
CR5 2ZP

Tel: +44 20 8660 9525
e-mail: rrab@completeclassics.fsnet.co.uk

Every effort has been made to ensure the information contained in this publication is as accurate as possible. Aircraft can and do, move from place to place and it is inevitable in a database consisting of many thousands of individual records, that some errors may have crept in during the editing process. Neither the authors, nor the publisher, can therefore accept liability for any errors or changes that may occur in the location or status of aircraft and neither can they be held responsible for subsequent use made of information extracted from this publication.

Printed in the United Kingdom by:

Perfectaprint
Byfleet
Surrey
Tel: +1932 352340

Front Cover
This dramatic shot of G-AGSH, posing for the camera somewhere over southern England when in the ownership of Brian Haddican and Partners. Built by Brush Coachworks at Loughborough and first flown in April 1945 as one of a large contract placed for Dominie aircraft, construction number 6884 did not enter military service. Instead, sold to Channel Island Airways after conversion to Dragon Rapide standard by de Havilland at Witney 28.5.45. Only a very small number of Rapides remain airworthy but among them is G-AGSH, in the hands of Philip Meeson, Chief Executive of Dart Group PLC and kept at Bournemouth since June 1989. Now painted in full British European Airways livery and named James Keir Hardie – just as it was when serving with B.E.A.C. from formation in February 1947 until sale in May 1956.

Rear Cover
DH83 Fox Moth ZK-ADI construction number 4097, arrived in New Zealand during December 1934 and entered service with Tourist Air Travel & Transport Service N.Z. Co. Ltd., Christchurch and survived an unfortunate collision with a bull at Weheka just a couple of months later! Shipped to the U.S.A. in April 1974 and became, appropriately registered, N83DH in July 1975. Many will remember its time with Brian Woodford in England from 1984 to 1997, when reg'd G-ADHA and painted red and blue to represent H.R.H. The Prince of Wales machine c/n 4033. Now back in New Zealand and painted in the orange and silver colour scheme as it first appeared with Tourist Air Travel. (Phillip Treweek/Kiwi Aircraft Images)

DH84 Dragon G-ACIT construction number 6039, originally delivered to Highland Airways Ltd., Inverness and inaugurated Aberdeen to Orkney scheduled services in May 1934. Seen here when with British Executive & General Aviation Ltd. sporting the bronze and white house colours of Beagle Aircraft Ltd. 30.1.62. Was at the defunct Southend Historic Aircraft Museum from September 1971 and on closure, ownership passed to London's Science Museum and moved to their Air Transport Collection and Storage Facility at Wroughton, Wiltshire in August 1983. Now painted in the original Highland Airways livery and named Aberdeen.

DH86 G-ADUG construction number 2335 was originally delivered to Imperial Airways Ltd. at Croydon as a DH86A. Probably due to the model's rapid design and development, the DH86 proved not to be one of de Havilland's most successful aeroplanes. Unlike today, when rigorous testing is carried out before deliveries commence, the DH86 appeared at a time when market forces seemed to dictate a new model's introduction! Early DH86 aircraft suffered from a lack of stability at the rer end and the fix was the addition of vertical stabilisers on each tailplane. G-ADUG was flown back to Hatfield for these to be fitted during 1937. Impressed into military dervice as HK831 in November 1941, it was shot down by an enemy fighter in February 1942.

No less than a dozen Dominies awaiting collection at the Brush factory airfield at Loughborough. Wartime factory photographs are a rare commodity and with the aid of a magnifying glass, we have been able to identify NR721 (c/n 6809) at left and NR693 (c/n 6792) at right confirming that this photograph would have been shot around November 1944. At that stage in the war, there was a greater need for fighting aircraft and the new-build communications types often sat around for long periods awaiting collection by the Delivery Flight and Air Transport Auxiliary crews. Initially flown to maintenance units, the majority of late production Dominies were immediately placed into store and these aircraft "with delivery mileage only", of course, were the most sought after by the many eager civilian purchasers after hostilities ceased. However, NR721 remained in military service and was last recorded with the Royal Aircraft Establishment Farnborough in 1952. NR693 did become civil and as G-AHKV, many readers will remember the yellow and black Dragon Rapide of the Automobile Association!

The prototype DH90 Dragonfly, registered G-ADNA and first flown in August 1935. The ultimate development of the Dragon series, featured a wooden monocoque fuselage and was, to all intents and purposes, the world's first purpose built aircraft for the business user. Retained by the manufacturer until sold to Albert Batchelor of Ramsgate in January 1938, a year later, G-ADNA went to Western Airways Ltd. Impressed as X9452 in May 1940, the first Dragonfly subsequently flew with an anti-aircraft co-operation unit and then, briefly, with Air Service Training before being struck off charge after inspection by de Havilland at Witney, August 1942.

Contents

Preface & Acknowledgements

Some 35 years ago, Paul Hayes started work on a DH89 Dragon Rapide production history and amassed a collection of nearly 2000 photographs of the type. In the late 1960s and into the 1970s, he personally interviewed many people directly connected with de Havilland's most successful biplane transport, including buyers, testers, operators and maintenance personnel.

Following a period as an Air Traffic Control Assistant at Heathrow, still at London Airport, he joined a company specialising in providing information to the aviation insurance community. Trends in aircraft accidents have therefore become a major interest and this fact is reflected within the text.

Business commitments and family life, compelled placing his Dragon Rapide work on the back burner, but after many years of pestering by the joint author, Paul, a founding member of the Gatwick Aviation Society, finally handed over his life's work to the group in December 2001.

As Air Britain's Rapide specialist for some thirty years, he hoped that some form of co-operative project between the G.A.S. and Air Britain would be possible with publication of the work following in due course. However, an amicable arrangement could not be reached.

Bernard King's major interest has always been the British civil register, U.K. built aircraft such as the de Havilland Biplane Transports and the lightning growth of air transport operations in the 1930s. It is now hard to believe, but the sole regular British Isles internal air service in 1931 was across the Wash from Skegness to Hunstanton, operated twice daily during the summer only by de Havilland DH80A Puss Moth G-AAXL, construction number 2010. The route was just 19 miles and the fare was £1 return! Of great significance to airline service historians, is the fact that the route was across water and the short flight cut out a road journey of in excess of 60 miles.

When inputting all the material, the Gatwick team felt that other de Havilland transport types would have to be included as they were so closely connected. Therefore, included in the book, is detailed information on the DH84 Dragon, the un-named DH86, the DH90 Dragonfly - the world's first purpose-built executive aeroplane and, thrown in for good measure, the singularly unsuccessful DH92 Dolphin.

In the final stages of production, it was realised that the DH83 Fox Moth could not be left out. Edward Hillman, an energetic bus and coach operator based in Essex, was an early protagonist in the burgeoning air transport industry. Hillman's Airways Ltd. was founded in 1932 and scheduled passenger services commenced during the first half of the year, using a small fleet of de Havilland DH80A Puss Moths, supplemented by two Fox Moths in June of that year. Growth in passenger numbers necessitated larger capacity equipment and Hillman approached de Havilland to fulfil the requirement. The result was, to all intents and purposes, a scaled up Fox Moth, to become known at first as the DH84 Dragon Moth and first flown in November 1932.

Inclusion of the Fox Moth at the final hour, has meant that it has not been possible to research the Canadian built examples in any great detail within the time available. However, limited information on all 54 examples is included and hopefully, readers will feel compelled to add to the information in time for a possible second edition!

Equipped with four engines, the larger DH86 took to the air for the first time in January 1934 and effectively, the scaled down version with twin engines, the DH89, rapidly followed three months later. A number of early Rapides were sold to industrialists and to fulfil a new requirement, the ultimate development, the DH90 - a 4/5 seater transport geared to the executive user, was flown in August 1935. The DH92, a modernised version of the Rapide with accommodation for two crew and dual controls, was flown in September 1936.

Aficionados of this important period of aviation development are presented with the dreaded, "chicken or the egg" conundrum. Did the DH83 and DH84 types answer a need or did they make the need? Hitherto, former military types had been pressed into service by the commercial transport companies, supplemented by small numbers of airliners built by de Havilland and others for international operation by Imperial Airways. Whatever, the DH84/86/89 were at the forefront of airlines, before the DC2 which first flew in May 1934 and the follow-up and ubiquitos DC3, flown in December 1935.

Many airlines commenced operations using de Havilland built biplane products covered in this book. Airlines, their precursors or successors, that immediately spring to mind are: British European Airways, P.L.U.N.A. of Uruguay, Air Madagascar, East African Airways Corporation, QANTAS, Air Vietnam, Indian Airlines Corporation and Iraqi Airways.

The DH89 Dragon Rapide is the most important model covered with 729 produced, initially for airline service but also, in tremendous numbers for the British and Commonwealth military as the Dominie. On the cessation of hostilities, the surviving Dominies were offered for sale on the civil market.

Producing any work of this nature would not have been possible without assistance from a large number of individuals located around the world. It would be impossible to list the names of all those pestered over many years by Paul, but the following persons were unfailing with their enthusiasm to see the work published in more recent years:-

Australia: Particular mention of John Hopton must be made – as every question concerning civilian and military operation of de Havilland biplane transports in Australia, was instantly answered by forwarding the applicable pages of his momentous, but as yet, unpublished work *The Aeroplane in Australia*. John has fixed ideas on presentation of aeronautical history and we have tried to comply with his formatting ideals wherever possible. Our thanks also go to Tony Arbon – an enthusiastic researcher of the Australian civil register, Clive Lynch for detailed information on R.A.A.F. units and Steve Stuckey of the Australian National Archives in Canberra, for digging out the service records of the DH84A built in Sydney and for civilian aircraft impressed into service for the Royal Australian Air Force during the war years.
Italy: Dr. Alberto Filsi for detailed information on the personalities involved in Italian aviation between the wars, most of whom were also connected with motor racing, an area also of great interest to Alberto.
Taiwan: Clarence Fu of the China Project e-group for historical information on the seven DH89A aircraft supplied to the Nationalists.
United Kingdom: Special thanks are due to John Dyer, Michael Green and Adam Hawkins for inputting much of the Dragon Rapide material. Rod Page for checking recent information on the survivors. Ray Hoddinott and Kelvin Cross of LAAS International for access to their outstanding databases, encompassing the complete British Civil Aircraft Register. Ian Callier for his lighthearted "Fiery Ends" chapter. The late Denis Fox for assistance over many years with Royal Air Force/Royal Navy input, Peter Marson for illustrations, Peter Moss – in addition to his masterpiece, "Impressment Log" and the superb de Havilland Rapide in the Profile Publications series, for his kind assistance with this project over many years and to Keith A. Palmer, mainly for information on the DH86. To Ian Terry - Gatwick Aviation Society member number 1 for access to his home produced world registers and in particular, for extremely useful and very recent information on the seven Rapides operated by the Chinese Nationalists. Another, who did not want to be named, was the purchaser of a number of Rapide aircraft which were supplied to a country which ended up within the Communist sphere of influence after World War II, and enlightened us to the reason for purchase and the fleet's eventual demise. His input, recorded at a delightful lunchtime meeting in the 1960s, is included in the text by the appropriate construction numbers.

Photographs, unless otherwise acknowledged, are from Paul Hayes' collection.

1. de Havilland Aircraft Co. History

The son of the Reverend Charles de Havilland, Geoffrey, was a mechanically minded young man who built his own motor cycle with an engine to his own design, in order to commute from the family home situated near Highclere in Hampshire to Crystal Palace Engineering School in the southern suburbs of London.

Early employment was with the Motor Omnibus Construction Company, where he worked in the design department, but Geoffrey was captivated by man's attempts at free flight and following the Wright brothers first heavier-than-air flights, exactly 100 years ago, studied every written word about their triumph.

With the aid of a £500 loan from his grandfather, a small workshop was rented in London's West End and from it, in 1909, emerged a wire-braced biplane with front elevator and bicycle wheel undercarriage. Powered by a 45 h.p. flat-four water cooled engine designed by himself and with the power to weight ratio only one half of that used by the Wrights! The aircraft was transported to Seven Barrows near the family home in Hampshire and after waiting for weather conditions to be ideal, the first de Havilland built aircraft finally took to the air in December 1909. The euphoria was short-lived however, as the port wings folded shortly after lift-off and the machine hit the ground and was wrecked, but mercifully, Geoffrey de Havilland suffered only minor injuries.

Undaunted, he hastily built a second similar machine, this time utilising more suitable spruce and ash in the construction and the new craft flew for the first time on 1th September 1910 at Seven Barrows. Obviously, this machine was a success for within a month, his wife and 8 month old son had been taken for flights. Transported by road to Farnborough at the end of the year and demonstrated to the War Office on 14th January 1911, not only was the aircraft purchased for £400, but Geoffrey and his partner, F. T. Earle, were given employment at H. M. Balloon Factory, later to become the Army Aircraft Factory.

In June 1914, Geoffrey had moved on to become Chief Designer at the Aircraft Manufacturing Co. Ltd. at Hendon but on the outbreak of war he was called up and briefly served with No.2 Squadron at Farnborough. However, it was not long before the powers-that-be realised that enthusiastic pilots, there were many, but gifted aircraft designers, far fewer! So, promoted to Captain, he returned to work at what was to become Airco at Hendon.

After the war, George Holt Thomas, owner of Airco, decided to sell out to the Birmingham Small Arms Co. Ltd., later famed for their B.S.A. motorcycles. Even though Airco's first civil design, the DH18 was flown in March 1920 and entered service with Air Transport and Travel Ltd. the following month, the company was badly affected by the postwar slump and B.S.A. decided to close down the aircraft manufacturing business shortly after.

Unemployment was undoubtedly the catalyst for Geoffrey de Havilland who, aided by his brothers Ivon and Hereward, formed the de Havilland Aircraft Co. Ltd. on 25th September 1920. A number of Airco colleagues also joined the new company, among them, F. E. N. St. Barbe and A. E. Hagg, and of these two gentlemen we will hear later.

A large field was rented in Edgware, Middlesex at the end of Stag Lane and at an early juncture, it was decided to concentrate on the design and manufacture of aeroplanes for the almost non-existent civil market. An early private customer in 1921, was Alan Samuel Butler from a very wealthy family. Already the owner of Bristol Type 29 Tourer G-EAWB, Butler commissioned de Havilland to build a three seat tourer suitable for touring within the U.K. and on the Continent. Alan Butler monitored progress on his new 'baby' closely, spending a lot of time in the Stag Lane works and getting to know the small team assembled by Geoffrey de Havilland. At a time of crisis, when the landlord demanded that the company either, purchase the field outright or move out, Butler immediately came to the rescue with a substantial investment, enabling de Havilland to be secure in the knowledge of having a permanent home. Butler's aeroplane became the D.H.37 and registered G-ABDO, it flew for the first time in June 1922.

Alan Butler was not the only wealthy individual to put his money into the risky business of aeroplane manufacture, for Lord Wakefield of Castrol Oil, poured funds into de Havilland during the 1930s in the form of aircraft purchases for his British Empire Flying Club sponsorship scheme. Much more recently, King Ibn Saud of Saudi Arabia purchased a DH106 Comet 4C in 1962 for executive use, liberally coated in gold leaf, when sales of the world's first jetliner were trailing off.

The latter purchase is, of course, well outside the period covered by this book, but it does illustrate customer confidence in the management, design and manufacturing team, led by the amiable founder.

Returning to Alan Butler, in recognition of his financial input and his undoubted organisational skills, he was made Chairman of the company in 1924, a post he continued to hold until retirement in 1950.

Many notable de Havilland models first took to the sky from the turf at Stag Lane, including the Fox Moth and Dragon Moth. However, the once quiet and fairly isolated area outside of the North London suburbs, was rapidly being over-run by the need for housing. The London Underground system's Northern Line extension to Edgware allowed easy access to the city centre, further increasing the demand for commuter housing.

Besides the obvious need for a quieter place more suited to the testing of aeroplanes, the rapidly rising land value must have provided immense incentive to find a new location! In 1930, a green field site, well outside London's northern environs was acquired at Hatfield in Hertfordshire.

By then, series production of the DH60GIII Moth Major, DH80 Puss Moth, DH83 Fox Moth and the DH84 Dragon was in full swing at Stag Lane but by the end of 1932, all airframe manufacture had been transferred to Hatfield. Moving the world's foremost civilian aircraft maker would have been a major undertaking but a look at contemporary records, reveals that the transfer was achieved with remarkably little upheaval.

Hornet Moth G-ACTA was the last aeroplane to take-off from Stag Lane on 28th July 1934. Surely, a sad departure but the move was opening up new horizons for the Hornet's pilot, Geoffrey de Havilland. A recent editorial visit to Edgware, revealed little evidence of the area's previous use and only two road names, De Havilland Road and Mollison Way, after the pioneering aviator Jim Mollison, bear witness to days gone by.

Purpose built factory premises at Hatfield, ensured the continued and increased success of The de Havilland Aircraft Co. Ltd. and the 1930s saw the company producing their renowned models in greater numbers than ever before. Serving the burgeoning training, air taxi and airline markets, the management team swiftly reacted to customer demand, with the DH60 Gipsy Moth developing into the DH82 Tiger Moth, the DH80 Puss Moth metamorphising into the DH85 Leopard Moth, whilst on the transport front, the Dragon family was enlarged with the addition of the un-named DH86 four-engine airliner in January 1934 and just three months later, by its smaller sister, the DH89 Dragon Six, later to become known as the Dragon Rapide.

Renowned for their simple but strong plywood box structures and devoid of internal wire bracing, this style of construction was used exclusively until the mid 1920s. The ultimate development of the form appeared in September 1934 with the first flight of the D.H.88 Comet, specially designed for air racing and, in particular, for the MacRobertson Air Race from England to Australia departing from Mildenhall in Suffolk at dawn on 20th October. The revolutionary twin-engine machines, featured an all wood monocoque fuselage with accommodation for two persons and one of the five built, G-ACSS and named Grosvenor House after owner A. O. Edwards' prestigious hotel in London's Park Lane, is preserved by the Shuttleworth Trust at White Waltham.

Of consequence to our story, is the use of this form of construction for the DH90 Dragonfly, reminiscent of the DH89 Dragon Rapide, but scaled down slightly and designed exclusively for the private and business user, desiring the assurance of a twin engine installation! Unfortunately, just 67 examples left the Hatfield production line, before the declining situation in Europe, compelled de Havilland's designers to concentrate their efforts on the possible future need for fighting aircraft. It was not until 13th August 1962, when the DH125 twin jet transport first flew, that de Havilland were to again, have available a product created for the business user.

A monocoque form was similarly used for the DH91 Albatross, an airliner with four engines originally proposed as a competitor for the Douglas DC2, an example of which competed against the MacRobertson Race winning DH88 Comet G-ACSS. Somewhat surprisingly, the performance of the Santa Monica produced airliner was found to be only slightly inferior to that of the specially built racing monoplane! Two DH91s were laid down following an order from the Air Ministry for an experimental Transatlantic mailplanes and the prototype E.2/G-AEVV, was first flown on 20th May 1937. Five passenger transports were subsequently ordered by Imperial Airways, with the first, registered G-AFDI, delivered to Croydon in October 1938. Following proving trials when only mail was carried, this most handsome of airliners only saw limited service on Imperial's routes to Paris, Brussels and Zurich before the fleet was evacuated to Whitchurch on the outbreak of war. The company's expertise with wooden structures was put to good use for the DH98 Mosquito which was to come and made its maiden flight at Hatfield on 25th November 1940.

During wartime, de Havilland's major contribution was the development and production of the Mosquito for a wide variety of roles, though they did find time to build no fewer than 1,440 Airspeed Oxfords at Hatfield! Fully committed to production of these types, precluding much further involvement with their DH89, production of a substantial order for Dominies was switched to Brush Coachworks at Loughborough and full details are included in a chapter elsewhere.

This most versatile of fighting machines proved to be their 'piece de resistance', with nearly 8,000 examples produced at Hatfield, on a supplementary line established at Leavesden in Hertfordshire and at their overseas factories in Toronto, Canada and Sydney, Australia.

However, the story does not end there, as mention must be made of their Repair Unit, established at Witney in Oxfordshire. Not only did this important unit attend to repair and maintenance of mainly impressed types of their own manufacture, but they also specialised in Spitfires, Hurricanes and of course, Mosquitos. With the cessation of hostilities, Witney continued to fulfil an important function when large numbers of demobbed Dominies were flown in from Maintenance Units for preparation to civilian standard. Several hundred examples were eagerly snapped up by civilian purchasers and although some were prepared for the civil register by smaller concerns elsewhere, by far the majority were attended to at Witney. This work drew to a close during the winter of 1948-1949 and the freehold, comprising some 117,350 square feet of factory premises and the adjoining airfield - an area of approximately 140 acres, were auctioned in London on 21st September 1949.

Meanwhile, back at Hatfield, series production of the DH104 Dove was well under way. Designed to fulfil the Brabazon Committee's Type 5B specification for a light transport to replace the Rapide, the first flight of the prototype G-AGPJ took place on 25th September 1945. The first Heron four-engine airliner G-ALZL, flew on 10th May 1950 and this model can best be described as a modern day counterpart of the DH86B.

In 1959, the company merged with Hawker Siddeley Aviation, to whom we are indebted for unrestricted use of the comprehensive photographic archive assembled throughout the de Havilland Aircraft Company's existence. Of the company's founder, Geoffrey de Havilland was knighted in 1944 and died in retirement on 26th May 1965.

Right from the earliest days of the company, an important source of revenue was from foreign sales and overseas companies were soon established to look after local interests. First to be formed was in Australia with de Havilland Aircraft Pty. Ltd. incorporated on 7th March 1927 with Geoffrey's brother Major Hereward de Havilland at the helm. De Havilland Aircraft of Canada Ltd. followed on 5th March 1928 and in successive years, an Indian arm was founded in 1929, South Africa in 1930 and New Zealand in 1939.

Within the scope of this book, only the Australian and Canadian companies will be discussed in more detail, as they acted more than mere local assemblers of kits supplied by the parent company at Hatfield. Ongoing demand for de Havilland aircraft types out of production, was instrumental in production lines being set up in Australia to produce the DH84 Dragon during 1942, whilst in Canada, the bush flying fraternity were desperate for more DH83 Fox Moths and similarly, production commenced of a new batch in late 1945 at the Downsview, Ontario works.

de Havilland Australia Pty. Ltd. Initially set up to assemble imported DH60 Moths in rented accomodation at the back of the town of Melbourne in early 1927, the expanding concern later moved to more suitable premises at Sydney's Bankstown Aerodrome. Here, in excess of one thousand DH82A Tiger Moths were produced from 1940 to 1945, not only to fulfil the Royal Australian Air Force need for training aircraft, but also in large numbers for use by R.A.F. schools established in South Africa and Southern Rhodesian. In addition, to fulfil an urgent requirement for radio and navigation trainers, construction of a second generation of Dragon aircraft commenced with the first of 87 examples taking to the air on 29th September 1942. Also flown in 1942, utilising a Dragon nose section, was the D.H.A. G.2, a troop carrying glider. Two prototypes and six production examples were built but whilst successful, the ready availability of American made Waco Hadrian gliders, determined the cancellation of the project. Post war, de Havilland Australia built two Fox Moths but they are perhaps best known for their tri-engine D.H.A.3 Drover aircraft. Only 20 of the type were built, but as air ambulance aircraft operated by Australia's Royal Flying Doctor Service, there place in the annals of aeronautical history was assured.

The de Havilland Aircraft of Canada Ltd. The previously mentioned Francis E. N. St. Barbe, the company's sales manager, went to Canada in November 1927 to promote sales and set up a spares provisioning programme for the first ten DH60 Moths supplied to the government for flying club use. He returned to England early in the new year with further orders and communicated his enthusiasm for what he saw during his whirlwind visit, forecasting that the country would "open up" due to commercial aviation and that de Havilland should immediately organise a permanent presence in the vast country. His personal assistant, Robert A. Loader, was given the task and he arrived in Toronto during the first week of February 1928. Loader quickly located the field at Mount Dennis in Toronto's suburbs where Count Jacques de Lesseps had made the first flight in the city. The location was absolutely ideal, having a spur from the Canadian National Railway just a short distance away, allowing easy transfer of the Stag Lane products from the docks. Furthermore, the landowner was delighted that his field was to be used for aviation purposes again and even allowed the use of a former canning shed where aeroplane assembly could take place. Less than a month later on 5th March 1928, the company was formally incorporated. Realising that the rapidly growing company would soon outgrow de Lesseps Field, as it had become known, a new site at Downsview, to the north of the city was selected in October 1928. Moving swiftly on to the war years, de Havilland Canada built 25 DH82A Tiger Moths plus 1728 of their DH82C version with tailwheel and canopy and in excess of 1100 DH98 Mosquitos. After the war, production of a series of indigenous designs commenced but before the DHC-1 Chipmunk first flew on 22nd May, demand from the growing number of bush operators for a rugged light transport was met by building the DH83 Fox Moth in series, a type that had ceased production in England some eleven years previously. The long established company was purchased by the Boeing Commercial Airplane Company in 1986 but just six years later, they placed their de Havilland Division on the market and a sale agreement to Bombardier Inc. of Montreal was signed on 22nd January 1992. As these words are written, production of the DHC-8 continues at Downsview.

de Havilland
DH83 Fox Moth

DH83 c/n 4000. The prototype G-ABUO shown here with the starboard wing folded back demonstrating de Havilland's cunning method of saving hangar space. (Ian Terry Collection)

DH83 c/n 4033. Unusually for the period, this aeroplane was issued with two registrations. Firstly, as G-ACAJ and just a month later, as G-ACDD, a special allocation for H.R.H. The Prince of Wales.

DH83 c/n 4001. A delightful period shot of the first production aeroplane G-ABUP, on joy riding duty throughout its life. A family await their turn. (Ian Terry Collection)

DH83 c/n 4042. G-ACCB seen here on Southport Beach where it operated joy flights for nearly 20 years from delivery to Giro Aviation in January 1936. (Ian Terry Collection)

DH83 c/n 4002. Wearing the colours of Surrey Flying Services Ltd. and photographed at their Croydon base, G-ABUT proudly wears "1932 King's Cup Winner" titling. (Ian Terry Collection)

DH83 c/n 4042. After ditching in the sea off Southport in 1956 it was placed into store but in late 1971, the Midland Air Museum obtained the fuselage and used it for a time as a travelling exhibit.

DH83 c/n 4008. G-ABWF suffered a forced landing in Lancashire January 1933 and a mid-air collision with a DH60G over Ireland July 1933, before crashing in India March 1935. (Ian Terry Collection)

DH83 c/n 4056. Croydon based Provincial Airways used G-ACEX on their scheduled services to Portsmouth and the West Country from mid 1934 until sale to Pine's Airways, Porthcawl in April 1936.

2.1 de Havilland DH83 Fox Moth – Development

Following the immediate success of the DH80 Puss Moth first flown on 9th September 1929 and the DH82A which took to the air from Stag Lane on 26th October 1931, next off designer A. E. Hagg's drawing board was the DH83 Fox Moth.

Legend has it that Hagg required a suitable aeroplane to transport his family and that the cabin dimensions were paced out to suit! What resulted, was a light transport aircraft with the pilot located in an open cockpit behind an enclosed cabin with seats for up to four passengers, an ideal upgrade for Puss Moths and other types in use by the growing number of short domestic and feeder airlines in all parts of the world. To use the words of the respected C. G. Grey, editor of *The Aeroplane* magazine, "The Fox Moth, unquestionably the first British aeroplane to support itself financially in the air"; complimentary words indeed!

Low initial cost was a prime requirement and so standard Tiger Moth mainplanes, tail unit, undercarriage and engine bearer were used, the only totally new component being the fuselage. This was of spruce and plywood construction of simple box form covered in fabric, so successfully used by de Havilland in earlier days. Early production examples sold for approximately £1200.

The new model flew from Stag Lane on 29th January 1932 and a further 97 examples were built at Stag Lane and Hatfield after the move to the new location by the end of 1932. The first passenger to ride in a Fox Moth was Lt.-Colonel Francis Claude Shelmerdine, the former Director of Civil Aviation in India and the Director of Civil Aviation at the Air Ministry 1931-1934. He became Director-General of Civil Aviation in 1934 and was knighted for his service to the air in 1936.

Customer deliveries commenced in the following June with the first production machine going to British Hospitals Air Pageants Ltd. and used for joyriding. Also in June, Hillman's Airways accepted three aircraft and these were immediately pressed into service on their services from Maylands to Clacton and to Ramsgate replacing the Puss Moths used hitherto.

Delivery of the second production aircraft was delayed due to the installation of a sliding cockpit canopy, a repositioned fuel tank from the centre section of the top wing to the cabin and the fitment of a 130 h.p. Gipsy III engine, later known as the Gipsy Major. These drastic modifications aided W. L. Hope's third victory in the King's Cup Air Race at an average speed of 124.13 m.p.h. Doubtless, the handicappers were outwitted mainly due to the removal of the fuel tank to the Fox's interior, which would have reduced drag considerably. Subsequently delivered to Surrey Flying Services at Croydon and used extensively by them for joy riding, air taxi work and for freight carriage until impressment into R.A.F. service in April 1940. Following its race victory, G-ABUT proudly wore "1932 King's Cup Winner" titling and the aircraft is illustrated on page 8.

It is probable that around 30 aircraft were completed at Stag Lane before the production line moved to Hatfield and most of these went to British buyers. However, a few went to overseas customers with two for Australia and one each to Canada, Ireland, Japan and Canada. In February 1933, the prototype, registered G-ABUO, also went to Canada and there it was evaluated on both skis and floats by Canadian Airways.

A keen user, albeit as a passenger, was H.R.H. The Prince of Wales. Already the owner of Puss Moths, his personal pilot took delivery of Fox Moth G-ACAJ in November 1932, but unusually at that time, during the following month, it was re-registered G-ACDD as a special privelege to the future uncrowned King Edward VIII.

Fox Moths were soon busily employed around the world; five supplemented 25 DH60T Moth Trainers at the Escola de Aviacao Navale in Brazil and were used as navigation trainers, Misr Airwork commenced operations utilising SU-ABA and SU-ABG for their scheduled service from Cairo to Alexandria, Rhodesia and Nyasaland Airways employed their two aircraft, VP-YAD and VP-YAK on scheduled services radiating from Salisbury and for charter flying, whilst in Australia, the type was in use by a variety of operators for scheduled services, air taxi work and a number as air ambulances.

Quietly going about their business, making money for their operators, if Grey's usual words of wisdom are to be believed, but a couple of DH83s did make newsworthy flights. The Marquess of Clydesdale, the future 14th Duke of Hamilton, flew G-ACCS to India ex Heston on 16th February 1933, in support of the Mount Everest Flight Expedition. Clydesdale later became President of the British Air Line Pilots' Association in 1937 and was President of the Air League 1959-1968.

Another notable flight was carried out by the float equipped G-ACRK, which John Grierson flew off the River Medway at Rochester on 20th July 1934 bound for Canada. After many stops en route and traversing the Greenland Ice Cap, the Fox Moth finally landed, after 61 hours flying time, at Ottawa on the 30th August,

By now fully committed to Tiger Moth and Dragon production, the 98th and last Fox Moth was built for an overseas customer and it arrived in New Zealand in December 1934 for Tourist Air Travel & Transport Service NZ Co. Ltd. of Christchurch.

Two were built up by de Havilland Australia at Bankstown in late 1937 for air ambulance use. Also, in New Zealand, a new fuselage was built by the recently established de Havilland Technical School in early 1938, to replace the one badly damaged when ZK-ADH crash landed in fog near Wigram some two years earlier. The wings, undercarriage and tail unit from the crashed aircraft were used, together with the new fuselage identified as T/S 2810. The 'new' Fox Moth, registered ZK-AGM, was first flown by Bert Mercer's Air Travel (NZ) Ltd. at Hokitika in June 1938.

In order to keep the production line active, now that wartime need for Tiger Moths and Mosquitos had ended and to satisfy demand from bush fliers, production of the DH83C commenced in 1946. The new generation Canadian built aircraft featured a strengthened cabin area, port side door extended rearwards to allow easier loading and unloading of bulky items and a plexiglass sliding canopy. A wider cockpit opening was also included to allow the pilot to wear thick insulating clothing, necessary when flying in the cold northern reaches of Canada. Powered by the 145 h.p. Gipsy Major 1C, the DH83C had a cruising speed of 96 m.p.h. and a still air range of 375 miles but accommodation was limited to the pilot and up to 3 passengers. Fifty two aircraft were completed by de Havilland of Canada using many surplus DH82C Tiger Moth parts and were delivered to customers in Canada, India, Pakistan and Southern Rhodesia. The last two (FM.53 and FM.54) were not finished at Downsview but passed to Leavens Bros. of Toronto for completion, due to de Havilland of Canada's preoccupation with their locally designed DHC-1 Chipmunk. One Canadian built example, FM.42, eventually came to the U.K. when purchased by a British buyer in Pakistan and it arrived at Southend ex Karachi on 24th September 1955 and was registered G-AOJH.

A lookalike known as a KR-1 Chidorigo, which translates from the Japanese as plover (a wading bird), with a 150 h.p. 7 cylinder radial Gasden Jimpu engine modelled on the Armstrong Siddeley Mongoose, was built in Japan by Tokyo Gas and Electric Industry Co. First flown on 23rd December 1933 and at least three, including J-BBJI, J-BBMI and J-BBNI, flew alongside 4 British built examples in service as air taxis by the Japan Aerial Transport Co. A second version, the KR-2 was a sesquiplane, with the lower wings having an area some 46 square feet less than the earlier KR-1. First flown on 17th November 1934 and reportedly, 12 examples were built. The revised wing arrangement had the effect of increasing cruise speed from 99 m.p.h., in the case of the KR-1, to 112 m.p.h. for the KR-2. There is no record of any licence fee being paid to de Havilland and copying by the Japanese of the best western products, prevalent until the 1960s, even seems to have extended to aircraft!

2.2 de Havilland DH83 Fox Moth - Specifications

Type: Low-cost, light utility transport
Capacity: Pilot and either 3 or 4 passengers. (DH83C, pilot and 3 passengers)
Country of origin: Great Britain
Production period: 1934-1947
Engine: 1 X de Havilland Gipsy Major I in-line inverted air cooled piston engine 130 h.p. As an option for the DH83 and fitted to all DH83C aircraft, Gipsy Major IC 145 h.p.

First flight: 20th May 1932 (Stag Lane)
Total number built: 154
Production by: de Havilland Aircraft Co. Ltd., Edgware, Middlesex (later Hatfield, Hertfordshire) 98 (first delivery June 1932 and the last in late 1934)
                         de Havilland Aircraft Co. Pty. Ltd., Bankstown, New South Wales   2 (built late 1937 and second aircraft completed February 1938)
                         The de Havilland Aircraft Co. of Canada Ltd., Downsview, Ontario   54 (two passed to Leavens Bros. Air Services Ltd., Toronto, Ontario for completion)

Dimensions (all variants)
Wing span: 30' 11" (9.41m) – with wings folded, 9' 10" (3.20m)
Wing area: 261.4 sq. ft. (24.3 sq. m)
Length: 25' 9" (7.85m)
Height: 8' 5" (2.68m)

Weights:
Empty: 1,105lb (502 kgs)
Max take-off: 2,050lb (932 kgs)

Tankage:
Fuel   25 gallons
Oil $1\frac{3}{4}$ gallons

Performance:
Initial rate of climb: 492 ft. per minute (150m per minute)
Max speed: 113 m.p.h. (182 kms per hour)
Cruise speed: 96 m.p.h. (155 kms per hour)
Service ceiling: 12,700' (3,871m)
Range: 360 miles (579 kms)
Stalling speed: 52 m.p.h. (83.75 kms per hour)

2.3 de Havilland DH83 Fox Moth – U.K. Production Listing

4000 First flight at de Havilland's private aerodrome, Stag Lane 29.1.32. Reg'd **G-ABUO** [CofR 3639 19.3.32] for de Havilland Aircraft Co. Ltd., Stag Lane 20.5.32. Sold abroad 1.33. Evaluated on both floats and skis by Canadian Airways Ltd. reg'd **CF-API** 4.33 To General Airways, Noranda, PQ serving the local mining industry. Withdrawn from use Toronto, cancelled 1.50 and scrapped by Leavens Brothers Air Services that year. Parts built into CF-EVK (c/n FM.53).

4001 Reg'd **G-ABUP** [CofR 3787 6.6.32] for Aviation Tours Ltd., Skipton, Yorkshire. CofA no.3494 issued and operated by British Hospitals Air Pageants Ltd., Hanworth 17.6.32. Crashed Ashby, near Scunthorpe, Yorkshire 24.8.33. Cancelled as destroyed 1934.

4002 Reg'd **G-ABUT** [CofR 3957 15.9.32], fitted with a Gipsy IIIA engine and sliding canopy. Flown by W. L. Hope, won the 1932 King's Cup Air Race at an average speed of 124.13 m.p.h. To Surrey Flying Services Ltd., Croydon 15.9.32. Impressed as **X9304** 14.4.40 and delivered for military service 10.5.40. Scrapped 11.41.

4003 Export CofA issued 20.7.32 and reg'd **EI-AAP** for Iona National Airways Ltd., Dublin's Kildonan Airfield. To Everson Flying Services, Dublin-Kildonan 2.12.33 and operated for Lady Cathleen Nelson. Later re-named Free State Air Ferries and later still, Dublin Air Ferries on 1.1.35. Cancelled from Irish register 18.9.38 and reg'd **G-AFKI** [CofR 8767 27.9.38] on return to U.K. To Hugh Graham Aitcheson, Bexhill, Sussex but normally kept at Croydon. Later moved to Shoreham. Impressed 31.8.41 but no serial issued and as there are no records of use, it is unlikely to have entered military service.

4004 Reg'd **G-ABVI** for Hillman's Airways Ltd., Maylands 17.6.32 with CofA no.3495. Operated on route Clacton – Maylands – Ramsgate. To Essex Aero Club Ltd., Maylands 7.36. To Romford Flying Club Ltd., Maylands [CofR 8418 25.3.38]. Burned out in hangar fire at Maylands due enemy bombing 6.2.40 and cancelled 7.2.40.

4005 Reg'd **G-ABVK** 23.6.32 for Hillman's Airways Ltd., Maylands with CofA no.3456. To British Airways Ltd., Stapleford 1.36. To L. Lipton, Stapleford 4.36. To Pine's Airways Ltd., Porthcawl [CofR 7955 23.6.37]. Impressed as **X2867** 29.12.39. Scrapped 8.41.

4006 Reg'd **G-ABVJ** 24.6.32 for Hillman's Airways Ltd., Maylands with CofA no.3499. To Eastern Air Transport Ltd., Skegness 4.33. To Midland Airways Ltd., Sywell 9.35. To Clifford Wright, Ryde, Isle of Wight but normally kept at Brooklands [CofR 7220 28.7.36]. Destroyed by fire at Brooklands 1936 and removed from register 12.37.

4007 Reg'd **G-ABWB** 5.7.32 and retained by de Havilland Aircraft Co. Ltd. with CofA no.3500. To Blackburn Aircraft Ltd., Grimsby 1.37. To Graham Hippesley Jackson, Eastleigh [CofR 8367 3.3.38]. Sold abroad 12.38 and reg'd **VT-AKV** for D. J. Minwala, Karachi 27.2.39. Cancelled from register 30.7.41.

4008 Reg'd **G-ABWF** 8.7.32 for Scottish Motor Traction Co. Ltd., Renfrew with CofA no.3501. Damaged when in mid-air collision with de Havilland DH60G EI-AAI near Limerick 7.7.33 but repaired. Damaged during forced landing Haslingden, near Bury, Lancashire 31.1.33. Ownership changed to Arthur Hammond Dalton, Heston [CofR 5332 1.9.34]. Crashed near Belgaum, India 28.3.35 and cancelled as destroyed 5.35.

4009 Reg'd **G-ABWD** for de Havilland Aircraft Co. Ltd., Stag Lane [CofR 3721 16.7.32]. To Marcel Genens reg'd **CH-344** 7.32. Fate unknown.

4010 Ordered via de Havilland at Mascot, NSW for Holyman Brothers Pty. Ltd., Launceston. Reg'd **VH-UQM** [CofR 449 22.8.32] and CofA no.407 issued same day. Named *Miss Currie*. To Tasmanian Aerial Services Pty. Ltd., Launceston on amalgamation 18.10.32. To Holyman's Airways Pty. Ltd., Launceston 10.33. Merged to form Australian National Airways Pty. Ltd. 7.11.36 and re-named *Dromana*. Burnt out in hangar fire Broken Hill NSW 6.9.39.

4011 Reg'd **CF-ATV** 11.32. Cancelled from register 2.50.

4012 Reg'd **G-ABYO** 16.8.32, initially for the de Havilland Aircraft Co. Ltd., Stag Lane with CofA no.3550. To Norman Edgar, Whitchurch [CofR 4117 5.1.33] but commenced operation of twice daily scheduled services Bristol to Cardiff somewhat earlier on 26.9.32. Crashed Caerwent, Monmouthshire en route Cardiff to Whitchurch and burnt out 16.6.34. Cancelled 5.35.

4013 To Japan Aerial Transport Co., reg'n unknown.

4014 Reg'd **G-ABZA** [CofR 3900 26.8.32] for Thomas George Mapplebeck, London W1 with CofA 3565 issued. Taken by Mapplebeck to Belgrade, Yugoslavia and re-reg'd **UN-SAK** 9.32. Later, again re-reg'd as **YU-SAK**. Fate unknown.

4015 Reg'd **G-ABXS** 7.9.32 for H. G. Travers, Stag Lane with CofA no.3570. To P. A. Wills, Stag Lane 1.33. To the Hon. Brian Lewis, Heston [CofR 5762 2.4.35]. Cancelled as sold abroad 7.35. To H. C. Miller of MacRobertson-Miller Aviation Co. Ltd., Perth WA. Reg'd **VH-UVL** [CofR 541 6.9.35]. Operated almost exclusively in the "Flying Doctor" role for the Aerial Medical Service, Port Hedland WA from 30.10.35 named *John Flynn*. Aircraft extensively damaged when the hangar collapsed during a cyclone, Port Hedland. The rear fuselage was crushed and all four wings were twisted and broken. Repaired by MacRobertson-Miller in Perth and returned to Port Hedland. Sold to Sidney David Marshall, Bankstown 2.6.39. Impressed as **A41-2** 7.10.42. Served with 35Sqdn., 2AAU, 1RCS and 8CU. Returned to civil register as **VH-UVL**. Restored to flying condition by Ken Orrman, Blairgowrie VIC 27.7.00. To Dr. Robert Fox, Kellyville NSW 9.4.02 and presumed kept at Bankstown.

4016 To Japan Aerial Transport Co., reg'n unknown.

4017 Reg'd **G-ABYR** initially for de Havilland Aircraft Co. Ltd., Stag Lane [CofR 3891 11.8.32]. Transferred to de Havilland Aircraft Pty. Ltd., Sydney. Reg'd **VH-UQR** 22.11.32 [CofR 458 21.3.33] and CofA no.418 issued same day to Guinea Airways Ltd., Adelaide SA. Overturned on landing at unknown location in PNG 14.9.37 but repaired. Based Lae, PNG 3.11.39. Destroyed on the ground PNG during Japanese air strike 21.1.42. Struck off register 11.3.42.

4018 Reg'd **G-ABZM** initially for de Havilland Aircraft Co. Ltd., Stag Lane [CofR 3912 23.9.32]. Departed Heston for the Oslo, Norway customer flown by W. Omsted 23.1.33. Disappeared en route and a wing was washed up on the Norwegian coast 2.2.33. Reg'n **LN-ABP** intended but not taken up. Cancelled from register 4.33.

4019 To de Havilland Aircraft Pty. Ltd., Mascot NSW. Reg'd **VH-UQS** [CofR 457 21.3.33] and CofA no.417 issued same day. To Guinea Airways Ltd., Adelaide SA 31.10.33. Crashed Sandy Creek, PNG 14.10.35 and struck off register 5.11.35. Restored to Guinea Airways 11.37. Crashed and destroyed by fire near Surprise Creek, PNG 12.3.38.

4020 To W. R. Carpenter & Co. Ltd., Sydney NSW. Reg'd **VH-UQP** [CofR 452 9.12.32] and CofA no.413 issued 11.1.33. Named *Jacqueline*. Transferred to Carpenter owned Mandated Airlines Ltd., Wau PNG 16.10.36. Crashed in Bitoi Valley, PNG 30.10.41. Struck off register 17.11.41.

4021 To W. R. Carpenter & Co. Ltd., Sydney NSW. Reg'd **VH-UQQ** [CofR 453 9.12.32] and CofA no.414 issued 18.1.33. Transferred to Carpenter owned Mandated Airlines Ltd., Wau PNG. When proceeding up Bitoi Valley, PNG under a layer of clouds which began to close down, owing to continued loss of height, was unable to turn up the next valley to the right and pancacked on top of trees 15.12.34. The pilot E. D. Crisp was injured. Struck off register 5.35.

4022 Reg'd **G-ABZN** 1.11.32 for Airwork Ltd., Heston with CofA no.3593. To Misr Airwork Ltd., Cairo as **SU-ABA** 3.33. Restored to Airwork Ltd., Heston as **G-ABZN** [CofR 6134 29.7.35]. Sold abroad 2.9.36 and to **SE-AFL**. Written off but details unknown.

4023 Reg'd **ZS-ADH** to Capt. S. S. Halse 12.32. Sold abroad to **VP-YBD** 2.36. To **VP-RCE** 1951. To **VP-YLS** 1954. Sold abroad to **ZS-CFP** 1956. Written-off Oranjeville 24.1.58

4024   Reg'd **SU-ABG** 3.11.32 for Misr Airwork Ltd., Cairo. Reg'd **G-ADNF** for C. T. Berry, Hunstanton on return to the U.K. 13.8.35. Sold abroad to Australia. Reg'n **VH-ABQ** allocated 3.8.38 for Kevin Parer, Wewak PNG [CofR 16.2.39]. Destroyed on the ground PNG during Japanese air strike 1.42.

4025   To Southland Aero Club, Invercargill reg'd **ZK-ADC** late .32. Shipped to New Zealand and first flown there 21.1.33. Leased to A. J. Bradshaw, trading as Southland Airways 10.12.36. Stalled and crashed when landing Big Bay, West Coast 30.12.36. The pilot, Bradshaw and one passenger were killed.

4026   Reg'd **G-ABZD** [CofR 3903 26.9.32] to Anthony Gee of Winter Garden Garage, Stag Lane with CofA no.3626. To **NC12739** 12.32. Later re-registered **N12739**. With Geert E. Frank, East Kingston NH 1977. Crashed Fire Island NY (parallels southern side of Long Island) when flying in a severe storm. To K. F. Horton. To Joel M. Hirtle, Westerville OH 9.1.97 and currently undergoing rebuild to flying condition.

4027   Brazil

4028   Brazil

4029   Brazil

4030   Brazil

4031   Brazil

4032   Tata Sons Ltd., Bombay reg'd **VT-ADZ** 3.33. To Air Union Joy Riding Co., Bombay 5.39. Cancelled 10.41.

4033   First flown reg'd **G-ACAJ** [CofR 4009 19.11.32]. To Flt. Lt. Edward Hedley Fielden, Hendon on behalf of H.R.H. The Prince of Wales (the future uncrowned King Edward VIII), re-reg'd 6.12.32 in favour of a double letter sequence as **G-ACDD**. To Guy Hansez reg'd **OO-ENC** [CofR 287 3.33] although not cancelled from the U.K. register until 12.33. Indeed, it is reported that the aeroplane was involved in an accident at Colmorrell, Ayrshire 6.6.33! Certainly in Belgium from late 1933 and Hansez used it extensively within Europe and for a flight to the Belgian Congo. Returned U.K. & restored to Malcolm T. Farquharson Ltd., Heston as **G-ACDD** [CofR 5976 14.6.35]. However, kept at Croydon until sale abroad 7.35.. To Air Travel (NZ) Ltd., Hokitika reg'd **ZK-AEK** 10.5.36. Crashed on Franz Josef Glacier 29.10.43 but subsequently rebuilt by de Havilland at Rongotai using a new locally constructed fuselage. Returned to service 21.5.44 and to New Zealand National Airways named *Mohua*, when Air Travel absorbed 4.11.47. To W. K. Wakeman, Christchurch 1.10.53, Aerial Sowing (Canterbury) Ltd. 3.12.53 and C. A. Wornall 1.8.54. To B. N. McCook 26.3.57 who shipped the aircraft to Fiji 6.4.57. To **VQ-FAT** for B. N. McCook, trading as Air Viti Ltd., 10.4.57. CofA expired 29.10.57, struck off the register 26.11.59 and left to rot at Nausori, where noted derelict 1960. The remains were eventually returned to New Zealand and used for a major rebuild completed 5.93. Officially restored as **ZK-AEK**, it however received dispensation to wear **G-ACDD**. Taken to U.S.A. and the U.K. later in the year by Roger Fiennes. Sold to Sir Timothy William Wallis, whose father had been a frequent passenger, and he returned the aircraft to N.Z. Again wearing **ZK-AEK** and currently kept at Wanaka.

4034   To Rhodesia & Nyasaland Airways reg'd **VP-YAD** 6.33. Withdrawn from use after accident 22.5.37.

4035   Reg'd **VP-YAK** 3.33 To **ZS-AEW** 22.6.34. Impressed as **SAAF1413** 3.40. Restored as **ZS-AEW**. To Noon & Pearce Air Charters, Nairobi reg'd **VP-KDS** 1.47. Crashed Entebbe 15.3.52.

4036   Reg'd **G-ACBO** 17.1.33 for Mrs. E. J. Richardson, Stag Lane with CofA no.3697. To George Edge, Nairobi, Kenya [CofR 5378 1.10.34]. Re-reg'd in Kenya as **VP-KBH** 5.35. To Southern Rhodesia as **VP-YBM** 3.37. Impressed to Southern Rhodesian Air Service 1941. Fate unknown.

4037   Reg'd **CF-APF** 2.33. Cancelled from register 11.39.

4038   Reg'd **CF-APG** 2.33 to Ontario Provincial Air Service. Cancelled from register 10.42.

4039   Allocated in Germany as **D-2408** (not D-3408 as previously published elsewhere) but unusually, there is no date of issue shown and therefore, it is probable that it was not taken up. Instead, reg'd **G-ACID** [CofR 4402 23.6.33] for Leonard Ingrams, Heston. Sold abroad to de Havilland Aircraft Pty. Ltd. Reg'd **VH-UTF** [CofR 533 9.7.35] and CofA no.491 issued same day for MacRobertson-Miller Aviation Co. Ltd., Perth WA. Operated for the Flying Doctor Service, Wyndham WA and named *Dunbar Hooper*. To G. W. Lewis t/a Goldfields Airways, Kalgoorlie WA 14.9.38 and operated for the Australian Aerial Medical Service. To R. M. Edwards, Darwin NT 12.2.46. To H. V. Moss, Darwin NT 17.6.47 and often used for the transport of fish from Daly River situated some 150kms to the south-west of Darwin. To Max Bond, Parafield SA 10.2.50. At Robby's Aircraft Repair Co., Parafield SA 29.3.50, but withdrawn from service 14.7.50 and struck off register 6.8.51. Restored as **VH-RAL** to Robby's Aircraft 17.4.53. Again, struck off register 7.61 but restored to Austerserve Ltd., Bankstown NSW 10.62 and re-reg'd **VH-UAL** [CofR 5.5.63]. Ditched in sea off Carlisle Island QLD 1.8.68.

4040   Reg'd **G-ACBZ** [CofR 4068 24.1.33] for John Cuthill Sword, Craigwell, Ayrshire and operated by Midland & Scottish Air Ferries Ltd., Renfrew. Sold abroad 12.36. Reg'd **VH-UZD** [CofR no.631 1.4.37] and CofA no.588 issued same day for QANTAS Empire Airways Ltd., Archerfield QLD. Crashed on landing Tapini PNG 3.10.49.

4041   Reg'd **G-ACCA** 27.9.33 for Portsmouth, Southsea and Isle of Wight Aviation Ltd., Portsmouth with CofA no.3738. Sold abroad 6.35 and to G. W. Lewis t/a Goldfields Airways, Kalgoorlie WA as **VH-UTY** [CofR 531 4.6.35] and CofA no.487 issued same day. To Guinea Airways Ltd., Adelaide SA 18.10.40. To Kingsford Smith Aviation Service Pty. Ltd., Bankstown NSW 24.9.52. To Papuan Air Transport Ltd., Port Moresby PNG sometime in 1953. Crashed Lake Myola PNG 17.11.53. Struck off register 20.2.54.

4042   Reg'd **G-ACCB** 10.2.33 John Cuthill Sword, Craigwell, Ayrshire for o/b Midland & Scottish Air Ferries Ltd., Renfrew with CofA no.3734. To Giro Aviation Co. Ltd., Hesketh Park, Lancashire [CofR 6613 1.1.36] and used extensively for joyriding from Southport sands. Withdrawn from use Hesketh Park 4.4.40 prior to CofA expiry. As in storage, deemed unsuitable for impressment. Restored to Giro Aviation 25.1.48. Ditched in sea off Southport 25.9.56. Wreck still stored at Hesketh Park when Giro Aviation closed 7.64. To Midland Air Museum, Coventry and stored off-site but occasionally roaded to events, publicising the Museum's work. To I. B. Grace, Chilbolton 23.3.88. Fuselage only to E. A. Gautrey, Nuneaton, Warwickshire 17.8.88 and last noted on rebuild at his home using some Tiger Moth parts 10.95.

4043   To Bombay Flying Club reg'd **VT-AEA** 5.33. Cancelled from register 10.7.41.

4044   Reg'd as **G-ACCS** 8.2.33 for Mount Everest Flight Expedition, Heston with CofA 3759 and flown from Heston to India by Lord Clydesdale. To John Allen Mairs, Coleraine [CofR 5305 16.8.34] but kept at Portrush, Co. Antrim. Sold abroad 8.36 and to Mandated Airlines Ltd., Salamaua PNG reg'd **VH-UUS** [CofR 624 18.2.37] and CofA no.581 issued same day. Based Wau PNG 3.11.39. Overturned on landing at unknown location 15.5.41 but repaired. To QANTAS Empire Airways Ltd., Sydney NSW 26.6.42. Impressed as **A41-3** 8.8.43. Served with 35Sqdn., 2AAU, 1RCS and 8CU. Restored as **VH-UUS** to the Methodist Inland Mission, Kew VIC 22.2.46. Flown by the Rev. C. W. Lanham, Mt. Isa QLD to whom ownership was transferred 12.11.47. To J. & A. Bjelke-Petersen, Kingaroy QLD 13.4.55. To Cropcair Aviation Pty. Ltd. 13.10.60. Re-reg'd **VH-CCH** 31.3.64. Crashed Barney View QLD 6.12.65. Remains sold to Charles Miller, Canberra ACT during 1978 but further damaged when the shed in which it was stored at Geary's Gap ACT, was over run by a bush fire. Later with Max Horsecroft, Perth WA and trucked to Murwillumbah NSW for restoration by Greg Challinor of Mothcair 6.95.

4045   To the Government of Bengal reg'd **VT-AEB** 6.33. Cancelled from register 2.8.43.

4046   Reg'd **G-ACCF** 23.2.33 for C. W. A. Scott's Air Display concern with CofA 3746. To Provincial Airways Ltd., Croydon 11.33. To British Air Transport Ltd., Redhill 5.36. To Redhill Flying Club Ltd., [CofR 8458 14.4.38]. When inspected Gatwick prior to impressment, owner was annotated as Hugh Graham

Aitchison, Bexhill, Sussex. Impressed 31.8.41 but seemingly, did not enter military service and no serial issued.

4047 Reg'd **G-ACCT** 7.3.33 for Midland & Scottish Air Ferries Ltd., Renfrew with CofA no.3760. To West of Scotland Air Services Ltd., Renfrew [CofR 6106 24.7.35]. Sold abroad 20.11.37 and to V. H. James, Maylands WA allotted **VH-ABU** 18.1.38. Nominal change to James Taxiplanes Ltd. 8.2.38. Business offered as a going concern 2.40 but impressed as **A41-1** 16.7.41. Operated by 4CF, Pearce WA. SOC to the Methodist Inland Mission and restored as **VH-ABU** 12.3.46. Operated as an air ambulance, flown by Rev. C. W. Lanham, Mt. Isa QLD. Re-reg'd **VH-GAV**, date unknown. Struck off register 20.10.48.

4048 Reg'd **G-ACCU** [CofR 4088 13.2.33] for John Cuthill Sword, Craigwell, Ayrshire o/b Midland & Scottish Air Ferries Ltd., Renfrew. Sold abroad 12.36 and **VH-UZC** allotted 2.37 for QANTAS Empire Airways Ltd., Sydney NSW. CofA no.628 and CofA no.585 issued 23.3.37. Impressed as **A41-4** 8.8.43. Served with 35Sqdn., 2AAU, 1RCS and 8CU. Crashed 1944 – circumstances unknown. Approved for conversion 3.45.

4049 Reg'd **CF-ATX** for Prospector Airways 4.33. To Austin Airways 10.34. To H. Watt. To Elmer Ruddick. To Arthur Fecteau t/a A. Fecteau Transport Aerien Ltee, Senneterre PQ. Sank at unknown location 1945 and rebuilt by de Havilland of Canada. To J. N. Stevenson. To F. Larivierie. To W. F. McQuade. Cancelled from register 3.60.

4050 Reg'd **CF-APH** 2.33. Cancelled from register 10.37.

4051 Sold to Adastra Airways Ltd., Mascot NSW as **VH-UQU** [CofR 467 4.9.33] and CofA no.425 issued same day. To Guinea Airways Ltd., Lae PNG 25.3.38. Crashed on landing Sonia PNG 30.8.41. It is unclear whether the aircraft was repaired, but official records state "destroyed by enemy action 21.1.42". Struck off register 11.3.42.

4052 Reg'd **CF-APO** 9.33. Cancelled from register 3.50.

4053 Reg'd **G-ACFC** [CofR 4247 23.3.33] for Blackpool and West Coast Air Services Ltd., Squires Gate. CofA no.3823 issued & named *Progress I*. Name changed to West Coast Air Services Ltd. To Olley Air Service Ltd., Croydon 1.36. To Great Western and Southern Air Lines Ltd., Shoreham 20.4.39. Impressed as **AX859** 5.40. SOC and to **2583M**.

4054 Reg'd **G-ACDZ** 28.3.33 for Scottish Motor Traction Co. Ltd., Renfrew. CofA no.3808 issued. To West of Scotland Air Services Ltd., Renfrew 11.34. To Border Flying Club Ltd., Carlisle [CofR 8504 18.5.38]. Impressed as **X2865** 12.39. Scrapped 8.41.

4055 Reg'd **G-ACEA** 30.3.33 for Scottish Motor Traction Co. Ltd., Renfrew. To Sussex Aero Club, Wilmington 6.36. To Sandown and Shanklin Flying Services, Lea 17.7.36. To Isle of Wight Flying Club Ltd., Lea 20.9.39. Records show "change of ownership 29.12.39" and impressed as **AW124** 6.40. Allotted maintenance serial **4078M** 4.44 but SOC as scrapped 12.4.44.

4056 Reg'd **G-ACEX** for Alan Cobham's National Aviation Day Ltd., Ford. CofA no.3820 issued and named *Youth of Ireland*. Provincial Airways Ltd., Croydon named *Mercury* 5.34 and used on their Croydon to Portsmouth, Exeter and Plymouth route. To Pine's Airways Ltd., Porthcawl but normally kept at Cardiff [CofR 6912 15.4.36]. Impressed as **X2866** 29.12.39. Overturned on landing Wroughton, Wiltshire 6.4.41 and damaged beyond economical repair.

4057 Reg'd **G-ACEY** for Alan Cobham's National Aviation Day Ltd., Ford. CofA no.3821 issued and named *Youth of Newfoundland*. To Provincial Airways Ltd., Croydon named *Jupiter* 5.34. To Crilly Airways Ltd., Braunstone 4.35 and named *Athene*. To Utility Airways Ltd., Hooton Park [CofR 8240 25.11.37]. Badly damaged when attempting an uphill take-off from Walsall, Staffordshire 24.9.38. It is unlikely that the aircraft flew again as although reviewed for possible impressment 1.9.39, there is no record of it passing to the military. Burnt out Hooton 8.7.40.

4058 Reg'd **G-ACEB** 13.4.33 for Scottish Motor Traction Co. Ltd., Renfrew. First aircraft to land on Shetland, at Sumburgh 19.4.33. To Southend Flying Services Ltd., 6.34 and operated regular services across the Thames Southend to Rochester. To

W. S. Shackleton Ltd., Heston [CofR 5838 27.4.35]. Sold abroad 7.35. Reg'd **VH-USJ** [CofR 534 9.7.35] and CofA no.490 issued same day for MacRobertson-Miller Aviation Co. Ltd., Perth WA. Operated almost exclusively for the West Australian Section, Australian Aerial Medical Services at Port Hedland WA from 10.35 and named *John Flynn*. Sold to the Flying Doctor Service 7.41 and continued to be based Port Hedland. By now operated in reserve following the acquisition of a DH84, the Fox Moth forced landed due engine failure Port Hedland WA 13.4.42 and badly damaged. On inspection, water was found in the fuel but no blame was placed on the pilot. Repair undertaken by MacRobertson-Miller at Perth and returned to Port Hedland 2.43. To R. C. Currell, Maylands WA 17.5.61. To Bob Couper & Co., Cunderdin WA 5.5.62. To W. E. Dermody, Shackleton WA 8.7.63. Apparently "a would-be flyer", Dermody crash-landed 8.7.63 and the aircraft flipped over on to its back, causing extensive damage. Obviously repaired, for another accident occurred on 16.3.64. Sold to Bob Couper & Co., Cunderdin WA later in the year. With Cunderdin Branch of the Historical Society of Western Australia 10.68. To Barry Markham 1994 and to be rebuilt by Lyn Forster of Aerobuild. However, restored to Croydon Aircraft Company at Mandeville, New Zealand 11.11.02.

4059 Reg'd **G-ACEC** 13.4.33 for Scottish Motor Traction Co. Ltd., Renfrew with CofA no.3811. To West of Scotland Air Services Ltd., Renfrew [CofR 5817 15.4.35]. Sold abroad to Raymond John Paul Parer t/a Parer Air Transport, Wewak PNG 4.37. Reg'd **VH-AAX** [CofR 23.7.37] 4.37. Destroyed by enemy action at Lae PNG and struck off register 11.3.42.

4060 Reg'd **G-ACFF** [CofR 4259 24.4.33] for Blackpool and West Coast Air Services Ltd., Squires Gate and named *Progress II*. Name changed to West Coast Air Services Ltd. To Olley Air Service Ltd., Croydon and transferred to affiliate Great Western and Southern Air Lines Ltd., Shoreham 15.3.39, based at Land's End. Impressed as **X9305** 2.4.40. Withdrawn from use and issued **2613M**. Delivered to 402Sqdn. Air Training Corps, Gravesend, Kent 21.8.41. Fate unknown.

4061 Austria **A-129**, **OE-STA**, **D-OSTA**. No further information and fate unknown.

4062 Reg'd **G-ACGB** 29.4.33 for H. W. Noble, Heston. To Helen Marcel Barnes, Shoreham [CofR 4924 21.3.35]. Sold abroad as **VT-AGI** for Himalaya Air Transport & Survey Co., Delhi 3.35. Cancelled from register 5.8.38.

4063 Reg'd **G-ACGN** 18.5.33 for Gravesend Aviation Ltd. with CofA no.3899 and operated for a time by C. W. A. Scott's Air Display concern. To Launcelot John Rimmer, Hooton Park (CofR 6190 13.8.35]. Sold abroad 11.35. Reg'd **VH-UDD** [CofR 566 14.1.36] and CofA no.523 issued same day for MacRobertson-Miller Aviation Co. Ltd., Perth WA. Damaged Tanunda SA 29.3.36 but repaired. To Madang Aerial Transport Co., Madang PNG 13.1.40. Destroyed at Lae or Salamaua PNG by enemy action 21.1.42. Struck off register 11.3.42.

4064 Reg'd **G-ACED** 6.5.33 for Scottish Motor Traction Co. Ltd., Renfrew. To Northern & Scottish Airways Ltd., Renfrew [CofR 6045 5.7.35]. Sold abroad 3.37. Reg'd **VH-UZL** [CofR 639 27.5.37] for W. W. Pike t/a Light Aeroplanes Pty. Ltd., Brisbane QLD and CofA no.596 issued same day. To Guinea Airways Ltd., Adelaide SA 21.11.38. Based Lae PNG 3.11.39. Strafed by enemy aircraft on the ground 21.1.42. Struck off register 11.3.42.

4065 Reg'd **G-ACEE** [CofR 4204 12.4.33] for Scottish Motor Traction Co. Ltd., Renfrew. Crashed during a joyriding sortie Riverside Park, Dundee 31.7.34. Cancelled from register 11.34.

4066 Reg'd **EC-AVA**.

4067 Reg'd **G-ACGW** [CofR 4370 24.5.33] for Charles Lloyd, Heston. Crashed and burnt out on landing Jersey Race Course 1.10.33. Cancelled from register 4.2.34.

4068 Reg'd **G-ACEI** [CofR 4214 21.4.33] for Scottish Motor Traction Co. Ltd., Renfrew. Crashed at Alva, Clackmannanshire and burnt out 1.7.33. Cancelled from register 12.33.

4069 Reg'd **G-ACEJ** 30.5.33 for Scottish Motor Traction Co. Ltd., Renfrew with CofA no.3916. To Giro Aviation Co. Ltd., Hesketh Park, Lancashire [CofR 7206 22.7.36] and used

DH83 c/n 4057. When in service with Utility Airways, G-ACEY suffered a take-off accident at Walsall in Staffordshire. Unlikely to have been repaired and burnt out at Hooton Park July 1940.

DH83 c/n 4090. The only British registered float-equipped Fox Moth, G-ACRK was flown across the Atlantic from Rochester to Ottawa, Canada by owner John Grierson in July 1934.

DH83 c/n 4063. G-ACGN seems to be having a radio fitted at its Gravesend, Kent base. Later in Australia and eventually destroyed in New Guinea by Japanese bombing during January 1942.

DH83 c/n 4094. The second of two purchased by Imperial Airways when they commenced air mail services in Newfoundland, wears rare local registration VO-ADE.

DH83 c/n 4069. G-ACEJ visits the 1976 Popular Flying Association Rally. In the ownership of Tony Haig-Thomas at the time, who amassed a fine collection of most de Havilland types in the 1970s.

DH83 c/n 4097. But for a nine year period in the United States and twelve years in the U.K. as G-ADHA, this Fox Moth has spent the majority of its life in New Zealand.

DH83 c/n 4072. With P.S.I.O.W.A. titles, G-ACIG operated Portsmouth, Southsea and Isle of Wight Aviation's virtual shuttle service from Portsmouth to Ryde on the Isle of Wight.

DH83C c/n FM.42. The owner uses the Canadian built G-AOJH to visit his hometown of Shoreham from Blackpool, June 1978. John Lewery was an international ice skating champion in the 1950s.

extensively for joyriding from Southport sands. To Norman Herbert Jones (of the Tiger Club), Redhill 16.6.66. To Anthony Haig-Thomas, Kirby-le-Soken, Essex 26.10.72. Wrecked when struck on ground while parked Old Warden by landing Beech Sundowner G-AYWS 17.7.82. Cancelled 23.7.82. Remains purchased by Ben & Mrs. J. I. Cooper and rebuilt by their company, Newbury Aeroplane Co. at Hungerford – Denton Manor. Reflown 2.94 and re-painted in Scottish Motor Traction livery 2.96.

4070 To Eagle Oil, Argentina.

4071 To Madras Flying Club reg'd **VT-AEJ** 9.33. Cancelled from register 3.10.35.

4072 Reg'd **G-ACIG** [CofR 4405 10.7.33] for Portsmouth, Southsea and Isle of Wight Aviation Ltd., Portsmouth with CofA no.3978. Operated semi-scheduled shuttle service Portsmouth to Ryde, Isle of Wight. Impressed as **X9299** 14.4.40. In use as an instructional airframe with 779Sqdn. Air Training Corps, Haberdasher Aske's School, Hampstead. Damaged beyond repair during removal from their premises 1946 and SOC.

4073 Delivered as **EC-W19**.

4074 Delivered as **EC-W20**.

4075 Delivered as **EC-W21**.

4076 Delivered as **EC-W22**.

4077 Reg'd **G-ACIY** 17.8.33 for Brooklands Aviation Ltd., Sywell with CofA no.4005. To Henri Deterding of Shell Oil [CofR 5288 2.8.34] and though nominally based Sywell, regularly flown from a strip at Deterding's home, Newnham Grounds, Daventry, Northamptonshire. Impressed as **DZ213** and delivered to the Royal Navy at Lee-on-Solent 30.6.41. Cancelled by the Secretary of State 26.6.44.

4078 To Indian National Airways, Calcutta reg'd **VT-AEM** 12.33. Cancelled from register 26.3.41.

4079 To Japan Aerial Transport Co., reg'n unknown.

4080 To Japan Aerial Transport Co., reg'n unknown.

4081 To Indian Air Survey and Transport Ltd., Calcutta reg'd **VT-AEN** 2.34. Cancelled from register 7.5.34.

4082 To Madras Air Taxi Service reg'd **VT-AEQ** 11.33. Cancelled from register 14.4.34.

4083 Reg'd **G-ACKZ** [CofR 4473 27.10.33] for Robert Lester Palmer, Hatfield and used for a time by C. W. A. Scott's Air Display concern. Sold abroad as **VT-AJW** for Air Services of India 1.38. Cancelled from register 7.10.46.

4084 Sold to QANTAS Empire Airways Ltd., Brisbane QLD. Reg'd **VH-URI** [CofR 473 22.2.34] and CofA no.431 issued on same day. To N. R. Wilde, Wau PNG 30.4.52. To J. K. Gray, Goroka PNG 26.6.58. Crashed in PNG 13.11.58 but no further information known.

4085 Reg'd **ZK-ADH** .34. Arrived New Zealand 22.3.34 and test flown four days later for the Canterbury Aero Club, Christchurch. Leased to Air Travel (NZ) Ltd. 11.2.35 to 6.35. Damaged beyond repair when landing in fog near Wigram 7.6.36 and cancelled from register 11.3.37. The wings, undercarriage and tail unit were used, together with new fuselage built by de Havilland Technical School, identified as T/S 2810, to construct a 'new' Fox Moth. New reg'n **ZK-AGM** allocated and first flown by Air Travel (NZ) Ltd. at Hokitika 10.6.38. To New Zealand National Airways named *Matuhi* 1.12.47. To Wanaganui Aero Work 1.2.56. Delivered to T. A. Garnier, Christchurch 12.12.62 but not reg'd to him until 22.1.63. Crashed Freezing Flat, near Minaret Creek, West Wanaka 27.4.63. Cancelled from register 5.8.63. Remains stored until arrival in U.K. and in 2.03 was undergoing rebuild at Hungerford – Denton Manor.

4086 To Indian National Airways, Calcutta reg'd **VT-AFB** 5.34. Cancelled from register 22.7.43.

4087 Delivered to Spain as **EC-W23**. Operated on floats as **EC-VVA**, and later as **EC-AEI**. Transferred to the Spanish Air Force with serial **30-147**.

4088 To Tata and Sons Ltd., Bombay reg'd **VT-AFI** .34. Impressed as **MA959** 31.10.42 and cancelled from civilian register 4.8.43. SOC 2.6.44.

4089 Reg'd **G-ACRU** [CofR 5021 28.5.34] for the British Graham Land Expedition 1934-1937, Hatfield with CofA no.4381. Used for survey work in the Falkland Islands and Antartica until 7.37. Sold abroad via broker W. S. Shackleton Ltd., Heston 1.38 Reg'n **VH-AAZ** allocated 1.9.37. CofR issued 20.11.37 for Raymond John Paul Parer t/a Parer Air Transport, Wewak PNG. Crashed and destroyed Black Cat Ridge PNG 6.11.39.

4090 Reg'd **G-ACRK** [CofR 4998 10.7.34] for John Grierson, Rochester, Kent. However, first flown with test markings **E.10** to prove the interchangeable float undercarriage for Grierson's proposed flight from U.K. to Canada. CofA no.4379 issued and Grierson departed his Rochester, Kent base 20.7.34, flying via Iceland and Greenland and reached Ottawa 30.8.34. Sold abroad 5.35. Reg'd **VH-UBB** [CofR 546 7.10.35] and CofA no.504 issued same day for W. R. Carpenter & Co. Ltd., Sydney NSW. Operated by their company Mandated Airlines Ltd., Wau PNG. Destroyed by enemy action, probably on the ground at Lae 21.1.42. Struck off register 11.3.42.

4091 Ordered as a "Speed Model" for the MacRobertson Race to Australia and reg'd **G-ACSW** [CofR 5071 29.5.34] for Harry Frank Broadbent, Hanworth. CofA no.4323 issued. Placed eighth in the 1934 King's Cup Air Race at a speed of 121.03 m.p.h. Sold abroad as **VT-AFT** for Himalaya Air Transport & Survey Co., Delhi 9.34. Cancelled from U. K. register 1.35. Cancelled from Indian register 24.3.41.

4092 To Irrawaddy Flotilla & Airway Ltd., Rangoon, Burma as **VT-AFZ** 11.34. Cancelled from register 26.8.37.

4093 Reg'd **VO-ABC** and U.K. CofA issued to Newfoundland Government 26.9.34. Fitted with floats and used by Imperial Airways when they took over the Newfoundland air mail service in 1935. Fate unknown.

4094 Reg'd **VO-ADE** and U.K. CofA issued to Newfoundland Government 26.9.34. Fitted with floats and used by Imperial Airways when they took over the Newfoundland air mail service in 1935. To Newfoundland Government Air Services 4.41. To R.C.A.F. with serial **A145** on 17.6.41. Restored to Newfoundland Government Air Services as **VO-ADE** 24.10.45. Fate unknown.

4095 Reg'd **CF-AVE** .35. Involved in a fatal accident 1942 and cancelled.

4096 Sold to Arnhem Land Development Co., Sydney NSW and reg'n allocated 30.8.34. Reg'd **VH-USL** [CofR 500 28.12.34] and CofA no.457 issued same day. To QANTAS Empire Airwys Ltd., Sydney NSW 28.6.35. Damaged beyond repair on the ground during a severe dust storm, Winton QLD 1.1.38.

4097 Reg'd **ZK-ADI** .34. Arrived New Zealand 8.12.34 for Tourist Air Travel & Transport Service NZ Co. Ltd., Christchurch. Renamed Air Travel (NZ) Ltd. Damaged when in collision with a bull, Weheka 8.2.35, necessitating lease of c/n 4085. Impressed as **NZ566** 12.4.43. Served with Rongotai C.F. and 42sqn. Survived the war and restored to civil register as **ZK-ASP**.and sold to National Airways Corp. 16.7.48. To W. K. Wakeman, Christchurch .53. To M. P. Robertson, Auckland .72. Myles Robertson shipped the aircraft to the U.S.A. 4.74 and toured the country in it. Sold to Hamburg Airdrome Inc., Lakeview NY as **N83DH** 15.7.75. Sold to Brian Woodford and reg'd **G-ADHA** 3.12.84. Painted red and blue to represent the Prince of Wales machine c/n 4033. Nominal ownership change to Wessex Aviation and Transport Ltd.15.4.85. To G. Grocott, Switzerland (a New Zealander then flying for Swissair). Returned to New Zealand register as **ZK-ADI** 4.2.97 and reg'd to Croydon Aircraft Company, Gore. To Double U Anchor Ltd., Paraparaumu. Colour scheme is now orange/silver as it first appeared with Tourist Air Travel.

"134" Reg'd **G-AEPB** 5.11.36 for Essex Aero Ltd., Stapleford. This probable hybrid, of unknown origin, was not certificated and the reg'n was cancelled as sold abroad 11.38.

FM.99 Reg'd **G-BFOX** 13.2.78 for M. C. Russell, R. W. E. Lake, A. D. Raby & D. W. Brabham t/a The Fox Moth Syndicate, Duxford. This was intended to be a "new build" DH83C by Russavia, using many DH82A parts. Although it is believed that the project was not commenced, ownership changed to R. K. J. Hadlow, Bedford 6.3.81. Cancelled by the C..A..A. during a regular "clean-up" 2.9.91.

2.4 Overseas Production

Australian built aircraft

DHA.5 Built by de Havilland Aircraft Pty. Ltd., Mascot NSW for the Department of the Interior, Canberra ACT and reg'd **VH-UZS** [CofR no.672 dated 17.11.37]. Used by Dr. C. C. Fenton, Katherine NT in the aerial ambulance role. Stalled and crashed soon after departing Katherine NT 10.10.41. The aircraft was totally destroyed; the pilot, R. Edwards and the nursing sister D. Black were injured and the passenger Mrs. C. Hindley was killed.

DHA.6 Built by de Havilland Aircraft Pty. Ltd., Mascot NSW for the Bush Church Aid Society for Australia & Tasmania and to be based Ceduna SA. Reg'd **VH-AAA** [CofR no.692 dated 23.2.38] and CofA no.649 issued same day. Forced landed after engine failure on take-off Ceduna SA 8.43. Presumably after a period off the register, **VH-BYA** was allocated 11.48. Unhappy with this allocation the Bush Church Aid Society requested the more apt **VH-BCA**, but this had already been issued. Instead, **VH-CAS** was issued 9.9.49. Re-reg'd **VH-GAS** early 1950 when the Directorate of Civil Aviation appropriated the VH-CAA to VH-CAZ block for their own use. Reg'n cancelled 16.6.50. To Papuan Air Transport Ltd., Port Moresby PNG 12.53. Noted at an air show, Mildura VIC 30.9.62. Subsequently restored as **VH-AAA**. Fate unknown.

de Havilland DH83C Fox Moth – Canadian Production Listing

FM.1 Reg'd **CF-BFI** 11.45. To Arthur Fecteau t/a A. Fecteau Transport Aerien Ltee, Senneterre PQ. Cancelled from register 9.58.

FM.2 Reg'd **CF-BNI** 4.46. Cancelled from register 8.50. Note: a replica wearing the marks CF-BNI built up from various parts located throughout Canada, is exhibited at the Prince of Wales Northern Heritage Centre, Yellowknife NWT.

FM.3 Reg'd **CF-BNK** 2.46. Cancelled from register 10.48.

FM.4 Reg'd **CF-BNL** 3.46. Cancelled from register 10 48.

FM.5 Reg'd **CF-BNM** 2.46 to Newfoundland Airways.

FM.6 Reg'd **CF-BNN** 3.46. To Richard D. Jackson & Neil Walsten, Kenora ONT .68. Cancelled from register 2.79.

FM.7 Reg'd **CF-BNO** 3.46 to Parson's Airways, Kenora ONT. Said to have been used in the U.S.A. at some stage but no registration traced. Cancelled from Canadian register 10.63. On rebuild to display standard using DH82C parts at the Canadian Bushplane Heritage Centre, Sault Ste. Marie ONT.

FM.8 Reg'd **CF-BNP** 4.46. Reg'd to Robert R. Colley, Lake Caummit ONT .68. Cancelled from register 5.69.

FM.9 Reg'd **CF-BNQ** 3.46. Float equipped. Cancelled from register 1.56.

FM.10 Reg'd **CF-BNH** 4.46. Cancelled from register 8.50.

FM.11 Reg'd **CF-BNR** 4.46. Cancelled from register 9.52.

FM.12 Reg'd **CF-BNS** 4.46. Reg'd to Thomas Carr, Port Arthur ONT .68. Cancelled from register 2.69.

FM.13 Reg'd **CF-BNV** 6.46. Cancelled from register 5.56.

FM.14 Reg'd **CF-BNW** to Messrs. Spoarski and Roderick. Rainy River ONT 5.46. Crashed Lake Kagani ONT 30.8.46 and cancelled from register 3.47.

FM.15 Reg'd **CF-BNX** 7.46. Cancelled from register 7.47.

FM.16 Reg'd **CF-BNY** 6.46. Cancelled from register 6.58.

FM.17 Reg'd **CF-DIQ** 5.46 to Central British Columbia Airways. Crashed near Prince George BC 4.7.48 and cancelled from register 1.49.

FM.18 Reg'd **CF-DIR** 8.46. Cancelled on sale abroad to India 7.50. To Nalanda Airways Ltd., Patna reg'd **VT-CLS**.

FM.19 Reg'd **CF-DIS**.

FM.20 Reg'd **CF-DIT** 6.46. Cancelled from register 2.50.

FM.21 Reg'd **CF-DIU** 6.46. Cancelled from register 9.47.

FM.22 Reg'd **CF-DIW** 8.46. To Eugene Dolin, Asbestos PQ .75. Cancelled from register 9.79.

FM.23 Reg'd **CF-DIV** 8.46. Cancelled from register 10.60.

FM.24 Reg'd **CF-DIX**. Reg'd to Henry Boulanger, Winnipeg MB 20.11.61. Currently with the same owner and as not seen for many years, presumably stored at the owner's home.

FM.25 Reg'd **CF-DIY** 7.46. Cancelled from register 11.50.

FM.26 Reg'd **CF-DIZ** 7.46. Cancelled from register 8.68.

FM.27 Reg'd **CF-DJA** 10.46. Cancelled from register 3.52.

FM.28 Reg'd **CF-DJB**. As **CF-FGL** in very poor condition with Jack H. Edwards, Kenora ONT .75. A major rebuild commenced soon after. The result, virtually a completely new aeroplane, was flown in 1980. To Wardair Canada Inc., Edmonton MB and restored as **CF-DJB** 30.6.80. To Maxwell W. Ward, Edmonton MB 2.5.89. Donated to National Aviation Museum, Rockcliffe 1989.

FM.29 Reg'd **CF-DJC** 8.46. To Maxwell W. Ward/Polaris Charter Co. Ltd., Yellowknife. Flown by Ward, crashed on delivery flight from Toronto to Yellowknife but repaired. Charter aircraft used to support gold mining around Yellowknife. With a partner, Yellowknife Airways formed. Crashed 10.49, killing the pilot.

FM.30 Reg'd **CF-SAL** .46 to Saskatchewan Department of Natural Development. Destroyed in hangar fire Prince Albert SK 1947.

FM.31 Reg'd **CF-DJE** 7.46. Cancelled from register 4.50.

FM.32 Reg'd **CF-DJG** 8.46 to Photographic Survey Co. Ltd.. Crashed on lake south of Goose Bay 11.8.47. Cancelled from register 7.50.

FM.33 Reg'd **CF-DJF** .46. To Zambesi Airways reg'd **VP-RAY** .46. To **VP-YLK** .54. To **ZS-CFR** 4.57. To **ZS-CYW** 10.62. Crashed Baragwanath 28.11.64.

FM.34 Reg'd **CF-DJD** 11.46. Cancelled from register 7.48.

FM.35 Reg'd **CF-DJJ** 11.46. Cancelled from register 2.48.

FM.36 Reg'd **CF-DJK** 3.47. Cancelled from register 11.47.

FM.37 Reg'd **CF-DJL** 10.46. Cancelled from register 7.47.

FM.38 Reg'd **CF-EXW** 11.46. Badly damaged Ruperts House River, James Bay 30.8.47. Obviously repaired as not cancelled from register until 8.69.

FM.39 Reg'd **CF-DJM**. To Nalanda Airways Ltd., Patna reg'd **VT-CLT**. Written off but details unknown. Cancelled from register 1951.

FM.40 Reg'd **CF-DJN**.

FM.41   To Mr. Ataullah, Lahore reg'd **AP-ABN** .48. CofA expired 10.12.48 and presumably withdrawn from use as cancelled from register on unknown date.

FM.42   To Flt. Lt. W. Banach, Lahore reg'd **AP-ABO** .48. Flown to U.K. from Karachi and arrived Southend 24.9.55. To Blackpool & Fylde Aero Club Ltd., Squires Gate reg'd **G-AOJH** [CofR R5133/1 29.3.56]. Delivered to Barton 21.9.57 and reg'd to Henry Paterson, Barton 4.10.57. To John Shepherd Lewery, Squires Gate 16.4.63 and commenced pleasure flying from Southport Beach following the demise of Giro Aviation. To Victor Gauntlett, t/a Proteus Petroleum Aviation Ltd., Goodwood 4.5.90. To R. M. Brooks, London W9 and kept at Wycombe Air Park 8.7.91. To Torquil P. A. Norman, Rendcomb 18.4.97. To A. J. Norman t/a Norman Aeroplane Trust, Rendcomb 8.7.97.

FM.43   To Government of Pakistan reg'd **AP-ABP** and loaned to East Pakistan Flying Club, Dacca. Damaged beyond repair in storm Dacca 26.3.55.

FM.44   Believed to Government of Pakistan reg'd **AP-ABQ**. Struck by an Auster J/5 at unknown location and presumed damaged beyond repair 12.6.51. Cancelled from register 1953.

FM.45   Believed to Government of Pakistan and loaned to Lahore Flying Club reg'd **AP-ABR** .48. Cancelled from register after CofA expiry 23.4.54.

FM.46   Believed to Government of Pakistan and loaned to Karachi Aero Club reg'd **AP-ABS** .48. Written off Karachi 28.5.54.

FM.47   To Government of Pakistan and loaned to Lahore Flying Club reg'd **AP-AAM** .47. CofA expired 13.12.57 and removed from register.

FM.48   Reg'd **ZK-APT** 19.11.47 for the Marlborough Aero Club and CofA issued 24.11.47. Damaged at Bluff Station 3.48 but rebuilt. To H. J. Buchanan, trading as West Coast Flying School 27.11.56. To Coast Aviation 27.6.57. To Phoenix Airways. To T. B. Furse. Withdrawn from use and last reported in storage awaiting rebuild with G. S. Smith in Auckland. More recently, with Smith's Tech Air, North Shore undergoing restoration to flying condition.

FM.49   Arrived Auckland 13.10.47 and reg'd **ZK-AQB** 25.11.47 for Auckland Aero Club. To Tauranga Aero Club 17.12.55. To J. Paterson, Motiti Island 17.4.59. To W. Paterson, Tauranga 1.1.61. Crashed Motiti Island 28.6.72. Remains sold to M. P. Robertson, Auckland 15.10.76 and was awaiting rebuild. More recently, noted at the Croydon Aircraft Co., Mandeville undergoing restoration to flying condition.

FM.50   Imported by de Havilland Aircraft Co. of New Zealand Ltd. for D. H. McCarthy, Patea. Reg'd **ZK-AQM** 2.12.47 and CofA issued 17.12.47. Loaned to Hawera Aero Club 1948. Crashed Otautu River 27.9.53 and cancelled from register 21.4.54.

FM.51   To Nalanda Airways Ltd., Patna reg'd **VT-CLU**. Cancelled from register 1951.

FM.52   To Nalanda Airways Ltd., Patna reg'd **VT-CLV**. On the register dated 4.78.

FM.53   Fully committed to DHC-1 Chipmunk production, components passed to Leavens Bros. Ltd., Toronto ONT for completion. Allocated **ZK-ARQ** 23.3.48 for de Havilland Aircraft Co. of New Zealand Ltd. but not completed and eventually broken up in Canada by Leavens Bros. A 'new' Fox Moth is under construction by Jim Lawson at Manurewa, using mainly Tiger Moth parts. However, it is said that some parts of the original FM.53 are to be incorporated and on this basis, the D.C.A. have allowed the reg'n **ZK-ARQ** to be used!.

FM.54   Reg'd **CF-EVK** 3.47. Fully committed to DHC1 Chipmunk production, components passed to Leavens Bros. Ltd., Toronto ONT for completion. First flew 1952 and incorporated parts of the British built prototype CF-API (c/n 4000). Cancelled from register 11.64.

Japanese built Chindorigo lookalike aircraft

1   **J-BBJI**, KR-1 model, first flown 23.12.33 and delivered to Nihon Koku Yuso KK.

?   **J-BBMI**, KR-1 model, delivered to Nihon Koku Yuso KK.

?   **J-BBNI**, KR-1 model, delivered to Nihon Koku Yuso KK.

?   **J-BLIB**, KR-2 model, first flown 17.11.34 and delivered to Nihon Koku Yuso KK.

2.5 de Havilland DH83 Fox Moth Registration to Construction Number Cross Index

AUSTRALIA – CIVILIAN

VH-AAA	DHA.6
VH-AAX	4059
VH-AAZ	4089
VH-ABQ	4024
VH-ABU	4047
(VH-BCA)	DHA.6
(VH-BYA)	DHA.6
VH-CAS	DHA.6
VH-CCH	4044
VH-GAS	DHA.6
VH-GAV	4047
VH-RAL	4039
VH-UAL	4039
VH-UBB	4090
VH-UDD	4063
VH-UQM	4010
VH-UQP	4020
VH-UQQ	4021
VH-UQR	4017
VH-UQS	4019
VH-UQU	4051
VH-URI	4084
VH-USJ	4058
VH-USL	4096
VH-UTF	4039
VH-UTY	4041
VH-UUS	4044
VH-UVL	4015
VH-UZC	4048
VH-UZD	4040
VH-UZL	4064
VH-UZS	DHA.5

AUSTRALIA – MILITARY

A41-1	4047
A41-2	4015
A41-3	4044
A41-4	4048

AUSTRIA – CIVILIAN

OE-STA	4061

AUSTRIA - MILITARY

A-129	4061

BELGIUM

OO-ENC	4033

BRAZIL - MILITARY

?	4027
?	4028
?	4029
?	4030
?	4031

CANADA - CIVILIAN

CF-APF	4037
CF-APG	4038
CF-APH	4050
CF-API	4000
CF-APO	4052
CF-ATV	4011
CF-ATX	4049
CF-AVE	4095
CF-BFI-X	FM.1
CF-BFI	FM.1
CF-BNH	FM.10
CF-BNI	FM.2
CF-BNK	FM.3
CF-BNL	FM.4
CF-BNM	FM.5
CF-BNN	FM.6

CF-BNO	FM.7
CF-BNP	FM.8
CF-BNQ	FM.9
CF-BNR	FM.11
CF-BNS	FM.12
CF-BNV	FM.13
CF-BNW	FM.14
CF-BNX	FM.15
CF-BNY	FM.16
CF-DIQ	FM.17
CF-DIR	FM.18
CF-DIS	FM.19
CF-DIT	FM.20
CF-DIU	FM.21
CF-DIV	FM.23
CF-DIW	FM.22
CF-DIX	FM.24
CF-DIY	FM.25
CF-DIZ	FM.26
CF-DJA	FM.27
CF-DJB	FM.28
CF-DJC	FM.29
CF-DJD	FM.34
CF-DJE	FM.31
CF-DJF	FM.33
CF-DJG	FM.32
CF-DJJ	FM.35
CF-DJK	FM.36
CF-DJL	FM.37
CF-DJM	FM.39
CF-DJN	FM.40
CF-EVK	FM.54
CF-EXW	FM.38
CF-FGL	FM.28
CF-SAL	FM.30

CANADA - MILITARY

A145	4094

EGYPT

SU-ABA	4022
SU-ABG	4024

FIJI

VQ-FAT	4033

GERMANY

D-OSTA	4061
D-2408	4039

GREAT BRITAIN – CIVILIAN

E.10	4090
G-ABUO	4000
G-ABUP	4001
G-ABUT	4002
G-ABVI	4004
G-ABVJ	4006
G-ABVK	4005
G-ABWB	4007
G-ABWD	4009
G-ABWF	4008
G-ABXS	4015
G-ABYO	4012
G-ABYR	4017
G-ABZA	4014
G-ABZD	4026
G-ABZM	4018
G-ABZN	4022
G-ACAJ	4033
G-ACBO	4036
G-ACBZ	4040
G-ACCA	4041
G-ACCB	4042
G-ACCF	4046

G-ACCS	4044
G-ACCT	4047
G-ACCU	4048
G-ACDD	4033
G-ACDZ	4054
G-ACEA	4055
G-ACEB	4058
G-ACEC	4059
G-ACED	4064
G-ACEE	4065
G-ACEI	4068
G-ACEJ	4069
G-ACEX	4056
G-ACEY	4057
G-ACFC	4053
G-ACFF	4060
G-ACGB	4062
G-ACGN	4063
G-ACGW	4067
G-ACID	4039
G-ACIG	4072
G-ACIY	4077
G-ACKZ	4083
G-ACRK	4090
G-ACRU	4089
G-ACSW	4091
G-ADHA	4097
G-ADNF	4024
(G-AEPB)	"134"
G-AFKI	4003
G-AOJH	FM.42
G-BFOX	FM.99

GREAT BRITAIN - MILITARY

X2865	4054
X2866	4056
X2867	4005
X9299	4072
X9304	4002
X9305	4060
AW124	4055
AX859	4053
DZ213	4077
MA959	4088
2583M	4053
2613M	4060
4078M	4055

INDIA

VT-ADZ	4032
VT-AEA	4043
VT-AEB	4045
VT-AEJ	4071
VT-AEM	4078
VT-AEN	4081
VT-AEQ	4082
VT-AFB	4086
VT-AFI	4088
VT-AFT	4091
VT-AFZ	4092
VT-AGI	4062
VT-AJW	4083
VT-AKV	4007
VT-CLS	FM.18
VT-CLT	FM.39
VT-CLU	FM.51
VT-CLV	FM.52

IRELAND

EI-AAP	4003

JAPAN

J-	4013
J-	4016
J-	4079
J-	4080

J-BEIG	?

KENYA

VP-KBH	4036
VP-KDS	4035

NEWFOUNDLAND

VO-ABC	4093
VO-ADE	4094

NEW ZEALAND - CIVILIAN

ZK-ADC	4025
ZK-ADH	4085
ZK-ADI	4097
ZK-AEK	4033
ZK-AGM	T/S 2810
ZK-APT	FM.48
ZK-AQB	FM.49
ZK-AQM	FM.50
(ZK-ARQ)	FM.53
ZK-ASP	4097

NEW ZEALAND – MILITARY

NZ566	4097

NORTHERN RHODESIA

VP-RAY	FM.33
VP-RCE	4023

NORWAY

(LN-ABP)	4018

PAKISTAN

AP-AAM	FM.47
AP-ABN	FM.41
AP-ABO	FM.42
AP-ABP	FM.43
AP-ABQ	FM.44
AP-ABR	FM.45
AP-ABS	FM.46

SOUTH AFRICA - CIVILIAN

ZS-ADH	4023
ZS-AEW	4035
ZS-CFP	4023
ZS-CFR	FM.33
ZS-CYW	FM.33

SOUTH AFRICA – MILITARY

SAAF1413	4035

SOUTHERN RHODESIA

VP-YAD	4034
VP-YAK	4035
VP-YBD	4023
VP-YBM	4036
VP-YLK	FM.33
VP-YLS	4023

SPAIN - CIVILIAN		EC-W23	4087	SWITZERLAND		N?????	FM.7
		SPAIN - MILITARY		CH-344	4009	**YUGOSLAVIA**	
EC-AVA	4066						
EC-AEI	4087	30-147	4087	**UNITED STATES**		UN-SAK	4014
EC-VVA	4087					YU-SAK	4014
EC-W19	4073	**SWEDEN**		N83DH	4097		
EC-W20	4074			NC12739	4026		
EC-W21	4075	SE-AFL	4022	N12739	4026		
EC-W22	4076						

de Havilland DH84 Dragon

DH84 c/n 6006. One of eight military variants of the Dragon supplied to the Iraq Ministry of Defence which all left Hatfield on delivery on 13th May 1933. We wonder whether it recovered from this incident!

DH84 c/n 6067. Olley's G-ACNA at Croydon with the famous Aerodrome Hotel as a backdrop. Like many other de Havilland twin engine transports, later saw service with one of the Spanish factions.

DH84 c/n 6039. The only DH84 to join the British European Airways Corporation fleet on formation 1st February 1947. G-ACIT is seen here when in use as a company hack by Beagle Aircraft from 1962.

DH84 c/n 6072. An air to air of Allied Airways' G-ACNJ. Not impressed and remained in civilian service throughout the war operating from Aberdeen's Dyce Airport.

DH84 c/n 6041. G-ACIU was impressed as X9395 in April 1940, only to be damaged in France later in the month and purposely destroyed by fire before the airfield was over-run by advancing German forces.

DH84 c/n 6073. G-ACOR seen here in the colours of Northern & Scottish Airways. Sold to Australia February 1938 and destroyed on the ground in New Guinea by enemy bombing January 1942.

DH84 c/n 6058. Originally delivered to Jersey Airways, but sold to Western Airways in July 1938, G-ACMJ is seen here in the latter's distinctive colour scheme.

DH84 c/n 6075. Last in civil use by Western Airways, G-ACPX was impressed and received by No.6 Anti-Aircaft Co-operation Unit at Ringway. Unusually, records do not reveal its eventual demise.

3.1 de Havilland DH84 Dragon – Development

First commercial operator of the DH83 Fox Moth was Hillman's Airways of Maylands Aerodrome, Romford in Essex, who received three aircraft in June 1932. Having replaced unsuitable Puss Moths on their scheduled services to the seaside resorts of Clacton and across the Thames Estuary to Ramsgate in Kent, the DH83 proved an instant success. The transport entrepreneur Edward Hillman, was soon back at de Havilland's offices demanding more seats and perhaps, twin engines, more suited to frequent over water sorties. Low initial cost and economy of operation completed his specification.

Designer A. E. Hagg, had already commenced work on what was termed the Dragon Moth, as a similar requirement had been received from the Iraqi Air Force. Hagg was therefore able to show the excitable Mr. Hillman that a project which would aid the Essex airline's expansion, was already under way. Calmer now, he ordered four straight from the drawing board!

The first flight of what by now was known simply as the DH84 Dragon, took place at Stag Lane on 12th November 1932 (some sources give the first flight date as 24th November, but the 12th is believed correct) with Captain H. S. Broad at the controls in the single seat cockpit. Wearing E.9, one of a series allocated to de Havilland for testing purposes, the Dragon was soon on its way to Martlesham Heath for certification test flying to be carried out. Just over a month later, on the 16th December, the all important certificate of airworthiness was issued and now marked as G-ACAN, the prototype Dragon was delivered to Maylands.

During testing, the Dragon was found to offer economics even more superior to the outstanding Fox Moth. With six seats, a luggage compartment permitting each passenger a 45lb allowance and a cruising speed of 109 m.p.h. - 13 m.p.h. more than the Fox, the twin Gipsy Major engines drank a mere 13 gallons of fuel per hour. Compared to the Fox, which gave 17 ton-miles per gallon, the Dragon achieved 19 ton-miles per gallon and quickly gained the reputation as being the world's first multi-engine transport that could pay its way without subsidy.

Hillman was absolutely delighted with his purchase and all four of the initial order were delivered in time for the commencement of the airline's cut price scheduled flights to Paris on 1st April 1933. One-way tickets were £3-10-0, far lower than the fares charged by rival operators such as Imperial Airways and Air France ex Croydon. So successful was Hillman's first international route that the Freddie Laker of olden times, purchased two more Dragons and these were delivered in May and June 1933. To further increase capacity, the fleet of six aircraft were modified to 8-seaters by the removal of the rear luggage compartment. In spring 1934, a service was commenced from Maylands to Belfast and the airline was awarded the first contract for the domestic carriage of air mail by the Post Office, to be carried on this route. The first of eight Dragon Rapides was added to the fleet in June 1934, which compelled a move to nearby Abridge, Romford's Maylands being unsuitable for the larger aircraft. The old airfield is now a golf course. On 1st December 1934, the Belfast service was extended to Glasgow but during the following month, Edward Hillman died. Although the staff received minimum wages they had deep respect for their employer who's dream was low-cost air travel for the masses. The airline never recovered from his passing, and merged with Railway Air Services and United Airways to form British Airways Ltd. on 1st October 1935.

Returning to the aircraft, early deliveries were to the Iraqi Air Force who received eight and de Havilland enjoyed good sales to the new, rapidly expanding operators in Scotland. Among them were John Sword of Midland and Scottish Air Ferries and the Scottish Motor Traction Co. who were foremost bus and coach operators in the Lowlands. Like Edward Hillman in the south, who had also been weaned in the bus and coach world, the two Scottish operators progressed from Fox Moths to Dragons.

Island based airlines with flights to the mainland enjoyed early financial reward. Links from the Isle of Man to Blackpool and Liverpool, from Jersey and Guernsey in the Channel Islands to south coast towns such as Shoreham and Southampton with some flights extended to Croydon, serving London's metropolis, were immediately successful. Such was the demand for seats during the summer months that Jersey Airways often had to schedule more than one Dragon. One contributor to this book, recalls seeing a loose formation of no less than five Dragons crossing the south coast inbound from Jersey one sunny afternoon!

From the sixty-third aircraft, all were built to Dragon 2 standard with individually framed windows and faired undercarriage struts. Other less noticeable changes from the Dragon 1 to Dragon 2 included shorter exhausts, the door handle repositioned, louvres on the top cowling deleted and when fitted, larger spats. These modifications enhanced the cruising speed by 5 m.p.h. and gave a useful increase to the maximum take-off weight of 300lb (136 kgs), with only the rate of climb being sacrificed to the tune of approximately 8%.

Three Dragons went to Canadian buyers. The aircraft were shipped, assembled at Downsview and the first, CF-APJ (6024) entered service with Canadian Airways whilst the third to cross the Atlantic, CF-AVI (6093), started out with Consolidated Mining and Smelting before moving on to Howard Watt's North Shore Airways company. Operated on Fairchild made metal floats and with the extended dorsal fin as fitted to the DH84M, North Shore operated in direct competition to Quebec Airways, who were using float-equipped Dragon Rapides on the St. Lawrence River. Quebec Airways' Rapides had replaced their Dragon CF-AVD which had floats and the revised fin fitted in February 1935.

Other British Empire countries to receive Dragon aircraft were India and Kenya, each with three, South Africa with four, New Zealand with two and Southern Rhodesia with one.

By far the biggest overseas importer, however, was Australia with 25 British built machines registered. Of these, VH-UZG crashed in Australia (still wearing its British marks G-ACFG) when on delivery to North Queensland Airways, VH-UZQ was not delivered, VH-UZX (c/n 6084) crashed prior to delivery, 800 yards west of Waddon Railway Station at Beddington, Surrey when on approach to Croydon. Furthermore, de Havilland Australia Pty. Ltd. went on to build 87 Dragons at Bankstown in answer to an urgent need for radio and navigation trainers and general transports in Australia during the Second World War and further details may be found at chapter 3.3. Incredibly, taking this local production into consideration, over 55% of all Dragons built at the two locations, served civil and military organisations in Australia.

Glowing reports of the prototype's performance were received in Australia within a few days of the first flight and by April 1933, Norman Brearley of West Australian Airways had placed the first order, directly with the parent company in England. A second order quickly followed from Ivan Holyman of Tasmanian Aerial Services Pty. Ltd., then a third order for two machines to be fitted with Williamson cameras for photographic survey in connection with gold mining at Kalgoorlie, Western Australia by the Western Mining Corporation. These first four Dragons were all in operation by the end of 1933, followed by another seven in 1934. After a lapse of 15 months, five more were registered in 1936, one in 1937, three in 1938 and the last pair in 1940.

Shipped to Australia, the first two aircraft arrived at Maylands (Perth) and Mascot (Sydney) in August 1933. After assembly and test flying, followed by brief demonstration flights, the two Dragons were placed into service in the first week of September. E. C. Johnston, Controller of Civil Aviation in Australia, visited Mascot at the time of trials with Tasmania bound VH-URD and he stated "It is really a beautiful thing to travel in". Meanwhile, on the other side of the country, Brearley commented "The Dragon is really delightful in every way and is the nicest thing I have ever flown". At the end of the first week of operations with West Australian Airways, Brearley commented, "It has certainly given me a new zest for flying and I think it is the most delightful machine I have ever handled. One of the most remarkable things about it, is the view of the country ahead of the machine which is given to passengers from their seats looking past the pilot". Those familiar with the Spartan arrangements of the Dragon might pause to consider these remarks in relation to the earlier types then operated by the airlines, all effectively designed as World War 1 types or being their lineal descendents – the Dragon was clearly a great leap forward.

Surprisingly, Hudson Fysh of QANTAS offered a dissenting view, noting "The Dragon is impressive except that I feel they have erred too much on the side of economy in construction, and (it) will not fly on one engine under service conditions with a full load". These observations were made during a visit to England in August 1933 and it is clear that Fysh was much more impressed by the Spartan Cruiser , which although with a higher purchase and operating cost, offered an increased safety factor by virtue of its three engines – this latter point being his main criteria. These views may indicate the reasoning behind the fact that QANTAS Empire Airways, of all the major operators, did not use the type prior to the outbreak of war.

Twenty Dragons had been delivered to Australia by the time hostilities commenced; of these, two had been written-off in accidents and so 18 of the type were available for possible military use and these were joined by two late arrivals in 1940. In the event, nine aircraft received call-up notices. Notice of a further three required from Mandated Airlines in New Guinea was dated 24th February 1941. These were intended as replacements for No.1 Air Observers School as the result of an Air Board decision to transfer three impressed DH86 aircraft, operated by the school, to the newly-formed Air Ambulance Unit which the War Cabinet had recently decided would be transferred to the Middle East. However, Mandated's owner Sir Walter Randolph Carpenter was not at all taken with the idea that he would lose three of his Dragons and protested vociferously! In the end, a compromise was reached and Mandated retained VH-UVB and the proposed R.A.A.F. serial number A34-12 was eventually used on the first locally built Dragon. Six of the impressed aircraft were returned to civil operators as the war drew to a close.

Other overseas operators were Viacao Aerea de Sao Paulo SA (V.A.S.P.) with Dragon 2 PP-SPC (6085), YI-AAC (6044) operated in Iraq by Airwork Ltd., OE-FKD (6101) for the Austrian Aero Club and EC-TAT (6020), delivered as EC-W14 to a Barcelona based air taxi operator.

Another major user was Misr Airwork who acquired three aircraft SU-ABH (6028), SU-ABI (6031) and SU-ABJ (6051) all delivered in 1933. The last mentioned was burnt out at Almaza in June 1938 and SU-ABZ was purchased second hand to replace it, arriving March 1939.

Production continued alongside the DH89 for some time, but Dragon production finally ceased in April 1936. A few stood around for a time at Hatfield pending sale, until the last departed for service with the Portugese Air Force in May 1937.

Some would query the inclusion of a project to build a twin-engined (2 X Walter Mikron) Currie Wot to represent a DH84! However, plans were already drawn up for this amazing project and the required material was being gathered for its construction. Only a change in personal circumstances prevented the work commencing. Designed by the Popular Flying Association's former Chairman, David Faulkner-Bryant, only slight change in profile would have have been necessary for the Currie Wot fuselage to closely resemble that of a Dragon and it was intended to glaze the cockpit and side windows like the de Havilland original. Accommodation was planned for the pilot and one passenger seated in tandem, their heads protruding from the mini-Dragon's fuselage top!

3.2 de Havilland DH84 Dragon – Specifications

Type:	Utility transport
Capacity:	Single pilot and up to 6 passengers
Country of origin:	Great Britain
Production period:	1932-1942
Engines:	2 X de Havilland Gipsy Major I 4-cylinder in-line inverted air cooled piston engines each of 130hp
First flight:	12th November 1932 (at Stag Lane). DH84A 29th September 1942 (at Bankstown)
Price:	£4200 to £4400, depending on individual equipment requirements
Total number built:	202
Production by:	de Havilland Aircraft Co. Ltd., Stag Lane, Edgware, Middlesex 115 (first, delivered December 1932 and the last, ex Hatfield in May 1937. Later deliveries were ex Hatfield after the production line moved from Stag Lane).
	de Havilland of Australia Pty. Ltd., Bankstown, New South Wales 87 (first, delivered February 1943 and the last, in June of the same year!)

Dimensions:	Mk1	Mk2	MkII Seaplane
Wing span:	47' 4" (14.4m)	47' 4" (14.4m)	47' 4" (14.4m)
Wing area:	376 sq' (34.95 sq. m)	376 sq' (34.95 sq. m)	376 sq' (34.95 sq. m)
Length:	34' 6" (10.5m)	34' 6" (10.5m)	36' 6" (11.9m)
Height:	10' 1" (3.07m)	10' 1" (3.07m)	10' 1" (3.07m)

Weights:			
Empty:	2,300 lb (1,045.5 kg)	2,336 lb (1,061.8 kg)	2,795 lb (1,270.5 kg)
Max take-off:	4,200 lb (1,909.1 kg)	4,500 lb (2,041.2 kg)	4,500 lb (2,041.2 kg)

Tankage:	
Petrol:	60 gallons
Oil:	4¾ gallons

Performance:			
Initial rate of climb:	612' per minute	565' per minute (172.2m per minute)	500' per minute
Max speed per hour:	128 m.p.h. (205.9 km)	134 m.p.h. (215.6 km)	120 m.p.h. (193 km)
Cruise speed per hour:	109 m.p.h. (175.4 km)	114 m.p.h. (183.4 km per hour)	95 m.p.h. (152.8 km)
Service ceiling:	12,500'	14,500' (4,419.6m)	-
Range with full payload:	-	364 miles (585.8 km)	-
Range with full fuel:	460 miles	545 miles (877.1 km)	-

3.3 de Havilland DH84 Dragon – U.K. Production Listing

6000 First flown 12.11.32 at Stag Lane as **E.9**. CofA no.3689 issued 16.12.32. Reg'd **G-ACAN** to Hillman's Saloon Coaches and Airways Ltd. (later Hillman's Airways), Maylands. Allocated fleet no.9 and later named *Maylands* by aviatrix Amy Johnson after the Hillman's Maylands Aerodrome, Romford, Essex base. To Aberdeen Airways 16.8.34 & named *The Starling* after Aberdeen Airways' chief pilot, Eric Allen Starling 7.9.34. Company re-named Allied Airways (Gandar Dower) Ltd. [CofR 5359 17.9.34] Reviewed for possible impressment 31.8.39 but listed for the N.A.C. fleet, continuing in use with Allied Airways. En route Aberdeen to Wick, the port engine failed due to fuel starvation over the Moray Firth 21.5.41. The aircraft reached land but stalled and crashed at Hilltown Farm, near Dunbeath. The pilot died of his injuries 9 days after the accident, but the 5 passengers suffered little more than minor scrapes and bruises. Cancelled from register 5.11.45 (1945 census).

6001 CofA no.3742 issued 3.2.33. Reg'd **G-ACAO** to Hillman's Saloon Coaches and Airways Ltd. (later Hillman's Airways), Maylands. Named *Goodmayes*. To Lady Apsley, Whitchurch 10.35. [note: wife of Lord Apsley, Chairman of Western Airways, the Dragon continued in operation for much of the time with Western, but also between Whitchurch and the Apsley home at Badminton] To Norman Edgar (Western Airways) Ltd. [CofR 8617 8.7.38]. Cancelled from register 2.4.40 and impressed into R.A.F. service as **X9398** 10.5.40. Initially to 6AACU, Ringway. At 7AACU 3.5.40. En route Church Fenton to Usworth, the pilot lost his bearings in poor visibility and forced landed at Parliament Oak, Ollerton, Nottinghamshire 21.10.40. During the landing run, the aircraft hit a hedge damaging the undercarriage which collapsed on contact with the ground. The port wing tip and both starboard mainplanes were damaged. Removed to de Havilland 24.10.40 but deemed beyond economical repair and SOC as Cat.E1 21.2.41. Dismantled for spares use .

6002 CofA no.3743 issued 9.2.33. Reg'd **G-ACAP** to Hillman's Saloon Coaches and Airways Ltd. (later Hillman's Airways), Maylands. Named *Romford*. To Commercial Air Hire Ltd., Croydon [CofR 6717 8.2.36]. Whilst engaged on army co-operation operations at night in stormy weather conditions 26.6.36, the aircraft was seen to dive into the ground at Lyndhurst, Hampshire. The 5 occupants were killed and the reason for the accident could not be determined.

6003 DH84M. Export CofA issued 7.4.33. To Iraq Ministry of Defence with military serial **16**. Delivered ex Hatfield 13.5.33. Operational details and eventual fate unknown.

6004 DH84M. Export CofA issued 20.4.33. To Iraq Ministry of Defence with military serial **17**. Delivered ex Hatfield 13.5.33. Operational details and eventual fate unknown.

6005 DH84M. Export CofA issued 8.4.33. To Iraq Ministry of Defence with military serial **18**. Delivered ex Hatfield 13.5.33. Operational details and eventual fate unknown.

6006 DH84M. Export CofA issued 8.4.33. To Iraq Ministry of Defence with military serial **19**. Delivered ex Hatfield 13.5.33. Operational details and eventual fate unknown.

6007 DH84M. Export CofA issued 25.4.33. To Iraq Ministry of Defence with military serial **20**. Delivered ex Hatfield 13.5.33. Operational details and eventual fate unknown.

6008 DH84M. Export CofA issued 24.4.33. To Iraq Ministry of Defence with military serial **21**. Delivered ex Hatfield 13.5.33. Operational details and eventual fate unknown.

6009 CofA no.3856 issued 13.4.33. Reg'd **G-ACBW** to Hillman's Saloon Coaches and Airways Ltd. (later Hillman's Airways), Maylands. Named *Gidea Park* and allocated fleet no.9. To Commercial Air Hire Ltd., Croydon 7.34. Known to have been used by Provincial Airways Ltd. named *Neptune* and presumably leased from Commercial. To Air Dispatch Ltd. and converted to air ambulance by Airwork Ltd. at Croydon 11.35. Ownership changed to Anglo European Airways Ltd., Croydon [CofR 8468 22.4.38] but continued in use with Air Dispatch. Evacuated to Cardiff. To Commercial Air Hire Ltd., Cardiff 11.12.39. Impressed into R.A.F. service as **BS816** at Ringway 2.11.40. With

6AACU Ringway 2.11.40. Flown to de Havilland for major inspection 6.9.41. SOC as Cat.E1 22.10.41 and donated to 115Sqdn. Air Training Corps, Peterborough, Northamptonshire. Fate unknown.

6010 Reg'd **G-ACCE** [CofR 4073 24.3.33] to The Hon. Brian Edmund Lewis, eldest son of Sir Frederick William Lewis, Bt., chairman of shipping company Furness, Withy & Co. Ltd. CofA issued 21.4.33. Leased to Highland Airways Ltd., Inverness for five days July 1933 and sold to them 25.4.34. Named *Caithness*. Operated first British Internal Air Mail Service 26.5.34. Failed to get airborne on take-off Kirkwall and hit the stone perimeter wall 29.8.34. The pilot and seven passengers received only minor injuries. The subsequent report blamed sodden grass following a downpour which retarded the aircraft from gaining enough speed to successfully take-off.

6011 CofA no.3846 issued 3.4.33. To W. A. Rollason, Croydon reg'd **G-ACCR**. To Barnstaple and North Devon Aero Services 10.33. To Robert T. Boyd, trading as Atlantic Coast Air Service. Badly damaged in accident on Lundy Island in the Bristol Channel 3.34 but repaired. To Doris Godley t/a Commercial Air Hire Ltd., Croydon [CofR 5497 13.12.34]. Damaged at Paris-Le Bourget 27.2.35 but repaired. Written-off when ditched in the Channel off the French coast 22.1.36.

6012 Export CofA issued 1.5.33. To Iraq Ministry of Defence with military serial **22**. Delivered ex Hatfield 13.5.33. Operational details and eventual fate unknown.

6013 Export CofA issued 1.5.33. To Iraq Ministry of Defence with military serial **23**. Delivered ex Hatfield 13.5.33. Operational details and eventual fate unknown.

6014 Initial CofA issued 4.3.33. However, following extensive modifications, a supplemental CofA was issued 2.6.33. Delivered to Mrs. Jim Mollison C.B.E. (Amy Johnson) reg'd **G-ACCV** [CofR 4089 4.3.33] and named *Seafarer*. Heavily laden with fuel, the undercarriage collapsed at Croydon at the start of an attempt on the first westbound trans Atlantic flight to New York 8.6.33. Repaired and the record breaking flight eventually took place on 22.7.33, departing from Pendine Sands, South Wales. After the successful crossing, when landing in the dark at Bridgeport CT 23.7.33, the pilot mistook the wind direction and on landing down wind, the aircraft turned over and was wrecked. Damaged beyond repair, but the engines and special fuel tanks were salvaged and incorporated into the Mollisons' replacement G-ACJM (c/n 6049). Cancelled from register 11.33.

6015 Reg'd **G-ACCZ** [CofR no.4093 21.4.33] & CofA no.3872 issued 11.5.33. Delivered ex Stag Lane to Midland and Scottish Air Ferries Ltd., Renfrew 13.5.33. Fitted with 8 passenger seats but later modified to enable a stretcher to be accommodated if necessary. Shortly after take off from Belfast's Aldergrove Airport on a scheduled flight to Campbeltown and Renfrew, an engine failed necessitating a forced landing in a field near Antrim, Northern Ireland 14.9.33. Substantially damaged and returned to Glasgow by sea for repair, flying again on 14.12.33. Leased to Crilly Airways Ltd., Leicester 2.4.35. To Western Airways 1938. To Eric Noddings, Croydon [CofR 8450 12.4.38]. To Air Dispatch Ltd., Cardiff 22.1.40. Impressed into R.A.F. service as **AW154** 1.7.40. To Station Flight Ringway 6.7.40. At 8AACU 10.8.40. To Carlax Ltd., Hooton Park for the installation of night flying equipment. Loaned to 7AACU 16.9.40. Allotted to 7AACU 1.41. Donated to 635Sqdn. Air Training Corps, West Hartlepool 26.8.41 but SOC as Cat.C 10.11.41. To West Hartlepool Technical School and reduced to spares there 20.12.42.

6016 Reg'd **G-ACDL** 21.4.33 and CofA no.3873 issued 12.5.33. Delivered to Midland and Scottish Air Ferries Ltd., Renfrew together with G-ACCZ 13.5.33. To Provincial Airways Ltd., Croydon 9.34. To Luxury Air Tours Ltd., Croydon [CofR 6984 2.5.36]. Acquired for Spain by Union Founders Trust Ltd. Cancelled from the U.K. register as sold abroad 8.36 & delivered ex Croydon to Barcelona 15.8.36. Used by the Republican forces as **LD-002**. Fate unknown.

6017 Reg'd **G-ACDM** [CofR 4167 21.4.33] and CofA issued 18.5.33. To Scottish Motor Traction Co. Ltd., Edinburgh-Turnhouse. Sold abroad, cancelled 11.33. To Aircraft Operating Co. reg'd **ZS-AEI** 11.33. Fitted with curved dorsal fin. Impressed to South African Air Force 3.40 as **SAAF1570**. Fate unknown.

6018 Reg'd **G-ACDN** 21.4.33 and CofA issued 29.5.33. Delivered to Scottish Motor Traction Co. Ltd., Edinburgh-Turnhouse 31.5.33 but later based at their Glasgow-Renfrew station. To Midland and Scottish Air Ferries Ltd. 22.9.33. To Crilly Airways Ltd., Leicester 5.35. To Commercial Air Hire Ltd., Croydon [CofR 7886 21.5.37]. Impressed into R.A.F.service as **AW170** at Ringway 7.7.40. With 8AACU 10.8.40. At 4MU for inspection by de Havilland 28.8.40. En route from St. Eval to Exeter, the aircraft suddenly dived into the ground near Trewithen Farm, St. Wenn, Cornwall and destroyed 27.11.40. SOC 21.7.41.

6019 CofA no.3890 issued 11.5.33. To William Lindsay Everard, a brewer and Conservative Member of Parliament for the Melton division of Leicestershire from 1924. Reg'd **G-ACEK** and named *Leicestershire Vixen II* and operated from a private strip at Everard's home, Ratcliffe Hall in Leicestershire. To Olley Air Service Ltd. 6.36. To Anglo-European Airways Ltd., Croydon [CofR 8470 23.4.38]. To Commercial Air Hire Ltd., Cardiff 22.1.40. Impressed into R.A.F. service at Ringway 21.7.40 but retained its civil identity for a time. With 7AACU 23.8.40. To de Havilland for repair 23.8.40 and returned to Ringway, marked as **AX867** 8.9.40. To de Havilland again for major inspection 15.7.41 but SOC as Cat.E1 21.7.41.

6020 Export CofA issued 29.5.33. To Automobiles Fernandez, Barcelona with ferry markings **EC-W14**. Re-reg'd **EC-TAT** after delivery and used by Fernandez for their new Aerotaxi service. Requisitioned by Commandante Diaz Sandino at Prat de Llobrenat Airport, Barcelona 7.36 and used by the Republican Air Force as **LD-001**. Fate unknown.

6021 Reg'd **G-ACET** [CofR 4228 21.4.33] To Scottish Motor Traction Co. Ltd., Edinburgh-Turnhouse. CofA no.3922 issued 3.6.33. To Midland and Scottish Air Ferries Ltd. 15.2.34. To Highland Airways Ltd., Inverness 26.9.34 and named *Kirkwall*. Traded-in to de Havilland Aircraft Co. Ltd. in part-exchange for DH89 G-AEWL. To Eric Noddings, Croydon [CofR 8128 8.10.37]. Evacuated to Cardiff. To Air Dispatch Ltd., Cardiff 22.1.40. Impressed as **AW171** 7.7.40 although records show to Station Flight, Ringway on the previous day! To 6AACU 13.7.40. Returned to de Havilland for major inspection 6.9.41 and SOC as Cat.E1 22.10.41. Donated to 328Sqdn. Air Training Corps, Kingston-upon-Thames, Surrey and Maintenance Serial **2779M** allocated. Somewhat surprisingly, although the fuselage was scrapped 6.9.41, it is said that the wings and some other parts survived and **G-ACET** was restored to the civil register for Michael C. Russell t/a The Russavia Collection, Bishops Stortford 10.1.89. Using a new fuselage constructed in New Zealand, on rebuild by Ron & Michael Such of Aero Antiques & Aerotech Ltd. at Hedge End, Southampton.

6022 Reg'd **G-ACEU** and CofA no.3887 issued 12.5.33. To Hillman's Airways Ltd. named *Brentwood*. To Airwork Ltd., Heston [CofR 6634 13.1.36]. Cancelled as sold abroad 3.37 and presumed to Spain.

6023 Reg'd **G-ACEV** and CofA no.3900 issued 12.6.33. To Hillman's Airways Ltd. named *Ilford*. To Airwork Ltd., Heston [CofR 6665 23.1.36]. Cancelled as sold abroad 8.36 and delivered ex Croydon to Spain 15.8.36 for use by the Republican forces.

6024 Export CofA issued 26.4.33. Shipped to Canada and reg'd to de Havilland Aircraft of Canada Ltd., Toronto as **CF-APJ**. To Canadian Airways Ltd. and delivered 18.5.33. Name changed to Canadian Pacific Airlines 1942. Reduced to spares 10.42.

6025 Reg'd **G-ACGG** [CofR 3.5.33] to Flt. Lt. Edward Hedley Fielden, Hendon for operation by the King's Flight and CofA issued 6.6.33. To Richard O. Shuttleworth, Old Warden 2.35. To Leonard Harry Stace, Heston [CofR 6960 29.4.36]. Sold abroad to W. R. Carpenter & Co. Ltd., Sydney NSW. Reg'd as **VH-AAC** [CofR 690 18.2.38] and CofA no.647 issued on same day. Named *Alice*. Transferred to Carpenter's company Mandated Airlines Ltd., Lae, PNG 4.11.40. Formally impressed as **A34-10** 24.2.41. To Australian National at Essendon VIC for air observer conversion 18.4.41. Issued to 2AOS 19.8.41 then to de Havilland for sample purposes 14.12.41. Suffered an accident on operational transport flight 17.6.43. Issued to School of Photography, Canberra ACT 10.1.44. Just four days later, forced landed after engine failure causing 100% damage to starboard lower mainplane and 20% to the upper. Said to be repairable within unit, but on 23.2.44 "under consideration for disposal to Civil Aviation".

Issued to Department of Civil Aviation 21.6.44. Restored as **VH-AAC** to Aircrafts Pty. Ltd. 29.8.44. To Mandated Airlines Ltd., Lae, PNG 4.11.44. To Taylor's Air Transport 15.6.48. To Guinea Air Traders 15.3.49. To Wewak Air Transport 23.5.50. To Mandated Airlines 12.11.50. Crashed and badly damaged on approach to Slate Creek, PNG 29.1.51. Transported to Lae. Reg'd to Territory Airlines Ltd., Goroka PNG 1952 who intended to rebuild it but this did not happen. Struck off register 16.6.54.

6026 Export CofA issued 26.5.33. To de Havilland Aircraft of South Africa Ltd. reg'd **ZS-AEF**. Shipped to South Africa and erected at Baragwanath 6.33. To Aircraft Operating Co. Destroyed when crashed at Baragwanath 26.9.33, 2 fatalities.

6027 CofA no.3891 issued 28.6.33 and initially registered to de Havilland Aircraft Co. Ltd. as **G-ACFG**. Flown by Hubert Broad, finished last in the 1933 King's Cup Air Race at 132.7 m.p.h. To G. Nicholson, trading as Northern Airways, Renfrew 7.34. Became Northern and Scottish Airways Ltd. [CofR 5495 11.12.34]. Reported to have been owned by an Italian Count who used it to visit Vienna, Belgrade, Bucharest and Constantinople. Cancelled as sold abroad 2.37 but *Flight* magazine of 25.2.37 provides more information, "A Dragon aircraft has just been sold to an Australian company". Although allocated **VH-UZG** for North Queensland Airways, the registration was not taken up before the aircraft crashed approximately 22 miles north of Cairns QLD 7.5.37.

6028 Export CofA no.3939 issued 14.6.33. Delivered to Misr Airwork reg'd **SU-ABH** 26.6.33. Returned to U.K. 1936 and reg'd **G-AEKZ** for Airwork Ltd., Heston 7.36. To Leonard Harry Stace, Heston [CofR 7295 25.8.36]. To Mildred Mary Bruce (The Hon. Mrs. Victor Bruce) t/a Air Dispatch Ltd., Croydon 19.4.39. Impressed as **AW163** 30.6.40. Delivered to 110(AAC) Wing 7.40. Transferred to 7AACU 23.8.40. When attempting to overshoot at Castle Bromwich 18.11.40, the pilot turned to avoid a parked aircraft and collided with a wire fence. Conveyed to de Havilland as Cat.B 19.1.41 but SOC as Cat.E1 4.2.41.

6029 Export CofA issued 13.6.33. To West Australian Airways Ltd., Perth WA reg'd **VH-URE** [CofR 465 29.8.33] and CofA no.423 issued same day. Hit fence on take-off Geraldton WA and badly damaged 25.4.36 but repaired at Maylands. Taken over by Adelaide Airways Ltd. 1.7.36. Merged to form Australian National Airways Pty. Ltd., Essendon VIC 1.11.36. Named *Yannana*. To Airlines of Australia Ltd., Sydney NSW 26.2.38. Forced landed on beach at Cardwell 10 miles north of Cardwell QLD 13.6.38. Crashed at Mt. Sunrise Station 27.4.39 and the pilot and two passengers were injured. Repaired and to Australian Aerial Medical Services (N.S.W. Section) 5.2.40. Name changed to Flying Doctor Service of Australia (N.S.W. Section) 23.7.42. Re-reg'd in the Flying Doctor batch as **VH-FDB** and named *L. M. Pattison*. Based at Broken Hill NSW and remained in service until replaced by a Drover aircraft in late 1955. To Muir Aviation, Darwin NT for agricultural use and re-registered **VH-DMA** 1.11.56. Crashed and damaged beyond repair 4 miles south of Katherine NT 11.12.57 and struck off register 5.58.

6030 Export CofA issued 17.6.33. To de Havilland Aircraft of South Africa Ltd. reg'd **ZS-AEG**. Shipped to South Africa and erected at Baragwanath 7.33. To African Air Transport Ltd. Later modified to Mk II standard. To Rhodesia and Nyasaland Airways as **VP-YBY** 6.38. Impressed into Southern Rhodesia Air Force service as **260**. Written-off and cancelled 1940.

6031 Export CofA issued 21.6.33. To Misr Airwork, Cairo reg'd **SU-ABI** and delivered 26.6.33. Crashed 10 miles west of El Arish 15.3.35.

6032 Reg'd **G-ACIE** and CofA no.3960 issued 27.6.33. To V. A. Schmidt, Zlin, Czechoslovakia and operated on behalf of the Bata Shoe Co. Re-reg'd **OK-ATO** at Stag Lane 4.10.33 but did not fly with these marks until 11.5.34. Restored to register as **G-ACIE** for Airwork Ltd., Shoreham [CofR 8527 28.5.38]. To Misr Airwork from 11.9.38 and finally reg'd locally as **SU-ABZ** 3.39. Scrapped at Almaza 12.46.

6033 CofA no.3968 issued 30.6.33. To E. C. Gordon England, Hanworth reg'd **G-ACGK**. Gordon England was a test pilot, aircraft designer and successful racing driver, before setting up a coachbuilding business mainly on Austin car chassis in 1922. To Highland Airways Ltd., Inverness [CofR 5227 11.7.34]. Named *Loch Ness*.

Shortly after take off from Longman Aerodrome, Inverness for Orkney 8.1.35 and while at a height of less than 100', the aircraft began to lose height in a right hand turn and made a forced landing in the Moray Firth. It came to rest on an even keel in shallow water just 20 yards from the shore with the wheels on the sea bed. The pilot and his two passengers were picked up by a fishing boat some half hour later and though cold and wet, were none the worse for their spectacular arrival! The aircraft was later salvaged but deemed beyond economical repair due to the effects of sea water. The subsequent inquiry blamed severe icing to the wings and carburetters.

6034 To Blackpool and West Coast Air Services Ltd., Squires Gate reg'd **G-ACGU**. [CofR 4368 1.6.33]. CofA issued 28.6.33. To British American Air Services Ltd., Heston Stalled shortly after take off from Heston 16.7.35, crashed just outside the airfield boundary and destroyed by fire. The aircraft was operating a charter to view the fleet assembled at Spithead for the Royal Review and 2 of the 8 occupants were fatally injured. Cancelled from register 12.35.

6035 CofA no.3972 issued 4.7.33. To Anglo-Persian Oil Co. Ltd., Abadan reg'd **G-ACHV**. Returned to U.K. 1935 and to Railway Air Services Ltd., Croydon 8.35. To de Havilland Aircraft Co. 19.8.36 and intended for the Spanish Air Force but the sale was prohibited. To Air Taxis Ltd., Croydon [CofR 8944 10.12.38]. Impressed as **X9379** 30.3.40 and delivered to 6AACU on the following day. Transferred to 7AACU 3.5.40. To de Havilland for major inspection 29.5.40 and SOC as Cat.E1 7.8.40.

6036 CofA no.3975 issued 11.7.33. To R. V. Wrightson trading as Wrightson & Pearce Ltd., Heston reg'd **G-ACHX**. Nominal change to Wrightways Ltd., Croydon [CofR 6034 3.7.35]. Whilst preparing to land at Croydon after carrying out a flight in connection with Anti Aircraft Defence, the aircraft made a missed approach but failed to overshoot due to loss of power and stalled in a right hand turn 25.4.38. Crashed at Woodcote Lane, Purley and aircraft destroyed. Cancelled from register 25.4.38 (1938 census).

6037 Export CofA issued 3.7.33. To de Havilland Aircraft Pty Ltd. reg'd **VH-URD** [CofR 466 29.8.33] and CofA no.424 issued same day. Delivered to Tasmanian Aerial Services Pty. Ltd., Launceston. Became Holyman's Airways Pty. Ltd. 1.10.34. Named *Miss Launceston*. Merged to form Australian National Airways Pty. Ltd. 2.11.36 and re-named *Yoorana*. Impressed as **A34-7** 26.8.40 and struck off civil register 30.8.40. Completion of modifications delayed due to non-receipt of wireless, but to 1AOS 14.12.40. Issued to 2AOS 26.4.41. Damaged port lower mainplane during forced landing 14.10.41. Converted to air ambulance by Australian National, Melbourne-Essendon VIC 23.3.42. Issued to 33Sqdn. 19.4.42. To 1WAGS "only to be used for conversion of pilots to DH84 type". Disposed of to Department of Civil Aviation 5.10.44. Restored as **VH-URD** with Aircraft Pty. Ltd. 16.3.45. To the Catholic Mission of the Holy Ghost, Alexishafen PNG 8.48. To QANTAS Empire Airways Ltd. 3.5.50. Badly damaged on landing near Manyamya NSW 24.12.51 and struck off register 2.5.52.

6038 To William Nathan McEwen, Stag Lane reg'd **G-ACIW** [CofR 4420 28.7.33]. CofA no.3993 issued 29.7.33. Sold abroad 2.7.34. To J. Germain, Mouzaiaville, Algeria and reg'd **F-ANGE** 18.9.34. The fate is not recorded and one wonders whether this was yet another Dragon that ended its days on the Iberian Peninsula at the time of the Spanish Civil War.

6039 CofA issued 29.7.33. To Highland Airways Ltd., Inverness reg'd **G-ACIT** and named *Aberdeen*. Inaugurated Aberdeen to Orkney scheduled services 7.5.34. Became Scottish Airways Ltd. 16.6.38 and re-named *Orcadian*. To Associated Airways Joint Committee 6.40. To British European Airways Corporation, Inverness on formation 1.2.47. Transferred to Speedbird Flying Clubs Ltd. 10.3.49 and in service with Airways Aero Associations Ltd. 1.4.49. To Air Navigation & Trading Co. Ltd., Blackpool-Squires Gate 10.11.51. To British Executive & General Aviation Ltd. t/a Beagle Aircraft Ltd., Rearsby 30.1.62. To J. Beaty, Sywell 3.9.69. Purchased by the Southend Historic Aircraft Museum 6.71 and delivered to them 19.9.71. CofA expired 25.5.74 and cancelled as withdrawn from use 19.8.81. On closure of the Southend museum, ownership changed to The Science Museum, South Kensington, London SW7 26.5.83 and it was moved to the Science Museum's Air Transport Collection and Storage Facility at Wroughton, Wiltshire 8.83. Cancelled as permanently withdrawn from use 26.4.02 but continues on display at Wroughton, wearing Highland Airways livery.

6040 To Sydney Thomas Weedon, Stag Lane (presumed an aircraft dealer) reg'd **G-ACJH** [CofR 4431 9.8.33]. CofA issued 23.8.33. Sold abroad 11.33. To A. Garric, Leyrac reg'd **F-AMTM** 4.12.33. Cancelled as destroyed 11.38 with a total time of 1177 hours.

6041 CofA no.3995 issued 5.8.33. To the shipping magnate Viscount Furness reg'd **G-ACIU** [25.7.33]. To Maddox Airways Ltd., Brooklands 4.35. To Surrey Flying Services Ltd., Croydon [CofR 6022 29.6.35] and named *Blue Mist*. Impressed as **X9395** 4.4.40 but military serial not used. Operated by 24Sqdn. based at Reims/Champagne. Damaged on take off Mourmelon 29.4.40 and intentionally burnt there 28.5.40 before the airfield was abandoned.

6042 CofA no.3996 issued 4.8.33. To Midland and Scottish Air Ferries Ltd., Renfrew reg'd **G-ACJS**. Fitted out with executive accoutrements such as toilet and radio and mainly for the personal use of John Cuthill Sword, founding owner of Midland & Scottish Air Ferries. Interestingly, this is one of the first uses of a contrived British aircraft registration. To Northern and Scottish Airways Ltd., Renfrew [CofR 5529 8.1.35]. Reg'n cancelled 11.36 and presumed to have ended its days in Spain.

6043 CofA no.4011 issued 26.8.33. To Norman Edgar trading as Western Airways Ltd., Whitchurch reg'd **G-ACJT**. Nominal change shortly after delivery to Norman Edgar (Western Airways) Ltd. Purchased to replace a DH80 Puss Moth on the Bristol (Whitchurch) to Cardiff (Splott) scheduled service. To Sir Derwent Hall Caine, Ronaldsway (Caine was a publisher and Labour M.P.for the Everton Division of Liverpool 1929-1931) 9.33. Reverted to Western Airways Ltd. [CofR 5876 16.5.35]. Stalled in a turn and crashed shortly after take off from Weston-Super-Mare on a ferry flight 20.12.39. The aircraft was destroyed and the pilot, the sole occupant, was killed.

6044 Export CofA no.4019 issued 5.9.33. To Airwork Ltd., Heston and to Iraq as **YI-AAC**. Reg'd **G-ACLE** on return U.K. To Crilly Airways Ltd., Braunstone 9.35. To North Eastern Airways Ltd. 2.37. To Allied Airways (Gandar Dower) Ltd., Aberdeen [CofR 8258 7.12.37]. Named *Old Bill*. Crashed at St. Margaret's Hope strip at Berriedale during 1939 and returned to Aberdeen for repairs. To Western Airways Ltd., Weston-super-Mare 18.5.39. Impressed as X9397 2.4.40. Delivered to 6AACU. Transferred to 7AACU and based on detachment at Odiham, Hampshire 5.5.40. Struck on the ground by a runaway fuel bowser and badly damaged 8.4.41. Transported to Witney for inspection by de Havilland and was SOC 12.5.41.

6045 Export CofA issued 3.10.33. Arrived Perth per *SS Largs Bay* 14.11.33. To Western Mining Corporation Ltd., Perth WA and operated by MacRobertson-Miller Aviation Co. Ltd. Reg'd **VH-URF** [CofR 471 15.12.33] and CofA no.430 issued same day. Named *Gay Prospector*, later *Golden Prospector*. Aircraft used for aerial survey and fitted with Williamson Eagle 4 cameras. To MacRobertson-Miller Aviation Co. Ltd. Perth WA 27.11.34. Named *The Kimberley*. Officially impressed as **A34-9** 5.5.41 and arrived on that date Australian National at Essendon VIC for air observer conversion. Issued to 2AOS 12.8.41. To Australian National Melbourne-Essendon for conversion to air ambulance 18.1.42. To 34Sqdn., Darwin NT 17.2.42. Destroyed on the ground Wyndham WA during a Japanese air raid 3.3.42 and declared a write-off 16.4.42.

6046 Export CofA issued 3.10.33. Arrived Perth per *SS Largs Bay* 14.11.33. To Western Mining Corporation Ltd., Perth WA and operated by MacRobertson-Miller Aviation. Reg'd **VH-URG** [CofR 470 9.12.33] and named *Golden West*, this aircraft was similarly used for aerial survey and fitted with the same Williamson Eagle 4 cameras. To Holyman's Airways Pty. Ltd., Launceston TAS 14.12.34. Merged to form Australian National Airways Pty. Ltd. 2.11.36 and named *Yuptana*. "Accident" at Skipton VIC due engine failure 18.2.37. "Accident" at Cowell SA, again due to engine failure 5.5.37. To Airlines of Australia Ltd., Sydney NSW 9.6.39. Badly damaged at Inverleigh Station 21.2.40 but repaired. Damaged at Cairns QLD when collided with a truck on landing 26.9.40. Repaired but suffered yet another accident at Bald Hill Station 17.2.41 due to a fuel blockage. Finally, crashed and destroyed by fire Wenlock QLD 4.2.42. Struck off register 18.2.42.

6047 Export CofA issued 1.9.33. To Wilson Airways Ltd., Nairobi reg'd **VP-KAW**. Crashed at Mombasa 8.12.33.

6048   Export CofA issued 20.10.33. To Indian National Airlines Ltd. reg'd **VT-AEL** and delivered ex Heston 2.11.33. Crashed while undertaking a mail flight 26.8.39 and the two crew aboard were killed.

6049   Engines and special fuel tanks incorporated during construction from the ill-fated G-ACCV (c/n 6014). CofA no.4018 issued 6.9.33. To Mrs. J. A. Mollison C.B.E. (Amy Johnson) reg'd **G-ACJM** and named *Seafarer II*. Shipped to Canada per *SS Duchess of York* to attempt first non-stop crossing of the Atlantic from Canada to England. However, the aircraft failed to become airborne from Wasaga Beach on departure for the attempt and was slightly damaged. Returned to de Havilland at Stag Lane for repairs. To Capt. J. R. Ayling and Leonard Gillespie Reid, Hatfield [CofR 5072 15.5.34]. Named *Trail of the Caribou*. Shipped back to Canada and departed Wasaga Beach 8.8.34 to again attempt the distance record. Forced to land en route due to severe icing over the Atlantic. Eventually reached Heston, only to be damaged beyond repair in a heavy landing at Hamble 12.8.34.

6050   Export CofA issued 21.10.33. To Indian National Airlines Ltd. reg'd **VT-AEK** and delivered ex Heston 2.11.33. Cancelled from register 26.5.37, reason unknown.

6051   Export CofA issued 21.10.33. To Misr Airwork, Cairo reg'd **SU-ABJ**. Burnt out at Almaza 22.6.38.

6052   CofA no.4026 issued 15.9.33. Reg'd **G-ACKD** to the Honorable Brian Edmund Lewis, eldest son of Sir Frederick William Lewis, Bt., chairman of shipping company Furness, Withy & Co. Ltd. To Provincial Airways Ltd., Croydon 7.34. To League of Nations Union, Croydon [CofR 6598 14.12.35]. Converted by Airwork Ltd. at Croydon to an ambulance aircraft. Presented to the Ethiopian Red Cross and departed Croydon 12.35 and arrived Addid Ababa 21.1.36. Failed to become completely airborne on take off Akaki Airport, Addid Ababa 24.2.36 and struck eucalyptus trees, crashed and destroyed by fire. The two crew, Capt. Haytrer and Haile Giorghis were injured.

6053   Modified on the production line 9.33 and became the prototype Dragon Mk II. Reg'd to de Havilland Aircraft Co. Ltd. as **G-ACMC** and CofA no.4096 issued 24.11.33. To Jersey Airways Ltd. and named *St. Brelade's Bay*. Was in service with Northern & Scottish Airways Ltd. 8.35, presumably on lease. To Airwork Ltd., Heston [CofR 6666 23.1.36]. Sold abroad 8.36 and reg'd to North Queensland Airlines Pty. Ltd., Cairns QLD as **VH-UXK** [CofR 607 1.10.36] and CofA no.574 issued same day. Named *Cairns*. Operated first Cairns to Brisbane service 8.4.37. Stalled on approach to Innisfail and crashed at Mundoo QLD 29.8.38. The pilot and 4 passengers were killed and the other 4 passengers injured. Wreck transported to Airlines of Australia Ltd., Sydney 20.2.39 and struck off register 15.11.39.

6054   Export CofA issued 19.10.33. Reg'd **ZS-AEH**, shipped to South Africa for African Air Transport and erected at Baragwanath. To Stewart & Lloyds of South Africa Ltd. .33. To Aircraft Operating Company .38. Impressed 1940 as **SAAF1414**. Cancelled from register 27.4.47, reason unknown.

6055   CofA no.4074 issued 6.11.33. To Iraq Petroleum Transport Co. Ltd. reg'd **G-ACKB**. Returned to de Havilland and intended for onward sale to the Spanish Air Force, but prohibited. Instead, to Commercial Air Hire Ltd., Croydon [CofR 7321 3.9.36]. Impressed as **AX863** 7.7.40 and delivered to Ringway. To 6AACU 13.7.40. Flown to de Havilland for major inspection but SOC and scrapped for spares 1.2.41 having total time 3545 hours.

6056   CofA no.4082 issued 9.11.33. To Iraq Petroleum Transport Co. Ltd. reg'd **G-ACKC**. Returned to U.K. and to Commercial Air Hire Ltd., Croydon [CofR 6950 27.4.36]. Acquired by Union Founders Trust Ltd. together with others for operation by the Spanish Republican forces. Cancelled as sold abroad 9.36 and departed Croydon for Barcelona 15.8.36. Transferred to the new flying ground at Sarinena near Zaragoza 18.8.36 and incorporated into a squadron of mixed types known as Alas Rojas (Red Wings). Fate not recorded.

6057   Export CofA issued 6.11.33. To G. Descampes (a dealer?) reg'd **F-AMTR**. To R. Germain, Algeria 26.1.34. To H. Germain, Algeria 9.35. To ETAT Francais 10.37. Cancelled from the register 2.38 as destroyed.

6058   CofA no.4105 issued 7.12.33. Departed Stag Lane via Portsmouth on delivery to W. L. Thurgood trading as Jersey Airways Ltd. 15.12.33. Reg'd **G-ACMJ** and named *St. Aubin's Bay*. In service with United Airways Ltd., Stanley Park 1935. To Airwork Ltd., Heston 1.36. To Western Airways Ltd., Weston-super-Mare [CofR 8601 1.7.38]. Impressed as **X9396** 2.4.40 and delivered to 24Sqdn. on the following day. Transferred to 1CU at Hendon 26.7.41. To de Havilland for major inspection 3.11.41 and SOC as Cat.E1 12.11.41.

6059   Export CofA issued 21.12.33. To Wilson Airways Ltd., Nairobi as **VP-KBA**. Impressed to Kenya Auxiliary Air Unit as **K-15**. Fate not recorded.

6060   Export CofA issued 12.2.34. Delivered to Haerens Hyrestrapper (Danish Army Air Force) as **S-21** 27.2.34. In use for observer training and as staff transport. Crashed near Ringsted, Zealand 24.2.36; three persons killed.

6061   Export CofA issued 12.2.34. Delivered to Haerens Hyrestrapper (Danish Army Air Force) as **S-22** 24.3.34. In use for observer training and as staff transport. Crashed on take off following engine failure Vaerlose Air Force Base 9.8.39. No injuries to the crew and five passengers.

6062   CofA no.4164 issued 31.1.34. To Jersey Airways Ltd. reg'd **G-ACMO** and named *St. Ouen's Bay*. To Northern & Scottish Airways Ltd., Renfrew [CofR 6043 4.7.35]. Became Scottish Airways Ltd. 1937. Sold to Australia 3.38. Reg'd **VH-ABK** [CofR 722 27.10.38] and CofA no.679 issued same day for South Queensland Airways Pty. Ltd. 4.7.40. Named *City of Toowoomba*. Impressed as **A34-4** 4.7.40 and issued to 3EFTS. To Australian National for modifications 13.10.40. To 1AD 20.10.40. To 1AOS 9.12.40. Forced landed after engine cut out 4.2.41 but no damage. To 2AOS 19.2.41. To Australian National 16.2.42 for conversion to air ambulance. To 35Sqdn. 30.4.42. Mainplane spars damaged as the result of a heavy landing 25.6.42 and as repair was beyond the capacity of the unit, remained grounded until issued to MacRobertson-Miller Airlines 8.10.42. On completion of repairs, restored as **VH-ABK** by 21.5.43 and loaned to MacRobertson-Miller. Again as **A34-4** 31.8.43 and returned to 35Sqdn. 2.9.43. Issued to No.7 Conversion Unit 10.11.43. Although details are not recorded, presumably a further accident meant another visit to MacRobertson-Miller where the aircraft was "for inspection" 27.3.44. Obviously deemed beyond economical repair and given "Approval for Conversion" 12.9.44.

6063   To Jersey Airways Ltd. reg'd **G-ACMP** [CofR 4842 31.1.34]. CofA issued 20.2.34. Named *St. Clements Bay*. Leased to Western Airways Ltd., Weston-super-Mare 1935 and while inbound to Cardiff on a flight from Whitchurch, the aircraft stalled and crashed on to mud flats at Rumney, near Splott 23.7.35, about a mile short of Cardiff Airport. Three persons killed. Finally cancelled from register 30.12.37.

6064   Export CofA issued 22.2.34. To G. Descampes (probable dealer) as **F-ANUZ**. To H. Germain, Algiers 5.3.34. To ETAT Francais 10.37. Cancelled as destroyed 7.38 but more than likely ended up with one of the factions in Spain.

6065   Export CofA issued 17.3.34. To Indian National Airways Ltd. reg'd **VT-AES** and named *Sapphire*. To QANTAS Empire Airways reg'd **VH-UZF** [CofR 773 19.7.40] and CofA no.728 issued same day. Intended for their Brisbane to Mt. Isa route nut noted as a "spare aircraft" 6.7.40. Impressed as **A34-8** 16.8.40. Issued to 1AOS 3.2.41 after long delay awaiting radio installation. To 2AOS 24.2.41. Collided with a truck 17.4.41 causing major damage to port lower mainplane and spar but quickly back in service with 2AOS. Converted to air ambulance by Australian National at Melbourne-Essendon VIC 16.2.42. Issued to 33Sqdn. 30.3.42. Forced landed due engine failure 8.6.42 and suffered major damage to both lower mainplanes, undercarriage and fuselage. To de Havilland, Sydney 3.7.42 where it was declared beyond economical repair and reduced to produce.

6066   CofA no.4094 issued 24.11.33. To William Lindsay Everard reg'd **G-ACKU**, Unionist MP for Melton 1924-45, Chairman of Everards Brewery Ltd. & director of the vinegar maker John Sarson & Son Ltd. and Alliance Assurance Ltd. Based at Everard's private strip at Ratcliffe Hall, Leicestershire. Won the Oases Circuit Race in Egypt 12.33, flown by W. D. MacPherson. To Wrightways Ltd., Croydon 2.34. Departed Croydon on delivery to the Spanish Air Force 17.8.36, but returned with engine problems and impounded on arrival. To Anglo-European Airways Ltd., Croydon [CofR 8465 22.4.38]. Evacuated to Cardiff. To Commercial Air Hire Ltd., Cardiff 18.1.40. Impressed as **AW172** 7.7.40 and delivered to 110AAC Wing the same day. Transferred to 7AACU 15.11.40. Whilst on army co-operation duties over Shrivenham, Wiltshire 10.2.41, the port engine failed and the pilot could not maintain height. Crashed at Hanney Fields near Wantage, Berkshire and badly damaged. Conveyed by road to de Havilland for inspection. SOC as Cat.E 26.2.41.

6067 To Olley Air Service Ltd., Croydon reg'd **G-ACNA**. [CofR 4755 25.1.34]. CofA issued 28.2.34. Acquired by Union Founders Trust and cancelled as sold abroad 2.9.36 but had already departed Croydon 15.8.36 en route Barcelona for delivery to the Spanish Republican forces. Fate not recorded.

6068 Export CofA issued 10.3.34. Arrived Fremantle WA per *SS Moreton Bay* 17.4.34. To West Australian Airways Ltd., Perth WA and reg'd **VH-URO** [CofR 478 27.7.34] and CofA no.436 issued same day. Ran out of fuel and forced to land 8 miles west of Forrest WA 22.5.34. Another incident is recorded at Zanthus WA 4.12.34 due to a vapor lock in the starboard engine. To W. R. Carpenter & Co. Ltd., Sydney NSW 28.12.34. Transferred to their Mandated Airlines, Salamaua PNG 26.1.35. Crashed and destroyed at Black Cat Creek, near Wau PNG 30.9.35. The pilot was killed and struck off register 1.10.35.

6069 CofA no.4223 issued 23.3.34. To Jersey Airways Ltd., reg'd **G-ACNG** and named *Portelet Bay*. To Spartan Airlines Ltd., Cowes, Isle of Wight 6.35. Officially to British Airways, Abridge 3.36 but had been delivered to them 1.10.35!. To Northern & Scottish Airways Ltd., Renfrew 17.2.37. To Scottish Airways Ltd., Renfrew [CofR 8552 14.6.38]. Crashed and destroyed Hatston, Kirkwall when caught in a downdraught 19.4.40. Cancelled from register 7.5.40.

6070 CofA no.4231 issued 26.3.34. To Jersey Airways Ltd., reg'd **G-ACNH** and named *Bouley Bay*. To Northern and Scottish Airways Ltd., Renfrew [CofR 6042 4.7.35]. Registration cancelled 1.37 and assumed to have departed for operation in Spain.

6071 First flown at Stag Lane 22.3.34 and CofA issued 28.3.34. To Jersey Airways Ltd., reg'd **G-ACNI** and named *Bonne Nuit Bay*. Believed used by Railway Air Services for a time on lease. To British Airways Ltd., Eastleigh 2.36. To Airwork Ltd., Heston [CofR 7571 31.12.36]. Modifiied by Airwork to Eire's military use specification; fitted with wireless, bomb racks, a camera and accommodation for a towed target. To Irish Army Air Corps as **DH18**. Crashed at Baldonnel 16.12.41.

6072 CofA issued 28.3.34. To Jersey Airways Ltd. and reg'd **G-ACNJ**. Named *Rozel Bay*. To Allied Airways (Gandar Dower) Ltd., Dyce [CofR 8252 6.12.37] and named *Sir Rowland Hill* – founder of The Post Office. Withdrawn from use at Dyce after CofA expiry 28.5.43 and stored. To Air Taxis Ltd., Croydon 29.6.45 but "unlikely to be reconditioned for CofA renewal" according to *The Aeroplane Spotter* 7.46 and dismantled for spares at Dyce prior to 11.46.

6073 Reg'd **G-ACOR** to G. Mackinnon, Hatfield and named *Fiona*. CofA no.4292 issued 19.5.34. To British Continental Airways Ltd., Croydon 10.35 and named *St. Christopher*. Officially to British Airways Ltd., Gatwick 3.37 but already delivered to them 1.8.36. To Northern & Scottish Airways Ltd., Renfrew 8.3.37. Sold abroad 2.38. Reg'd **VH-AEA** [CofR 707 23.6.38] and CofA no.664 issued same day for Kevin A. Parer t/a Wewak Air Transport, Wewak PNG. Damaged in PNG 11.38 but repaired. Caught on ground prior to take off at Salamaua PNG by Japanese fighters 21.1.42 and the pilot was killed. Struck off register 11.3.42.

6074 Export CofA issued 29.5.34. To W. R. Carpenter & Co. Ltd., Sydney NSW reg'd **VH-USA** [CofR 481 27.7.34] and CofA no.439 issued same day. Named *Grace*. Transferred to Carpenter's company Mandated Airlines Ltd. and arrived Salamaua PNG 3.8.34. Rebuilt late 1941 using component from VH-UVB (c/n 6102). Caught on ground by Japanese fighters at Salamaua and destroyed 21.1.42. Struck off register 11.3.42.

6075 CofA no.4272 issued 26.4.34. To Railway Air Services Ltd., Croydon reg'd **G-ACPX**. To Air Taxis Ltd., Croydon 1.35. To Brian Allen Aviation Ltd., Croydon 7.35. Acquired by Western Airways Ltd.,

Weston-super-Mare [CofR 8652 23.7.38] to replace the ill-fated G-ACMP. Impressed as **X9399** 2.4.40 and delivered to 6AACU 4.4.40. Fate unknown.

6076 CofA no.4286 issued 10.5.34. To Olley Air Service Ltd., Croydon reg'd **G-ACPY**. In service with Railway Air Services 7.34. To Blackpool and West Coast Air Services Ltd., Squires Gate 2.35. To Aer Lingus Teoranta, Baldonnel reg'd **EI-ABI(1)** and named *Iolar* 26.5.36. This was the first aircraft to be owned and operated by the newly formed Irish National carrier and the Dragon, titled Irish Sea Airways, commenced Dublin to Bristol servces in July 1936 . Restored to Olley Air Service Ltd., Croydon as **G-ACPY** [CofR 8371 1.3.38]. Later to A.A.J.C. and whilst operating a Great Western and Southern Airlines Ltd. service from Scilly to Land's End, believed shot down by a Luftwaffe Junkers Ju.88 fighter off the Scilly Isles 3.6.41. Cancelled from register 11.6.41. (Also see EI-ABI(2) c/n 6105).

6077 To Portsmouth, Southsea and Isle of Wight Aviation Ltd. reg'd **G-ACRF** [CofR 4989 30.4.34]. CofA no.4291 issued 18.5.34. Sold abroad 2.36. To Aircrafts Pty. Ltd., Brisbane QLD and reg'd **VH-UXG** [CofR 582 27.4.36] with CofA no.539 issued same day. Named *Riama*. To Queensland Flying Services, Brisbane QLD 30.11.48. To S. J. Porter, Tingalpa QLD 24.1.53. Crashed and damaged by fire Archerfield QLD 19.4.54 and struck off register the same month. Restored to the register as **VH-UXG** 1.1.70. To Desmond Robert Porter, Wynnum QLD 2.12.99 and was undergoing restoration with Greg Challinor of Mothcair at Murwillumbah NSW 9.02.

6078 CofA no.4349 issued 16.6.34. to Aberdeen Airways Ltd., Dyce reg'd **G-ACRH** [CofR 4995 16.6.34] and named *Aberdonian*. Positioning to Hatfield with guests to view the King's Cup Air Race, the aircraft swung on take off Dyce 13.7.34 and struck a heap of earth and stones on the north side of the airfield and was destroyed by fire. The subsequent inquiry noted that the pilot had little experience on type.

6079 CofA no.4281 issued 3.5.34. Initially reg'd to de Havilland Aircraft Co. Ltd., Hatfield as **G-ACRO**.[CofR 5007 3.5.34]. To Wilson Airways Ltd., Nairobi as **VP-KBG** 10.34. Written-off in forced landing shortly after take-off from Wilson Aerodrome 14.4.37.

6080 Export CofA issued 4.7.34. Delivered to MacRobertson-Miller Aviation Co. Ltd., Perth WA as **VH-URW** [CofR 487 31.8.34] and CofA no.442 issued same day. Named *The Pilbara*. Overturned on landing Wyndham WA 8.3.35 and transported to Maylands for repair. To W. R. Carpenter & Co. Ltd., Sydney NSW 22.3.39 and transferred to their company Mandated Airlines Ltd., Salamaua PNG. Crashed into Little Wau Creek PNG near Wewak 30.1.40. The pilot R. E. Doyle and two native passengers were killed. Remains purchased by Kevin Parer of Parer Air Transport Co. Wewak 24.6.40 as spares for his VH-AEA (c/n 6073).

6081 Export CofA issued 13.7.34. Shipped to Australia and delivered to MacRobertson-Miller Aviation Co. Ltd., Perth WA reg'd **VH-URX** [CofR 488 11.9.34] and CofA no.444 issued same day. Named *Gascoyne*. Damaged on the ground Ord River WA by a cyclone 23.10.34 but repaired. Impressed 27.12.39 and allocated serial **A34-1** 3.1.40. Issued to No.1 Advanced Training School 26.1.40. Issued to Signals School, Point Cook VIC 14.7.40. To Butler Air Transport, Sydney-Mascot for modifications 9.8.40. To 4EFTS 7.11.40 but to 3EFTS same day. Temporarily used by Civil Aviation Department 30.11.40 to 18.12.40. To 2AOS 26.2.41. Forced landed 26.6.41 but no damage. To Australian National for conversion to air ambulance 9.2.42. Issued to 35Sqdn. 20.3.42. Slightly damaged when aircraft swung off runway and struck an obstruction 20.5.42. Nine days later, the starboard engine failed due to water in the fuel system, but a "normal" landing was possible and no damage suffered. However, on 14.6.42, the starboard engine failed necessitating ditching in the sea 18 miles from Dongara WA. The aircraft turned over on impact in 4ft water depth and was extensively damaged. Officially written-off 21.6.42 and approved for conversion to components two days later.

6082 CofA issued 13.7.34. Shipped to Australia for MacRobertson-Miller Aviation Co. Ltd. reg'd **VH-URY** [CofR 489 11.9.34] and CofA no.445 issued same day. Named *Murchison*. Crashed and damaged Hall's Creek WA 7.11.34. Damaged whet fit fence Port Hedland WA 5.4.35. Forced to land due fuel exhaustion at unknown location 21.11.36. Sold to Airlines (Western Australia) Ltd., Perth WA 13.8.38. Impressed 15.9.40 and allocated serial

DH84 c/n 6076. G-ACPY was operated by Great Western & Southern Airlines Ltd. during the war years, but was lost on 3rd June 1941; believed shot down by a Luftwaffe Junkers Ju.88 aircraft.

DH84 c/n 6096. One of ten Dragons owned by Railway Air Services and remained civilian registered as G-ADDI throughout the war, although in service for a time with 24 Squadron at Hendon.

DH84 c/n 6079. Delivered new from the factory to Wilson Airways of Nairobi, VP-KBG suffered this accident on 14th April 1937 and as no further information is available, believed written-off as a result.

DH84 c/n 6096. Many readers will have enjoyed their first Dragon flight when in this guise! Now as N34DH, seen here November 1970 prior to flying to Rotterdam, dismantling and shipping to California.

DH84 c/n 6086. The float equipped CF-AVD was with Canadian Pacific from February 1942. Stalled shortly after taking off from Comeau Bay, Quebec and was destroyed on impact with the water.

DH84 c/n 6105. G-AECZ, seen shortly after demobilisation with Air Taxis Ltd. of Croydon. Sold on to the Wiltshire School of Flying at Thruxton in April 1948, who in turn sold it to Ireland February 1950.

DH84 c/n 6090. ZK-ADR was the second Union Airways Dragon to be impressed by the Royal New Zealand Air Force and as NZ551, was deemed beyond repair after a forced landing February 1940.

DH84 c/n 6105. Here with the original registration EI-AFK, this Dragon now flies officially marked EI-ABI to represent the first aeroplane operated by Aer Lingus. (Also see c/n 6076)

A34-6 15.9.40. At Guinea Airways for modifications but as work badly delayed, to Australian National for the work to be carried out 12.5.41. Issued 2AOS 5.7.41. Forced landed 31.7.41 but suffered no damage. Still at 2AOS, major repairs were reported 12.10.41 and again 7.12.41. Issued to Civil Aviation Department 24.5.43 and passed to QANTAS Empire Airways Ltd. for use of Flying Doctor Service, Cloncurry QLD. Named *John Flynn*. Sold to Trans Australian Airlines, Melbourne VIC 22.7.49. Crashed Cheviot Hills QLD 20.10.53 and struck off register 23.10.53.

6083   CofA issued 21.6.34. To Roger Levy reg'd **F-ANES**. Actual fate unknown but probably passed to Spain for use during the Spanish Civil War.

6084   Reg'd to de Havilland Aircraft Co. Ltd. as **G-ACVD** 29.6.34 and CofA no.4048 issued 24.7.34. Hired to Railway Air Services Ltd., Croydon until 10.34. Eventually sold to Railway Air Services [CofR 7285 19.8.36] and named *Star of Cheshire*. Returned to de Havilland 1937 and sold to Australia for Air Transport & Survey Pty. Ltd. Reg'n **VH-UZX** allotted 27.9.37. Crashed, still marked as **G-ACVD** at Beddington, Surrey 26.2.38 prior to delivery.

6085   CofA issued 30.7.34. To Viacao Aerea Sao Paulo SA (VASP) as **PP-SPC**. Fate unknown.

6086   CofA issued 24.1.34. To de Havilland Canada Ltd., as **CF-AVD**. To Quebec Airways Ltd. Subsequently fitted with floats and extended dorsal fin 2.35. To Canadian Airways 8.35. Absorbed by Canadian Pacific Airways 2.42. Stalled on take-off Baie Comeau, Que and damaged beyond repair 26.5.44.

6087   CofA no.4465 issued 28.8.34. Intended for Railway Air Services Ltd., Croydon but to de Havilland Aircraft Co. Ltd. reg'd as **G-ACXI** [CofR 5401 20.10.34]. Sold abroad 12.35 and delivered ex Hatfield to the Ministry of National Defence, Ankara, Turkey. Fate unknown.

6088   CofA issued 18.8.34 and shipped to Australia. Reg'd to de Havilland Aircraft Pty Ltd. as **VH-URU** [CofR 495 8.11.34] and CofA no.452 issued same day. To Butler Air Transport Co. Ltd., Perth WA and named *Charleville*. Impressed 11.1.40 and allocated serial **A34-2**. Issued to No.1 Advanced Training School 26.1.40. Although tied down, a wing tip hit the ground during a storm 30.3.40; repaired. Aircraft flew into the ground near Cootamundra NSW and was totally destroyed by fire 11.11.40. Pilot Officer Hearne and four crew were killed and one was critically injured.

6089   CofA issued 5.9.34 and shipped to Australia. Reg'd to de Havilland Aircraft Pty Ltd. as **VH-URV** [CofR 496 9.11.34] and CofA no.453 issued same day. To Butler Air Transport Co. Ltd., Perth WA 21.12.34 and named *Cootamundra*. At Butler Air Transport Pty. Ltd., Mascot NSW 30.6.46. To QANTAS Empire Airways Ltd. 1946. Crashed and destroyed by fire Yaramunda PNG 13.12.51 and struck off register the same month.

6090   CofA issued 22.1.35 and shipped to New Zealand. Assembled at Hobsonville and made its first flight in New Zealand 25.3.35. To East Coast Airways reg'd **ZK-ADR** and named *Muia*. Re-reg'd **ZK-AER** 30.12.37. Transferred to Union Airways 1.7.38. Impressed by the Royal New Zealand Air Force 25.10.39, allocated serial **NZ551** and used by Electrical & Wireless Flight at Wigram from early 1940. Damaged undercarriage and propellers after a forced landing 21.2.40.

6091   CofA issued 23.1.35 and shipped to New Zealand. Assembled at Hobsonville and made its first flight in New Zealand 29.3.35. To East Coast Airways reg'd **ZK-ADS** and named *Tui*. Transferred to Union Airways 1.7.38. Impressed by the Royal New Zealand Air Force 13.10.39 and allocated serial **NZ550**. Fate unknown.

6092   CofA no.4723 issued 30.3.35. To Blackpool and West Coast Air Services Ltd., Blackpool reg'd **G-ADCP**. To Isle of Man Air Services Ltd., Derbyhaven [CofR 8153 19.10.37]. Impressed by the R.A.F. as **X9440**. Fate unknown.

6093   Export CofA issued 2.11.34 and delivered to Consolidated Mining & Smelting Ltd. reg'd **CF-AVI**. To North Shore Airways Ltd., Toronto 12.37. Operated on floats, damaged beyond repair when

swept from its moorings and over a dam at Godbout PQ 13.1.41.

6094   CofA no.4717 issued 6.3.35. To Blackpool and West Coast Air Services Ltd., Squires Gate reg'd **G-ADCR** [CofR 5607 6.3.35]. Whilst attempting to land in poor visibility and low cloud at Lands End, inbound from St Mary's, Scilly Isles 25.6.38, the aircraft lost height and struck the ground during a turn. Totally destroyed and 1 occupant killed. Cancelled from register 1.1.39 (1938 census).

6095   CofA no.4747 issued 26.5.35. To Highland Airways Ltd., Inverness reg'd **G-ADCT** and named *Orcadian*. Crashed into trees Westness, Ronsay, Orkneys due downdraught 6.9.35. Dismantled and transported to Inverness, said by rowing boat! Rebuilt and reflown by 10.11.35. To Scottish Airways Ltd., Inverness [CofR 8557 16.6.38]. Reviewed by the Air Ministry for impressment, under N.A.C. 1.9.39 but crashed on take off Longman Aerodrome, Inverness 14.12.39. Insured value £1500. Cancelled from the register 7.5.40.

6096   CofA no.4836 issued 18.5.35. To Railway Air Services Ltd., Croydon reg'd **G-ADDI** [CofR 5655 18.3.35] and named *City of Cardiff*. Re-named *Island Maid* when the Shoreham to Ryde and Southampton service was inaugurated 7.3.37. To Great Western and Southern Air Lines Ltd., Shoreham 31.1.39 but normally based Land's End. Impressed into R.A.F. service with 24Sqdn. Hendon but no military serial issued 22.9.39. To National Air Communications, later known as the Associated Airways Joint Committee. Via W. S. Shackleton Ltd. to Vickers-Armstrongs Ltd. , Castle Bromwich 15.7.43. Officially restored to the civilian register as **G-ADDI** for Gilbert Anthony Phelps 23.5.46 and was being operated by British European Airways at Inverness 2.47. To Air Charter Ltd. , Croydon 22.8.47. To Air Navigation and Trading Co. Ltd., Blackpool 8.3.51 and used for pleasure flights from Squires Gate. To Aero Enterprises (JHS) Ltd., Charing 26.4.63 and operated by Mrs. Claire M. Roberts t/a Chrisair, Charing, Kent for joy riding throughout the U.K. Sold to Irving Perlitch t/a Perlitch Transportation Museum, Morgan Hill CA. Reg'd **N34DH** and shipped to Los Angeles. To Michael G. Kimbrel, a former Western Air Lines DC10 pilot, and flown from his private airstrip at Oakville near Olympia WA 29.5.81. Last CofA 9.5.84 but believed still in storage at Oakville.

6097   CofA no.4847 issued 1.3.35. Delivered to Railway Air Services Ltd. reg'd **G-ADDJ** [CofR 5656 18.3.35] and named *City of Plymouth*. Sold to Aircrafts Pty Ltd., Brisbane QLD reg'd **VH-UZZ** [CofR no.644 dated 21.6.37] and CofA no.601 issued same day. Named *Riada*. Impressed 11.1.40 and issued to No.1EFTS as **A34-3**. Served with C.F.C. 26.1.40 to 12.8.40. Issued to 1AOS 22.9.40. Collided with two aircraft on the ground, including Anson N4996, at Cootamundra, NSW 20.9.40. Suffered damage to port & starboard lower wing tips, port airscrew & fabric torn underneath the nose. Intended to 3EFTS 27.9.40 for repair by Australian National, but eventually with 4EFTS and thence by road to Butler Air Transport, Perth WA 11.11.40. Repairs completed 10.2.41 and to 1AD 7.3.41 for fitting of Sperry equipment and w/t wiring. Issued to 2AOS 19.4.41. Forced landed due to engine failure 9.1.42. Issued to Australian National for repair and modification to air ambulance 16.2.42. Issued to 34Sqdn. 11.3.42 and intended to 33Sqdn. 3.5.42 but to 1EFTS ex Daly Waters NT 8.5.42. Departed Brisbane-Parafield QLD for Ansett Airways, Melbourne-Essendon VIC 3.6.42. Issued to 36Sqdn. 4.9.42. Crash landed and badly damaged Musgrove Station QLD 13.10.42. Repairs commenced at 12RSU Garbutt QLD 21.12.42 but then to 13ARD for completion 22.7.43. The records dated 11.10.43 then state "beyond economical repair" and eventually "Approved for Conversion" 18.12.43. Remains sold by the Commonwealth Disposals Commission to Airlines (Western Australia) Ltd. 29.6.45, presumably for spares use.

6098   CofA no.4848 issued 13.4.35. To Railway Air Services Ltd., Croydon reg'd **G-ADED** [CofR 5682 13.4.35]. Crashed on take off from Ronaldsway temporary airfield 1.7.35 when failed to become airborne, brushed through hedges on top of the airfield's north boundary wall, sank to the ground and finally crashed in to a fenced wall on far side of a field adjoining the airfield. Totally destroyed in the ensuing fire. Cancelled from register 11.35.

6099   CofA no.4849 issued 15.4.35. To Railway Air Services Ltd., Croydon reg'd **G-ADEE** [CofR 5683 15.4.35]. Whilst en route Liverpool to Blackpool in poor weather, the aircraft hit the slopes of Fairsnape Fell, 19 miles east northeast of Blackpool 26.10.35. Destroyed on impact and the two occupants were killed. Cancelled from register 5.36.

6100   CofA no.5058 issued 4.9.35. To Allied Airways (Gandar Dower) Ltd., Aberdeen reg'd **G-ADFI** [CofR 5731 5.9.35] and named *The Silver Ghost*. Burnt out in take off crash Thurso, Caithness 3.7.37. The pilot and 7 passengers escaped but 3 passengers were slightly injured. Cancelled from register 22.1.38.

6101   Export CofA issued 10.7.35. To Osterreichischer Aero Club reg'd **OE-FKD**. Passed to the Austrian Air Force with serial **64** and reportedly used for clandestine operations. Fate not recorded.

6102   Export CofA issued 29.10.35. To the Air Board, Commonwealth of Australia reg'd **VH-UVB** [CofR 573 24.2.36] and CofA no.529 issued same day. To W. R. Carpenter & Co. Ltd., Sydney NSW 4.36 and named *Helen*. Transferred to Carpenter's Mandated Airlines Ltd., Salamaua PNG 6.10.36. "Intention to impress the aircraft" was advised 11.2.41 but the Australian Government was informed that it was not in flying condition and currently undergoing CofA renewal! Impressment therefore rescinded and the allocated serial **A34-12** was not taken up. Withdrawn from use Salamaua 6.41 and gradually dismantled for spares use. Finally destroyed during an air raid by Japanese fighters 21.1.42. Struck off register 11.3.42. (Note: Also see DH84A c/n 2001 for actual use use of serial A34-12).

6103   First flown using test markings **E.4**. CofA no.5060 issued 2.10.35. To Smith's Aircraft Instruments (a branch of S. Smith & Sons Motor Accessories Ltd.), Hatfield and reg'd **G-ADOS** [CofR 6206 21.10.35]. Used as a flying showroom. Impressed into R.A.F. service as **HM569** 6.6.42. Saw service with No.3 School of General Reconaissance, Blackpool. Undershot on landing Squires Gate and struck a low bank on the airfield's perimeter 24.6.42. To de Havilland for repair, but SOC as Cat.E1 7.8.42, having flown just 577 hours. Deleted from civil register 1.1.46 (1945 census).

6104   Export CofA issued 4.36. To the Air Board, Commonwealth of Australia reg'd **VH-UTX** [CofR 583 17.4.36] and CofA no.540 issued same day. To W. R. Carpenter & Co. Ltd., Sydney NSW and named *Hope*. Transferred to their company Mandated Airlines Ltd., Salamaua PNG 6.10.36. Impressment advised 11.2.41 and serial **A34-11** allotted. To Australian National, Melbourne-Essendon VIC for air observer conversion 25.3.41. Issued to 2AOS 23.6.41. To Australian National, Essendon VIC for conversion to air ambulance 24.1.42. Issued to 34Sqdn. 17.2.42. To 1EFTS 17.4.42. To 36Sqdn. 24.7.42. On a proposed flight to Alice Springs NT 17.11.42, due to prevailing conditions, compelled to return to Oodnadatta SA but the aircraft stalled when 10 feet off the ground and the port undercarriage collapsed during the subsequent heavy landing. On site repairs carried out by No.1RSU. To 34Sqdn. 13.2.43. Destroyed on the ground Oodnadatta SA during 87 m.p.h. gale 15.2.43. Struck off charge 26.3.43.

6105   CofA no.5394 issued 18.4.36. To Air Cruises Ltd., Hatfield as **G-AECZ** 11.3.36. To Ramsgate Airport Ltd. [CofR 8215 15.11.37]. Believed operated briefly by Western Airways Ltd. 1938 (note: both Ramsgate Airport Ltd. & Western Airways were owned by the Straight Corporation at the time). To Southern Airways Ltd., Ramsgate 14.2.39. Impressed as **AV982** 8.5.40, initially with 24Sqdn. To 110 (AAC) Wing Ringway 12.5.40. With 7AACU 16.5.40. At 4MU 2.10.40. At 18MU 30.6.41. Damaged Cat.B at West Bromwich 4.11.41 and repaired. To the English Electric Co. for communications duties with inspectors of the Ministry of Aircraft Production 13.10.42. At 5MU 31.8.44. SOC to Air Taxis Ltd., Kenley as **G-AECZ** 18.6.46. Nominal change to Air Taxis (Croydon) Ltd., Croydon 18.3.47. To Frederick Thomas Bingham 13.1.48. To Wiltshire School of Flying Ltd., Thruxton 30.4.48. Sold to J. Cleary, Weston Ltd. 16.3.50. To D. Kennedy, Weston Air Services 1.8.50 & reg'd **EI-AFK**. Withdrawn from use at Weston & cancelled from the register 11.3.66. Donated to Aer Lingus Teoranta 1.9.67 and subsequently placed on display within Dublin's terminal building, painted as **EI-ABI** to represent the first aircraft operated by the national carrier. Restored to flying condition 1985 and in order to legally wear the "new" marks, the Dragon was registered to Aer Lingus PLC 12.8.85. First flown after restoration 10.4.86. Christened *Iolar*, like the original and re-enacted the first Aer Lingus flight 50 years before from Dublin to Bristol 5.7.86. Now regularly flown by current and former Aer Lingus aircrew from its Dublin base.

6106   CofA no.5448 issued 5.5.36. To W. S. Shackleton Ltd.,

Hanworth reg'd **G-AEFX** [CofR 6904 23.4.36]. Sold abroad 5.36. To MacRobertson-Miller Aviation Co. Ltd., Perth WA reg'd **VH-UVN** [CofR 597 10.7.36] and CofA no.554 issued same day. Named *The Ashburton*. Based at Wyndham WA, operated as an air ambulance and renamed *Dunbar Hooper II* 1.8.38. Extensively damaged at Neda Station WA 11.12.40 but repaired. Crashed and destroyed by fire near Broome WA en route Broome to Perth for overhaul 7.1.42. The pilot and 3 passengers were not injured. Struck off register 19.1.42.

6107   CofA no.5498 issued 13.6.36. In "semi-military condition". Initially reg'd to de Havilland Aircraft Co. Ltd. as **G-AEIS** [CofR 7018 14.5.36] for delivery to Ministry of National Defence, Ankara, Turkey. Cancelled from U.K. register 12.36 as sold abroad. Turkish serial, service details and eventual fate, unknown.

6108   CofA no.5499 issued 13.6.36. In "semi-military condition". Initially reg'd to de Havilland Aircraft Co. Ltd. as **G-AEIT** [CofR 7019 14.5.36] for delivery to Ministry of National Defence, Ankara, Turkey. Cancelled from U.K. register 12.36 as sold abroad. Turkish serial, service details and eventual fate, unknown.

6109   CofA no.5500 issued 13.6.36. In "semi-military condition". Initially reg'd to de Havilland Aircraft Co. Ltd. as **G-AEIU** [CofR 7020 14.5.36] for delivery to Ministry of National Defence, Ankara, Turkey. Cancelled from U.K. register 12.36 as sold abroad. Turkish serial, service details and eventual fate, unknown.

6110   DH84M. CofA no.5624 issued 5.9.36. Sold to Union Founders Trust Ltd. Heston reg'd **G-AEMI** [CofR 7250 14.8.36] and intended for the Spanish Air Force, but sale prohibited. Instead, to Commercial Air Hire Ltd., Croydon [CofR 7315 2.9.36]. Impressed as **AW173** but serial not painted on the aircraft. To 110 (AAC) Wing Ringway 7.7.40. With 7AACU 19.8.40. Stalled and crashed during attempted forced landing on the Fosse Way, near Bury Farm, Pillerton Hersey, Warwickshire 14.12.40.

6111   DH84M. Sold to Union Founders Trust Ltd., Heston reg'd **G-AEMJ**. [CofR 7251 14.8.36] and intended for the Spanish Air Force, but sale prohibited. Cancelled from register 1.37. and CofA eventually issued 13.4.37. To Portugese Air Force and allotted serial **504**. Fate unknown.

6112   DH84M. CofA issued 3.9.36. Sold to Union Founders Trust Ltd., Heston reg'd **G-AEMK** [CofR 7252 14.8.36] and intended for the Spanish Air Force, but sale prohibited. Instead, to Commercial Air Hire Ltd., Croydon 9.36. To Mutual Finance Ltd., Croydon, probably for operation by Air Dispatch [CofR 7736 5.3.37]. Sold abroad 6.38 and flown to Australia by Denzil and Andrew MacArthur-Onslow, directors of Air Travel & Survey Pty. Ltd. Reg'd **VH-AAO** [CofR 754 15.2.40] and CofA no.711 issued same day. Fitted with autopilot and special camera equipment for survey work. Impressed as **A34-5** 15.7.40 and struck off register 20.7.40. To Butler Air Transport Pty. Ltd. at Mascot for modifications but the work was cancelled and aircraft continued in use for survey work with Survey Flight. Damaged, believed at Canberra ACT when a tyre blew after heavy landing causing a ground-loop 28.10.40. To 2AAU at Canberra ACT by 31.8.42. Issued to 36Sqdn. 11.12.42 but instead, to 34Sqdn. same day. At sometime wore the radio call-sign **VHC-SB** in large letters on fuselage sides. Issued to Guinea Airways 28.1.43 for overhaul. SOC to Director of Civil Aviation and restored as **VH-AAO** 30.7.43 but remained on strength of 34Sqdn. 23.8.43. Disposed of to Butler Air Transport Ltd., Perth WA 22.10.43. With Butler Air Transport Pty. Ltd., Mascot 30.6.46. Damaged beyond repair when blown by a windstorm into the Castlereagh River, Coonamble, NSW 23.12.47. Struck off register 3.5.48.

6113   DH84M. CofA issued 10.5.37. To Portugese Air Force and allocated serial **505**. Fate unknown.

6114   DH84M. CofA issued 20.5.37. To Portugese Air Force and allocated serial **506**. Fate unknown.

3.4 de Havilland DH84 Dragon - Australian Requirement

As already described, Dragon sales to Australia were excellent and over half of the aircraft imported were impressed into Royal Australian Air Force service during the war, with the decision made to "grab" the first three at a meeting of the Impressment Committee on 24th November 1939. Eight more aircraft joined them with the last two, via requisition numbers 8195 and 8196 dated 24th February 1941, with instructions to be delivered to Ansett and Australian National at Melbourne

The eleven impressed aircraft were mainly used by the two Air Observer Schools situated at Cootamundra, New South Wales (No.1 A.O.S.) and Mount Gambier, South Australia (No.2 A.O.S.) but a few were used as general transports. When war broke out in the Pacific, all but one of the impressed Dragons remained in service and from January 1942, seven were converted to ambulance aircraft. These were subsequentrly used by newly formed transport squadrons for casualty evacuation work in New Guinea, Queensland and the Northern Territory.

An urgent requirement by the R.A.A.F. for further twin engine navigation trainer and general transport aircraft, would have been ably met by the DH89, but de Havilland facilities at Hatfield were fully stretched fulfilling Mosquito and Dominie orders for the Royal Air Force. It was therefore decided to contract de Havilland Australia Pty. Ltd. at Bankstown, to build 87 DH84. The decision to build the Dragon in preference to its larger sister, was because of its simpler construction which would speed service entry. Furthermore, the Dragon was powered by the ubiquitous Gipsy Major – an engine which was readily available locally, being produced under licence by General Motors Holden for fitment to DH82A Tiger Moth training aircraft then in series production at Bankstown.

Drawings and various jigs, out of use since production ceased in England during 1936, were shipped to Sydney and a production line was swiftly set up. Known as the DH84A, the Australian built aircraft were based on the Dragon 1 but with the framed windows as introduced on the Dragon 2.

The first, A34-12 flew at Bankstown on 29th September 1942 and the newly built Dragons began to be accepted the following month. Deliveries were completed just eight months later with the final aircraft handed over at the factory on 28th June 1943..

Although a few were used by training units, the majority of the 87 built, entered service with transport squadrons for use as communications aircraft. Australian National at Melbourne's Essendon Airport, converted a number to air ambulances. Four of these were lost, in accidents A34-66 was the first of ten to be delivered to WAGS - Wireless & Gunnery School (also known as Wireless Air Gunners School in some documentation). 1WAGS was based at Ballarat in Victoria, 2WAGS at Parkes New South Wales and 3WAGS at Maryborough Queensland.

One rather exotic role was given to A34-25, which was issued to No.3 Communications Flight for exclusive use by the U.S. Army Services of Supply - Horse Purchasing Board, giving rise to the romantic notion of some beleaguered garrison in the jungle being rescued at the last moment by the Seventh Cavalry, in true Hollywood tradition! It remained with the U.S. Army, later with Base Section 2 at Townsville, until it went missing when carrying radar equipment out of Garbutt, Queensland.

Dragons operated into some very primitive airstrips both in Australia's outback and in Papua-New Guinea and some suffered casualties as a result, although few proved fatal. So remote were some of these strips, if damaged, aircraft often had to be abandoned as being too difficult to recover for repair. If that was not enough, the wooden structures did not stand up well to the tropical conditions experienced in New Guinea and a few were "approved for conversion", to use the R.A.A.F. parlance for "struck off charge", due to deterioration. Probably due to their frequent use of unprepared strips, it proved necessary for the fleet to be returned to the manufacturer or other large repair and maintenance organisations for floor strengthening work to be carried out.

It was intended to dispose of surplus Dragon aircraft prior to the end of the war and the Commonwealth Disposals Commission were informed in October 1944, that the Department of Air proposed to release 59 DH84s and 38 Gipsy Major 1 engines. In December 1944, the total number to be disposed off was very much reduced to just nine aircraft. Only A34-68 of this batch was sold, to Butler Air Transport in March 1945. The number for disposal changed again in June 1945, when in a letter from the Department of Air to the Disposals Commission they advised that after the disposal of A34-68, another (A34-98) written-off in the interim and 17 retained for immediate operation by the R.A.A.F., 40 were available for immediate release. When new, each DH84A had cost the Government A£6000, but it was intended to sell them at a top price of A£750! Even at this low price, sales were slow due to procrastination by the Department of Civil Aviation in the award of certificates of airworthiness. At this time, hangarage was at a premium and on 5th February 1946, the Commonwealth Disposals Commission advised their regional managers "that all Dragon aircraft must be disposed of within two weeks" and an unbelievable A£50 each was to be charged for the remaining 17 aircraft! Needless to say, the storage hangars were quickly cleared at this ridiculously low price! It was thought that the afore-mentioned certification difficulties would preclude their sale other than to a buyer breaking the Dragons for spares use. The chief beneficiary however, was the wily Sir Walter of W. R. Carpenter & Co., who subsequently found a market for the transports he had obtained at a give-away price!

Despite the rigours of operating in a harsh climate and usually in primitive conditions, 47 eventually saw post-war service with a wide variety of operators and a further 3 were sold off for spares use. The Queensland Air Transport Brigade and Flying Doctor service acquired a few Dragons from the R.A.A.F. during the war and supplemented these when the type was taken out of service. Others were purchased by airlines for use in the outback and at least two were fitted for crop spraying. A number went to missionary societies for operation in New Guinea.

Only three Australian built DH84As have appeared on overseas registers and all are extant:-
A34-59 (2048) was in storage with Sid Marshall for many years at Sydney-Bankstown as VH-AQU. Made airworthy during the 1980s by de Havilland Australia Ltd. at Sydney-Bankstown, re-reg'd VH-DHX (initially for test/ferrying purposes only) though painted as A34-59 coded 'A-XJ'. Sold abroad to Torquil P. A. Norman, Rendcomb, Gloucestershire as G-ECAN January 2001. Currently undergoing restoration in Cliff Lovell's Hampshire Light Plane Services workshop at Chilbolton Airfield and expected to fly in England for the first time in the month of publication of this book.
A34-68 (2057) went to Rolvin Airways, Palmerston North as ZK-AXI July 1953. Damaged beyond repair during forced-landing after the port engine failed with six parachutists aboard at Ardmore in April 1967. Donated by the insurance company to the Museum of Transport and Technology and stored Auckland-Ardmore. Traded to Stan and Gilly Smith 1982 and rebuilt to flying condition at their Tech-Air facility at North Shore, flying again on 22nd April 1997.
A34-92 (2081) was sold to W. R. Carpenter Co. Ltd. of Sydney on 15th February 1946 for just A£50. Registered to Butlins Ltd. as G-AJKF in March 1947 and intended for pleasure flying from their Skegness Holiday Camp. Unfortunately, it was not imported and cancelled in August 1948 as "Incorrect registration". Subsequently civilianised as VH-BDS with QANTAS Empire Airways Ltd. but re-registered VH-AML in September 1963. Noted by the authors in open store at Perth's Jandakot Aerodrome in February 1976 when with Mike W. Hockin, Capel WA. Re-built to flying condition by Lyn Forster & others and used in the 1984 A.B.C. film 'Flight Into Hell'. Currently in flying condition at Point Cook, Victoria, painted in original colours and wears serial A34-92.
Another that went overseas is A34-13 (2002), though still wearing VH-SNB. Currently dsplayed at the Royal Museum of Scotland's Museum of Flight at East Fortune since 1981, after purchase at the Strathallan Aircraft Collection sale.

Ten Dragons are known to survive, five each from the Hatfield and Bankstown production lines.

de Havilland (Australia) DH84A – Production Listing

2001   Royal Australian Air Force serial **A34-12**. First flown 29.9.42. Received by 2AD 21.2.43. Issued 33Sqdn. 7.3.43. To 1RCS 25.10.43. To 9CU 4.11.43. Crashed on landing Berry Strip PNG 9.12.43. To 15ARD 13.12.43. Damage repair was beyond capacity of unit and owing to the machine's location, recommended for conversion to spares. Finally, write-off approved 30.5.44.

2002   Royal Australian Air Force serial **A34-13**. Received by 2AD 12.10.42. Issued 1AD 25.10.42. To Australian National Airways Pty Ltd., Essendon VIC for ambulance transport modifications 5.4.43. Issued to 6CF 22.5.43. At de Havilland for complete airframe overhaul 11.8.44. Issued to CMU Evans Head NSW for storage 25.7.45. Approved for disposal 16.5.46 for A£7600. Sold to the Commonwealth Department of Health, Canberra ACT for just A£50 and reg'd **VH-ASK** [CofR 1044 19.8.46]. Nominal ownership change to Director-General of Health, Canberra ACT 31.7.50. Withdrawn from use 4.1.54. Restored to J. G. & G. Schulz, Prairie QLD as **VH-SNB** [CoR 2178]. Noted at Bankstown 5.60, also Tamworth NSW and Camden NSW 10.60. To L. G. Nixon, Les Nixon Evangelist Mission, Bexley NSW 15.9.62. Stored at Camden NSW c.1973. To Sir William J. Roberts of the Strathallan Aircraft Collection in Scotland. On closure, auctioned for £7000. Moved late 1981 to Royal Scottish Museum – Museum of Flight at East Fortune. Now part of the National Museums of Scotland.

2003   Royal Australian Air Force serial **A34-14**. Received by 2AD 12.10.42. Issued 1RCF Port Moresby, New Guinea and passed through 12RSU Garbutt QLD 21.10.42 en route. Crashed Popondetta PNG 17.1.43 suffering extensive damage to forward fuselage, lower mainplanes, port engine and undercarriage. Although issued to 15RSU to arrange salvage & repair, deemed not economical and "approval given for conversion" 11.2.43.

2004   Royal Australian Air Force serial **A34-15**. Received by 2AD 25.10.42. To 33Sqdn. 11.11.42. Badly damaged on take-off 18.6.43 Terapo PNG, believed due structural failure of a compression leg. Fuselage, undercarriage and probably port wing damaged. Issued to 15ARD 24.6.43 and though deemed repairable, recommended for conversion to spares 4.2.44 and finally, write-off approved 30.5.44.

2005   Royal Australian Air Force serial **A34-16**. Received by 2AD 28.10.42. Issued 33Sqdn. 11.11.42. Issued Australian National Airways 19.6.43 for modifications to ambulance transport and trial re-positioning of fuel tank. Re-issued to 33Sqdn. 23.8.43. To 8CU 26.10.43, but received by 9CU 4.11.43. Operated in Papua New Guinea where tropical conditions did not suit the wooden construction and on 24.3.44, recommended for return to mainland. However, the condition was obviously too severe and write-off was approved 6.5.44.

2006   Royal Australian Air Force serial **A34-17**. Received by 2AD 5.11.42. Issued 1RCF 17.11.42. Damaged Ward's strip (one of about seven airstrips around Port Moreby PNG) 5.12.42. To de Havilland 14.2.43 for repair. Issued 35Sqdn. 28.10.43. To 7CU 10.11.43. Badly damaged in storm during night of 20/21.2.44 at Broodit Fosdage. To 17RSU for repairs 26.2.44. Returned to 7CU 22.3.44. Whilst on a non-operational flight from Onslow WA to Exmouth WA 12.5.44, the starboard mainplane and undercarriage were damaged in a 'collision'. To 5AD for storage 16.9.44. Sold to W. R. Carpenter & Co. Ltd. Sydney NSW for A£400 28.9.45. Civilianised as **VH-AOS** [CofR 943]. To R. L. Farquharson t/a Farquharson Bros., Brisbane QLD. To Mandated Airlines Ltd., Lae PNG by 11.3.46 and in service with them 29.4.46. Carrying freight, whilst en route Lae to Kerowagi in bad weather, hit Mount Kerowagi 29.1.47 and the pilot was killed.

2007   Royal Australian Air Force serial **A34-18**. Received by 2AD 10.11.42. Issued 1RCF 30.11.42. Failed to rise even after 1,000 yard take-off run at an unknown location in New Guinea 19.2.43. When the aircraft finally came to rest, port upper and lower wings, the starboard lower wing, both engines & propellers were damaged and the under-carriage wrecked. To de Havilland for repairs 25.4.43. To 6CF 24.9.43. To 14ARD 23.10.43. Aircraft broke from moorings Katherine NT during a storm 22.10.43 and damage was so severe, that approval was given for conversion to produce 22.11.43.

2008   Royal Australian Air Force serial **A34-19**. Received by 2AD 11.11.42. Issued 35Sqdn. 19.11.42. To Australian National for modifications 15.2.43. Allotted to 6CF but instead to 3CF 14.3.43. To 2AAU 31.5.43. A non-operational accident occured 17.9.43 but 3 days later the aircraft was severely damaged when it crashed at Toogoolawah QLD. Recommended for conversion to salvage but the official records do not state whether this was done and it is therefore assumed that the wreck was abandoned at the crash site.

2009   Royal Australian Air Force serial **A34-20**. Received by 2AD 16.11.42. Delivered to 1CF 30.11.42. Starboard compression strut collapsed on landing 26.3.43. Finally repaired 21.6.43 and delivered to 6CF 11.8.43. Crashed at Narrakaiang PNG 26.8.43; severe damage necessitated a write-off which was approved 14.9.43.

2010   Royal Australian Air Force serial **A34-21**. Received by 2AD 16.11.42. Fitted out as an air ambulance by Australian National Airways at Melbourne-Essendon 26.11.42. Delivered 2AAU 17.12.42. To 5AD for storage 16.11.44. Sold to W. R. Carpenter & Co. Ltd. for A£400 24.1.46 and departed 30.1.46. Reg'd **VH-AOP** [CofR 899] to R. L. Farquharson t/a Farquharson Bros., Brisbane QLD. To Mandated Airlines Ltd., Salamaua PNG by 14.3.46 and in service with them 29.3.46. Swung during take-off and use of the brakes failed when the pilot tried to correct the swing, Heyfield PNG 9.8.54. The aircraft ran into a ditch and was destroyed by fire. SOC 2.55.

2011   Royal Australian Air Force serial **A34-22**. Received by 2AD 22.11.42. To Australian National at Melbourne-Essendon for air ambulance conversion 26.11.42. Issued 2AAU 18.12.42. To 5AD 14.11.44 for storage. Sold to W. R. Capenter & Co. Pty. Ltd. 24.1.46. To R. L. Farquharson t/a Farquharson Bros., Brisbane QLD by 11.3.46, perhaps acting as buying agent for Mandated Airlines. Civilianised as **VH-AOQ** with CofR no.900 issued 15.3.46 to Mandated Airlines Ltd., Salamaua PNG. To New Guinea Co. Ltd. 26.6.59. WFU 12.60 and handed over to the D.C.A. for fire practice.

Royal Australian Air Force serial **A34-23**. Received by 2AD 22.11.42. Issued 34Sqdn. 29.11.42. Forced to land 5 miles north of Diopur 1.12.42 but no damage sustained. To 6CF and on strength by 9.1.43. Forced-landed into sea off Goulburn Island NT 5.9.43. Damage was little more than superficial but owing to partial submersion in sea water, to de Havilland, via 14ARD and 6CU, 24.6.44 for repairs. Issued 2AD 28.1.45. To 5AD 12.2.45. To 6CU 17.9.45. To R.A.A.F. Darwin NT via 60TU 5.2.46. At sometime wore call-sign **VHC-SF** in large letters on fuselage sides. Aircraft swung and crashed on take-off 21.3.46 and was severely damaged at unrecorded location. Remains sold to the Commonwealth Department of Health 29.5.46 for A£25 and used for spares by the Northern Territory Medical Service.

2013   Royal Australian Air Force serial **A34-24**. Received by 2AD 25.11.42. Issued 5CF 15.12.42. Went missing on a flight from Cairns QLD to Mareeba QLD 7.3.43. Wreck discovered five days later at Freshwater Gorge, 2 miles north of Crystal Cascades QLD. Allotted to 12RSU and approval given for conversion 4.6.43.

2014   Royal Australian Air Force serial **A34-25**. Received by 2AD 26.11.42. Issued to 3CF 4.1.43 "For exclusive use of U.S.A. Army Horse Purchasing Board". Temporarily transferred to 5CF at Townsville 6.6.43 but still used by Base Section 2 of U.S. Army Services of Supply. Went missing on a non-operational flight carrying radar equipment ex Garbutt QLD 6.12.43 and crash site subsequently located 15 miles south of Croydon QLD. Approval given for write-off 20.12.43.

2015   Royal Australian Air Force serial **A34-26**. Received by 2AD 3.12.42. Issued to 36Sqdn. 15.12.42. Crashed at indecipherable location New Guinea 16.2.43. Severe damage to the fuselage underside, lower mainplanes and undercarriage completely gone. To Guinea Airways for repairs 1.4.43. To 6CU 14.12.43. At sometime wore radio call-sign **VHC-SG** in large letters on fuselage sides. Landed on beach Merets Island 16.1.44 and pilot then found the sandy beach too soft to allow a successful take-off! Presumably it was a precautionary landing as it is recorded that "Engineer Officer states that extensive repairs necessary to make aircraft serviceable". Airframe deemed beyond economical repair 22.10.44 and approval given for conversion.

2016 Royal Australian Air Force serial **A34-27**. Received by 2AD 30.11.42. Issued to 34Sqdn. 4.12.42. To 6CF 16.12.42. Following a complete overhaul by de Havilland, to 6CU 9.4.44. Crashed Darwin Civil Aerodrome 3.12.44. The undercarriage was destroyed causing major damage to underside and engines wrenched from mountings. Although said to be repairable by the unit, using available replacement parts, deemed beyond economical repair and approval for conversion finally given 19.3.45.

2017 Royal Australian Air Force serial **A34-28**. Received by 2AD 2.12.42. Issued 5CF 15.12.42. To 12RSU 5.1.43. Starboard undercarriage damaged landing Charters Towers QLD 8.1.43. Again to 5CF 28.1.43. Taxying accident Horn Island 10.9.43 sustaining severe damage to port upper & lower mainplanes. To 1RSU for repairs 13.9.43. To 5AD for storage 18.9.44. Sold to Rev. T. Jones/Bush Church Aid Society for Australia & Tasmania, Sydney NSW 24.9.45 for A£750. Civilianised as **VH-AGI** [CofR 893 15.3.46]. Forced-landed and damaged beyond repair Bateman's Bay, NSW 1.10.61. Struck off register 1.62.

2018 Royal Australian Air Force serial **A34-29**. Received by 2AD 6.12.42. Issued 33Sqdn. 4.1.43. Damaged on landing Terapo PNG 12.9.43 and although recovered by 15ARD, deemed beyond economical repair. Approval finally given for conversion 12.1.45.

2019 Royal Australian Air Force serial **A34-30**. Received by 2AD 14.12.42. Fitted out as an air ambulance by Australian National at Essendon 28.12.42. Issued 2AAU 29.12.42. Heavy landing Cairns QLD 11.3.43 but repaired by 12RSU before returning to 2AAU 5.8.43. To 5AD for storage 14.11.44. Sold to Queensland Ambulance Transport Brigade 27.5.46 for A£50 and civilianised as **VH-AON**. To Territory Airlines Ltd., Goroka PNG by 30.6.54 & eventually with the Joe Drage Collection, Wodonga VIC. To Rural City of Wangaratta VIC 20.10.98 for exhibition at the now defunct Drage's Airworld. Named *Puff* and later, *Puff the Magic Dragon*.

2020 Royal Australian Air Force serial **A34-31**. Received by 2AD 14.12.42. Issued 36Sqdn. 15.12.42. Crash landed 24.12.42 shattering port mainplane, rear spar and undercarriage. Received 1RSU 5.1.43 for repairs. To 34Sqdn. 1.2.43. At sometime wore call-sign **VHC-SH** in large letters on fuselage sides. Forced landed due engine failure at 400' and undercarriage totally destroyed when it struck a ditch, 1 mile from Oodnadatta SA 26.2.43. Repaired and issued to 6CF 18.6.43. Records are sketchy at this point but known to have forced landed due engine failure through oil loss from the front main bearing of one engine 8.10.43. Allocated to de Havilland 5.5.44 for extensive repairs and overhaul. Sold to the Commonwealth Department of Health, Canberra ACT by 11.7.46. Civilianised as **VH-ASL** and CofR issued 22.11.46. Nominal change of ownership to Director-General of Health, Canberra ACT 31.7.50. Further nominal change to Department of Health, Canberra ACT 30.6.54. To L. A. Wall, Townsville QLD 11.56 and re-reg'd **VH-SJW** 19.11.56. Crashed Mt. Douglas QLD 15.8.57 and struck off register 20.2.58.

2021 Royal Australian Air Force serial **A34-32**. Received by 2AD 14.12.42. Issued to 33Sqdn. 20.12.42. Non-operational crash on take-off 23.7.43. Repaired and to 8CU 26.10.43. To 9CU 4.11.43. Swung on landing whilst on operational transport flight to an unnamed airstrip in New Guinea 18.1.44. Damaged beyond economical repair and approval given for conversion 14.2.44.

2022 Royal Australian Air Force serial **A34-33**. Received by 2AD 16.12.42. Issued to Parachute Training Unit 20.12.42. To 4CU 6.4.44. At sometime wore call-sign **VHC-RM** in large letters on fuselage sides. To 5AD for storage 29.8.44. Surveyed prior to disposal 29.9.45 and sold to W. R. Carpenter & Co. Ltd. for A£50 by 11.2.46 and delivered 9.4.46. Civilianised as **VH-ALL**. To K. A. Virtue, Yeerongpilly QLD 23.5.47.. Operated by Trans- Australia Airlines on behalf of the Queensland Flying Doctor Service. Crashed Moothandilla QLD 6.2.51.

2023 Royal Australian Air Force serial **A34-34**. Received by 2AD 17.12.42. Modified to air ambulance configuration by Australian National at Essendon and Issued to 2AAU 31.12.42. Operated in New Guinea March – October 1943 and tropical conditions necessitated a complete re-build of the structure by de Havilland. To 5AD for storage 16.11.44. Sold to Queensland Ambulance Transport Brigade (Cairns

Centre), Cairns QLD 10.10.45 for A£670 and collected 16.10.45. Reg'd **VH-AMB** with [CofR 849 28.11.45]. Crashed Palmerville QLD 6.2.51.

2024 Royal Australian Air Force serial **A34-35**. Received by 2AD 17.12.42. Issued 1CF 20.12.42. To 6CF 30.7.43. Rendered unserviceable Port Keath 15.12.43 when an eye bolt sheared on port undercarriage, causing major damage to port lower mainplane, engine bearer and undercarriage. To de Havilland for repairs 4.8.44. To 5AD 14.5.45 for storage. Sold to Bridgwater Amplivox Sound Systems, Sydney NSW 8.10.45 for A£750 and collected 22.11.45. Civilianised as **VH-AFK** with [CofR 890 7.3.46]. Operated by Shark Patrol Service Co., Sydney NSW. Crashed Bena Bena PNG 8.9.48. Obviously repaired as listed with Taylor's Air Transport, Lae PNG 31.7.50. Struck off register 8.56.

2025 Royal Australian Air Force serial **A34-36**. Received by 2AD 22.12.42 and issued 1RCS same day. Undercarriage collapsed on landing Goodenough Island PNG 1.4.43. Shipped per *SS Wanaka* 7.7.43 and after re-build by de Havilland, issued to 5CU 11.3.44. Whilst returning from a non-operational transport flight to Horn Island QLD, an engine failed and the aircraft was forced to return to the island where it crashed at Higgins Field (now known as Bamaga Strip) 13.5.44. Major damage and although received by 1RSU 16.5.44, approval given for write-off on or about 17.7.44.

2026 Royal Australian Air Force serial **A34-37**. Received by 2AD 26.12.42 and issued to Parachute Training School on the following day (flown by 36Sqdn. crews). At sometime wore call-sign **VHC-RN** in large letters on fuselage sides. Whilst flying a non-operational survey in connection with training paratroop batallions 14.10.43, aircraft was last seen flying low and apparently then spun into wooded area, Limeburner's Creek NSW. The pilot, Ian Holllingdale, was killed. Although allocated to de Havilland for repair work to be carried out, the fuselage was deemed beyond economical repair and subsequently approved for conversion 15.11.43.

2027 Royal Australian Air Force serial **A34-38**. Received by 2AD 27.12.42. Issued 34Sqdn. 7.1.43. Very soon after delivery, on 11th January, the tailwheel collapsed on landing Tennant Creek NT and the rear fuselage was badly smashed. Repairs effected by 1RSU before returning to 34Sqdn.. To 3CF 11.6.43 as replacement for the crashed A34-19. To R.I.M.U. for special duty 23.8.43 until 22.11.43. Issued 14ARD 18.7.44 and wireless and navigation equipment removed. To 6CU 26.8.44. To 5AD 28.1.45 for storage. Sold to R. J. Knight & A. J. McCarthy of K.M.H. Service, Bowen Hills, Brisbane QLD 15.3.46 for A£480 and collected 9.4.46. Ferried to Mackay QLD. Reg'd as **VH-BAF**. Delivered to QANTAS Empire Airways Ltd. 28.5.47. Crashed Zenag PNG 14.7.47. Struck off register 11.47.

2028 Royal Australian Air Force serial **A34-39**. Received by 2AD 4.1.43. Issued Parachute Training Unit (flown by 36Sqdn. crews) 22.1.43. To 2CU 29.11.43. To 7SFTS 3.4.44. To 14ARD 5.9.44. To 6CU 10.10.44. At sometime wore call-sign **VHC-RO** in large letters on fuselage sides. To 5AD for storage 3.12.45. Sold to W. R. Carpenter & Co. Ltd., Sydney NSW 12.2.46 for just A£50 and collected 8.4.46. Civilianised as **VH-ARJ** reg'd 18.7.46. In service with Mandated Airlines Ltd., Salamaua PNG 30.6.47. Struck off register 1.9.60 as "withdrawn from service".

2029 Royal Australian Air Force serial **A34-40**. Received by 2AD 3.1.43. To Australian National Airways for air ambulance conversion 7.1.43. Issued 1RCS 2.2.43 and received by them fourteen days later. Crashed North-East of Milne Bay 26.6.43 and airframe considered beyond salvage. Approved for conversion 26.8.43. However, it has been reported as sold to W. R. Carpenter & Co. Ltd. for just A£50 and delivered 9.4.46. To Mandated Airlines Ltd., Lae PNG, civilianised as **VH-ARI** and reg'd 1.11.46. Hit ground after engine failure on take-off Wewak PNG due contaminated fuel 31.8.46 and destroyed in the ensuing fire. The crew and passengers were uninjured.

2030 Royal Australian Air Force serial **A34-41**. Received by 2AD 10.1.43. To Australian National Airways for air ambulance conversion 21.1.43. Received 33Sqdn. 28.2.43. At sometime wore call-sign **VHC-SJ** in large letters on fuselage sides. Badly damaged landing 3.7.43 and although allotted to 15ARD for salvage and repair, approval finally given for conversion more than two years later on 4.8.45. Official records state "withdrawn from service due to tropical deterioration"!

2031 Royal Australian Air Force serial **A34-42**. Received by 2AD 10.1.43. To Australian National Airways for air ambulance conversion 13.1.43. Received 35Sqdn. 4.2.43. Damaged by high winds Maylands SA 15.3.43. Repaired, but damaged during landing accident 29.4.43. Repaired at 17RSU and returned to 35Sqdn. 6.6.43. To 7CU 10.11.43. Allotted for use by A.W.C. 24.4.44 and available for collection 6.6.44. Presumably not used and next issue record 27.9.44 states to 5AD for storage. Sold to W. R. Carpenter & Co. Ltd., Sydney for just A£50 by 11.2.46. Reg'd **VH-AYM** and delivered to QANTAS Empire Airways Ltd. 1.11.46. Caught fire on starting starboard engine Canobie Station, QLD (this may actually have been at Canoble NSW) 24.11.48. Struck off register 1.49.

2032 Royal Australian Air Force serial **A34-43**. Received by 2AD 10.1.43. To Australian National Airways for air ambulance conversion 21.1.43. Issued 33Sqdn. 1.2.43. Damaged on landing Berry strip, PNG 7.5.43, but repaired locally within 48 hours of the required parts being made available. Badly damaged on landing Terapo, PNG 12.7.43 but repaired by 15ARD. Again damaged in crash landing 18.5.44 and owing to tropical deterioration, deemed beyond economical repair and approved for conversion 4.8.44.

2033 Royal Australian Air Force serial **A34-44**. Received by 2AD 15.1.43. Received by Australian National for air ambulance conversion 31.1.43. Issued to 34Sqdn. 18.2.43 for service on behalf of Flying Doctor Service, Broken Hill NSW. To 1RCS 13.5.43. At sometime wore call-sign **VHC-SK** in large letters on fuselage sides. Crashed on take-off Berry strip, PNG 26.7.43. Approval given for conversion 12.1.45.

2034 Royal Australian Air Force serial **A34-45**. Received by 2AD 17.1.43. To Australian National Airways for air ambulance conversion 21.1.43. Issued 34Sqdn. 14.2.43. At sometime wore call-sign **VHC-SL** in large letters on fuselage sides. Forced to land, reason unknown, 35 miles north of Tennant Creek SA 1.4.43 and completely destroyed by fire. Approval given for conversion 5.5.43.

2035 Royal Australian Air Force serial **A34-46**. Received by 2AD 17.1.43. To Australian National Airways for air ambulance conversion 22.1.43. Altitude control equipment fitted and issued 1RCS 8.4.43. Crashed between Hope Island and Coomera 13.4.43. Repairs quickly carried out at 3AD and returned to 1RCS. Crashed again following starboard engine failure on take-off 27.7.43. Not repairable and approval given for conversion 18.8.43.

2036 Royal Australian Air Force serial **A34-47**. Received by 2AD 19.1.43. To Australian National Airways for air ambulance conversion 22.1.43. Allotted for use by 33Sqdn. but instead issued to 34Sqdn. 23.2.43. At sometime wore call-sign **VHC-SN** in large letters on fuselage sides. Disappeared in the region of Prospect NSW 19.4.43 whilst en route Sydney-Mascot to Melbourne-Essendon via Forest Hill NSW. Not found and approval given for write-off 4.5.43. 'Exercise Dragon-Fly' was mounted by over 60 members of the Confederate Air Force to locate the remains in March 1980.

2037 Royal Australian Air Force serial **A34-48**. Received by 2AD 22.1.43. Received by 34Sqdn. 25.1.43. At sometime wore call-sign **VHC-SM** in large letters on fuselage sides. Damaged undercarriage and wing tip whilst landing on the following day! Quickly repaired, but flying at low level on 11.3.43, aircraft appeared to stall and dived into ground, 1 mile East of Adelaide-Parafield SA. Totally destroyed and approval given for conversion 4.4.43.

2038 Royal Australian Air Force serial **A34-49**. Received by 2AD 31.1.43. Allocated to 3CF but instead to 4CF 11.2.43 for use by General Officer Commanding 1st Army. Flying in poor visibility 2.3.43, hit trees then pancaked on its belly and finally was totally destroyed by fire. "Ordered to components" 18.3.43.

2039 Royal Australian Air Force serial **A34-50**. Received by 2AD 29.1.43. Records missing until delivery 3CU 4.1.45. To 5AD for storage 18.7.45. Sold to Flying Doctor Service (W.A. Section), Perth WA by 11.7.46. Civilianised as **VH-ASN**. Ferried Sydney-Mascot to Guildford WA by Dr. H. G. Dicks 27.7.46. Re-regd with the same owner as **VH-ASX** 9.4.52. To Territory Airlines Ltd., Goroka PNG 15.9.53. Owner/operator listed as Mandated Airlines

Ltd., Lae PNG 14.9.54. Struck off register 1.11.56 as "withdrawn from service".

2040 Royal Australian Air Force serial **A34-51**. Received by 2AD 29.1.43. To Australian National Airways, Melbourne-Essendon for air ambulance conversion 11.2.43. Issued 6CF 28.2.43. Crashed into sea south-west of Goulburn Island NT 31.5.43. Approval given for conversion 19.6.43.

2041 Royal Australian Air Force serial **A34-52**. Received by 2AD 4.2.43. To Australian National Airways for ambulance conversion 15.2.43. Issued 6CF 8.3.43. Ground looped on landing Gorrie strip 15.10.43. Repairs beyond capability of unit so to 14ARD for repairs. Forced landed Port Keats 7.12.43 with only superficial damage. Allocated to 5CU for exclusive use of Allied Works Commander but not received as unairworthy at 5EFTS whilst en route to de Havilland for major overhaul 9.2.44. To 6CU 25.8.44. Crashed in sea off Mendell Beach (has also been recorded as Misdil Beach) NT 3.9.44 and totally destroyed.

2042 Royal Australian Air Force serial **A34-53**. Received by 2AD 4.2.43. To Australian National for transport/ambulance conversion 12.2.43. Originally allotted to 6CF but instead to 2AAU 24.3.43 and operated in PNG. Owing to fabric and woodwork deterioration, result of tropical service, despatched to Kingaroy QLD for substantial work 2.4.44. To 5AD for storage 14.12.44. Sold to W. R. Carpenter & Co. Ltd., Sydney 24.1.46 for A£400. To R. L. Farquharson, t/a Farquharson Bros., Hamilton QLD (perhaps operating as a purchasing agent) 30.8.46. Reg'd as **VH-AOR** 30.8.46. To QANTAS Empire Airways Ltd. 8.47. Noted in storage 9.3.53. To S. J. Porter, Air Express Co. Brisbane-Archerfield QLD by 30.6.54. Crashed Doboy Creek, near Tingalpa QLD 24.10.54. Struck off register 5.55.

2043 Royal Australian Air Force serial **A34-54**. Received by 2AD 4.2.43. To Australian National for transport/ambulance conversion 12.2.43. Received 2AAU 27.3.43. To 5AD for storage 16.11.44. Sold to Royal Aero Club of New South Wales, Sydney-Bankstown 12.2.46 for A£50 and collected 9.4.46. Reserved as **VH-API** but ntu so presumably unsuitable for civilianisation.

2044 Royal Australian Air Force serial **A34-55**. Received by 2AD 7.2.43. To Australian National, Melbourne-Essendon VIC for transport/ambulance conversion 15.2.43. Issued 35Sqdn. 25.3.43. To 7CU 10.11.43. To 5AD for storage 19.9.44. Sold to W. R. Carpenter & Co. Ltd. for just A£50 by 11.2.46. To Airways Pty. Ltd. Brisbane-Archerfield QLD 26.2.46 and collected by them 4.3.46. Civilianised as **VH-BJH** 28.9.48. Struck off register 27.9.49 due CofR expiry. However, owner/operated listed as Guinea Air Traders Ltd., Lae at 31.7.50. Listed with A. Earle, Dalby QLD by 30.6.55. With C. R. Laver, Mackay QLD by 11.57. Struck off register 13.9.60 as "withdrawn from service".

2045 Royal Australian Air Force serial **A34-56**. Received by 2AD 11.2.43. To Australian National Airways, Melbourne-Essendon for transport/ambulance conversion 15.2.43. Issued 6CF 1.4.43. Allotted to 2AAU 16.12.43 but to de Havilland for complete overhaul instead 17.4.44. To 2AP 20.10.44 and to 5AD 15.11.44 for storage. To Flying Doctor Service (N.S.W. Section) by 11.7.46. Civilianised as **VH-ASO** 10.3.47. Re-reg'd **VH-FDA** still with the Flying Doctor Service 30.09.48. To Adastra Airways Pty. Ltd. 1.6.53. Re-reg'd **VH-AGC** 7.8.56. To R. S. & S. R. MacDonald, Clermont QLD 2.9.58. Withdrawn from service 20.7.62. Later in use with the Newcastle Sport Parachute Club, until the pilot lost control on take-off, wiping off the undercarriage and causing other other serious damage late 1968. Cancelled from register 1.12.68. James O'Connell purchased the remains and transported them to Berwick VIC. Later, moved to Point Cook, where O'Connell completed the rebuild Formally registered to James O'Connell 12.4.76. Based Point Cook VIC, but when being moved to a new base at Kyneton 15.12.79, an engine apparently failed shortly after take-off. The pilot elected to turn back to the airfield, where it crashed, disintegrated and burst into flames. Totally destroyed and the pilot was killed. As an aside, the tailwheel unit was incorporated into a DH88 Comet replica.

2046 Royal Australian Air Force serial **A34-57**. Received by 2AD 11.2.43. To Australian National for transport/ambulance conversion 17.2.43. Received 12RSU 10.4.43. To 1RCS 13.5.43. To 8CU 5.11.43. To 9CU 23.11.43. To 2AAU 8.3.44. Deemed unfit for further tropical service 27.3.44. To 10RSU 30.3.44 but returned to 2AAU

2.4.44. After overhaul by de Havilland to 5AD for storage 26.12.44. Sold to Flying Doctor Service (W. A. Section) 24.9.45 for A£750. Civilianised as **VH-AGI** 15.10.45 with CofR no.837. Delivered Sydney-Mascot to Maylands WA by Dr. H. G. Dicks 17-20.10.45. Struck off register 14.6.51 as "withdrawn from service".

2047　Royal Australian Air Force serial **A34-58**. Received by 2AD 2.3.43. Issued to 5OTU 3.3.43 and delivered 6.4.43. An accident due to engine failure recorded 4.11.43, but damage must have been slight as no rectification action noted. Received 4CU 27.12.43. Aircaft crashed on edge of Toowoomba QLD aerodrome 20.3.44 killing Flight Sergeant Jack Hume Bird, Sqd. Ldr. Terence Cantor Oswald and Sqd. Ldr. Joseph Henry James. LAC John Royal Twyford later died of his injuries. Approval given for conversion 19.4.44.

2048　Royal Australian Air Force serial **A34-59**. Received by 2AD 2.3.43. Issued 5OTU 3.3.43. At de Havilland 19.3.43 to 6.4.43, pre-sumably for floor strengthening. To 2CU 21.12.43. Suffered taxying accident 6.2.44 with 70% damage to starboard lower mainplane and front spar inboard of bracing "badly bruised and split" reported. Repairs carried out and to 5SFTS 17.3.44. To 14ARD 30.8.44. Like the other DH84s, presumably then to 5AD for storage. Sold to S. D. Marshall/Marshall Airways, Sydney-Mascot by 11.3.46 and reg'n **VH-AOF** allocated but ntu. Instead, civilianised as **VH-AQU** by 24.5.46. Struck off register 28.9.48 as "withdrawn from service". Remained in storage with Marshall for many years at Sydney-Bankstown. Made airworthy 1980s by de Havilland Australia Ltd. at Sydney-Bankstown, re-reg'd **VH-DHX** (initially for test/ferrying purposes only) though paint-ed as A34-59 coded 'A-XJ'. Later based South Australia. Sold abroad to Torquil P. A. Norman, Rendcomb Gloucestershire as **G-ECAN** 11.1.01. Currently undergoing restoration in Cliff Lovell's Hampshire Light Plane Services workshop at Chilbolton Airfield. To fly 4.03.

2049　Royal Australian Air Force serial **A34-60**. Received by 2AD 7.3.43. Delivered 5OTU 11.3.43. Received 5CF 17.10.43. Made air-worthy for ferry flight to 5AD 28.8.44 and placed into storage. Sold to W. R.Carpenter & Co. Ltd., Sydney NSW for just A£50 by 11.2.46. Reg'n **VH-GAU** reserved but ntu. Eventually civilianised as **VH-BMX** 24.2.49. Listed with Guinea Air Traders Ltd., Lae PNG 31.7.50. Struck off register 8.51.

2050　Royal Australian Air Force serial **A34-61**. Received by 2AD 9.3.43. Issued to 1AD for trial installation of radio equipment 28.5.43. To 7AD 26.6.43 for further modification to radio installation. Allocated to 1WAGS 17.7.43 but instead to 3WAGS 16.8.43. To 5AD for stor-age 19.9.44. Sold to Howard K. Norris, Rose Bay, NSW 24.1.46 for A£570 and collected following day. Civilianised as **VH-AOT** [CofR 901 21.3.46]. Acquired by QANTAS Empire Airways Ltd., 20.1.49. Listed with Riverlea Market Gardens Ltd., Madang PNG 30.6.54. Whilst operating a charter flight, the pilot failed to gain height on take-off and collided with trees, Togoba PNG 2.8.55. The pilot was killed, one pas-senger seriously injured and the other two occupants had minor injuries. The accident report stated "due pilot error in attempting to take-off with the aircraft overloaded in regard to the airstrip's condi-tion".

2051　Royal Australian Air Force serial **A34-62**. Received by 2AD 21.3.43. Issued 5SFTS 29.3.43. To 14ARD RP 18.9.44. Repainted in camouflage at 1AD 25.9.44 and returned to 14ARD RP. To 6CU 4.10.44. To 5AD for storage 9.11.44. Sold to W. R. Carpenter & Co. Ltd., Sydney NSW by 11.2.46. Civilianised as **VH-APL** [CofR no.942 issued 29.4.46]. To Mandated Airlines Ltd., Lae PNG. Damaged at Lae when the undercarriage collapsed on landing 2.47 but repaired. Sold to Territory Airlines Ltd., Goroka PNG 15.12.51. Crashed Chimbu PNG 23.9.52 and struck off register 2.53.

2052　Royal Australian Air Force serial **A34-63**. Received by 2AD 15.3.43. Delivered to 7SFTS 26.3.43. To 14ARD RP 5.9.44. To 6CU 10.10.44. Crashed into the sea in Darwin area 15.3.45 – damage could not be ascertained as it was totally submerged. "Write-off approval requested".

2053　Royal Australian Air Force serial **A34-64**. Received by 2AD 16.3.43. Issued to 4CF for exclusive use of the Australian Army 6.4.43. To 5AD for storage 6.9.44. Sold to R. A. Virtue 14.2.46 for just A£50 and delivered 9.4.46. Reg'd **VH-AYZ** 1.11.46. Listed with E. D. Hill, Wyandra NSW on 30.6.47. Nominal change to Edward D. Hill &

Co. 11.57. Noted named *Rosevale* 4.62. Struck off register 22.6.64 as "withdrawn from service".

2054　Royal Australian Air Force serial **A34-65**. Received by 2AD 19.4.43. Issued 5OTU 25.6.43. To 6CU 19.10.43 for exclusive use of Allied Works Council. To 5CU 4.5.44 but later in the month the records state "badly deteriorated due to tropical conditions". To de Havilland for complete overhaul 29.5.44. Crashed Plumbton, near Mount Druitt NSW 6.1.45 and was totally destroyed. Approval given for conversion 20.2.45.

2055　Royal Australian Air Force serial **A34-66**. Received by 2AD 28.3.43. To 7AD for wireless modifications. Issued 3WAGS 6.8.43. To 5AD for storage 19.9.44. Sold to Namoi Walgett District Ambulance Service by 11.7.46. **VH-ASM** reserved but ntu. Reg'd to Queensland Aerial Ambulance & Taxi Services Pty. Ltd. reg'd **VH-BAH** 23.5.47. Sold to QANTAS Empire Airways Ltd. 1.6.48. To Australian National for operation by Trans Australian Airlines 13.5.49. To Schutt Aviation t/a Schutt Airfarmers Pty. Ltd., Melbourne-Moorabbin VIC 11.55. Crashed on take-off Brewarrina NSW 1.7.56, destroyed by fire and the pilot Michael Driscoll Hart, the sole occupant, later died of his injuries. Apparently, the aircraft was bound for Weilmoringle Station NSW with flood relief supplies, was overweight for take-off, probably badly loaded and outside centre of gravity limits.

2056　Royal Australian Air Force serial **A34-67**. Received by 2AD 23.3.43. To 7AD for wireless modifications. Allocated 1WAGS 17.7.43 but owing to delay due accident at 7AD, instead to 3WAGS 15.12.43. To 5AD for storage 19.9.44. Sold to Newcastle Aero Club NSW by 11.3.46. Civilianised as **VH-AOK** 4.7.46. Listed with Queensland Flying Services, Brisbane QLD 30.6.47. To QANTAS Empire Airways Ltd. 6.4.50. Struck off register 6.8.51 as "withdrawn from service".

2057　Royal Australian Air Force serial **A34-68**. Received by 2AD 24.3.43. Wireless fitment modified by de Havilland 20.5.43. Received via 7AD by 1WAGS, Ballarat VIC 2.8.43. Damaged undercarriage dur-ing heavy landing 3.8.43. To 5AD for storage 30.10.44. Sold to Butler Air Transport Pty. Ltd., Sydney-Mascot NSW on/about 16.3.45. Reg'd **VH-AEF** [CofR 805 29.4.45. To QANTAS Empire Airways Ltd. 18.6.48 for use in New Guinea. Chartered by Trans Australian Airlines for services in NSW. Sold to Fawcett Aviation Pty. Ltd., Sydney-Bankstown 14.5.53. To Rolvin Airways, Palmerston North as **ZK-AXI** 14.7.53. To Nelson Aero Club 17.5.54 and used for charters and air ambulance duties. To Arthur J. Bradshaw, Nelson 7.63 for aerial sur-vey and photography work. To Auckland Flying School, Ardmore 4.67. Damaged beyond repair during forced-landing after the port engine failed with six parachutists aboard 23.4.67. Donated by the insurance company to Museum of Transport and Technology and stored Auckland-Ardmore. Traded to Stan and Gilly Smith 1982 and rebuilt to flying condition at their Tech-Air facility at North Shore. Test flown 22.4.97 and the now immaculate aircraft is named *Taniwha,* a Maori word meaning a monstrous creature.

2058　Royal Australian Air Force serial **A34-69**. Received by 2AD 24.3.43. Issued to 1WAGS 27.7.43. To 5AD for storage 30.10.44. Sold to S. D. Marshall/Marshall Airways, Sydney-Mascot by 29.10.45. Reg'd **VH-AOE** [CofR 897 5.3.46]. To Catholic Mission of the Holy Ghost, Alexishafen PNG 24.2.48. To Madang Air Charters, Madang PNG 3.3.54. Possibly the aircraft which suffered engine failure on take-off Madang 29.10.55 necessitating a ditching into Madang Harbour. The pilot suffered minor injuries and the aircraft was destroyed. The subsequent report identified water in a fuel filter being the cause. Struck off register as "withdrawn from service" 25.7.57.

2059　Royal Australian Air Force serial **A34-70**. Received by 2AD 8.4.43. To 7AD for wireless fitment modifications 30.6.43. To 1WAGS 2.8.43. To 5AD for storage 30.10.44. Sold to K. A. Virtue, Yeerongpilly QLD 25.10.45. Reg'd **VH-AMN** [CofR 861 4.12.45]. To QANTAS Empire Airways Ltd. 7.46. To Australian National for operation by Trans Australian Airlines 2.4.49. To Schutt Aviation t/a Schutt Airfarmers Pty. Ltd., Melbourne-Moorabbin VIC 11.55. To Ross International Fisheries for air shipment of crayfish 7.60. Damaged 25.7.61 but further information not available.

2060　Royal Australian Air Force serial **A34-71**. Received by 2AD 8.4.43. To 7AD for wireless fitment modifications 28.6.43. To 1WAGS

2.8.43. Undercarriage collapsed following a heavy landing Ballarat VIC 3.3.44. Although damage was apparently superficial, the last record 9.5.44 notes "awaiting parts".

2061 Royal Australian Air Force serial **A34-72**. Received by 2AD 8.4.43. Retained for floor strengthening, wireless installation modifications and attention to nose heaviness. Issued to 35Sqdn. 20.7.43. To MacRobertson Miller Aviation for repairs 19.8.43. To 7CU 10.11.43. Allotted 6CU but considered unsuitable for operation in tropical conditions. To 5AD for storage 22.8.44. To W. R. Carpenter & Co. Ltd., Sydney NSW for just A£50 by 11.2.46. Reg'n **VH-APK** reserved but ntu. To Mandated Airlines Ltd., Lae PNG reg'd **VH-AKX** by 5.2.47. Whilst en route Lae back to Sydney for annual CofA renewal, the aircraft forced-landed on Turnagain Island, PNG 12.5.48 and was damaged beyond repair. Struck off register 5.51.

2062 Royal Australian Air Force serial **A34-73**. Received by 2AD 8.4.43. To 7AD for wireless modifications 30.6.43. To 3WAGS 13.9.43. Aircraft destroyed 19.9.43, when just after take-off, "a sudden up current forced starboard wing up and port wing down, aircraft stalled into ground and looped after striking ground". Approval given for conversion 14.10.43.

2063 Royal Australian Air Force serial **A34-74**. Received by 2AD 8.4.43. Allocated to 3CF for special undisclosed tests by Sqd. Ldr. McGilvery. To 7AD for wireless modifications 30.6.43. To 2WAGS 12.8.43. Transferred To 3WAGS 6.1.44. To 5AD for storage 19.9.44. Sold to W. R. Carpenter & Co. Ltd., Sydney NSW by 11.2.46. Civilianised as **VH-BDB** 20.5.47 and to Mandated Airlines Ltd., Lae. Crashed on take-off Kerowagi PNG due to aircraft being overloaded 3.4.51. Two of eight passengers were seriously injured. Struck off register 6.51.

2064 Royal Australian Air Force serial **A34-75**. Received by 2AD 11.4.43. To 7AD for wireless modifications 28.6.43. To 2WAGS 25.8.43. Forced to land, reasons unknown, 9.12.43 but negligible damage. To 3WAGS 6.1.44. Sold to Royal Aero Club of New South Wales, Sydney-Bankstown by 11.3.46. Civilianised as **VH-APJ** 28.10.47. Possibly spent a time on lease to Mandated Airlines Ltd., Lae PNG. Re-reg'd **VH-RSZ**, still with the Aero Club, 12.6.57. Re-reg'd **VH-PSZ** 1.9.58. Whilst en route Quirindi to Sydney, the aircraft ran short of fuel and forced-landed near Rutherford NSW 10.6.61. The pilot, Joe Palmer, was not injured but the aircraft was badly damaged. Struck off register 1.9.61.

2065 Royal Australian Air Force serial **A34-76**. Received by 2AD 15.4.43. To 7AD for wireless modifications 1.7.43. To 2WAGS 16.8.43. Transferred to 3WAGS 6.1.44. To 5AD for storage 19.9.43. Sold to W. R. Carpenter & Co. Ltd., Sydney NSW for just A£50 by 11.2.46. Civilianised as **VH-AYB** by 21.10.46. In service with Mandated Airlines Ltd., Lae PNG 21.2.47. Crashed in sea off Lae PNG 20.8.47.

2066 Royal Australian Air Force serial **A34-77**. Received by 2AD 15.4.43. To 7AD for wireless modification 1.7.43. To 1WAGS Ballarat VIC 26.8.43. To 5AD for storage 30.10.44. Sold to K. A. Virtue for A£520 7.11.45. Reg'd **VH-AOM** [CofR 898 28.2.46]. However, Virtue is unlikely to have taken delivery, as official records also show to R. T. Knight & R. J. McCarthy, Mackay QLD by 11.3.46. Crashed Mackay QLD 20.7.46. Struck off register 5.47.

2067 Royal Australian Air Force serial **A34-78**. Received by 2AD 20.4.43. Issued 5CF 17.5.43 for the exclusive use of the Allied Works Council. Allotted to 14ARD RP 20.9.44 and received by 6CU for inspection. Not delivered to 14ARD RP and instead to storage with 5AD 9.11.44. Sold to N. H. Blackman, Corinda QLD for A£520 5.10.45. Reg'd **VH-AMO** [CofR 860 23.12.45] for T. H. McDonald, Cairns QLD. Eventually collected from the C.M.U. at Evans Head NSW 25.2.46 and flown to Brisbane-Archerfield. Listed with the Catholic Mission of the Holy Ghost, Alexishafen, PNG 30.6.47. Crashed Mingende, PNG 31.12.48. Struck off register 3.49.

2068 Royal Australian Air Force serial **A34-79**. Received by 2AD 20.4.43. Issued 2CF 2.7.43. Substantial damage after crash on take-off 9.11.43. To de Havilland for repair 20.12.43. To 6CU 21.6.44. To 5AD for storage 9.11.44. To C.M.U. Evans Head NSW 5.9.45 for further storage. Sold to Zinc Corporation, Broken Hill NSW by 4.10.45.

Reg'd **VH-AQW** [CofR 991 1.7.46]. Later listed with Silver City Airways (Australia) Pty. Ltd. To QANTAS Empire Airways Ltd. 7.3.49. To Madang Air Charters, Madang, PNG 23.4.53. Nominal change to Madang Air Services Ltd. 9.56. Company absorbed by Mandated Airlines Ltd. 1.4.60. Mandated themselves taken over by Ansett Transport Industries 12.1.61, the company becoming known as Ansett-MAL. Sold to Territory Airlines Ltd., Goroka PNG for spares use .and struck off register 19.6.61.

2069 Royal Australian Air Force serial **A34-80**. Received by 2AD 22.4.43. Issued 5CF 16.7.43. Damaged Cooktown QLD 11.8.43. Badly damaged on landing 22.9.43. Owing to location and oncoming wet season, approval given for conversion 22.11.43.

2070 Royal Australian Air Force serial **A34-81**. Received by 2AD 26.4.43, but returned to de Havilland for modifications to wireless fitment 2.6.43. Issued 1RCS without floor strengthening modification incorporated 15.8.43. To 8CU 5.11.43. To 9CU 24.11.43. Damaged beyond repair after engine cut during take-off 23.12.43. Approval given for conversion 28.12.43.

2071 Royal Australian Air Force serial **A34-82**. Received by 2AD 28.4.43. Issued 5CF 16.7.43. Damaged on landing Meruake 30.11.43. Crashed between Vion (?) Range and Cairns 28.2.44. After repair at 13ARD again issued to 5CU replacing the crashed A34-36 15.5.44. To de Havilland for complete overhaul 8.8.44. To 5AD 5.7.45. To 6CU 5.11.45. With R.A.A.F. Darwin 5.3.46. According to official records sold to Flying Doctor Service for A£50 14.6.46 and issued to them 5.8.46, but listed with E. J. Connellan, Alice Springs NT when registered **VH-AXL** 1.9.46. Damaged on take-off, date uknown, Hermannsburg Mission NT but repaired. To QANTAS Empire Airways Ltd. 9.5.47. Crashed Koranka, PNG 21.9.51 and struck off register 10.51.

2072 Royal Australian Air Force serial **A34-83**. Received by 2AD 28.4.43. Returned to de Havilland for wireless fitment modifications 16.6.43. Issued 5CF 16.7.43. To 5AD for storage 2.11.44. Sold to W. R. Carpenter & Co. Ltd., Sydney NSW (as agent) for Shark Patrol Service Co. of Sydney at a price of just A£50 and issued to them 9.4.46. Reg'd **VH-APP** [CofR 994 6.7.46] to Airflite Pty. Ltd., Sydney-Mascot NSW for operation by their offshoot New England Airways. To Brown & Dureau Ltd., Melbourne VIC 26.3.47. Damaged at Bathurst Harbour TAS when overturned on take-off after striking soft ground 27.2.48. Re-registered **VH-CCP** 26.11.48 due to conflict with standard radio call signs. Aircraft noted August 1951 on charter to Victorian Railways for aerial survey work between Ballarat and Mildura. To D. C. Muir t/a Muir Aviation, Darwin NT and re-reg'd **VH-DMB** but date of sale/change unknown. Crashed Darwin NT 26.2.59 and struck off register 9.59.

2073 Royal Australian Air Force serial **A34-84**. Received by 2AD 1.5.43. Returned to de Havilland for wireless fitment modifications 16.6.43. Issued 5CF 16.7.43. Complete overhaul by de Havilland 3.7.44. To 3CU 29.3.45. To 5AD for storage 19.6.45. Sold to Bridgwater Amplivox Sound System, Sydney NSW for A£750 8.10.45 and issued to them 30.11.45. Reg'd **VH-AHY** CofR 956 24.5.46] with owner given as Shark Patrol Service Co., c/o Airflite Pty. Ltd., Sydney-Mascot NSW. To Taylor's Air Transport Ltd., Lae PNG by 7.47. Crashed Hope Creek PNG 20.5.48 and struck off register 8.48.

2074 Royal Australian Air Force serial **A34-85**. Received by 2AD 7.5.43. Allotted to 3DF for modified wireless installation trials and nose heaviness tests 13.7.43 and then to 1RCS after floor strengthening 16.9.43. Neither allotment went ahead and instead to 6CF 3.11.43. To 5AD for storage 30.11.44. Sold to Butler Air Transport Pty. Ltd., Sydney NSW via W. R. Carpenter Co. Ltd., Sydney NSW for just A£50 15.2.46 and collected 21.2.46. Civilianised as **VH-AVU** 21.11.46. To Catholic Mission of the Holy Ghost, Alexishafen PNG 11.8.48. Struck off register 23.5.51 as "withdrawn from service".

2075 Royal Australian Air Force serial **A34-86**. Received by 2AD 18.5.43. Returned to de Havilland for wireless fitment modifications 26.6.43. Following floor strengthening modification, allotted to 1RCS but instead to 6CF 3.11.43. A slight accident occurred during that month but was not reported until 17.4.44. To 2CRD 27.10.44 and transported by road to 5AD for storage 27.11.44. Sold to W. R. Carpenter & Co. Ltd., Sydney NSW for just A£50, as agent for the

Queensland Ambulance Transport Brigade on 22.2.46. Not civilianised, so presumably purchased for spares use.

2076   Royal Australian Air Force serial **A34-87**. Received by 2AD 17.5.43. Allotted to 1RCS after floor strengthening but instead received by 6CF 24.11.43. To 5AD for storage 6.12.44. Aircraft in need of complete overhaul and sold for spares use to W. R. Carpenter Co. Ltd., Sydney NSW for just A£50 on 21.2.46.

2077   Royal Australian Air Force serial **A34-88**. Received by 2AD 13.5.43. Allotted to 1RCS and then 9CU following floor strengthening. Eventually to 5CU 22.12.43. Shortly after take-off Coffs Harbour NSW 23.12.43, flew into wires and was substantially damaged. Approval given for conversion 7.1.44.

2078   Royal Australian Air Force serial **A34-89**. Received by 2AD 20.5.43. Allotted to 1RCS following floor strengthening but instead to 7CU 2.2.44. To 6CU 1.7.44. Crashed and badly damaged Batchelor NT 3.2.45. Approval given for conversion 27.2.45.

2079   Royal Australian Air Force serial **A34-90**. Received by 2AD 20.5.43. Painted in camouflage and received 33Sqdn. 7.6.43. To 8CU 4.11.43. Crashed on landing Bulldog Strip, PNG 14.12.43 but although quite severe, repairs carried out in unit. To 8CU 19.5.44. To 5AD for storage 21.11.44. Sold to W. R. Carpenter & Co. Co. Ltd., Sydney NSW for just A£50 by 11.2.46. Civilianised as **VH-ASU** 27.9.46. Listed with A. B. Browning, Bellevue Hill NSW on 30.6.47. Struck off register 19.12.47 but with QANTAS Empire Airways Ltd. 1.6.48. To Australian National for Trans Australian Airlines 13.5.49. To Schutt Aviation t/a Schutt Airfarmers Pty. Ltd., Melbourne-Moorabbin VIC 11.55. Re-reg'd **VH-APJ** 3.5.60. Struck off register 9.10.64 as "withdrawn from service".

2080   Royal Australian Air Force serial **A34-91**. Received by 2AD 25.5.43. After floor strengthening modification, allocated to 33Sqdn. but instead eventually to 6CU 24.1.44. To C.M.U. Evans Head NSW for storage 5.10.45. Sold to W. R. Capenter Pty. Ltd. for just A£50 12.2.46 and collected by them 12.3.46. Although the reg'n **VH-ARJ** was reserved, it was not taken up and therefore, presumably was purchased for spares use.

2081   Royal Australian Air Force serial **A34-92**. Received by 2AD 30.5.43. After floor strengthening modification, allocated to 33Sqdn. but instead, eventually to 6CU 25.12.43. To 5AD for storage 6.9.44. Sold to W. R. Carpenter Co. Ltd., Sydney NSW 15.2.46 for just A£50 and collected 9.4.46. Reg'd to Butlins Ltd., London W1 as **G-AJKF** [CofR 11370/1 28.3.47] for intended pleasure flying from their Skegness Holiday Camp. Not imported and cancelled 19.8.48 as "Incorrect registration". Civilianised as **VH-BDS** 28.4.48 for QANTAS Empire Airways Ltd. To E. E. Condon, c/o Wagga Flying School, Wagga Wagga NSW by 30.6.54. To N. R. Thompson, c/o North Australian Aviation Service, Darwin NT. Re-reg'd **VH-AML** 19.9.63. Noted in open store Perth-Jandakot 2.76 when with Mike W. Hockin, Capel WA. Re-built to flying condition by Lyn Forster & others and used in the 1984 A.B.C. film 'Flight Into Hell'. To Michael Howard Hockin, Castlecrag NSW 27.3.98. In flying condition at Point Cook VIC, painted in original colours and wears serial A34-92.

2082   Royal Australian Air Force serial **A34-93**. Received by 2AD 30.5.43. After floor strengthening modification, allocated to 1RCS but instead to School of Photography 13.2.44. To 5AD for storage 27.8.44. Sold to Flying Doctor Service of Australia (N.S.W. Section) for A£750 28.9.45 and issued to them 4.10.45. Reg'd **VH-AGM** [CofR 875 7.12.45]. Struck off register 31.7.46. Dismantled and parts used in the re-builds of VH-AQW (2068) and VH-URE (6029).

2083   Royal Australian Air Force serial **A34-94**. Received by 2AD 10.6.43. After floor strengthening modification, allocated to 1RCS but instead to 9CU 29.11.43. To 5AD for storage 5.10.44. Sold to W. R. Carpenter Co. Ltd., Sydney NSW 15.2.46 for just A£50 and collected 9.4.46. Civilianised as **VH-BDC** 13.6.47 for Mandated Airlines Ltd., Lae PNG. To Territory Airlines Ltd., Goroka PNG sometime in 1951. Struck off register 11.7.57 as "withdrawn from service".

2084   Royal Australian Air Force serial **A34-95**. Received by 2AD 11.6.43. After floor strengthening modification, allocated to 33Sqdn. but instead to 1CU 16.1.44 for bush fire patrol duties. Camouflaged

and to 9CU 23.4.44. Repairs and complete overhaul effected at 10RSU completed by 2.11.44. To 5AD for storage. Sold to Newcastle Aero Club, Broadmeadow NSW for A£670 by 11.3.46. Civilianised as **VH-AOL** 3.7.47. Damaged Orange NSW 10.5.53 and struck off register 7.53.

2085   Royal Australian Air Force serial **A34-96**. Received by 2AD 20.6.43. After floor strengthening modification, allocated to 33Sqdn. but instead to 1CU 16.1.44 for bush fire patrol duties. Accident on landing 4.2.44 but no damage. Camouflaged and to 9CU 23.4.44. To 5AD for storage 30.9.44. Sold to A. T. Reid c/o James Hardie & Co. Ltd., Sydney NSW for A£690 1.11.45 and issued to him 6.11.45. Reg'd **VH-AFH** [CofR 856 12.12.45]. Listed with North Australian Aviation Services, Darwin NT by 11.57. Struck off register 22.9.59 as "withdrawn from service".

2086   Royal Australian Air Force serial **A34-97**. Received by 2AD 24.6.43. After floor strengthening modification, allocated to 33Sqdn. but instead to 9CU 1.4.44. At 5AD for storage 8.1.45. Sold to Aircrafts Pty. Ltd., Brisbane-Archerfield QLD for A£1000 3.9.45 and issued to them 18.9.45. Reg'd **VH-AIA** [CofR 836 31.10.45]. To Butler Air Transport Pty. Ltd., Sydney-Mascot NSW 1.7.47. To QANTAS Empire Airways Ltd. 7.48. Struck off register 6.10.48 as "withdrawn from service". Restored to QANTAS 23.6.50. Sold 16.3.53, presumably to Territory Airlines Ltd., Goroka PNG as it was in their hands by 30.6.54. To Mitchell Aerial Services Pty. Ltd., Cairns QLD by 11.57. Ultimate fate unknown but struck off register 2.9.63.

Royal Australian Air Force serial **A34-98**. Received by 2AD 23.6.43. After floor strengthening modification, allocated to 33Sqdn. but instead to 1APU for tests 5.2.44. To 9CU 22.7.44. Crashed on take-off Daru Island PNG following engine failure 27.9.44. Approval given for conversion 5.7.45.

Three accidents are reported to unidentified Dragons and they are detailed below for completeness.

On 2.4.55, whilst operating a private flight at Narrandera NSW, the aircraft swung towards the end of the landing run and gound-looped. There were no injuries to the occupant(s) but the aircraft was substantially damaged. The accident report identified the cause as excessive cross-wind and the pilot's limited experience on type.

At Goroka PNG on 22.4.55, presumably a Territory Airlines aircraft on a charter flight, stalled during the final approach, struck bushes and crashed onto the airstrip. Again, there were no injuries but there was substantial damage to the aircraft. The subsequent report noted the pilot's limited local experience which contributed to his failure to maintain safe airspeed during the final stages of approach.

Substantial damage to a further Papua New Guinea based aircraft occurred on 26.7.56, when operating a charter flight to Faita. The pilot over-corrected a swing on landing and the aircraft ran off the strip and nosed over.

DH84A c/n 2042. Photographed 1946/47 when with Farquharson, VH-AOR later saw service with QANTAS who had previously rejected operation of the type due to its perceived single engine handling.

DH84A c/n 2079. Operated by Schutt Airfarmers of Melbourne as VH-ASU from November 1955 until re-registered VH-APJ in May 1960, this Dragon was cancelled as withdrawn in October 1964.

DH84A c/n 2045. In service with Newcastle Sport Parachute Club in New South Wales. Re-build and based for a time at Point Cook, where it was eventually destroyed in a fatal accident.

DH84A c/n 2081. Purchased by the British holiday camp entrepreneur Billy Butlin in 1947 and G-AJKF reserved, however it failed to make the U.K. As VH-AML seen here in open store at Perth's Jandakot Airfield.

DH84A c/n 2048. Actually VH-DHX but wearing its original serial A34-59, this Dragon is now owned by Torquil Norman in the U.K. and is currently undergoing restoration by Cliff Lovell at Chilbolton.

DH84A c/n 2002. After languishing in open storage at Camden, New South Wales, purchased by Sir William Roberts for his burgeoning Strathallan Aircraft Collection but now displayed at East Fortune.

DH84A c/n 2057. In New Zealand since 1953, ZK-AXI was stored for many years by the Museum of Transport and Technology at Ardmore following an accident, but was restored to flying condition in 1997.

DH84A c/n 2019. One of 87 aircraft built by de Havilland of Australia at Sydney's Mascot Airport. Presently owned by the Rural City of Wangaratta, Victoria and was displayed at their Air World attraction.

AUSTRALIA - CIVILIAN

Reg	C/N
VH-AAC	6025
VH-AAO	6112
VH-ABK	6062
VH-AEA	6073
VH-AEF	2057
VH-AFH	2085
VH-AFK	2024
VH-AGC	2045
VH-AGI	2017
VH-AGJ	2046
VH-AGM	2082
VH-AHY	2073
VH-AIA	2076
VH-AKX	2061
VH-ALL	2022
VH-AMB	2023
VH-AML	2081
VH-AMN	2059
VH-AMO	2067
VH-AOE	2058
(VH-AOF)	2048
VH-AOK	2056
VH-AOL	2084
VH-AOM	2066
VH-AON	2019
VH-AOP	2010
VH-AOQ	2011
VH-AOR	2042
VH-AOS	2006
VH-AOT	2050
(VH-API)	2043
VH-APJ (1)	2064
VH-APJ (2)	2079
(VH-APK)	2061
VH-APL	2051
VH-APP	2072
VH-AQU	2048
VH-AQW	2068
VH-ARI	2029
VH-ARJ	2028
(VH-ARJ)	2080
VH-ASK	2002
VH-ASL	2020
(VH-ASM)	2055
VH-ASN	2039
VH-ASO	2045
VH-ASU	2079
VH-ASX	2039
VH-AVU	2074
VH-AXL	2071
VH-AYB	2065
VH-AYM	2031
VH-AYZ	2053
VH-BAF	2027
VH-BAH	2055
VH-BDB	2063
VH-BDC	2083
VH-BDS	2081
VH-BJH	2044
VH-BMX	2049
VH-CPP	2072
VH-DHX	2048
VH-DMA	6029
VH-DMB	2072
VH-FDA	2045
VH-FDB	6029
(VH-GAU)	2049
VH-PSZ	2064
VH-RSZ	2064
VH-SJW	2020
VH-SNB	2002
VH-URD	6037
VH-URE	6029
VH-URF	6045
VH-URG	6046
VH-URO	6068
VH-URU	6088
VH-URV	6089
VH-URW	6080
VH-URX	6081
VH-URY	6082
VH-USA	6074
VH-UTX	6104
VH-UVB	6102
VH-UVN	6106
VH-UXG	6077
VH-UXK	6053
VH-UZF	6065
(VH-UZG)	6027
(VH-UZQ)	See 01
(VH-UZX)	6084
VH-UZZ	6097

AUSTRALIA - MILITARY

Reg	C/N
A34-1	6081
A34-2	6088
A34-3	6097
A34-4	6062
A34-5	6112
A34-6	6082
A34-7	6037
A34-8	6065
A34-9	6045
A34-10	6025
A34-11	6014
(A34-12)	6102
A34-12	2001
A34-13	2002
A34-14	2003
A34-15	2004
A34-16	2005
A34-17	2006
A34-18	2007
A34-19	2008
A34-20	2009
A34-21	2010
A34-22	2011
A34-23	2012
A34-24	2013
A34-25	2014
A34-26	2015
A34-27	2016
A34-28	2017
A34-29	2018
A34-30	2019
A34-31	2020
A34-32	2021
A34-33	2022
A34-34	2023
A34-35	2024
A34-36	2025
A34-37	2026
A34-38	2027
A34-39	2028
A34-40	2029
A34-41	2030
A34-42	2031
A34-43	2032
A34-44	2033
A34-45	2034
A34-46	2035
A34-47	2036
A34-48	2037
A34-49	2038
A34-50	2039
A34-51	2040
A34-52	2041
A34-53	2042
A34-54	2043
A34-55	2044
A34-56	2045
A34-57	2046
A34-58	2047
A34-59	2048
A34-60	2049
A34-61	2050
A34-62	2051
A34-63	2052
A34-65	2054
A34-66	2055
A34-67	2056
A34-68	2057
A34-69	2058
A34-70	2059
A34-71	2060
A34-72	2061
A34-73	2062
A34-74	2063
A34-75	2064
A34-76	2065
A34-77	2066
A34-78	2067
A34-79	2068
A34-80	2069
A34-81	2070
A34-82	2071
A34-83	2072
A34-84	2073
A34-85	2074
A34-86	2075
A34-87	2076
A34-88	2077
A34-89	2078
A34-90	2079
A34-91	2080
A34-92	2081
A34-93	2082
A34-94	2083
A34-95	2084
A34-96	2085
A34-97	2086
A34-98	2087

Radio Call Signs

These are included here as they were painted on the aircraft. As they have the appearance of civilian type registrations, we have made the break after the VHC!

Reg	C/N
VHC-RM	2022
VHC-RN	2026
VHC-RO	2028
VHC-SB	6112
VHC-SF	2012
VHC-SG	2015
VHC-SH	2020
VHC-SJ	2030
VHC-SK	2033
VHC-SL	2034
VHC-SM	2037
VHC-SN	2036

AUSTRIA - CIVILIAN

Reg	C/N
OE-FKD	6101

AUSTRIA - MILITARY

Reg	C/N
64	6101

BRAZIL

Reg	C/N
PP-SPC	6085

CANADA

Reg	C/N
CF-APJ	6024
CF-AVD	6086
CF-AVI	6093

DENMARK - MILITARY

Reg	C/N
S-21	6060
S-22	6061

EGYPT

Reg	C/N
SU-ABH	6028
SU-ABI	6031
SU-ABJ	6051
SU-ABZ	6032

FRANCE

Reg	C/N
F-AMTM	6040
F-AMTR	6057
F-AMUZ	6064
F-ANES	6083
F-ANGE	6038

GREAT BRITAIN - CIVILIAN

Reg	C/N
E.4	6103
E.9	6000
G-ACAN	6000
G-ACAO	6001
G-ACAP	6002
G-ACBW	6009
G-ACCE	6010
G-ACCR	6011
G-ACCV	6014
G-ACCZ	6015
G-ACDL	6016
G-ACDM	6017
G-ACDN	6018
G-ACEK	6019
G-ACET	6021
G-ACEU	6022
G-ACEV	6023
G-ACFG	6027
G-ACGG	6025
G-ACGK	6033
G-ACGU	6034
G-ACHV	6035
G-ACHX	6036
G-ACIE	6032
G-ACIT	6039
G-ACIU	6041
G-ACIW	6038
G-ACJH	6040
G-ACJM	6049
G-ACJS	6042
G-ACJT	6043
G-ACKB	6055
G-ACKC	6056
G-ACKD	6052
G-ACKU	6066
G-ACLE	6044
G-ACMC	6053
G-ACMJ	6058
G-ACMO	6062
G-ACMP	6063
G-ACNA	6067
G-ACNG	6069
G-ACNH	6070
G-ACNI	6071
G-ACNJ	6072
G-ACOR	6073
G-ACPX	6075
G-ACPY	6076
G-ACRF	6077
G-ACRH	6078
G-ACRO	6079
G-ACVD	6084
G-ADCP	6092
G-ADCR	6094
G-ADCT	6095
G-ADDI	6096
G-ADDJ	6097
G-ADED	6098
G-ADEE	6099
G-ADFI	6100
G-ADOS	6103
G-ADXI	6087
G-AECZ	6105

G-AEFX	6106
G-AEKZ	6028
G-AEIS	6107
G-AEIT	6108
G-AEIU	6109
G-AEMI	6110
G-AEMJ	6111
G-AEMK	6112
(G-AJKF)	2081
G-ECAN	2048

GREAT BRITAIN - MILITARY

X9379	6035
(X9395)	6041
X9396	6058
X9397	6044
X9398	6001
X9399	6075
X9340	6092
AV982	6105
AW154	6015
AW163	6028
AW170	6018
AW171	6021
AW172	6066
AW173	6110
AX863	6055
AX867	6019
BS816	6009
HM569	6103
2779M	6021

INDIA

VT-AEK	6050
VT-AEL	6048
VT-AES	6065

IRAQ - CIVILIAN

YI-AAC	6044

IRAQ - MILITARY

16	6003
17	6004
18	6005
19	6006
20	6007
21	6008
22	6012
23	6013

IRELAND - CIVILIAN

EI-ABI (1)	6076
EI-ABI (2)	6105
EI-AFK	6105

IRELAND - MILITARY

DH18	6071

KENYA

VP-KAW	6047
VP-KBA	6059
VP-KBG	6079

NEW ZEALAND - CIVILIAN

ZK-ADR	6090
ZK-ADS	6091
ZK-AKT	6090
ZK-AXI	2057

NEW ZEALAND - MILITARY

NZ550	6091
NZ551	6090

PORTUGAL - MILITARY

504	6111
505	6113
506	6114

PORTUGESE EAST TIMOR

CR-ABT	See 02

SOUTH AFRICA - CIVILIAN

ZS-AEF	6026
ZS-AEG	6030
ZS-AEH	6054
ZS-AEI	6017

SOUTH AFRICA - MILITARY

SAAF1414	6054
SAAF1570	6017

SOUTHERN RHODESIA - CIVILIAN

VP-YBY	6030

SOUTHERN RHODESIA - MILITARY

260	6030

SPAIN – CIVILIAN

EC-W14	6020
EC-TAT	6020

SPAIN – MILITARY

Republican

LD-001	6020
LD-002	6016
?	6023
?	6056
?	6067

Side Unknown

?	6022
?	6038
?	6042
?	6057
?	6064
?	6070
?	6083

TURKEY - MILITARY

?	6087
?	6107
?	6108
?	6109

UNITED STATES

N34DH	6096

3.7 Unknown DH84s

The identities of just two Dragons are unknown and these are detailed below:-

1.   **VH-UZQ** was reserved, presumably for a U.K. built machine, but in the event was not imported. It seems likely that negotiations were at an advanced stage and therefore a registration was requested. Conjecture may be, but both the Spanish Nationalist and Republican forces were actively purchasing second hand aircraft in the U.K. at inflated prices during 1936/37 when the registration was reserved and it is believed that the Australian purchaser was gazumped!

2.   **CR-ABT** was registered on 14th December 1946 to the Portugese East Timor Government for use by Transportes Aereos de Timor. Although thought to be an Australian built DH84A, it has proved impossible to identify the actual aircraft.

de Havilland
DH 86

DH86 c/n 2300. An early photograph of the prototype G-ACPL shows the original cockpit glazing for intended single pilot operation. Just a few months later it had been modified for two crew.

DH86 c/n 2306. VH-UUA was originally laid down for Imperial Airways but switched to the Australian airline prior to delivery, to replace their ill-fated VH-USG.

DH86 c/n 2302. G-ACVY was the first delivered to Railway Air Services in July 1934. When in service with Skytravel after the war, the main spar broke but miraculously, it landed safely!

DH86 c/n 2307. Impressed for operation by the R.A.A.F. with serial A31-5 but restored as VH-USC in March 1942. Damaged beyond repair when crashed Darwin October 1944.

DH86 c/n 2303. Flying an Imperial Airways service from Strasbourg to Venice March 1937, the pilot lost his bearings. Fuel exhaustion necessitated a forced landing and G-ACVZ was destroyed by fire.

DH86 c/n 2309. There was considerable disquiet in Australia about safety aspects of the DH86. Perhaps to quell this, QANTAS proudly announced in July 1941 that VH-USE had flown 1 million miles.

DH86 c/n 2304. Based, at various times, variously at Imperial Airways outstations at Khartoum and Bangkok, G-ACWC was eventually cancelled as destroyed after a crash in Nigeria June 1941.

DH86 c/n 2313. Jersey Airways' G-ACYF takes on another load at their base during the late 1930s. After a period in Singapore, it was later written-off in R.A.A.F. service near Maryborough, Queensland.

4.1 de Havilland DH86 - Development

Designed and built in just four months, the unnamed DH86, was primarily intended for the long awaited through airmail and passenger service from England to Australia. The type's specification was laid down jointly by the British and Australian Governments and the state sponsored airline Imperial Airways would operate the route from Croydon to Singapore and the recently formed QANTAS Empire Airways would operate the connecting service from Singapore, via Darwin to Cootamundra in New South Wales. The plan was to commence operations in September 1934.

Structurally, the DH86 followed standard de Havilland practice, the fuselage being a plywood box with spruce stiffening members and sound proofing on the outside. A fabric outer covering was then applied to give a slightly rounded appearance, similar to that achieved for later model DH85 Leopard Moths.

The prototype first flew at Stag Lane on 14th January 1934, flown by the company's test pilot Hubert S. Broad and wearing E.2 in the company's allocated test series. After a number of successful test flights, a week later, the aircraft was flown to the Aircraft and Armament Experimental Establishment at Martlesham Heath for certification trials. A certificate of airworthiness was issued on 30th January 1934, just one day prior to the Australian Government's deadline for aircraft manufacturers to provide suitable machines to operate safely on the long over water stretches between stops on the route Singapore to Darwin.

Unfortunately, de Havilland's first four-engine transport did not quite match the QANTAS Managing Director Hudson Fysh's ideal specification to operate the ambitious new route. As we saw previously in the DH84 development history, he had strong feelings about multi engine reliability and he was obviously well satisfied with that aspect of the forthcoming DH86. In a letter to E. C. Johnston, Controller of Civil Aviation in Australia dated 15th February 1934, he provided cuttings from a Brisbane newspaper showing the possibilities of a forced landing worked out on a mathematical basis:-

Single engine – risk of forced landing	1 in 100
Twin engine – able to fly on one engine	1 in 5,000
Three engines – able to fly on any two	2 in 1,650
Four engines – able to fly on any two	2 in 41,350

In other respects he was not so happy and despite severe weight difficulties that would ensue, he put pressure on Johnston and directly to the manufacturer to provide an aircraft with cockpit accommodation for two crew, increased fuel tankage and for flaps to be installed as he could not contemplate a permanently fixed landing speed of 69 m.p.h., far higher than any other type in airline service at that time.

While de Havilland strove to comply with these requirements, QANTAS placed an order for five aircraft and their Chief Pilot, Lester Brain departed Australia by sea for England on 23rd May 1934 to carry out acceptance trials and fly the first DH86 home to his airline's base established at Longreach in Queenland.

In the meantime, Launceston, Tasmania based Holyman's Airways had placed an order for three aircraft and the first, a single pilot type, arrived by sea in late August 1934. The certificate of airworthiness was issued on 27th September 1934 and VH-URN entered service on the Launceston to Melbourne route on 3rd October. The pride of Holyman's fleet named *Miss Hobart* was short-lived as it crashed into the Bass Strait off Wilson's Promonotory just 16 days later with the loss of all 12 souls on board, including the airline's founder Victor Holyman. Unfortunately, no trace of the wreck could be found and therefore the later Aircraft Accident Investigation Committee inquiry had to rely heavily on testimony received from pilot's rather limited experience of flying the type. Noteworthy, were Holyman's K. M. Frewin, who reported oscillations in the directional plane and Lester Brain, who had flown the first QANTAS DH86 VH-USC into Australia a few days prior to the accident, commented on the type's behaviour during turns.

As the investigation continued, QANTAS decided to ship their 2nd and 3rd aircraft instead of flying them to Australia and these duly arrived in January, too late to tie in with the Imperial service to Singapore. As an interim measure, Imperial extended their service through to Darwin and QANTAS operated the onward link from Darwin to Brisbane, which was the revised destination of the Empire Route. However, on 25th February 1935, their service was extended from Darwin to Singapore.

The fourth QANTAS aircraft, VH-USF, was retained in England for further trials at Hatfield and Martlesham Heath as a result of the various reports to the Holyman accident inquiry. Although no abnormal behaviour or structural weakness was found, various precautionary modifications were taken including fin strengthening, the removal of the rudder servo tab and the filling of the gap left after its removal.

Two more fatal accidents occurred to Australian registered DH86s. VH-USG c/n 2311 crashed in open country on Barradale Station QLD 15th November 1934, 15 miles south-east of the QANTAS base at Longreach QLD, whilst on delivery from the U.K. All 4 occupants, 3 crew under Capt. D. R. Prendergast and 1 passenger were killed and on 2nd October 1935, Holyman's VH-URT c/n 2312 crashed off Flinders Island with the loss of crew & 10 passengers.

Notwithstanding three serious accidents in Australia, QANTAS proudly announced that VH-USE c/n 2309 had flown 1 million miles in their service by July 1941.

Another tragedy occurred on 15th September 1936, when British Airways G-ADYF was taking-off from Gatwick on a mail flight to Hanover via Cologne. The aircraft entered a normal left hand turn, but failed to take up the required heading for Cologne, continuing to turn and lose height until crashing into a field in the vicinity of Lowfield Heath. The DH86 caught fire on impact and was totally destroyed.

A sister ship G-ADYH was immediately dispatched to Martlesham Heath for extensive trials, specifically looking at possible control problems during turns. Their report was scathing and led to major modifications to the tail end as illustrated on pages 50 and 52. In this form, the aircraft was known as the DH86B and even after all surviving aircraft had been modified to this standard, the handling qualities were merely described as acceptable!

Surely one of the quickest passenger aircraft ever to come from the drawing board into service, but also the subject of a series of major design modifications throughout the first years of its life and these are detailed below.

DH86 (single pilot)
Four aircraft only. Featured a second crew member, responsible for radio operation and as navigator with a seat stationed at the forward end of the passenger cabin. Two later returned to the manufacturer for front fuselage modification to accommodate two crew and dual controls.

DH86 (dual control)
Modified for two crew operation and provision of split trailing edge flaps on the upper mainplanes.

DH86A

Pneumatic undercarriage legs, larger brakes and tail wheel, metal rudder

Two versions: with Gipsy Six 1 engines driving two bladed wooden props – all-up weight of 10250lb

Gipsy Six II high compression engines driving de Havilland variable pitch airscrews. The only example of this version was c/n 2342, tested at Martlesham Heath as E.2. Reverted to Gipsy Six I engines and fixed pitch propellers prior to delivery to Misr Airwork as SU-ABV

DH86B

Following the crash of G-ADYF near Lowfield Heath, after take-off from Gatwick in September 1936, sister ship G-ADYH was sent to Martlesham Heath for a new series of flight tests. The report that followed, criticised rudder and aileron control and de Havilland's fix was the addition of large auxiliary fins attached to the tailplanes. The last ten aircraft were the DH86B model, with the tailplanes having increased chord at the tips , higher gearing in the aileron circuit and the afore mentioned auxiliary fins. All surviving DH86As were subsequently modified to DH86B standard.

Notwithstanding all the trials and tribulations, the type was successfully operated

Aer Lingus	Two purchased second hand and used Dublin to Bristol, Croydon, Isle of Man and Speke
Australian National Airways	The two surviving Holyman aircraft flew A.N.A.'s first flights, operated daily Melbourne to Sydney from formation in July 1936
Blackpool and West Coast	Two aircraft operated a virtual shuttle service Blackpool to Ronaldsway, Isle of Man
British Airways	Short-lived operation of daytime passenger and night time mail services ex Gatwick to Continental destinations used eight DH86 aircraft
Carpenter, W. R.	The last three built, operated the 3,000 mile service from Sydney to Rabaul, via Townsville, Thursday Island and Port Moresby
Devlet Hava Yollari	Four aircraft delivered to the Turkish State Airline and operated ex Istanbul to Ankara and Izmir, also Ankara to Adana
Gulf Aviation	Two purchased second hand and used thrice daily Bahrain to Dhahran, first flight on 25th July 1951
Hillman's Airways	Three DH86s replaced Dragons on the popular cut-price route from Stapleford to Paris
Jersey Airways	Six DH86s replaced Dragons on the Heston, Southampton and Channel Islands services
Misr Airwork	Four DH86s also superseded Dragons on services from Cairo to Alexandria, Assuit, Baghdad, Cyprus and Haifa
P.L.U.N.A., Uruguay	Two aircraft connected the Uruguayan capital Montevideo to Artigas and Rivera
Railway Air Services	After route proving carried out by the prototype, two single pilot DH86s entered service on the R.A.S. trunk routes connecting Croydon with Castle Bromwich (serving Birmingham), Barton (serving Manchester), Belfast-Harbour, and Renfrew
Union Airways of New Zealand Dunedin	Scheduled passenger and mail services from Palmerston North to Blenheim, Christchurch and
Wearne's Air Services	Two aircraft operated ex Singapore to Kuala Lumpar and Penang

4.2 de Havilland DH86 – Specifications

Type:	Airliner
Capacity:	Pilot(s) and 8 (QANTAS) to 18 (Blackpool and West Coast Air Services) passengers
Country of origin:	Great Britain
Production period:	1934-1947
Engines:	4 X de Havilland Gipsy Six 6 cylinder in-line air cooled piston engines each of 200hp
First flight:	14th January 1934 (at Stag Lane, Edgware, Middlesex)
Total number built:	62
Production by:	de Havilland Aircraft Co. Ltd., Hatfield, Hertfordshire (first delivery April 1934 and the last in November 1942)

Dimensions	DH86 Single pilot	DH86 Two pilot	DH86A/I	DH86A/II	DH86B
Wing span:	64' 6"	64' 6"	64' 6"	64' 6"	64' 6"
Wing area:	641 sq ft	641 sq ft	641 sq ft	641 sq ft	641 sq ft
Length:	43' 11"	46' 11"	46' 11"	46' 11"	46' 11"
Height:	13' 0"	13' 0"	13' 0"	13' 0"	13' 0"
Weights:					
Empty:	5,520 lb	6,303 lb	6,140 lb	7,228 lb	6,489 lb
Max take-off:	9,200 lb	10,000 lb	10,250 lb	11,000 lb	10,250 lb
Tankage:					
Petrol:	114 gallons	183 gallons	183 gallons	183 gallons	183 gallons
Performance:					
Initial rate of climb:	1,140' per m	1,200' per m	925' per m	1,100' per m	925' per m
Max speed:	170 m.p.h.	170 m.p.h.	166 m.p.h.	150 m.p.h.	166 m.p.h.
Cruise speed:	145 m.p.h.	145 m.p.h.	142 m p.h.	135 m.p.h.	142 m.p.h.
Service ceiling:	-	20,500'	17,400'	18,000'	17,400'
Range:	450 miles	760 miles	760 miles	748 miles	800 miles
Aircraft built:	4	28	20	1	10
Construction numbers:	2300 [1], 2301, 2302, 2303 [1]	2304 - 2327 2329 - 2332	2328 [2] 2333 – 2351 [2]	2342 [3]	2352 - 2361

Notes:	
[1]	Forward fuselage subsequently modified for two crew operation
[2]	All returned to Hatfield for conversion to DH86B standard in 1937
[3]	Tested with the higher compression Gipsy Queen II engines and variable pitch propellers but returned to standard configuration prior to delivery to Misr Airwork

4.3 de Havilland DH86 Production

2300 Single pilot. First flown in test marks as **E.2** at Stag Lane 14.1.34. After trials at Martlesham Heath, CofA no.4162 issued 30.1.34. To Imperial Airways Ltd., Croydon reg'd **G-ACPL** [CofR 4954 23.4.34] and named *Delphinius*. Used by Railway Air Services Ltd., Croydon for route proving named *Diana*. Returned to Hatfield for 2-crew cockpit conversion 8.34. Transferred to Imperial's Karachi station 15.2.36. Moved on to Imperial's Bangkok station 11.37. To British Overseas Airways Corporation, Whitchurch on formation 1.4.40 but remained based at Bangkok. Actually based at Whitchurch 22.8.40 according to official records. Transferred to Khartoum station 10.40. Impressed as **HK844** 15.12.41 at Cairo and served with 206Grp. Middle East, initially with B flight of 117Sqdn. from 4.3.42. Used by 1AAU, R.A.A.F. Starboard engines cut on take-off Maaten Bagush (Landing Ground L.G.14) 10.4.42 causing a violent swing and the undercarriage collapsed. SOC as Cat.E1 1.12.42.

2301 Single pilot. Export CofA issued 25.7.34 and delivered by sea to Australia arriving late 8.34. Assembled at R.A.A.F. Laverton, reg'd **VH-URN** [CofR 490 27.9.34] and CofA no.446 issued on the same day. Delivered to Holyman's Airways Pty. Ltd., Launceston on 1.10.34 and named *Miss Hobart*. To be used by Holyman's exclusively for their Melboune VIC to Hobart TAS route with first service operated 3.10.34. With 12 souls including the airline's founder Victor Holyman aboard, the aircraft ditched in the Bass Strait, off Wilson's Promontory VIC 19.10.34. No trace of the wreck found.

2302 Single pilot. CofA no.4464 issued 15.8.34. Reg'd to Railway Air Services Ltd., Croydon as **G-ACVY** [CofR 5234 21.4.34]. Handed over 18.7.34 and named *Mercury*. Continued in civilian service throughout the war under the aegis of A.A.J.C. To Skytravel Ltd., Speke 22.10.46. En route Dublin to Liverpool 8.8.46, the main spar broke but the aircraft landed safely. All DH86 were grounded for a time while the matter was investigated. Continued in service with Skytravel until the company went into liquidation 15.8.47. Cancelled from the register 5.11.48 and broken up Langley.

2303 Single pilot. CofA issued 7.12.34. To Railway Air Services Ltd., Croydon reg'd **G-ACVZ** [CofR 5235 21.7.34] and named *Jupiter*. Returned to Hatfield for 2-crew cockpit conversion. Transferred for operation by Imperial Airways Ltd., Croydon. During a night flight Strasbourg to Venice, the pilot became lost and because of fuel exhaustion, attempted to land on the old airfield at Elsdorf near Cologne 15/16.3.37. However, he undershot, the aircraft's right wing struck the top of a tree and crashed, catching fire on impact with the ground. Three persons were killed in the conflagration. [Note: *Flight* magazine gives accident location as a wood near Bergheim]. Cancelled from the register 4.37.

2304 Two crew. For Imperial Airways Ltd., Croydon and reg'd **G-ACWC** [CofR 5241 29.1.35], named *Delia*. CofA no.4713 issued 5.3.36. Transferred to Khartoum station 1936. To Bangkok station 1938. To British Overseas Airways Corporation, again at Bangkok station 1.4.40 but nominal ownership change not recorded until 22.8.40. To Khartoum station 10.40. Crashed Minnaa, Nigeria 17.6.41 and cancelled following day.

2305 Two crew. For Imperial Airways Ltd., Croydon and reg'd **G-ACWD** [CofR 5242 29.1.35], named *Dorado*. CofA no.4706 issued 28.2.35. Based at their Penang station from 4.10.35 and operated first Penang – Saigon – Hong Kong service 14.3.36. On 3.6.38, the port inner engine backfired on start up and the port wing and centre section fabric was damaged. One occupant broke a leg during the hurried evacuation and repairs to the aircraft took 6 weeks, whilst the unfortunate party was immobilised for somewhat longer! To British Overseas Airways Corporation 1.4.40 at Bangkok station but nominal ownership change not recorded until 22.8.40. Impressed into R.A.F. service Heliopolis with serial **HK829** 22.11.41. Initial use by 216Sqdn., then B Flight 117Sqdn. at Bilbeis from 4.3.42. Transferred to 1AAU R.A.A.F. at Heliopolis from 29.5.42. Undercarriage collapsed on landing Neffatia North 17.2.43 and SOC as Cat.E1 28.2.43.

2306 Two crew. Intended for Imperial Airways Ltd., Croydon reg'd **G-ACWE** [CofR 5243 29.1.35] but diverted for operation by QANTAS Empire Airways Ltd. to replace their VH-USG, lost on 15.11.34. Export CofA issued 14.2.35. Reg'd **VH-UUA** [CofR 506 22.1.35], named *R.M.A. Adelaide*. CofA no.474 issued 8.4.35. To

Tata Group Ltd., Bombay reg'd **VT-AKM** 8.9.38. Impressed for military service with serial **HX789** 3.7.42 and flown by No.5 Flt. Indian Air Force Voluntary Reserve at Cochin. Swung on take-off and undercarriage collapsed Cochin 15.9.42. SOC as Cat.E 2.7.43.

2307 Two crew. Export CofA issued 13.9.34. Reg'd **VH-USC** for QANTAS Empire Airways Ltd. [CofR 483 1.9.34]. Handed over 10.9.34 and departed on delivery ex Croydon 24.9.34 and arrived Darwin 11.10.34. Named *R.M.A. Canberra*. To MacRobertson-Miller Aviation Co. Ltd., Perth WA 22.7.38. Impressed into R.A.A.F. service as **A31-5** 30.9.40. To 1AOS 13.1.41. Issued to Department of Civil Aviation for loan to QANTAS 30.3.42 and restored to civil register as **VH-USC**. Long range tanks and altitude controls fitted by QANTAS to allow supply dropping missions over the 12,000' mountains in the Bismarck Range in PNG. Badly damaged when crashed Darwin NT 9.10.44, finally being struck off register 6.1.45.

2308 Two crew. Export CofA issued 2.10.34. Shipped to Australia per *SS Bendigo*. To QANTAS Empire Airways Ltd. reg'd **VH-USD** [CofR 503 22.1.35], named *R.M.A. Brisbane*. CofA no.460 issued same day. To MacRobertson-Miller Aviation Co. Ltd. 9.8.38. To Tata Group Ltd., Bombay as **VT-AKZ** 8.38. Impressed as **AX800** 21.6.40 and modified to carry two 250lb anti-submarine bombs. Initially served with 2CDF at Bombay-Juhu, later with 5CDF at Wilmington Island, Cochin, No.105 Flt. and finally, 1SFTS at Ambala. Crashed on take-off Ahmedabad 18.12.41 for an intended ferry flight to Bombay, due to an uncontrollable swing and the port undercarriage collapsed. Remains transferred to Director of Civil Aviation for spares use 1.9.43.

2309 Two crew. Export CofA issued 27.10.34. To QANTAS Empire Airways Ltd. reg'd **VH-USE** [CofR 504 22.1.35], named *R.M.A. Sydney*. CofA no.465 issued the same day. By July 1941, the aircraft had flown 1 million miles in QANTAS service. En route from Archerfield to Darwin, crashed into Mount Petrie, near Brisbane QLD 20.2.42 and the 7 occupants were killed.

2310 Two crew. After extensive flight trials at Martlesham Heath, export CofA issued 27.12.34. As a result of the trials, fin strengthening work and removal of the rudder servo tab was undertaken. Delivered ex Croydon 7.1.35. To QANTAS Empire Airways Ltd. reg'd **VH-USF** [CofR 505 22.1.35], named *R.M.A. Melbourne*. CofA no.466 issued 14.3.35. Operated a sector from Singapore to Brisbane 30th April 1935 and carried first through passengers from the U.K. to Australia, two Anglo-Persian Oil Co. geologists. Impressed as **A31-6**. Initially with 3EFTS but to 1AOS 25.1.41. Allocated to 1AAU 7.2.41 but remained with 1AOS. Loaned to Department of Civil Aviation 27.3.42, for use by QANTAS, modified like c/n 2307 and restored as **VH-USF**. Crashed on take-off Blackall QLD 9.7.44 sustaining severe damage to starboard undercarriage, wings, outer wing struts and propellers. Wreck returned to R.A.A.F. less parts required by QANTAS to keep other aircraft serviceable and stored Amberley. To MacRobertson-Miller Aviation Co. Ltd., Perth 13.2.45 and restored to flying condition. Crashed Geraldton WA 24.6.45 killing both occupants.

2311 Two crew. Export CofA issued 18.10.34. To QANTAS Empire Airways Ltd. reg'd **VH-USG** [CofR 506]. Crashed in open country on Barradale Station QLD 15.11.34, 15 miles south of the QANTAS base at Longreach QLD, whilst on delivery from the U.K. All 4 occupants, 3 crew under Capt. D. R. Prendergast and 1 passenger were killed.

2312 Two crew. Export CofA issued 18.10.34 or 8.11.34?. To Holyman's Airways Pty. Ltd. reg'd **VH-URT** [CofR 507 29.1.35] and named *Loina*, an Aboriginal work meaning "the sun". CofA no.461 issued on the same day. Crashed off Flinders Island with the loss of crew & 10 passengers 2.10.35.

2313 Two crew. For Jersey Airways Ltd., St. Helier (but based Heston) reg'd **G-ACYF** [CofR 5352 7.12.34] and named *The Giffard Bay*. CofA no.4668 issued 6.2.35. To Wearne's Air Services Ltd., Singapore 6.38 reg'd **VR-SBD** and named *Governor Murchison*. To W. R. Carpenter & Co. Ltd., Sydney NSW reg'd **VH-ADN** [CofR 771 24.6.40]. To Ansett Airways

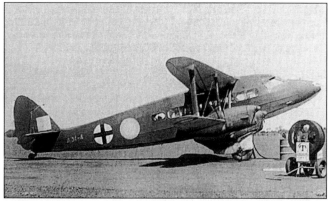

DH86 c/n 2315. Last noted at Amberley in "crashed condition" during 1946, one wonders whether A31-4 is the mysterious DH86 of which parts were reported still in existence in the 1980s.

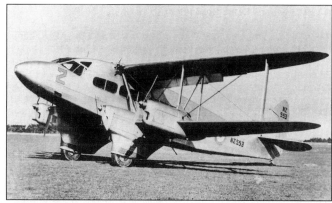

DH86 c/n 2331. Following an accident, major repairs to NZ553 were undertaken by de Havilland. It was subsequently known as DHNZ2332 and obviously incorporated major parts of that aircraft.

DH86 c/n 2321. The last flying DH86 G-ACZP when with Hampshire Aeroplane Club. A tyre burst on landing Madrid September 1958 and the undercarriage collapsed, damaging the aircraft beyond repair.

DH86A c/n 2333. G-ADUE delivered to Imperial Airways but returned to DH for conversion to DH86B standard 1937. The additional tailplane fins, may be clearly seen in this photograph.

DH86 c/n 2322. G-ACZR was delivered new to Jersey Airways and it served them for five years until impressment. Destroyed when spun into the ground at R.N.A.S. Donibristle March 1943.

DH86 c/n 2336. EI-ABT served Aer Lingus throughout the war and later with two Gatwick based companies, before sale by Aerocontacts, also of Gatwick to Gulf Aviation in Bahrain.

DH86 c/n 2323. Originally delivered to Hillman's Airways, G-ADEA subsequently saw service with British Airways, Wearne's Air Services in Singapore and, as A31-7, as an air ambulance in the Middle East.

DH86 c/n 2338. Like c/n 2336, operated by Aer Lingus but seen here as G-ADVJ during the period 1947-1951 when operated by Bond Air Services from Gatwick. Similarly, subsequently to Gulf Aviation.

and possibly operated very briefly by South Queensland Airways. Impressed as **A31-2** 7.40. Initially with 3EFTS but to 1AOS 2.12.40. To Point Cook, VIC. 13.3.42. To 1AD 21.3.42. To Signals School 29.5.42 but declared "indefinitely unserviceable due to undercarriage". Repairs carried out at 1SFTS and to 36Sqdn. 21.9.42. Ground looped 2.12.42 and to de Havilland, Sydney-Mascot for repairs 26.12.42. To 34Sqdn. 3.4.43. To 2AAU for air ambulance modifications 3.44. Forced landed approximately 1 mile north-west of Maryborough QLD when ran out of fuel 1.5.44 sustaining major damage to spats, port outer propeller, ailerons & fuselage. Although it was intended to salvage the remains, moving the wreck by rail to a repair centre, the aircraft was deemed beyond economical repair and finally written-off 1.8.44.

2314   Two crew. For Jersey Airways Ltd., St. Helier (but based Heston) reg'd **G-ACYG** [CofR 5351 7.12.34] and named *The St. Grouville Bay*. CofA no.4722 issued 8.3.35 and handed over 20.3.35. Impressed by the military as **AX840** 21.7.40. Served with 782Sqdn. Fleet Air Arm at R.N.A.S. Donibristle. Damaged 8.12.43 and to de Havilland Witney for repairs 25.9.44. Re-categorised as Cat.E and finally scrapped 6.3.45 or 14.3.45.

2315   Two crew. Export CofA issued 6.3.35. To Holyman's Airways Ltd. reg'd **VH-USW** named *Lepena*, an Aboriginal word meaning "the eye". Carried out a precautionary landing on Hunter Island and the undercarriage collapsed, following suspected structural failure, en route Launceston to Melbourne 13.12.35. Recovered and repaired. Merged to form Australian National Airways Pty. Ltd. 2.11.36. Impressed as **A31-4** 13.9.40. Initially with 3EFTS, to 1AD 19.12.40. Damaged 27.12.40 when torn from moorings during a gale sustaining damage to all main-planes and outer starboard inter-plane strut. Allotted after repair to 1AAU but not delivered. Instead to 1AOS 16.4.41. Loaned to QANTAS 30.3.42 – 4.5.42 and restored temporarily to the civil register as **VH-USW**. Modified to air ambulance and again as **A31-4**, issued to 2AAU 3.7.42. With air ambulance fittings removed, issued to Department of Civil Aviation at Brisbane-Archerfield, Qld 7.9.44. However to 3AD at Amberley and stored there in "crashed condition" 2.2.45. To MacRobertson-Miller Aviation Co. 14.2.45 and returned to Australian National Airways 5.45. Sale to Universal Flying Services Ltd. in England late 1946 was stillborn. Eventual fate unknown.

2316   Two crew. CofA no.4752 issued 22.3.35 and handed over to Jersey Airways Ltd., Southampton 26.3.35. Named *The St. Catherine's Bay*. Somewhat belatedly, reg'd **G-ACZN** [CofR 6695 31.1.36]. The aircraft took off in bad weather en route to Southampton and after about one minute, the pilot apparently got disorientated in cloud and lost control. It dived into the ground within the Jersey Airport perimeter 4.11.38 and was destroyed in the ensuing fire. All occupants and one person on the ground were killed. Cancelled from register 7.1.39.

2317   Two crew. CofA issued 30.3.35. Handed over to Imperial Airways Ltd., Croydon 31.3.35. Reg'd **G-ADCM** and named *Draco*. After encountering severe icing, a forced landing was attempted at Zwettl, Austria 22.10.35. The ground proved unsuitable and the aircraft was destroyed.

2318   Two crew. For Jersey Airways Ltd., Portsmouth and reg'd **G-ACZO** [CofR 5440 7.12.34]. CofA no.4771 issued 9.4.35 and handed over 13.4.35, named *The Ouaine Bay*. Impressed for military service as serial **AX841** 21.7.40. To Fleet Air Arm at R.N.A.S. Donibristle? Destroyed by enemy action R.N.A.S. Lee-on-Solent 16.7.40.

2319   Two crew. For Imperial Airways Ltd., Croydon and reg'd **G-ADCN** [CofR 5604 15.2.35]. CofA no.4783 issued 15.4.35. Handed over 13.4.35 and named *Daedalus*. To Bangkok station. Destroyed by fire when starting engines at Bangkok 3.12.38. Cancelled from register 2 days later.

2320   Two crew. Handed over to Misr Airwork Ltd., Cairo reg'd **SU-ABN** named *Khartoum*, 25.5.35. Export CofA issued 27.5.35 and delivered ex Hatfield 10.6.35. Forced landed at Ruthah and was written-off 11.1.39.

2321   Two crew. For Jersey Airways Ltd., Portsmouth and reg'd **G-ACZP** [CofR 5441 7.12.34]. CofA no.4830 issued 11.5.35. and handed over 15.5.35 named *The Belcroute Bay*. Impressed as **AX843** 21.7.40 but released swiftly to Railway Air Services Ltd.,

Speke 29.8.40 and operated by Scottish Airways throughout the war with civil marks, under the aegis of A.A.J.C. To Skytravel Ltd., Speke 10.40. To Bowmaker Ltd., Bournemouth 2.7.48. To Lancashire Aircraft Corporation Ltd., Samlesbury 20.4.51. To Silver City Airways Ltd. 28.10.57. To Vivian Hampson Bellamy of Hampshire Aeroplane Club Ltd. 21.2.58. A tyre burst on landing Madrid-Barajas 21.9.58, causing a ground loop and the undercarriage collapsed. Although Continental Aircraft Services of Croydon were considering repairs in early 1959, the work did not commence and the mortal remains could still be seen at Madrid during the 1970s.

2322   Two crew. For Jersey Airways Ltd., Southampton reg'd **G-ACZR** [CofR 6669 27.1.34]. CofA no.4879 issued 29.5.35. Handed over 31.5.35 and named *The La Saline Bay*, 31.5.35. Impressed into military service with serial **AX844** 21.7.40. Served with 782Sqdn. Fleet Air Arm at R.N.A.S. Donibristle. Spun into ground at Donibristle and destroyed 31.3.43.

2323   Two crew. CofA no.4844 issued 5.6.35. Handed over to Hillman's Airways Ltd., Maylands reg'd **G-ADEA** and named *Drake*, 3.6.35. Operated by British Continental Airways Ltd., Croydon 1935. To British Airways Ltd., Heston .36. To Airwork Ltd., Heston [CofR 8132 11.10.37]. Sold to Wearne's Air Services Ltd., Singapore 6.38 reg'd **VR-SBC**. Sold to W. R. Carpenter & Co. Ltd., Sydney NSW and reg'd **VH-UZX** 17.7.40. Impressed as **A31-7** 2.1.41. Initially with 3EFTS, but to 1AAU 25.3.41 for service in the Middle East. Damaged during air raid 28.8.42 but repaired. Last recorded with the British Aircraft Repair Unit, Heliopolis 25.2.44. SOC 22.10.48.

2324   Two crew. CofA no.4845 issued 20.6.35. To Hillman's Airways Ltd., Maylands as **G-ADEB**. Operated by British Continental Airways Ltd., Croydon 1935. To British Airways Ltd., Heston [CofR 6851 24.3..36]. When operating a mail flight from Hanover to London via Cologne, the aircraft descended through cloud and hit high ground near Altenkirchen, approximately 35kms south-east of Cologne 12.8.36. Caught fire on impact and destroyed. Cancelled from register 12.36.

2325   Two crew. CofA no.4846 issued 1.7.35. To Hillman's Airways Ltd. reg'd **G-ADEC**. Operated by British Continental Airways Ltd., Croydon 1935. To British Airways Ltd., Gatwick .36. Sold to Airwork Ltd., Heston [CofR 8100 2.9.37]. Sold to Cia. Primeras Lineas Uruguayas de Navegacion Aerea (PLUNA) 10.38 reg'd **CX-AAH** and named *Santa Rosa de Lima*. Damaged landing Artigas 22.10.45 and believed not repaired, although it still appeared on the 1950 official register!

2326   Two crew. Export CofA issued 15.7.35. To Holyman's Airways reg'd **VH-UUB** named *Loila*, an Aboriginal word meaning "the sky". CofR no.542 and CofA no.499 issued 27.9.35. Merged to form Australian National Airways Pty. Ltd. 7.11.36. Impressed as **A31-3** 13.9.40. Initially with 3EFTS but to 1AOS 10.11.40. To 1AAU 24.4.41. Destroyed by fire on the ground at Heliopolis 19.4.42, when hit by Bristol Beaufighter X7804 which swung on take-off following an engine failure.

2327   Two crew. CofA no.5303 issued 10.8.35. Handed over to Wrightways Ltd., Croydon reg'd **G-ADMY** 28.8.35. To British Continental Airways Ltd., Croydon named *St. George* 2.37 To L.H.G. Ltd., Heston [CofR 8928 2.12.38]. To British-South American Air Services Ltd., Croydon 2.12.38. Again reg'd to L.H.G. Ltd. 26.6.39. Impressed for military service as **X9442** 4.4.40. Initially at 4MU, but to 9MU 29.11.40. Served with 782Sqdn. Fleet Air Arm at R.N.A.S. Donibristle. Damaged twice and repaired at de Havilland 14.2.42 and again, 30.12.42. SOC 4.4.44.

2328   DH86A. For Imperial Airways Ltd., Croydon and reg'd **G-ADFF** [CofR 5728 7.12.35]. CofA no.5303 issued 13.1.36. Named *Dione*. Tranferred to Khartoum station. To British Overseas Airways Corporation on formation 1.4.40, but transferred 22.8.40 according to offical records. Handed over to the R.A.F. at Cairo 15.8.41 and officially impressed for military service as **AX760** 13.9.41. Used by R.A.F. Lydda Communications Flight. The undercarriage collapsed whilst taxiing Lydda 26.11.41 and eventually SOC as Cat.E1 30.7.42.

2329   Two crew. Export CofA issued 20.9.35. To Misr Airwork Ltd. reg'd **SU-ABO** named *Al Fostat*. Later, re-named *Beyrouth*. Reg'n cancelled and believed dismantled.

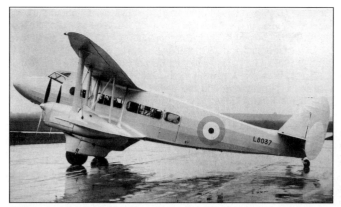

DH86 c/n 2340. Another Gatwick based carrier, British Airways, took delivery of the brand new G-ADYC February 1937 but only operated it briefly prior to selling the aircraft on for military service as L8037.

DH86 c/n 2349. Impressed in the Middle East as HK843 and wearing red cross markings when in use by the R.A.A.F.'s No.1 Air Ambulance Unit in Egypt.

DH86 c/n 2342. Ordered as a DH86A but completed on the production line to DH86B standard, the first to fly of the new variant. Registered G-AJNB, but operated in Egypt by Peacock Air Charter.

DH86 c/n 2352. G-AENR wears the colours of Blackpool and West Coast Air Services prior to impressment as AX842. In service with Skytravel Ltd. after the war until scrapped at their Langley base 1948.

DH86 c/n 2344. Here wearing West Coast Air Service titles, G-ADYH was not impressed but used throughout the war under the aegis of the Associated Airways Joint Committee.

DH86 c/n 2353. Here seen in Western Airways livery, G-AETM eventually went to Finland as an air ambulance and was damaged beyond repair when in ground collision with another aircraft in 1940.

DH86 c/n 2348. Like the previously seen L8037, sister ship L7596 was delivered to British Airways but only saw limited service before being sold to the military in October 1937.

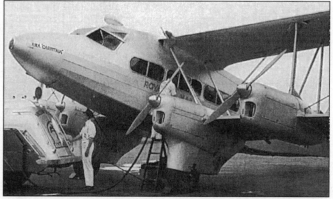

DH86 c/n 2361. The 62nd and last DH86 produced was delivered to W. R. Carpenter in Australia and used almost exclusively in New Guinea before crashing into the sea off New Ireland in March 1940.

2330 Two crew. Export CofA issued 23.9.35. For Union Airways of New Zealand Ltd. reg'd **ZK-AEF** named *Kotuku*. Transported per MV *Waipawa* together with c/n 2331 and arrived Lyttleton 20.11.35. Erected at Wigram. Impressed into R.N.Z.A.F. service as **NZ552** 20.9.39. To Air Gunners & Air Observers School, Ohakea 14.11.39 coded '1'. To 3SFTS, Ohakea 20.10.40. To 2GR Sqdn., Nelson 1.41. Overseas service, to Nadi, Fiji 13.3.41. To 4GR Sqdn., Fiji 8.10.41. To Communications Flight, Nausori 25.6.42. Damaged taxying Nausori 7.12.43. Written-off 12.7.44 and subsequently broken up.

2331 Two crew. Export CofA issued 8.10.35. For Union Airways of New Zealand Ltd. reg'd **ZK-AEG** named *Karoro*. Transported per MV *Waipawa* together with c/n 2330 and arrived Lyttleton 20.11.35. Erected at Wigram. Impressed into R.N.Z.A.F. service as **NZ553** 17.10.39. To Air Gunners & Air Observers School, Ohakea 14.11.39 coded '2'. To 3SFTS, Ohakea 28.10.40. To 2GR Sqdn., Nelson 1.41. Overseas service, to Nadi, Fiji 13.3.41. To 4GR Sqdn., Fiji. Returned to New Zealand for overhaul 11.9.41. To 1SFTS Wigram and used by Electrical & Wireless School 12.41. To Communications Flight, Nausori 12.42. Crashed on take-off Nausori 19.12.42. To de Havilland for repair 23.2.43. Returned to service 16.11.44. Stored Woodbourne. Loaned to Union Airways reg'd **ZK-AHW** 28.2.45 – 30.9.46 but civil reg'n cancelled 21.10.46. Engines removed for use in DH89Bs and airframe broken up for spares at Ohakea (has also been reported as Palmerston North) 4.47. [Note: After rebuild in February 1943, the construction number was quoted as DHNZ2332 and when subsequently loaned to Union Airways, named *Korinako* previously used on c/n 2332; therefore, in the eyes of the N.Z. authorities, ZK-AHW was previously NZ554 and ZK-AEH!]

2332 Two crew. Export CofA issued 31.10.35. For Union Airways of New Zealand Ltd. reg'd **ZK-AEH** named *Korinako*. Transported per MV *Port Wyndham* and arrived Lyttleton 12.35. Erected at Wigram. Impressed into R.N.Z.A.F. service as **NZ554** 30.10.39. To Air Gunners & Air Observers School, Ohakea. Broken up for spares Ohakea.

2333 DH86A. For Imperial Airways Ltd., Croydon and reg'd **G-ADUE** [CofR 6344 19.12.35]. Named *Dardanus*. CofA no.5309 issued 20.1.36. Converted to DH86B standard 1937. Aircraft was machine gunned and forced down at Wai Chow Island 8.11.39 by Japanese fighters. Detained on the ground there until some time after 15.11.39, the aircraft was eventually flown out. Repair necessary to the 92 bullet holes found and to British Overseas Airways Corporation, Whitchurch on formation 1.4.40, although official records show transfer date as 22.8.40. Handed over to the R.A.F. at Cairo 20.8.41 and officially impressed as **AX762** 24.9.41 but marked **"AX672"** in error! Served with B Flight 117Sqdn. at Bilbeis from 4.3.42 and with 1AAU, R.A.A.F. at Heliopolis from 29.5.42. Destroyed when the undercarriage collapsed on landing Siwa, Egypt 24.6.42. SOC as Cat.E1, date unknown, but still marked as AX672!

2334 DH86A. For Imperial Airways Ltd., Croydon and reg'd **G-ADUF** [CofR 6345 1912.35]. CofA no.5314 issued 24.1.36 (later amended to A.649). Named *Dido*. Converted to DH86B standard 1937. To British Overseas Airways Corporation, Croydon on formation 1.4.40, although official records show transfer date as 27.8.40. Allocated serial **HK828** on impressment at Cairo 22.11.41 but did not enter service with the R.A.F. Instead, sold to Misr Airwork Ltd., Cairo reg'd **SU-ACR** and named *Beirut*. Restored to Field Aircraft Services Ltd. as **G-ADUF** 24.5.48. To John Alexander Walter Hill, Jersey 3.6.49. To Air Navigation & Trading Co. Ltd., Blackpool 28.12.50. To Gulf Aviation Ltd., Bahrain 17.10.51. CofA expired 3.5.52 and broken up Bahrain later in the year. Cancelled from register 17.6.52.

2335 DH86A. For Imperial Airways Ltd., Croydon and reg'd **G-ADUG** [CofR 6346 19.12.35]. CofA no.5321 issued 7.2.36. Named *Danae*. Converted to DH86B standard 1937. To British Overseas Airways Corporation on formation 1.4.40, although official records show transfer date as 22.8.40. Cancelled from register 5.11.41 on impressment as **HK831**. Shot down by enemy fighter when with 216Sqdn. and SOC 15.2.42.

2336 DH86A. To Imperial Airways Ltd., Croydon as **G-ADUH** [CofR 6347 19.12.35]. CofA no.5381 issued 7.3.36 and named *Dryad*. Converted to DH86B standard 1937. To Aer Lingus Teoranta reg'd **EI-ABT** 14.10.38 named *Sasana*. Irish reg'n cancelled 30.12.46 but already restored as **G-ADUH** to Domino Louis Steiner trading as

Steiner's Air Service Ltd., Liverpool 26.11.46. To C. & H. D. C. Treen t/a Union Air Services Ltd., Gatwick 24.1.47 but ownership transferred to Bond Air Services Ltd. 11.10.47, when Union's owners purchased the latter company. To Aerocontacts Ltd., Gatwick 30.1.51. To Gulf Aviation Ltd., Bahrain 3.4.51. Destroyed at Bahrain, very shortly after delivery, in ground collision with Auster J/1 Autocrat G-AIBO prior to 23.5.51. Cancelled from register 13.8.51.

2337 DH86A. To Imperial Airways Ltd., Croydon as **G-ADUI** [CofR 6348 19.12.35]. CofA no.5329 issued 24.1.36 and named *Denebola*. Converted to DH86B standard 1937. To British Overseas Airways Corporation on formation 1.4.40, although official records show transfer date as 22.8.40. Handed over to the R.A.F. at Heliopolis 5.11.41 and officially Impressed as **HK830** 22.11.41. Served with B Flight 117Sqd. Whilst taxiing at Bilbeis Airfield 11.3.42, the port tyre burst, causing severe damage to the aircraft. SOC as Cat.E1 31.12.42.

2338 DH86A. For Blackpool and West Coast Air Services Ltd., Squires Gate reg'd **G-ADVJ** [CofR 6396 4.2.36]. CofA no.5430 issued 8.4.36 and named *Ronaldsway*. To Aer Lingus Teoranta reg'd **EI-ABK** 16.09.36 named *Eire*. Converted to DH86B standard 1937. Irish reg'n cancelled 20.11.46 but already restored as **G-ADVJ** to C. & H. D. C. Treen t/a Union Air Services Ltd., Gatwick 20.10.46 but ownership subsequently transferred to Bond Air Services Ltd., when Union's owners purchased the latter company. To Aerocontacts Ltd., Gatwick 30.1.51. To Gulf Aviation Ltd., Bahrain 1.8.51 and used on a thrice daily Bahrain to Dhahran service with the first flight on 25.7.51. Cancelled from register 18.3.52 and noted derelict Bahrain 8.52.

2339 DH86A. CofA no.5318 issued 8.4.36. To Blackpool and West Coast Air Services Ltd., Blackpool reg'd **G-ADVK** and named *Ronaldsway*. Converted to DH86B standard 1937. Name changed to Isle of Man Air Services Ltd. To Jersey Airways Ltd., [CofR 8950 21.12.38]. To Guernsey Airways Ltd., Jersey 22.4.39. Whilst on CofA renewal at Jersey, abandoned when the Channel Islands were occupied by German forces 6.40 and cancelled from register 20.8.40.

2340 DH86A. For British Continental Airways Ltd., Gatwick and CofA no.5502 issued 14.5.36. To British Airways Ltd., Gatwick reg'd **G-ADYC** [CofR 7665 16.2.37]. Converted to DH86B standard 1937. Sold to R.A.F. as **L8037** 11.37 and with Electrical & Wireless School, Cranwell 18.7.38 and later with 24Sqdn. Damaged 22.2.42 but repaired by de Havilland engineers on site. Returned to 24Sqdn. 2.7.42. To 782Sqdn. Fleet Air Arm at Donibristle 26.6.42. SOC date unknown.

2341 DH86A. For British Continental Airways Ltd., Gatwick and CofA no.5512 issued 19.5.36. To British Airways Ltd., Gatwick reg'd **G-ADYD** [CofR 7666 16.2.37]. Converted to DH86B standard 1937. Sold to R.A.F. as **L8040** 11.37 and with Electrical & Wireless School, Cranwell 11.8.38. To 24Sqdn. 20.2.42. Overhauled by de Havilland 8.6.42. To No.3 School of General Reconnaissance 9.9.42. To R.N.A.S. Donibristle 1.10.42. SOC date unknown.

2342 Completed on the line to DH86B standard. Test flown marked as **E.2** at Martlesham Heath with Gipsy Six Series II engines and variable pitch aircscrews. Export CofA no.5743 issued 1.1.37. To Misr Airwork Ltd., Cairo reg'd **SU-ABV** named *Al Mahroussa*. To Lawrence Azzopardi t/a Peacock Air Charter, Alexandria reg'd **G-AJNB** [CofR 11440 8.4.47]. Named *Paul* . Withdrawn from use and noted derelict Wadi Halfa 1949.

2343 DH86A. Intended for British Continental Airways Ltd., Gatwick as a srs.II but delivered to British Airways Ltd., Gatwick as **G-ADYG** [CofR 6528 21.5.36] CofA no.5563 issued 30.6.36. Converted to DH86B standard 1937. Sold to R.A.F. as **N6246** 6.38 and with 24Sqdn., Hendon 27.8.38. Listed as Cat.B at Hendon 20.2.42. Destroyed in hangar fire at Hendon 5.5.42.

2344 DH86A. Intended for British Continental Airways Ltd., Gatwick as a srs.II but delivered to British Airways Ltd., Gatwick as **G-ADYH**. CofA no.5599 issued 21.7.36. To West Coast Air Services Ltd., Liverpool [CofR 8261 13.12.37]. To Railway Air Services Ltd., Croydon 8.40 and operated throughout the war in camouflage on the skeleton services of the Associated Airways Joint Committee. To Skytravel Ltd., Speke 22.10.46. To Henry

Warren Grindrod Penney, Croydon 27.10.47. Apparently trading as Intercontinental Airlines Pty. Ltd., and flown to Australia 10.48 by Bill Mellor. Cancelled from U.K. register 3.4.49. Subsequently sold to Frank Gregnare (an American national) and flown from Darwin to Penang. Later, in use by Indonesian Republican forces marked as **RI-008**. Captured by Dutch forces at the rebel base of Manguwo 12.12.48. Broken up Bandoeng 1949.

2345 DH86A. Intended for British Continental Airways Ltd., Gatwick as a srs.II but delivered to British Airways Ltd., Gatwick as **G-ADYI**. CofA no.5631 issued 26.8.36. Converted to DH86B standard 1937. To Wrightways Ltd., Croydon [CofR 8292 5.1.38. Sold to R.A.F. for 24Sqdn., Hendon 6.38 as **AX795**. To No.1 Signals School 14.10.40. To R.A.E. Farnborough for fitment of unspecified equipment 22.11.40 and returned to No.1 Signals School 31.3.41. To R.A.F. Halton Station Flight 10.6.42. Loaned to Royal Navy (D.A.) for two months from 27.10.42. Declared Cat.E1 by de Havilland 24.5.43. SOC 27.5.43 and scrapped at R.A.F. Halton.

2346 DH86A. Intended for British Continental Airways Ltd., Gatwick as a srs.II but delivered to British Airways Ltd., Gatwick as **G-ADYE** [CofR 7667 16.2.37]. CofA no.5605 issued 28.7.36. Converted to DH86B standard 1937. To Cia. Primeras Lineas Uruguayas de Navegacion Aerea (PLUNA) 11.37 reg'd **CX-ABG** named *San Felipe y Santiago*. No further information but still on 1950 official register!

2347 DH86A. For British Continental Airways Ltd., Croydon reg'd **G-ADYF**.[CofR 6527 29.1.36]. CofA no.5647 issued 2.9.36. Crashed on night take-off at Gatwick 15.9.36. After take off on a mail flight to Hanover via Cologne, the aircraft entered a normal left hand turn, but failed to take up heading for Cologne, continuing to turn and lose height until crashing into a field ? mile south-west of the airport; caught fire on impact and was destroyed. Cancelled from register 4.37.

2348 DH86A. Intended for British Continental Airways Ltd., Gatwick as a srs.II but delivered to British Airways Ltd., Gatwick as **G-ADYJ** [CofR 6531 15.5.36] Converted to DH86B standard 1937. Sold for military service as **L7596** 12.10.37 and operated by 24Sqdn.. On a flight from Biggin Hill to Belfast 29.7.39 carrying the Secretary of State for Air and others, on arrival at Belfast and whilst flying in cloud, the blind flying equipment failed. The pilot elected to return southwards in the belief that the weather conditions were better in that direction and intended to land at Squires Gate. However, on descending below the clouds and flying in heavy rain, it was discovered that the aeroplane was over a mountainous area. With the fuel by now becoming dangerously low, the pilot decided to carry out a forced landing but the aircraft stalled at a height of about 50' and it crashed on Kirkby Moor, at a point about 3 miles north-west of Ulverston, Lancashire. The aircraft came down on rough ground at an altitude of 1000', the starboard wing making contact with the ground first and then continued for only about 20 feet before slewing round to the right through some 180 degrees and coming to rest. The starboard wing was crumpled and damage was sustained to the nose, undercarriage and starboard side of the fuselage but there were no serious injuries. In view of the severe damage and the wreck's location, no possibility of retrieval and repair could be considered and it was therefore SOC. Total time 980 hours.

2349 DH86A. For Imperial Airways Ltd., Croydon as **G-AEAP** [CofR 5964]. CofA no.5408 issued 17.3.36 and named *Demeter*. Converted to DH86B standard 1937. To British Overseas Airways Corporation on formation 1.4.40, although official records show transfer date as 22.8.40. . Impressed as **HK843** at Cairo with 206Grp. Headquarters Middle East and served with B Flight 117Sqdn. at Bilbeis. To Iraq Command 1.7.42. To Middle East Command 30.9.42 and served with 1AAU, R.A.A.F. Evacuating patients from Sicily, a Very signalling pistol apparently combusted spontaneously in its holster and the aircraft was destroyed by fire Pachino, Sicily 23.7.43.

2350 DH86A. CofA no.5437 issued 10.8.36. For Railway Air Services Ltd., Croydon reg'd **G-AEFH** [CofR 6865 15.4.36]. Named *Neptune*. Converted to DH86B standard 1937. Continued in civilian service until ordered to France, together with sister ship G-AEWR and Rapides G-AEBW and G-AEPF, to aid the evacuation of forces. Lost when on the ground in Bordeaux when the French city was over-run by German forces 6.40. Cancelled from register 18.6.40.

2351 DH86A. To Wrightways Ltd., Croydon reg'd **G-AEJM** [CofR 7044 6.7.36] CofA no.5669 issued 24.9.36. Converted to DH86B standard 1937. Sold to the R.A.F. 14.4.40. To 24Sqdn. at Hendon with serial **X9441** and affectionately known as *The Cathedral*. To 4MU 13.6.40 and in use by Air Taxis (Croydon) Ltd. for a 6 week period on unrecorded special operations. Returned to 24Sqdn. 25.7.40. Damaged beyond repair by fire on engine start up Hendon 17.2.42. Total time 1597 hours. Finally SOC 31.3.43.

2352 DH86B. CofA no.5787 issued 8.2.37. To Blackpool and West Coast Air Services Ltd., Blackpool. Operated by affiliate, Isle of Man Air Services Ltd., Derbyhaven reg'd **G-AENR** [CofR 8147 19.10.37]. To Guernsey Airways Ltd., Jersey 21.3.39. Impressed as **AX842** 7.40 but not used and restored as **G-AENR** for civilian operation by Railway Air Services Ltd., Speke 29.8.40 under the aegis of A.A.J.C. To Skytravel Ltd., Gatwick 22.10.46. Cancelled from register 5.11.48 and scrapped Langley.

2353 DH86B. To Allied Airways (Gandar Dower) Ltd., Aberdeen reg'd **G-AETM** [CofR 7650 6.4.37]. CofA no.5962 issued 29.6.37 and named *The Norseman*. To Western Airways Ltd., Weston-super-Mare 18.5.39. To Henry McGrady Bell, Gatwick 1.2.40 and donated by him to the Finnish Government for use as an ambulance aircraft. Modified by Airwork Ltd., Gatwick with positions for 12 stretchers and 2 attendants. Cancelled from U.K. register 20.2.40. Reg'd **OH-SLA** (already in unofficial use on a Waco ZQC-6) and named *Silver Star* 12.39. Allocated the Finnish Air Force serial **DH-1** but not taken up. Re-reg'd **OH-IPA** 2.40 and operated by Finnish Naval Coastguard Service. Written-off Helsinki-Malmi 2.5.40 after ground collision with a Brewster aircraft serialled BW-394. Although damage to the DH86 was said not to be severe, the necessary replacement parts could not be obtained from de Havilland, due to more urgent commitments to the war effort.

2354 DH86B. CofA no.5900 issued 10.8.36. To Railway Air Services Ltd., Croydon reg'd **G-AEWR** [CofR 7780 7.5.37] Named *Venus*. Continued in civilian service until ordered to France, together with sister ship G-AEFH and Rapides G-AEBW and G-AEPF, to aid the evacuation of forces. Lost when on the ground in Bordeaux when the French city was over-run by German forces 6.40. Cancelled from register 18.6.40.

2355 DH86B. Allocated U.K. ferry markings **G-AFAJ** [CofR 8011 22.7.37] for delivery to Turkey. Export CofA no.6018 issued 18.8.37. U.K. reg'n cancelled 9.37. To Devlet Hava Yollari reg'd **TC-ERK**. To Hurkus Airlines, Ankara 5.59. If the report that this aircraft was still operational in 1963 is correct, it would have been the last of the model in flying condition. To B. N. Oznur 11.64. Eventual fate unknown. (Also see the Survivors chapter, reference DH89A 'TC-ERK').

2356 DH86B. Allocated U.K. ferry markings **G-AFAK** [CofR 8012 22.7.37] for delivery to Turkey. Export CofA no.6043 issued 22.7.37. U.K. reg'n cancelled 9.37. To Devlet Hava Yollari reg'd **TC-FER**. To Hurkus Airlines, Ankara 5.59. Fate unknown.

2357 DH86B. Allocated U.K. ferry markings **G-AFAL** [CofR 8013 22.7.37] for delivery to Turkey. Export CofA no.6068 issued 30.9.37. U.K. reg'n cancelled 12.37. To Devlet Hava Yollari reg'd **TC-GEN**. To Hurkus Airlines, Ankara 5.59. Fate unknown.

2358 DH86B. Allocated U.K. ferry markings **G-AFAM** [CofR 8014 22.7.37] for delivery to Turkey. Export CofA no.6109 issued 29.10.37. U.K. reg'n cancelled 12.37. To Devlet Hava Yollari reg'd **TC-HEP**. To Hurkus Airlines, Ankara 5.59. Fate unknown.

2359 DH86B. Export CofA no.6141 issued 30.11.37. To W. R. Carpenter & Co. Ltd., Sydney NSW as **VH-UYU** [CofR 696 10.3.38]. Named *R.M.A. Carmania* and CofA no.653 issued same day. Impressed as **A31-8** 20.6.41. Modified to air ambulance by Australian National Airways at Melbourne-Essendon, VIC and received at 1AD 22.8.41. To 1AAU on same day for operation in the Middle East. Destroyed, believed shot down by the enemy 8.12.41.

2360 DH86B. Export CofA no.6167 issued 18.12.37. To W. R. Carpenter & Co. Ltd., Sydney NSW reg'd **VH-UYV** [CofR 698 12.4.38]. Named *R.M.A. Caronia* and CofA no.655 issued same day. Impressed as **A31-1** 11.12.39. Received by 1FTS Signals School, Point Cook VIC. Major overhaul by Ansett 17.3.41 – 13.6.41. To 36Sqdn. 14.9.42. Complete overhaul by Australian

National 6.11.42. Returned to 36Sqdn. To 34Sqdn. 2.1.43. At Guinea Airways for repairs 14.1.43. To 35Sqdn. 13.5.43. To 2AAU 19.1.44 and modified by them to air ambulance configuration. Badly damaged on take-off when port tyre suffered blow-out 15.8.44, main spar broken, starboard undercarriage wiped off and three propellers bent. Remains to 6AD 23.8.44 and written off 12.9.44.

2361   DH86B. Export CofA no.6172 issued 30.12.37. To W. R. Carpenter & Co. Ltd., Sydney NSW reg'd **VH-UYW** [CofR 703 9.5.38]. Named *R.M.A. Carinthia* and CofA no.660 issued same day. Crashed in sea off Kavieng, New Ireland, PNG 15.3.40. No casualties.

4.4 de Havilland DH86 - Registration to Construction Number Cross Index

AUSTRALIA - CIVILIAN	
VH-ADN	2313
VH-URN	2301
VH-URT	2312
VH-USC	2307
VH-USD	2308
VH-USE	2309
VH-USF	2310
VH-USG	2311
VH-USW	2315
VH-UUA	2306
VH-UUB	2326
VH-UYU	2359
VH-UYV	2360
VH-UYW	2361
VH-UZX	2323

AUSTRALIA - MILITARY	
A31-1	2360
A31-2	2313
A31-3	2326
A31-4	2315
A31-5	2307
A31-6	2310
A31-7	2323
A31-8	2359

EGYPT	
SU-ABN	2320
SU-ABO	2329
SU-ABV	2342
SU-ACR	2334

FINLAND - CIVILIAN	
OH-IPA	2353
OH-SLA	2353

FINLAND - MILITARY	
(DH-1)	2353

GREAT BRITAIN - CIVILIAN	
E.2 (1)	2300
E.2 (2)	2342
G-ACPL	2300
G-ACVY	2302
G-ACVZ	2303
G-ACWC	2304
G-ACWD	2305
G-ACWE	2306
G-ACYF	2313
G-ACYG	2314
G-ACZN	2316
G-ACZO	2318
G-ACZP	2321
G-ACZR	2322
G-ADCM	2317
G-ADCN	2319
G-ADEA	2323
G-ADEB	2324
G-ADEC	2325
G-ADFF	2328
G-ADMY	2327
G-ADUE	2333
G-ADUF	2334
G-ADUG	2335
G-ADUH	2336
G-ADUI	2337
G-ADVJ	2338
G-ADVK	2339
G-ADYC	2340
G-ADYD	2341
G-ADYE	2346
G-ADYF	2347
G-ADYG	2343
G-ADYH	2344
G-ADYI	2345
G-ADYJ	2348
G-AEAP	2349
G-AEFH	2350
G-AEJM	2351
G-AENR	2352
G-AETM	2353
G-AEWR	2354
G-AFAJ	2355
G-AFAK	2356
G-AFAL	2357
G-AFAM	2358
G-AJNB	2342

GREAT BRITAIN - MILITARY	
L7596	2348
L8037	2340
L8040	2341
N6246	2343
X9441	2351
X9442	2327
"AX672"	2333
AX760	2328
AX762	2333
AX795	2345
AX800	2308
AX840	2314
AX841	2318
(AX842)	2352
AX843	2321
AX844	2322
HK828	2334
HK829	2305
HK830	2337
HK831	2335
HK843	2349
HK844	2300
HX789	2306

INDIA	
VT-AKM	2306
VT-AKZ	2308

INDONESIA REPUBLICAN REBELS - MILITARY	
RI-008	2344

IRELAND	
EI-ABK	2338
EI-ABT	2336

NEW ZEALAND - CIVILIAN	
ZK-AEF	2330
ZK-AEG	2331
ZK-AEH	2332
ZK-AHW	2331

NEW ZEALAND - MILITARY	
NZ552	2330
NZ553	2331
NZ554	2332

STRAITS SETTLEMENTS/ SINGAPORE	
VR-SBC	2323
VR-SBD	2313

TURKEY	
TC-ERK	2355
TC-FER	2356
TC-GEN	2357
TC-HEP	2358

URUGUAY	
CX-AAH	2325
CX-ABG	2346

de Havilland
DH89 Dragon Rapide

DH89 c/n 6250. First flown at Hatfield on 17th April 1934 and very soon after on to Martlesham Heath for CofA trials. The prototype awaits delivery to Aero St. Gallen as CH-287 in July the same year.

DH89 c/n 6258. G-ACTU was delivered to Personal Airways at Heston in September 1934. Purchased by Whitney Straight in October 1938 and later served at his Western Airways company.

DH89 c/n 6253. G-ACPO seen being refuelled at Hatfield prior to delivery to Hillman's Airways. It later served with Guinea Airways as VH-ABN and crashed into high ground in bad weather July 1944.

DH89 c/n 6261. The famous Olley aircraft that flew Franco from the Canary Islands to Spanish territory during the Civil War and now displayed at Cuatro Vientos.

DH89 c/n 6256. Sold via de Havilland Aircraft of South Africa P/L, the seventh aircraft built was handed over to African Air Transport at Hatfield on 14th December 1934.

DH89 c/n 6263. In service with Wrightways of Croydon, G-ADAL wears camouflage. Impressed as X9448 in April 1940, however it continued to fly wearing the civil marks until November of that year.

DH89 c/n 6257. Originally built for Anglo-Iranian Oil, G-ACTT was handed over to Flt. Lt. E. H. Fielden, personal pilot of H.R.H. The Prince of Wales. Dragon G-ACCG was briefly retained as a back-up.

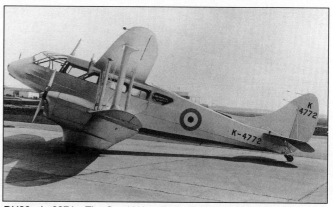

DH89 c/n 6271. The first U.K. military Rapide was K4772, built as a contender for a coastal reconnaissance aeroplane and also used for comparative tests with the Avro Anson. Broken-up Witney July 1942.

5.1 de Havilland DH89 Dragon Rapide – Development

Airline customers for the DH84 Dragon were forever knocking at de Havilland's door, requesting a new model that would offer increased capacity and better performance but still to be as economical in operation as its predecessor.

A. E. Hagg's small design team had formulated the four engine DH86, sometimes unofficially referred to as the Dragon Express, to fulfil a joint Australian and British requirement for a long range 10-seater for the proposed Empire Air Route from England to Australia. For this ambitious project, another de Havilland team, led by Major F. B. Halford, came up with the now famous Gipsy Six engine, a six cylinder version of the Gipsy Major giving 200 h.p. The first of these new engines was rushed through Air Ministry testing in time for the prototype DH86 to make its first flight in January 1934.

For shorter routes, a 'down-sized' version of the DH86 with two Gipsy Six engines, was on the drawing board in the late summer of 1933. Initially known as the Dragon Six, the DH89 closely resembled its larger sister, as it employed the same fuselage structure, tapered mainplanes, engine nacelles and faired undercarriage.

To more clearly differentiate the new model from the DH84 Dragon and to better reflect the new model's greatest enhancement, particularly in regard to speed, the name was changed to Dragon Rapide in February 1934.

The prototype, wearing E.4 in de Havilland's test series, flew for the first time at Hatfield on 17th April 1934. Flown to Martlesham Heath for certification trials during the first week of May 1934 and the only problem encountered during testing was when the Rapide was conducting a high speed trial and at about 175 m.p.h., the nose buckled with a loud bang! As a direct result, the DH89's maximum permissible speed was restricted to 160 m.p.h. and a certificate of airworthiness was then speedily issued on 10th May. With the all-important certification granted, the prototype was returned to Hatfield and prepared for delivery to Switzerland. In a six-place layout and a rear luggage area able to take up to 140lb, registered CH-287, the aircraft departed for Altenrhein on 18th July. The very first Rapide was soon earning its keep on the routes of Aero St. Gallen to Berne and Zurich.

It had become traditional that new de Havilland models made their debut at the King's Cup Air Race. This very popular annual public event, took place at Hatfield on 13th July 1934 and the first production Rapide, G-ACPM, was entered by Viscount Wakefield of Castrol Oil and flown by de Havilland's test pilot Captain Hubert S. Broad. The Rapide did well in the early heats, averaging 158 m.p.h., but was forced to withdraw when the wings were severely damaged in a hail storm encountered near Waddington. Repaired and subsequently delivered to Hillman's Airways, the ill-fated aircraft flew into the English channel 3 miles off Folkestone on 3rd October 1934 while on a scheduled flight from Stapleford to Paris, killing all seven on board. The accident report gave disorientation and subsequent loss of control whilst flying in cloud as the probable cause

Even before certification of the DH89 had been gained, orders for the new model began to flood in and series production was in full swing. Besides numerous examples for British based customers, aircraft were delivered to civil operators throughout the world as follows:-

In Africa, Angola, Kenya, Mozambique, South Africa and Southern Rhodesia
In the Americas, Brazil and Canada
In Australasia, Australia and New Zealand
In Europe, Belgium, Finland, France, Italy, Latvia, Nederland, Roumania, Spain, Switzerland, Turkey and Yugoslavia
In Far East, China (Nationalist), India and Singapore
In Middle East, Egypt, Iran and Iraq

Aviation enthusiasts born after the war, the authors' chain of thought automatically connects the numerous Dragon Rapides in service as wartime surplus aircraft. We were somewhat surprised to learn therefore during the preparation of this book, that the last civil delivery before the outbreak of war was the 203rd Dragon Rapide aircraft (c/n 6454), built for airline use for Air Services of India Ltd.

Small numbers of the DH89M military variant were sold to Lithuania and Spain. In addition, the R.A.F. acquired two aircraft in 1935; K5070 (6267) was operated as a V.I.P. transport by 24Sqdn. at Hendon and K4772 (6271), supplied as de Havilland's contender for a coastal command and general reconnaissance requirement, which was eventually won by the Avro Anson. From small beginnings, wartime requirements for the training, general transport and communication roles, ensured contracts for in excess of 400 Dominies, as the type was known in British and Empire military service.

By 1942, DH89B Dominie output at Hatfield was approximately 15 aircraft per month, but since factory space was required for increased DH98 Mosquito production, manufacture was transferred to Brush Coachworks Ltd. at Loughborough, Leicestershire. Brush went on to build 336 Dominies. Two additional aircraft, given the special construction numbers W.1001 and W.1002, were built up from parts at de Havilland's Repair Unit at Witney in Oxfordshire during 1947.

Only nine impressed DH89 aircraft were returned after the war but several hundred surplus R.A.F. aircraft, many in new condition, were sold by public tender 1946/47 and so the poor return to civilian use was hardly noticed! Preparation to Dragon Rapide standard, entailed the addition of sound proofing, upholstered seating, new interior décor and a coat of paint and the majority of conversions were carried out, as previously detailed, at de Havilland's Repair Unit at Witney. The Royal Navy had received 64 of the type during the war years and 14 of these remained on charge into the 1960s for communication duties and sea cadet familiarisation flights. Sold by public tender at R.N.A.S. Lossiemouth in 1963, only four were civilianised.

Listed below are the various civil and military production versions. Also included are the versions, modified post-war by various civil organisations.

Models – Civilian

DH89	Initial production version.
DH89	From 1936, with the addition of nose landing light, cabin heating and wing tips modified - slightly thicker in profile.
DH89A Mk1	Introduced 1937 with small trailing edge flaps outboard of the engine nacelles. Many DH89s were later modified to DH89A standard.
DH89A Mk2	Civilianised DH89B Dominie Mk.I for pilot, radio operator and up to 6 passengers.
DH89A Mk3	Civilianised DH89B Dominie Mk.II for pilot and eight passengers. (Note: Although the official designations, they were rarely used in practice)
DH89A Mk4	200hp Gipsy Queen 2 engines driving de Havilland constant speed propellers. These variable pitch propellers had successfully been used on the Percival Proctor communications aircraft. The installation allowed an increase in maximum take-off weight to 6,000lb and offered a significant improvement in climb, cruising and single engine performance. The prototype installation was carried out on G-AHGF (6903) by Flightways Ltd. at Southampton-Eastleigh in 1953.

DH89A Mk5	A one-off carried out by de Havilland to their company communications aircraft G-AHKA (6839) in 1948. The Mk5 featured modified Gipsy Queen engines with manually operated variable pitch propellers.
DH89A Mk6	Aircraft using the Fairey Aviation fixed pitch propeller especially developed for the Rapide. Replacement by the Fairey produced propeller allowed a performance increase similar to that offered by the Mk4, but without the maintenance cost of the complex variable pitch mechanism. The following 24 aircraft are known to have been converted:-

G-AGSH, G-AGUG, G-AGZO, G-AHED, G-AHKU, G-AHKV, G-AHLM, G-AHRH, G-AIBB, G-AIDL, G-AIUL, G-AJCL, G-AJHP, G-AKNN, G-AKSE, G-AKZB, G-ALBC, G-ALBI, G-ALGC, G-ALWK, G-AMJK, G-ANZP, G-APBM and G-ASKO.

Models – Military

DH89M	Under Air Ministry design specification G-18/35, a single prototype was built for the R.A.F. to fulfil a Coastal Command requirement for an armed general reconnaissance aircraft. Featuring a Vickers E type gun on the starboard side of the nose, a bomb bay for two 100lb and four 20lb bombs, a Lewis gun on a flexible mounting on top of the fuselage, extra cabin windows and a long curved dorsal fin. First flown in spring 1935, c/n 6271 was supplied to the Air Council under contract no.352854/34 and received the serial K4772. Delivered to Martlesham Heath for trials on 13.4.35, comparative tests with the Avro Anson were then conducted at Coastal Defence Development Unit, Gosport from 13.5.35. The Anson was selected as the more suitable type for the role and it was to be some years before the British military purchased the DH89A in great numbers. However, Spain ordered three modified DH89Ms for police operations in Spanish Morocco. These aircraft had the nose gun, a Vickers F type mounted on mid upper fuselage and a further gun fired downward through the floor. Racks mounted under the fuselage carried twelve 27lb bombs. Transferred to the mainland for Republican use during the Spanish Civil War, the three aircraft were later operated by the other side, after capture by Nationalists forces. At Zaragoza in July 1936. Two other DH89Ms were built for the Lithuanian Air Force.
DH89B Dominie Mk.I	Navigation trainer variant with accommodation for pilot, radio operator and up to 6 passengers
DH89B Dominie Mk.II	Communications aircraft with accommodation for pilot and 8/10 passengers
DH89B Dominie Mk.III	None built – order changed to Mk.I and Mk.II versions (see Chapter 5.3)

5.2 de Havilland DH89 Dragon Rapide – Specifications

Type:	Utility transport
Capacity:	Pilot and up to 8 passengers
Country of origin:	Great Britain
Production period:	1934-1947
Engines:	DH89/89M: 2 X de Havilland Gipsy Six, 6 cylinder in-line air cooled piston engines each of 200hp
	DH89A Mk1/2/3/6: 2 X DH Gipsy Queen 3, 6 cylinder in-line air cooled piston engines each of 200hp
	DH89A Mk4: 2 X DH Gipsy Queen 2, 6 cylinder in-line air cooled piston engines each of 200hp
	DH89A Mk5: 2 X DH Gipsy Queen 3, 6 cylinder in-line air cooled piston engines each of 200hp (with manually operated variable pitch propellers)
	DH89B Dominie Mk1: 2 X DH Gipsy Queen 3, 6 cylinder in-line air cooled piston engines each of 200hp
	DH89B Dominie Mk2: 2 X DH Gipsy Queen 3, 6 cylinder in-line air cooled piston engines each of 200hp
First flight:	17th April 1934 (at Hatfield)
Total number built:	729 (excludes c/n 6400 used out of sequence for the sole DH92 Dolphin but includes c/n 6462 for static testing)
Production by:	de Havilland Aircraft Co. Ltd., Hatfield, Hertfordshire 391 (first delivery July 1934 and the last in November 1942)
	Brush Coachworks Ltd., Loughborough, Leicestershire 336 (first delivery May 1943 with last in May 1946 but includes works number 89232 supplied as a fuselage only to Canada, early 1942)
	De Havilland Repair Unit, Witney, Oxfordshire 2 (c/ns W.1001 & W.1002 built up from parts 1947)

Dimensions

Wing span:	48 0" (14.63m)
area:	336 sq. ft. (31.59m2)
loading:	12.8 lb/sq. ft.
aspect ratio:	11.7
dihedral:	3 degrees
Length:	34' 6" (10.51m)
Height:	10' 3" (3.12m)

Tankage (fuel):	2 X 38 gallons

	DH89	DH89A/B	DH89M	Mk.4/6	Mk.5
Weights					
Empty:	3,368lb (1,531kg)	3,276lb (1,489kg)	3,368lb (1,531kg)	3,230lb (1,468kg)	3,500lb (1,591kg)
Max take-off:	5,500lb (2,495kg)	5,500lb (2,495kg)	5,372lb (2,442kg)	6,000lb (2,727kg)	5,750lb (2,614kg)

	DH89	DH89A/B	DH89M	Mk.4/6	Mk.5
Performance					
Take-off run	245 yards	290 yards			
Initial rate of climb:					
(ft. per minute)	1,000'	867'	890'	1,200'	955'
Max speed:	157mph (252kph)	157mph (252kph)	148mph (238kph)	150mph (241kph)	145mph (233kph)
Cruise speed:	132mph (212kph)	132mph (212kph)	125mph (201kph)	140mph (225kph)	141mph (226kph)
Service ceiling:	19,500' (5,943m)	19,500' (5,943m)	17,700' (5,395m)	1,6000' (4,877m)	-
Range:					
(nautical miles)	578nm (1,071km)	556nm (1030km)	550nm (1,019km)	530nm (982km)	520nm (964km)
Landing speed:	64mph (103kph)	65mph (104kph)	64mph (103kph)	65mph (104kph)	65mph (104kph)
Landing run:	220 yards	170 yards			

Weights and performance figures quoted for the first prototype and the seaplane variant, equipped with floats manufactured by the Edo Aircraft Corporation in Canada, vary slightly.

5.3 Brush Coachworks Ltd.

In 1941 all factory space at de Havilland's Hatfield factory was fully committed to DH98 Mosquito production, which meant that contracts expected from the Air Ministry for other de Havilland designs, had to be awarded to able organisations located elsewhere. Morris Motors of Cowley, Oxfordshire and Brush Coachworks of Loughborough, Leicestershire were the main beneficiaries, with the former building a grand total of 3,214 Tiger Moths, exceeding de Havilland's own ouput in the U.K. by 149. The latter company was the recipient of three major contracts for Dominie aircraft, eventually leading to their manufacture of 336 of the type.

Founded by Charles Francis Brush (1849-1929) in Cleveland, Ohio, U.S.A. during 1881, Brush's invention of a sensational arc lamp ensured the immediate success of the newly established company. A little later, a revolutionary electric dynamo was developed which was instrumental in the link, that survives today, of the Brush name to mass transport undertakings.

A British subsidiary named Brush Anglo Electric Light Company was established in London during 1879 with a showroom in Lambeth to exhibit American made electrical products, but it was not long before a small manufacturing facility was built up at the premises. Since the invention of the wheel, electricity has to be considered one of man's greatest achievements and companies involved with its development and making products powered by it, continue to be among the world's most successful. General Electric in the United States springs to mind, whilst in this country, Frederick Henry Royce made enough money when making electric switches and bell pushes, to finance the manufacture of his first three automobiles in 1904.

Company growth prompted a move from the capital and following a merger in 1889 with Falcon Engine and Car Works Ltd., the company base moved northwards to the Falcon premises at Loughborough. Founded in 1965 as Henry Hughes & Co., a carriage builder and horse drawn bus maker, the company name had changed to Falcon Engine & Car Works in 1883.

To better describe the company's trade, the newly merged company changed their name to Brush Electrical Engineering Company Ltd. Brush's expertise in lighting and transformers and Falcon's in coachbuilding, were a brilliant combination and by 1885 a subsidiary, Brush Traction Co. Ltd., was building steam trams and railway locomotives. By the late 1800s, many of Britain's larger towns were building tramways and Brush were at the forefront when local councils and city corporations were requesting proposals to equip their new systems with rolling stock. Among them, was Blackpool Corporation and their year round sea front tram service, remains both an attraction and an effective form of transport along the promenade, to the present day. From around 1910, trolleybuses were seen as offering a more flexible system of transportation and Brush once again, were a major suppliers. First deliveries were made to Stockport in Cheshire in 1913 and up until 1952, when the motorbus displaced them, Brush supplied many hundreds to local government operatives around the country. The systems operated by Darlington and Newcastle in the north, Southend-on-Sea in the south-east and Llanelli and the Rhonda Valley in Wales to the west, all used Brush made trolleybuses. Much more recently, locomotives for London's Dockland Light Railway and the Channel Tunnel have been built in Loughborough.

During the first world war, Winston Churchill, who at that time was first Sea Lord of the Admiralty, approved the expansion of the Royal Naval Air Service. Existing manufacturers were unable to increase their production further and the government therefore commenced a search for companies with the expertise and high quality of workmanship in order to build the aircraft required by the expanded R.N.A.S. Brush were one of the first concerns to receive contracts to build aircraft, with an order for 12 Maurice Farman F.7 Longhorns in late 1915. This initial order, was followed up by further orders and a total of 97 were expected to be built, but it seems that the last 30 were cancelled prior to work commencing. In addition, a requirement for a twin engine bomber was fulfilled by Brush in 1916/17. Although an order for ten was placed, only a single example of the Henry Farman designed Astra was actually built in England. Other aircraft to emerge from Brush's Falcon Works, were 20 Short Type 827 reconnaissance/bomber seaplanes and 142 Short 184 anti-submarine seaplanes. There then followed, three contracts for a total of 500 Avro 504 type aircraft, although the final 100 were subsequently cancelled in the days leading up to the armistice.

Their aircraft related work recommenced during the second war, initially with building nose sections for Armstrong Whitworth Albemarles and sub-contract work received from the Derby Locomotive Works. This amounted to Handley Page Hampden fuselage repairs and 100 of the type for attention passed through the Brush works at Loughborough during the period, March 1941 to December 1943. Brush also fabricated Avro Lancaster wing sections throughout the war and it is probable that this work too, was subcontracted from Derby Locomotive.

Following de Havilland's notification of their inability to produce further Dominies, a contract numbered 6/AIRCRAFT/2580/C20a Requisition 3/E11/42 was awareded to Brush for 275 aircraft. After production had been transferred from Hatfield, their first aircraft with serial HG644, had been towed tail-first by tractor from Falcon Works to the now defunct Loughborough Aerodrome on Derby Road in March 1943. However, prior to that, perhaps as a trial, a fuselage only was built in November 1941 and supplied to Canada. This received the Brush works number 89232 but apparently, was not allotted a de Havilland construction number. On arrival in Canada, the new aircraft was assembled at Downsview by de Havilland Aircraft of Canada, presumably using wings and tailplane built at Hatfield and the aircraft was then delivered for service with Maritime Central Airways in June 1942.

On 2nd November 1943, a second contract for a further 100 Mk.II and Mk.III aircraft was awarded to Brush but just a few days later, on the 8th of the month, the contract had been amended to the Mk.I version and the order substantially reduced to 40 aircraft on the 10th. In a further change to the original contract on 8th June 1945, the final 29 (c/ns 6929 through to 6957), were re-ordered to the Mk.II specification.

Bearing in mind the afore-mentioned reduced number of aircraft in the second batch, somewhat surprisingly, a new contract reference number 6/AIRCRAFT/5072/C20a Requisition DA/3//E23/44, was placed for a further 50 aircraft, of which 6 were to be incomplete airframes. The total number of complete airframes was later increased to 74 but in the event, the programme was abandoned at the completion of the twentieth airframe.

A table of all Dragon Rapides completed at Loughborough follows on the next two pages. As previously advised, the "trial" airframe was allotted Brush works number 89232 and a layman (or someone without so much time to spare!) would immediately surmise that the number signified that it was the 232rd DH89 built. However, the actual 232nd Hatfield built Rapide was delivered to the R.A.F. in May 1940, a long while before the Brush built fuselage was rolled out in November 1941 for onward delivery to Canada. It is unthinkable that the very efficient Brush concern at a time of conflict, would take 18 months to finish their first effort . The digital problem is further compounded by the first Brush aircraft having a probable works number of 89294, when if our theory is correct, it should have been around 89392. Furthermore for reasons of incompatibility, with hand on heart, we cannot definitely state that the Brush numbers ran consecutively in synchronisation with the de Havilland construction numbers! However, the few Brush numbers that are definitely confirmed are shown in "bold" in the following table and tend to indicate that they did indeed run in series, with a direct correlation with the series initiated at Hatfield!

The company was taken over by Hawker Siddeley Group in 1957 and subsequently trades as Hawker Siddeley Brush Traction. By a strange coincidence, the merger in 1959, of the original design and manufacturer of the Dragon Rapide/Dominie type, into Hawker Siddeley Aviation found the two manufacturers of the DH89, members of the same group!

Brush Works No.	DH c/n	Original. reg'n or serial	Remarks
89232	Nil	CF-BNJ	Fuselage only built 11.41
89294	6643	HG644	Delivered May 1943
89295	6644	HG645	
89296	6645	HG646	
89297	6646	HG647	
89298	6647	HG648	
89299	6648	HG649	
89300	6649	HG650	
89301	6650	HG651	
89302	6651	HG652	
89303	6652	HG653	
89304	6653	HG654	
89305	6654	HG655	
89306	6655	HG656	
89307	6656	HG657	
89308	**6657**	**HG658**	
89309	6658	HG659	
89310	6659	HG660	
89311	6660	HG661	
89312	**6661**	**HG662**	
89313	6662	HG663	
89314	6663	HG664	
89315	6664	HG665	
89316	6665	HG666	
89317	6666	HG667	
89318	6667	HG668	
89319	6668	HG669	
89320	6669	HG670	
89321	6670	HG671	
89322	6671	HG672	
89323	6672	HG673	
89324	6673	HG674	
89325	6674	HG689	
89326	6675	HG690	
89327	6676	HG691	
89328	6677	HG692	
89329	6678	HG693	
89330	6679	HG694	
89331	6680	HG695	
89332	6681	HG696	
89333	6682	HG697	
89334	6683	HG698	
89335	6684	HG699	
89336	6685	HG700	
89337	6686	HG701	
89338	6687	HG702	
89339	6688	HG703	
89340	6689	HG704	
89341	6690	HG705	
89342	6691	HG706	
89343	6692	HG707	
89344	6693	HG708	
89345	6694	HG709	
89346	6695	HG710	
89347	6696	HG711	

Brush Works No.	DH c/n	Original. reg'n or serial	Remarks
89348	6697	HG712	
89349	6698	HG713	
89350	6699	HG714	
89351	6700	HG715	
89352	6701	HG716	
89353	6702	HG717	
89354	6703	HG718	
89355	6704	HG719	
89356	6705	HG720	
89357	6706	HG721	
89358	6707	HG722	
89359	6708	HG723	
89360	6709	HG724	
89361	6710	HG725	
89362	6711	HG726	
89363	6712	HG727	
89364	6713	HG728	
89365	6714	HG729	
89366	6715	HG730	
89367	6716	HG731	
89368	**6717**	**HG732**	
89369	6718	NF847	
89370	6719	NF848	
89371	6720	NF849	
89372	6721	NF850	
89373	6722	NF851	
89374	6723	NF852	
89375	6724	NF853	
89376	6725	NF854	
89377	6726	NF855	
89378	6727	NF856	
89379	6728	NF857	
89380	6729	NF858	
89381	6730	NF859	
89382	6731	NF860	
89383	6732	NF861	
89384	6733	NF862	
89385	6734	NF863	
89386	6735	NF864	
89387	6736	NF865	
89388	6737	NF866	
89389	6738	NF867	
89390	6739	NF868	
89391	6740	NF869	
89392	6741	NF870	
89393	6742	NF871	
89394	6743	NF872	
89395	6744	NF873	
89396	6745	NF874	
89397	**6746**	**NF875**	
89398	6747	NF876	
89399	6748	NF877	
89400	**6749**	**NF878**	
89401	6750	NF879	
89402	6751	NF880	
89403	6752	NF881	
89404	6753	NF882	

Brush Works No.	DH c/n	Original. reg'n or serial	Remarks
89405	6754	NF883	
89406	6755	NF884	
89407	6756	NF885	
89408	6757	NF886	
89409	6758	NF887	
89410	6759	NF888	
89411	6760	NF889	
89412	6761	NF890	
89413	6762	NF891	
89414	6763	NF892	
89415	6764	NF893	
89416	6765	NF894	
89417	6766	NF895	
89418	6767	NF896	
89419	6768	NF669	
89420	6769	NF670	
89421	6770	NF671	
89422	6771	NF672	
89423	6772	NF673	
89424	6773	NF674	
89425	6774	NF675	
89426	6775	NF676	
89427	6776	NF677	
89428	6777	NF678	
89429	6778	NF679	
89430	6779	NF680	
89431	6780	NF681	
89432	6781	NF682	
89433	6782	NF683	
89434	6783	NF684	
89435	6784	NF685	
89436	6785	NF686	
89437	6786	NF687	
89438	6787	NF688	
89439	6788	NF689	
89440	6789	NF690	
89441	6790	NF691	
89442	6791	NF692	
89443	6792	NF693	
89444	**6793**	**NF694**	
89445	**6794**	**NF695**	
89446	**6795**	**NF696**	
89447	6796	NF697	
89448	6797	NF698	
89449	6798	NF699	
89450	6799	NF700	
89451	6800	NF701	
89452	6801	NR713	
89453	6802	NR714	
89454	6803	NR715	
89455	6804	NR716	
89456	6805	NR717	
89457	6806	NR718	
89458	6807	NR719	
89459	6808	NR720	
89460	6809	NR721	
89461	6810	NR722	

Brush Works No.	DH c/n	Original. reg'n or serial	Remarks
89462	6811	NR723	
89463	6812	NR724	
89464	6813	NR725	
89465	6814	NR726	
89466	6815	NR727	
89467	6816	NR728	
89468	6817	NR729	
89469	6818	NR730	
89470	6819	NR731	
89471	6820	NR732	
89472	6821	NR733	
89473	6822	NR734	
89474	6823	NR735	
89475	6824	NR736	
89476	6825	NR737	
89477	6826	NR738	
89478	6827	NR739	
89479	6828	NR740	
89480	6829	NR741	
89481	6830	NR742	
89482	6831	NR743	
89483	6832	NR744	
89484	6833	NR745	
89485	6834	NR746	
89486	6835	NR747	
89487	6836	NR748	
89488	6837	NR749	
89489	6838	NR750	
89490	6839	NR751	
89491	6840	NR752	
89492	6841	NR753	
89493	6842	NR754	
89494	6843	NR755	
89495	6844	NR756	
89496	6845	NR769	
89497	6846	NR770	
89498	6847	NR771	
89499	6848	NR772	
89500	6849	NR773	
89501	6850	NR774	
89502	6851	NR775	
89503	6852	NR776	
89504	**6853**	**NR777**	
89505	6854	NR778	
89506	**6855**	**NR779**	
89507	6856	NR780	
89508	6857	NR781	
89509	6858	NR782	
89510	**6859**	**NR783**	
89511	6860	NR784	
89512	6861	NR785	
89513	6862	NR786	
89514	6863	NR787	
89515	6864	NR788	
89516	6865	NR789	
89517	6866	NR790	
89518	6867	NR791	

Brush Works No.	DH c/n	Original. reg'n or serial	Remarks
89519	6868	NR792	
89520	**6869**	**NR793**	
89521	6870	NR794	
89522	6871	NR795	
89523	6872	NR796	
89524	**6873**	**NR797**	
89525	6874	NR798	
89526	6875	NR799	
89527	6876	NR800	
89528	**6877**	**NR801**	
89529	6878	NR802	
89530	6879	NR803	
89531	6880	NR804	
89532	6881	NR805	
89533	6882	NR806	
89534	6883	NR807	
89535	6884	NR808	
89536	6885	NR809	
89537	6886	NR810	
89538	6887	NR811	
89539	6888	NR812	
89540	6889	NR813	
89541	6890	NR814	
89542	6891	NR815	
89543	6892	NR828	
89544	6893	NR829	
89545	6894	NR830	
89546	6895	NR831	
89547	6896	NR832	
89548	6897	NR833	
89549	6898	NR834	
89550	6899	NR835	
89551	6900	NR836	
89552	6901	NR837	
89553	6902	NR838	
89554	6903	NR839	
89555	6904	NR840	
89556	6905	NR841	
89557	6906	NR842	
89558	6907	NR843	
89559	6908	NR844	
89560	6909	NR845	
89561	6910	NR846	
89562	6911	NR847	
89563	6912	NR848	
89564	6913	NR849	
89565	6914	NR850	
89566	6915	NR851	
89567	6916	NR852	
89568	6917	NR853	
89569	6918	RL936	
89570	6919	RL937	
89571	6920	RL938	
89572	6921	RL939	
89573	6922	RL940	
89574	6923	RL941	
89575	6924	RL942	

Brush Works No.	DH c/n	Original. reg'n or serial	Remarks
89576	6925	RL943	
89577	6926	RL944	
89578	6927	RL945	
89579	**6928**	**RL946**	
89580	6929	RL947	MkII
89581	6930	RL948	MkII
89582	6931	RL949	MkII
89583	6932	RL950	MkII
89584	6933	RL951	MkII
89585	6934	RL952	MkII
89586	6935	RL953	MkII
89587	6936	RL954	MkII
89588	6937	RL955	MkII
89589	6938	RL956	MkII
89590	6939	RL957	MkII
89591	6940	RL958	MkII
89592	6941	RL959	MkII
89593	6942	RL960	MkII
89594	6943	RL961	MkII
89595	6944	RL962	MkII
89596	6945	RL963	MkII
89597	6946	RL964	MkII
89598	6947	RL965	MkII
89599	6948	RL966	MkII
89600	6949	RL967	MkII
89601	6950	RL968	MkII
89602	6951	RL980	MkII
89603	6952	RL981	MkII
89604	6953	RL982	MkII
89605	6954	RL983	MkII
89606	6955	RL984	MkII
89607	6956	RL985	MkII
89608	6957	RL986	MkII
89609	6958	TX300	MkII
89610	6959	TX301	MkII
89611	6960	TX302	MkII
89612	6961	TX303	MkII
89613	6962	TX304	MkII
89614	6963	TX305	MkII
89615	6964	TX306	MkII
89616	6965	TX307	MkII
89617	6966	TX308	MkII
89618	6967	TX309	MkII
89619	6968	TX310	MkII
89620	6969	TX311	MkII
89621	6970	TX312	MkII
89622	6971	TX313	MkII
89623	6972	TX314	MkII
89624	6973	TX315	MkII
89625	6974	TX316	MkII
89626	6975	TX317	MkII
89627	6976	TX318	MkII
89628	6977	TX319	MkII

5.4 de Havilland DH89 Dragon Rapide – Production Listing

6250 First flew as **E.4** at Hatfield on 17.4.34, then moved to Martlesham Heath for CofA trials in 5.34. CofA no.4306 issued 10.5.34. Handed over to dealer Ostschweiz Aero Gessellschaft on 16.7.34 and flown to Altenrhein two days later. Reg'd **CH-287** to R. Herzig for Aero St. Gallen 19.7.34, and named *Aero le Gallen*. Re-reg'd **HB-ARA** 1.11.34. Damaged in an accident in Switzerland which required the despatch of a de Havilland engineer there on 26.3.35, who described the airframe as 'recently crashed'. To Swissair 20.3.37 and re-reg'd **HB-APA** while with them on 19.4.48. To Farner Werke AG of Grenchen in 1954, and to Motorfluggruppe Zurich des Ae.C.S in 1955. Last flight was on 3.10.60 and was officially withdrawn from use during 1961. Dismantled in 1962, then dumped on the approach to Zurich-Kloten airport, where it was burnt in 1965.

6251 Reg'd **G-ACPM** [CofR 4955 7.6.34] for Hillman's Airways Ltd., Stapleford 7.6.34, CofA no.4365 issued 5.7.34 and handed over 27.7.34. Before Hillmans took delivery, entered in the July 1934 King's Cup Air Race by Viscount Wakefield of Hythe (head of Castrol Oil) and was averaging 158 m.p.h., but was unable to complete the race due to sustaining damage in a hailstorm over Waddington. Flew into the English Channel 3 miles off Folkestone while on a scheduled flight from Stapleford to Paris, killing all seven on board on 2.10.34. The accident report gives disorientation and subsequent loss of control whilst flying in cloud as the probable cause.

6252 Reg'd **G-ACPN** for Hillman's Airways Ltd., Stapleford 12.7.34, CofA no.4389 issued 2.8.34 and handed over 1.8.34. Merged to form Allied British Airways Ltd. 30.9.35 and aircraft based at Heston. Name changed to British Airways Ltd. 29.10.35 [CofR 6890 8.4.36]. Leased to Highland Airways 19.4.36 to 9.8.36. Reported as 'sold abroad' 9.36. Actually purchased by the autogyro developer Juan de la Cierva and his partner Louis Bolin for the Spanish Nationalists. The aircraft was flown non-stop (presumably with extra tanks fitted) from Heston to Burgos 14-15.8.36 to join the 'Fokker/Dragon' Spanish Nationalist group. Variously reported as shot down 27.8.36 and destroyed by fire at Aragon 13.9.36.

6253 Reg'd **G-ACPO** for Hillman's Airways Ltd., Stapleford 12.7.34. CofA no.4390 issued 4.9.34 and handed over 5.9.34. Loaned to de Havilland for demonstration to Highland Airways 9.11.34 to 4.12.34 and arrived Longman Aerodrome 19.11.34. Damaged in gale at Ronaldsway IoM 25.1.35 and again damaged at an Essex aerodrome, necessitating repairs by de Havilland 27.3.35. Merged to form Allied British Airways Ltd. 30.9.35 and aircraft based Liverpool-Speke. Name changed to British Airways Ltd. 29.10.35 [CofR 6850 24.3.36]. Sold to Australia 5.36 and to Rockhampton Aerial Services, Rockhampton QLD reg'd **VH-ABN** 17.8.36. Impressed by R.A.A.F. as **A33-5** 12.8.40, initially to 3EFTS and to Australian National together with impressed c/ns 6439 & 6466 for modifications. Issued to 1AOS and ready for collection by them from 1AD 11.12.40. SOC 16.4.42 to Civil Aviation Department and restored as **VH-ABN** for Guinea Airways. Crashed at Mount Kitchener 20.7.44 whilst operating scheduled service Broken Hill NSW - Adelaide SA. The weather was poor and all seven occupants were killed.

6254 Reg'd **G-ACPP** [CofR 4958 20.2.35] for Railway Air Services Ltd., Croydon 20.2.35. CofA no.4730 issued 12.3.35 and handed over 4.4.35. Delivered to Croydon 18.5.35 named *City of Bristol*. Exhibited at a Royal Aeronautical Society Garden Party, Harmondsworth during 1935. Whilst operating a scheduled service from Le Touquet to Shoreham 25.8.35, the pilot got lost in conditions of low cloud and the gathering dusk. Hunting a ship to ditch near to, one of the passengers sighted a lighthouse and the aircraft was quickly aimed towards a patch of rough ground behind! The Rapide came to an abrupt halt when hitting a hedge and the four occupants were very surprised to learn from onlookers that quickly gathered, that their spectacular arrival was near Shanklin on the Isle of Wight!. Retrieved from the temporary airstrip and repaired. To Great Western and Southern Airlines Ltd., Shoreham, 31.1.39. Impressed 17.9.39 and was delivered on 22.9.39 to 'C' Flt of 24Sqdn., though no military serial was issued. Returned to Great Western and Southern at Speke in 6.40 and was operated under the aegis of A.A.J.C. Operated by Scottish Airways, Renfrew from 22.2.41. Handed over to British European Airways Corporation on formation 1.2.47. To Sqdn. Ldr. Kenneth James Nalson t/a Aircraft and Engineering Services Ltd.,

Croydon 16.4.48. To Yellow Air Taxi Company Ltd., Elmdon 22.6.48. To Air Couriers (Properties) Ltd., 4.9.51. To Hawker Aircraft Ltd., Dunsfold 7.5.52 and CofA renewed 7.5.52. To William Herbert Wetton 1.58 for operation by 600 (City of London) Sqdn. Flying Group. To Aviation Traders Ltd. 23.4..59 but already delivered to Stansted 2.3.59 for storage, having been taken in part exchange for Prentice G-APPL. CofA lapsed 4.9.59, and registration cancelled as WFU. Flown from Stansted to Blackpool 10.3.60 under a Permit to Fly and officially restored, now as a DH89A having been modified, to Air Navigation and Trading Co. Ltd. 29.11.60. Sold abroad 19.5.61 and an export CofA was issued 12.6.61 and it left Blackpool by road for onward shipment to Canada 15.6.61. Purchased by North-Air Services Ltd. who intended to use the aircraft as a floatplane at Lac L'Orange but in fact, it was not used by them and remained unmarked at Toronto-Malton airport. To Jack R. Bowdery reg'd **CF-PTK** at Bradford, ONT 2.3.64. CofA lapsed 2.3.65. Displayed at Reynolds Heritage Preservation Foundation, Wetaskiwin ALB by 5.02.

6255 Reg'd **G-ACPR** [CofR 4959 20.2.35] for Railway Air Services Ltd., Croydon 20.2.35. CofA no.4743 issued 18.3.35 and handed over 30.3.35. Named *City of Birmingham*. Loaned to Imperial Airways during 1936 for pilot training purposes. To Great Western and Southern Airlines Ltd., Shoreham 31.1.39. Impressed 17.9.39 and was delivered on 21.9.39 to 'C' Flt of 24Sqdn., though no military serial was issued. Returned to Great Western and Southern 7.12.39 and was operated under the aegis of N.A.C. Damaged beyond repair in an accident at Burford, Shropshire 19.2.40, when it was caught in a snowstorm and made a forced landing on snow covered ground, nosed over and sustained severe damage to the front end.

6256 Export CofA issued 10.12.34, supplied via Cyril Hull of the de Havilland Aircraft Co. of South Africa (Pty) Ltd., to African Air Transport. Reg'd **ZS-AES** 12.34, handed over 14.12.34 and departed Hatfield on delivery to Baragwanath 29.12.34 named *Mau-Hea-Tom*. Sold in Rhodesia, reg'd **VP-YBZ** 26.9.38 to Rhodesia and Nyasaland Airways, RANA. Rhodesian military serial **302** was allocated by 11.39, the aircraft flew in either civil or military marks depending on circumstances. Assets of RANA acquired by the Southern Rhodesian Gov't. 1.2.40 to form Southern Rhodesian Air Services to act as a communications squadron for the Air Force. Reverted to **VP-YBZ** by 4.42. Destroyed in a crash 11.43.

6257 For Anglo-Iranian Oil Co. Ltd., Abadan reg'd **G-ACTT** but not delivered and CofA no.4475 issued 20.10.34. To Flt. Lt. Edward Hedley Fielden for operation by The King's Flight, Hendon, 2.35 and handed over 26.4.35. To Olley Air Service Ltd., Croydon [CofR 6872 30.3.36]. Sustained damage in France 27.9.37 but flown back to Hatfield for repairs. Impressed 8.3.40 and delivered to 24Sqdn. 9.2.40, becoming **X8509** soon after. Continued in use with 24Sqdn. until involved in an accident 14.7.41. Initially conveyed to de Havilland on 27.7.41 for repair but was SOC 29.8.41 with damage assessed as Cat.E1.

6258 For Anglo-Iranian Oil Co. Ltd., Abadan reg'd **G-ACTU** but not delivered and instead, to C. R. Anson, Heston 3.9.34. CofA no.4477 issued 24.9.34. Operated by Personal Airways Ltd., Croydon on behalf of Viscount Forbes 1936. (Resident at Castle Forbes in Ireland and at a home in Paris, the Viscountcy was an Irish courtesy title for the eldest son of the 8th Earl of Granard. The Viscount succeeded his father 1948. Forbes was an experienced pilot, gaining the A.F.C. during the war and later owned a Lockheed 12 and an Aero Commander, normally based at Toussus-le-Noble and often flown to a substantial private airstrip at Castle Forbes until his death in 1992). To Straight Corporation for operation by Western Airways Ltd., Weston-super-Mare [CofR 8854 1.11.38]. Taken over by N.A.C., delivered to 24Sqdn. 30.9.39 and based at Paris-Le Bourget from 8.11.39. Returned to Western Airways 5.40. Impressed 4.6.40, allocated **AW115** and delivered to 8AACU at Weston, although initially operated with the civil marks. Destroyed shortly after take-off from Cardiff 15.2.41 when it stalled, crashed and was burnt out en route to St. Eval. SOC 28.2.41 with Cat.E2 damage.

6259 Handed over to the Melbourne Centenary Air Race Committee 3.10.34. Reg'd **ZK-ACO** and named *Tainui* (after the first Maori canoe to reach New Zealand). Export CofA issued 9.10.34. Eleventh aircraft to depart Mildenhall in the Air Race

20.10.34 flown by Sqd. Ldr. J. D. Hewett and C. E. Kay with E. Stewart as radio operator. Three extra fuel tanks within the fuselage extended range to 1000 miles. Arrived Melbourne 3.11.34 coming fifth in race. To New Zealand 14.11.34 but no buyer found there so shipped to Sydney per SS Wanganella and arrived 27.5.35. Assembled Melbourne-Essendon VIC and test flown 5.6.35. Reg'd **VH-UUO** 10.6.35. To West Australian Airways 7.35 named Malonga. Taken over by Adelaide Airways Ltd. 7.36. Merged to form Australian National Airways Pty. Ltd. 11.36. To Guinea Airways Pty. Ltd. 8.39. Impressed R.A.A.F. as **A33-1** 2.7.40 and delivered to 3EFTS Melbourne-Essendon. Served with 1AOS Cootamundra NSW. Restored as **VH-UUO** to Airlines of Australia 20.4.42. To Australian National Airways 5.47. To Butler Air Transport, Sydney 2.50. Crashed on Warrumbungle Mountain NSW whilst en route Baradine - Tooraweenah NSW 23.5.52. Heavy rain and low cloud was to blame but mercifully, the pilot and his four passengers only sustained minor injuries.

6260   CofA issued 27.12.34 and reg'd **I-DRAG** 29.1.35 for ALA Littoria SA. Handed over at Hatfield 8.2.35. Sold to Franco Mazzotti Biancinelli, Milan, 6.36. (Note; a Dragonfly was later also registered I-DRAG to an owner shown as Franco Mazzotti on 12.36). Acquired by the Spanish Republicans via Rollason Air Service, Croydon, it was delivered to Barcelona 14.8.36, and was finally cancelled from the Italian register on 3.9.37. Known to have been damaged beyond repair in Spain when it collided with a Fiat Cr32 while taxiing, but actual date and location unknown.

6261   Reg'd **G-ACYR** [CofR 5375 15.10.34] to Olley Air Service Ltd., Croydon. CofA no.4534 issued 2.2.35, and handed over 7.2.35 with a non-standard cabin fit. Described by The Aeroplane as 'one of the most comfortably furnished Dragon Rapides', it had just five permanent seats, though two more could be provided if required. Chartered to fly General Franco from Las Palmas in the Canary Islands to Tetuan, Spanish Morocco 17.7.36, where he took command of the successful Spanish uprising. To Miles Aircraft Ltd., Woodley 6.4.45. To Reid and Sigrist Ltd., Desford & Braunstone 15.8.46. CofA expired 23.8.47 and was reported in storage at Desford 4.53. Dismantled and transported to Croydon 7.53 where it continued in storage. In view of its history, presented by Mr Griffiths, the Managing Director of Air Couriers, to General Franco in 5.57. Shipped per Monte Urbosa to Bilbao 6.57 and then conveyed to Cuatro Vientos for display at the Museo del Aeronautica y Astronautica, where it remains on show.

6262   CofA issued 27.11.34. Reg'd **EC-W27** as ferry marks for Lineas Aereas Postales Espanolas – L.A.P.E., it was handed over to Senor Escario, acting on their behalf, on 8.12.34. After delivery re-reg'd **EC-AZZ**, later wore **EC-AGO** and allocated L.A.P.E. fleet number 41. Little is known of this aircraft but it was certainly in use by the Republican side during the Spanish Civil War as a bomber on the Madrid and Aragon fronts.

6263   Reg'd **G-ADAL** for Hillman's Airways Ltd., Abridge. CofA no.4715 issued 2.3.35 and handed over 4.3.35. Merged to form Allied British Airways Ltd. 30.9.35. Name changed to British Airways Ltd. 29.10.35. To Wrightways Ltd., Croydon [CofR 7109 4.6.36]. Impressed and allocated **X9448** 14.4.40 but delivered to 6AACU still marked as **G-ADAL**. To 7AACU 6.40. Damaged whilst landing at night at Abingdon 1.7.40 and taken to Air Taxis Ltd. for repairs. Flown to 9MU after repair 26.8.40, and released to 3FPP as **X9448** 2.11.40. To Station Flight Andover 31.11.40, to 7FPP 5.2.41. While on a ferry flight to 11SFF at Dumfries on 25.3.41 bad weather was encountered, and eventually a forced landing due to fuel starvation was made in a boggy field at Standish, near Wigan, where it overran into a hedge. The aircraft was initially conveyed to de Havilland for repair, but was SOC 21.4.41 with damage assessed as Cat.E1.

6264   Reg'd **G-ACZE** [CofR 5408 20.11.34] for Anglo-Iranian Oil Co. Ltd., Abadan. CofA no.4684 issued 15.12.34. Handed over to Airwork Ltd., Heston for operation on behalf of Anglo-Iranian and delivered ex Heston 19.12.34, arriving at Almaza, Cairo, 25.12.34. Used for communication flights between the oil shipping base at Abadan and the oil fields. Returned to Airwork Ltd., Heston 17.3..39 and converted to 'flying classroom' configuration by de Havilland for operation by subsidiary Air Service Training Ltd., Perth on behalf of 7AONS and then by 6AONS at Staverton from 5.40. Impressed 15.7.40 and allocated **Z7266**. Delivered to de Havilland 22.8.40 for conversion to air ambulance configuration; initial allotment to 24Sqdn. was cancelled and instead delivered to 48MU. To 3FPP 8.12.40 and later loaned to Allied Airways (Gandar Dower) Ltd., Aberdeen from 21.9.41. SOC on sale to Allied Airways and restored to **G-ACZE** 9.2.42, named The Don (or The Dawn). However, the aircraft remained on charge with the R.A.F. and served as a replacement for Allied's G-ADAH which had been taken over by the Secretary of State. The aircraft crashed and was badly damaged at Grimsetter, Orkney, on 27.12.45 when, shortly after take-off on a scheduled service to Dyce, the starboard engine failed. An attempt was made to regain the field, but the aircraft stalled and crashed. Of the nine on board, two passengers and the radio operator were slightly injured. Cancelled from register 12.5.47. Salvaged parts from this aircraft were used at Witney in 1947 to build c/n W.1001 reg'd G-AJGS (q.v.).

6265   Export CofA issued 8.1.35. Handed over Hatfield to the Asiatic Petroleum Co. Ltd. 15.1.35. Reg'd **VH-UVS** and named The Spirit of Shell. Shipped to Australia and test flown Sydney-Mascot 27.3.35. Aircraft used by the Aviation Department of Shell Company of Australia Ltd. for testing new aviation fuels and oils in a working environment and was fitted with auxiliary fuel tanks, a set of thermometers to record fuel tank, carburetter and oil temperatures and unusually, the cockpit glass was fitted with sun blinds and windscreen wiper. Leased to Airlines of Australia early '37 and destroyed by fire on start up when in their service Sydney-Mascot 12.5.37. Illustrated "The Aeroplane" 23.1.35 p111.

6266   Reg'd **G-ADAG** for Hillman's Airways Ltd., Abridge, CofA no.4675 issued 6.2.35, handed over 7.2.35. Damaged on landing in fog at Speke 2.3.35 but repaired. Merged to form Allied British Airways Ltd. 30.9.35. Name changed to British Airways Ltd. 29.10.35. Delivered to Northern and Scottish Airways Ltd., Renfrew 30.7.36. To Airwork Ltd., Heston [CofR 8099 2.9.37] and used by 6AONS at Shoreham, though at Renfrew by 7.12.39. Impressed 15.7.40 and allocated **Z7264** but remained at 6AONS. To A.T.A. HQ White Waltham 3.41, operated by 11 Service Ferry Flight, Dumfries for a short period during May and June 1941, and then returned to A.T.A. Conveyed to de Havilland 20.8.43 with Cat.B damage. SOC 13.9.43 after reassessment as Cat.E.

6267   Allocated **K5070** for the Air Council and handed over 29.3.35, allocated to 24Sqdn. for service trials during 1935, the Rapide was found to be faster than any of the R.A.F.'s twin-engined bombers, and it was used by the Air Council as a six-seater for official journeys, being replaced by a DH86 in October 1937. Loaned by the MoD to Imperial Airways until 1.7.41, a UK CofA no.6098 was issued 22.10.37, and on the same date reg'd **VP-KCK** to Wilson Airways Ltd., Nairobi. Impressed locally 9.39 it was used by the Kenya Auxiliary Air Unit as either **K-11** or **K-16**. Not restored to the civil register, the aircraft was cannibalised during 1946 at Eastleigh by EAAC, its remains noted there in late 1946. (Also see c/n 6357 reference serial).

6268   Reg'd **G-ACZF** [CofR 5408 20.11.34] for Anglo-Iranian Oil Co. Ltd., Abadan. CofA no.4684 issued, handed over 12.2.35 and delivered ex Heston 19.12.34. Departed Abadan 8.11.38 and arrived back at Heston 24.11.38 prior to sale to Airwork Ltd. , Heston 17.3.39. To Allied Airways (Gandar Dower) Ltd., Dyce, 16.5.40, and named Carina. Badly damaged at Wideford, Orkney, late 1941 and returned to Dyce by sea for repairs. Although noted in derelict condition at Witney 28.10.46, ownership changed to B.E.A.C. 12.4.47 but cancelled from register 12.5.47. To Lancashire Aircraft Corporation Ltd., Samlesbury 7.48 for spares use only as the aircraft had already been 'dumped' at Witney. Dismantled and used for spares by 8.48. Wings only were noted with Lancashire Aircraft at Squires Gate in 1950.

6269   Reg'd **G-ACYM** [CofR 5368 10.1.35] for Olley Air Service Ltd., Croydon. Handed over 4.3.35 and CofA no.4649 issued 6.3.35. To Great Western and Southern Air Lines Ltd., Shoreham 6.4.39. Impressed 12.3.40, allocated **X9320**, delivered to 'C' Flt 24Sqdn. 3.40 and cancelled from register 17.6.40. While on a passenger and freight flight to Amiens on 12.2.40 (sic) a snowstorm forced a landing at Moyenneville near Abbeville, but on arrival the tail 'collapsed' due to a rough landing on frozen ground. SOC 4.4.40 with Cat.W damage. The aircraft was intentionally set alight and abandoned during the evacuation from France in May/June 1940.

6270   Export CofA issued 2.7.35. To Royal Australian Air Force as **A3-1**. Operated by 1Sqdn. and, flown by Sqdn. Ldr. G. Jones, used for a geological survey of the outback attached to the

DH89 c/n 6272. G-ADAE was supplied to United Airways and operated by their subsidiary Northern & Scottish Airways Ltd. Broken-up by Air Charter Experts, probably as spares for G-AEMH.

DH89 c/n 6317. Showing fleet no.5 of the Istanbul based airline, Devlet Hava Yollari, together with c/ns 6315 and 6316, the new fleet was delivered in May 1936.

DH89 c/n 6276. Three second hand Rapides were purchased by Air France in 1948. F-BEDY (6276), F-BEDX (6547) and F-BEDZ (6522) were certificated at Le Bourget, before flying on to Madagascar.

DH89 c/n 6334. Originally delivered to Cook Strait Airways in September 1936 and registered ZK-AEC, this was the first of 5 to be impressed locally. In addition, nine aircraft came new from the U.K.

DH89 c/n 6284. Originally registered to Aberdeen Airways, the owner-ship of G-ADDF was quickly changed to Hillman's. One of many Rapides to end up in Spain - this one with the Republican side.

DH89 c/n 6336. After withdrawal in late 1961, G-AEMH was abandoned in the open at Ipswich. The weather and vandalism soon took their toll but mercifully, this early model has survived at Chirk.

DH89 c/n 6303. One of seven, operated by Misr Airwork on domestic schedules. The survivors were sold in the late 1940s and Syria and Yemen each received two former Egyptian aircraft.

DH89 c/n 6344. Many oldies will remember the jingle "208 metres on the medium Wave – Radio Luxembourg". Personal Airways' G-AEPE provided a revolutionary method of commercial advertising.

North Australian Survey Flight. To Holyman's Airways as **VH-UFF** 30.12.35 named *Memma*. Merged to form Australian National Airways Pty. Ltd. 2.11.36. Impressment Requisition no.12536 12.7.40 and allocated serial **A33-3** [note the A3- prefix previously used for DH89 aircraft had been re-allotted to Commonwealth Wackett training aircraft]. Initially received by 3EFTS, but to Australian National for modifications 18.7.40. Issued to 1AOS by 14.10.40. Wings recovered by de Havilland 24.7.42. To 3CF Sydney-Mascot NSW 24.8.42. To 36Sqdn. Brisbane-Archerfield QLD 25.9.42. Damaged on landing 28.11.42 when hit pot holes in runway. Repaired by Ansett and noted as serviceable with 36Sqdn. 29.12.42. Briefly to 34Sqdn. 2.1.43. To Guinea Airways 20.1.43 but not completed until 10.11.43. SOC 15.11.43 and restored to Guinea Airways as **VH-UFF** 21.11.43. To Airlines (Western Australia) Ltd. 2.45. Ownership transferred to Australian National Airways 30.6.45. To Brown & Dureau Ltd. Melbourne VIC 1.10.48 and converted to survey aircraft at Geelong VIC. To James Air Charter, Wollongong NSW 4.55. Sold abroad 4.56. To Ste. Caledonienne de Transport Aeriens reg'd **F-OAVG** 10.8.56. Operated last flight 11.6.57, CofA suspended at Noumea 3.59 and used for spares.

6271 Allocated **K4772** for the Air Council under contract No.352854/34, this aircraft was built as a contender for Air Ministry Specification G.18/35 for a coastal reconnaissance aircraft. Conducted trials at Martlesham Heath from 13.4.35, being officially handed over on 15.4.35 and also engaged on comparative tests with the Avro Anson at the Central Defence Development Unit at Gosport from 13.5.35. The aircraft was stripped of its military equipment 6.6.35 and delivered to R.A.E. Farnborough 19.6.35 for experimental flying with automatic controls. Allocated to the Instrument and Photographic Flight by 7.35 and then transferred in 9.35 to the Wireless and Electrical Flight for radio telephony experiments and also trials with different types of landing lamps. During 7.36, used for autopilot trials, and then returned to the Instrument and Photographic Flight for work on stability under gyroscopic control. During the early part of the war it was used as a 'hack' at Farnborough, and then later by the A. & A.E.E. Boscombe Down. Broken up for spares by de Havilland at Witney 6.42 and finally SOC 15.7.42.

6272 Supplied via Brian Lewis & Co. Ltd. of Stanley Park Airfield, Blackpool, to United Airways Ltd. for operation by Northern & Scottish Airways Ltd., Renfrew. CofA no.4699 issued 17.4.35 and reg'd **G-ADAE** 19.4.35. Merged to form Allied British Airways Ltd., Southampton 30.9.35. Name changed to British Airways Ltd. 29.10.35. To Airwork Ltd., Heston [CofR 8092 28.8.37]. Sold to Det Danske Luftfartselskap, operated by Provinsluftfartselskabet AS and arrived Copenhagen 18.5.38. Reg'n **OY-DIN** issued 28.5.38. Acquired by Southampton Air Services Ltd. and departed Copenhagen 8.5.46. Restored to Stewart, Smith & Co. Ltd., Croydon as **G-ADAE**. To Airborne Taxi Services Ltd. (of Bracknell, Berkshire) 12.9.46. We assume that Southampton Air Services operated the aircraft on behalf of insurance company Stewart, Smith as they seem to have done when with Airborne as it was "often operated by Southampton Air Services". Sold to Air Charter Experts Ltd., Ronaldsway 6.6.47. Renamed Manx Air Charters Ltd. 9.8.47 and aircraft broken up 8.48. Cancelled from register as permanently withdrawn from use 20.8.48. (Note: Manx Air Charters are reported to have acquired only one Rapide, G-AEMH c/n 6336. As G-ADAE was apparently already WFU, it is presumed that Air Charter Experts acquired the aeroplane purely as a spares source for their G-AEMH. Also see c/n 6677 for details of another Rapide acquired for spares use).

6273 Initially allocated **OO-APO** for Le Compte de Mahieu, but this was not taken up and the aircraft was reg'd **OO-JFN** on 13.3.35 when Belgian CofA no.325 was issued. Handed over 15.3.35 to the Belgian aircraft manufacturer Stampe and Vertongen acting on behalf of John Mahieu Aviation, Brussels. Count Mahieu was a director of The Belgian Bank, and used the Rapide for flights between Brussels and the Belgian Congo, replacing it in 1937 into a DH90. Noted visiting the Royal Aero Club Week-End Aerien at Heston in July 1936. (Illustrated *'The Aeroplane'* 27.7.36 p.161). Cancelled as 'sold in France' 25.5.37 but never aspired to a French reg'n and was thought to have ended up in Spain. Fate remains unknown.

6274 Reg'd **G-ACZU** 25.3.35 and handed over the same day to 1st Viscount Furness of Melton Mowbray (Chairman of the family shipbuilding concern and numerous other companies involved with the iron and steel industries and coal mining) and flown on his

behalf ex Croydon by Dan Cameron. Replaced by Lockheed 12 G-AEOI and sold to S. Harris of Cinema Press Ltd. [CofR 7616 22.1.37] for operation by subsidiary, Croydon Airways. After the failure of Croydon Airways, the aircraft was offered for sale by auction at Hanworth 9.6.37. Cancelled as 'sold abroad' 7.37 but nothing further is known. Once again it is thought that the aircraft may have ended up in Spain.

6275 Reg'd **G-ADAO** [CofR 5499 16.2.35] for Thomas Raymond Anthony Bevan of Ethyl Export Corporation, Heston. CofA no.4697 issued 5.4.35 and handed over the same day to Bevan, Ethyl Export's business manager in Europe. The aircraft was acquired for use in Europe, Africa and the Middle East, and was therefore fitted with additional cockpit equipment, including a Sperry artificial horizon and directional gyro, an airlog, a Marconi 41/42 radio set and a constant speed generator. More significantly for the company, the engines were fitted with special heads which allowed them to be run on ethyl fuels. The aircraft was based at Brooklands, and embarked on a long tour of Ethyl's facilities on 21.9.35, including visits to oil refineries at Karachi, Suez, Persia, Assam and Palembang before returning to the UK on 18.11.35. The British registration was cancelled as 'sold abroad' 9.36. Yet again, this aircraft went to Spain, but in this case served the Nationalist side. Fate unknown.

6276 Reg'd **G-ADAJ** for Hillman's Airways Ltd., Abridge, CofA no.4829 issued 5.6.35 and handed over the same day. Merged to form Allied British Airways Ltd. 30.9.35, name changed to British Airways Ltd. 29.10.35. To Highland Airways Ltd., Inverness, 9.36, named *Inverness* and delivered 26.12.36. Merged into Scottish Airways Ltd., Inverness 12.8.37 [CofR 8565 18.6.38]. To B.E.A.C., Renfrew on formation 1.2.47. Cancelled as sold abroad 21.11.47, the aircraft departed the U.K. bound for Tananarive, Mozambique 21.4.48. A French CofA was issued en route at Le Bourget 22.4.48 and reg'n **F-BEDY** was taken up for Air France at Ivato, Mozambique. Re-reg'd **F-OADY**, still to Air France with new CofA on 31.5.49. Returned to France and new CofA and reg'n **F-BAHY** were issued 21.10.50, still to Air France but now at Orly. Sold to Cie. D'Autrex, Hanoi Saigon 6.52 and arrived 10.7.52. The aircraft crashed and was destroyed when it hit tree tops whilst taking off from Seno, near Savannakhet, Laos on 20.8.54, though the reg'n was not cancelled until 22.12.56.

6277 Reg'd **G-ADCL** [CofR 5602 16.4.35] for Anglo-American Oil Co. Ltd., Heston. CofA no.4784 issued 4.5.35 and handed over to Brian Lewis & Co. Ltd., de Havilland's UK agent acting on behalf of Anglo-American 8.5.35. Damaged at Redhill 26.6.35 in a crash caused by a poorly executed 'side-slip' approach, killing the pilot. Repaired. To Airwork Ltd., Heston, 12.35. Cancelled as sold 8.36 and flown non-stop Heston-Burgos 14-15.8.36 by L'Estrange Malone to join the Spanish Nationalists and became **40-2**. Re-reg'd as **EC-AAY** 2.10.45 to Iberia CA, at Madrid-Barajas. Written off in a crash at unknown location in Spanish Guinea 22.6.46.

6278 Reg'd **G-ADAH** for Hillman's Airways Ltd., Abridge and CofA no.4690 issued 19.2.35. Handed over 23.2.35. Merged to form Allied British Airways Ltd. 30.9.35, name changed to British Airways Ltd 29.10.35. To Northern and Scottish Airways Ltd., Renfrew 30.6.36 and delivered to them 10.8.36. To Airwork Ltd., Shoreham 8.37. To Allied Airways (Gandar Dower) Ltd, Dyce [CofR 8843 26.10.38]. Named *The Thurso Venturer* and later as *Pioneer*. Crashed at Wideford, Orkney, in the summer of 1940 but repaired by Air Dispatch at Cardiff. Registered to the Secretary of State for Air 2.12.42 but continued in operation by Allied Airways and transferred back to them 31.10.44. To Eric Leslie Gandar-Dower 25.7.46 and noted with Island Air Services (Gandar Dower) Ltd. titles. After overhaul for CofA renewal at Kenley in summer 1946, it was grounded 6.47 and placed in storage in a hangar at Dyce. Reg'n cancelled as withdrawn from use 6.54. **G-ADAH** remained in storage until 8.66 when moved by road to Booker. The CofA was not renewed, however, and it remained disassembled until donated to The Aeroplane Collection, and the fuselage went by road for storage at Peel Green, Manchester 11.10.70 to be followed on 25.10.70, by the wings and other parts. Moved to East Fortune 11.73 for display at the Royal Scottish Museum of Flight. Moved again 4.89 to Manchester for display at the Manchester Museum of Science and Industry.

6279 To Quebec Airways Ltd., Montreal PQ as **CF-AEO**. Temporary CofR issued 28.6.35. Featured an extended dorsal fin for increased longitudinal stability whilst operating on floats during summer and skis during winter. To Canadian Airways, Winnipeg 11.7.35 but destroyed seven days later when wing dropped on take-off Moncton NB. Aircraft crashed and totally consumed by fire.

6280   CofA no.4794 issued 29.4.35 and handed over same day to United Airways Ltd., Stanley Park reg'd **G-ADBU**. Became part of Allied British Airways Ltd., Stanley Park 1.10.35. Name changed to British Airways Ltd. 29.10.35. To Northern & Scottish Airways Ltd., Renfrew [CofR 7276 19.8.36]. Damaged beyond repair 11.36 but further details of the accident are unknown.

6281   Originally ordered by Hillman's Airways Ltd. but released from contract. CofA no.4827 issued 14.5.35 and handed over to British Continental Airways Ltd., Croydon, Surrey on the following day reg'd **G-ADAK** and named *St. Patrick*. To British Airways Ltd. 8.36. To C. H. Stone, Croydon 9.36 and intended for onward sale to Spanish Republicans but sale prohibited. Purchased by the Hon. Mrs. Victor Bruce from United Founders Trust 29.1.37 and used briefly by her company, Air Dispatch. Leased by Provinsluftfartselskabet AS in Denmark briefly 9.37 but no local marks issued. To John Wormald, Croydon [CofR 8408 22.3.38]. To Mutual Finance Ltd., Croydon 19.1.39. To the Hon. Mrs. Victor Bruce t/a Air Dispatch Ltd., Cardiff 2.12.39. Briefly with Anglo-European Airways Ltd., Cardiff 1.2.40 but returned to Air Dispatch 14.5.40. Impressed as **AW155** 7 7.40 and delivered to 8AACU. To Carlux Ltd., Hooton Park for installation of night flying equipment 26.11.40. Later to 18MU 6.41, to Overseas Aircraft Dispatch Unit, Kemble 4.42, 6AOS 8.42 (becoming No.6 [O] AFU 4.43) and to RAF Halton 9.43. To de Havilland for inspection 11.9.44 and subsequently SOC as Cat.E1. (Note: many ownership changes occurred during the period 9.36 to 5.40 but it seems likely that this aircraft was in continuous service with the Hon. Mrs. Victor Bruce's company Air Dispatch Ltd.).

6282   To Aberdeen Airways Ltd. reg'd **G-ADDE** named *The Aberdonian*. CofA no.4815 issued 31.5.35 and handed over on the following day. On 10.9.36 en route Aberdeen to Shetland, the weather closed in and the pilot became lost in fog. Whilst descending the aircraft touched down in a field and nosed over, but all five on board were uninjured and the aircraft was repaired. To North Eastern Airways Ltd., Croydon [CofR 8158 21.10.37]. Impressed as **X9386** 27.5.40 and delivered to 110(AAC) Wing the same day. To 6AACU 25.5.40, to 24Sqdn. 5.40, to A.T.A. HQ White Waltham, to 39MU 1.10.41, to 26Sqdn 5.42, to Farnborough 6.44 and then to 5MU 11.45. Sold to E. L. Gandar Dower Ltd. for spares use 24.3.47, but not restored to the register.

6283   Reg'd **G-ADDD** for Edward, Prince of Wales. CofA no.4802 issued 8.6.35, and handed over the same day to the Prince's Chief Air Pilot Flt. Lt. Edward Hedley Fielden, Hendon. Based at Hendon, the aircraft was hangared free of charge by the R.A.F. Apart from Fielden, the operation was supported by a clerk and two mechanics. Repairs and more major maintenance were carried out by, it is believed, Vickers and these arrangements cost the Prince £2000 per annum. When Edward became King, the operation of the aircraft was rearranged such that the R.A.F. would take over the responsibility and cost of operations on behalf of His Majesty. Fielden was retained as his pilot, and by the summer of 1936, 'DDD and its establishment had become the King's Flight, based at Hendon and attached to 24Sqdn. for administration purposes. On his abdication, the aircraft remained with the King's Flight but was only flown occasionally. In February 1937 Edward, by now the Duke of Windsor, requested the return of his aircraft so that it could be sold on the open market, and this was agreed. It was therefore sold to The Channel Trust Ltd. for £3345 25.5.37 and operated by Western Airways Ltd., Weston-super-Mare for use on their Weston to Birmingham services. Delivered by Fielden to Weston-super-Mare on Whit Sunday 1937 to be met by a large party of local councillors, many of whom were given rides on the day [CofR 8856 1.11.38]. Impressed 4.6.40 and delivered from Weston to 8AACU still marked **G-ADDD** but soon after, became **AW116**. Flown to de Havilland for maintenance 7.4.41. SOC as Cat.E1 22.5.41.

6284   Reg'd **G-ADDF** for Aberdeen Airways Ltd., Dyce, CofA no.4994 issued 8.8.35 and handed over 10.8.35, the CofR was quickly amended, on 15.8.35, to show Hillman's Airways Ltd., Abridge and ownership was transferred to Hillman's in 9.35, presumably without entering Aberdeen Airways service. Merged to form Allied British Airways Ltd. 30.9.35. Name changed to British Airways Ltd. 29.10.35.

Delivered to Northern and Scottish Airways Ltd. Renfrew 29.6.36 and officially reg'd to them 8.36. To Airwork Ltd., Heston [CofR 8098 31.8.37]. Cancelled as sold abroad 9.37, in fact the aircraft had been sold by Airwork a month earlier via Malcomson and Farquarson Ltd. to M. Vandervelde who was acting on behalf of Lejeune Aviation of Esbly, France. Lejeune Aviation was one of the companies set up to obtain aircraft from foreign countries for the Spanish Republican Air Force, and it also set up flying schools at various locations in France to train Spanish pilots. This aircraft presumably ended up in Spain, though its eventual fate is unknown.

6285   Reg'd **VP-YAU** for Rhodesia and Nyasaland Airways Ltd., an export CofA was issued 20.7.35 and handed over 29.7.35. Departing Hatfield on delivery 1.8.35, the aircraft entered service with RANA in 11.35, having been ordered as a replacement for the company's Westland Wessex. The assets of RANA were acquired by the Southern Rhodesian Government on 1.2.40 to form Southern Rhodesian Air Services which acted as a communications squadron for the Air Force. Military serial **301** was allocated, possibly as early as 11.39, although it may never have been carried. The aircraft was reported as SOC 7.8.44 and dismantled.

6286   Reg'd **G-ADBV** for Jersey Airways Ltd., CofA no.4795 issued 6.6.35 and handed over 9.6.35 named *St. Ouen's Bay II*. To J. Dade (a pilot with Olley Air Service), Croydon, 5.37. To Weston Airport Ltd. 9.38. To Western Airways Ltd., Weston-super-Mare [CofR 8855 1.11.38]. Taken over by N.A.C. and delivered to 24Sqdn. 30.9.39, the aircraft was impressed 12.1.40 and allocated **X8511**, though it remained in civilian marks until it took up this military serial in 2.41. The last recorded service flight was on 29.9.41 and it is next noted when returned to de Havilland for repair as Cat.B on 22.10.41 but was SOC as Cat.E1 2.11.41.

6287   Reg'd **G-ADAI** to an order from Hillman's Airways Ltd, but not delivered and instead, sold via Rollason Aircraft Services to British Continental Airways Ltd., Croydon. CofA no.4828 issued 20.6.35 and handed over 23.6.35, named *St Andrew*. Merged with British Airways Ltd., Gatwick, 8.36. To Airwork Ltd., Heston [CofR 8091 28.8.37] and used by 6AONS at Shoreham until impressed 15.7.40 as **Z7262** and issued to 7AACU. Before actually taking up the military serial, it crashed and was extensively damaged at Shawbury 31.7.40. SOC as Cat.E1 2.12.40.

6288   Reg'd **G-ADBW** [CofR 5916 28.5.35] for Jersey Airways Ltd. CofA no.4796 issued 27.6.35. To Isle of Man Air services Ltd. 10.37. To Airwork Ltd., Heston 30.1.39 and used by 6AONS at Shoreham. Impressed 15.7.40 and allocated **Z7265**. Delivered to RAF Ringway, then to 7AACU. To 8AACU 1.41. SOC 17.11.41 for reasons unknown.

6289   Reg'd **G-ADBX** for United Airways Ltd., Heston. CofA no.4797 issued 4.7.35. Merged to form Allied British Airways Ltd 30.9.35. Name changed to British Airways Ltd. 29.10.35 [CofR 6789 2.3.36]. Crashed into a hangar on landing at Ronaldsway 16.5.36 and written off.

6290   Reg'd **G-ADFX** for British American Air Services Ltd., Heston. CofA no.4903 issued 22.7.35 and handed over 25.7.35. A receiver was appointed 6.1.37 and ownership passed to L.H.G. Ltd., Heston [CofR 7708 23.2.37]. L.H.G. was a company registered 18.1.37 to carry passengers, goods and mail and took the unusual name from the initials of one of it's subscribers, Mrs. Lillian Hartigan Gibbs. Impressed 27.4.40 (reportedly directly from British American, so it may never have flown with L.H.G.) and was allocated **X9457**. Used by 6AACU and then by 24Sqdn. in 5.40 still as 'DFX. Later took up the military serial and joined 1ADF at Hendon 4.41. To 24Sqdn. 7.41. To de Havilland for maintenance 17.9.41. To 79(S) Wing 5.42. To 77(S) Wing 11.42. To 79(S) Wing 1.43. The aircraft landed in a rough field at Sywell 17.5.43 and was badly damaged when it struck a ridge and tipped onto it's nose. Conveyed to de Havilland for repair but was SOC 5.6.43 as Cat.E1.

6291   Reg'd **G-ADFY** for W. H. Rhodes-Moorhouse, Heston. CofA no.4928 issued 26.7.35 and handed over on the same day. To Charles Eaton Gardner, Hamsey Green [CofR 6599 14.12.35]. Cancelled as sold abroad 8.36 and to Conde Cimera Garcia Gutierrez, Madrid. Flown to Burgos by R. V. L'Estrange Malone from Heston on 4.8.36 for use by the Spanish Nationalists. Fate unknown.

6292 An export CofA was issued 30.8.35, and the aircraft was delivered as **PH-AKV** from Croydon on 31.8.35 to Rotterdam for The Asiatic Petroleum Co. Ltd., though the registration date was 4.9.35. At Rotterdam, KLM engineers carried out extensive modifications to this and the other two Asiatic Petroleum aircraft acquired for aerial survey missions. Airframe changes included, metal airscrews, a glass-covered hole in the floor and 30 gal. auxiliary fuel tanks. Internally there were blind-flying instruments and an extensive camera fit, including one nine-lens panoramic camera and three wide-angle cameras. The fuel tanks were covered for use as working tables. Departed Holland September 1935 and it flew to Makassar in 34 stages and was then shipped to New Guinea. Re-reg'd **PK-AKV** and operated by K.N.I.L.M. from 24.1.36, this aircraft was nicknamed *Vera* and was flown between oil prospecting sites in Netherlands New Guinea. Although K.N.I.L.M. was the operator, the owner was actually N.N.G.P.M. - Nederlandsch Nieuw Guinea Petroleum Maatschappij, a joint venture between Standard Oil Company and Texaco, managed by Shell and operated under contract. The aircraft was destroyed by the owner at the request of the Army in either February or March 1942 'at Andir at capitulation'. The two surviving Rapides, replaced by two Sikorsky S38Bs, were due to be shipped to Java to continue their survey work. (Note: see also c/ns 6294 and 6296).

6293 Reg'd **G-ADIM** for British Continental Airways Ltd., Croydon. CofA no.4972 issued 31.7.35 and handed over the same day, named *St. David*. Company taken over by British Airways Ltd, Gatwick, 8.36. To Airwork Ltd., Heston [CofR 8093 28.8.37] and operated by 6AONS at Shoreham. Impressed 15.7.40 and allotted **Z7263**. Transferred to RAF Ringway. To 8AACU 11.40 (released by 110 Wing). To RAF Old Sarum 9.41. To 4Sqdn. 3.42. Taking off from Doncaster 11.4.42, the aircraft made a half circuit of the field when the port wing appeared to stall and it went into a vertical dive. Although control was partly regained, the aircraft hit a tree and burst into flames, before coming to rest on a roadway. SOC 9.5.42 as Cat.E2.

6294 An export CofA was issued 2.9.35, and the aircraft was delivered as **PH-AKW** from Croydon 31.8.35 to Rotterdam for The Asiatic Petroleum Co. Ltd., though the registration date was 4.9.35. Then followed same history as c/ns 6292 and 6296 (q.v.), including re-registration to **PK-AKW** 24.1.36 for KNILM, until it was damaged beyond repair on landing at Babo, New Guinea 5.3.36 inbound from Efman. One main wheel dug into a water filled rut in the sandy surface of the airstrip, and the aircraft turned over.

6295 Reg'd **CF-AVJ** for Canadian Airways Ltd. 24.9.35. Sold to Quebec Airways Ltd., Montreal PQ 30.3.38 when CofA no.168 was issued. During an engine run-up at St John, NB, on 17.5.39 the port engine exhaust started a fire and the aircraft was burnt out and destroyed.

6296 An export CofA was issued 30.8.35, and the aircraft was delivered as **PH-AKU** from Croydon 31.8.35 to Rotterdam for The Asiatic Petroleum Co. Ltd., though the registration date was 4.9.35. Then followed same history as c/ns 6292 and 6294 (q.v.), including re-registration to **PK-AKU** 24.1.36 for KNILM. Forced landed in the sea at Ketapangdaja, off Madura, and was destroyed 16.8.38.

6297 Reg'd **G-ADNG** [CofR 6157 15.8.35] for Iraq Petroleum Transport Co. Ltd., Haifa. CofA no.5156 issued 5.10.35. Destroyed when it hit a building whilst on approach to land 30 miles east of Rutba, Iraq 10.3.36. Cancelled 8.36.

6298 Reg'd **SU-ABP** for Misr Airwork Ltd., CofA issued 27.8.35 and handed over to Airwork 28.8.35. Misr Airwork was a joint venture company set up with the Egyptian Government to open scheduled services to and within Egypt. Named *Al Kahira*. Crashed and destroyed near Mariut airport 6.2.45.

6299 Reg'd **SU-ABQ** for Misr Airwork Ltd., CofA issued 11.9.35 and handed over to Airwork 12.9.35. Named *Thebes*. Believed delivered from Heston 18.9.35. Crashed and destroyed 9.10.41 on approach to Port Sudan, 18 miles north of the town.

6300 Reg'd **G-ADNH** for Iraq Petroleum Transport Co. Ltd., Haifa. CofA no.5164 issued 11.10.35. To Mutual Finance Ltd. [CofR 8571 22.6.38]. To The Hon. Mrs. Victor Bruce t/a Air Dispatch Ltd., Cardiff 5.2.40. Impressed as **W6423** 1.3.40 and delivered to 24Sqdn. Hendon but still marked as **G-ADNH**.

Damaged by enemy action at Coulommiers, France 16.5.40. The engines and other equipment were salvaged but the airframe was abandoned. SOC 3.6.40.

6301 Reg'd **G-ADNI** for Iraq Petroleum Transport Co. Ltd., Haifa. CofA no.5166 issued 17.10.35 and handed over 21.10.35. To Mutual Finance Ltd. [CofR 8572 22.6.38]. To Anglo-European Airways Ltd., Cardiff 27.2.40. Impressed as **W9365** 12.4.40 and delivered to 24Sqdn. Hendon. Similarly damaged in an air raid at Coulommiers, France. To be collected by 21AD but abandoned when German forces over-ran the area. SOC 22.6.40.

6302 Reg'd **SU-ABR** for Misr Airwork Ltd., CofA issued 20.9.35 and handed over to Airwork 21.9.35. Named *Memphis*. Sold on dates variously reported as 4.47 or 5.49 to an unknown customer, possibly in Syria or the Yemen.

6303 Reg'd **SU-ABS** for Misr Airwork Ltd., CofA issued 25.9.35 and handed over to Airwork 27.9.35. Named *Helwan*. Reg'n cancelled. Nothing further known, but possibly one of the aircraft later operated by Syria or in the Yemen.

6304 Reg'd **CF-AYE** 11.4.36 to de Havilland Aircraft of Canada Ltd., and used as a demonstrator. At the request of the National Research Council, de Havilland Canada developed new, experimental self-aligning skis for this Rapide and commenced testing them 3.36. They apparently performed well but were too weak structurally for regular use. To British North American Airways, CofA no.34 issued 13.5.37. To Canadian Airways 5.9.38 and named *City of Zeballos*. (The name *Zeballos Express* has also been reported but the former seems more likely.) Merged into Canadian Pacific 1942. To Central Northern Airways 31.7.47. To Queen Charlotte Airlines, Vancouver BC 4.49. Withdrawn from use after the CofA expired 24.8.51 and the arcraft was dismantled. The engines were removed and the remains burnt by the Vancouver Airport Fire Department.

6305 Reg'd **ZK-AED** for Cook Strait Airways Ltd., on 5.12.35, an export CofA was issued 18.10.35 and the aircraft was named *Venus*. Impressed by the R.N.Z.A.F. 15.10.39 as **NZ556** and passed to the Air Gunners and Air Observers School at Ohakea, carrying code '6'. Later fitted with bomb racks and dispatched to Fiji 10.40, arriving 5.11.40 for use as a general reconnaissance aircraft. Destroyed by gales at Nadi, Fiji, 20.2.41 and SOC 4.7.43.

6306 Reg'd **ZK-AEE** for Cook Strait Airways Ltd., an export CofA was issued 22.10.35 and the aircraft was named *Jupiter*. Impressed by the R.N.Z.A.F. 15.10.39 as **NZ559** and passed to Rongotai CF. Later, to Air Gunners and Air Observers School at Ohakea, carrying code '5'. Later still, fitted with bomb racks, the history then mirrored that of c/n 6305 above, being sent to Fiji and destroyed there in the same gales of 20.2.41.

6307 Reg'd **CF-BBC** for Canadian Airways Ltd., Vancouver, on 2.11.36. To Quebec Airways Ltd., Montreal PQ, on issue of CofA no.165 on 28.3.38. To Canadian Pacific Airlines 1942. On 23.12.46, whilst en route across the lower St. Lawrence, both engines failed, probably as a result of fuel exhaustion after ground crew at Seven Islands failed to refuel as requested and the pilot failing to dip the tanks. A distress call was broadcast and a forced landing was carried out on floating ice some distance off Matane. A good landing was made without damage, but at the end of the landing roll the skis went through the ice. The pilot and his six passengers were able to disembark onto the ice before the aircraft sank completely, but sadly one passenger died before rescuers arrived over the next few days.

6308 Reg'd **VT-AHB** and CofA issued 11.12.35 for His Highness the Maharajah of Jammu and Kashmir. The aircraft was fitted out for VIP use and the cockpit included the latest in blind-flying instruments and a precision altimeter, while the colour scheme featured the Kashmir state colours of red and yellow with the state flag on both sides. To Air Services of India Ltd., Bombay 5.37 and named *City of Bhavnagar*. This company suspended operations in February 1941 and the aircraft passed to Indian National Airways Ltd. at Calcutta. Nosed over on landing Kanpur, extensively damaging both port mainplanes, the port engine and both propellers 30.12.45. Reg'n cancelled 2.2.46.

6309 CofA no.5206 issued 9.11.35. Originally reg'd to the de Havilland Aircraft Co. Ltd., for trials and demonstration purposes, as **G-ADWZ**. To Personal Airways Ltd., Croydon 3.36. Converted to

DH89A standard. Sold to Marc Pierre Cayre, a Paris hotelier and reg'd **F-APES** 10.36 but reportedly, actually bound for the Spanish Republicans. Reg'n painted on the aircraft at Gatwick, night of 15/16.10.36 & export CofA no.4888 issued 16.10.36. Deal not completed & aircraft not delivered. French reg'n cancelled 1.37. Restored as **G-ADWZ** to North Eastern Airways Ltd., Croydon [CofR 8893 21.11.38]. Impressed as **X9449** 12.4.40 but serial not painted on aircraft. Operated by 6AACU and 7AACU. Crashed owing to fuel starvation at Llanrhaiadr-ym-Mochnant, North Wales 2.8.40 and SOC 7.9.40.

6310   DH89M.   Reg'd **G-ADYK** [CofR 6540 2.12.35] to de Havilland Aircraft Co. Ltd., Hatfield. CofA no.5252 issued 10.12.35. Cancelled as sold abroad 2.36 after sale to the Spanish Government 1.36. Delivered, with c/ns 6311 and 6312, to El Jete de Aviacion Militar, arriving in Spain on 9.1.36. Probably as **22-1**, used for a time on police duties in Morocco. Captured at Zaragoza by the Nationalists 7.36 but has been reported as destroyed by Nationalist bombing at Santander-Albericia 6.4.37! See the notes under c/n 6312 for an alternative!

6311   DH89M.   Reg'd **G-ADYL** [CofR 6541 2.12.35] to de Havilland Aircraft Co. Ltd., Hatfield. CofA no.5253 issued 10.12.35. Sold to the Spanish Government and it then followed the same history as c/ns 6310 and 6312. Probably as **22-2**, captured at Zaragoza by the Nationalists 7.36. Reportedly shot down by a Heinkel He.51 of their own Condor Legion 19.10.36, but see the notes under c/n 6312 for an alternative! (Also see c/n 6895 for second use of the British registration).

6312   DH89M.   Reg'd **G-ADYM** [CofR 6542 2.12.35] to de Havilland Aircraft Co. Ltd., Hatfield. CofA no.5254 issued 10.12.35. Sold to the Spanish Government it then followed the same history as c/ns 6310 and 6311 above. Probably as **22-3**, captured at Zaragoza by the Nationalists 7.36 and continued in use, later with the serial **40-5**. Reportedly shot down near Segovia by a Heinkel He.51 of their own Condor Legion 26.8.36 in error, but see notes under for an alternative!

(Note: c/ns 6310 to 6312 were supplied to Spain as DH89M Military Rapides. They were equipped to carry four stretchers, and could also carry three machine-guns with one backward firing, one forward firing Vickers 'E' gun in the cockpit, and one in the floor of the cabin which was also modified for camera use. Up to twelve 27lb bombs could be carried under the belly. Performance improvements included cruising speeds of 130mph, climb rates of 900ft per min and 4hr 30min duration, but only with all hatches closed. (Pictured *The Aeroplane* 11.12.35 p710). All three were captured by Nationalist forces in July 1936 and used as bombers during that month in the fighting for the Somosierra Passes near Madrid. In July or early August they were incorporated into a new group known as Grupo 20. In the middle of August, two second hand aircraft arrived at Burgos from England to bring the number of aircraft in Nationalist service to five, and at this stage 'military' serials were issued, **1** through to **5**, later changed to **40-1** through to **40-5**, although which aircraft wore which serial is uncertain. What is known, is that **40-5** was shot down on the Madrid front near Segovia 26.8.36 by a Heinkel He.51 of the Condor Legion in mistake for a Republican aircraft, killing the two crew and another suffered exactly the same fate 19.10.36. A further Rapide crashed on take-off at Zaragoza during the first week of September 1936 and was burnt out. The two remaining aircraft were then named after the pilots of the aircraft shot down in error, **40-1** becoming *Capitan Pouso* and **40-2**, *Capitan Vela*. It is reported, that when the group disbanded, the two Rapides remained on strength. (Also see c/n 6277 reference 40-2, passed to Iberia as EC-AAY).

6313   Export CofA issued 16.11.35. To Misr Airwork Ltd. reg'd **SU-ABU** and named *Heliopolis*. Apparently crashed on approach to unknown airfield 22.4.39 but obviously repaired, as was surveyed by the A.R.B. in September 1946. Reg'n cancelled, date unknown

6314   Export CofA no.5304 issued 17.1.36. To de Havilland (Pty.) Co. Ltd. reg'd **VH-UVG**. To R.A.A.F. early 1936 and initially wearing its civilian marks, used for survey flights of the outback. To **A3-2**. Returning from a training flight, the aircraft banked sharply on finals to Laverton VIC 3.2.38. The wing dug in and the aircraft was totally destroyed, though there were no injuries to the three persons on board.

6315   Initially reg'd to de Havilland Aircraft Co. Ltd., Hatfield as **G-ADUM** [CofR 6361 16.3.36]. CofA no.5474 issued 30.4.36. To Devlet Hava Yollari, Istanbul, with fleet no.3, reg'd **TC-ARI** 5.36. Commenced scheduled operations Istanbul-Ankara 25.5.36. To V. Hurkus of Hurkus Airlines 7.57. Withdrawn from use 1959 and scrapped.

6316   Initially reg'd to de Havilland Aircraft Co. Ltd., Hatfield as **G-ADUN** [CofR 6362 16.3.36]. CofA no.5475 issued 30.4.36. To Devlet Hava Yollari, Istanbul, with fleet no.4, reg'd **TC-BAY** 5.36. Believed damaged beyond repair in an accident 25.3.40.

6317   Initially reg'd to de Havilland Aircraft Co. Ltd., Hatfield as **G-ADUO** [CofR 6363 16.3.36]. CofA no.5476 issued 30.4.36. To Devlet Hava Yollari, Istanbul, with fleet no.5, reg'd **TC-CAN** 5.36. Fate unknown.

6318   Export CofA no.5323 issued 7.2.36. Shipped to Australia; assembled and test flown Adelaide-Parafield SA 7.4.36. To Adelaide Airways Pty. Ltd. reg'd **VH-UVI** and named *Moogana*. Merged into Australian National Airways Pty. Ltd. on formation 2.11.36. To Guinea Airways 8.39. Impressed as **A33-2** 12.7.40 and initially to 1EFTS at Parafield. Issued to 1AOS Cootamundra NSW. Crashed into trees after engine failure on take-off 20.6.41. The pilot was killed and four passengers were injured.

6319   Reg'n **G-ADUP** [CofR 6364, undated] allocated but not taken up. Export CofA no.5324 issued 11.2.36. Shipped to Australia; assembled and test flown Adelaide-Parafield SA 8.4.36. To Adelaide Airways Pty. Ltd. reg'd **VH-UVT** and named *Monana*. Merged into Australian National Airways Pty. Ltd. on formation 2.11.36. Badly damaged when struck a windmill when attempting to avoid cows on the airstrip Mount Gambier SA 30.6.37. Conveyed to Melbourne-Essendon for rebuild 7.37, but owing to extent of damage and the intervention of the war, did not return to service, by now re-named *Memma*, until 4.41. To Butler Air Transport (Pty) Ltd., Sydney 2.50. To Connellan Airways Ltd., Alice Springs NT 2.53. Withdrawn from service 11.54 and scrapped as CofA renewal deemed uneconomical.

6320   Reg'd **G-AEAJ** for Railway Air Services Ltd, Croydon, CofA no.5349 issued 14.3.36 and delivered the same day. Named *Star of Lancashire*. Damaged in an accident at Croydon 24.4.36 but repaired. To Isle of Man Air Services Ltd, Derbyhaven [CofR 8148 19.10.37] and renamed *RMA Castletown*. Impressed 4.1.40 as **W6425**. A long military history started with 24Sqdn., then 9MU, RAF Andover, A.T.A. HQ White Waltham, 271Sqdn., 9MU again, RAF Exeter, 18MU, 55OTU, 530OTU and 3 "T.B.U." To de Havilland at Witney and SOC 26.9.44 as Cat.E1.

6321   Ordered by the Imperial Iranian War Ministry in 3.36 and reg'd **EP-AAA** to the Government of Persia (Ministry of Posts and Telegraphs) but operated by Iranian State Airlines. CofA no.5503 issued 13.5.36. Seized by the R.A.F. and impressed as **HK917** 8.41. Operated throughout the war period by B.O.A.C. Returned post war to Iranian State Airlines and restored to **EP-AAA**. Fate unknown.

6322   Ordered by the Imperial Iranian War Ministry in 3.36 and reg'd **EP-AAB** to the Government of Persia (Ministry of Posts and Telegraphs). CofA no.5449 issued 18.4.36, the aircraft was operated by Iranian State Airlines. Seized by the R.A.F. and impressed as **HK916** 8.41. Written off while in military service, details unknown.

6323   Ordered by the Imperial Iranian War Ministry in 3.36 and reg'd **EP-AAC** to the Government of Persia (Ministry of Posts and Telegraphs). CofA no.5450 issued 18.4.36, the aircraft was operated by Iranian State Airlines. Seized by the R.A.F. and impressed as **HK915** 8.41. Written off while in military service, details unknown.

6324   Reg'd **G-AEAK** for Railway Air Services Ltd., CofA no.5350 issued 4.4.36 and named *Star of Mona*. To Isle of Man Air Services Ltd., Derbyhaven, [CofR 8149 19.10.37]. Whilst approaching to land at Speke on 25.4.39 after a searchlight co-operation flight at night, the aircraft struck a tree near the airfield boundary and was completely wrecked. Cancelled as destroyed 18.5.39.

6325   Reg'd **G-AEAL** for Railway Air Services Ltd., CofA no.5351 issued 25.4.36 and named *Star of Yorkshire*. To Isle of

Man Air Services Ltd., Derbyhaven [CofR 8150 19.10.37]. Continued in civilian service throughout the war and intended for operation in Sweden as **SE-BAL** at some juncture but not delivered. To Field Consolidated Aircraft Services, Croydon 29.5.45. To Hunting Aerosurveys Ltd., Luton 1.4.46. While with Hunting, the aircraft was modified for survey work in climatic extremes, a 21" camera aperture was made, with the cameras being enclosed in a glass dome for protection from the heat. In 1947, it left Croydon for oil survey work in the Persian Gulf. To Wolverhampton Aviation Ltd. 20.3.53, when it was restored to an 8-passenger interior. To aircraft broker R. K. Dundas Ltd. 13.3.56 for export and the U.K. reg'n was cancelled as sold abroad 10.4.56. In the meantime, however, it had been delivered to France via Lydd 9.3.56. Reg'd **F-OAUE** with CofA issued 26.4.56 for Cie. des Transports Aeriens Intercontinentaux (T.A.I.) and operated by Air Ivoire. To SGAA Algiers 6.60 and later with Air Fret. CofA was suspended 1.62.

6326   Reg'd **G-AEAM** for Railway Air Services Ltd., Croydon and CofA no.5352 issued 5.5.36. Named *Star of Ulster*. Sustained major damage in an accident near Bolton 6.6.36, but repaired. To Isle of Man Air Services Ltd., Derbyhaven [CofR 8151 19.10.37]. Impressed as **W6424** 4.1.40 and used by 24Sqdn. Damaged in a forced landing due to fuel shortage at St. Philbert, near Clisson, 25kms south-east of Nantes 23.3.40. Dismantled and transported to Bouguenais for repair. Last reported when abandoned Amiens 16.5.40.

6327   Reg'd **G-AEBW** for Railway Air Services Ltd., Croydon and CofA no.5353 issued 13.5.36. Named *Star of Renfrew*. Damaged in an accident at Ronaldsway 25.6.36 but repaired. To Isle of Man Air Services Ltd., Derbyhaven [CofR 8152 19.10.37]. Impressed 4.9.39 but not allocated a military serial, becoming part of the A.A.J.C. fleet. On 15.6.40, all services were suspended and A.A.J.C. aircraft were flown to Exeter to help with the evacuation of troops from France. Together with another Rapide G-AEPF and two DH86s G-AEFH and G-AEWR, abandoned at Bordeaux due to lack of fuel needed to fly home. Cancelled 18.6.40.

6328   Reg'd **G-AEBX** [CofR 6710 22.2.36] for Railway Air Services Ltd., Croydon. CofA no.5354 issued 20.5.36 and named *Star of Scotia*. Arriving at Belfast Harbour airport at about 1840, the aircraft was seen losing height in a left hand circuit and just beyond the eastern boundary of the airfield, control was lost and it spun in, catching fire on impact 3.7.38. The aircraft was totally destroyed and both occupants perished.

6329   Export CofA no.5539 issued 12.6.36, and reg'd **YR-DRA** for Linile Aeriene Romane Exploate cu Statul – L.A.R.E.S., with Romanian CofA no.117. Written off in an accident 29.4.37, and cancelled the same day.

6330   Export CofA no.5546 issued 19.6.36, and reg'd **YR-DRI** for Linile Aeriene Romane Exploate cu Statul – L.A.R.E.S., with Romanian CofA no.119. Fate unknown.

6331   Export CofA no.5568 issued 3.7.36, and reg'd **YR-DRO** for Linile Aeriene Romane Exploate cu Statul – L.A.R.E.S. Fate unknown.

6332   Reg'd **G-AEKF** [CofR 7062 15.6.36] to Thomas George Mapplebeck, Belgrade, with CofA no.5538 issued on 15.6.36. Cancelled almost immediately in 6.36 as sold in Yugoslavia, and reg'd **YU-SAS** 7.36 for Societe de Navigation Aerienne Yougoslave, Aeroput. Aeroput had purchased the Rapide to replace a Spartan Cruiser lost in an accident near Ljubljana in July 1936. In March 1941, the Aeroput fleet was formed into a special squadron which, in time of war, could act in a communication role, and although most 'older types' were destroyed in air raids on Belgrade airport during April 1941, the Rapide survived. In May 1941, all the airline's remaining assets were placed under German control and the company was subsequently liquidated by order of the military commander of Serbia. Although some reports claim the aircraft's destruction in the air raids of April 1941, mentioned above, it was certainly noted at Belgrade airport in May 1941, after the take over by German forces and was apparently in good condition. A photograph of a Breda 44 taken at Podgorica, Yugoslavia, in May 1943, shows a Rapide in the background and it is highly probable that it was this machine. No later reports of the aircraft are known and it is thought that it did not survive the war,

6333   U.K. export CofA no.5581 issued. To Ministerio de Salud Publica, Montevideo and reg'd **CX-ABL** 8.7.36 and used as an air ambulance by the Amulancia Aeria equipped with four stretchers and four folding seats. Damaged beyond repair in an accident 1943 but still appeared on the 1950 civil register.

6334   Reg'd **ZK-AEC** 16.9.36 for Cook Strait Airways Ltd., Wellington, CofA no.5597 was issued 22.7.36 and named *Mercury*. Impressed into the R.N.Z.A.F. 17.9.39 as **NZ555** and allocated to the Air Gunners and Air Observers School at Ohakea, coded '4'. Fitted with bomb racks and despatched to Fiji 11.40 as a general reconaissance aircraft. Scrapped due to deterioration 19.9.45 at Nausori, Fiji, and SOC 19.11.45.

6335   Reg'd **G-AEGS** [CofR 6936 13.5.36] for Iraq Petroleum Transport Co. Ltd., Haifa. CofA no.5497 issued 7.8.36 and delivered via Croydon. On 30.12.36, while executing a forced landing at Affule, Palestine, the aircraft ran into soft ground and overturned. The two occupants were killed.

6336   Reg'd **G-AEMH** for Personal Airways Ltd., Croydon. CofA 5639 issued 5.9.36. Intended for operation by the Spanish Republicans, but the sale prohibited. To North Eastern Airways Ltd., Croydon [CofR 8892 21.11.38]. Impressed as **X9387** 27.3.40. Operated by 6AACU, 7AACU, 110 (AAC) Wing, 6AACU, 20MU, 22MU, 410TU. Stn Flt Old Sarum, Wiltshire & 5MU. Damaged at Witney 20.12.41, but repaired. Restored as **G-AEMH** to L. E. Hamson t/a Air Charter Experts Ltd. Ronaldsway 11.3.47. CofA renewed 16.7.47. Company renamed Manx Air Charters Ltd. 9.8.47. To George Clifton, Spalding, Lincolnshire 9.3.49. De-converted to DH89 standard 5.50! To East Anglian Flying Services Ltd., Southend 4.6.52. Renamed Channel Airways Ltd. ca. 9.56. CofA expired 15.4.60 and WFU at Ipswich, Suffolk. By road to Southend 10.64 and reported as "for rebuild using parts of G-AKRN". However, departed by road 19.8.72 to a farm at Latchington near Burnham-on-Crouch, Essex for storage pending sale. Registration cancelled as 'destroyed' 14.2.73, and remained in store at Latchington (together with G-AKRN) but sometime later, was noted in store at Chirk.

6337   Reg'd **G-AEML** [CofR 7260 1.9.36] for Wrightways Ltd., Croydon. First flew 26.9.36 and CofA no.5643 issued the same day. Damaged in an accident at Croydon 13.12.37 but was repaired. Impressed 9.4.40 as **X9450**. Operated by 6AACU, AFEE, then to Armstrong Whitworth Aircraft Ltd. 7.4.43. Restored to **G-AEML** 13.3.46 for Sir W. G. Armstrong Whitworth Aircraft Ltd. at Witney, moving with the company to Baginton 10.61. CofA renewed 17.5.46 after test flights with Gipsy Queen 3s. Company name changed to Whitworth Gloster Aircraft Ltd 16.10.61. To Neil Tool Co. Ltd., Panshanger 29.8.62. To Stanley John Lines, Denham 10.11.65. To Liverpool Aero Engineering Co. Ltd., Speke 26.1.68. To Spartan Group, Booker 1966. To Liverpool Aero Club, Speke, and delivered there 16.12.67. To J. P. Filhol Ltd., Baginton 19.12.69. CofA extension expired 2.4.71 and application for renewal was cancelled. Remained stored inside at Baginton with G-AKOE (c/n 6601) until transported to V. H. Bellamy at St. Just for rebuild in 1980, though damaged by a fork lift truck during loading for the road journey to Cornwall. Sold at auction from store at St. Just 1984 to I. Jones, and re-sold to H. Orde-Powlett 1986, it was taken to Barrow-in-Furness for continued rebuild. Sold prior to completion 19.11.87 to M. Victor Gauntlett t/a Proteus Petroleum for finishing by Barrow Aviation. This company ceased trading and the aircraft was subsequently moved by road to Rush Green, for continuation of the rebuild by Bowker Air Services 1988. Nominal ownership change to Proteus Holdings Ltd., Goodwood 1.4.92. First flown after 22 years from Rush Green 16.4.93. To K. Whitehead of Amanda Investments Ltd., Rendcomb 14.6.95 and named *Proteus*.

6338   Export CofA no.5630 issued 25.8.36 and reg'd **YR-DNC** for Linile Aeriene Romane Explotate cu Statul – L.A.R.E.S., with Romanian CofA no.118. Written off in an accident 17.7.42 and cancelled 28.7.42.

6339   Reg'd **G-AEMM** [CofR 7262 31.8.36] for Anglo-Iranian Oil Co. Ltd., Abadan. CofA no.5640 issued 10.10.36. To Airwork Ltd., Heston 17.3.39. Converted to 'flying classroom' configuration by de Havilland 13.3.39, then operated by Airwork for 6 Civil Air Navigation School, Staverton from 10.39. Reached the Middle East sometime in 1940 but operational details were not recorded. In any event, possibly a total loss while with the R.A.F. in that area

3.5.40 and the CofA expired 12.10.40. Reg'n finally cancelled on 30.3.46 (1945 census).

6340   Reg'd **G-AENN** to C. W. Wood, Dar-es-Salaam, and CofA no.5677 issued 25.11.36. (Note: C. W. F. Wood was 'one of Olley Air Service's pilots' and he reportedly actually used the aircraft in Spain before returning to the U.K. 1937). To Olley Air Service Ltd. [CofR 8262 13.12.37]. Impressed 23.1.40 and allocated **W6455**. Issued to 24Sqdn. on this date but did not take up military marks until 3.41. To R.A.F. Skeabrae 27.5.42 and later used by 8(C) OTU at R.A.F. Dyce. Whilst flying over Rosehearty, Aberdeenshire, the aircraft suffered engine failure and crash landed near R.A.F. Fraserburgh 13.12.42. Conveyed to de Havilland for repair but SOC 18.1.43 as Cat.E1.

6341   Reg'd **G-AENO** [CofR 7345 22.9.36] to Blackpool & West Coast Air Services Ltd., Squires Gate. CofA no.5667 issued 10.11.36. Merged into Isle of Man Air Services Ltd. 27.9.37. Operated almost exclusively Douglas IoM to Dublin from 14.5.37 to 4.9.37 when service suspended for the winter. To Aer Lingus Teoranta reg'd **EI-ABP** and named *Iolar II* 24.2.38. Sustained major damage in accident at Croydon 21.5.38 but repaired. Withdrawn from use at Dublin on declaration of war in Europe 1.9.39. Sold overseas 8.2.40, delivered to Liverpool and shipped to Port Adelaide. Assembled and test flown as **VH-ADE**, Adelaide-Parafield SA 19.6.40. CofA issued 21.6.40 and to Guinea Airways Ltd. named *Morobe*. Impressed as **A33-7** 25.8.40. Initially to 1EFTS and then issued to 1AOS. SOC 15.4.42 and CofA renewed at Melbourne-Essendon for Australian National Airways Pty. Ltd., again as **VH-ADE** 23.4.42. Forced landed on beach at Princess Charlotte Bay, 13 miles south of Cape Sidmouth QLD 26.1.44. Stripped of usable spare parts and abandoned.

6342   Prototype DH89A, first flown as **E.4** at Hatfield 11.36. CofA trials at Martlesham Heath, Suffolk flown by R. Waite 2.37. Reg'd **G-AEOV**, CofA no.5806 issued 3.3.37 and delivered to Viscount Forbes (see c/n 6258 for biography). To Mrs. Helen Wood, Croydon [CofR 8297 14.1.38]. To Scottish Airways Ltd., Renfrew 1.5.39. To William Douglas Thompson Gairdner, Renfrew 27.7.39. Impressed 10.1.40 as **W6456** and operated by 24Sqdn. Badly damaged at Hendon when a tyre burst whilst taxiing 11.4.42. Transported to de Havilland for repair but SOC as Cat.E1.

6343   Reg'd **ZK-AEW** for Cook Strait Airways Ltd., Wellington. CofA no.5723 issued 30.11.36 and named *Mars*. Impressed into the R.N.Z.A.F. 15.10.39 as **NZ557** and issued to the Air Gunners and Air Observers School at Ohakea. Fitted with bomb racks 10.40 and despatched to Fiji for general reconnaissance duties. Broken up at Nausori, Fiji due to deterioration 4.7.43.

6344   Reg'd **G-AEPE** for Personal Airways Ltd., Croydon. CofA no.5718 issued 24.2.37 and named *Luxembourg Listener* later *Windermere*. To Olley Air Service Ltd., Croydon [CofR 8001 17.7.37]. To Scottish Airways Ltd., Speke 12.7.40. Impressed 24.7.40 as **BD143** and operated by 24Sqdn. Badly damaged in a forced landing 20.4.42 at Breston Farm, near Glengal Hospital, Dalmellington. SOC 30.4.42 as Cat.E1.

6345   Reg'd **G-AERN** [CofR 7536 15.1.37] to Blackpool and West Coast Air Services Ltd., Squires Gate. CofA no.5820 issued 24.3.37. Renamed West Coast Air Services Ltd. and base changed to Inverness. Merged into Isle of Man Air Services Ltd., 27.9.37. To Olley Air Service Ltd. but operated by affiliate Great Western and Southern Air Lines Ltd., Derbyhaven, 10.39. In use when with the A.A.J.C., by Scottish Airways, Inverness from 1.7.40 until 4.1.44. To West Coast Air Services, Speke, 5.46. To B.E.A.C., Northolt on formation 1.2.47. Transferred to Gibraltar Airways Ltd. 17.11.47. To Roger Antony Peacock, Croydon 29.6.53. To Iguacio Saler de la Riva, Sabadell, 1.12.53 and reg'd **EC-AKO**. Although the British registration was cancelled 18.1.54, the aircraft reportedly continued to wear the British reg'n when operating a contract carrying seafood from Ibiza to Barcelona. A Spanish CofA no.265 was finally issued 7.6.56 when ownership changed to Metamar SA. Sometime used in a taxiing role in the film 'The Tin Duck', filmed at Sabadell. Reported stored at Sabadell in 1969, 1973 and 1978 it finally arrived at Cuatro Vientos for restoration in 1998.

6346   Export CofA no.5862 issued 2.4.37. Shipped to Australia per S.S. *Moreton Bay* 4.37; assembled and test flown Melbourne-Essendon reg'd **VH-UXT** 25.5.37. To Australian

National Airways Pty. Ltd. named *Mundoora*. Impressed, initially with 3EFTS, as **A33-4** 19.7.40. Issued to 1AOS. SOC 15.4.42 and restored to Australian National Airways, as **VH-UXT**, although operated by Airlines of Austalia for a time, until finally absorbed into A.N.A. during 1943. Over-ran on landing Wynard TAS 18.8.43, ending up in a ditch. Aircraft badly damaged and broken up for spares. Some useful parts eventually shipped to Perth per S.S. *Lowana* to aid rebuild of c/n 6384.

6347   Ordered 22.10.36 by Aero Oy of Finland, according to *The Aeroplane* magazine issue 23rd December 1936 p812, "for experiments with internal services". Reg'd **OH-BLA** 9.3.37 and delivered 13.4.37. Aircraft named *Salama* (Lightning). To Ilmavoimat 14.10.39 for hospital and communication flights. Returned to Aero Oy 19.3.40. To Veljekset Karhumaki Oy 18.6.41 and operated on behalf of the Finnish Government for ambulance flights. Re-reg'd **OH-VKH** 20.6.46. To Savon Lentolinjat Oy 27.11.50. To Lentohuolto Oy 8.52. Re-reg'd **OH-DHA** 31.5.54. To Pasanen & Pasanen, Turku 4.55. Cancelled as sold 21.5.55 and reg'd to Sylvest Jensen as **OY-DAS** 17.8.55. Sold abroad and reg'd to Nico Rupke Vermessungsburo, Hamburg as **D-IGEL** 27.3.56. CofA no.354 issued. Nosed over on landing at grass strip Mannheim 26.3.61 and not returned to service until a year later. To U. W. Reszka, Flensburg 9.65. To Gert Seuffert, Bremen 12.66. Visited Gatwick 16.4.68 but WFU after CofA expiry 29.4.68. Finally burnt at Weser Wumme Airfield near Bremen 27.4.72. Reg'n cancelled as withdrawn from use 10.8.73.

6348   Export CofA no.5875 issued 17.4.37 and delivered the same month to the Lithuanian Air Force and reg'd **701**. Captured by Russian forces when they overran Lithuania 15-17.6.40.

6349   Export CofA no.5876 issued 17.4.37 and delivered the same month to the Lithuanian Air Force.and reg'd **702**. Captured by Russian forces when they overran Lithuania 15-17.6.40.

(Notes ref. C/ns 6348/6349: In turn, Lithuania overrun by German forces 4.42 and it is possible that both Rapides then saw service with Luftflotte 2).

6350   Reg'd **G-AEPW** [CofR 7475 1.12.36] for Olley Air Service Ltd., Croydon, 1.12.36. CofA no.5819 issued 15.3.37. Impressed 4.3.40 as **X8510**, and flown by 24Sqdn., then to 27MU and R.A.F. Andover. SOC 11.12.41 as Cat.E1.

6351   Export CofA no.5893 issued 30.4.37 and reg'd **YL-ABC** to Valsts Gaisa Satiksme, the Post and Telegraph Department of the Ministry of Commerce, Latvia. Delivered via Lympne, Amsterdam, Berlin and Konigsberg 15-16.5.37 and used by an unidentified airline from 15.6.37 on services between Riga and Liepaja. See further notes under c/n 6352 below.

6352   Export CofA no.5894 issued 30.4.37 and reg'd **YL-ABD** to Valsts Gaisa Satiksme, the Post and Telegraph Department of the Ministry of Commerce, Latvia. Delivered via Lympne, Amsterdam, Berlin and Konigsberg 15-16.5.37 and used by an unidentified airline from 15.6.37 on services between Riga and Liepaja.

(Notes ref. c/ns 6351 and 6352: both aircraft were seized by Russian forces in June 1940 and used for communications flights. One is reported to have been grounded very soon after this having sustained damage. The other is reported to have been collected from Riga in 5.42 and flown to Tallinn in a drab olive colour scheme with radio call-sign SB+AH and used thereafter for courier flights to Konigsberg, and as a bread- and mail-bomber to the island of Tuttarsaare in the spring of 1943 when with NSGr11 unit).

6353   Reg'd **G-AEPF** [CofR 7448 10.3.37] for Air Commerce Ltd., Heston. CofA no.5822 issued 17.4.37. Damaged 8.39, at which time it was insured with Olley Air Service Ltd., both Olley and Air Commerce were wholly owned subsidiaries of British and Foreign Aviation. Impressed 18.4.40, but not allocated a military serial and joined the A.A.J.C. fleet. On 15.6.40, all their services were suspended and the fleet was flown to Exeter to assist with the evacuation of troops from France. However, together with DH89A G-AEBW and two DH86s G-AEFH and G-AEWR, abandoned at Bordeaux as the area was over-run by enemy forces. Cancelled 18.6.40.

6354   Delivered to de Havilland Canada in disassembled condition, CofR no.1985 issued 10.6.37 and reg'd **CF-BBG** for The

Globe and Mail Ltd., Toronto. Named *The Flying Newsroom*, the aircraft was equipped with floats. Caught fire and burnt out while refuelling at Toronto Air Harbour, ONT 21.8.37.

6355   Reg'd **G-AERE** for L.H.G. Ltd., Heston and CofA no.5903 issued 11.5.37. To Mrs. Lillian Hartigan Gibbs (nee Falk) [CofR 8586 25.6.38] for British-American Air Services, Heston. Whilst en route Heston to Newcastle, the aircraft struck high ground in cloud west of track and crashed, catching fire on impact at Ettersgill, Fell Head, Yorkshire, six miles north-west of Middleton-in-Teesdale 20.6.39. The three on board were killed. Cancelled 27.6.39.

6356   Reg'd **G-AERZ** [CofR 7577 10.3.37] for Air Commerce Ltd., Heston and CofA no.5823 issued 7.5.37. Under the aegis of A.A.J.C., operated by Scottish Airways Ltd. from 15.11.40 to 26.8.43. While operating the 0830 departure from Liverpool the aircraft was approaching Belfast airport in fog when it flew into high ground, crashed and caught fire Royal Belfast College, Clulo, Craigavad, County Down 1.4.46. All six on board were killed. At the time of the accident, although still owned by Air Commerce, the aircraft was being operated by Railway Air Services. Cancelled as destroyed 4.5.46.

6357   Export CofA no.5902 issued 7.5.37, and reg'd **VP-KCG** 31.5.37 for Wilson Airways Ltd. Impressed locally 9.39 and used by the Kenyan Auxiliary Air Unit as either **K-11** or **K-16**. Fate unknown. (Also see c/n 6267 reference serial number).

6358   Export CofA no.5921 issued 21.5.37, and reg'd 8.6.37 **VP-YBJ** for Rhodesia and Nyasaland Airways Ltd. Named *Bulawayo*, and handed over at Hatfield 26.5.37. Departed on delivery the following day and arrived Salisbury ten days later. Re-reg'd 9.39 as **303** to the same owner, joined Southern Rhodesia Air Services 1.2.40. Reverted to civilian marks **VP-YBJ** 4.42, still with Southern Rhodesia Air Services. Reportedly 'written off during 1944' and 'SOC after an accident' but also has been reported 'to Central African Airways 1.6.46, believed acquired for spares'. It would seem likely that some of these notes actually apply to a sistership VP-YBU c/n 6412 which saw service with Central African. Whatever, VP-YBJ was finally removed from the register in 1949.

6359   Export CofA no.5922 issued 24.5.37, and reg'd 8.6.37 as **VP-YBK** for Rhodesia and Nyasaland Airways Ltd. Named *City of Salisbury*, handed over at Hatfield 26.5.37 and departed on delivery the following day, arriving at Salisbury ten days later. Re-reg'd 9.39 as **304** to the same owner, joined Southern Rhodesia Air Services 1.2.40. Reverted to civil marks **VP-YBK** 4.42 still with Southern Rhodesia Air Services. To Central African Airways 1.6.46. Damaged beyond repair at Balovale, Northern Rhodesia, 13.12.47 and broken up for spares June 1948.

6360   Export CofA no.5930 issued 28.5.37, and reg'd **VR-SAV** to Wearne Brothers Ltd, trading as Wearne's Air Services Ltd. Named *Governer Raffles*, first services were operated 28.6.37. Wearne's Air services became 'B' Flight of the Malayan Volunteer Air Force 1.12.41. Just after landing at Ipoh 18.12.41 the aircraft was caught on the ground in an air raid and was hit by a fragmentation bomb which destroyed it and killed the two crew on board.

6361   Export CofA no.5941 issued 9.6.37, and reg'd **CR-AAD** for Divisao de Exploracao dos Transportes Aereos, DETA, on 16.2.38. Fate unknown.

6362   Export CofA no.5942 issued 9.6.37, and reg'd **CR-AAE** for Divisao de Exploracao dos Transportes Aereos – D.E.T.A., Lourenco Marques on 11.2.38. Reportedly sold in South Africa as **ZS-AVY**. This is not confirmed, and indeed, the reg'n was actually worn by a Miles Messenger in 12.52. Fate unknown.

6363   Reg'd **G-AESR** [CofR 7604 18.3.37] for Iraq Petroleum Transport Co. Ltd., Haifa and CofA no.5954 issued 25.6.37. To Airwork Ltd., Perth 18.10.47. To Air Kruise (Kent) Ltd., Lympne, 18.3.53. Wore 'Trans Channel Airways' titles for services between Ramsgate and Le Touquet. Reported 'gone abroad and taken-off the approved maintenance schedule', the engines were changed to Gipsy Queen 3s and delivered to Oilfields Supply and Trading Inc., Benghazi, 1.56, returning to Ramsgate for CofA renewal 14.5.56. Whilst taking off on 22.7.56 at Gerdes el Abid, near Barce, 30 miles from El Marj, Libya, at the beginning of a flight to

Benina, the aircraft ran into soft sand and nosed over, then fell back onto its tail, sustaining major damage. Subsequently declared a total loss and the reg'n was cancelled 9.56 as 'withdrawn from use in Libya'.

6364   Export CofA no.5970 issued 7.7.37, and reg'd **VR-SAW** to Wearne Brothers Ltd., trading as Wearne's Air Services Ltd. Named *Governor Fullerton*, the aircraft had been delivered by 27.9.37. Wearne's Air Services became 'B' Flight of the Malayan Volunteer Air Force 1.12.41. Just after arrival at airfield P1, near Pladjoe, 10 miles from Palembang circa 10.2.42, an air raid started. Hurricanes were scrambled, and one collided with the Rapide, shearing off its starboard wings. The two crew were unhurt, but the aircraft was damaged beyond repair.

6365   Export CofA no.5964 issued 1.7.37. Shipped to Australia; assembled and test flown Melbourne-Essendon 11.9.37. To Australian National Airways Pty. Ltd. and reg'd **VH-UXZ(1)** - see c/n 6801. Whilst attempting to regain the Flinders Island, TAS, airstrip following engine failure, the aircraft came down in Tanners Bay 29.5.42 and four occupants were killed. (Also see c/n 6801).

6366   Export CofA no.5965 issued 2.7.37, and reg'd **VP-KCJ** for Wilson Airways Ltd. 30.7.37. Impressed locally 9.39 and used by the Kenyan Auxiliary Air Unit, almost certainly as **K-4**. Restored to **VP-KCJ** 13.12.46 for East African Airways Corp. To Stirling Astaldi Ltd., 4.8.48. To Caspair Air Charters and Agencies Ltd. , Mazinde 6.5.52, the reg'n was cancelled the following day as 'broken up' but it was restored to the register 10.11.52 and ownership passed to J. E. F. Wilkins, Mazinde 20.11.52. Ownership returned to Caspair Air Charters 22.11.55, who re-sold the aircraft back to East African Airways Corporation the following day! Caspair was shown as the owner again by 1960. Crashed on landing at Entebbe 7.10.62 after the pilot became incapacitated. One person died.

6367   Ordered by North Eastern Airways but reg'd **G-AEWL** to Highland Airways Ltd., Inverness. CofA no.5926 issued 18.6.37, delivered Hatfield-Perth-Inverness 27.6.37 and named *Zetland*. Merged to form Scottish Airways 8.37, remaining at Inverness [CofR 8566 18.6.38]. Damaged on landing Kirkwall, Orkney, in poor visibility, when it overran and nosed over in a ditch 8.7.38. There were no injuries, and the aircraft was repaired at Hatfield, returning to service 26.10.38. Merged into B.E.A.C. on formation 1.2.47. To Charles W. J. Allen t/a Allen Aircraft Services, Old Coulsdon 25.5.48. To Michael George Humphrey Fletcher, t/a Aircraft and Engineering Services, Croydon 27.9.48. To Wng. Cmdr. Hugh Charles Kennard, t/a Air Kruise (Kent) Ltd. 13.4.50. Nominal change to Air Kruise (Kent) Ltd., Lympne 13.4.55, and named *Nicole*, despite remaining unflown between 2.55 and 15.9.55 after an overhaul. To Aviation Supplies Co. Ltd., Hounslow, Middlesex 14.12.55. Sold in the Ivory Coast via Hants and Sussex Aviation Ltd., Portsmouth 24.1.56. CofA issued and reg'd **F-OATT** 26.4.56 for Ste. Navale Delmas et Vieljeux - Air Ivoire, Abidjan. To S.F.A.T.A.T. (parachuting club) and based Biscarosse reg'd **F-BJUY** 2.11.61. Destroyed Gaillac 30.7.62.

6368   To North Eastern Airways Ltd., Donaster reg'd **G-AEXO** [CofR 7839 19.5.37]. CofA 5915 issued 19.7.37. Impressed as **X8507** 26.3.40 and flown by 24Sqdn. Hendon. SOC 13.6.41 with total time 976hrs.

6369   To North Eastern Airways Ltd., Doncaster reg'd **G-AEXP** [CofR 7840 19.5.37]. CofA 5916 issued 19.7.37. Impressed as **X8505** 26.3.40 flown by 24Sqdn. at Hendon. Damaged beyond repair during air raid St. Omer, France 21.5.40 and abandoned there. SOC 28.5.40.

6370   Reg'd **CF-BBH** 26.8.37 for de Havilland Canada Ltd., and delivered by sea in disassembled condition to Canada. To Consolidated Mining and Smelting, Trail, BC., 7.1.38. Returned in part exchange to de Havilland Canada in 1939 when Consolidated Mining acquired a Dragonfly. To Canadian Airways Ltd., 23.5.39, named *City of Victoria*. Became Canadian Pacific Airlines 1942. Damaged beyond repair Pentecost, PQ., when it stalled on its third attempt to take-off from 'sticky' snow 19.3.47.

6371   Reg'd **CF-BFM** 26.11.37 for de Havilland Canada Ltd., and delivered by sea in disassembled condition to Canada. Sold 13.1.38 and reg'd 3.38 as **CX-ABI** to Berto Scaglione, t/a Campagnia Aeronautica Expreso del Plata, Montevideo. Equipped

DH89A c/n 6345. Although sold abroad to Spain in 1953, G-AERN continued to wear the British marks for a time, hauling fish from Ibiza to Barcelona. Aircraft survives at Cuatro Vientos.

DH89A c/n 6398 registered CR-AAN and c/n 6397 as CR-AAM were delivered ex Hatfield to the airline, Divisao de Exploracao dos Transportes Aereos of Mozambique (D.E.T.A.), in April 1938.

DH89A c/n 6354. The short lived float-equipped CF-BBG operated by a Toronto based newspaper, caught fire whilst refuelling and despite the water in the immediate vicinity, total destruction was swift!

DH89A c/n 6399. G-AFEN, delivered for the personal use of steel manufacturer Sir William Firth. Sold abroad to Argentina at the end of 1948 and served with the airline T.A.A.S.A. until CofA expiry 1960.

DH89A c/n 6363. With just a brief interlude with Air Kruise at Lympne, G-AESR served as oil company transport in Iraq and Libya. In the latter country, the aircraft was written-off in July 1956.

DH89 c/n 6401. Fitted with skis, OH-BLB was probably unique on this side of the Atlantic, though a number of Canadian examples swapped floats for this form of landing gear during the winter months.

DH89A c/n 6381. Bullock carts remain a common sight in India, but not so the Dragon Rapide! VT-AJB was used by Tata Airlines, forerunner of the state owned airline of today, Air India.

DH89 c/n 6403. Built for a French customer and operated in the Middle East, this aircraft was registered in the U.K. as G-AGDP. Seen here when stored Wolverhampton from 1958 to 1969.

with floats and named *Nuestra Senora del Carman*. Cancelled after an accident at Colonia 6.40.

6372   Registered to de Havilland Aircraft Co. Ltd., Hatfield as **G-AFAO** [CofR 8016 21.7.37] and CofA no.6007 issued 4.8.37. Cancelled 9.37 and to Devlet Hava Yollari, Istanbul reg'd **TC-DAG** with fleet no.6. Fate unknown.

6373   Reg'd **CF-BFL** for de Havilland Canada Ltd. and delivered by sea in disassembled condition to Canada. To Canadian Airways Ltd. 22.10.37. To Quebec Airways Ltd., Montreal PQ, 17.2.38. Damaged at Matane, PQ, after stalling in a turn just after take-off 23.2.38. Sent to de Havilland for rebuild but this was not proceeded with and cancelled as 'damaged beyond repair'.

6374   Reg'd **CF-BFP** for de Havilland Canada Ltd. and delivered by sea in disassembled condition to Canada. To Quebec Airways Ltd., Montreal PQ, 23.8.38 and CofA issued the same day. To Canadian Pacific Airways 1942. Destroyed by fire 5.7.45 at Walker Lake PQ, when port engine caught fire during starting.

6375   Reg'd **CF-BND** for de Havilland Canada Ltd. and delivered by sea in disassembled condition to Canada. To Quebec Airways Ltd., Montreal PQ, 8.9.39. Leased to Central Northern Airways Ltd., Winnipeg MB, 2.6.47. Leased to Queen Charlotte Airlines, Vancouver BC 5.49 and named *Tsimpsean Queen*. Both engines failed due to fuel starvation, shortly after take-off from Prince Rupert for a scheduled flight to Queen Charlotte and the aircraft hit trees while attempting a forced landing on Digby Island BC 29.7.49. There were no casualties, but the aircraft was written off. Many years later, in 1984, the remains were reported at the Western Canada Aviation Museum.

6376   Reg'd **CF-BNE** for de Havilland Canada Ltd. and delivered by sea in disassembled condition to Canada. To Quebec Airways Ltd., Montreal PQ, 4.11.39. To Canadian Pacific Airways 1941. Damaged beyond repair when the aircraft broke through the ice and sank at Lake George MB 3.12.43.

6377   Reg'd **G-AFAH** For Personal Airways Ltd., Croydon, CofA no.6025 issued 26.8.37. To Capt. Graham S. L. Whitelaw, Croydon 7.6.38 and named *Bit it Ben*. To Capt. William Ledlie, c/o Personal Airways, Barton 2.5.40. Impressed as **X8508** 24.6.40, and used by 24Sqdn. Damaged in an accident at Merville 21.5.40 and abandoned after deliberately being set on fire by R.A.F. personnel.

6378   Reg'd **VT-AIZ** for Tata and Sons Ltd., Bombay 7.37. CofA no.6039 issued 8.9.37. Company became Tata Airlines 1938. Reg'n cancelled 15.12.41 on impressment locally as **AX806** and used by 2 Flight, Indian Air Force Volunteer Reserve. Stalled and crashed on landing at Juhu aerodrome, Bombay, 22.10.42. SOC as beyond repair 1.7.43.

6379   Reg'd **VT-AJA** for Tata and Sons Ltd., Bombay 7.37. CofA no.6040 issued 8.9.37. Company became Tata Airlines 1938. Aircraft landed outside the aerodrome boundary at Juhu, Bombay and was written off 20.11.38. Reg'n cancelled 9.12.38.

6380   Export CofA no.6047 issued 13.9.37, and reg'd **ZS-AKT** 11.10.37 for de Havilland Aircraft Co. of South Africa. To African Flying Services 1.38. Impressed locally 1939 as **SAAF1560** and subsequently used by 61Sqdn., South African Air Force from at least 1.41 until 7.45. Restored as **ZS-AKT** 13.3.46, again to African Flying Services. To Trans-Oranje Air Services (Pty) Ltd. 1954. To Drakensberg Air Services 1954. Damaged on landing at Mokholong, Basutoland, 29.11.55 but repaired. Reg'n cancelled 5.8.57, and re-reg'd 7.12.57 as **OO-CJU** to Air Brousse SPRL, Leopoldville-Ndolo. Re-reg'd **9O-CJU**, still with Air Brousse, 17.3.61. Later re-reg'd **9Q-CJU**, still with Air Brousse. Reported current with Air Congo in 1969 but ownership later changed to A.M.A.Z., Kinshasa, date unknown.

6381   Reg'd **VT-AJB** for Tata and Sons Ltd., Bombay 7.37. Export CofA no.6041 issued 8.9.37. Company became Tata Airlines 1938. Reg'n cancelled 1941 on impressment locally as **HX790**. Transferred to the Director of Civil Aviation in India, 1.9.43. SOC 31.5.45.

6382   Export CofA no.6145 issued 2.12.37, and reg'd **F-AQIL** 13.12.37 for P. Legastelois [a dealer for Caudron, Renault and Potez], when CofA no.5513 was issued. To A. J. Rodier [the owner of an imitation pearl factory], Coulommiers, 12.37. To Societe Francaise de Transports Aeriens 5.38. Reg'n cancelled 1939 and the aircraft is assumed to have gone to Spain for use in the civil war. Actual fate unknown.

6383   Export CofA no.6143 issued 1.12.37, and reg'd **F-AQIM** 8.12.37 for P. Legastelois, when CofA no.5497 was issued. To A. J. Rodier, Coulommiers, 12.37. To Societe Francaise de Transports Aeriens 5.38. Reg'n cancelled 1939 and the aircraft is assumed to have gone to Spain for use in the civil war. Actual fate unknown.

6384   Export CofA no.6125 issued 25.1.38. Shipped to Australia; assembled and test flown Sydney-Mascot 17.1.38. Reg'd to W. R. Carpenter & Co. Ltd., Sydney NSW as **VH-UZY** 25.1.38. Impressed into the R.A.A.F., initially to 3EFTS, as **A33-6** 12.8.40. Issued to 1AOS. To 32Sqdn. Port Moresby 15.6.42. Transferred to 33Sqdn. New Guinea shortly afterwards. To 2AAU New Guinea 9.3.43. Crashed at Cape Sidmouth QLD 27.1.44. Stored in damaged condition Sydney-Mascot until sold to Airlines (WA) Ltd. and shipped to Perth per *SS Madura* 17.3.44. Restored to the register as **VH-UZY** and named *R.M.A. Perth* with fresh CofA issued 19.11.44. To Connellan Airways, Alice Springs 22.10.48. Struck trees on take-off Coolibah Station NT 21.10.49. The pilot was killed and the aircraft totally destroyed by fire.

6385   Export CofA no.6127 issued 15.11.37. To Military Council of the Nationalist Government of China. Serial unknown but see notes within the operations chapter.

6386   First flew 13.1.38, and reg'd **G-AFFF** for de Havilland Aircraft Co. Ltd., CofA no.6222 issued 16.3.38. To Railway Air Services Ltd., Renfrew [CofR 8660 27.7.38] and named *Juno*. Whilst inbound to Renfrew in IMC, and navigating on QDMs received from Renfrew, the aircraft flew into high ground at Craigton Hill, Milngavie, about 7 miles north of the airfield 27.9.46. Completely detroyed, and the pilot, radio operator and all six passengers were killed. It was later established that a 'wait' signal had been sent to, and acknowledged by, 'FFF, and QDMs were then passed to a second aircraft which had declared an emergency due to fuel shortage. It is believed that 'FFF then used these QDMs for its own navigation which led to the crash. Cancelled as destroyed 31.12.46.

6387   Export CofA no.6129 issued 24.11.37. Reg'd **ZS-AME** 22.12.37 to The Anglo-American Corporation of South Africa. Impressed locally 1939 as **SAAF1402** and used by the S.A.A.F., its detailed military history is unknown, but it was noted with 'B' Flight of 61Sqdn. 10.40 to 6.41, with THQ Communication Flight 4.42 to 11.42, back with 61Sqdn. in 1943, 1944 and 1945, and with 1AD for inspection and overhaul 3.45. Restored as **ZS-AME** 1946, and cancelled as 'exported' 29.10.49. To Tank Aircraft Co. Ltd. reg'd **VP-KHJ** 29.10.49. Re-reg'd **ZS-DFL** 15.8.51, still in the ownership of Tank Aircraft. Sold to Banco Nacional Ultramarino and reg'd **CR-ADH** 19.2.52. Cancelled 17.7.56 as 'broken up'.

6388   Export CofA no.6130 issued 19.11.37. To Military Council of the Nationalist Government of China. Serial unknown but see notes within the operations chapter..

6389   Export CofA no.6134 issued 24.11.37. To Military Council of the Nationalist Government of China. Serial unknown but see notes within the operations chapter.

6390   Export CofA no.6154 issued 11.12.37. To Military Council of the Nationalist Government of China. Serial unknown but see notes within the operations chapter.

6391   Export CofA no.6155 issued 13.12.37. To Military Council of the Nationalist Government of China. Serial unknown but see notes within the operations chapter.

6392   Export CofA no.6163 issued 16.12.37. To Military Council of the Nationalist Government of China. Serial unknown but see notes within the operations chapter.

6393   Export CofA no.6176 issued 4.1.38. Reg'd **F-AQIN** 10.1.38 for P. Legastelois when CofA no.5545 was issued. To A. Rodier, Coulommiers, 1.38. To Societe Francais de Transports

DH89 c/n 6404. Delivered to Rhodesia and Nyasaland Airways of Salisbury as VP-YBT, but impressed by the Southern Rhodesia Government on 1st January 1940. Restored to R.A.N.A. April 1942.

DH89 c/n 6423. Originally operated as ZK-AGT by Cook Strait Airways, after impressment as NZ558, the Rapide was restored as ZK-AHS. Currently displayed at M.O.T.A.T. in Auckland.

DH89 c/n 6405. North Eastern Airways' G-AFEO was impressed as X8506 in March 1940 and is thought to have been abandoned in France a couple of months later.

DH89 c/n 6430. Wearing FAP2307 and currently in store at the Museo do Ar storage facility at Sintra, a Portugese Air Force base. Built up from two Rapides and sometimes, the other's c/n is quoted.

DH89 c/n 6409. G-AFFB was supplied to Iraq Petroleum Transport but is seen here soon after the war in the colours of Air Transport Charter (C.I.) Ltd. Finally broken-up at Coventry during the 1960s.

DH89 c/n 6432. Supplied to Airwork and operated for military training purposes, initially at Shoreham and later at Staverton. Crashed in Northumberland February 1954 after encountering icing in cloud.

DH89 c/n 6414. Although sold to "Iraq Aeroplane Society", YI-ZWA and two sister ships were collected by Royal Iraqi Air Force pilots and are said to have been used by the first civil airline in Iraq.

DH89 c/ns 6434 and 6436. The two aircraft presented to the R.A.F. at Hendon by Lady Carnegie on behalf of the Silver Thimble Fund. Named *Women of the Empire* & *Women of Britain* respectively.

Aeriens. Reg'n cancelled 1939 and the aircraft is assumed to have gone to Spain for use in the civil war. Actual fate unknown.

6394 Export CofA no.6188 issued 8.1.38. Reg'd **VP-KCL** for Wilson Airways Ltd. 27.1.38. Impressed locally 9.39 and used by the Kenyan Auxiliary Air Unit, almost certainly as **K-10**. Never restored, the aircraft is reported as having been broken up by East African Airways Corporation at Eastleigh Aerodrome during 1946, 'remains' having been noted there late that year.

6395 Export CofA no.6193 issued 21.1.38. Reg'd **F-AQJH** 21.2.38 for R. Arbeltier, Coulommiers {a Town Councillor for Coulommiers and also the Vice-President of the Aero Club de Coulommiers et la Brie} and CofA no.5580 was issued. To Societe Francais de Transports Aeriens 5.38. Reg'n cancelled 1939 and the aircraft is assumed to have gone to Spain for use in the civil war. Actual fate unknown.

6396 Export CofA no.6221 issued 16.3.38. Reg'd **F-AQJI** 4.4.38 for A. Rodier, Coulommiers amd CofA no.5653 was issued. To Societe Francais de Transports Aeriens 5.38. Reg'n cancelled 1939 and the aircraft is assumed to have gone to Spain for use in the civil war. Actual fate unknown.

6397 CofA no.6239 issued 12.4.38. To Divisao de Exploracao dos Transportes Aereos – D.E.T.A., Lourenco Marques and reg'd **CR-AAM** 4.5.38. Fate unknown.

6398 CofA no.6240 issued 12.4.38. Divisao de Exploracao dos Transportes Aereos – D.E.T.A., Lourenco Marques and reg'd **CR-AAN** 4.5.38. Named *Porto Amelio*. Fate unknown.

6399 Reg'd **G-AFEN** [CofR 8312 13.4.38] to Sir William (John) Firth, Chairman & Managing Director of steel maker Richard Thomas & Co. Ltd. and hangared at Heston. CofA no.6256 issued 25.4.38. Sold abroad 12.38. To Palestine Air Transport Ltd. as **VQ-PAC** 9.39. Impressed locally by the R.A.F. as **Z7188**, but not taken up and the impressment was cancelled at Lydda. Restored as **G-AFEN** to The Secretary of State for Air 25.7.40 at Heliopolis, and operated by B.O.A.C. from 7.40 until 2.42. Impressed again 17.2.42 as **HK864** and used by 173Sqdn. 9.42. To Iraq and Persia Communication Flight after 10.42 and remained with them until 1945. Reg'd **TJ-AAI** 1946 for Arab Airways but not taken up. Restored to **G-AFEN** 21.4.47 for W. A. Rollason Ltd. and shipped to Croydon for conversion. The CofA was renewed 18.11.48 but aircraft sold abroad 30.12.48. Reg'd **LV-AGV** 23.3.49 to the importer Speddo y Paolini Ltda., Zonda. To TAASA 7.5.57. CofA expired 29.4.60 and reported WFU. (Note: See

6400 Construction number not used for a Dragon Rapide as it had been previously used for the first DH92 Dolphin during summer 1936.

6401 Ordered by Aero Oy of Finland 25.10.37. Allocated reg'n **OH-BLB** 12.4.38 and U.K. export CofA no.6262 issued 2.5.38 and delivered 8.5.38. Aircraft named *Lappi* (Lapland) but renamed at an unknown juncture as *Silver Star*. To Ilmavoimat 14.10.39 for hospital and communication flights. Returned to Aero Oy 19.3.40. To Veljekset Karhumaki Oy 18.6.41 and operated on behalf of the Finnish Government for ambulance flights. On 8.11.41, whilst en route Kuusamo to Kiestinki, attacked by four Me109s and shot up wounding some of the occupants. However, the pilot was able to make a forced landing on a frozen lake and taxied under some trees for cover. The aircraft was later repaired and flown back to base. Stored 1944-46. Re-reg'd **OH-VKH** 17.4.47. To Savon Lentolinjat Oy 11.50. To Lentohuolto Oy 8.52. Re-reg'd **OH-DHB** 31.5.54. To Pasanen & Pasanen, Turku 4.55. Cancelled as sold abroad 21.5.55 and to Sylvest Jensen in Denmark but no Danish marks issued. Sold and reg'd **LN-BFB** to Skogbruksfly AS, Eggermoen 20.7.55. To Nor Flyselskap, Eggermoen 21.4.59. WFU after CofA expiry 30.12.60 but remained at Eggermoen for a number of years in a derelict condition until finally burnt.

6402 Reg'd **G-AFEY** [CofR 8342 7.3.38] for Scottish Airways Ltd., Renfrew. CofA no.6325 issued 11.4.38. Crashed and damaged beyond repair at Kirkwall-Wideford, Orkney 18.3.40.

6403 Export CofA no.6267 issued 6.5.38, and reg'd **F-AQOH** for Societe de Transports du Proche Orient 12.5.38 when CofA no.5741 was issued. Based in the Middle East, either at Tripoli or

in the Lebanon. Reg'd **G-AGDP** [CofR 9349 26.11.41] for Iraq Petroleum Transport Co. Ltd., Haifa, and CofA no.6267 was renewed 1.12.41. Damaged in a taxiing accident 23.5.44 at Vileiat airport, Tripoli, Lebanon but repaired. To Short Brothers and Harland Ltd., Rochester 12.1.49. To Modern Transport (Wolverhampton) Ltd., 7.4.49. This company was owned by Don Everall, and it was renamed Don Everall (Aviation) Ltd., Elmdon 29.1.52. Suffered tail wheel damage on take-off 12.5.52, and main undercarriage damage in a hard crosswind landing 7.6.52 but repaired on both occasions. Although a report claims that this aircraft was offered for sale by W. S. Shackleton Ltd. at Kidlington 26.4.58, it was withdrawn from use at Wolverhampton on CofA expiry 24.7.58. Permanently withdrawn from use 7.60 although not notified until 3.5.63. It lingered on at Wolverhampton until 8.69 when it was finally burnt, though some small components were noted at Shobdon in 1972 while other parts were used in the repair of F-BFPU c/n 6796 during 1974.

6404 CofA no.6258 issued 25.4.38, reg'd **VP-YBT** for Rhodesian and Nyasaland Airways Ltd. 11.1.39. Impressed locally 1.1.40 and allocated serial **305** by the Southern Rhodesia Government. Restored to **VP-YBT** 4.42. Reported to have been broken up 12.44.

6405 Reg'd **G-AFEO** [CofR 8319 11.4.38] for North Eastern Airways Ltd., Croydon. CofA no.6251 issued 9.5.38. Impressed as **X8506** 26.3.40 and operated by 24Sqdn. Hendon. Last service flight recorded Hendon to Amiens & return. Presumed abandoned in France 5.40 and SOC 22.6.40.

6406 Reg'd **G-AFEP** [CofR 8320 11.4.38] for North Eastern Airways Ltd., Croydon. CofA no.6252 issued 13.5.38. Impressed as **X9388** 23.3.40 and delivered to R.A.F. Benson, Oxfordshire. To 6AACU 4.40. To Stn. Flt. RNAS Donibristle 5.40. Restored to Air Commerce Ltd., Speke as **G-AFEP** 13.11.40. Absorbed by Olley Air Service Ltd. 30.12.46. To Sir Brograve Campbell Beauchamp Bt. t/a Demolition & Construction Co. Ltd. 19.5.47. To Frederick Arthur White & Herbert Cecil Douglas Haytor, London W1 2.9.47. Sold abroad 15.4.48. To Mrs. E. M. Noon, Nairobi t/a Noon & Pearce Air Charters Ltd. reg'd **VP-KFV** 6.48. Destroyed by fire on start-up Masindi 29.11.49.

6407 Export CofA no.6283 issued 19.5.38 and reg'd **F-AQOI** for Societe de Transports du Proche Orient 8.6.38, when CofA no.5813 was issued. Converted to a medical aircraft and used in support of Middle Eastern oil fields. Fate unknown, though Air Britain note that 'it was grounded in 8.40 presumably due to strained relations between Britain and the Vichy French, possibly subsequently destroyed in 5.41 during the allied invasion of Syria.

6408 Reg'd **G-AFEZ** [CofR 8343 31.5.38] for Wrightways Ltd., Croydon. CofA no.6296 issued 21.6.38. Impressed for use by the Royal Navy 14.4.40 and allocated **X9451**. Restored as **G-AFEZ** to Isle of Man Air Services Ltd., Derbyhaven 7.9.40 and operated under the aegis of A.A.J.C.. Absorbed by B.E.A.C. on formation 1.2.47 and later named *Lord Shaftesbury*. To Hants and Sussex Aviation Ltd., Portsmouth 7.6.56 and converted to Mk4 standard. CofA renewed 2.11.56 and officially sold in France on the following day. Reg'd **F-LAAL** for Laos Air Service and delivered ex Portsmouth 15.11.56, a fresh CofA being issued 21.1.57. Not delivered to Laos and flown to Algeria 1.58. Reg'd **F-OBHI** to Societe Generale d'Affretements Aerien, Algiers with CofA issued 9.7.58. Crashed on landing at Fort Flatters airfield, Sahara 24.8.60.

6409 Reg'd **G-AFFB** [CofR 8345 12.4.38] for Iraq Petroleum Transport Co. Ltd., Haifa. CofA no.6293 issued 27.5.38. To Air Transport (Charter) (C.I.) Ltd., Jersey 30.6.47 and named *Saint Peter*. Air Transport Charter was taken over by Lambert's Trust 27.10.50 but the aircraft continued to be operated in Air Transport's colours. To Aerocontacts Ltd., Gatwick 21.1.52 despite being unflown from 6.51 to 4.52. To Harry James Rose, Bournemouth 4.11.52. To Henry Cockburn Gresley Heathcote Stisted, Southampton 17.7.53. To I.A.S. (London) Ltd., Heathrow, 12.4.54. As Island Air Services, operated pleasure flights at Heathrow. To Air Couriers (Transport) Ltd., Croydon 19.3.59. To Trans European Aviation Ltd., Swansea 29.5.59 and ferried from Croydon to Fairwood Common 30.5.59. Eventually moved on to Baginton and withdrawn from use there 2.62 prior to CofA expiry 23.6.62. Offered for sale at auction 26.10.63 but failed to reach the reserve. Permanently withdrawn from use 11.11.64. Dismantled and stored at Baginton 1965 and still noted there 8.66.

6410   Reg'd **G-AFFC** [CofR 8346 12.4.38] for Iraq Petroleum Transport Co. Ltd., Haifa. CofA no.6297 issued 2.6.38. Taken over by the British Military Forces at Haifa 28.5.41 but not officially impressed into the R.A.F. until 15.2.42. Allocated **HK862** and used by 206 Group until transferred to Iraq and Persia Communications Flight. SOC in Iraq 31.8.44.

6411   Export CofA no.6338 issued 1.7.38, and reg'd **ZS-AOM** for Stewarts and Lloyds of South Africa Ltd. 30.8.38. Impressed into the S.A.A.F. 1939 as **SAAF1401** and noted in use with 61Sqdn. 8.40 and 7.45. SOC and reg'd **ZS-CAB** for the Department of Civil Aviation 7.12.46. Re-reg'd **ZS-DDX** for Pretoria Light Aircraft Co. Ltd. 13.5.50. To Drakensberg Air Services (Pty) Ltd. 1951. Crashed on landing at Mokhotlong, Basutoland 24.6.55.

6412   Export CofA issued 4.7.48, and reg'd **VP-YBU** for Southern Rhodesia Government 16.8.38 and named *Southern Rhodesia*. It was fitted out as a VIP aircraft, and was transferred to the Southern Rhodesia Air Unit as **SR-8** 6.39, though it carried both this and its civil mark simultaneously. To Rhodesia and Nyasaland Airways Ltd. as **300** by 9.39. Merged into Southern Rhodesia Air Services 1.2.40. Restored as **VP-YBU**, still with Southern Rhodesia Air Services 4.42. To Central African Airways 1.6.46. To Royal Rhodesia Air Force as **SR-23** 13.6.47. Reg'd **VP-YNJ** for Fish Air (Pty) Ltd., Salisbury, 10.55. Sold and re-reg'd **F-OBOD**. CofA issued for Cie Aerien Brouillet, Libreville, 22.7.59. Destroyed at Libreville 27.4.65.

6413   Export CofA no.6358 issued 23.7.38, and reg'd **VP-KCR** for Wilson Airways Ltd. 16.8.38. Impressed into the Kenyan Auxiliary Air Unit, almost certainly as **K-8** 9.39. Never restored to the civilian register but reported broken up at Eastleigh by E.A.A.C. in 1946.

6414   First flew 23.7.38 and CofA no.6359 issued 25.7.38, reg'd **YI-ZWA** for the Iraq Aeroplane Society. This society was actually a section of the Royal Iraqi Air Force and the aircraft were delivered ex Hatfield by Air Force pilots, although reports state that they were actually used 'by the first civil airline in Iraq'. Fate unknown.

6415   CofA no.6360 issued 25.7.38 and reg'd **YI-HDA** for the Iraq Aeroplane Society. This company was owned by the Royal Iraq Air Force and the aircraft were delivered ex Hatfield by Air Force pilots, although reports say that they were actually used 'by the first civil airline in Iraq'. Fate unknown.

6416   CofA no.6366 issued 22.9.38 and reg'd **YI-FYA** for the Iraq Aeroplane Society. This company was owned by the Royal Iraqi Air Force and the aircraft were delivered ex Hatfield by Air Force pilots, although reports say that they were actually used 'by the first civil airline in Iraq'. Fate Unknown.

6417   Reg'd **G-AFHY** [CofR 8546 1.7.38] for Anglo-Iranian Oil Co. Ltd., Abadan. CofA no.6387 issued 1.9.38. To Aircraft and Engineering Services Ltd., Croydon (a Charles Allen company) 23.9.46. To Air Charter Ltd., Haddenham 28.3.47. Damaged at Croydon 22.4.47 and again at Rotterdam 10.10.47 but repaired on both occasions. Sold abroad 9.6.50 and possibly to Compagnie Belge de Transports for spares use. (see also c/n 6463).

6418   Reg'd **G-AFHZ** [CofR 8547 1.7.38] for Anglo-Iranian Oil Co. Ltd., Abadan. CofA no.6393 issued 15.9.38. To W. A. Rollason Ltd., Croydon, 23.6.47 (sic, should probably read 23.7.46). Cancelled as sold abroad 30.4.47, reg'd **VP-UAX** for Uganda Co. 9.47. Reg'd **VP-KFH** for Noon and Pearce Air Charters Ltd., Nairobi 4.48. Cancelled 26.6.52 and broken up 8.52 at Nairobi.

6419   Reg'd **G-AFIA** [CofR 8548 1.7.38] for Anglo-Iranian Oil Co. Ltd., Abadan, 1.7.38. CofA no.6398 issued 22.9.38. Destroyed by fire Abadan 20.8.42. Cancelled 30.10.42.

6420   Export CofA no.6431 issued 11.11.38, and reg'd **F-ARII** for P. Legastelois, Paris, 2.12.38 on issue of CofA no.6226. Ownership transferred the same month to Societe Francaise de Transports Aeriens. Cancelled 1939 and the aircraft went to Spain for use in the civil war. Reg'd **EC-BAC** for Iberia CA, 2.6.42. Re-reg'd **EC-AAR** 9.7.51, still to Iberia. Reported still current in 1957. Fate unknown.

6421   Reg'd **E.9** to de Havilland Aircraft Co. Ltd. 9.38, and used for testing a Dowty made levered suspension undercarriage during autumn 1938. Allocated **P1764** for The Air Council, and delivered to them 29.11.38. Used by 24Sqdn. Damaged beyond repair by enemy action in an air raid at Coulommiers, the engines and equipment were salvaged and the aircraft abandoned 16.5.40. SOC 3.6.40 while still on strength with 24Sqdn.

6422   Allocated **P1765** for the Air Council, and delivered to them 29.11.38. Used by 24Sqdn. Written off in 'a flying accident' and SOC 4.4.40.

6423   CofA no.6395 issued 19.9.38, shipped to New Zealand per *Rangitata* arriving 16.11.38. Reg'd **ZK-AGT** for Cook Strait Airways Ltd 24.11.38, erected and first flew 30.11.38. Named *Neptune*. Impressed into the R.N.Z.A.F. 10.11.39, serial **NZ558** allocated 18.2.40. Used by 42Sqdn., and by the Communications Flight at Rongotai. SOC to Air Travel (NZ) Ltd. 1943 and overhauled by de Havilland Aircraft Co. of NZ Ltd. during late 1943/early 1944. Reg'd **ZK-AHS** for Air Travel (NZ) Ltd. 29.9.44. Taken over by New Zealand National Airways Co. 10.47. Named *Huia* and later *Mokai*. To West Coast Airways Ltd. (a subsidiary of Sothern Scenic Air Services) 22.1.57. Taken over by New Zealand Tourist Air Travel Ltd. 1.5.65. Taken over by Mount Cook and Southern Lakes Tourist Co. Ltd. 3.67. Withdrawn from use 1973 and stored at Hokitika until donated to the Museum of Transport and Technology, Auckland, and ferried to Auckland 8.74. Currently displayed at MoTAT.

6424   U.K. CofA issued 22.11.38, and reg'd **F-ARIJ** for P. Legastelois, Paris. On issue of CofA no.6446, ownership transferred 12.38 to Societe Francaise de Transports Aeriens. Cancelled 1939 and the aircraft went to Spain for use in the civil war. Reg'd **EC-AAS (2)** for Iberia CA 29.12.53. Cancelled as sold abroad 12.2.57 and reg'd **F-OBAQ** for Cie. Aerien J. C. Brouillet, Libreville, 27.5.57. Reg'n cancelled 9.58. Fate unknown.

6425   UK CofA no.6448 issued 25.11.38, and reg'd **F-ARIK** for P. Legastelois, Paris, on issue of CofA no.6243 20.12.38. Ownership transferred the same month to Societe Francaise de Transports Aeriens. Cancelled 1939 and the aircraft went to Spain for use in the civil war, initially wearing serial **LR-007** and later, would have worn a serial in the **40-** range. Reg'd **EC-AAS** (1) in the 2nd series for Iberia CA 18.3.41. Damaged Tetuan 18.1.43 but repaired. Re-reg'd **EC-AAV** (2) in the 3rd series 9.7.51, still with Iberia. Cancelled as sold abroad 20.6.54 or 30.6.54 (other sources show the more likely "withdrawn from use"). Actual fate unknown but cancelled from register 20.10.59.

6426   Reg'd **G-AFLY** [CofR 8878 22.11.38] for Airwork Ltd., Heston. CofA no.6443 issued 30.11.38. Impressed as **Z7253** 15.7.40 and sometime coded '1', used by 6AACU, 9MU, 10B&GS, 10AOS, 10 (O) AFU, 9 (O) AFU and 18MU. Then used by the Royal Navy at RNAS Stretton coded ST-9A before returning to 18MU. SOC 22.12.45 at Dumfries as Cat.E2 and scrapped.

6427   Export CofA no.6449 issued 28.11.38, and reg'd **F-ARIL** for P. Legastelois, Paris, on issue of CofA no.6254 on 3.1.39. Cancelled 1939 and the aircraft is yet another one assumed to have gone to Spain for use in the civil war. Fate unknown.

6428   Export CofA no.6457 issued 7.12.38, and reg'd **F-ARIM** for P. Legastelois, Paris, on issue of CofA no.6258 on 16.1.39, ownership transferred the same month to Societe Francaise de Transports Aeriens. Cancelled 1939, the aircraft is assumed to have gone to Spain for use in the civil war. Fate unknown.

6429   Reg'd **G-AFLZ** [CofR 8879 22.11.38] for Airwork Ltd., Heston. CofA no.6444 issued 14.12.38. Impressed as **Z7254** 15.7.40 and sometime coded '2', used by 6AONS and 5MU. Reg'd **G-AHPX** [CofR 10269 22.5.46] for Field Consolidated Aircraft Services Ltd., Croydon. However, reg'n cancelled as not taken up and instead the aircraft was restored as **G-AFLZ**. Civilianised by Fields for the Aircraft Operating Co. of South Africa and British reg'n cancelled 12.8.46. Reg'd **ZS-AYF** 19.10.46. Cancelled 28.8.56 and delivered to Air Brousse SPRL, Leopoldville-Ndolo reg'd **OO-CJS** [CofR 264 31.7.56]. Re-reg'd **9O-CJS** on independence 1.1.61. Reg'n cancelled 23.5.60. Fate unknown.

6430   Reg'd **G-AFMA** [CofR 8880 22.11.38] for Airwork Ltd., Heston. CofA no.6445 issued 3.1.39. Used under an Air Ministry

Shoreham which eventually became 6CANS. Base moved to Staverton 9.39 and renamed 6AONS. Impressed as **Z7255** 15.7.40 and sometime coded '3', used by 7AONS and at R.A.F. Halton wearing 'THA:B'. To Dumfries for disposal 26.8.46. SOC on sale to Ciro's Aviation Ltd., Gatwick and restored as **G-AFMA** 30.6.47. To the United Nations Organisation 1948 as **UN73** and operated in Palestine. Restored as **G-AFMA** to William Dempster Ltd., Heathrow, 24.1.49. Cancelled as 'sold abroad' 13.4.50 and reg'd **CS-AEB** for Durval Ferreira da Costa Mergulhao, Luanda 4.50. Eventually re-reg'd **CR-LCO** to the same owner 1951. To Divisao de Exploracao dos Transportes Aereos de Angola – D.T.A., Beira. Withdrawn from use 1961. Recovered by Portugese Air Force and now beautifully restored, stored at Sintra for the Museo do Ar, marked as **FAP2307**.

6431 Reg'g **G-AFME** [CofR 8902 9.12.38] for Airwork Ltd., Heston. CofA no.6459 issued 13.1.39. Used under an Air Ministry type 'A' contract by C. W. Martin's School of Navigation at Shoreham which eventually became 6CANS. Base moved to Staverton 9.39 and renamed 6AONS. Impressed as **Z7257** 15.7.40 and sometime coded '4', used by 7AONS and Station Flight Skeabrae. Loaned to Allied Airways 31.12.42 - 12.7.43. Stored Kemble 25.9.43 to 23.4.44 and then to Witney for inspection 20.2.45. SOC as Cat.E1 3.3.45 and dismantled.

6432 Reg'd **G-AFMF** [CofR 8903 9.12.38] for Airwork Ltd., Heston. CofA no.6460 issued 20.1.39. Used under an Air Ministry type 'A' contract by C. W. Martin's School of Navigation at Shoreham which eventually became 6CANS. Base moved to Staverton 9.39 and renamed 6AONS. Impressed as **Z7256** 15.7.40 and sometime coded '5'. With Gloster Aircraft 13.10.42 to 10.45 and then stored Kemble. Restored as **G-AFMF** 26.1.46 for Norman Ray Harben, Burnaston, for use by Air Schools Ltd. and CofA renewed 20.8.46. To Kennings Ltd., Burnaston 24.8.46. To Domino Louis Steiner t/a Steiner's Air and Travel Services Ltd., Speke 17.1.47. To Reginald Jones t/a Belle Vue Flying Service, Ringway for use by British Cellulose Co. Ltd. 9.9.47. Ownership transferred to British Cellulose Industries (Manchester) Ltd. 4.3.48. To Roy Charles Jarvis, Leicester 19.1.49. To Adie Aviation Ltd., Croydon 23.3.49 and rebuilt using parts from G-AHXY (c/n 6808). To John Weston Adamson t/a Oldstead Aircraft, Sunderland 18.4.50. Shortly after departure from Newcastle at the start of a flight to Dublin, the aircraft encountered icing in cloud and turned back 19.2.54. Control was lost soon after and it crashed and was destroyed by fire near Simonburn, 7 miles from Hexham, Northumberland. Reg'n cancelled 17.9.54.

6433 Reg'd **G-AFMG** [CofR 8904 9.12.38] for Airwork Ltd., Heston. CofA no.6461 issued 1.2.39. Used under an Air Ministry type 'A' contract by C. W. Martin's School of Navigation at Shoreham which eventually became 6CANS. Base moved to Staverton 9.39 and renamed 6AONS. Impressed as **Z7259** 15.7.40 and sometime coded '6'. To storage 5MU 21.12.44. Restored as **G-AFMG** 11.12.46 for Portsmouth Aviation Ltd., and CofA renewed 11.1.47. Cancelled as sold abroad 21.5.48 and reg'd **EI-AEA** for Weston Ltd., operating as Weston Air Services 26.7.48. Whilst attempting a night landing at a private airfield using a flare path of straw bales the aircraft overshot and hit buildings at Highfield Farm, Hutton Cranswick, near Driffield, Yorkshire 4.10.49. The aircraft was dismantled 10.11.49 and conveyed to Manchester but was later noted with W. A. Rollason Ltd. at Croydon. Later reported 'exported to Israel'.

6434 Reg'd **G-AFMH** [CofR 8905 9.12.38] for Airwork Ltd., Heston. CofA no.6462 issued 6.2.39. Used under an Air Ministry type 'A' contract by C. W. Martin's School of Navigation at Shoreham which eventually became 6CANS. Base moved to Staverton 9.39 and renamed 6AONS. Impressed as **Z7258** 15.7.40 and sometime coded '7'. Used by 1680 Flt Abbotsinch, and named *Women of the Empire*, in ambulance configuration. SOC as Cat.E1 25.7.45. (Also see c/n 6436 for details on the second Silver Thimble Fund Rapide and c/n 6862 which was painted to represent Z7258).

6435 Reg'd **G-AFMI** [CofR 8906 9.12.38] to Airwork Ltd., Heston. CofA no.6463 issued 20.2.39. Used under an Air Ministry type 'A' contract by C. W. Martin's School of Navigation at Shoreham which eventually became 6CANS. Base moved to Staverton 9.39 and renamed 6AONS. Impressed as **Z7260** 15.7.40 and sometime coded '8'. Continued in use by 6AONS until passing to 63MU for storage. SOC as Cat.E2 23.4.46 and scrapped Carluke.

6436 Reg'd **G-AFMJ** [CofR 8907 9.12.38] for Airwork Ltd., Heston. CofA no.6464 issued 27.2.39. Used under an Air Ministry type 'A' contract by C. W. Martin's School of Navigation at Shoreham which eventually became 6CANS. Base moved to Staverton 9.39 and renamed 6AONS. Impressed as **Z7261** 15.7.40 and sometime coded '9'. Used by 6AONS, then flown to de Havilland for conversion to ambulance configuration 22.8.40. After conversion, delivered to 24Sqdn. at Hendon 17.5.41. On 21.5.41 at a special ceremony, it was 'presented' to the R.A.F. at Hendon by Lady Maud Carnegie (daughter of H.R.H. the late Princess Royal and the Duke of Fife) on behalf of the Silver Thimble Fund, named *Women of Britain*. Delivered to Communications Flight Wick 22.8.41, to Kinloss Stn. Flt.5.46 and finally, to 18MU for storage 5.47. SOC and restored as **G-AFMJ** for Air Enterprises Ltd., Gatwick 11.12.47, named *The Shanklin Flyer*. CofA renewed 27.7.48. During 1948, the aircraft was painted white overall with '3' on the tail and carried United Nations titling for use in Palestine. To Airwork Ltd., Heston 13.4.53. Cancelled as sold abroad 17.9.56 and reg'd **ZP-TDH** for Aero-Carga SRL, Paraguay 10.56. Later reportedly to Roland Degli Ubertti. Destroyed when a hangar collapsed at Asuncion 10.62.

6437 Export CofA no.6524 issued 22.3.39, and reg'd **HB-AME** for Alpar Schweizerische Luftverkehrs AG, Bern, 3.39. Merged with other operators to form Swissair 10.47. Re-reg'd **HB-APE**, still for Swissair 19.4.48. To Farner-Werke AG, Grenchen, 1954. To Motorfluggruppe Zurich des Ae.CS 1955. Reg'd **D-IGUN** for Gunter Nitzsche 15.4.69, CofA no.4382 issued 4.69. Noted dumped at Saarbrucken-Ensheim 26.5.73. Acquired by Air Classik (part of the Kurfiss Group) 5.74 and displayed on the roof terrass, Frankfurt Airport. Noted at Dusseldorf 1982, still with Air Classic, displayed in the open with other aircraft near the freight terminal. Returned to Frankfurt and more recently, displayed inside the terminal painted **'G-RCYR'** to represent the aircraft that was used by Franco to return to Spanish soil during the Civil War. Aircraft not seen on a visit to Frankfurt 2.03. (Also see c/n 6261).

6438 Export CofA no.6532 issued 29.3.39, and reg'd **HB-AMU** for Alpar Schweizerische Luftverkehrs AG, Bern, 3.39. Merged with other operators to form Swissair 10.47. Re-reg'd **HB-APU** 19.4.48, still for Swissair. To Farner-Werke AG, Grenchen, 1954. To Motorfluggruppe Zurich des Ae.CS 1955. Cancelled as 'cannibalised' 1968.

6439 Export CofA no.6561 issued 25.4.39. To Divisao de Exploracao dos Transportes Aereos – D.E.T.A., Lourenco Marques and reg'd **CR-AAT** 1.7.39. Named *Mocambique*. Fate unknown.

6440 Export CofA no.6571 issued 4.5.39. To Divisao de Exploracao dos Transportes Aereos – D.E.T.A., Lourenco Marques and reg'd **CR-AAU** 1.7.39. Named *Sofala*. Noted at Lourenco Marques in early 1970s but believed broken up prior to end '74.

6441 Reg'd **G-AFRK** for Isle of Man Air Services Ltd., Derbyhaven, 9.3.39. First flew and CofA no.6517 issued 8.5.39. To Scottish Airways Ltd., Renfrew, 12.7.39. To B.E.A.C. on formation 1.2.47 and later named *Rudyard Kipling*. To Airviews Ltd., Barton, 16.5.56. To W. S. Shackleton Ltd. prior to 12.58, and to T. H. Marshall, Christchurch 25.2.59. Withdrawn from use on CofA expiry 10.3.59 and broken up for spares at Christchurch 3.59 with parts used during the rebuild of G-ALAX c/n 6930.

6442 Reg'd **G-AFNC** [CofR 8965 1.2.39] for Aircraft Operating Co. Ltd., Hatfield. CofA no.6654 issued 21.6.39. Delivered to 24Sqdn. 8.9.39, then impressed as **V4724** 16.10.39. To 1CU at Baginton 27.11.39, to 24Sqdn. 2.40, to 22MU 10.40, to 1AONS 10.40, to 1CU at Hendon 1.41, to Skeabrae (Orkney Islands) Com. Flt. 12.42, to R.A.F. Halton 10.43, to 18MU 7.45 and finally, to 5MU for storage 2.4.46. SOC on sale to Field Consolidated Aircraft Services Ltd., Croydon 24.5.46 and restored as **G-AFNC** Hanworth Park 24.6.46. Cancelled on sale abroad 14.8.46. The CofA was renewed 23.10.46, but in the meantime reg'd **OO-CCD** [CofR C.61 13.6.56] for A. Camelbeek, Elizabethville, Belgian Congo. Declared unairworthy 5.7.47 and reg'n cancelled 8.7.47.

6443 Reg'd **G-AFND** [CofR 8966 1.2.39] for Aircraft Operating Co. Ltd., Hatfield. CofA no.6658 issued 29.6.39. Delivered to 24Sqdn. 8.9.39, then impressed as **V4725** 16.10.39. To 1CU at Baginton 27.11.39, to 24Sqdn. 2.40, to 1CU at Hendon 3.40, to

DH89 c/n 6437. The Air Classik collection's Rapide displayed on the roof at Frankfurt Airport. Subsequently moved inside and is now painted G-RCYR, to represent Franco's plane preserved at Madrid.

DH89 c/n 6458. In Belgium since 1955 with Avions Fairey SA and passed to a private owner at Wevelgem in 1964. The photograph shows preparation for transfer to the Brussels museum.

DH89 c/n 6441. Operated by Scottish Airways when absorbed into British European Airways Corporation on 1st February 1947, G-AFRK was eventually broken-up at Christchurch.

DH89 c/n 6469. Operated for one year by Air Navigation & Trading at Blackpool, G-AKNW was sold to Lebanon where it eventually succumbed in a start-up fire in Syria July 1954.

DH89 c/n 6447. The earliest Dominie to survive the war, G-AKJY was struck off charge to Brooklands Aviation. It was later sold via W. S. Shackleton to Algeria where the CofA expired March 1960.

DH89 c/n 6470. Photographed at Dakar March 1965, 6V-AAC was operated at the time by Senegalaise des Transports Aeriens. Later, reserved as F-BOHL for a parachute club at Chalon but not taken up.

DH89 c/n 6455. G-AGHI remained in airline service throughout the war with Allied Airways and it is seen here wearing obligatory camouflage and named *The Shetlander*.

DH89 c/n 6472. In service with Canadian Pacific, the float-equipped CF-BNG forced landed on ice in the St. Lawrence River following an in flight engine fire and was destroyed.

R.A.F. Stapleford Tawney 6.42, to 19Grp. Com. Flt. 10.42, to 18Grp. Com. Flt. Leuchars, 10.44, to 12FU at Melton Mowbray 10.45, to 18MU 2.46. SOC on sale to W. A. Rollason Ltd. 1947 and reg'n G-AKOG reserved. However, error realised and correctly restored as **G-AFND** at Croydon 4.12.47 and CofA renewed to Rollason 7.6.48. Cancelled on sale abroad 15.7.48. Reg'd as **TJ-AAP** for Arab Airways Association Ltd., Amman, 13.7.48. CofA renewed 6.3.51. To Arab Legion Air Force as **R301**. Fate unknown.

6444   Export CofA no.6583 issued 11.5.39. To Military Council of the Nationalist Government of China as **'38'**. Destroyed when the Eurasia company's hangar caught fire, Sanhupa Airfield Chungking 27.1.40. (Note: the China National Airways Corp. hangar was adjacent and it is possible that the Rapide was situated in that hangar, which also burnt).

6445   Reg'd **G-AFSO** [CofR 9076 21.4.39] for Western Airways Ltd., Weston-super-Mare. CofA no.6554 issued 22.5.39. Delivered to 24Sqdn. 10.10.39, then impressed as **W6457** 4.1.40. While still with 24Sqdn. during the evacuation from France, the aircraft made a forced landing near Aneuil 31.5.40 and came under concentrated machine gun fire from German troops. The Rapide caught fire and was destroyed.

6446   Supplied to the Air Council with military serial **R2485**. Initially at 8MU 8.39, then to 2E&WS 10.39, to de Havilland for 'MR' 9.42. SOC as Cat.E 12.9.42.

6447   Supplied to the Air Council with military serial **R2486**. Initially at 8MU 7.39, then RAE 9.39, and 2E&WS 10.39. In use by Wrightways Ltd., Croydon 1.42. To No.2 Signals School 8.42, A.T.A. HQ White Waltham 3.43, Coastal Command. Communications Flight Northolt 1.45, Coastal Command Communications Flight Leavesden 4.45, Coastal Command Communications Flight Northern Ireland at Sydenham (date unknown) and 5MU 11.46. SOC on sale to Brooklands Aviation Ltd. 25.8.47 and reg'd **G-AKJY** [CofR 11996 22.12.47]. CofA no.9937 issued 13.5.48. To broker W. S. Shackleton Ltd. 18.2.54. Cancelled on sale to French Algeria 7.4.54. To Societe Aerotechnique, Algiers and reg'd **F-OAPT** 11.6.54. To Societe General d'Affretements Aeriens (S.G.A.A.) Algiers '57. CofA suspended at Algiers 3.60 but reported to C.G.T.A. 9.60. Fate unknown.

6448   Supplied to the Air Council with military serial **R2487**. Initially at 8MU 7.39, then RAE 9.39, returned to 8MU 10.39, to 2E&WS 5.40, to 18MU 2.43, to Halton ATC Flight 3.43, to 59OTU 9.43, to Millfield Fighter Leader School 1.44, to A&AEE 3.46, to 5MU 1.50. SOC on sale to Herts and Essex Aero Club 919460 Ltd., Broxbourne 13.4.50. Reg'd **G-ALZH** [CofR 14965 24.3.50] for Le Bryan Group Products (Great Britain) Ltd., London N17. CofA no.10874 was issued. To William James Edward Lee, London N21 24.5.50. To Aerocontacts Ltd., Gatwick 6.4.51. Cancelled as sold abroad to Madagascar 2.4.52. Reg'd **F-OAKF** for Societe Air Madagascar and CofA issued 25.10.52. CofA suspended 4.62 as withdrawn from use.

6449   Export CofA no.6751 issued 23.8.39, and reg'd **PP-LAA** for Cia Fabril de Juta 30.3.40 and named *Maristella*. (de Havilland records show the first owner as Dr. Mario B. Andra, possibly he was the de Havilland agent in Brazil). To Varig 22.7.42. Re-reg'd **PP-VAN(1)** 28.7.42 still for Varig, and named *Chui*. Stored unflown by Varig 1942-45 due to legal difficulties and passed to OMTA 5.11.45. Re-reg'd **PP-OMA** still for OMTA 11.2.46. Last inspection was on 8.7.48, eventually cancelled as damaged beyond repair 24.10.62 although it was believed to have met with an accident sometime prior to 7.7.49!

6450   Reg'd **G-AFOI** [CofR 8995 28.7.39] for Scottish Airways Ltd., Renfrew. CofA no.6720 issued 28.8.39. Absorbed into B.E.A.C. on formation 1.2.47. Transferred to Gibraltar Airways Ltd. 20.1.49. To James Henry Hoggart Hill, Taunton 18.5.50. To Airmotive (Liverpool) Ltd. 28.6.50. To Handley Page Ltd., Radlett 5.6.52. Withdrawn from use at Sywell on CofA expiry 20.9.57, dismantled 4.58 and conveyed by road to Luton for use as spares by Luton Airways. Fuselage had been stripped and dumped outside by 3.60.

6451   Export CofA no.6752 issued 24.8.39. To Divisao de Exploracao dos Transportes Aereos de Angola - D.E.T.A.,

Lourenco Marques and reg'd **CR-LAV** 7.40. Crashed, but details unknown.

6452   Export CofA no.6755 issued 29.8.39. To Divisao de Exploracao dos Transportes Aereos de Angola - D.E.T.A. and reg'd **CR-LAU** 7.40. Withdrawn from use at Luanda.

6453   Export CofA no.6760 issued 29.8.39. To Divisao de Exploracao dos Transportes Aereos de Angola - D.E.T.A. and reg'd **CR-LAT** 7.40. To Transport Aerien de Gabon reg'd **F-OAVZ** 7.56. Hit trees on flight Kribi - Douala and crashed on the Sanaga River, 35kms from destination 18.9.56. Aircraft not found until 10.57.

6454   Reg'd **VT-ALO** for Air Services of India Ltd., Bombay 6.39, and export CofA no.6715 issued 26.7.39. Dismantled and prepared for shipment to India by de Havilland 14.9.39. Impressed locally as **HX791** 1941. Transferred to the Director of Civil Aviation of India, 1.9.43, and SOC 29.3.45. [Note: it has been suggested that this aircraft became VT-ASQ in 1943, but the identity of 'ASQ is normally given as 'BCL 89445' which would make it c/n 6794].

6455   Supplied to the Air Council with military serial **P9588**. To 10MU 21.9.39, to 2E&WS 13.12.39. Leased to Air Taxis Ltd. 1.9.42, then to 18MU 21.11.42. SOC to Allied Airways (Gandar Dower) Ltd., Aberdeen 30.4.43. Reg'd **G-AGHI** [CofR 9441 2.12.43] and CofA no.7047 issued 18.3.44, named *The Shetlander*. To B.E.A.C. 13.11.47. To Charles W. J. Allen t/a Allen Aircraft Services, Old Coulsdon 15.6.48. To Christopher Leake Burton t/a International Airways Ltd., Croydon 1.7.48. Leased to Jersey Airlines for the summer 1949 season. Withdrawn from use at Croydon on CofA expiry 31.8.50, the aircraft was dismantled and conveyed to Portsmouth, being noted dumped there in 1952. Finally cancelled as permanently withdrawn from use 31.8.59.

6456   Supplied to the Air Council with military serial **P9589**. Initially to 10MU 9.39. Served with No.2 E&WS 12.39, No.1 Signals School 10.41, 18MU 1.43, 15Grp. Com. Flt. 4.43 and to 5MU for storage 12.44. SOC on sale to Wng. Cmdr. Resland, London, representing the R.A.F. Flying Club 25.11.46. Reg'd as **G-AIYP** [CofR 11084 9.12.46] to Wng. Cmdr. W. H. Wetton, Manging Director of Garden Corner, London SW3 and CofA no.8806 issued 17.1.47. To Roy Walter Marsh, London WC2 8.9.47, but in fact the aircraft was operated throughout this period by St. Christopher Travel-Ways Ltd. from Croydon. Operated, probably on lease, by Island Air Services 4.48. To Autowork (Winchester) Ltd. 11.3.49. To V. H. Bellamy t/a Flightways Ltd., Eastleigh 29.3.50. To Murray Chown Aviation Ltd., Staverton 28.3.52. Leased to Dragon Airways for joy-riding during the 1953 summer season at Pwllheli. The aircraft hit a hedge 5.7.53 whilst attempting a forced landing in a cornfield in thick fog at Pentre Uchaf, 5 miles from Pwllheli, and was burnt out.

6457   Supplied to the Air Council with military serial **R5921**. To 2E&WS 9.39, to 34 Wing 12.42, to No.2 Signals School 1.43, operated by Wrightways Ltd. for undisclosed flights 7.43. To Stn. Flt. Old Sarum 4.44, to 7Grp. Com. Flt. 10.44, to 18MU 12.45, to Valley TC 4.46, to 18MU 5.46. SOC on sale to Lancashire Aircraft Corporation Ltd., Samlesbury 10.3.47. Reg'd **G-AJKX** [CofR 11387 22.3.47] and CofA no.9438 issued 18.7.47. Cancelled 9.11.50 as "In long term storage" but restored 9.4.51. Cancelled on sale abroad to Pakistan 7.1.53 and reg'd **AP-AGI** for Crescent Air Transport Ltd., Karachi 5.53. Arrived back at Croydon from Pakistan in a crate 7.56, but remained dismantled. Transported by road to Biggin Hill on Croydon's closure 1959 but scrapped 1962.

6458   Supplied to the Air Council with military serial **R5922**. To 2E&WS 10.39, to Halton A.T.C. Flight 3.43, to No.2 Delivery Flight 4.44, to No.1 Delivery Flight 7.44, to Redhill 11.44, to 12FU at Melton Mowbray 10.45 and to 18MU for storage 2.47. SOC on sale to Lancashire Aircraft Corporation Ltd., Samlesbury 9.12.47. Reg'd **G-AKNV** [CofR 12083 2.12.47] and CofA no.9979 issued 24.3.48. Cancelled as sold abroad to Ireland 11.12.53. To J. J. Crowley reg'd **EI-AGK** 16.12.53 and operated by Republic Air Charters Ltd., named *Marian*. Cancelled 12.6.55 and restored as **G-AKNV** to Derby Aviation Ltd., Burnaston 20.6.55. To Fairey Aviation Co. Ltd., Hayes 12.7.55. Cancelled on sale abroad to Belgium 27.9.55, the aircraft went to Charleroi for rebuild before being reg'd **OO-AFG** for Avions Fairey SA 27.2.57. CofA no.1179 issued. Fitted with large Dragon-type windows. To Air Affairs Jumet, Charleroi, 10.4.62. Re-reg'd **OO-CNP** to L. Huybrechts,

Wevelgem, 10.4.64 and CofA no.1496 issued. Cancelled 10.8.70 as withdrawn from use and donated to the Musee de l'Armee et d'Histoire Militaire, Brussels 4.10.73.

6459 Supplied to the Air Council with military serial **R5923**. To 2E&WS 10.39, to 43Grp. Com. Flt. 4.41. The aircraft swung on take off from Yatesbury 22.4.41, struck a wire fence and crashed. SOC 29.4.41 with 638.55 hours total time.

6460 Supplied to the Air Council with military serial **R5924**. To 2E&WS 10.39, to 5MU 7.42, to 7AGS 8.42, to HQ R.A.F. Croydon 8.42, to 18MU 10.42, to No.2 Signals School 11.42, to School of Technical Training Halton 12.42, to 5MU 2.47. Although reserved by V. H. Bellamy's Flightways concern at Eastleigh, SOC on sale to Southern Aircraft (Gatwick) Ltd. Reg'd **G-AKFO** [CofR 11878 3.9.47]. CofA never issued, and the reg'n was cancelled as dismantled 4.8.49. The aircraft remained unconverted from its military state and was eventually dismantled at Gatwick for spares.

6461 Supplied to the Air Council with military serial **R5925**. To 2E&WS 10.39, to 24Sqdn. 5.43, to Metropolitan Com. Sqdn. at Hendon 9.44. SOC as Cat.E 31.12.45.

6462 Static test airframe.

6463 Supplied to the Air Council with military serial **R5926**. To 2E&WS 10.39, to 18MU 9.42. SOC on sale to Airwork Ltd., Heston 21.10.42. Shipped to Basrah per S.S. *Salawati* arriving there 29.6.43. Reg'd **G-AGFU** [CofR 9402 26.11.42] for Anglo- Iranian Oil Co. Ltd., Abadan. CofA no.6951 issued 4.8.43. To Aircraft and Engineering Services Ltd., Croydon 20.8.47. To Air Charter Ltd., Croydon 29.8.47. Cancelled as sold abroad 9.6.50. Purchased by Compagnie Belge de Transports Aeriens for use as spares and noted derelict at Brussels, still with its British marks, in 1952 and eventually scrapped there. [See also c/n 6417].

6464 Supplied to the Air Council with military serial **R5927**. To 2E&WS 10.39. Hit balloon cables 14.2.42 and crashed in flames at Wiggins Field, Horton, Bucks, 7 killed. SOC as Cat.E 14.3.42.

6465 Supplied to the Air Council with military serial **R5928**. To No.2 E&WS 10.39, to No.1 Signals School 10.41, to Abbotsinch Station Flight 10.42, to 1680 Flt 6.43. The pilot became lost while flying in a snowstorm 1.3.44 and was unable to maintain height due to icing, and the aircraft hit the ground and nosed over at Carrick Knowe golf course, Corstorphine, near Turnhouse, Edinburgh. SOC as Cat.E 2.3.44.

6466 Supplied to the Air Council with military serial **R5929**. To 2E&WS 10.39. Stalled in a turn whilst low flying 27.5.41, crashed and caught fire at Bishops Cannings, near Devizes, Wilts. One person was killed. SOC as Cat.E 3.6.41.

6467 Supplied to the Air Council with military serial **R5930**. Served with 2E&WS 11.39, No.1 Signals School 10.41, No.2 Signals School 7.42, 57OTU 6.43, 58OTU 9.43, 60OTU, 13OTU 3.45 until placed into storage 18MU 5.46. SOC on sale to Air Schools Ltd., Burnaston, Derbyshire and reg'd **G-AIUO** [CofR 10983 20.11.46]. SOC 9.1.47. CofA applied for by Field Aircraft Services on behalf of Air Schools and no.9011 issued 20.6.47. To Hornton Airways Ltd. 26.6.47. Sold abroad to Sweden 19.7.51 and to Jumex Konfektions reg'd **SE-BTT**. To Sylvest Jensen, Hillerod and reg'd **OY-ACV** 13.4.53. Sold to Hamburg Aero-Lloyd as **D-IDAK** 26.3.56. To Hanseatische Flugdienste GmbH 28.6.60. Company later liquidated and thence to Deutsche Nah-Luftverkehr AG, later re-named Air-Lloyd. CofA expired 29.10.60. Deemed uneconomic to renew the certificate and the aircraft was cancelled as withdrawn from use 15.11.62.

6468 Supplied to the Air Council with military serial **R5931**. Served with 2E&WS 11.39, 24Sqdn. 3.43, Metropolitan Com. Sqdn. 9.44, Technical Training Command Halton 4.46 until placed into storage 18MU 6.47. SOC on sale to Southern Aircraft (Gatwick) Ltd. 15.12.47. Reg'd **G-AKOO** [CofR 12102 8.12.47] and CofA no.10056 issued 2.12.48. Sold abroad 13.12.48, presumably to Chile where it was reported 4.52. U.K. reg'n actually cancelled 1.5.52. Fate unknown. This is thought to be the aircraft that became CC-CIC-0034 – see note 1, immediately following the reg'n to construction number cross-index.

6469 Supplied to the Air Council with military serial **R5932**. To 2E&WS 11.39, to 83Grp. Com. Flt. 4.43, to 3 Delivery Flight 5.43, to 13Grp. Com. Flt. 12.43, to 15Grp. Com. Flt., Speke 10.44, to 18MU 10.46. SOC on sale to Lancashire Aircraft Corporation Ltd., Samlesbury 9.12.47. Reg'd **G-AKNW** [CofR 12084 2.12.47] and CofA no.9980 issued 7.4.48. To Russell Littledale Whyham of Air Navigation & Trading Co. Ltd., Squires Gate 25.4.49. To Skyways Ltd., Langley 5.5.50. Reg'n cancelled on sale to Lebanon 23.6.50. Reg'd **LR-ABH** the same day for Arab Contracting and Trading Co. and operated by Saad Transport Co. Re-reg'd **OD-ABH,** still for Saad Transport 5.51. The aircraft caught fire and was burnt out 30.7.54 due to overpriming the port engine while starting up at Iraq Petroleum's H3 pumping station in Syria.

6470 Supplied to the Air Council with military serial **R5933**. To 2 E&WS 12.39, to BW Flight 10.42, to 54OTU 1.44, to 18MU 1.46. SOC on sale to Air Enterprises Ltd., Gatwick 4.12.47. Reg'd **G-AKNY** [CofR 12086 11.12.47] and CofA no.10014 issued 25.3.48. To Patrick Motors Ltd., Birmingham 22.1.49. Operated a proving flight from R.A.F. Chivenor to Lundy Island on 16.8.50, and was then used on a daily service to the island under the Devon Air Travel umbrella. To Wrafton Flying Club Ltd., Wrafton Gate, near Braunton 25.3.52 but actually merged with North Devon Flying Club Ltd. during the month and later formed a new charter company named Devonair 19.12.52. To Air Couriers (Transport) Ltd., Croydon 29.7.53. Cancelled on sale to France 3.10.60. and delivered ex Biggin Hill 4.10.60, arriving in Dakar, Senegal 17.10.60. Reg'd **F-OBRX** for Societe Ardic Aviation, Dakar, 13.10.60. Re-reg'd **6V-AAC** for Cie. Senegalaise des Transports Aeriens 4.63. Sold to Centre de Parachutisme Sportif de Dakar mid 1965. (Believed to have been rebuilt utilising parts obtained from G-AKJS c/n W.1002, as c/n was amended at this stage to 5933/W.1002. However, the reason for the prefix 5933 is unknown). Reserved as **F-BOHL** for Para Club, Chalon, 1970 but not taken up. Noted dismantled at Chalon 14.8.70 but it had disappeared by 5.71.

6471 Supplied to the Air Council with military serial **R5934**, sometime coded MD:X. To 2E&WS 12.39, to BW Flight, to 526Sqdn. 8.43, to 527Sqdn. 5.45, to Watton RWE F.C. 4.46, to 5MU 12.46. SOC on sale to Brooklands Aviation Ltd., Sywell 25.8.47. Reg'd **G-AKSH** [CofR 12169 31.1.48] and CofA no.9962 issued 14.5.48. To W. S. Shackleton Ltd. 15.11.51. Cancelled as sold abroad 22.11.51. Reg'd **VQ-FAM** for Katafanga Estates Ltd. t/a Fiji Airways Ltd. 11.2.52. Withdrawn from use on CofA expiry 17.3.55 and used as a spares source for VQ-FAN, c/n 6577.

6472 Reg'd **CF-BNG** for de Havilland Aircraft of Canada Ltd. 12.9.40, and shipped disassembled and without engines to Canada. To Ginger Coote Airways Ltd. 6.1.41. Taken over by Canadian Pacific Airways 1.2.41. Forced landed 9.3.46 due to an in-flight engine fire on floating ice on the St. Lawrence River at Great Lake, PQ, and destroyed by fire.

6473 Supplied to the Air Council with military serial **R9545**. Served with 2E&WS 1.40, A.T.A. HQ White Waltham 3.43, at 18MU 2.45, to A. & A.E.E. Boscombe Down 9.45. While parked at Boscombe, hit by a fuel bowser 17.12.47 and badly damaged. Initially assessed as Cat.B but later, SOC as Cat.E1 20.4.48.

6474 Supplied to the Air Council with military serial **R9546**. To 2E&WS 1.40, to Old Sarum 4.43, to A.T.A. HQ White Waltham 5.43, to Vickers 8.45, to 18MU 4.46. SOC on sale to W. A. Rollason Ltd., Croydon 19.12.47. Reg'd **G-AKOK** [CofR 12098 4.12.47] and CofA no.10138 issued 2.6.48. To Mannin Airways Ltd., Ronaldsway 18.6.48 but in service with North-West Airlines (IoM) Ltd. around this time. Change of ownership notified 20.3.52 and cancelled as sold abroad 1.4.52. Reg'd **F-BGPK** to Soc. Aigle Azure Indochine, Hanoi 30.4.52. CofA expired 2.5.53 but permit issued for single flight to Saigon 15.9.53. Sold to Cie. Laotienne de Commerce et Transport 6.54, presumably for spares use. Reg'n cancelled as withdrawn from use 23.9.54.

6475 Supplied to the Air Council with military serial **R9547**. To 2E&WS 1.40, to 2BW Flt 11.42, to 1680 Flt 3.44. SOC 1.12.45.

6476 Supplied to the Air Council with military serial **R9548**, and sometime coded THA:A. To 2E&WS 1.40, to 43Grp. Com. Flt. 6.41, to Halton A.T.C. Flt., 3.43, to 5MU 4.47. SOC on sale to Denham Air Services 11.3.48 but cancelled. Reg'd as **G-AKVU** [CofR 12255 10.3.48] for Surrey Financial Trust Ltd., Croydon, one of Charles Allen's many companies! To Aircraft & Engineering Services Ltd., Croydon 19.3.48. CofA no.10397 issued 24.2.49. To Patrick Motors Ltd., Birmingham 30.9.49. To W. S. Shackleton Ltd. 30.5.50. To Goodhew Aviation Ltd., Kidlington 26.10.50. To Transair Ltd., Croydon 17.3.52. Reg'n cancelled as sold abroad to France 1.4.52. Reg'd **F-BGPM** to Soc. Aigle Azur Indochine, Hanoi and French CofA issued 25.6.52. Destroyed by fire 13.2.53 whilst starting engines at Siem Reap, Cambodia and reg'n cancelled 17.6.53.

6477   Supplied to the Air Council with military serial **R9549**. To 20MU 2.40, to 44MU 10.41, to 24Sqdn. 8.42, to 18MU 11.42, to 47MU 1.43. SOC as sold in South Africa. And shipped per S.S. *Clan McNairn* 2-3.43. Reg'd **SAAF1363** for the South African Air Force 3.43. Used by Signals School, and then to 61Sqdn. 11.44. Disposed of at 15AD 2.7.46, and reg'd **ZS-BCD** for Owenair (Pty) Ltd. 21.10.46. To O. G. Davies, Youngsfield, but still operated by Owenair. Cancelled on sale abroad '53 and reg'd **VP-YKJ** for Fishair (Pvt) Ltd. 23.5.53. Reg'd **F-OBKH** for Societe Franco Africaine d'Exploitation, Libreville, 10.58. To G.A.A. 1959. Reported destroyed 8.61.

6478   Supplied to the Air Council with military serial **R9550**. To 20MU 3.40, to A.T.A. HQ White Waltham 12.41, to Royal Aircraft Establishment, Farnborough 4.44, to Hendon, to 5MU 1.46. SOC on sale to Field Consolidated Aircraft Services Ltd., Croydon. Reg'd **G-AHPT** [CofR 10265 22.5.46]. To Island Air Charters Ltd., Jersey 24.8.46 and CofA no.7912 issued 6.10.46. To Aerocontacts Ltd., Gatwick 11.5.51. To Wright Aviation Ltd., Speke 25.3.52. Taken over by Dragon Airways Ltd., Speke 16.2.54 and named *Peter Tare*. To Don Everall (Aviation) Ltd., Birmingham 10.2.56 and operated almost exclusively for Tarmac Ltd. Whilst operating a Tarmac flight inbound to Leverstock Green from Wolverhampton, the Rapide overshot when attempting to land on the partially completed St. Albans by-pass 7.7.59. The aircraft hit a lorry and burnt out on the A414, 2 miles east of Leverstock Green. One passenger killed. Cancelled 18.8.59.

6479   Supplied to the Air Council with military serial **R9551**. Initially to 12MU 4.40 but to 18MU 8.40. Served with No.1 Com. Flt. Hendon, 12.40, to 43Grp. Com. Flt. 3.41 and to No.1 Camouflage Unit. Ran out of fuel in bad visibility 25.3.41 and crashed at Yoxall, Staffordshire. SOC 14.4.41.

6480   Supplied to the Air Council with military serial **R9552**. Initially at 12MU 4.40 but to 18MU 8.40. Served with 1CF at Hendon, 12.40, Halton 8.42, 58OTU 8.42, 57OTU 6.43, 18MU 12.43, 13Grp. Com. Flt. 7.45, to No.1 Flying Unit, Pershore, 1.46. To storage 18MU 4.46. SOC on sale to Air Navigation and Trading Co. Ltd., Squires Gate 15.12.47 but cancelled. Instead, reg'd as **G-AKRO** to East Anglian Flying Services Ltd., Southend [CofR 12151 17.1.48]. Collected from Dumfries 27.1.48 and CofA no.9994 issued 11.5.48 entering service with East Anglian the same day. To Inter-City Air Services Ltd. 4.49. To Lancashire Aircraft Corporation Ltd., Samlesbury 11.51. Cancelled when sold abroad 10.3.54. Reg'd as **F-OAOY** for Aero Club de Colomb-Bechar, Algeria 16.3.54. Burnt out 22.10.54 while starting engines at Colomb-Bechar. Reg'n cancelled 27.12.54.

6481   Supplied to the Air Council with military serial **R9553**. Initially to 12MU 5.40 but to 18MU 8.40 and to 27MU 4.41. Served with 10FPP 4.41, to 9MU 12.41, to Honeybourne Ferry Training Unit 12.41, to 24Sqdn. 5.42. The aircraft was destroyed while attempting to regain the airfield, it crash landed and overturned at Rednal, Shropshire 27.4.43. SOC as Cat.E 27.4.43 with 295.05 hours total time.

6482   Supplied to the Air Council with military serial **R9554**. Delivered to 5MU 5.40. Served with 7FPP 11.40, 10FPP 4.41, HQ FPP 5.41 and thence to 29MU. To Northolt 6.42, No.2 Delivery Flt 3.43, 5MU 8.44, Stn. Flt. Gatwick, Stn. Flt. Redhill 10.44 and to 5MU for storage 3.46. SOC on sale to Denham Air Services Ltd. 11.3.48 but cancelled. Instead reg'd **G-AKTZ** to Derek John Hayles, Portsmouth [CofR 12211 3.3.48] and CofA no.10057 issued 5.5.48. To Airwork Ltd., Croydon 9.6.48. To Birkett Air Service Ltd., Croydon 25.10.50. This company operated joy flights at London Air Port until about 1952, but ceased operations in 4.53 due to 'lack of joy flight contracts'. To Morton Air Services Ltd., Croydon 14.5.53. To Iraq Petroleum Transport Co. Ltd., Haifa 25.8.54. To Gordon, Woodroffe and Co. Ltd., London W1 4.9.56. To Bahamas Helicopters (U.K.) Ltd. 12.4.57 and used on an oil survey contract in North Africa. Later renamed World Wide

Helicopters (U.K.) Ltd. The aircraft suffered a burst tyre on landing in the desert near Benghazi, Libya 27.5.57 and the damaged airframe was returned to Croydon, arriving there 23.10.58. However, it was not repaired and noted, still in dismantled condition 12.58. Reg'n cancelled 23.4.63.

6483   Supplied to the Air Council with military serial **R9555**. To 5MU 4.40, to 7FPP 11.40, to 2FPP 2.41, to 37MU 4.42, to No.2 Signals School 7.42, to No.4 Del. Flt. Turnhouse 3.43. SOC as Cat.E 20.3.46.

6484   Supplied to the Air Council with military serial **R9556**. Delivered to 5MU 5.40. Served with 7FPP 11.40, A.T.A. HQ White Waltham 9.41, at 27MU 3.42, to 24Sqdn. 6.42 and 4 Radio School 11.43 until moved to 18MU for storage 1.46. SOC on sale to Tyne Taxis Ltd., Newcastle-upon-Tyne 27.5.48. Reg'n **G-ALAS** allocated [CofR 12378 1.6.48] but not taken up at the owner's request due to the unfortunate connotations. Instead, received reg'n **G-ALEJ** [CofR 12469 1.6.48] and CofA no.10173 issued 1.4.49. To Lancashire Aircraft Corporation Ltd., Samlesbury 24.6.49. While en route Birmingham to Blackpool 14.9.56 the cockpit filled with smoke and the aircraft forced landed at Eccleshall, 10 miles south of Newcastle-under-Lyme, sustaining extensive damage to wings and undercarriage. Cancelled as destroyed 22.11.56.

6485   Supplied to the Air Council with military serial **R9557**. To 9MU 5.40, to 3FPP 11.40. SOC as Cat.E 11.1.45.

6486   Supplied to the Air Council with military serial **R9558**. To 9MU 5.40, to 3FPP 11.40, to 18MU 4.44, to Vickers 5.44. Reg'd **G-AHJA** [CofR 10098 8.4.46] for Vickers-Armstrongs Ltd. and CofA no.7624 issued 8.5.47. Company name changed to Vickers-Armstrong (Aircraft) Ltd. 22.8.55 and again, to Vickers-Armstrong (Supermarine) Ltd. 1958. To Conway Hunt Ltd., Fairoaks 10.6.59 and operated by Universal Flying Services Ltd. To Swansea Airways Ltd. 11.60. To Mexfield Aviation Co. (Ireland) Ltd., Dublin 22.11.61. Seized by H.M. Customs at Luton 6.12.61 and believed remained unflown until 28.6.63. To Air Navigation and Trading Co. Ltd., Squires Gate 18.6.63. To David John Moores, Castle Donington 6.6.67. To Trent Valley Aviation Ltd., Castle Donington 28.3.68. The aircraft nosed over on landing 20.5.69 after a training flight at Castle Donington due to overbraking when it had TT 3211.10. Conveyed to Nipper Aircraft's hangar for survey and possible repair, but the cost was more than the insured value of the aircraft. Remained hangared until October when moved outside, but in November, Trent Valley went into liquidation and Nipper Aircraft put a lien on the aircraft to cover the cost of five months hangarage. The aircraft then remained at Castle Donington until 7.70 when it was sold 'as is' to the R.A.F. Sports Parachute Association for use as spares. Dismantled and conveyed to Abingdon 19.7.70 by Halton apprentices as a training exercise, before being moved to the fire dump there and presumably subsequently burnt.

6487   Supplied to the Air Council with military serial **R9559**. Delivered to 9MU 5.40. Served with 3FPP 11.40, Halton 8.43, Technical Training Command Com. Flt. 8.45, Technical Training Staff College Flt. White Waltham 3.46, Radio Calibration Com. Sqdn. 11.46. Into storage at 18MU 1.47. SOC on sale to D. J. Adie 31.5.47. Reg'd **G-AKED** for A. Hamson and Son Ltd. t/a Air Charter Experts, Sywell 25.8.47 and CofA no.9702 issued 20.1.48. Company taken over by Manx Air Charter 8.47. To L. E. H. Airways Ltd., London WC2 3.2.48. To Walter Maurice Andrews, Tollerton 16.12.49. To Patrick Motors Ltd., Birmingham 21.11.50. To Airlines (Jersey) Ltd. 9.4.51. Converted to Mk4 standard 2.54 and to Eric Bemrose Ltd., Speke, 10.3.55. Cancelled on sale to France 26.11.55. Reg'd **F-DABY** for Societe Norafor, Casablanca and French CofA issued 14.3.56. Reg'd **F-OBHH** for Societe Generale d'Affretements Aeriens - CMTA and further CofA issued 31.3.58. To CGTA 9.60. Returned to CMTA 1.61. CofA suspended 8.62 but actual fate unknown.

6488   Supplied to the Air Council with military serial **R9560**. Delivered to 12MU 5.40, moved on to 18MU 8.40 and to 8MU 2.41. Served with HQ SFPP 6.41, at 9MU 1.42 and to Sealand 12.42 before passing into store 5MU 7.44. SOC on sale to Cambrian Airways 11.3.48. Reg'd **G-AKUB** [CofR 12213 3.3.48] to S. K. Davis, Bridgend, acting for Cambrian and CofA no.10038 issued 2.4.48. To J. H. Watts t/a Cambrian Air Enterprises, Pengam Moors 4.48 and named *Glamorgan*. To Airwork Ltd., Croydon 25.1.55. Cancelled as sold abroad to Persia 11.6.55. Reg'd **EP-ADN** to to Iraanse Aardolie Exploratie en Productie

DH89 c/n 6474. G-AKOK in service with North-West Airlines (Isle of Man) Ltd. Sold abroad early 1952, it briefly operated airline services in Indochina and Laos until French certification expired late 1953.

DH89 c/n 6505. Unusually, X7332 served with both the R.A.F. and Royal Navy. Although sold to Hants & Sussex Aviation, deemed uneconomical to transport it south and burnt at Lossiemouth 1960.

DH89 c/n 6483. Delivered to 5MU at Kemble in April 1940 and R9555 initially served with 7 Ferry Pilots Pool at Sherburn-in-Elmet. Written-off in an accident and struck off charge March 1946.

DH89 c/n 6530. G-AJXB served Eagle Aviation for 10 months until sold to Sweden. The owner emigrated to Australia and flew the aircraft out with the family and doubtless, the kitchen sink aboard!

DH89 c/n 6492. Operated by East African Airways Corporation from January 1956 until 1960, as 5H-AAM, was destroyed by fire on engine start-up September 1966. (Keith Butcher/Old Aero Prints).

DH89 c/n 6532. From delivery at 18MU, Dumfries in June 1941, served throughout at Abbotsinch until categorised as beyond repair there and struck off charge in April 1946.

DH89 c/n 6494. Served with Westland Aircraft at Yeovil on communication duties throughout the war and struck off charge to them April 1946. An ignominious demise at Portsmouth's tip 1962!

DH89 c/n 6539. Modified when in civilian hands as a nine passenger transport with the cockpit bulkhead removed and extra windows installed. Seen here with Westair, sometime between 1957 & 1963.

Maatschappij N.V. (Iranian Oil Exploration and Producing Co.) 6.55. Fate unknown.

6489   Supplied to the Air Council with military serial **R9561**. To 12MU 5.40, to 18MU 7.40, to 7FPP 11.40. Taking off from Prestwick 22.2.41 for Kemble, the aircraft swung and control was not regained before it hit the perimeter fence. SOC as Cat.E 3.3.41.

6490   Supplied to the Air Council with military serial **R9562**. Delivered to 12MU 5.40 and then commenced a tour of Maintenance Units, at 18MU 7.40, to 15MU 2.41 and finally to 48MU 10.41! Served at No.4 Signals School 8.42, 43Grp. Com. Flt. 3.43, Northolt Stn. Flt. 10.43, Metropolitan Com. Sqdn. 10.45, Halton 9.46 before being placed into store at 18MU 6.47. SOC on sale to Air Navigation and Trading Co. Ltd., Squires Gate 15.12.47 but cancelled. Instead, reg'd as **G-AKSF** [CofR 12167 14.2.48] to Scottish Aviation Ltd., Prestwick and CofA no.10032 issued 23.6.48. Caught fire and burnt out while running up engines at Prestwick 23.7.49, there were no casualties. The register records "destroyed by fire" 25.7.49 but reg'n not actually cancelled until 8.8.49.

6491   Supplied to the Air Council with military serial **R9563**. To 9MU 5.40. Officially transferred to the Royal Navy 29.8.40, but noted already at Donibristle a couple of days earlier. Flew into high ground in bad visibility on a local flight from Donibristle and was wrecked 7.41.

6492   Supplied to the Air Council with military serial **R9564**. Delivered to 9MU 5.40. Served with 3FPP 11.40, Kenley 2.44 and Gatwick 8.44 before passing into storage at 18 MU 4.46. SOC as sold to Air Enterprises Ltd., Gatwick, 9.12.47. Reg'd **G-AKOB** [CofR 12089 11.12.47] and CofA no.9964 issued 19.3.48. Named *The Sandown Flyer*. To Eagle Aviation Ltd., Blackbushe 2.10.52. Transferred to Dragon Airways Ltd., Speke 20.3.54. Cancelled on sale to Kenya 30.11.55. Reg'd **VP-KNS** to East African Airways Corporation 12.55 and painted up at Croydon. To Seychelles-Kilimanjaro Air Transport Ltd. 1960. Re-reg'd **5H-AAM** still for Seychelles-Kilimanjaro 1.65. Burnt out on start up Dar-es-Salaam 13.9.66.

6493   Supplied to the Air Council with military serial **X7320** but retained by de Havilland 8.40. Eventually to 18MU 2.42 and served with 4 Radio School 4.42. SOC as Cat.E 30.10.45.

6494   Supplied to the Air Council with military serial **X7321**. To 9MU 8.40. Operated by Westland Aircraft Co. Ltd., Yeovil 10.40. SOC on sale to Westland Aircraft and reg'd **G-AHLF** [CofR 10153 26.4.46] and CofA no.7706 issued 20.6.46. Reg'd to Hants and Sussex Aviation Ltd. 27.5.58 but delivered to Portsmouth earlier on 19.5.58. Thought to be destined for a French operator, in fact to Agricultural Aviation Co. Ltd., Panshanger 1.1.59. Leased to Luton Airways during the summer of 1959, but Agricultural Aviation failed and the aircraft was repossessed by Hants and Sussex Aviation, being delivered back to Portsmouth 2.11.59. Reg'd to Hants & Sussex Aviation again 4.12.59. Delivered to Skycraft Services, Southend, 6.1.60, but ownership to Robert Alan Short, Biggin Hill 15.2.60. CofA expired 22.2.60. To F. A. Frampton Ltd., Biggin Hill 18.7.60. Taken to Portsmouth 9.60, where it was officially withdrawn from use 1.11.62. Subsequently stripped for spares and thrown on the Portsmouth Corporation municipal rubbish tip and was burnt there 12.62. Notified to registration authorities 8.4.63.

6495   Supplied to the Air Council with military serial **X7322**. Delivered to 9MU 8.40, to 6FPP 11.40, to 19MU 2.41, to 43Grp. Com. Flt. 4.41, to de Havilland 5.41. SOC 12.6.41.

6496   Supplied to the Air Council with military serial **X7323**. Delivered to 9MU 8.40. Served with A. & A.E.E. 12.40 and then briefly with 43Grp. Com. Flt. To 9MU 3.41, Hendon Com. Flt. 5.41, No.1 Signals School 9.42, to Staverton 9.44 and finally, to storage at 18MU 6.46. SOC on sale to Field Aircraft Services Ltd., Croydon 18.2.47. Reg'd **G-AJFM** [CofR 11252 29.1.47]. Sold abroad to Kenya 15.4.47. CofA no.8981 issued 6.9.47 and reg'd **VP-KEE** for East African Airways Corporation 1947. Cancelled on sale to Israel 30.9.51, the aircraft had, in fact, been delivered to Israel in 1948, being reg'd **4X-AEH** for Arkia Israel Inland Airways 13.11.49. Later with the Israeli Defence Force as **IDFAF 1310**. Shortly after take-off 2.7.54 from Lydda, both engines failed, compelling a forced landing. The Rapide overturned and was destroyed. At the subsequent inquiry, it was reported that water

was discovered in the fuel tanks. Some parts used during the rebuild of 4X-AEI (c/n 6895).

6497   Supplied to the Air Council with military serial **X7324**. Delivered to 9MU 8.40, to 3FPP 11.40, to A.T.A. HQ White Waltham 12.42, to Skeabrae Stn. Flt. 8.43, to Metropolitan Com. Sqdn. 11.44, to 5MU 1.45. SOC on sale to North Sea Air Transport Ltd., Hanworth 8.11.46. Reg'd **G-AIWG** [CofR 11025 20.11.46] and CofA 8812 issued 6.1.47. Later moved to Brough. Sold abroad 25.1.50. To E. J. Connellan, Alice Springs NT reg'd **VH-AIK** 2.50. Nominal ownership change to Connellan Airways Ltd. 31.1.51. Caught fire when starting engines Turkey Creek NT 29.9.51 and totally burnt out. Reg'n cancelled the same month.

6498   Supplied to the Air Council with military serial **X7325**. Delivered to 9MU 9.40, 7FPP at Sherburn-in-Elmet 1.41 where it was attached to Blackburn Aircraft for use as a Swordfish delivery crew ferry aircraft. To 18MU 3.41, HQ FPP 4.41, 10MU 8.41, No.2 Signals School 8.42, 18MU 2.44, 1680 Flt 3.44, Prestwick TC 4.46. Handed over to the Ministry of Supply and passed to A.A.J.C. at Prestwick 16.4.46. Reg'd **G-AIHN** [CofR 10684 5.9.46] to Railway Air Services Ltd., Speke and CofA no.8512 issued 25.10.46 following conversion to civil configuration at Speke. Absorbed by B.E.A.C. on formation 1.2.47. Transferred to Gibraltar Airways Ltd. 26.11.47. To A. J. Whittemore (Aeradio) Ltd., Croydon 7.1.54. To General Mining and Finance Corporation Ltd., Johannesburg 24.3.54. U.K. reg'n cancelled as sold in South Africa 23.7.54 and reg'd **ZS-DJT** as a Mk4 21.4.55. To African Air Photo (Pty) Ltd. by 1959, and sometime with Ladysmith Air Charter. Crashed and ground-looped at Ladysmith 11.10.63. Dismantled, used for spares and some remains were still visible at Ladysmith in 1974, consisting of the tail section and empennage and the main cabin structure. Presented to the SAAF Museum 1975 and was stored dismantled at Lanseria.

6499   Supplied to the Air Council with military serial **X7326**. Delivered to 18MU 9.40 and to 6MU 2.41. Served with A.T.A. HQ White Waltham from 12.41 until returned to 18MU 8.43. SOC to A.A.J.C. 10.43. Reg'd **G-AGJF** [CofR 9486 25.10.43] to Scottish Airways Ltd., Renfrew and CofA no.7029 issued 29.10.43. Absorbed by B.E.A.C. on formation 1.2.47. Crashed on take off Isle of Barra, Outer Hebrides 6.8.47. Reg'n cancelled 4.9.47.

6500   Supplied to the Air Council with military serial **X7327**. Delivered to 18MU 9.40. Served with 7FPP 11.40, 9MU 10.41, Macmerry 11.42, 18MU 1.43, 1680Flt 8.43, 510Sqdn. 9.43, 526Sqdn. 2.44, 527Sqdn. 5.45, Watton RWE FC 4.46. Into storage 5MU 1.47. Sold to Field Aircraft Services Ltd., Croydon 29.5.47. Reg'd **G-AJSK** [CofR 11549 8.5.47] but cancelled as sold abroad 16.6.47. Restored to Field Aircraft 17.1.48 and CofA no.9373 issued 27.4.48. To British European Airways Corporation 17.5.49 and later named *Lord Lister*. Transferred to Gibraltar Airways Ltd. 1.1.53. To A. J. Whittemore (Aeradio) Ltd., Croydon 13.1.54. Cancelled as sold in East Africa 14.2.54. To J. E. F. Wilkins, Mazinde t/a Caspar Air Charters and Agencies 9.53 as **VP-KMD**. To Airspray (East Africa) Ltd. in 1955. To Richard Costain (Africa) Ltd. 25.4.56 and reg'd **VP-YOE**. Cancelled 2.2.59 "at owner's request".

6501   Supplied to the Air Council with military serial **X7328**. Delivered to 18MU 9.40, then HQ SFPP 1.41, No.11 Ferry Flt. On landing at Abbotsinch 8.6.41, the aircraft struck a ridge, "ballooned" and stalled into ground nose first. SOC as Cat.E 15.6.41.

6502   Supplied to the Air Council with military serial **X7329**. Delivered to 18MU 10.40. Served with 7FPP 11.40, A.T.A. HQ White Waltham 7.41, 18MU 1.44, de Havilland 2.44. SOC as Cat.E 20.5.46.

6503   Supplied to the Air Council with military serial **X7330**. Delivered to de Havilland 1.41, then 18MU 8.41 and to 47MU 2.42. To India from Birkenhead Dock per *SS City of Hong Kong* 18.3.42. Known to have been with 1SFTS, India 3.43. SOC on sale to India National Airways 9.5.46 and reg'd **VT-ARR** 12.43. Sold to Indian Air Supply and Transport Co. Ltd., Calcutta 4.6.46. Name changed to Air Survey Co. of India Ltd. in 1948. Reduced to produce by Air Survey at Calcutta the following year and reg'n cancelled.

6504   Supplied to the Air Council with military serial **X7331**. Initially to No.2 Del. Flt. 3.41, then Colerne Stn. Flt. 10.41,

418Sqdn 2.42, No.3 Del. Flt. 11.42, 18MU 8.43, No.4 Radio School 5.44. SOC on sale to Russell Littledale Whyham of Air Navigation and Trading Co. Ltd., Squires Gate 15.12.47. Reg'd as **G-AKOY** [CofR 12111 31.12.47] and CofA no.10016 issued 21.5.48. To Lancashire Aircraft Corporation Ltd., Samlesbury 3.5.49. Sold abroad to Pakistan 11.4.53. To Crescent Air Transport Ltd., Karachi 5.53, reg'd **AP-AGM**. Sold abroad 9.56. To Ste. Tunisienne de Reparations Aeronautique et de Construction, operated as Aero Sahara and reg'd **F-OAYN**. CofA issued 27.6.57. Badly damaged by fire in hangar at Tunis 12.12.57. Reported as a total loss and reg'n cancelled 31.3.58.

6505   Supplied to Air Council with military serial **X7332**. Initially to No.3 Del. Flt. then No.4 Signals School 4.42, 18MU 11.44. To Royal Navy 17.10.45. To Evanton 12.45. Stored at Crail about 10.46. With Lossiemouth Stn. Flt. by 4.48. Further service with GN 1.49 to 1.50, de Havilland 7.50 to 1.51, AO 7.51 to 1.53 (delivered to Arbroath ex de Havilland 12.2.51), LM 7.53 to 7.54. Joined Midlands Air Division 24.8.55. Noted with Bramcote 1844Sqdn. BR/890 6.56. On charge with Bramcote Stn. Flt. by 7.57 still as BR/890. To Lossiemouth AHU 15.1.58 and ordered to be reduced to spares on site 13.1.59. Parked awaiting disposal at Lossiemouth (no wheels) early 1960. Put up to tender as scrap and purchased with others by Hants and Sussex Aviation Ltd. 8.60. Reportedly few usable components due to bad condition of aircraft and therefore cut up and burnt at Lossiemouth 8.60.

6506   Supplied to the Air Council with military serial **X7333**. Initially to No.4 Del. Flt. 3.41. On taking off from Acklington on a ferry flight to Grangemouth, the aircraft swung and struck a hedge on the airfield boundary, caught fire and burnt 8.6.41. Total time when accident occurred, just 91:55. SOC as Cat.E 8.6.41. Salvage to No.1MPRU (Metal Produce and Recovery Unit at Cowley) 6.41.

6507   Supplied to the Air Council with military serial **X7334**. Delivered to 18MU 3.41 but moved on to 47MU 4.41. Passed to South African Air Force as **SAAF1353** 25.5.41. Del to 9AD 5.41. Served with 2AS 27.8.41, 62AS 7.41 until at least 10.42. Recommended for overhaul 9.44. Records suggest that the aircraft be issued to 25Grp. Com. Flt. after overhaul. To 61Sqdn. 3.45. Surplus to requirements at 61Sqdn. 1.46. To 15AD for storage 12.4.46. Offered for sale and a figure of £1485 from Maj. J. W. O. Billingham of Capetown was accepted 31.10.46. To Aviation Industries and Associated Services (Pty) Ltd., Cape Town. Reg'd **ZS-BEF** 18.12.46. To South West Air Transport (Pty) Ltd in 1954. Still owned in 1957. Sold abroad 12.58 and registration concelled 28.6.59. To Societe Air Madagascar and reg'd **F-OBIO**. CofA issued 27.4.59. Re-reg'd **5R-MAO** still with Societe Air Madagascar 1.63. Reg'n cancelled 7.67.

6508   Supplied to the Air Council with military serial **X7335**. Delivered to 18MU 3.41 but moved to 47MU 4.41. SOC as sold in South Africa. Del to 9AD 5.41. To South African Air Force as **SAAF1354** 25.5.41. Served with 2AS 27.8.41, 62AS 7.41 until at least 11.42 and 61Sqdn. 11.44. Surplus to requirements at 61Sqdn. 1.46. To 15AD for storage 23.3.46 until 26.3.46. To 28Sqdn. 12.4.46. Offered for sale at 15AD and sold to African Flying Services Ltd., Grand Central 26.8.46 for £1386. Reg'd **ZS-BCS** 8.10.46. "Cancelled 26.9.50 as scrapped". To Victoria Falls Airways Ltd. 5.56 and reg'd **VP-YNU**. To Air Brousse SPRL and reg'd **OO-CJW** 16.2.59. CofA no.302. Re-reg'd **9O-CJW** still with Air Brousse 17.3.61. Re-reg'd again, as **9Q-CJW** with Air Brousse after 8.9.62. Ownership later changed to A.M.A.Z., Kinshasa, date unknown.

6509   Supplied to the Air Council with military serial **X7336**. Delivered to 18MU 3.41, then 614Sqdn. 4.41, 225Sqdn. 9.42, Macmerry 12.42, 18MU 6.43. Reg'd **G-AGIF** [CofR 9462 15.7.43] to Great Western and Southern Airlines Ltd., Liverpool but normally kept at Inverness. CofA no.7012 issued. To Scottish Airways Ltd., Renfrew 6.3.44. To British European Airways Corporation on formation 1.2.47. Ground-looped and nosed over on the ramp at Hatston, Orkney, but repaired. To Ulster Aviation Ltd., Newtownards 23.4.48. Ulster Aviation was absorbed into North-West Airlines (IOM) Ltd. during 1948/49. CofA expired at Newtownards 24.1.50 and cancelled from register 13.10.50. Finally burnt at Newtownards 4.54.

6510   Supplied to the Air Council with military serial **X7337**. Initially to 18MU 3.41, then 47MU 5.41. To South African Air Force as **SAAF1356** 7.6.41. Del to 9AD. To 2AS 28.8.41. To 62AS

8.41. High altitude performance tests 25.9.41. To 61Sqdn. 4.45. Surplus to requirements at 61Sqdn. 1.46. To 15AD for short term storage. To 28Sqdn. 18.3.46. Disposed of at 15AD to Copper and Kotze 5.7.46 for £1350 and reg'd **ZS-BCI** 2.9.46. To South West Air Transport 11.46. Became South West African Airways Ltd. To Resident Motors Ltd. To Anglo-Transvaal Consolidated Investment Co. Ltd. and operated by Africair Ltd. by 1951. Whilst on lease to Commercial Air Sevices Ltd., the aircraft caught fire on starting engines and burnt out at Welkom 6.9.52.

6511   Supplied to the Air Council with military serial **X7338**. Initially to 9MU 3.41, then HQ SFPP 5.41, No.10 Ferry Flt. 6.41, 12MU 6.41, 19MU 10.41, No.2 Signals School 10.42, A.T.A. HQ White Waltham 3.43, 19Grp. Com. Flt. 7.44. At Witney awaiting disposal 5.46. To 5MU 2.47 - "repairs cancelled" recat E and sold 5.47. SOC as sold to Aircraft and Engineering Services Ltd., Croydon 29.5.47. Reg'd **G-AJMY** [CofR 11437 13.6.47]. CofA No.9901 issued 17.2.48 after conversion at Croydon. TTSN 641hr. To Siverwright Airways Ltd., Manchester 30.3.48. Siverwright Airways ceased operations in March 1951 and all aircraft ownership was transferred to Silverwright Transport and Storage Ltd. and stored at Barton. To Melba Airways Ltd., Manchester-Barton 6.6.51. To Wolverhampton Aviation Ltd. 17.7.51. Sold abroad to Portugese Guinea 21.8.52. CofA renewed at Elstree 23.10.52. TTSN 20.10.10. CofA records state that the aircraft "had not flown since 5.12.51, except for a delivery flight to Elstree under a Permit to Fly at time of CofA renewal". To Government of Portugese Guinea, Bissau 8.52 reg'd **CR-GAK**. Withdrawn from use, date unknown and used as a spares source for CR-GAI & CR-GAJ.

6512   Supplied to the Air Council with military serial **X7339**. Initially to 8MU 3.41, then 47MU 4.41. To South African Air Force as **SAAF 1355** 7.6.41. TOC 4.9.41 and delivered to 9AD. To ZAS 28.8.41. To 62AS 9.41. Aircraft placed before a Board of Survey at No.1 Air Depot, Voortrekkerhoogte 9.6.43. After examination of the airframe, the board found that it was damaged through wear and tear to an overall package of 45%. It was felt that repair was not an economical proposition, particularly in view of a shortage of spares and it was recommended that it be written off charge and reduced to produce - all serviceable and repairable components to be taken on charge with a view to repairing other aircraft and all scrap metal disposed of through the "Q" Salvage Organisation. SOC 12.43. SOC 1.1.47 in South Africa in general clear up of Air Historical Branch files.

6513   Supplied to the Air Council with military serial **X7340**. Delivered to 9MU 4.41 but to 6MU 5.41. Served with A.T.A. HQ White Waltham 6.41, No.2 Radio School 8.43 and No.4 Radio School 3.45. To storage 18MU 8.46. SOC on sale to Air Navigation and Trading Co. Ltd., Squires Gate 15.12.47 but cancelled. Instead to East Anglian Flying Services Ltd., Southend and reg'd **G-AKRN** [CofR 12150 17.1.48]. Collected from Dumfries 27.1.48. CofA No. 9993 issued 24.3.48. Withdrawn from use at Ipswich after CofA expired 27.6.60. Company name changed to Channel Airways Ltd. 5.11.60 but reg'n cancelled 4.61. In Tradair hangar at Southend 10.64 to be used as spares for East Anglian's sole DH89 G-AEMH. No action taken and still in store at Southend in 1972. Reported as owned by I. Jones and moved by road from Southend to Burnham-on-Crouch 19.8.72 for storage pending sale. Cancelled as "destroyed" 14.2.73. Acquired by J. E. Pierce, Chirk by late 1978 for rebuild, possibly with G-AHAG and G-AIUL to make one aircraft in 1979.

6514   Supplied to the Air Council with military serial **X7341**. Initially to 9MU 4.41, then 53OTU 5.41, 58OTU 4.43, 18MU 12.43. To Royal Navy 3.4.45. Delivered into storage at Lee on Solent 3.5.45. To Christchurch 4.6.45. From storage at Lee on Solent to 736Sqdn. B Flt at Woodvale 14.7.45. To Hatston Stn. Flt. 18.8.45. Later to Donibristle Stn. Flt. and to de Havilland at Witney (for overhaul?) 27.9.45. To 782Sqdn., Donibristle 20.6.46. To Crail 26.6.46 then to 701Sqdn., Heston 29.8.46. To Crail 25.10.46, then to 781Sqdn., Lee on Solent 7.11.46, To storage at Stretton 8.7.47 and to Evanton Stn. Flt. 3.9.47. To AHU, Stretton 14.10.47, then Eglinton 14.1.48. To Stretton (No. 2 Ferry Flt?) 19.2.48 and to de Havilland at Witney again (for overhaul?) 25.10.48. To Stretton 18.5.49 and thence to de Havilland 25.10.48 until 1.49 at least. To ST 18.5.49. To AO 16.5.50. With 728Sqdn. Donibristle 14.7.51. Cat4 to de Havilland for repair 4.9.51. To AO 30.1.52. To Lossiemouth AHU 17.3.53. To Shorts Ferry Flt. Rochester. To Lossiemouth AHU 24.5.55 and to Lossiemouth Stn. Flt. 9.55. To Brawdy HQ Flt. 30.11.55. To 7FTS, Valley 7.56 to 9.56. Returned to Brawdy by 1.57. To Shorts Ferry Flt. Rochester 3.3.58. To

Lossiemouth AHU 18.7.58. Stored at Lossiemouth until WOC 22.6.63. Sold to Anglo Diesel Co., Poplar High Street, London E14 and left Lossiemouth 5.7.63. Ultimate fate not recorded.

6515   Supplied to the Air Council with military serial **X7342**. Initially to 9MU 4.41, then 56OTU 6.41, 54OTU 8.44, 53OTU 9.44, 18MU 2.45. SOC on sale to Oxford Aircraft 11.12.47. To Wng. Cmdr. Barry Thomson Aikman t/a Aikman Airways Ltd., Croydon and reg'd **G-AKND** [CofR 12066 29.11.47]. CofA No. 9978 issued 1.4.48. Probably not operated by Aikman Airways on their joy riding and charter services but converted by them, perhaps at Thame, for onward sale. To William and Henry Charles Victor Hext, London SW9 13.4.48. Forced landed on beach 110 miles North of Mombasa 28.6.48. Obviously any damage was light as sold abroad 12.8.48. To Jivraj's Air Service as **VP-KGE** in 1948. Reduced to spares in 1950.

6516   Supplied to the Air Council with military serial **X7343**. Initially to 9MU 4.41, then 52OTU 6.41, Inverness 9.41, St. Mawgan 1.44, 5MU 11.46. SOC on sale to Field Aircraft Services Ltd., Croydon 30.5.47. Had already been reg'd **G-AJNA** [CofR 11439 8.5.47] and CofA no.9372 issued 23.7.47. To Franco-British Commercial & Industrial Co. Ltd. 15.7.47. Departed U.K. as **G-AJNA** 10.10.47 for Toussus le-Noble en route to Antananarivo. Cancelled as sold abroad 10.12.47 and reg'd **F-BEDI** to Soc. Air Madagascar 12.47. CofA issued 3.1.48. Later named *Antalaha*. Struck a tree and crashed into a swamp whilst landing in poor visibility at Tamatave 30.5.48. One killed.

6517   Supplied to the Air Council with military serial **X7344**. Initially to 9MU 16.4.41, then No.1 Com. Flt. Hendon 10.5.41, 18MU 10.10.42. To A.A.J.C. and reg'd **G-AGJG** [CofR 9487 25.10.43] to Scottish Airways Ltd., Renfrew. Delivered to Inverness 7.1.44 and CofA no.7030 issued 15.2.44. First revenue service 1.3.44. Absorbed by B.E.A.C. on formation 1.2.47. To Adie Aviation Ltd., Croydon 14.10.48. At some stage named *Isles of Scilly*. Transferred to Adie's offshoot Mediterranean Air Services Ltd., Cyprus 10.1.49. Returned to Adie 4.8.50. To Ernest Arthur Taylor, Croydon 9.6.53. To I.A.S. (London) Ltd., 2.4.54 and operated joy rides at Heathrow airport as Island Air Services. Via Morton Air Services to Thomas Hutton Marshall, Christchurch for Christchurch Aero Club 13.3.59, and departed Croydon on delivery 19.3.59. Delivered to Swansea 10.9.60 and reg'd to Ernest Percy Jones t/a Swansea Airways Ltd. 26.9.60. Returned to T. H. Marshall, Christchurch 18.12.61. To Gerald Austin Dommett, Thruxton 11.5.62 but continued to be operated by Christchurch Aero Club for a time. Also in use by the British Skydiving Club 1962 to 1967. To John Alexander Galt, Booker 8.6.67. To Aerial Enterprises Ltd., Booker 25.3.68 and later moved to Halfpenny Green and used by South Staffs Skydiving Club. Aerial Enterprises quoted a sale price of £1800 in 8.69. CofA expired 15.11.74. Noted at Biggin Hill 3.75 to 8.75. Had been destined for breaking up, but was saved and CofA renewed during 8.75. Leased to Duxford for 25 years and arrived at Duxford by 24.8.75. To be painted in Island Air Services colours. To Emanuel (Ted) Wein, London SW19 3.1.84. To Mike Russell of the Russavia Collection, Duxford by 10.85. To Mark J. and D. J. T. Miller, Duxford 20.3.86 and a slow rebuild continues.

6518   Supplied to the Air Council with military serial **X7345**. Initially to 18MU 4.41, then No.4 Del. Flt. 6.41, 43Grp. Com. Flt. 9.41, No.4 Del. Flt. 11.41, 18MU 6.43. SOC and sold to Island Air Charters Ltd., Southampton 9.12.47. Reg'd **G-AKNF** [CofR 12068 29.11.47]. To Robert James Martin of Airlines (Jersey) Ltd. 5.49, CofA no.10019 issued 2.5.49 and delivered to Jersey 3.5.49. Nominal ownership change to Airlines (Jersey) Ltd. 11.5.49. Converted to Mk4 standard 1954. To Airwork Ltd., Croydon 25.1.55. Sold abroad to Persia 18.7.55. To Iraanse Aardolie Exploratie en Productie Maatschappij N.V. (Iranian Oil Exploration and Producing Co., Abadan as **EP-ADP** 7.55. Fate unknown.

6519   Supplied to the Air Council with military serial **X7346**. Initially to 9MU 4.41 then 57OTU 6.61, 43Grp. Com. Flt. 7.41, 57OTU 4.42, 58OTU 4.42, 18MU 4.42, 41OTU 10.42, Old Sarum 12.42, U.S.A.F. Alconbury 5.44, 5MU 8.44. SOC on sale to Air Schools Ltd., Burnaston 22.11.46 but had already been reg'd to them as **G-AIUM** [CofR 10981 20.11.46]. CofA applied for 25.11.46 and no.8778 issued 19.2.47. To Southern Aircraft (Gatwick) Ltd. 27.11.46 and operated as Southernair. To Hunting Flying Clubs Ltd., Luton 7.5.47 but continued to wear Southernair titles!. To Frank Cecil Gold, Southall, Middlesex 30.6.50. Sold

abroad 25.7.50. To Duells Aero AB, Gotenburg 25.8.50 and reg'd **SE-BTA** and later named *Vastan Vind*. To Bolidens Gruv AB in 1953. Cancelled from Swedish Register 12.7.63 on sale to England. Returned to Portsmouth "before Easter 1963" but apparently "beyond economical repair". Noted mouldering away outside Hants and Sussex Aviation hangar 23.12.63. Last seen dumped behind Hants and Sussex hangar 4.4.64.

6520   Supplied to the Air Council with military serial **X7347**. Initially to 18MU 4.41, then 59OTU 6.41, No.4 Signals School 12.41, returned to 59OTU 12.41, 18MU 2.44, 44Grp. Com. Flt. 2.44, 1FWTC 8.46, thence R.A.F. Pershore and to storage at 18MU 8.46. SOC on sale to Field Aircraft Services Ltd., Croydon and reg'd **G-AJFN** [CofR 11253 29.1.47]. Cancelled as sold abroad 29.4.47 and allocated **OO-CDE** but not taken up. CofA no.8982 issued 23.7.47. Restored as **G-AJFN** for Franco-British Commercial & Industrial Co. Ltd., London W1 15.7.47. Destined for Air Madagascar 7.47, both G-AJFN and its travelling companion, G-AJFO c/n 6756, were burnt out on engine start up at Kosti, Anglo-Egyptian Sudan 3.12.47!

6521   Supplied to the Air Council with military serial **X7348**. Initially to 9MU 4.41, then No.4 Signals School 12.41, 18MU 3.45. To Royal Navy 17.10.45. To Evanton 26.10.45. To Crail 23.9.46 and to 782Sqdn., Donibristle 10.10.46. To de Havilland at Witney for overhaul 29.9.47 and delivered to Stretton 2.2.48 for "embalming". Served at Stretton 1948 to 1951 and again in 1952, 1953 and 1954. Noted in store at Stretton in 1955. WOC and reduced to scrap on site at Stretton 12.6.58.

6522   Supplied to the Air Council with military serial **X7349**. Initially to HQ SFPP 5.5.41, then 10 FPP 26.5.41. To de Havilland 3.2.42. Awaiting collection 17.4.43. To 18MU 23.4.43. Delivered Renfrew to Inverness 28.5.43 and reg'd **G-AGIC** [CofR 9459 6.7.43] to Scottish Airways Ltd., Inverness. CofA no.7011 issued 20.8.43. First revenue service 1.9.43. To British European Airways Corporation on formation 1.2.47. Cancelled as sold abroad 20.11.47 and departed U.K. for Tananarive via Le Bourget 21.4.48. To Air France, Le Bourget as **F-BEDZ**. CofA issued 22.4.48. To Air France, Ivato as **F-OADZ** 1.6.49. Transferred to Algeria end 1949. Transferred to Le Bourget and reg'd **F-BAHZ** 10.10.50. Crashed at La Madelaine de Nonencourt, France 24.2.51 and reg'n cancelled 31.3.51.

6523   Supplied to the Air Council with military serial **X7350**. Initially to 18MU 5.41, then 57OTU 6.41, 43Grp. Com. Flt. 6.41, 9MU 10.41. To Royal Navy 17.2.42. To 781Sqdn. Lee on Solent 12.2.42. To de Havilland for repairs (Cat.B) 24.12.42 until 2.43. Back as Cat B 10.43 to 1.44. To Donibristle 27.8.45. At Stretton 1.49 to 1.50. With 782Sqdn., Donibristle 7.50 and at de Havilland again 1.51. SOC 18.6.51 and reduced to produce.

6524   Supplied to the Air Council with serial **X7351**. Initially to 18MU 17.5.41, then 55OTU 6.41, 43Grp. Com. Flt. 7.41, 24Sqdn. 11.41, 9MU 1.42, 271Sqdn. 3.42, 1680 Flt. 1.44. Possibly served with 64Grp. Com. Flt. and coded RCH-F. Handed over to the Ministry of Supply. SOC 25.4.46 and arrived at the A.A.J.C. pool, Prestwick 16.4.46. Not civilianised and used for spares by Allied Airways.

6525   Supplied to the Air Council with military serial **X7352**. Initially to 18MU 5.41, then 58OTU 6.41, No.2 Signals School 8.42 and coded 214, later 219. To Metropolitan Com. Sqdn. 10.45, 18MU 8.46. SOC on sale to Scottish Aviation Ltd., Prestwick 24.5.48. Reg'd **G-ALBI** [CofR 12394 7.6.48] and CofA no.10217? issued 14.7.48. Cancelled on sale abroad to Luxembourg 1.6.49. To Cie Luxembourgosie de Navigation Aerienne in 1949 and reg'd **LX-LAD** 12.6.49. Restored to Scottish Aviation Ltd., Prestwick as **G-ALBI** 14.9.50. To Airwork Ltd., Croydon 19.5.53 and to Air Couriers (Transport) Ltd., Croydon 25.6.55. Converted to Mk6 by Air Couriers at Biggin Hill. Sold abroad to Senegal and reg'n cancelled 16.8.60. Departed Biggin Hill 16.8.60 and arrived at Yoff 30.8.60. To Societe Ardic Aviation, Dakar as **F-OBRV**. CofA issued 29.8.60. Destroyed at Boglie 4.8.61

6526   Supplied to the Air Council with military serial **X7353**. Initially to 9MU 5.41, then 43Grp. Com. Flt. 6.41, 52OTU 8.41, 63OTU 8.43, 54OTU 4.44, No.2 Del. Flt 4.44, 5MU 11.44, A&AEE 1.48. SOC on sale to Air Navigation and Trading Co. Ltd., Squires Gate 30.11.49. Reg'd **G-ALVU** [CofR 14877 27.10.49] to George Carhill Sergenson Whyham, Blackpool. Aircraft remained unconverted and no application was made for issue of a CofA.

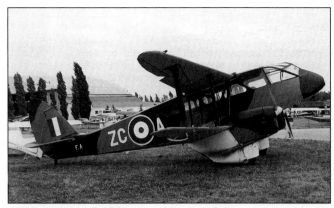

DH89 c/n 6541. F-AZCA, owned by Jean Salis and restored by his team at La Ferte Alais, was first away in the 1981 Air Transat Paris to New York to Paris Air Race.

DH89 c/n 6575. As F-BHFM, fulfilled a parachuting role with Aero Club Republique Francais Strasbourg under the aegis of S.F.A.T.A.T. Certification expired late 1966 and broken-up at La Ferte-Gaucher.

DH89 c/n 6542. From delivery in July 1941 until storage exactly three years later, X7382 was used exclusively by the Air Transport Auxiliary and based at their White Waltham headquarters.

DH89 c/n 6583. In service with Hawker Aircraft at the end of the war and struck off charge to them March 1946. Saved from Hawker's Guy Fawkes bonfire at Dunsfold in 1965,. it contined flying until 1968.

DH89 c/n 6558. X7398, coded 209, is seen nearer the camera and behind, X7386 c/n 6546 coded 205. The two aircraft were photographed when in service with No.2 Radio School.

DH89 c/n 6584. G-AGDM when with Airviews of Manchester from 1951 to 1956. Shipped to French Guyana in April 1957 and certification finally suspended there December 1965.

DH89 c/n 6573. Continued in R.A.F. service after the war and X7413 was resident at Staverton from November 1945 until January 1950. Last noted in derelict condition at Tunis 1973.

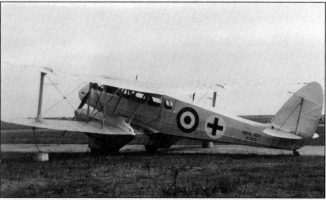

DH89 c/n 6594. Operated as an air ambulance from R.N.A.S. Donibristle from January 1949, X7452 continued in military service until April 1955 when cancelled due to "general deterioration".

Dismantled and placed in storage at Squires Gate. Although the reg'n was cancelled 10.11.56, the fuselage could still be seen in the Blackpool and Fylde Aero Club hangar in 1962, but it was finally burnt later that year.

6527 Supplied to the Air Council with military serial **X7354**. Initially to 9MU 5.41, No.3 Del. Flt. 6.41. In the course of a ferry flight between Litchfield and Hawarden, and while flying in a snowstorm, the aircraft was struck by lightning rendering "blind flying" instruments unserviceable. The pilot ordered his passengers to bail out and the aircraft subsequently struck ground and caught fire at Hordley, Shropshire.

6528 Supplied to the Air Council with military serial **X7368**. Initially to 18MU 6.41, then 10AGS 9.41, 2(O)AFU 8.42, 18MU 9.42, 51OTU 12.42. Whilst on approach to land at Cranfield, the aircraft was struck by Beaufighter R2252 - both aircraft crashed to the ground and caught fire 11.11.43.

6529 Supplied to the Air Council with military serial **X7369**. Initially to No.1 Del. Flt. 6.41 and with the flt. at Croydon 2.42, 21Grp. Com. Flt. 10.46, 23Grp. Com. Flt. 4.47 and then stored 18MU 8.47. SOC on sale to Herts and Sussex Aeroclub (1946) Ltd., Broxbourne 24.5.48. Reg'd **G-AKZH** [CofR 12343 19.5.48] and CofA no.10153 issued 11.4.48. To Kenning Aviation Ltd., Burnaston 8.9.49. Sold abroad to Portugese Guinea 7.5.52 and reg'n cancelled 1.6.52. Painted at Elstree as **CR-GAJ** for Government of Portugese Guinea Bissau for operation by Transportes Aereos da Guine Portuguese - T.A.G.P. Cancelled 11.80.

6530 Supplied to the Air Council with military serial **X7370**. Initially to 18MU 6.41, then 60OTU 7.41, 52OTU 9.42, No.2 Del. Flt., also in 9.42. To No.1 Radio School 9.43, Halton coded THA-D 3.45, and then to 5MU 12.46 for storage. Sold to Field Aircraft Services Ltd., Croydon 29.5.47. Reg'd **G-AJXB** [CofR 11665 14.6.47] but CofA no.9479 not issued until 15.12.48 when being readied for a new owner. To British European Airways Corporation 21.12.48 and later named *William Gilbert Grace* after the noted cricketer. To Eagle Aviation Ltd., Blackbushe 29.4.55. To Independent Air Travel Ltd., Bournemouth 20.2.56. Sold in Sweden 4.3.56 and reg'd **SE-CBU** to Dragon Aviation AB 2.8.56. To Peter Ahrens 8.60 and flown by him with his family to Australia, being noted at Nicosia 5.9.60, Singapore 17.9.60 and Darwin 29.9.60. Re-reg'd **VH-CBU** to W. A. R. Ahrens, Burleigh Heads QLD 5.61 and operated by him as East Coast Airways. Re-reg'd **VH-ECW** with same owner 6.62. To R. Healey t/a Darwin Air Taxis Ltd. 1.63. Out of service at Darwin 12.63 for a protracted overhaul not completed until 6.66. Caught fire on engine start-up and burnt out Bluckall QLD 30.3.68.

6531 Supplied to the Air Council with military serial **X7371**. Initially to No.2 Del. Flt. 6.41. Pilot failed to locate aerodrome, misjudged forced landing and overshot at Old Sodbury, Glos 20.10.41. Declared Cat.B, but changed to Cat.E2 and SOC 13.11.41.

6532 Supplied to the Air Council with military serial **X7372**. Initially to 18MU 6.41, then Abbotsinch 7.41 and with 1680 Flt. there 6.43. Declared Cat.B 8.11.45, but changed to Cat.E 4.4.46. SOC 5.4.46.

6533 Supplied to the Air Council with military serial **X7373**. Initially to 33MU 6.41, then 51OTU 8.41, No.1 Del. Flt. 8.42 and with the flt. at Redhill 11.44. SOC as Cat.E 2.10.45.

6534 Supplied to the Air Council with military serial **X7374**. Initially to 18MU 6.41, then 24Sqdn. 7.41. Damaged beyond repair in hangar fire at Hendon 21.4.42. SOC as Cat.E 6.5.42.

6535 Supplied to the Air Council with military serial **X7375**. Initially to 9MU 6.41, then 61OTU 7.41, 18MU 2.44, RAE 7.45. Broken up at R.A.F. Colerne during 1947. SOC as Cat.E 31.8.48.

6536 Supplied to the Air Council with military serial **X7376**. Initially to 33MU 6.41, then 57OTU 7.41, 18MU 7.45, Valley T.C 5.46, 18MU 6.46. SOC on sale to Adie Aviation Ltd., Croydon 31.5.48. Reg'd **G-AKZI** [CofR 12344 19.5.48] and CofA no.10174 issued 29.7.48. Probably purchased by Adie purely for coversion and onward sale. To Mayfair Air Services Ltd., Croydon 11.8.48. Delivered surreptitiously to Palestine (Israeli Air Force). By then wearing the serial S-76, the Rapide was forced down by anti-aircraft fire near Wadi Robin, Egypt 20.10.48 (although reports at the time gave the location as "in Indo-China"). Captured by Egyptian forces and flown to a strip near Gaza but recaptured by the Israeli a couple of months later, repaired and flown back to Israel. The official U.K. register records "written off" 16.5.50 as destroyed in Palestine. Reg'n finally cancelled 29.5.50. However, these entries could be merely a clearing-up exercise and the aircraft may well have soldiered on for considerably longer.

6537 Supplied to the Air Council with military serial **X7377**. Initially to 9MU 6.41, then HQ SFPP 7.41, 55OTU 4.42, 18MU 7.43, 3Grp. Com. Flt. 10.44. Noted at Ringway in 1946 coded BB3. Written off in flying accident 24.4.46 and SOC as Cat.E2 (scrap) 16.9.46.

6538 Supplied to the Air Council with military serial **X7378**. Initially to 9MU 5.41, then 55OTU 8.41, 18MU 7.42, 271Sqdn. 8.42, Doncaster 2.44, Staverton 2.44, 44Grp. Com. Flt. 5.44, Old Sarum 1.45, Fighter Command Com. Flt. 1.45, 10Grp. Com. Flt (no date), returned to Fighter Command Com. Flt. 5.45, No.1 Del. Flt. 8.45, 18MU 10.45 (flew about 800 hours). Officially SOC on sale to W. A. Rollason Ltd., Croydon 19.12.47. Already reg'd **G-AKOF** [CofR 12093 4.12.47] and CofA no.9954 issued 18.6.48. To Mannin Airwys Ltd., Ronaldsway 18.6.48. Ditched in River Mersey after running out of fuel 11.11.48. The aircraft had been en route Dublin to Ronaldsway, but due to bad weather at Ronaldsway, the pilot elected to divert to Speke. Due to fuel exhaustion the aircraft came down in the River Mersey. After ditching, the aircraft remained afloat for some 25 minutes with tclinging desperately to the floating hulk. When it sank, they were forced to swim in icy cold water, with only one successfully reaching the shore. The aircraft was salvaged next day and some remains built into the wall of the Manchester Ship Canal! Reg'n cancelled 17.1.49. TT 917 hours.

6539 Supplied to the Air Council with military serial **X7379**. Initially to 9MU 7.41, then A.T.A. HQ White Waltham 10.41, 3FPP 12.41, No.1 Radio School 7.43, 27Grp. HQ 7.44, No.1 Radio School 2.45, 18MU 5.46. SOC on sale to Lancashire Aircraft Corporation Ltd., Samlesbury 10.3.47 and reg'd **G-AJKW** [CofR 11386 22.3.47]. Test flown 28.7.48 and CofA issued at Kidlington 30.7.48. TTSN 1856.35 hours. Modified with "bulkhead removed, extra windows and radio". On 6.4.50 the aircraft made a hard landing and nosed over, at unknown location and was then out of use. Reportedly delivered to Westair 7.53 but not officially sold to Walter Westoby t/a Westair Flying Services, Squires Gate, until 17.6.57. To Air Navigation and Trading Co. Ltd., Blackpool 21.5.63. To Mid-Fly Ltd., Birmingham prior to 6.65. To Peter John Amor and Donald John Allan Smith, trustees of the assets of Skydivers Flying Club 22 Air Special Air Services Regiment, Shobdon 12.5.66. The aircraft was badly damaged when it ground looped on landing at Halfpenny Green inbound from Shobdon 7.5.67. Later conveyed to Tacair for possible repairs, but was deemed too badly damaged and was cancelled 10.7.67.

6540 Supplied to the Air Council with military serial **X7380**. Initially to 9MU 7.41, then No.1 Del. Flt. 9.41, 1ADF 3.42, 18MU 10.42, No.2 Radio School coded 211 11.42, 18MU 4.45. SOC as Cat E.2 29.3.46.

6541 Supplied to the Air Council with military serial **X7381**. Initially to 9MU 7.41, 43Grp. Com. Flt. 7.41, A.T.A. HQ White Waltham 10.41, 9MU 3.42, No.2 Radio School coded 201 9.42, A&AEE 11.45, 5MU 1.50. SOC on sale to Herts and Essex Aero Club (1946) Ltd., Broxbourne 30.3.50. Reg'd **G-ALZF** [CofR 14963 24.3.50] and CofA no.10919 issued 5.7.50. To East Riding Flying Club (Speeton) Ltd., Bridlington 2.8.50. To Frank Joseph Rand Elliott, Middlesborough 2.8.51. Sold abroad to France 5.9.51. To C.I.C. Parachutisme as **F-BGON** and French CofA issued 24.9.52. To SALS at Buc, Gisy-les-Nobles prior to 1953, La Ferte Gaucher 1958 and Nantes 1965 (some time registered to C.I.C. Parachutisme de l'Ouest). Aircraft was still flying in 1971 and had been placed in storage at Etampes by about 1974 and was noted there in 1975. At La Ferte Alais in poor condition 6.77, and then again in 6.79, painted in overall drab green with French tricolor on rudder and French roundel. Re-reg'd **F-AZCA** early 1981 and took part in the Air Transat Paris-New York-Paris race being the first official starter 6.6.81. Sponsored by Blueway (formerly Gauloises) and flown by Jean Salis and Pierre Dague. The aircraft had been "beautifully restored" and "lavishly equipped" with the latest Badin Crouzet avionics. In flying condition with Jean Salis, la Ferte Alais.

6542 Supplied to the Air Council with military serial **X7382**. Initially to 9MU 7.41, then A.T.A. HQ White Waltham 10.41, 5MU 7.44, RAE 1.48. SOC as scrap/spares 14.4.50.

6543 Supplied to the Air Council with military serial **X7383**. Initially to 18MU 7.41 and to Leuchars 8.41 until stored 5MU 12.44. SOC on sale to R. N. D. Miller, chief pilot for E. J. Connellan as **VH-BKM** 2.48. Whilst on delivery to Connellan Airways of Alice Springs NT, in company with another DH89 VH-BKR, power was lost on both engines at a height of approximately 150' following take-off from Daly Waters NT 6.5.48. The pilot attempted a forced landing in scrub outside the aerodrome boundary, but whilst in the flare for landing, power on one engine returned and he lost control. The aircraft crashed and was completely burnt out.

6544 Supplied to the Air Council with military serial **X7384**. Initially to 18MU 7.41, then 55OTU 7.41, 43Grp. Com. Flt. 8.41, 54OTU 3.42, Northolt 8.42, 18MU 2.43. SOC to Airwork Ltd., Croydon for Misrair 25.3.43. Reg'd **SU-ACS** to Misrair in 1943 and named *Jerusalem*. Damaged beyond repair by fire at Zaafarene 27.7.48.

6545 Supplied to the Air Council with military serial **X7385**. Initially to 18MU 7.41, then Central Flying School 8.41, 4AOS 5.42, 18MU 9.42, No.4 Radio School 4.43, Flight Refuelling 5.45. Continued in service with Flight Refuelling Ltd., Tarrant Rushton until shortly prior to sale. Reg'd **G-AHFJ** to Skyways Ltd., Langley [CofR 10008 25.3.46]. CofA no.7592 issued 28.5.46. Named *Sky Trail*. Cancelled as sold abroad 26.6.48. Damaged on landing at Mauritius 8.8.48 still marked as **G-AHFJ**. Presumably damaged beyond repair as the allocated marks **VP-KFW** were not taken up. Aircraft had been on delivery to Skyways (East Africa) Ltd. at the time of its loss. Cancelled from register 28.10.48.

6546 Supplied to the Air Council with military serial **X7386**. Initially to 18MU 7.41, then Central Flying School 8.41, 4AOS 6.42, 18MU 9.42, No.2 Radio School (coded 205) 10.42, 5MU 11.45, 18MU 3.46. SOC on sale to W. A. Rollason Ltd., Croydon 19.12.47. Reg'd as **G-AKOI** [CofR 12096 4.12.47] and CofA no.10098 issued 5.5.48. Cancelled as sold abroad 7.7.48. To Arab Airways Ltd. reg'd as **TJ-AAQ** 7.48. Shot down by an Israeli fighter aircraft 8 miles inside Transjordan whilst en route Beirut to Amman 23.9.48. Three killed. Aircraft had maintained a flight path across Israeli territory before the attack.

6547 Supplied to the Air Council with military serial **X7387**. Delivered to 18MU 7.41 but did not enter service. Instead to the Director General of Civil Aviation for A.A.J.C. 7.9.41. Passed for operation by Scottish Airways Ltd., Inverness 11.9.41 as **G-AGDG** and CofA no.6941 issued 21.10.41. First revenue service 3.11.41. To British European Airways Corporation on formation [CofR 9340 1.2.47]. Cancelled as sold abroad 21.11.47. Departed U.K. for Tananarive via Le Bourget 21.4.48. To Air France, Ivato reg'd as **F-BEDX** 14.4.48 and CofA issued 22.4.48. Re-reg'd **F-OADX** to Air France, Ivato 31.5.49. CofA issued 31.5.49. To Air France, Le Bourget as **F-BAHX** 10.10.50. Based at Ecole de l'Aviation for crew training by 31.10.50. At Dreux 6.2.51 and Toulouse 26.2.52. To Cie. D'Autrex, Hanoi 10.7.52. Damaged in crash 29.6.53 and later, voluntarily destroyed at Nam Dinh airfield, 100 miles SW of Hanoi during the French evacuation of Vietnam. Reg'n cancelled 22.12.56.

6548 Supplied to the Air Council with serial **X7388** but did not enter military service. Initially to 18MU 7.41, but transferred to the Director-General of Civil Aviation 9.41. Reg'd **G-AGDH** [CofR 9341 11.9.41] to Scottish Airways Ltd., Inverness. CofA no.6909 issued 10.10.41. Destroyed by 95 m.p.h. winds in gale at Stornoway 25.11.41.

6549 Supplied to the Air Council with military serial **X7389**. Initially to 9MU 8.41, then 3FPP 12.41, 18MU 4.43, No.2 Radio School 4.43, 18MU 4.45. SOC on sale to Adie Aviation Ltd., Croydon 10.6.48. Reg'd **G-AKZJ** [CofR 12345 19.5.48] and CofA no.10175 issued 29.6.48. Probably only purchased by Adie for conversion and onward sale. To Mayfair Air Services Ltd., Croydon 5.7.48. Transferred to their sister company Mediterranean Air Services Ltd., Nicosia, Cyprus 17.12.48. Cancelled by the Minister of Civil Aviation 6.5.49 and reg'n cancelled 12.6.50. Almost certainly served with the Israeli Air Force, serialled 1308. Fate unknown.

6550 Supplied to the Air Council with military serial **X7390**. Initially to 9MU 8.41, then A.T.A. HQ White Waltham 10.41, 27MU 10.41, 3FPP Hawarden 12.41, 18MU 8.43, No.1 Del. Flt., Redhill 12.44, 18MU 10.45. SOC on sale to Air Enterprises Ltd., Gatwick 9.12.47. Reg'd **G-AKNZ** [CofR 12087 11.12.47] and CofA no.9940 issued 9.3.48. To W. A. Rollason Ltd., Croydon 29.11.48. Sold abroad to South America 30.12.48. Reg'd **LV-AGY** to importer Speddo y Paolini Ltda., Zonda 23.3.49. Re-reg'd **LV-FEP** to Ricardo Alvares, Moron 25.9.51. Supposedly crashed during a smuggling operation 3.11.52 but precise details unknown.

6551 Supplied to the Air Council with military serial **X7391**. Initially to 18MU 8.41, then 10AOS 8.41. SOC to Airwork Ltd., Croydon for Misrair 25.3.43. Probably the Rapide reg'd **SU-ACT** to Misrair 3.43. Later named *Al Alamein*. Destroyed by fire at Almaza Airport, Cairo 25.2.51 whilst undergoing maintenance.

6552 Supplied to the Air Council with military serial **X7392**. Initially to 18MU 8.41, then 10AOS 8.41, 3(Pilot)AFU South Cerney 8.42, 18MU 9.42, 54OTU 2.43, Chartershall 1.44, 18MU 3.44, 7Grp. Com. Flt. 11.44, 18MU 1.46, Halton 3.46, 18MU 8.46. At some time coded THA/I. SOC on sale to Field Aircraft Services Ltd., Croydon 14.2.47. Reg'd **G-AJFK** [CofR 11250 29.1.47]. To Island Air Charters Ltd., Jersey 19.2.47. CofA no.8979 issued 29.4.47. Flew 567.40 hrs in 1950 and nil in 1951. To Aerocontacts Ltd., Gatwick 21.5.51. CofA test flight at Barton 12.12.51 and renewed 13.12.51. At time of CofA renewal, aircraft had not flown for about a year following Island Air Charters cessation of operations. Aircraft was found to be in poor condition due to water ingress and required extensive replacement of wooden structure. TTSN 3262 hrs. Sold abroad to Pakistan 21.2.52 and U.K. reg'n cancelled 1.4.52. Reg'd **AP-AFN** to Crescent Air Transport Ltd., Karachi 2.52. Badly damaged by fire at Karachi 28.9.52. Cancelled from register on CofA expiry 17.9.53.

6553 Supplied to the Air Council with military serial **X7393**. Initially to 10AOS 8.41, then 1(O)AFU 8.42, 18MU 11.42, No.1 Signals School 1.43, 6(O)AFU 10.44, 44Grp. Com. Flt. 11.44, Netheravon 1.46 and to storage 18MU 5.46. SOC on sale to Lancashire Aircraft Corporation Ltd., Samlesbury 10.3.47. Reg'd **G-AJKY** [CofR 11388 22.3.47] and CofA no.9303 issued 25.7.47. Reg'n lapsed 9.11.50 due to "long term storage". Valid again from 9.4.51. CofA renewed 8.4.54. TTSN 3958 hrs. To Aeroservices Ltd., Croydon 12.4.54. Cancelled as sold to Indo China 23.6.54. Reg'd **F-OAQZ** to Compagnie de Transports Aeriens Autrex (Lopez-Loreta et Cie), Hanoi 14.7.54. CofA issued 7.10.54. Certification suspended 16.4.55, possibly after an accident at Sam Neua. Reg'n finally cancelled 31.3.58.

6554 Supplied to the Air Council with military serial **X7394**. Initially to 9MU 8.41, then 782Sqdn., Donibristle 25.9.41 and equipped as an ambulance. Named *Merlin V*. Returned to de Havilland several times for repair. SOC to Royal Navy 21.7.44. Flew into Broad Crag, Scafell Pike in bad weather and wrecked 31.8.46 whilst still operating with 782Sqdn. Five killed. Owing to location, the wreckage was abandoned at the site.

6555 Supplied to the Air Council with military serial **X7395**. Initially to 9MU 8.41 and then served with Stn. Flt. Northolt 9.41, 18MU 4.45, Halton 10.45, Stn. Flt. Northolt again from 1.46 and to storage at 5MU 10.46. SOC on sale to C. W. Potter of Middlesex 10.3.47. Reg'd **G-AJKE** [CofR 11369 12.3.47] to Private Air Hire Service Ltd., Croydon and CoA no.9646 issued 28.8.47. To W. A. Rollason Ltd., Croydon 29.11.48. Cancelled on sale to France 20.5.52. Fitted with Graviner fire supression system (a French requirement) and CoA issued 23.5.52. To Societe Violet Freres (the Byrrh drinks company), Perpignan reg'd **F-BEFU**. To Aerosud, Bone, Algeria 1.56. Destroyed at M'Laqa 30.4.60 and cancelled 15.6.60.

6556 Supplied to the Air Council with military serial **X7396**. Initially to 9MU 22.8.41, then 24Sqdn. 5.10.41, No.4 Delivery Flight 6.11.41, No.3 Delivery Flight 8.42, A.T.A. HQ White Waltham 21.2.43, 18MU 2.45, 12FU 7.10.45, 18MU 2.46 and R.A.E. 19.9.46 to 11.52. Reg'd **G-APSD** [CofR R6558 4.2.59] to Air Navigation and Trading Co. Ltd., Blackpool. First flew after conversion 19.7.60 and CofA issued same day. To Stramsway Ltd., Shoreham 24.5.63. Noted at Shoreham 15.5.63, though reported still with the previous owner on that date. Commenced services 12.7.63. Later named *Cookie*. Withdrawn from use at Shoreham after CofA expiry 10.7.64. Burnt at Shoreham 4.5.66 and finally cancelled from register as permanently withdrawn from use 22.5.69!

6557 Supplied to the Air Council with military serial **X7397**. Initially to 9MU 8.41, then A.T.A. HQ White Waltham 11.41, 18MU 2.43, to R.N.D.A. 13.4.45. To Royal Navy, 782Sqdn., Donibristle 2.5.45. To Stretton for storage 4.46. To de Havilland, Witney 25.9.46. Again to Stretton 14.3.47 and possibly used by the Test Flight. To Ferry Flight at Stretton as 901/JA 20.1.48. To Stretton Stn. Flt. by 6.49. To de Havilland at Leavesden, Cat.B for repair 19.7.49. Delivered from Leavesden to Arbroath 12.5.50. Still at Arbroath 1.53. To Lossiemouth 24.3.53. To RN Air Unit (School of Land/Air Warfare), Old Sarum 6.11.53. To Yeovilton 7.54 (believed to be parent Stn. for aircraft at Old Sarum). Reported delivered to Yeovilton 14.4.56 and coded 421/VL, later as 921/VL. Still in service 5.56. Nosed over whilst taxying at Yeovilton 3.8.56 and ordered to be reduced to spares. WOC 13.9.56.

6558 Supplied to the Air Council with military serial **X7398**. Initially to 10AOS 8.41, then 9(O)AFU 8.42, No.2 Radio School (coded 209) 10.42, 18MU 7.45, No.1 Radio School 1.46, Staff Com. Flt., White Waltham 8.46, 18MU 1.47. SOC and sold to John Ernest Coxon, Salfords t/a Southern Aircraft (Gatwick) Ltd. Reg'd **G-AJTU** [CofR 11583 21.5.47]. CofA no.9530 issued 7.10.47. Actually reg'd to Southern Aircraft alone 19.5.48. Sold abroad 31.12.48 and reg'd **VP-KGS** to Jivraj's Air Service 12.48. To Air Travel (Charters) Ltd. 1950. Noted at Mombasa 7.51 out of use. Colours were silver and black. Broken up for spares 10.52.

6559 Supplied to the Air Council with military serial **X7399**. Initially to 10AOS 8.41, then 1(O)AFU 8.42, No.2 Radio School 12.42, 18MU 7.45, 4Grp. Com. Flt. 11.45, 18MU 10.47. SOC on sale to Robert Alan Short 2.2.49 but reg'd **G-ALGM** [CofR 12522 17.2.49] to Sqdn. Ldr. Kenneth James Nalson, Croydon. Reported with Adie Aviation Ltd. in 1950 but as not in official records, presumed only leased. Sold abroad 21.7.52 and CofA issued 22.8.52. Reg'd **F-BGOL** to Transportes Aereos Waldberg, Nice. CofA issued 26.8.52. To Aero Club Paul-Tissandier, St Cyr in 1954. Returned to Croydon 9.55 and French reg'n cancelled 5.10.55. Painted **OO-CRS** at Croydon 8.9.55, but the French marks were re-applied for the delivery flight to Belgium. Reg'd **OO-CRS** [Belgian CofR no.1058 11.10.55] for Air Brousse SPRL, Leopoldville-N'dola. Wrecked at Masimahimba 5.7.56, but obviously repaired as re-reg'd **OO-CJW** (a series used by Congo based aircraft) with CofA no.302 issued 16.2.59. The earlier Belgian Congo reg'n cancelled 16.8.59. Re-reg'd **9O-CJW** 17.3.61. Used throughout by Air Brousse in the Congo until damaged beyond repair in a heavy landing. Cannibalised by 1962.

6560 Supplied to the Air Council with military serial **X7400**. Initially to 10AOS (coded A7) 8.41, then 18MU 10.42, No.2 Signals School (coded 209) 10.42, 18MU 8.45. To R.N.D.A. 17.10.45. To Royal Navy, Evanton 12.45. With 782Sqdn., Donibristle 1.49. Suffered engine failure over Dun Rig, Peebles, hit mountainside and wrecked 2.49. SOC at Donibristle 28.2.49.

6561 Supplied to the Air Council with military serial **X7401**. Initially to 10AOS 9.41, then 6AOS 7.42, 18MU 12.42, 32 Wing 2.43, Macmerry 6.43, 32 Wing 3.44, 56OTU 1.45, 18MU 3.46. SOC on sale to Field Consolidated Aircraft Ltd. and reg'd **G-AHPY** [CofR 10270 22.5.46]. CofA applied for by Tollerton Aircraft Services Ltd. 19.6.46. Reg'n cancelled as sold abroad 12.8.46. CofA no.8014 issued 18.10.46. Reg'd **ZS-BCP** to O. G. Davies. t/a Owenair (Pty) Ltd., Wynberg, Cape Province 14.8.46. Still with Owenair 4.62. Broken up as spares for ZS-DLS (c/n 6773) at Natal, believed in 1967.

6562 Supplied to the Air Council with military serial **X7402**. Initially to 18MU 9.41, then 10AOS 9.41. Some time coded A8. Whilst on naval exercise and when low flying over Derwent Water, a wingtip or wheel struck the surface and the aircraft cartwheeled into the lake 28.11.41. SOC 10.12.41 as Cat.E2 (scrap).

6563 Supplied to the Air Council with military serial **X7403**. Initially to 18MU 9.41, then 24Sqdn. 8.42, U.S.A.A.F. 8th Air Force 12.42, 5MU 9.44. SOC on sale to Denham Air Services 11.3.48. Reg'd **G-AKTY** [CofR 12210 3.3.48] to Leslie Ernest Gisborne and Derek John Hayles t/a Ocean Airways, Portsmouth. To Herts and Essex Aero Club (1946) Ltd. 15.4.48 and CofA no.10081 issued 5.5.48. Sold abroad to France 11.5.51. Reg'd **F-BFVR** to Ste. Comm. d'Aviation, Toussus and French CofA issued 11.8.51. To Societe Air Madagascar 8.53. Re-reg'd **5R-MAM** still with Air

Madagascar 1.63. Leased to Societe Air Djibouti as **F-OCBX** and CofA issued 13.3.64. Restored as **5R-MAM** on return to Air Madagascar 5.65. Cancelled from register.

6564 Supplied to the Air Council with military serial **X7404**. Initially to 18MU 9.41, then 10AOS 9.41, 3(Pilot)AFU South Cerney 8.42, 18MU 9.42, 47MU 10.42. To Liverpool Docks 11.42. To South Africa per *SS Priam* and arrived 3.2.43. To **SAAF1362** 2.4. Known to have served with 62AS, then returned to AFS, Congella 12.44. Disposed of ex 15AD to Ninham Shand 17.7.46 for £1921. SOC as "sold in South Africa" 26.9.46. Reg'd **ZS-BCR** to Ninham Shand, Youngsfield 22.8.46. To **CR-ADT** with Celestino de Avmincao Neves, Quelimane 26.6.53. Cancelled 31.12.57 as broken up.

6565 Supplied to the Air Council with military serial **X7405**. Initially to HQ. FPP 9.41, then A.T.A. HQ White Waltham 5.43 and passed into store 5MU 7.44. SOC on sale to Cambrian Air Services Ltd., Cardiff 11.3.48. Reg'd **G-AKUC** [CofR 12214 3.3.48] to Stanley Kenneth Davis (founder of Cambrian Airways Ltd.) 3.3.48. CofA no.10036 issued 14.5.48. To John Hylton Watts, Stanley Kenneth Davies, Edward Keith Davies and Care Lines Ltd. t/a Cambrian Air Enterprises, Pengam Moors 13.4.49. Later named *Monmouth*. To Cambrian Air Services Ltd., Cardiff 25.1.52. To Airwork Ltd., Croydon 26.2.55. Converted to Mk4. Sold abroad to Persia 13.6.55 and U.K. reg'n cancelled 10.9.55. To Iraanse Aardolie Exploratie en Productie Maatschappij N.V. (Iranian Oil Exploration and Producing Co.), Abadan as **EP-ADM** 6.55. Fate unknown but the reg'n EP-ADM is known to have been allocated to a Cessna 310 in 1960.

6566 Supplied to the Air Council with military serial **X7406**. Initially to 18MU 9.41, then 10AOS 9.41, 2(O)AFU 8.42, 18MU 9.42, No.1 Signals School 9.42, Fairwood Common 10.44, 84Grp. Com. Flt. 3.45, at Fairwood Common 7.45, No.1 Ferry Unit 1.46, 18MU 4.46. SOC on sale to Darlington and District Aero Club Ltd. 9.12.47. Reg'd **G-AKOD** [CofR 12091 3.12.47] but CofA not issued and presumably remained unconverted. To Lancashire Aircraft Corporation Ltd., Samlesbury 26.5.49. Reg'n lapsed 24.11.50 due to "placed in long term storage". Restored to Lancashire Aircraft 4.7.51 and CofA no.2036 finally issued 10.1.52. To Aeroservices Ltd., Croydon 12.4.54. Sold abroad to Indo China 23.6.54. Reg'd **F-OAQY** to Cie. D'Autrex, Hanoi 1.7.54 and CofA issued 31.8.54. To Societe Laos Air Service 8.55. Destroyed at Sam Neua 9.4.57 and reg'n cancelled 17.6.57.

6567 Supplied to the Air Council with military serial **X7407**. Initially to 18MU 9.41, then No.3 Del. Flt. 10.41, 18MU 8.42, Abbotsinch 9.42, 1680 Flt. 6.43. Cat.E (write-off) 10.1.46 and SOC 29.1.46.

6568 Supplied to the Air Council with military serial **X7408**. Initially to 18MU 9.41, then 47MU 1.42. To India per SS *Streefkirk* ex Birkenhead 3.42. SOC Karachi 16.12.44.

6569 Supplied to the Air Council with military serial **X7409**. Initially to 18MU 10.41, then 47MU 3.42. To India per *SS City of Hong Kong* ex Birkenhead 18.3.42. Used by Radio School, Bombay during 1942. Transferred to Director of Civil Aviation 9.43. To R.A.F. SEA.AC 6.44. Reg'd **VT-ARF** for Air Services of India Ltd. 6.43. Probably then impressed, perhaps as **MA961**, for which the c/n is unknown. SOC on sale to Indian National Airways Ltd., Calcutta 25.4.46 and restored as **VT-ARF** 26.6.46. To Indian Air Survey and Transport Co. Ltd., Calcutta 5.6.47. Name changed to Air Survey Co. Ltd. 1948 and dismantled at Calcutta the following year. Cancelled 6.6.50 - "declared unairworthy"

6570 Supplied to the Air Council with military serial **X7410**. Initially to 18MU 10.41, then 41OTU 10.41, 53OTU 2.43, 18MU 7.45. SOC as Cat.E2 (scrap) 18.10.45.

6571 Supplied to Air Council with military serial **X7411**. Initially to 9MU 10.41, then A.T.A. HQ White Waltham 10.41, 271Sqdn. 3.42, 24Sqdn. 1.44, Metropolitan Com. Sqdn. 9.44, A. & A.E.E. 11.45 and to storage at 5MU 1.50. SOC on sale to Adie Aviation Ltd., Croydon 31.3.50. Reg'd **G-AMAM** [CofR 14995 11.4.50] but probably only for conversion by Adie for onward sale. To Martin-Baker Aircraft Co. Ltd., Chalgrove 3.51 and CofA no.2869 issued 29.3.51. To Fieldair Ltd., Croydon 24.11.59. Withdrawn from use at Wymeswold after CofA expiry 20.11.60. Overturned by severe winds during night of 4/5.2.62. Cancelled as destroyed 13.2.62 and aircraft cut up by the owner during the year.

6572   Supplied to the Air Council with military serial **X7412**. Initially to No.2 Del. Flt. 10.41, then 18MU 8.43, HQ No.27 Com. Flt., Aston Down (coded TSO-A) 10.44 and to storage 18MU 1.47. SOC on sale to Arthur Wesley Coombs t/a Aeroways, Croydon 21.5.48. Reg'd **G-ALBC** [CofR 12388 25.5.48] and CofA no.10188 issued 2.7.48. To Sir Robert McAlpine and Sons Ltd., Fairoaks 24.7.48. To Malcolm Hugh Dees McAlpine, Fairoaks 28.7.49. To Kenneth McAlpine, Luton 24.3.55. Used by Luton Airways at least during 1958. Converted to Mk6 prior to 1963. To Solair Flying Services Ltd., Birmingham 26.6.5.63. Crashed on high ground Edale, Derbyshire whilst on approach to Manchester Airport, returning from a photographic mission, due to repeatedly being caught in downdraughts 30.12.63. The remains were buried on Kinder Scout at accident site to prevent it being eaten by sheep! Cancelled as permanently withdrawn from use 9.1.64.

6573   Supplied to the Air Council with military serial **X7413**. Initially to 24Sqdn. 10.41, then R.A.F. Talbenny 10.44, 18MU 9.45, and Gloucester Airport 11.45. Placed into store 5MU 1.50. SOC on sale to Cambrian Air Services Ltd., Cardiff. Reg'd **G-ALZJ** [CofR 14967 27.3.50] and CofA no.10855 issued 20.4.50. Named *Caernarvon*. Nominal change to John Hylton Watts & Partners t/a Cambrian Air Enterprises, Cardiff 7.7.50. Again to Cambrian Air Services Ltd., 251.52. Name changed to Cambrian Airways Ltd. 12.3.56. To Independent Air Travel Ltd., Bournemouth 24.4.56. Sold abroad to French Morocco 30.4.56. To Societe Tunisienne de Reparation Aeronautique et de Construction (S.T.R.A.C.), Tunis for operation by Aero Sahara reg'd **F-OAME** 2.6.56. Re-reg'd locally as **TS-BME** 3.60 but it is not confirmed that the new reg'n was painted on the aircraft. Withdrawn from use and abandoned at Tunis well before '73 and remains finally disappeared by 4.74.

6574   Supplied to the Air Council with military serial **X7414**. Initially to 9MU 10.41, then A.T.A. HQ White Waltham 10.41, 18MU 9.43. SOC 11.10.44 to Royal Navy.   Crashed and wrecked on unknown airfield 1.45.

6575   Supplied to the Air Council with military serial **X7415**. Delivered to 9MU 10.41, then No.4 Signals School, Madley (coded 485) 1.42 until moved to storage 18MU 1.46. SOC on sale to J. Nesbit-Evans & Co. Ltd. Wednesbury 21.5.48. Reg'd **G-AKZO** [CofR 12350 20.5.48] and CofA no.10205 issued 21.7.48. To Don Everall (Aviation) Ltd., Wolverhampton 11.4.53. Sold abroad to France 9.8.60 and U.K. reg'n cancelled 9.60. Reg'd **F-BHFM** to Aero Club d'Alsace 4.61. To Aero Club RF at Strasbourg. CofA expired 11.66 and later broken-up at Le Ferte-Gaucher.

6576   Supplied to the Air Council with military serial **X7416**. Initially to 20MU 17.10.41, then 24Sqdn. 7.1.42, R.A.F. Croydon 1.42, 1ADF 28.1.42 and with the del. flt. at Redhill 11.44, 18MU 20.6.45, 1680 Flt. 14.12.45. Possibly some time with No.2 Radio School coded 202. Handed over to Ministry of Supply and transferred to A.A.J.C. at Prestwick 16.4.46. Reg'd **G-AHLL** [CofR 10159 8.5.46] to Scottish Airways Ltd., Renfrew and CofA no.7779 issued 28.6.46. Absorbed into B.E.A.C. on formation 1.2.47. Later named *Sir Henry Lawrence*. Skidded on landing and struck hedge at St. Just 21.5.59. Reg'n cancelled 30.7.59. Not repaired and dismantled for spares. Total Time 10747 hrs. Remains noted at Exeter with No.3 CAACU 10.68.

6577   Supplied to the Air Council with military serial **X7417**. Initially to 9MU 10.41, then A.T.A. HQ White Waltham 11.41, Leuchars Communication Flight 5.45, 18MU 10.46. SOC on sale to William Alfred Webb, Croydon 19.12.47.   Reg'd **G-AKOR** [CofR 12104 31.12.47] and CofA No.9918 issued 1.3.48. To Morton Air Services Ltd., Croydon 9.3.48. To John Mowlem and Co. Ltd., London SW1 5.5.48. Returned to Morton 11.7.49. To Skyways Ltd., Dunsfold 25.5.50. To broker W. S. Shackleton Ltd. 5.5.52. Sold abroad to Fiji 4.12.52. Reg'd **VQ-FAN** to Katatanga Estates t/a Fiji Airways Ltd. 20.2.53. To Noumea per *Thors Isle* 9.10.56. Reg'd **F-OAZT** to Societe Caledonienne de Transports Aeriens and CofA issued 12.7.57. CofA suspended 11.3.58. Reg'n cancelled 25.3.59 and notified as withdrawn from use 10.4.59.

6578   Supplied to the Air Council with military serial **X7437**. Initially to 9MU 24.10.41, then No.4 Signals School, Madley 12.12.41, 18MU 12.43. To Royal Navy 13.4.45. To Donibristle 27.4.45. At Lee on Solent (781Sqdn?) by 10.45 until at least 3.46. With Test Flight at Donibristle in 1946 and 1947 (probably stayed until 1.49). At Stretton 1.49 to 7.54, but in storage there by 4.50). SOC at Stretton 21.2.55. To Speke for civil conversion and noted there 21.2.55. A wit daubed **'G-AZZZ'** on the fuselage during its

long sojourn unconverted in the hangar at Speke! To Croydon by road 3.56 and stored for a further period. Reg'd **G-APJW** [CofR R6235 2.1.58] to Stephen John Stevens, Mrs. Kathleen Stevens and Herbert James Adams, trustees of the assets of Missionary Aviation Fellowship. To Tarmac Ltd., Wolverhampton 16.4.58. Converted to civilian standard at Croydon by Continental Aircraft Services. CofA issued 20.5.58. Reg'd to Plascom (1909) Ltd., Wolverhampton (an associate company) 29.4.59 and continued to be operated by Tarmac Ltd.. To Desert Air Ltd., Elstree 13.9.60. To Keegan Aviation Ltd. prior to 6.61 but not officially reg'd to them. Reg'n cancelled to France 9.8.62. CofA issued 3.10.62. Reg'd **F-BHOB** to C. Rousseau, Dinard 3.10.62. To A.C Centre, Alsace, Colmar in 1963. To Michel Rouchaud, Bordeaux (later Belle Isle) in 1968. CofA suspended 2.70.

6579   Supplied to Air Council with military serial **X7438**. Delivered to 9MU 10.41. Served with A.T.A. HQ White Waltham 11.41, 33 Wing R.A.F. York 3.43, Church Fenton Stn. Flt. 10.43, Grimister 12.45. SOC as Cat.E2 (scrap) 18.2.46.

6580   Supplied to the Air Council with military serial **X7439**. Delivered to 9MU 11.41 and then served at No.4 Signals School from 12.41 and continuously with with the School until storage at 18MU 3.46. SOC on sale to W. A. Rollason Ltd., Croydon 19.12.47. Reg'd **G-AKOJ** [CofR 4.12.47] and CofA no.9955 issued 20.4.48. Sold abroad 14.5.48 and reg'n cancelled 28.6.48. Reg'd **TJ-AAJ** to Arab Airways Ltd. 5.48. Damaged when machine gunned by an Israeli Air Force Harvard whilst en route to Beirut but returned safely to Amman 14.7.48. To Arab Airways (Jerusalem) 8.53. Reg'd **F-OARH** to Societe Air Madagascar. CofA issued 29.12.54. Destroyed 14.11.62.

6581   Supplied to the Air Council with military serial **X7440**. Delivered to 9MU 11.41 and then served at No.4 Signals School from 12.41 and continuously with the School until storage at 18MU 3.46. SOC on sale Derek John Hayles, Portsmouth 27.5.48.   Reg'd **G-AKYW** [CofR 12332 18.5.48]. Sold on to W. A. Rollason Ltd., Croydon 24.6.48 and CofA no.10199 issued to them 2.11.48. Sold abroad 23.11.48 and reg'n cancelled 27.12.48. Reg'd in Argentina as **LV-AGR** to STP Ltda, Zonsa 26.2.49. To Centro Universida de Aviacion, Moron 30.5.57. CofA expired 28.9.65.

6582   Supplied to the Air Council with military serial **X7441**. Delivered to 9MU 11.41. Served with No.4 Signals School 12.41, 18MU 10.45 and No.1 Ferry Unit 1.46. Placed into storage 18MU 4.46. SOC on sale to W. A. Rollason Ltd., Croydon 19.12.47. Reg'd as **G-AKOH** [CofR 12095 4.12.47] and CofA no.9992 issued 21.5.48. To Mannin Airways Ltd., Ronaldsway 21.5.48. Reg'n lapsed 14.12.50 due to "aircraft placed in long term storage". Restored to North-West Airlines (Isle of Man) Ltd., Ronaldsway 21.5.51. Cancelled on sale to France 12.5.53. Reg'd **F-BGXH** to Aero Club de Dauphine, Grenoble 6.53. CofA issued 18.6.53. To Aero Club du Rhone et Sud Est, Lyon in 1959. Damaged beyond repair during take-off accident 11.10.64.

6583   Supplied to the Air Council with military serial **X7442**. Delivered to 9MU 11.41. Served with No.4 Signals School 12.41, 18MU 4.44, 16 Wing Hendon 12.44, 18MU 2.45, Hawker Aircraft, Langley 12.45. SOC 30.4.46. Reg'd **G-AHGC** to Hawker Aircraft Ltd., Langley [CofR 10026 28.3.46] and CofA no.7591 issued 25.6.46. Later moved to Dunsfold and later still, with Hawker Siddeley Aviation Ltd., Hawker Blackburn Division 18.7.63. Withdrawn from use on expiry of CofA 21.6.65 at Dunsfold. Strangely, the ownership changed to Hawker Siddley (Leasing) Ltd., Brough 20.7.65 but was said to be destined to be burnt on Dunsfold's Guy Fawkes bonfire on November 5th! Mercifully, this did not happen and subsequently repaired at Redhill and to Blackbushe 1.5.66. To Kenneth Bryan Neely 5.4.66. Painted with Scillonia Airways titles at Booker 5.66 and named *Tresco*. CofA expired 4.7.68 but reportedly still with Scillonia Airways in 5.70 when the company's assets were sold. Bought for spares use by The Army Parachute Association at Netheravon in 1970. Cancelled as permanently withdrawn from use 16.5.72. Some parts said to be with the Durney Collection at Andover.

6584   Reg'd **G-AGDM** [CofR 9346 11.11.41] to Allied Airways (Gandar Dower) Ltd., Dyce. CofA no.6913 issued 8.11.41. Later named *Eldorado*. Noted in Southern Aircraft's hangar at Gatwick in wartime civil colours and with Allied Airways titles on nose 9.47. Handed over to B.E.A.C. 15.11.47. To Charles W. J. Allen t/a Allen Aircraft Services, Old Coulsdon 25.5.48 (but "sold prior to delivery"). To Robert Alan Short, Martha Marodeen & Derek John

Hayles, Croydon 29.12.48. To Sqdn. Ldr. Kenneth James Nalson, Croydon 24.1.59. To Silverwright Airways Ltd., Barton 23.6.49 (ceased operations 3.51). To Airviews Ltd., Barton (later Ringway) 11.9.51. To Hants and Sussex Aviation Ltd., Portsmouth 1.11.56. Modified to Mk4 22.3.57. Major overhaul at CofA renewal 29.3.57 at Portsmouth. TTSN 4654.35 hrs. Aircraft had not flown in 1957. Reg'n cancelled as sold in France 30.3.57. Reg'd F-OAXK to Societe Aerien de Transports Guyane-Antilles. Del via London Docks 1.4.57. French CofA issued 6.6.57. Damaged at Sophie Inin airfield, Cayenne 18.9.58. CofA suspended 12.65.

6585 Supplied to the Air Council with military serial **X7443**. Initially to 33MU 11.41, then B.W Flt. 9.42 (with No.2 Radio School 5.44), 22Grp. Com. Flt. Ternhill 7.45, 43Grp. Com. Flt. 8.46. Declared surplus to requirements 10.46 and to 5MU 2.47 for disposal. SOC on sale to Field Aircraft Services Ltd., Hanworth 29.5.47. Reg'd **G-AKBW** [CofR 11785 18.7.47] but not converted and subsequently broken up. Cancelled 5.5.48. Some parts may have gone to Belgium.

6586 Supplied to the Air Council with military serial **X7444**. Initially to 9MU 11.41, No.4 Signals School 12.41. Classified Cat.E 20.4.43 and SOC 25.4.43 with a TT 545 hrs.

6587 Supplied to the Air Council with military serial **X7445**. Initially to 9MU 11.41, then A.T.A. HQ White Waltham 12.41, HQ Army Co-operation Com. Flt. 12.41, Com. Flt., White Waltham 6.43, Technical Training Command Com. Flt., Wyton (date?), Northolt 11.45, Metropolitan. Com. Sqdn. 7.46, Kirkbride 10.46, 18MU 10.46. SOC on sale to Field Aircraft Services Ltd., Croydon. Reg'd **G-AJFJ** [CofR 11249 29.1.47] and CofA no.8978 issued 27.6.47 following test flight 16.6.47 - TTSN 969.20 hrs. To Thomas Loel Evelyn Bulkeley Guinness, London 17.3.47. To Airwork Ltd., Croydon 29.10.47. To Charles William John Allen, Old Coulsdon 20.12.49. Nominal change to Allen Aircraft Services Ltd. 4.5.50. Dismantled at Croydon prior to 7.51. Reg'n finally cancelled as permanently withdrawn from use 20.4.59.

6588 Supplied to the Air Council with military serial **X7446**. Initially delivered to 18MU 11.41 but moved to 47MU 2.42. To India per *SS Steefkirk* 10.3.42 ex Birkenhead Docks. Was with Com. Flt., Delhi 11.43. SOC on sale to Indian National Airways Ltd., Calcutta and reg'd as **VT-ASA** to them 9.44. To Indian Air Survey & Transport Co. Ltd., Calcutta (probably during 1947). Name changed to Air Survey Co. of India Ltd. 1948. Badly damaged when aircraft ran into a ditch while taking off at Ondal 24.3.59. Still owned by Air Survey, noted stored 18.3.77 at Calcutta's Dum Dum Airport in Hangar 11, all in one piece and in good condition. Reg'd **N2290B** to Elmer J. Gothard, Chelis, WA 7.78. To Michael G. Kimbrel, Oakville, WA by 7.79. Kimbrel, a Western Air Lines DC10 captain, kept the aircraft on a strip at his farm and it was noted there 5.81. Visited the Experimental Aircraft Association's Convention at Oshkosh later in 1981. To John Cournoyer and Albert Stix I of the Historic Aircraft Restoration Museum, St. Louis, MO 6.2.03.

6589 Supplied to the Air Council with military serial **X7447**. Initially to 9MU 12.41, No.4 Signals School 12.41, No.1 Signals School 7.42, No.4 Signals School 12.42 until stored 5MU 12.44. SOC on sale to A. Hamson and Son Ltd t/a Air Charter Experts Ltd., Ronaldsway 6.1.47. Reg'd **G-AJGV** [CofR 11285 11.2.47]. CofA no.9149 issued 30.4.47. Named *Glen Helen* by 5.47. Taken over by Manx Air Charters Ltd. 26.8.47. Became Manx Airlines Ltd. 24.8.53. CofA renewed at Ronaldsway probably 4.6.54 when TTSN 3534.15 hrs and time since last CofA, 1953 66.40 hrs. At time of CofA renewal, it was noted that the "engine and aircraft log books were found to be inaccurately kept by Pine's Airways (maintenance operator?) during previous summer". Reg'n cancelled as sold to Paraguay 5.5.55. Reg'n details and ultimate fate unknown.

6590 Supplied to the Air Council with military serial **X7448**. Initially to 9MU 1.42. To Royal Navy 16.2.42. At Lee on Solent with 781Sqdn. and to de Havilland for repairs etc a couple of times. Later with RNAY Donibrislte and del from there to Crail 24.6.46. To 781Sqdn. Lee On Solent 2.8.46. Coded 854/LP with Lee on Solent Stn. Flt. some time between 1946 and 1948. To Stretton by 1.49. SOC at Stretton 8.49.

6591 Supplied to the Air Council with military serial **X7449**. Initially to 18MU 12.41, No.4 Signals School (coded 492) 3.42, 18MU 9.46. SOC on sale to Ronald James Martin t/a Island Air

Charters Ltd., Jersey 9.12.47. Reg'd **G-AKNE** [CofR 12067 29.11.47] and CofA no.10018 issued 30.5.49. To Vivian H. Bellamy t/a Flightways Ltd., Southampton 23.6.49. To Maldwyn Lewis Thomas of Airlines (Jersey) Ltd. and delivered to Jersey 15.2.50. To Hants and Sussex Aviation Ltd., Portsmouth 30.5.57. Sold abroad to Madagascar 23.9.57. Reg'd **F-OBDV** to Societe Air Madagascar 9.57. Re-reg'd **5R-MAN** still with Societe Air Madagascar 1.63. Total loss in Madagascar 18.5.68.

6592 Supplied to the Air Council with military serial **X7450**. Initially to 47MU 2.42. To India 10.3.42 per *SS Streefkirk* ex Birkenhead Docks. Was with 172 Wing Com. Flt. 9.43 and 173 Wing 12.43. Caught fire while refuelling at Vizacpatam, India 23.12.43. Actual extent of damage unknown but SOC 31.8.44 in India.

6593 Supplied to the Air Council with military serial **X7451**. Initially to 18MU 12.41, then 47MU 2.42. To India 18.3.42 per *SS City of Hong Kong* ex Birkenhead Docks. Was with No.2 Flt., India 8.42, R.A.F. Stn. Flt., Chaklala 2.43 and 152OTU 11.43. SOC 1.1.47 in clear up of files.

6594 Supplied to the Air Council with military serial **X7452**. Initially to 18MU 12.41. To Royal Navy, Donibristle 3.42. To 782Sqdn. 13.3.42. To Lee on Solent (781Sqdn?) 21.6.44. After 10.45 was coded L9B with 781Sqdn.. In service at Donibristle as an air ambulance by 1.49. With 782Sqdn. Donibristle coded 802/DO. With de Havilland 7.50 and 1.51 and at Stretton 2.51. To 782Sqdn., Donibristle by 7.51 and coded 809/DO (recoded 804/DO by 10.51). At Donibristle until 7.53 at least. To Airwork Ltd., still at Donibristle by 31.3.54. WOC 27.4.55 due to general deterioration.

6595 Supplied to the Air Council with military serial **X7453**. SOC 29.3.45 as "to Royal Navy" and delivered to 782Sqdn., Donibristle 22.12.41. . Wrecked in mid-air collision with Seafire SW822 over Wimboldsley, Cheshire 11.2.46. Cat.E 12.2.46.

6596 Supplied to the Air Council with military serial **X7454**. Initially to A.T.A. HQ White Waltham 1.42, then 18MU 11.43, Abbots Ripton 4.44 (U.S.A.A.F. 8th Air Force), 57OTU 8.44, 10Grp. Com. Flt. 9.44. To Vickers-Armstrong Ltd., South Marston 1.45. SOC, still with Vickers, as **G-AHKB** [CofR 10124 16.4.46] and CofA no.7640 issued 11.5.46. To Vivian Hampson Bellamy (of the Hampshire Aeroplane Club), Eastleigh and del 2.4.59. Sold abroad to France 16.10.61. Reg'd **F-BEKB** to Atelier Aerien de la Cote d'Emeraude (i.e. Rousseau), Dinard and CofA issued 29.11.61. RF SFATAT, Bergerac 8.62. CofA expired 12.65. (See also c/n 6794).

6597 Supplied to the Air Council with military serial **X7445**. Initially to A.T.A. HQ White Waltham 12.41, then 18MU 12.44, No.1 Del. Flt. 7.45, Hawarden 9.45, 5MU 1.47. Cat.E2 (scrap) 30.5.47

6598 Supplied to the Air Council with military serial **X7446**. Initially to de Havilland 12.41, then 9MU 1.42, No.4 Signals School 3.42, 18MU 8.46. SOC on sale to West Cumberland Air Services Ltd., Kingstown Airport, Carlisle 11.2.47. Reg'd **G-AKNN** [CofR 12076 8.12.47] to William Arthur Herbert and Esther Cope Wilson t/a West Cumberland Air Services 8.12.47. CofA no.9981 issued 22.4.48. To Astral Aviation Ltd., Newcastle 26.5.48. To Air Couriers Ltd., Croydon 26.2.49. To Air Couriers (Properties) Ltd., Croydon 16.4.51. Changed to Air Couriers (Transport) Ltd., Croydon 12.10.53. To Marshall Flying Services Ltd., Cambridge 18.5.54. Converted to Mk6 prior to 7.60. To Williams Tomkins Ltd., Peterborough 18.1.62 and kept on their private airstrip at Apethorpe. Deconverted from Mk6 2.62. To British Sky-Diving Ltd. 4.4.67. To Geoffrey Harry Smale t/a Trak-Air, Dunkeswell 9.10.68. CofA expired at Castle Donington 29.8.69. Parked in Sagittair's hangar and used for spares for G-AHAG. Ownership changed 28.10.70 and noted outside hangar 1971/72, Finally cancelled as "permanently withdrawn from use" at Castle Donington" 10.9.73.

6599 Supplied to the Air Council with military serial **X7482**. Initially to 9MU 1.42, then No.3 Del. Flt. 4.42, No.2 Signals School 9.42, 18MU 9.45. SOC to Royal Navy, Evanton 5.11.45. At Old Sarum with the RN Air Unit in 1949. Stored at Stretton by 7.49 to 4.50 at least. At Arbroath by 7.50 . With 782Sqdn., Donibristle by 7.51? At Old Sarum 1.52 and with 782Sqdn., Donibristle. Ran

DH89 c/n 6596. Ended the war in service with Vickers-Armstrong and struck off charge to them. Later, with Viv Bellamy and ended its days with a parachuting school at Bergerac in France.

DH89 c/n 6635. Based at Manchester, Sivewright operated both charter and scheduled services to Jersey and the Isle of Man during the summer months. G-AKMG ended up in Indochina as F-BGPI.

DH89 c/n 6609. Operated by Tuyavion from July 1965, but LV-AER is seen here after being abandoned at Ascuncion, capital of neighbouring Paraguay in March 1972.

DH89 c/n 6641. X7524 was captioned on the Hatfield production line as "Dominie for Iraq". However, instead shipped to Egypt for operation by Misr Airwork, believed as SU-ACS, but lost en route.

DH89 c/n 6622. TF-KAA soon after delivery to Flying School Thytur in July 1953. Said to be still in good order 10 years later, but finally burnt after withdrawal from use in 1966.

DH89 c/n 6653. Originally HG654, but shipped to New Zealand and operated by the RNZAF as NZ525. Seen here wearing just the last three of its civil registration, allowed if used purely domestically.

DH89 c/n 6629. G-AKNX was one of eight Rapides operated by a Birmingham based group under various names including Patrick Aviation, Patrick-Duval Aviation or Patrick Motors!

DH89 c/n 6655. Similarly, not operated by the military in the U.K. but shipped to New Zealand. Seen here when in service with Ritchie Air Services sometime between July 1961 and December 1964.

into soft ground at end of runway at Donibristle and wrecked - airframe scrapped 3.53. SOC at Donibristle 25.3.53.

6600   Supplied to the Air Council with military serial **X7483**. Initially to 9MU 1.42, then No.4 Signals School 3.42, Technical Training Command Com. Flt. 3.46, Halton 8.46, 5MU 12.46. SOC on sale to Airwork Ltd., Croydon 29.5.47. Reg'd **G-AJVA** [CofR 11614 29.5.47]. To Iraq Petroleum Transport Co. Ltd., Haifa 30.6.47 and CofA no.9596 issued 1.3.48. Cancelled from U.K. register 13.12.51. To Arab Airways Association reg'd **TJ-ABM**. Burnt out in Arab Airways hangar fire at Amman Airport 9.5.53. Reg'n cancelled 5.6.53.

6601   Supplied to the Air Council with military serial **X7484**. Initially handed over to R.A.F. at Hatfield 3.1.42. To Ringway 3.1.42 for parachute training. Converted to Dominie Mk II in 1945. To 18MU 29.10.46. SOC on sale to Darlington and District Aero Club Ltd., Croft 9.12.47 and delivered same day. Reg'd **G-AKOE** [CofR 12092 3.12.47] and CofA no.10023 issued 26.5.48. To Lancashire Aircraft Corporation Ltd., Samlesbury 18.5.49. Cancelled when placed in long term storage 9.11.50. Restored to L.A.C. 3.2.51. Delivered to Silver City Airways Ltd., Stansted 12.56, but actually registered to that company 28.10.57. Subsequently used in Libya on charters for oil companies in Libya. Delivered to Hants and Sussex Aviation Ltd. 4.9.58 and reg'd to them 16.10.58. Converted to Mk4 at Portsmouth and first flew as such 10.12.58. To Air Rectification Ltd., Bournemouth 6.11.59, positioning a few miles along the coast to its new home a couple of days earlier. Named *The Water's Edge* about this time. Noted resident at Baginton 6.10.61. To Edward Maurice Brain and Stanley Martin Harley, Baginton 8.1.62. To Rapid Flying Group Ltd., Baginton 31.5.62. To John Elvet Pierce, Ley Farm, Chirk 31.10.62. Kept at Baginton and last flew 4.7.65 before withdrawal from use 11.69. Air Britain reported that it was "being stripped by Alvis for parts to rebuild G-AEML in 6.71 but that Alvis hoped to rebuild **G-AKOE** as well". Noted at Baginton 11.74 and again on 28.3.76, stored with G-AEML - neither aircraft had wings outboard of the engines and one had no fabric. Transported by road to Chirk, Clwyd 4.2.78. Expected to fly again summer 1978, painted in B.E.A.C. colours and to be based at Heathrow for public relations work for the Corporation. First flew after rebuild 17.10.78 and CofA renewed 27.7.79. Painted up at Heathrow with a "speedbird" under the cockpit window 6.79. The aircraft spent summer 1979 at Biggin Hill, but had returned to Heathrow by November 1979. Painted in British Airways colours with current logo type on fuselage and tail, rest all white and spinners red. Named *Sir Henry Morgan*. Noted at Chirk 20.6.87 complete, recently overhauled and airworthy. Cancelled by the C.A.A. 18.6.02.

6602   Supplied to the Air Council with military serial **X7485**. Initially to No.4 Signals School 1.42. On loan to B.O.A.C. Training Flt. 3.46, then 18MU 4.46. Reg'd **G-AIUN** [CofR 10982 20.11.46] to Air Schools Ltd., Burnaston and CofA no.9614 issued 7.8.47. To Domino Louis Steiner t/a Steiner's Air and Travel Services Ltd., Liverpool 30.7.47. To Mayfair Air Services Ltd., Croydon 25.5.48 and operated in Palestine. To Israeli Air Force as S-75 9.48 but not cancelled until 16.5.50 as "disappeared in Palestine".

6603   Supplied to the Air Council with military serial **X7486**. Initially to 18MU 2.42. To Royal Navy at Donibristle 13.3.42. To de Havilland 7.49 to 1.50. To Arbroath by 7.50. To 782Sqdn., Donibristle by 1.51 until 1954 at least (coded 805/DO at some time). With Airwork Ltd. still at Donibristle as an ambulance aircraft 1.54 to 7.54 at least. Arrived at Portsmouth for civil conversion by Hants and Sussex Aviation Ltd. 2.2.57. Reg'd to Hants and Sussex Aviation Ltd. as **G-AOZG** [CofR R5841 23.1.57] To Roy Eric Webb, Eastleigh 11.3.57. To Albert Victor Boella and William Bogatto, Eastleigh 22.7.57. CofA issued 5.10.57. Converted to Mk4 by 11.11.57. Sold abroad to Sierra Leone 10.12.57 and U.K. reg'n cancelled 10.2.58. To West African Airways Corporation, Lagos. Reg'd **VR-LAC** to Sierra Leone Airways Ltd. 2.58. Later named *Mount Mamba*. Reportedly all three Sierra Leone Airways Rapides (also see c/ns 6827 and 6963) were eventually burnt at Hastings Airfield, Freetown.

6604   Supplied to the Air Council with military serial **X7487**. Initially to 18MU 2.42. To Royal Navy at Donibristle 13.3.42. Named *Merlin VII*. Deteriorated in service and reduced to produce 8.48. Wings noted at Balado 3.52.

6605   Supplied to the Air Council with military serial **X7488**. Initially to 18MU 2.42. To Royal Navy at Donibristle 13.3.42. At Donibristle 1.49 to 7.49 at least. At Yeovilton with 50TAG 1.50 and with 767Sqdn. at Yeovilton 7.50 to 1.52 at least and coded 51/VL. At Arbroath 7.52 to 7.53 at least. At Lossiemouth 7.54. Noted in store at Stretton in 1955. Reported parked outside without wheels at Lossiemouth early 1960 awaiting disposal.

6606   Supplied to the Air Council with military serial **X7489**. Initially to 18MU 2.42, then No.4 Signals School 3.42, 18MU 7.45. SOC on sale to D. J. Adie, Croydon 30.6.47. Reg'd **G-AKRE** [CofR 12141 21.1.48] to L. E. H. Airways Ltd., London. CofA no.9945 issued 16.2.48. Sold in French Indo China 7.1.49. Reg'd **F-OABH** to Cie. D'Autrex, Hanoi 21.4.49. CofA issued 12.5.49. Destroyed by fire 4.6.52 at Gia-Lam Airport, Hanoi; fire started in the cockpit whilst the aircraft was in a hangar. Reg'n cancelled 22.7.52.

6607   Supplied to the Air Council with military serial **X7490**. Initially to School of Aircraft Flying Control 3.42, then 18MU 12.42, Old Sarum 3.43, 18MU 10.45, Metropolitan Com. Sqdn. 12.45, 18MU 8.46. SOC on sale to Scottish Aviation Ltd., Prestwick 24.5.48. Reg'd **G-ALBH** [CofR 12393 7.6.48] and CofA no.10212 issued 6.8.49. Reg'd **LX-LAC** to Luxembourgoise de Navigation Aerienne 12.6.49. Reg'n not taken up and remained as **G-ALBH**. To Mitchell Engineering Ltd., Peterborough 20.3.54. To Morton Air Services Ltd., Croydon 26.7.57. Base amended to Gatwick 27.1.60. To Aerocontracts [Aircraft Distributors] Ltd., Gatwick 23.6.60. Sold to Congo and cancelled 28.9.60, but CofA extended for one month up to 10.10.60. Reg'd **OO-CJD** to Air Brousse SPRL 15.11.60 and CofA no.C323 issued. Re-reg'd **9O-CJD** still with Air Brousse. Noted at Leopoldville-N'Dola 15.8.62. Re-reg'd again as **9Q-CJD** with Air Brousse and noted as such 4.4.63. Crashed on take-off Boma 7.6.62. Repaired, utilising parts of the wrecked OO-CJT c/n 6925 and also of VP-YOL c/n 6666. Subsequently, it is believed to have become **9Q-CJT** 6.63, apparently due to a mix up during re-build. Ownership changed to A.M.A.Z., Kinshasa, date unknown.

6608   Supplied to the Air Council with military serial **X7491**. Initially to School of Flying Control 3.42 and then used by No.1 Beam Approach School, Watchfield in 1942. To 41OTU 11.42, No.3 Tactical Exercise Unit Aston Down 11.44, Fighter Command Com. Sqdn. Northolt 8.45, No.4 Del. Flt. 9.45 and finally, to the manufacturer General Aircraft Ltd, Feltham 11.45. SOC on sale to General Aircraft Ltd. 28.3.46. Reg'd **G-AHTY** [CofR 10344 5.6.46] to Air Training (Fair Oaks) Ltd. 5.6.46 and CofA no.7865 issued 1.8.46. To Universal Flying Services Ltd., Fairoaks 26.2.47. Merged into North-Sea Air Transport Ltd., Brough 31.10.49. Cancelled as "owner changed" 21.7.52. Reg'd as **F-BGIS** to Ste. Turbomeca, Pau and CofA issued 28.8.52. To Societe Air-Ouest, Nantes 9.56. To S.G.A.A. 2.60 and then Ste Transport Air Sahara, Colomb Bechar during 1961 but the CofA had been suspended 11.60!

6609   Supplied to the Air Council with military serial **X7492**. Initially to School of Flying Control 3.42 and then used by No.1 Beam Approach School, Watchfield in 1942. To 81Grp. Com. Flt. 11.42, 61OTU 2.44, 18MU 1.47. SOC on sale to William Alfred Webb, Croydon 27.5.48. Reg'd **G-ALAU** [CofR 12380 26.5.46] and CofA no.10235 issued 21.9.48. Sold abroad by W. A. Rollason Ltd., Croydon 5.10.48. Reg'd **LV-AER** to the importer Sfreddo y Paolini Ltda., Zonda 31.12.48. To Aero Express Barcella and then to Tuyavion SRL 15.7.65. Withdrawn from use and abandoned at Ascunsion, Paraguay some time prior to 3.72 - not seen 2.79.

6610   Supplied to the Air Council with military serial **X7493**. Initially to School of Flying Control 2.42 and then used by No.1 Beam Approach School, Watchfield in 1942. To 18MU 11.42, then 24Sqdn. 9.43 and Metropolitan Com. Sqdn. 9.44. Cat.B 9.45 but later re-classified as Cat.E2. SOC 20.11.45.

6611   Supplied to the Air Council with military serial **X7494**. Delivered to Royal Navy, Lee on Solent 16.2.42. Crashed on landing at Lee 8.42.

6612   Supplied to the Air Council with military serial **X7493**. Initially to 32MU 2.42, then 18MU 5.47, 32MU 6.47. SOC on sale to Air Navigation and Trading Co. Ltd., Blackpool 15.12.47 but A.N.T. did not take delivery. Instead, reg'd **G-AKOV** [CofR 12108 17.12.47] to East Anglian Flying Services Ltd., Southend 17.12.47.

Collected from Dumfries 27.1.48. Air tested after civil conversion 15.9.48 and CofA no.10112 issued same day. To Inter-City Air Services Ltd., Hereford 4.4.49. To Wolverhampton Aviation Ltd. 9.8.50 and operated on behalf of Derby Air Services Ltd. Sold abroad to Kenya 7.2.55. Reg'd **VP-KNC** to J. E. F. Wilkins t/a Caspair, Mazinde 2.55. Sold 1956 and reg'd **F-OAHH** to Societe Air Madagascar 5.56. Burnt out on the ground at unknown location in Madagascar 14.11.56.

6613 Supplied to the Air Council with military serial **X7496**. Delivered to Royal Navy at Lee on Solent 2.42. With 782Sqdn. 6.43 and at Donibrislte 5.44. No further records.

6614 Supplied to the Air Council with military serial **X7497**. Delivered to Royal Navy at Donibristle 13.3.42. At Stretton 1.49 to 7.49 at least. With 781Sqdn. at Lee on Solent 1.50 to 7.51 at least, Arbroath 1.52 to 7.53 at least and Stretton 1.54 to 7.54 at least. Still in service in 1955. Reported as "embalmed" at Stretton until at least mid 1955, then believed scrapped.

6615 Supplied to the Air Council with military serial **X7498**. Delivered to Royal Navy at Donibristle 13.3.42. At Lee on Solent 7.42 and Donibristle 11.44. Reported at 18MU 7.45 and with 782Sqdn. at Donibristle 7.46. At Stretton 1.49 to 7.54 at least. Involved in accident at Stretton. SOC 2.2.55 and deleted 21.2.55. Noted in store at Stretton in 1955. Sold ex Stretton 6.55 and flown to Speke early 1955 for Federated Fruiterers Ltd. Advertised by Federated Fruiterers in 6.56 for £1500 "as is" at Speke. Not civilianised and eventually broken-up at Speke.

6616 Supplied to the Air Council with military serial **X7499**. Delivered to Royal Navy at Donibristle 13.3.42. In service at Stretton 1.49 to 7.54 at least. Reported "embalmed" at Stretton mid 1955, then believed scrapped.

6617 Supplied to the Air Council with military serial **X7501**. Served with No.4 Signals School 3.42. To storage at 5MU 8.44. SOC on sale to Capt. Charles Francis Cockburn, Chief Pilot of Goodhew Aviation Ltd., Kidlington 11.3.48. Reg'd **G-AKMF** [CofR 12043 23.2.48] and CofA no.10074 issued 11.5.48. To Mayfair Air Services Ltd., Thame 26.5.48. To Israeli Air Force soon after as S-74. Cancelled from U.K. register 17.5.50 as "disappeared in Palestine".

6618 Supplied to the Air Council with military serial **X7501**. Initially to No.4 Signals School, then 18MU 7.45. SOC on sale to Air Enterprises Ltd., Croydon 9.12.47. Reg'd **G-AKOA** [CofR 12088 11.12.47] and CofA no.10024 issued 18.3.48. To Patrick Motors Ltd., Birmingham 22.1.49. To Maldwyn Lewis Thomas t/a Airlines (Jersey) Ltd. 8.12.50. Overhauled at Jersey, converted to Mk4 and test flown 11.2.55. To Airwork Ltd., Croydon 25.2.55. Cancelled on sale to Persia 15.6.55. Reg'd **EP-ADO** to Iraanse Aardolie Exploratie en Productie Maatschappij N.V. (Iranian Oil Exploration and Producing Co.), Abadan 6.55. Damaged when the cabin filled with smoke causing the pilot to brake violently and aircraft nosed over Masjid-i-Sulaiman 3.1.56. Remained on the official register 1.2.58, but removed by 1.6.59.

6619 Supplied to the Air Council with military serial **X7502**. Initially to 9MU 3.42, then 47MU 5.42 and to Glasgow 8.42. Shipped to South African Air Force 18.8.42 per SS *Empire Migh*t, arriving 11.9.42. To **SAAF1357** and with 9AD 9.42, 62AS 10.42 and noted in operation by 61Sqdn. 12.44 and 4.45. Offered for sale 12.4.46. SOC as sold locally 31.10.46 and reg'd **ZS-BMV** 13.1.47, then to **VP-UBB** in 1947 and **VP-KFI** with Jivraj's Air Service, Mombasa 1.4.48. To Air Travel (Charters) Ltd, Mombasa in 1951. Broken up in 1952.

6620 Supplied to the Air Council with military serial **X7503**. Initially to 9MU 3.42, then No.2 Signals School 4.42 and 18MU 2.46. SOC on sale to Southern Aircraft (Gatwick) Ltd. 15.12.47. Reg'd **G-AKON** [CofR 12101 8.12.47] and CofA no.9910 issued 29.1.48. To John Ernest Coxon, Gatwick 29.1.48. Sold abroad 8.7.48 and reg'n cancelled 19.7.48. Reg'd **VP-KFX** to Noon and Pearce Air Charters Ltd., Nairobi 1952. Sold as **F-OAOS** to Societe Air Madagascar 1.54. CofA issued 11.1.54. Still with Air Madagascar, re-reg'd **5R-MAP** 1.63. Cancelled 1968.

6621 Supplied to the Air Council with serial **X7504** but did not enter military service. Passed to Associated Airways Ltd., Speke 3.42. Reg'd **G-AGED** [CofR 9362 21.4.42] to Scottish Airways

Ltd., Renfrew and CofA no.6923 issued 25.4.42. Ran into soft ground on take-off and overturned Renfrew 2.2.43.

6622 Supplied to the Air Council with serial **X7505** but did not enter military service. Passed to A.A.J.C. 3.42 and reg'd **G-AGEE** [CofR 9363 16.4.42] to Great Western and Southern Airlines Ltd., Speke. CofA no.6924 issued 15.5.32. To B.E.A.C. on formation 1.2.47. Transferred to Gibraltar Airways Ltd. 26.11.47. To A. J. Whittemore (Aeradio) Ltd. 7.53 and cancelled as sold abroad 1.7.53. Reg'd **TF-KAA** [CofR no.74 1.7.53] for Flugskolinn Thytur N.F (Flying School Thytur) and delivered 4.7.53. "Still in good order 1963". Scrapped and burnt some time during summer 1966.

6623 Supplied to the Air Council with military serial **X7506**. Initially to 9MU 4.42, then No.1 Signals School 4.42 and 18MU 12.43. To Royal Navy at Donibristle 29.4.45. At Stretton 1.49 to 7.54 at least. Involved in accident at Stretton 21.2.55 and noted in store there in 1955. Deleted 21.2.55 and broken up.

6624 Supplied to the Air Council with military serial **X7507**. Initially to 9MU 4.42, then to Lee on Solent 4.42. To Royal Navy 6.5.42 and to 787Sqdn., Duxford. At Stretton 1.49 to 7.49 at least. With de Havilland 1.50 and at Arbroath 7.50 to 7.51 at least and Donibristle 1.52 to 7.52 at least. Noted with 782Sqdn. at Donibristle 1.53 and then at Lossiemouth 7.53 to 7.54 at least. SOC at Lossiemouth in the late 1950s. Oil tank from this aircraft placed in NF857 8.56. Parked outside at Lossiemouth without wheels early 1960 awaiting disposal. Put up for tender as scrap at Lossiemouth and purchased with others by Hants and Sussex 8.60 as usable components. Due to bad condition of aircraft, cut up and burnt at Lossiemouth 8.60.

6625 Supplied to the Air Council with military serial **X7508**. Initially to 9MU 4.42 and then served briefly with No.2 Signals School 4.42. To Royal Navy, Lee on Solent 12.5.42. With CH 1.49. At Stretton 7.49 to 7.50 at least, Arbroath 1.51 to 7.51 at least, Machrihanish 1.52 and de Havilland 7.52. At Arbroath 1.53 and then Lossiemouth 7.53 to 7.54 at least. SOC at Lossiemouth in the late 1950s.

6626 Supplied to the Air Council with military serial **X7509**. Initially to 9MU 4.42, then 47MU 5.42. Shipped ex Glasgow to South Africa per SS *Empire Might* 18.8.42, arriving 11.9.42. To **SAAF1358**. With 9AD 9.42, then 62AS 10.42, 11OTU 'A' Flt. 9.44. Surplus to requirements 6ISqdn. 1.46. To 15AD for storage. Offered for sale 12.4.46. Disposed of at 15AD to Aircraft Operating Co. 5.7.46 for £2250. Reg'd **ZS-BEA** to Trans Oranje Air Services, Zastron 10.8.46. SOC by SAAF 26.9.46. With Aircraft Operating Company of Africa Ltd. in 1954. With O.F.S. Air Service (Pty) Ltd, Bloemfontein in 1953. Operated by Maluti Air Services in 1954. Crashed Leribe, Basutoland 24.7.54 while en route Ficksburg to Tlokoeng. Reg'n cancelled 24.7.54. Reported operated with South West Air Transport (Pty) Ltd. in 1955. Starboard engine caught fire on start up at Otjimarongo, S.W. Africa 22.2.55 and believed written off.

6627 Supplied to the Air Council with military serial **X7510**. Initially to 9MU 4.42, then 47MU 8.42. Shipped ex Glasgow to South Africa per SS *Empire Might* 18.8.42, arriving 11.9.42. To **SAAF1359**. With 9AD 9.42, then 62AS 10.42, 61Sqdn. 3.45. At 62AS available for collection by 61Sqdn. 13.1.45. Allotted to 1AD 2.45. Surplus to requirements at 61Sqdn. 1.46 and to 11AD for storage 11.1.46, 28Sqdn. 1.2.46 and 15AD 20.6.46. SOC 26.9.46. Sold to African Flying Services for £1386. Reg'd **ZS-BCT** to African Flying Services 29.1.47. To Aircraft Operating Co of Africa (Pty) Ltd 5.49. Sold in 1949. Reg'd **VP-KHF** to Caspar Air Charter 23.5.49. Pilot lost control in a climbing turn shortly after take-off from Garissa Airfiled, Kenya 23.1.55. Aircraft stalled, crashed and caught fire one mile north of the runway

6628 Supplied to the Air Council with military serial **X7511**. Initially to 18MU 5.42 then 47MU 8.42. Shipped from Glasgow to South Africa per SS *Empire Might* 18.8.42, arriving at Cape Town 16.9.42. To **SAAF1361** and with 9AD 9.42, then to 62AS 10.42. Crashed during a training flight at Bloemfontein 22.10.42 and sustained extensive damage. As the aircraft took-off from Bloemfontein, the aileron control jammed and the pilot elected to land, but the field was too soft and the aircraft overturned. A Board of Survey was held at 10AD at Voortrekkerhogte 3.12.42 for the purpose of examining the aircraft. The Board assessed the damage as approximately 40% and were of the opinion that repair was not economical. The aircraft was written off charge 12.43 and reduced to produce.

6629 Supplied to the Air Council with military serial **X7512**. Initially to R.A.F. Abbotsinch 5.42, then No.2 Signals School (coded 212) 1.43, No.4 Radio School 3.45 and to storage at 18MU 6.46. SOC on sale to Air Enterprises Ltd., Croydon 9.12.47. Reg'd as **G-AKNX** [CofR 12085 4.12.47] and CofA no.9911 issued 13.2.48. To Patrick Motors Ltd., Birmingham 14.2.49. To Airlines (Jersey) Ltd. 24.4.52. Sold abroad to France 13.9.55 and reg'n cancelled 1.10.55. Painted at Jersey 10.9.55 and **G-AKNX** re-applied for delivery flight via Croydon. Reg'd **F-OATD** to Transports Aeriens du Gabon and CofA issued 20.9.55. To Boularne-Lafond, Port Gentil 1.58 and to GAA 9.58. Destroyed 1.61.

6630 Supplied to the Air Council with military serial **X7513**. Initially to R.A.F. Abbotsinch 5.42, then 1680 Flt. 6.43. Whilst flying in a snow storm, the aircraft was unable to maintain height due to loss of power caused by icing. Flew into ground at Braehead 1.3.44. SOC as Cat.E (write off in flying accident) 1.3.44.

6631 Supplied to the Air Council with military serial **X7514**. Initially to 9MU 6.42, then No.1 Signals School 6.42, 18MU 10.44, Tactical Training Command Flt. White Waltham 6.45, to H.Q. Tactical Training Command Com. Flt., Wyton 10.45, 18MU 6.46. Noted at Ringway in 1946, coded TWY-C. SOC on sale to Field Aircraft Services Ltd., Croydon 19.2.47., somewhat later than the registration date! Reg'd **G-AJFL** [CofR 11251 29.1.47] and CofA no.8980 issued 30.4.47. Cancelled as sold abroad 28.3.47. Reg'd **VP-UAW** to The Uganda Company Ltd. 3.47. Starboard wing burnt out and fuselage also damaged, when starting engines at Zanzibar 21.9.47. Not repaired.

6632 Supplied to the Air Council with military serial **X7515**. Initially to 9MU 6.42, then 47MU 6.42. Transported ex Liverpool per *SS Nigerian* 29.8.42. Arrived in Middle East 3.10.42 and in West Africa 1.8.43.

6633 Supplied to the Air Council with military serial **X7516**. Initially to 18MU 6.42. Issued to No.2 Radio School (coded 206) 6.42 and remained with them until stored 18MU 7.45. SOC on sale to Flying Training Ltd., Hanworth reg'd **G-AHLU** [CofR 10167 2.5.46]. To North Sea Air Transport Ltd., Hanworth (owned by Blackburn Aircraft Ltd.) and CofA no.7792 issued 30.7.46. Sold abroad 21.11.49. Arrived Australia 8.12.49 for Edward John Connellan, Alice Springs NT and reg'd as **VH-AHI** 14.12.49. Nominal change to Connellan Airways Ltd. 31.1.51. Over ran on take-off and crashed into trees at unknown location 1952. Recovered by road to Connellan's base and repairs carried out over a period of 12 months. Withdrawn from use 13.5.58 and broken up, as the major overhaul that was due deemed not economically viable.

6634 Supplied to the Air Council with military serial **X7517**. Delivered to 18MU 6.42, then No.2 Signals School (coded 207) 6.42, 18MU 4.45. SOC as Cat.E2 3.9.45.

6635 Supplied to the Air Council with military serial **X7518**. Delivered to 18MU 6.42. Served with No.1 Signals School 7.42 until placed into store 5MU 9.44. SOC on sale to Aircraft and Engineering Services Ltd., Croydon 25.3.48. Reg'd **G-AKMG** [CofR 12044 24.2.48]. To Sivewright Airways Ltd., Barton 9.4.48 and CofA no.10061 issued 13.5.48. Transferred to Sivewright Transport and Storage Co. 31.8.51 for disposal. To Transair Ltd, Croydon 3.3.52. Sold abroad to France 23.4.52 for operation in Indochina. Reg'd **F-BGPI** to Soc. Aigle Azur Indochine, Hanoi and French CofA issued 25.6.52. To Cie. D'Autrex in 10.53. Destroyed 21.5.58 and reg'n finally cancelled 30.11.59.

6636 Supplied to the Air Council with military serial **X7519**. Delivered to 18MU 6.42. Served with 271Sqdn. 7.42, Metropolitan Com. Sqdn. 9.44. Placed into storage 18MU 4.46. SOC on sale 19.12.47. Reg'd **G-AKOP** [CofR 12103 11.12.47] to Theodore William Morton, Croydon. To William Alfred Webb 8.1.48 and CofA no.9909 issued 14.1.48. To Denham Air Services Ltd 9.2.48. Sold to France 3.5.48 and U.K. reg'n cancelled 24.1.49. No further French connection and thought to have been flown on to Israel.

6637 Supplied to the Air Council with military serial **X7520**. Delivered to 18MU 7.42, then 27MU 7.42. Shipped ex Glasgow to

South Africa per *SS Empire Might* 18.8.42, arriving 11.9.42. To **SAAF1360**? With 9AD 9.42, then 62AS 10.42, 11OTU 'A' Flt. 9.44 and 61Sqdn. 5.45. Offered for sale 12.4.46. SOC 31.10.46 as "sold to civil operator". Reg'n **ZS-BMW** allocated but not taken up and it is presumed that the aircraft was unsuitable for civilianisation.

6638 Supplied to the Air Council with military serial **X7521**. Delivered to 18MU 7.42. Served with No.2 Signals School 12.42, 5MU 9.44, Church Fenton 4.47, 64Grp. Com. Flt. 6.47 and then placed into storage 18MU 1.49. SOC on sale to Short Bros. & Harland Ltd., Rochester "for scrap" 28.4.49. Reg'd **G-ALOV** [CofR 12728 29.4.49] and CofA no.10583 issued 30.5.49. Cancelled as sold abroad to French Equatorial Africa 1.3.54. Reg'd **F-OAPS** to Societe Transportes Aeriens du Gabon and CofA issued 1.4.54. Caught fire whilst starting engines at Ekouata and destroyed 16.3.55. Reg'n cancelled 11.10.55.

6639 Supplied to the Air Council with military serial **X7522**. Delivered to 18MU 2.42 and served with 24Sqdn. 8.42. Transferred for service with U.S.A.A.F. 8th Air Force as "7522". Delivered to VIII Air Force 1.12.42. Known to have been based at Alconbury during 1944. Returned to R.A.F. 17.5.44 and to 5MU for storage 8.44. SOC on sale to Denham Aviation Services 11.3.48. Reg'd **G-AKTX** [CofR 12209 1.3.48] to Leslie Ernest Gisborne of Denham Aero Club and CofA no.10048 issued 8.4.48. To Mayfair Air Services Ltd., Croydon 22.4.48. Cancelled as "disappeared in Palestine" and "written-off" 17.5.50. With the Israeli Air Force, serial S-72.

6640 Supplied to the Air Council with military serial **X7523**. Initially to 18MU 8.42, then 24Sqdn. 8.42. To U.S.A.A.F. 8th Air Force 12.42, returned to R.A.F. at Old Sarum 6.44 and 18MU 4.46. SOC on sale to Kenning Ltd., Derby 17.1.47. Reg'd **G-AIUK** [CofR 10979 8.11.46] to Kenning Aviation Ltd., Burnaston and CofA no.9012 issued 26.9.47. Sold to Derby Airways and operated by their subsidiary Air Schools Ltd. 18.6.48. Sold abroad to Kenya 14.2.55. Reg'd **VP-KND** to J. E. F. Wilkins, t/a Caspair Ltd., Mazinde 3.55. Badly damaged by fire on starting engines Kisumu, Kenya 18.3.55. Reg'n cancelled 1964 as "scrapped".

6641 Built as part of the original contract for the Air Council and allotted serial **X7524** but deleted from the contract and not taken on charge. A de Havilland photograph dated 1.9.42 shows X7524 in full military marks, with the caption "Dominie for Iraq". Converted to Rapide by de Havilland at Witney and CofA no.6948 issued 4.11.42. Intended for Misr Airways, probably as **SU-ACS**, but reported lost at sea on board ship when on delivery to Egypt. Replaced by c/n 6544.

6642 The final Dominie completed by de Havilland at Hatfield. Built as part of the original contract for the Air Council and allotted serial **X7525** but deleted from the contract and not taken on charge. Instead, converted to Rapide by de Havilland at Witney and CofA no.6949 issued 4.11.42. Intended for Misr Airways, probably as **SU-ACT**, but reported lost at sea on board ship when on delivery to Egypt. Replaced by c/n 6551.

6643 Built as part of the original contract for the Air Council and the first Dominie completed by Brush Coachworks at Loughborough. Allotted serial **HG644** but deleted from the contract and not taken on charge. Instead, converted to Rapide by de Havilland at Witney. To J. Park and Son for packing 3.5.43. SOC 5.7.43 to Turkish Air Force. Arrived 21.8.43 per Liberty Ship no.320. Reg'd **TC-LAV** to Devlet Hava Yollari 4.44. Fate unknown.

6644 Built as part of the original contract for the Air Council by Brush Coachworks at Loughborough. Allotted serial **HG645** but deleted from the contract and not taken on charge. Instead, converted to Rapide by de Havilland at Witney. To J. Park and Son for packing 18.5.43. SOC 5.7.43 to Turkish Air Force. Arrived 21.8.43 per Liberty Ship 322. Reg'd **TC-MUT** to Devlet Hava Yollari 4.44. Fate unknown.

6645 Built as part of the original contract for the Air Council by Brush Coachworks at Loughborough. Allotted serial **HG646** but deleted from the contract and not taken on charge. Instead, converted to Rapide by de Havilland at Witney. To J. Park and Son for packing 31.5.43. SOC to Turkish Air Force. Arrived 20.9.43 per Liberty Ship 1053. Reg'd **TC-NUR** to Devlet Hava Yollari 4.44. Fate unknown.

6646 Built as part of the original contract for the Air Council by Brush Coachworks at Loughborough. Allotted serial **HG647** but deleted from the contract and not taken on charge. Instead, converted to Rapide by de Havilland at Witney. SOC 11.9.43 to Turkish Air Force. Arrived 10.10.43 per Liberty Ship 1063. Reg'd **TC-ZOR** to Devlet Hava Yollari 4.44. Fate unknown.

6647 Supplied to the Air Council with military serial **HG648**. Initially to 76MU 5.43, then to New Zealand per *SS Sussex*. Sailed 4.8.43 and arrived 5.9.43 (though RNZAF records says 8.9.43). To RNZAF **NZ523** and taken on charge 8.9.43. Assembled at Hobsonville & served with 42Sqdn. Reg'd **ZK-AKS** to New Zealand National Airways Corporation 25.7.46 and named *Teoteo* (Tern). To Southern Scenic Air Services Ltd., Queenstown 11.9.56. Taken over by NZ Tourist Air Travel Ltd. 5.65. Crashed at Macetown on Mount Soho, 23 miles NE of Queenstown 15.6.65 whilst on a sheep spotting flight after "pilot became disorientated". Reg'n cancelled 29.6.65. In 1998, the aircraft was undergoing restoration with Colin F. Smith, Mandeville.

6648 Supplied to the Air Council with military serial **HG649**. Delivered to 76MU 5.43. Passed to the Royal New Zealand Air Force and shipped per *SS Sussex* ex U.K. 4.8.43 and arrived New Zealand 5.9.43. Assembled Hobsonville and taken on charge as **NZ524** 8.9.43. Sold to Airwork (NZ) Ltd. and reg'd **ZK-BCP** 17.12.53. To South Island Airways Ltd. .54. To Trans Island Airways 5.56. To Coastal Airways Ltd. 9.58. To B. G. Chadwick t/a Air Charter (NZ) Ltd. 9.59. To Southern Scenic Air Services Ltd. .64. Taken over by New Zealand Tourist Air Travel Ltd. 5.65 and they in turn, taken over by Mount Cook Airlines Ltd. 1.68. In storage by 1974 when sold to C. Tracey & Co. Pty, Melbourne. Allocated reg'n **VH-BGP** applied in New Zealand but **ZK-BCP** was taped over the top for delivery flight via Auckland, Kaitaia, Norfolk Island, Brisbane, Tamworth, Albury to Kyneton arriving there 22.1.75. To Joseph G. Drage, Wodonga VIC. Flown in formation with DH89A VH-IAN and DH84 VH-AON 22.2.75 to commemorate the 50th anniversary of the first flight of the DH60 Moth. To Drage's Air World, Wangaratta VIC. Ownership changed to the Rural City of Wangaratta 20.10.98.

6649 Supplied to the Air Council with military serial **HG650**. Delivered to 76MU 3.6.43 where dismantled for shipping to India per *SS Fort Camouson*. Sailed 16.8.43 and arrived Bombay 23.9.43. Reg'd **VT-ARK** to Government of India 10.43 and operated by Air India. Impressed as **MA963** 12.43. Completely submerged in water and SOC 31.2.46.

6650 Supplied to the Air Council with military serial **HG651**. Delivered to 76MU 3.6.43 where dismantled for shipping to India per *SS Fort Camouson*. Sailed 16.8.43 and arrived Bombay 23.9.43. Reg'd **VT-ARL** to Government of India 10.43 and operated by Air India. Impressed as **MA964** 12.43. Sold by Director General of Aircraft Disposals 4.46. Restored to **VT-ARL** for Air Services of India Ltd. 9.4.47. To Madras Residency Airways Ltd. 31.7.48, then Vavadavaja Airways Ltd., also of Madras 19.10.49. Returned to Madras Residency Airways 27.8.57. Fate unknown.

6651 Supplied to the Air Council with military serial **HG652**. Initially to 76MU 11.6.43, then to India per *SS Fort Camouson*. Sailed 16.8.43 and arrived at Bombay 23.9.43. Reg'd **VT-ARM** to Government. of India 10.43 and operated by Air India. Impressed as **MA965** 12.43. Believed sold by Director General of Aircraft Disposals 4.46.

6652 Supplied to the Air Council with military serial **HG653**. Delivered to 76MU 23.6.43, then to India per *SS Fort Camouson*. Sailed 16.8.43 and arrived at Bombay 23.9.43. Reg'd as **VT-ARN** to Govt. of India 10.43 and operated by Air India. Impressed as **MA966** 12.43. 12.43. Sold by Director General of Aircraft Disposals 4.46. Restored as **VT-ARN** to Government of Bengal 29.3.47. Cancelled from register 24.2.48.

6653 Supplied to the Air Council with military serial **HG654**. To 76MU for dismantling and packing 7.43. Shipped to New Zealand per Liberty Ship no.732 *Port Chalmers* 26.8.43, arriving 6.10.43. To RNZAF as **NZ525**. Assembled at Hobsonville and TOC 13.10.43. Served with 24 Sqdn. Reg'd **ZK-AKY** to New Zealand Airways Corp 12.8.46 and named *Tui* (Parson Bird). To Ritchie Air Services Ltd, Te Anau 19.5.64. Taken over by NZ Tourist Air Travel Ltd 12.64. Taken over by Mount Cook Airlines 1.68. Used as back-up baggage aircraft by Mount Cook when

required. Based at Queenstown and still in use 3.75. To T. C. Williams, Masterton 28.3.78. Had acquired a semi-military colour scheme by mid 1981 with serial NZ525 and roundel apparently applied over its civil colours. Noted under "rebuild" for CofA renewal at Masterton 6.82; apparently, a major job due to "woodworm infestation". Aircraft listed with value of NZ$1000. Airworthy again after 3.5 year rebuild by early 1986. Painted in N.A.C. colours and named *Tui* again. With Croydon Air Service in 1998 (airworthy?).

6654 Supplied to the Air Council with military serial **HG655**. To 76MU for dismantling and packing 7.43. Shipped to New Zealand per Liberty Ship no.732 *Port Chalmers* 26.8.43, arriving 6.10.43. To RNZAF as **NZ526**. Assembled at Hobsonville and TOC 13.10.43. Served with 1 Sqdn. Sold 8.4.52 and to **ZK-BAU** for the Auckland Aero Club 28.4.52. CofA issued 14.5.52. To Southern Scenic Air Services 1.3.56. Overshot the runway at Milford Sound on a training flight 22.4.64 and wrecked. Broken up at Queenstown for spares during 1964.

6655 Supplied to the Air Council with military serial **HG656**. To 76MU for dismantling and packing 7.43. Shipped to New Zealand per Liberty Ship no.732 *Port Chalmers* 26.8.43, arriving 6.10.43. Assembled Hobsonville and taken on charge as **NZ527** 13.10.43. Issued to 42Sqdn. To New Zealand National Airways Corp., reg'd **ZK-ALB** 30.8.46 and named *Tikaka* (Blue Heron). To Trans Island Airways Ltd. 22.7.57. To G. L. McLatchie 29.7.57. To Coastal Airways Ltd., 7.58. To Marlborough Aero Club, Blenheim 2.6.59. To Ritchie Air Services Ltd., Gore 2.7.61. Taken over by New Zealand Tourist Air Travel Ltd. 12.64, who in turn, were taken over by Mount Cook Airlines Ltd. 1.68. Withdrawn 4.11.71 and stored until sale in Australia. Imported via Kaitaia, Norfolk Island and Brisbane by C. Tracey & Co. Pty, Melbourne and painted as **VH-IAN** at Essendon by 23.7.74, although reg'n not official until 2.8.74! Delivered to Kenneth E. Orrman, Shepparton VIC 8.9.74. Unflown for 5 years but restored early 1999 and to new owner Dr. Robert Fox, based at Sydney-Bankstown NSW re-reg'd **VH-UTV** 11.6.99.

6656 Supplied to the Air Council with military serial **HG657**. Delivered to 76MU 7.43 where dismantled for shipping to India. Reg'd **VT-ART** 3.44 and loaned to Tata Airlines, Bombay 12.45. To Indian National Airways Ltd., Calcutta. Forced landed during ferry flight due to weather conditions at Pastabgath, 30 miles from Allahabad and burnt out 8.4.46. Both crew killed.

6657 Supplied to the Air Council with serial **HG658** but did not enter military service. Delivered to 76MU 23.8.43 where dismantled for shipping to Karachi per *SS Chyebassa* 3.12.43 and arrived 22.1.44 (also quoted as 12.1.44). Reg'd **VT-ARV** in 1944. To Indian National Airways Ltd., Calcutta 1.7.46. To Indian Air Survey and Transport Co. Ltd., Calcutta 5.6.47. Name changed to Air Survey Co. of India Ltd. in 1948. Reg'd **G-AMJK** [CofR R3279 17.5.51] to Fairey Aviation Co. Ltd., Hayes and CofA no.3279 issued 14.10.51. Nominal change to Fairey Aviation Ltd. 24.9.59. Converted to Mk6 prior to 1.60. To Hants and Sussex Aviation Ltd., Portsmouth 17.8.60. Cancelled on sale to France 9.10.61. Reg'd as **F-OBVL** to the French Department of Guyane, Cayenne and delivered ex Portsmouth 21.10.61. CofA issued 15.12.61 and suspended 12.65.

6658 Supplied to the Air Council with serial **HG659** but did not enter military service. Converted to Rapide by de Havilland at Witney and CofA no.7035 issued 9.11.43. To J. Parks and Son for packing 11.43 and shipped to Cape Town per *SS Fort Jackson* 12.12.43, arriving 8.1.44. Reg'd **VP-YCI** to Southern Rhodesia Air Services 4.2.44. (This was the communications squadron for the R.R.A.F.). To Central African Airways 1.6.46. Sold 8.49 and reg'd **ZS-DDI** to Associated Manganese Mines of South Africa Ltd., Cape 19.10.49. Reg'n cancelled 30.11.59. Reg'd **OO-CJX** to Air Brousse SPRL, Leopoldville-Ndolo 10.11.59 with CofA no.C309. Following independence, re-reg'd **9O-CJX** 17.3.61 still with Air Brousse. Re-reg'd again as **9Q-CJX** after 8.9.62, also with Air Brousse. Ownership later changed to A.M.A.Z., Kinshasa. Fate unknown.

6659 Supplied to the Air Council with serial **HG660** but did not enter military service. Converted to Rapide by de Havilland at Witney and CofA no.7034 issued 9.11.43. To J. Parks and Son for packing 11.43 and shipped to Cape Town per *SS Roslin Castle* 20.11.43, arriving 11.12.43. Reg'd **VP-YCJ** to Southern Rhodesia Air Service 20.1.44. Operated in communications role for the

R.R.A.F. To Central African Airways 1.6.46. Reg'n cancelled 6.50 and reg'd as **VP-NAK** to Government of Nyasaland 3.50. Reg'n cancelled 12.51 and became **VP-RCP** with the Northern Rhodesian Government 12.51. Crashed on Nyasaland border 30.8.53.

6660   Supplied to the Air Council with military serial **HG660**. To de Havilland at Witney for conversion to Rapide 9.43 and CofA no.7036 issued 15.11.43. To J. Parks and Son for packing 11.43 and shipped to Cape Town per *SS Sandown Castle* 13.12.43, arriving 24.1.44. Reg'd **VP-YCK** to Southern Rhodesia Air Service 22.2.44. Operated in communications role for Royal Rhodesian Air Force. Sold 12.51 and reg'd **VP-RCI** to Zambesi Airways Ltd. 12.51 and then **VP-YLV** still with Zambesi Airways Ltd. in 1954. Destroyed at Victoria Falls when a hangar collapsed during a gale 6.1.55

6661   Ordered by the Air Council with military serial **HG661** but released from the contract and sold to de Havilland. Initially to 756MU 14.9.43. Shipped to Karachi per *SS Chyebassa* 3.12.43, arriving 12.1.44. Operated as **VT-ARW** by Indian National Airways Ltd., Calcutta. To Indian Air Survey and Transport Co. Ltd. 20.5.46. Name changed to Air Survey Co. of India Ltd. in 1948. Cancelled from register 16.5.47.

6662   Supplied to the Air Council with serial **HG662** but did not enter U.K. military service. Delivered to 76MU 9.43 where dismantled for shipping to New Zealand per *SS Glenberg* 28.9.43, arrived Auckland 21.11.43. To RNZAF as **NZ528**. Assembled at Hobsonville, taken on charge 22.11.43 and served with 42Sqdn. at Rongotai. Issued to NAC ex 42Sqdn. 30.8.46. Reg'd **ZK-AKU** to New Zealand National Airways Corporation 30.8.46 and named *Tawaka* (Grey Duck). Delivered to Nelson Aero Club 19.5.63. To Patchett Safaris Ltd., Christchurch 2.11.65. To Rotorua Aero Club 15.9.66 and to D. W. Gray, Auckland 22.7.68. Competed in the U.K. – Australia Air Race December 1969. Reportedly sold in the USA in 1971 for NZ$10000, however, in March 1975 the aircraft was still in New Zealand undergoing a complete rebuild at Ardmore at the hands of David Gray. On 23.1.77 the aircraft flew again after having spent over 5 years undergoing a complete rebuild at Ardmore. Ground-looped on landing at Te Kowhai, 27.1.80 - repairable. Repairs said to be almost complete at Ardmore in mid 1982 and airworthy with D. W. Gray and H. Noton, Ardmore in 1998.

6663   Supplied to the Air Council with serial **HG663** but did not enter U.K. military service. Delivered to 76MU 11.43 where dismantled for shipping per *SS Clan McBrayne* 7.12.43, arriving at Diego Suares, Madagascar 5.3.44. Taken on charge by French Air Force 1.10.44 and operated by ELA387. Crashed Tananarive 11.6.47.

6664   Supplied to the Air Council with serial **HG665** but did not enter U.K. military service. Delivered to 76MU 10.43, where dismantled for shipping to New Zealand per *SS Port Ahua* 17.10.43, arrived Auckland 26.11.43. To RNZAF as **NZ529**. Assembled at Hobsonville and taken on charge 22.11.43 serving with 42Sqdn. at Rongotai. Issued to NAC ex 42Sqdn. 30.8.46. Reg'd **ZK-ALC** to New Zealand National Airways Corporation 30.8.46 and named *Tiora* (Stitch Bird). Destroyed by fire at Rotorua 14.1.50 when engine exhaust ignited dry grass and fire spread to the aircraft. Reg'n cancelled 3.3.50.

6665   Supplied to the Air Council with serial **HG666** but did not enter military service. Instead, to de Havilland at Witney for conversion to Rapide 10.43 and CofA no.7043 issued 5.12.43. To J. Parks and Son for packing 11.43 and shipped to Cape Town per *SS Umtali* 22.12.43, arriving 30.1.44. Reg'd **VP-YCL** to Southern Rhodesia Air Service 1.3.44. Operated in communications role for the R.R.A.F. To Central African Airways Corporation 1.6.46. Sold 10.49 and reg'd **VP-RBT** to Northern Rhodesia Aviation Services Ltd. in 1950. Restored as **VP-YCL** to Northern Rhodesia Aviation Services Ltd., Lusaka 4.50. Destroyed during forced landing 11 miles S.E. of Fort Manning, Nyasaland 28.9.50 - no injuries.

6666   Supplied to the Air Council with serial **HG667** but did not enter military service. To de Havilland at Witney for conversion to Rapide 10.43 and CofA no.7044 issued 5.12.43. To J. Parks and Son for packing 12.43 and shipped to South Africa per *SS Empire Grace* 11.1.44, arrived Capetown 5.7.44. Reg'd **VP-YCM** to Southern Rhodesia Air Service 15.3.44. Operated in communications role for the R.R.A.F. To Central African Airways

Corporation 1.6.46. Sold 7.49 and became **SR-57** with the Royal Rhodesian Air Force in 1950. Re-serialled **RRAF-57**? Reg'd as **VP-YOL** to Victoria Falls Airways 5.56. Cancelled 15.8.62 as "sold". Reported reg'd as '9Q-CJD' with Air Brousse SPRL in 1962, but see c/n 6607.

6667   Supplied to the Air Council with serial **HG668** but did not enter military service. To de Havilland at Witney for conversion to Rapide 10.43 and CofA no.7053 issued 28.1.44. To J. Parks and Son for packing 1.44 and shipped to Cape Town per *SS Neleus* 29.1.44, arriving 26.2.44. Reg'd **VP-YCN** to Southern Rhodesia Air Service 28.4.44. Operated in communications role for the R.R.A.F. To Central African Airways 1.6.46. To Trevor Construction Co. Ltd. 4.50 and then Coleman Myers in 1950 and Air Carriers Ltd. also in 1950. Sold during 1951 and reg'd **ZS-DFG** to Africair Ltd. 4.6.51. To Anglo-Transvaal Consolidated Investments in 1952. Operated by Bechuanaland Air Services in 1954. Reg'd **VP-YMW** to Victoria Falls Airways (Pvt) Ltd. 25.2.55. To Zambesi Airways and R.U.A.C. Cancelled on sale to Belgian Congo 24.8.62. Arrived in the Congo 26.6.63 but no further information. (Note: the c/ns for Rapides 9Q-CPF/CQF/CQT/CYE are unknown and this is likely to be one of these).

6668   Supplied to the Air Council with military serial **HG669**. Initially to 76MU 11.43 for packing and preparation for shipping. To the Royal New Zealand Air Force and shipped per Liberty Ship *Port Huron* ex U.K. 1.12.43 and arrived Auckland 18.1.44. Assembled at Hobsonville and taken on charge as **NZ531** 25.1.44. Declared surplus 5.52 and sold to Airwork (NZ) Ltd., Christchurch. Reg'd **ZK-BBP** 4.9.52. To South Island Airways Ltd. .54. Shipped ex Lyttleton per SS *Kaitoke* to Sydney 1.57 but remained crated until late 1958. To Alpine Airways (Pty) Ltd. reg'd **VH-AAG** and named *Rapide* 19.8.58. To R. G. Carswell t/a Carsair Air Services (Pty) Ltd., Mount Pleasant QLD. 16.8.60. Leased to Darwin Air Taxis 10.61. Aircraft struck a kangaroo at Wolner Station airstrip NT 27.2.63 and although the lower centre section spar was broken, flown back to Darwin. However, deemed beyond economical repair and abandoned in the open. Remains taken over by Carswell on the liquidation of Darwin Air Taxis, radios and other useful items were removed and the hulk presented to R.A.A.F. for target practice. Finally destroyed in early 1964 when attacked by Sabre aircraft on the Leanyer Range near Darwin.

6669   Supplied to the Air Council with military serial **HG670**. Delivered to 76MU 11.43 where dismantled for shipping. To the French Air Force for service in Madagascar. Shipped per *SS Clan McBrayne* 7.12.43, arriving 5.3.44 at Diego Suares. No further information.

6670   Supplied to the Air Council with serial **HG671** but did not enter military service. To de Havilland at Witney for conversion to Rapide 12.43 and CofA no.7065 issued 12.4.44. To J. Parks and Son for packing 4.44 and shipped to Reykjavik per *SS Horsa* 9.4.44, arriving 22.4.44. Reg'd **TF-ISM** [CofR no.9 5.4.45] to Flugfleag Islands hf and named Sviffaxi. To Icelandair. Dismantled at Reykjavik Airport by 1955 and scrapped 1961.

6671   Supplied to the Air Council with military serial **HG672**. Initially to 76MU 11.43. Shipped per *SS Clan McBrayne* 7.12.43, arriving at Diego Suares, Madagascar 5.3.44. Taken on charge by French Air Force 1.10.44. Reg'd **F-OANU** to Air Madagascar and CofA issued 9.9.53. Destroyed 1.54 and reg'n cancelled 5.3.54.

6672   Supplied to the Air Council with military serial **HG673**. Initially to 18MU 12.43, then No.4 Radio School 2.44, 5MU 12.46. Sold to Airwork Ltd., Croydon 27.8.47. Reg'd **G-AKEU** [CofR 11858 5.9.47] and CofA no.9781 issued 3.6.48. To Iraq Petroleum Transport Co. Ltd., Haifa 29.9.47. Sold abroad to Lebanon 21.6.51 and reg'n cancelled 1.8.51. Reg'd **OD-ABL** to Saad Transport, Beirut 6.51. Operated by Contracting and Trading Co. (CAT) in 1955. Destroyed by fire whilst refuelling, Baghdad 26.7.55.

6673   Supplied to the Air Council with military serial **HG674**. Initially to 76MU 11.43 for dismantling. Shipped to Auckland per *SS Port Huron?* 1.12.43, arriving 18.1.44. To RNZAF as **NZ530**. Assembled at Hobsonville, TOC 25.1.44. Issued to NAC ex 42 Sqdn. 30.8.46. Reg'd as **ZK-AKT** to New Zealand National Airways Corp 30.8.46 and named *Tareke* (Quail). To West Coast Airways Ltd, Hokitika 17.1.56. To Southern Scenic Air Services Ltd 4.12.56. Taken over by NZ Tourist Air Travel Ltd 5.65. Crashed into the bed of the Shotover River while landing at Queenstown

DH89 c/n 6662. ZK-AKU was a competitor in the 1969 U.K. to Australia Air Race and here, proudly displays the many places visited en route from and back to the other side of the world.

DH89 c/n 6679. Seen at Newcastle on a sortie from Lossiemouth, HG694 was one of the longest serving Dominies. Although stored 1955-1961, it was noted visiting various locations in late 1962.

DH89 c/n 6668. A pity an audio cassette is not available to every reader of this book! The distinctive sound of twin Gipsy Queens just prior to landing is a joy and NZ531, in this mode, is seen here.

DH89 c/n 6679. Demobbed in February 1963, it joined the civil register with the R.A.F. Abingdon Sport Parachuting Club as G-ASFC and ended its days as a ground trainer at Weston-on-the-Green.

DH89 c/n 6670. Yet another Rapide that did not enter U.K. military service but sold to Iceland and operated scheduled domestic passenger services. Dismantled Reykjavik 1966.

DH89 c/n 6682. Wearing the colours of Federated Fruit Co., G-ANZP served them well for 10 years from 1955. Eventually broken up in France and provided parts for replicas built for the Blue Max film.

DH89 c/n 6676. G-AIYR when in service with Hunting Surveys at Leavesden. How many readers have circled the lighthouse off Land's End in this machine with Viv Bellamy at the controls?

DH89 c/n 6693. In service with the Royal Navy from 1945 until at least 1955, HG708 was last noted in open storage with several other Dominies at Lossiemouth, devoid of wheels!

after a flight from Glenorchy 15.4.67. No casualties. Cause was engine fire due to failure of an exhaust valve. Reg'n cancelled 12.5.67.

6674 Supplied to the Air Council with military serial **HG689**. Initially to 76MU 11.43 for packing and preparation for shipping. To Free French via Madagascar per *SS Atlantian* 3.44/5.44. Taken on charge by French Air Force 1.10.44. Fate unknown.

6675 Supplied to the Air Council with military serial **HG690**. Initially to 18MU 12.43, then No.2 E&WS (coded 208) 12.43 and to storage at 5MU 8.45. SOC on sale to Kenning Aviation Ltd., Burnaston 20.12.46. Reg'd **G-AIUI** [CofR 10977 8.11.46] and CofA no.8974 issued 29.5.47. To Hargreaves Airways Ltd., Elmdon 26.6.47. Whilst en route Elmdon to Ronaldsway, the aircraft descended below a safe altitude in a turn on the Ronaldsway VHF homer, 2 miles from the airport and flew into high ground in bad visibility at Dalby, near Peel 10.6.48. Five passengers and pilot killed but two passengers survived.

6676 Supplied to the Air Council with military serial **HG691** and initially to 18MU 12.43. To Flying Wing Yatesbury operated by No.2 Radio School coded '219'. To storage at 5MU 8.45. SOC on sale to Reid & Sigrist Ltd. 22.11.46 and reg'd **G-AIYR** 11.12.46. CofA no.8830 finally issued 26.2.48 although applied for 16.12.46!. To Rodney Reuben Carne, Elstree 3.52 but operated by Wolverhampton Aviation. To Hunting Aerosurveys, Elstree 1.53. (Moved to Leavesden .65 and name changed to Hunting Surveys & Consultants Ltd. 5.67). To V. H. Bellamy t/a Westward Airways, Land's End and operated pleasure flights from St. Just. To David & Mrs. C. A. Cyster and D. I. Rendall, Hawarden 10.1.79. Re-covered at Shipdham 3.80 and to Hatfield 4.80 for fitting of new engines. and flown to Capetown and back .80 to commemorate Sir Alan Cobham's trail blazing flight of 1925/26. Nominal change to David and Mrs. C. A. Cyster 2.10.85. To Clacton Aero Club (1988) Ltd. and delivered 28.3.91. Operates joy flights from Duxford during summer months and from .92, trades as Classic Wings with the aircraft named *Classic Lady*. Although still operated by Clacton Aero Club/Classic Wings, ownership changed to Fairmont Investments Ltd. 24.8.99. To Spectrum Leisure Ltd. 19.9.02 nd continues in service with the Clacton Aero Club..

6677 Supplied to the Air Council with military serial **HG692**. Delivered to 18MU 12.43. Served with No.1 Radio School 6.44. Returned to 18MU for storage 7.46. SOC on sale to A. Hamson & Son Ltd. 27.1.48. Not civilianised and possibly used by Air Charter Experts Ltd. as a spares source.

6678 Supplied to the Air Council with military serial **HG693**. Delivered to 18MU 1.44. Served with 87Grp. Com. Flt. 6.45. Returned to 18MU for storage 4.46. SOC on sale to Field Consolidated Aircraft Services Ltd., Croydon. Reg'd **G-AHPW** [CofR 10268 22.5.46] and CofA no.8160 issued 9.10.46. Cancelled as sold abroad 12.8.46. Reg'd to unknown operator as **ZS-BCO** 7.9.46. Cancelled as exported 22.8.47 and served with Southern Rhodesia Air Force with serial **SR-24**. To Gibb, Coyne & Sager (Kariba) Pvt. Ltd. reg'd **VP-YOY** .56. Name changed to Sir Alexander Gibb & Partners .57. Destroyed by fire Kariba 25.11.57.

6679 Supplied to the Air Council with military serial **HG694**. Delivered to 18MU 12.43 and then to Royal Navy service at RNAS Lee-on-Solent Stn. Flt. coded 'GN' 3.45, 782Sqdn. Donibristle 7.45, Evanton 9.45, until stored Stretton 6.48-10.49. Then to Lee-on-Solent 12.49 and Eglington 3.50. Taxied into obstruction 12.52 necessitating repairs at de Havilland Leavesden. To 782Sqdn. Donibristle 10.53 and to storage Lossiemouth 12.55-1.62. Visited Aberdeen 3.62 and Newcastle 10.62 operated by 700Z Flt Lossiemouth. Reg'd **G-ASFC** [CofR R7805 25.2.63] to Frederick Beresford Sowery, Michael Maurice Cecil Stamford & Bernard Willes Rigold, trustees of the assets of R.A.F. Abingdon Sport Parachuting Club. Last flown at Weston-on-the-Green, Oxfordshire 3.6.65 and CofA expired 27.8.65. Reg'n cancelled as permanently withdrawn from use 10.1.66. Wings burnt early '67 and fuselage last noted in use at Weston as a ground trainer.

6680 Supplied the Air Council with military serial **HG695**. Delivered to 76MU 1.44 where dismantled for shipment to South Africa. Shipped per *SS Ville d'Amiens* to Capetown and to the South African Air force as **SAF1364**. After assembly, to 62AS 6.44, 61Sqdn. 2.45, 28Sqdn. Com. Flt. Pretoria 3.46. To 15AD for storage 1.46 and offered for sale 12.4.46. Purchased by Southern Rhodesian Government for £3913 for operation by Central Africa

Airways and reg'd **VP-YEZ**. To C. A. Pritchard t/a Victoria Falls Airways (Pvt) Ltd. 4.50. Destroyed when hangar collapsed during gale at Victoria Falls 6.1.55.

6681 Supplied to the Air Council with military serial **HG696**. Delivered to 76MU 1.44 where dismantled for shipment to India. Shipped per *SS Custodian* 28.3.44. Sold to Indian National Airways Ltd., Calcutta 25.7.46, reg'd **VT-ARY** and in service by 12.9.46. To Indian Air Survey & Transport Co. Ltd., Calcutta 5.6.47. Name changed to Air Survey Co. of India Ltd. 1948. To Jokai (Assam) Tea Co. Ltd. 7.3.53. Aircraft hit the ground in a shallow dive near Mohanbari, Assam 9.2.59 and was destroyed by fire – two killed. Cancelled 7.4.59.

6682 Supplied to the Air Council with military serial **HG697**. To Royal Navy 3.3.45. Taken on charge 1.3.45. With Stretton by 1.49, 50TAG Yeovilton by 1.50, 767Sqdn., Yeovilton 7.50, Gosport by 7.51, Arbroath by 7.52 and Stretton by 7.53. Still at Stretton 7.54 and SOC 28.1.55. Reg'd as **G-ANZP** to Reginald James Gates t/a Federated Fruit Co. [CofR R4890 24.2.55]. Arrived at Speke by 4.55 and CofA issued 17.9.56. Converted to Mk6 9.61. Withdrawn from use at Speke after CofA expiry 30.7.62. To Harold Best-Devereux, Panshanger 13.5.65 and delivered south on 3.11.64 in part-exchange for an Aero Commander. Sold abroad to France 21.6.65. To Rousseau Aviation as a source of engines and other parts for Fokker D.VII replicas then being built for the film "Blue Max". Aircraft was dismantled at Dinard during 1965.

6683 Supplied to the Air Council with military serial **HG698**. To Royal Navy at Lee-on-Solent 1.2.45. At Stretton by 1.49, to Anthorn by 1.50, Gosport by 7.51 and to Arbroath by 1.53. To Shorts by 7.54 and used by the Shorts Ferry Service. Still on RN charge 2.60 and reported still flying 2.62. Stored inside at Lossiemouth mid 1960 but eventually broken up.

6684 Supplied to the Air Council with military serial **HG699**. Delivered to 18MU 1.44 and then served with 80OTU (French) 5.45. Taken on charge by the French Air Force 11.4.46 and with Ecole de Chasse Meknes 11.46. Served with BE703 at Pau and ELA56 at Persan-Beaumont. Still in service 10.50 but no further information after that date.

6685 Supplied to the Air Council with military serial **HG700**. To Royal Navy at Donbristle 27.3.45. Into storage "in reserve" 25.8.48. SOC 8.48 as deteriorated in service and reduced to produce 9.48.

6686 Built as part of the original contract for the Air Council and allotted serial **HG701** but deleted from the contract and not taken on charge. Converted to Rapide by de Havilland at Witney 1.44. Export CofA no.7066 issued 26.4.44. To J. Parkes & Son for packing and shipped to Turkey for operation by Devlet Hava Yollari. Reg'd **TC-AGA** 8.44. Fate unknown.

6687 Built as part of the original contract for the Air Council and allotted serial **HG702** but deleted from the contract and not taken on charge. Converted to Rapide by de Havilland at Witney 1.44. Export CofA no.7067 issued 26.4.44. To J. Parkes & Son for packing and shipped to Turkey for operation by Devlet Hava Yollari. Reg'd **TC-HAD** 8.44. To Hurkus Airlines 9.57. Wfu during 1959. Eventual fate unknown but see notes on unknown aircraft following the reg'n to c/n cross index.

6688 Built as part of the original contract for the Air Council and allotted serial **HG703** but deleted from the contract and not taken on charge. Converted to Rapide by de Havilland at Witney 1.44. Export CofA no.7068 issued 26.4.44. To J. Parkes & Son for packing and shipped to Turkey for Devlet Hava Yollari. Reg'd **TC-PER** 8.44. To Hurkus Airlines 9.57. Wfu during 1959. Eventual fate unknown but see notes reference unidentified aircraft following the reg'n to c/n cross index.

6689 Built as part of the original contract for the Air Council and allotted serial **HG704** but deleted from the contract and not taken on charge. Converted to Rapide by de Havilland at Witney 1.44. Export CofA no.7069 issued 26.4.44. To J. Parkes & Son for packing and shipped to Turkey for Devlet Hava Yollari. Reg'd **TC-VUR** 8.44. Fate unknown.

6690 Supplied to the Air Council with military serial **HG705**. Delivered to 18MU 1.44. Served with Metropolitan Com. Sqdn.

DH89 c/n 6704. Based in the Lebanon with the Arab Contracting & Trading Co. from 1955, however, G-AKMH wore Motherwell Bridge Contracting & Trading Co. titles when it visited Nicosia August 1960.

DH89 c/n 6718. Wearing the station code LM when with Lossiemouth Station Flight from September 1956, NF847 was sold to R.A.F. Abingdon Sport Parachuting Club as G-ASIA in May 1963.

DH89 c/n 6706. F-BHCD hangs from the roof as a "skydiving diorama" in the Musee de l'Air's Sporting and Light Aviation Hall which was inaugurated during the 1981 Paris Air Show.

DH89 c/n 6723. Manx Airlines' G-AKGY proudly wears the Isle of Man three-legged symbol on the fin. Sold abroad to France late 1956 but operated mainly in Algeria until certificate suspended June 1963.

DH89 c/n 6708. Operated by Marshall's of Cambridge for nearly 13 years, initially with their flying school from March 1948. In Mayflower service, destroyed in a take-off accident at St. Mary's July 1963.

DH89 c/n 6735. Operated by Mayflower Air Services only briefly from May to October 1964. From September 1965, with 20th Century Fox Productions and used as a camera ship for the Blue Max film.

DH89 c/n 6709. Formed to undertake ad-hoc passenger and freight charters, EI-AML was the first Aer Turas aircraft, delivered in June 1962. They went on to operate a range of large cargo aircraft.

DH89 c/n 6736. 4R-AAI photographed at Staverton shortly after arrival, following its epic flight from Sri Lanka. Purchased by the Science Museum in 1981 and displayed at Wroughton as G-ALXT.

8.45 (sometime coded CB-U), 18MU 11.46, 5MU 1.49. SOC on sale to Air Navigation and Trading Co. Ltd., Squires Gate 16.1.50. Reg'd **G-ALXI** [CofR 14916 31.1.50] to Mrs. D. Whyham and CofA no.10869 issued 4.5.50. To William Stevens, Exeter 3.2.51. Returned to Air Navigation and Trading Co. Ltd., Squires Gate 21.1.52. To Terence William Willans, Henley-on-Thames 13.5.55. Cancelled as sold in Austria 15.10.55. Reg'd **OE-FAA** to Oesterreichische Rettungsflugwacht 11.55. To Hans Heider, Vienna 8.59. Then to P. Givavdoni, Siegendorf 1960. Nominal change to Givavdoni & Cie, Vienna 1962. Reg'n cancelled 11.63. Aircraft at one time parked at Auto Metzker scrapyard on the Vienna to Styria road. Was in very bad condition there by 5.67 and had disappeared by 12.73.

6691   Supplied to the Air Council with military serial **HG706**. Delivered to 18MU 2.44. Served with Royal Navy at Donibristle 23.3.45, named *Merlin XXI*. At Stretton by 1.49, Donibristle by 7.49 and at de Havilland by 7.50. To Arbroath by 7.51, Machrihanish by 7.52, Arbroath by 1.53 and Stretton by 7.53. SOC at Stretton 17.7.54 and broken up there. At sometime wore codes 806/DO and 901/MA.

6692   Supplied to the Air Council with military serial **HG707**. To de Havilland at Witney for conversion to Rapide 8.2.44 and CofA no.7086 issued 22.8.44. To J. Parks and Son for packing prior to shipment per *SS Salawate?* to Alexandria 6.44. SOC on sale to Iran 8.44. Reg'd **EP-AAD** to Iranian State Airlines (Govt. of Persia, Ministry of Posts and Telegraphs). This was a replacement aircraft for an impressed aircraft written off during the war. To Aero Club (Doshan Teppeh) in 1955 or 1956. Still current in 1956, but cancelled by 1959.

6693   Supplied to the Air Council with military serial **HG708**. Initially to 18MU 2.44 and then to Royal Navy at Lee-on-Solent 20.4.45. At Crazies Hill (Upper Culham Farm), Henley-0n-Thmaes by 1.49 (sometime coded 601/CH), to Culdrose by 7.49 and with de Havilland 1.51. To Arbroath by 1.52, Anthorn by 1.53 and Arbroath again by 7.53. Still in service in 1955. SOC at Lossiemouth in late 1950s. Parked outside at Lossiemouth without wheels early 1960 awaiting disposal. Put up for tender as scrap and purchased with others by Hants and Sussex Aviation Ltd. 8.60. Few usable components due to bad state of aircraft and therefore, cut up and burnt at Lossiemouth 8.60.

6694   Supplied to the Air Council with military serial **HG709**. Delivered to 18MU 2.44. Into service with the Royal Navy, initially at Donibristle 11.4.45. At Stretton by 1.49, Old Sarum by 7.49 and with de Havilland 1.52. To Arbroath by 7.52, Anthorn by 7.53 and Abbotsinch by 1.54. Coded 801/VL with Yeovilton Stn. Flt. at sometime and 901/AC at Abbotsinch in 1955 and 1957. Coded 999/CU at Culdrose in 1960. Nosed over Roborough 31.8.61 and written off. "Brutally dismantled" and dumped at the repair yard at Fleetlands. Acquired by Hants and Sussex Aviation Ltd. circa 10.61 and transported by road to Portsmouth. Deemed repairable, but damaged further during the dismantling process after the accident. Noted Portsmouth in pieces 1962 but taken to Portsmouth Corporation rubbish tip and burnt 12.62.

6695   Supplied to the Air Council with serial **HG710** but did not enter military service. Instead, to de Havilland at Witney for conversion to Rapide 8.2.44 and CofA no.7087 issued 22.8.44. To J. Parks and Son 8.44 for packing prior to shipment per *SS Glenegle* ex Glasgow to Alexandria during 8.44. To Iranian Government 30.11.44 and reg'd **EP-AAE** to Iranian State Airlines (Govt. of Persia, Ministry of Posts and Telegraphs). This was a replacement for an impressed aircraft written off during the war. Still current in 1955, but cancelled by 1959.

6696   Supplied to the Air Council with serial **HG711** but did not enter military service. Instead, to de Havilland at Witney for conversion to Rapide 2.44 and CofA no.7088 issued 22.8.44. To J. Parks and Son 8.44 for packing prior to shipment per *SS Glenegle* from Glasgow to Alexandria during 8.44. To Iranian Govt. 30.11.44. Reg'd **EP-AAT** to Iranian State Airlines (Govt. of Persia, Ministry of Posts and Telegraphs). To Aero Club (Doshan Teppeh) in 1955 or 1956. Still current in 1956.

6697   Supplied to the Air Council with military serial **HG712**. Delivered to 18MU 2.44. Served with Metroploitan Com. Sqdn. 1.45. Port engine cut soon after take-off due to water contaminated fuel. Aircraft was unable to maintain height and

forced landed in a field 14.5.45. Location of accident given as B.78 (possibly Eindhoven Holland). SOC 17.5.45.

6698   Supplied to the Air Council with military serial **HG713**. To Royal Navy at Donibristle 6.4.45. At Lee-on-Solent by 1.49 and with de Havilland 1.50. Back at Lee-on-Solent by 7.50 and with 781Sqdn. at Lee-on-Solent by 1.51. Again returned to de Havilland 7.52. To Lossiemouth by 7.53, Gosport by 1.54 and Lee-on-Solent again by 7.54. Stored inside at Lossiemouth mid 1960. Noted in store with the Aircraft Holding Unit at Lossiemouth 1.62. Coded both 858/LP and 854/LP at some time.

6699   Supplied to the Air Council with military serial **HG714**. To Royal Navy at Lee-on-Solent 7.4.45 where it remained until at least 1.49. With de Havilland 1.50. To Arbroath by 7.50 and Lossiemouth by 7.54. Serving with Short's Ferry Division in 1954 and 1955. Coded 999 in 9.60. Noted in store at Lossiemouth coded 963/ST 1.62

6700   Supplied to the Air Council with military serial **HG715**. Initially to 18MU 3.44 and then with ETPS at Cranfield. Reg'd as **G-ANET** [CofR R4164 5.10.53] to Hants and Sussex Aviation Ltd., Portsmouth. CofA issued 16.11.53. To Silver City Aviation Ltd., Langley 8.3.54. To B.O.A.C. 17.3.55. Cancelled as sold in Aden 29.5.55. Converted to Mk4 in 1955. Reg'd **VR-AAL** to Aden Airways Ltd. 6.55 and named *Dhala*. Reg'n cancelled 5.9.58. Reg'd **ET-P-22** to Luisi Mascheroni and Christian Tonna, Asmara. Some time reportedly suffered an accident at Gondar. Joint owner Tonna was killed in a car accident and subsequent to that, the aircraft was reportedly abandoned at the "old airport" at Addis Ababa after the CofA expired 26.6.60. Grounded for a long time and consequently needing expensive repairs, the aircraft's resale value would not have covered the cost of restoration and it was decided to scrap the aircraft.

6701   Supplied to the Air Council with military serial **HG716**. To Royal Navy at Donibrislte 17.3.45, at Stretton by 1.49, Anthorn by 7.49, Arbroath by 1.50 and Short Brothers by 1.52. Still with Shorts 7.54 (used by Short's Ferry Division at Rochester). SOC at Rochester 12.7.54 and reduced to produce there 9.54. At some time coded 903/AO.

6702   Supplied to the Air Council with military serial **HG717**. Initially to 18MU 3.44. To Royal Navy at Lee-on-Solent 15.2.45, Culham by 1.49, possibly Arbroath by 7.49 and at de Havilland 1.50. Returned to Arbroath by 1.51 and with Short Brothers by 1.52. Still with Shorts 1.54. SOC at Lossiemouth 29.4.54 and reduced to produce 4.54.

6703   Supplied to the Air Council with military serial **HG718**. Delivered to 18MU 3.44. Served with No.4 Radio School 8.45 (coded TML-D, later TML-B) and to storage at 5MU 4.49. Sold to Short Brothers & Harland Ltd., Rochester 11.1.50. Reg'd **G-ALWI** [CofR 14891 21.1.50] and CofA no.10801 issued 28.3.50. To Transair Ltd, Croydon 20.2.52. Cancelled as sold in France 19.3.52. Reg'd **F-BGPJ** to Soc. Aigle Azur Indochine, Hanoi and CofA issued 28.4.52. Sold to Cie. D'Autrex, Hanoi 1.54. To Ste. Laos Air Service, Vientiane 8.55. CofA suspended 22.5.59 and withdrawn from use at Vientiane and broken up there.

6704   Supplied to the Air Council with military serial **HG719**. Delivered to 18MU 3.44. Served Staff College Flt. Bucknall, Staff College White Waltham coded TBR-D 3.46 and at Halton coded THA-B 8.46. To storage at 18MU 11.47. SOC on sale to Walter Westoby, t/a Westair Flying Services Ltd., Squires Gate 11.3.48. Reg'd as **G-AKMH** [CofR 12045 28.2.48] and CofA issued 16.6.48. To Isle of Wight Flying Club Ltd., Sandown 24.5.49. To Bees Flight Ltd., Sandown 11.2.53. To Sydney George Newport for t/a Arab Contracting and Trading Co., Beirut 30.3.55. In use by Motherwell Bridge Contracting & Trading Co. and visited Nicosia 3.8.60. To Aerocontacts (Aircraft Distributors) Ltd., Gatwick 3.4.64. Cancelled on sale abroad to Leopoldville, Congo 22.10.64. Reg'd **9Q-CJK** to A.M.A.Z., Kinshasa.

6705   Supplied to the Air Council with military serial **HG720**. Delivered to 18MU 3.44 but to 5MU 10.45. To French Air Force at Bordeaux 5.11.45. Served with BE703 at Pau and ELA56 at Persan-Beaumont. Noted on scrap heap at Villacoublay 1.56. SOC 11.5.56.

6706   Supplied to the Air Council with military serial **HG721**. Delivered to 18MU 3.44. Served with 527Sqdn. 4.45, Halton (or

Watton?) 4.46, 18MU 11.46, 61Grp. Com. Flt. 4.48 and 5MU pending sale 9.48. SOC on sale to George Carhill Sergenson Whyham, Blackpool 10.12.48. Reg'd **G-ALGB** [CofR 17.12.48] and CofA no.10443 issued 2.11.49. To Ronald Henry Braime and Arnold George Wilson t/a Yorkshire Aero Club 1.4.49. To R. A. Peacock (Aviation) Ltd., Croydon 7.5.54. Cancelled as sold abroad to France 26.10.54. Reg'd **F-BHCD** to S.A.L.S., St Cyr 12.54 and French CofA issued 10.12.54. To C.N. de Parachutisme, Biscarosse in 1956. At Biscarosse and Nantes in 1959, Biscarosse 1962, Nantes 1964 and Chalon in 1965. CofA expired in 1962. Stored at Villacoublay as part of the Musee de l'Air collection in 1979. Displayed in a "skydiving diorama" in the Musee de l'Air's Sporting and Light Aviation Hall which was inaugurated during the 1981 Paris Air Show.

6707 Supplied to the Air Council with military serial **HG722**. Delivered to 18MU 3.44. Served with Metropolitan Com. Sqdn. (coded CB-E) 9.45, 18MU 8.46, 5MU 1.49. SOC on sale to Allen Aircraft Services Ltd., Croydon 13.2.50. Reg'd **G-ALWP** [CofR 14898 23.1.50]to Allen Aircraft Services, Croydon 23.1.50. Nominal change to Charles W. J. Allen, Old Coulsdon 4.5.50. CofA no.10892 issued 26.7.50. To Airwork Ltd., Croydon 23.8.50. To broker W. S. Shackleton Ltd. 4.6.51. Sold abroad 28.6.51 and reg'd **VQ-FAL** to Katanga Estates Ltd, t/a Fiji Airways Ltd 21.8.51. Port engine failed shortly after take-off from Lambasa Airport. Aircraft forced landed in cane filed and burned out 24.4.54. No injuries to pilot or passengers.

6708 Supplied to the Air Council with military serial **HG723**. Delivered to 18MU 3.44, then 1680 Flt. 10.45. Handed over to Ministry of Supply and passed to A.A.J.C., Prestwick 16.4.46. Reg'd **G-AHLM** [CofR 10160 8.6.46] to Scottish Airways Ltd., Renfrew. CofA no.7780 issued 13.7.46. Absorbed by B.E.A.C. on formation 1.2.47. To Marshall's Flying School Ltd., Cambridge 6.3.48. Name changed to Marshall Flying Services Ltd. 9.4.52. Converted to Mk6 prior to 1961. Overhauled at Portsmouth and returned to Exeter 22.1.61. To Kenneth Philip Hubert Cleife, Plymouth t/a Mayflower Air Services 13.6.61. Ownership in the name of Mayflower 27.3.63. Aircraft swung at a late stage during take-off 20.7.63 and the pilot intentionally ground looped the aircraft. However, it was travelling too fast and the aircraft cartwheeled down a rough slope and caught fire when it came to rest at the top of cliffs at St Mary's, Scilly Isles. Cancelled from register 26.10.63.

6709 Supplied to the Air Council with military serial **HG724**. Delivered to 18MU 3.44. No record of any service history and placed into store 5MU 2.47! SOC on sale to Newman Aircraft Co. Ltd., Hatfield 25.8.47. Reg'd **G-AKPA** [CofR 12113 12.1.48] and CofA no.9919 issued 28.6.48. To Midland Metal Spinning Co. Ltd., Wolverhampton 16.3.51. Ownership change notified 17.5.62 and sold abroad to Eire 8.6.62. Reg'd **EI-AML** to F. J. Connolly, Dublin 15.6.62. To Aer Turas Teoranta 11.9.62. Cancelled on sale to France 19.6.64. Reg'd **F-BLHZ** to Aero Club de Lorraine, Lunneville 2.2.65 and French CofA issued same day. To Centre Ecole Regional de Parachutisme Sportif de Nancy-Lorraine 1968. Reg'n cancelled 27.11.72 and sold in the USA early 1973. Imported into USA by Geert E. Frank, East Kingston NH. Reg'd **N89DH** to Doyle W. Cotton Jr., Tulsa, OK 1.73. Last CofA dated 2.7.82. Sold at auction at Tulsa OK 3.10.87 for $75000 to Robert C. Hood, Jasper, MO. Reported at the time in dull camouflage colours and the buyer stated, "aircraft will be put into long term storage". CofR renewed 12.1.90.

6710 Supplied to the Air Council with military serial **HG725**. To Royal Navy at Donibristle 21.3.44. Made a forced landing on airfield after engine failure 3.45. Aircraft a complete wreck and SOC 6.3.45.

6711 Supplied to the Air Council with military serial **HG726**. To Royal Navy at Donibristle 21.3.44. Made a forced landing on airfield after engine fire 8.46. Aircraft a complete wreck.

6712 Supplied to the Air Council with military serial **HG727**. To Royal Navy at Donibristle 21.3.44. SOC to Royal Navy 21.7.45. Caught fire while on ground engine test and destroyed 4.47.

6713 Supplied to the Air Council with military serial **HG728**. Delivered to 18MU 3.44. Served with 527Sqdn. 4.45, 57OTU 4.45, 53OTU 6.45 and thence to 18MU 7.46 for storage. To 66Grp. Com. Flt. coded RCI-K 4.48, but returned to 18MU for further

storage 1.49. SOC on sale to Robert Alan Short & James Henry Tattersall, Croydon 15.4.49. Reg'd **G-ALNT** [CofR 12702 21.4.49] and CofA no.10604 issued 7.7.49. To Walter Hutchinson, Eastleigh 15.9.49. To Hampshire School of Flying Ltd., Eastleigh 2.12.50. Sold abroad to Australia 26.2.52 and dismantled for shipment. Assembled at Cairns QLD, initially allotted **VH-ATU** but instead to **VH-CFA (2)** and test flown 21.11.52. To Queensland Ambulance Transport Brigade named *Clive Jones* 11.52. En route from Iron Ridge to Cairns 26.10.53, the pilot became lost and when the fuel ran out, ditched in the Ocean 20 miles north of Ingham QLD, south-east of Brooke Island. The pilot and patient were killed, but the attendant was picked up by steamer *Fiona*. (Note: also see VH-CFA (1) c/n 6814).

6714 Supplied to the Air Council with military serial **HG729**. Served with No.1 Radio School 3.44, 18MU 1.47, 64Grp. Com. Flt 4.48 and 5MU 2.50. Sold to Short Brothers & Harland Ltd., Rochester and reg'd **G-AMCT** [CofR 15051 13.7.50]. Arrived Rochester 27.7.50 and CoA A.1559 issued 4.10.50. Stored out of use until prepared for sale abroad to France 13.8.56. To Groupement d'Etudes et de Consultations Aeronautiques (G.E.C.A.), trading as Air Nautic, Toussus-le-Noble reg'd **F-BHTH** and CofA issued 3.9.56. To Societe Generale d'Affretements Aeriens (S.G.A.A.), Algiers 8.57. To Aerosud, Bone, Algiers early '59. Noted at Perpignan 7.62. CofA expired 4.66 and canx from the register. Believed dismantled 9.67.

6715 Supplied to the Air Council with military serial **HG730**. Delivered to 18MU 4.44. Served with Metropolitan Com. Sqdn. 9.45, 18MU 8.46, 63Grp. Com. Flt. (date unknown). Into storage at 5MU 5.49. SOC on sale to Robert Allan Short, Croydon 2.1.50. Reg'd **G-ALXS** [CofR 14925 24.1.50] and CofA no.A2812 issued. To W. A. Rollason Ltd., Croydon 16.4.50. Intended for Arab Airways Ltd. as **TJ-AAU** 5.50, but not delivered, although registration chalked on for a short period. Cancelled as sold in France 22.5.51. Reg'd **F-OAIH** to J. M. Dulas, Port Gentil, Gabon and CofA issued 21.8.51. To Ste. Transportes Aeriens du Gabon 2.52. To J. C. Brouillet et Cie, Libreville 1.58, becoming Transgabon in 1960. Re-reg'd **TR-LKQ** to Cie Transgabon late 1965. CofA suspended 14.11.66 at Libreville and reg'n used on a Beechcraft Bonanza from 8.67.

6716 Supplied to the Air Council with military serial **HG731**. Initially to Halton coded THA-E 6.44, then to 5MU 2.47. Flying accident 24.2.46. Reclassified Cat.E 6.3.47 and sold to D. J. Adis, presumably for spares use, 29.5.47.

6717 Supplied to the Air Council with military serial **HG732**. Delivered to 76MU 12.4.44 for dismantling for shipment to India. Ex Middlesborough per *SS Fort Louisbourg* 18.6.44, arrived Bombay 3.8.44. Reg'd **VT-ARZ** to Government of Bihar, Patna 22.5.46. Sold to Tata and Sons Ltd., Bombay 25.7.46. Damaged beyond repair and cancelled 17.2.51.

6718 Supplied to the Air Council with military serial **NF847**. To Royal Navy at Lee-on-Solent 23.11.44. With 799 Flt. 7.45, at Donibristle in 1947, Stretton by 1.49, 781Sqdn. Lee-on-Solent by 1.50 and with DH 7.54. With Lossiemouth Stn. Flt. coded 931 in 9.56. Coded 903/AO at some time. Reg'd **G-ASIA** [CofR R7898 6.5.63] to Frederick Beresford Sowery, Michael Maurice Cecil Stamford & Bernard Willes Rigold, trustees of the assets of R.A.F. Abingdon Sport Parachuting Club. CofA supposedly issued 29.2.64, but aircraft remained unconverted at Abingdon. Seen at Abingdon open day 11.7.64 carrying both **NF847** and **G-ASIA** and in service colours but burnt soon after. Reg'n cancelled as permanently withdrawn from use 11.65.

6719 Supplied to the Air Council with military serial **NF848**. To Royal Navy at Donibristle 30.8.45. To Arbroath by 1.49, at de Havilland by 7.50, returned to Arbroath by 7.51 and at Stretton 7.53. Still at Stretton 7.54. Noted at Brawdy in 1954/55 and at that time, was still coded 902/ST with Stretton Stn. Flt. Reported stored at Stretton in 1955 and then parked outside at Lossiemouth without wheels early 1960.

6720 Supplied to the Air Council with military serial **NF849**. To Royal Navy at Lee-on-Solent 19.11.44. To Donibristle by 1.49. Possibly at Culham by 1.50 coded 602/CH. With de Havilland 1.51 and Shorts 7.51. At Lossiemouth by 7.54. SOC at Shorts, Rochester 5.7.54.

6721 Supplied to the Air Council with military serial **NF850**. Delivered 18MU 4.44. Taken on charge by Royal Navy at Lee-on-Solent 4.11.44. Used at Stretton from 1.49 until 7.54 at least. Noted in storage at Stretton in 1955.

6722 Supplied to the Air Council with military serial **NF851**. Delivered to 18MU 4.44, then 13OTU 4.45, 85Grp. Com. Flt. 10.45 but returned to 18MU for storage 12.46. SOC on sale to Butlins Ltd., London W1 14.9.48. Reg'd **G-AJCL** [CofR 11177 7.9.48] and CofA no.10364 issued 25.9.49. To Allgood Manufacturing Co. Ltd., Newport, Monmouthshire 2.7.49 and leased to Cambrian. Named *Flint*. Purchased by Cambrian Air Services Ltd., Cardiff 18.1.54. To B.E.A.C. 19.6.59 and named *Sir Henry Lawrence* (the second use of this name). Converted to Mk6 prior to 9.60. Reportedly no longer named by 12.60. Sold to British Westpoint Airlines Ltd., Exeter 20.5.64 and delivered to Exeter the following day. To Frank Herbert Mann, Torquay 16.7.65. To Kenneth Bryan Neely, t/a Scillonia Airways, St. Just 12.10.66 and named *Samson*. In 5.70, the assets of Scillonia Airways were seized to meet Neely's debts while he was imprisoned in Kuwait. The aircraft was sold for just £124-10-0! To John Peter Epplestone, trustee of the assets of the Rhine Army Parachute Association (a branch of the Army Parachute Association) 24.9.70. Withdrawn from use at Shobdon on CofA expiry 11.1.71. Cancelled as destroyed 24.5.71 and variously reported as broken up at Fairoaks, Shipdham and Shobdon! In any event, the lower wings were used for G-AKOE when re-built at yet another location, Chirk!

6723 Supplied to the Air Council with military serial **NF852**. Delivered to 18MU 4.44, the Metropolitan Com. Sqdn. 9.45 and 5MU 3.47. Sold to A. Hamson and Son Ltd., Sywell t/a Air Charter Experts Ltd. 25.8.47. Aircraft taken over by Manx Air Charters Ltd. Reg'd **G-AKGY** [CofR 11912 29.9.47] and CofA no.9797 issued 20.5.48. Renamed Manx Airlines Ltd. 20.8.53. Sold abroad to France 5.12.56. Reg'd **F-BFEH** to Societe Vignafribre France, Algiers 1.57. To Societe Generale d'Affretements Aerien (S.G.A.A.), Algiers 7.57. To Air Fret. CofA suspended 6.63.

6724 Supplied to the Air Council with military serial **NF853**. Delivered to 18MU 22.4.44, then 41OTU 3.10.44. The unit was at Hawarden until it moved to Chilbolton 25.3.45 and disbanded 25.6.45. To 5MU for storage 1.8.45. SOC on sale to Kenning Aviation Ltd., Burnaston 2.12.46. Reg'd **G-AIUJ** [CofR 10978 8.11.46] and CofA applied for 27.11.46. Reg'd to Air Services of India Ltd., Bombay and allocated **VT-CHZ** 22.1.47. CofA no.8779 issued 27.3.47. Sold 11.50 and reg'd **F-OAIL** to Compagnie Laotienne de Commerce et de Transport with CofA issued 15.2.57. Re-reg'd as **F-LAAB** to Cie Veha-Akat, Vientianne 10.55 and CofA issued 13.10.55. CofA suspended at Vientianne 27.3.61.

6725 Supplied to the Air Council with military serial **NF854**. Initially to 18MU 4.44, then to Royal Navy at Evanton 7.9.45. In use at Stretton by 1.49, Donibristle by 7.49, with 782Sqdn. at Donibristle in 1950 and 1951 and with de Havilland 1.51. To Lee-on-Solent by 7.51 until at least 7.54. SOC 30.12.54. In store at Stretton in 1955.

6726 Supplied to the Air Council with military serial **NF855**. Delivered to 18MU 4.44. To Royal Navy at Evanton 1.12.46. At Donibristle by 1.49 and with de Havilland by 1.50. At Arbroath by 7.50, Stretton by 7.51 and Anthorn by 7.54. Stored at Stretton by 1955 and still on Royal Navy charge 2.60. Stored at Lossiemouth in mid 1960 and still there, coded AH, 1.62.

6727 Supplied to the Air Council with military serial **NF856**. Delivered to 18MU 4.44. Served with R.A.F. Mission to Denmark Com. Flt. 11.45, 18MU 2.46, No.4 Radio School 4.48 and 5MU 6.48. SOC on sale to Darlington and District Aero Club Ltd. 12.1.50. Reg'd as **G-ALXA** [CofR 14908 16.1.50] and CofA no.10852 issued 8.6.50. To broker W. S. Shackleton Ltd. 14.12.51. Cancelled as sold abroad to Vietnam 25.2.52. Shipped to Indo China in a crate as **G-ALXA** ex Croydon 22.3.52. To Cie. D'Autrex, Hanoi. Destroyed by fire at Gia-Lam Airport, Hanoi 5.6.52 while still disassembled and crated. The fire started inside Rapide F-OABH c/n 6606 which was hangared nearby.

6728 Supplied to the Air Council with military serial **NF857**. Delivered to 18MU 4.44 and intended for Royal Navy, but movement cancelled when the aircraft was damaged in a flying accident 10.45. To 62Grp. Com. Flt. 4.48. Flew into high ground 1 mile north of Chipping Sodbury in poor visibility 18.1.49. Pilot killed. SOC as Cat.E2 18.1.49 as scrap to 49MU.

6729 Supplied to the Air Council with military serial **NF858**. Delivered to 18MU 4.44. Served with SHAEF Com. Flt., Denmark 6.45, 18MU 4.46 and 5MU 1.49. SOC on sale to Wilks and Chandler 1.50 but reg'd **G-ALWN** [CofR 14896 30.1.50] to V. H. Bellamy, t/a Flightways 30.1.50. CofA no.10889 issued 20.7.50. To Southern Aerowork Ltd., Eastleigh 24.10.50. To Transair Ltd., Croydon 28.2.52. Sold abroad to France 5.3.52. Reg'd **F-BGPG** to Soc. Aigle Azur Indochine, Hanoi and French CofA issued 7.4.52. To Cie. Laotienne de Commerce et de Transport, Hanoi 1954. Reg'd as **F-LAAC** to Cie. Veha-Akat, Vientianne and CofA issued 13.10.55. Destroyed 10.58 and CofA suspended at Luang Prabang 15.10.58 as written off.

6730 Supplied to the Air Council with military serial **NF859**. To de Havilland 8.5.44 and converted to Rapide with CofA no.7089 issued 22.8.44. To J. Parks and Son for packing prior to shipment to Iceland per *SS Nadir*, arriving Reykjavik 28.7.44. Reg'd **TF-ISO** [CofR no.10 5.4.45] to Flugfelag Islands HF. Pilot became lost whilst on a survey fight for herrings, ran out of fuel and ditched beside a herring boat in Bakkafjordur Bay, near Grimseyjarsundi 27.8.45. Aircraft lost but no casualties.

6731 Supplied to the Air Council with military serial **NF860**. Delivered to 18MU 5.44. Taken on charge by Royal Navy 11.44. To 18MU 11.45, St St Mawgan 17.5.46 and to French Air Force 22.5.46. To Pau 7.46 and served with BE703 at Pau and ELA56 at Persan-Beaumont. SOC 1951.

6732 Supplied to the Air Council with military serial **NF861**. Delivered to 18MU 5.44, then to Royal Navy at Lee-on-Solent 21.11.44. With Western Aircraft 7.45, 782Sqdn. Donibristle 3.46 and at Stretton by 7.49. With de Havilland 7.51, at Arbroath 1.52 and Eglinton 1.53. Still at Stretton 7.53. Crashed in Glendune Mountains, County Antrim while flying from Stretton to Eglinton 15.9.53 - pilot killed. SOC at Eglinton 25.9.53. At some time coded 002/LP with 781Sqdn. at Lee-on-Solent.

6733 Supplied to the Air Council with military serial **NF862**. Delivered to 18MU 5.44. Served with SHAEF Com. Flt., Denmark 6.45, 18MU 1.46, 62Grp. Com. Flt. 4.48. Declared Cat.E2 (Surplus) 2.49 and to 5MU pending sale 6.49. Sold to Short Bros. & Harland Ltd. 11.1.50 and conveyed to Rochester by road on the following day. Not civilianised and sold to Cumberland Air Services in 1954. Broken up for spares at Squires Gate during 1956. Some parts used in the re-conditioning of c/n 6757.

6734 Supplied to the Air Council with military serial **NF863**. Delivered to 18MU 5.44. Served with No.4 Radio School 10.44. SOC as Cat.E2 (Scrap) 13.4.48.

6735 Supplied to the Air Council with military serial **NF864**. Delivered to 18MU 5.44. Taken on charge by Royal Navy at Lee-on-Solent 21.11.44, to 782Sqdn. Donibristle by 4.46, Lee-on-Solent by 1.49, Arbroath by 1.50 and de Havilland 7.50. Returned to Arbroath by 7.51 and at Lossiemouth by 7.53. Noted coded 804/DO in 1954. Stored inside Lossiemouth mid 1960 but noted flying 1961 and again 7.62. Reported in use at Lee-on-Solent until 1963. Reg'd **G-ASKO** [CofR R7972 22.7.63] to Hants and Sussex Aviation Ltd., Portsmouth 22.7.63. Delivered to Portsmouth ex Lee-on-Solent 8.63. Converted to Mk6 and CofA issued 13.3.64. To Mayflower Air Services Ltd, Plymouth 25.5.64 but had already been delivered to Mayflower at Exeter 10.5.64. To British Westpoint Airlines Ltd, Exeter 8.10.64. To Hantsair Ltd., Eastleigh 15.6.65. To Twentieth Century Fox Productions Ltd., London W1 1.9.65 and used as a camera ship for filming the "Blue Max". Had titles "Demoiselle Airways" painted in small letters. Aircraft had acquired a German Iron Cross motif on tail by 1966. Cancelled as sold in France 17.3.66. Reg'd **F-OHCF** to Eurafair, Cayenne and CofA issued 29.8.67. CofA suspended 3.68

6736 Supplied to the Air Council with military serial **NF865**. Delivered to 18MU 5.44. Served with Metropolitan Com. Sqdn. 7.45. To 18MU for storage 8.46 but moved on for further storage 5MU 1.49. SOC on sale to Robert Allan Short, Croydon 2.1.50 and reg'd **G-ALXT** [CofR 14926 24.1.50]. To Arthur Robert Frogley, Broxbourne 24.2.50 and CofA no.10824 issued 2.5.50. Sold abroad 5.7.51 and reg'n cancelled 1.8.51. Reg'd **CY-AAI** to Directorate of Civil Aviation, Ceylon 3.7.51. Re-reg'd **4R-AAI** still with the Directorate of Civil Aviation 1.12.53 and operated by Ceylon Air Academy. Returned to U.K., arriving at Biggin Hill 10.3.74 and Staverton 30.3.74 where it was offered for sale at a reported £9000. Returned to Biggin Hill 22.7.75 and performed a

DH89 c/n 6738. NF867 was based on a farm at Culham for a three year period until January 1954. With many other Dominies, at the Aircraft Holding Unit at Lossiemouth in 1961 and broken up there.

DH89 c/n 6754. No, not the Minneapolis based carrier but an Isle of Man airline linking the Island with towns in the North of England and Scotland. G-AHLN was one of five Rapides operated.

DH89 c/n 6740. Purchased in 1945 and, but for a short time employed by the United Nations in Israel, in Holland ever since, V3 is now at the Royal Netherlands Air Force Museum at Soesterberg

DH89 c/n 6767. A poor reproduction maybe, but it shows the demise of G-AKME on engine start-up at Lympne in June 1950. So many were lost this way, mercifully, rarely causing more than a red face!

DH89 c/n 6745. Another Benelux government to snap up redundant aircraft was Belgium who received D2 in September 1946. It soldiered on until struck off charge in 1957.

DH89 c/n 6775. Used by Falcks as an air ambulance, OY-AAO survives and after many years in storage at a variety of locations, is now displayed at Danmarks Flyvemuseum, Helsingor.

DH89 c/n 6748. Some will remember the Air Couriers Rapide fleet at Croydon and later, at Biggin Hill. This one was G-APBM until sold to Societe Ardic Aviation for operation in Senegal.

DH89 c/n 6779. Demolition and construction was a highly lucrative game immediately after the war. Owned by a Baronet, one company purchased this and another Rapide from the proceeds!

test flight 3.8.75. Ferried to Strathallan 4.8.75. Aircraft was reportedly not in very good condition and was back at Biggin Hill in 8.75 but was delivered back to W. J. D. Roberts at Strathallan by 16.9.75. Painted as **G-ALXT** to represent a pre-war Railway Air Services aircraft and carried name *Star of Scotia*. Noted on static display at Strathallan 27.5.79. Purchased by the Science Museum for its collection at Wroughton during the auction of the Strathallan Collection 14.7.81.

6737   Supplied to the Air Council with military serial **NF866**. Delivered to 18MU 5.44. SOC to Royal Navy 6.11.44. Made a forced landing in a field after engine failure. Complete wreck 11.45.

6738   Supplied to the Air Council with military serial **NF867**. Delivered to 18MU 5.44. Taken on charge by Royal Navy at Donibristle 23.2.45. At Anthorn 1.49 and with de Havilland 7.50. To Culham by 7.51 and St. Davids? by 1.54. At Benson by 7.54 and coded 905. Still on Royal Navy charge and in flying condition 2.60. Noted in store with the Aircraft Holding Unit at Lossiemouth 1.62.

6739   Supplied to the Air Council with military serial **NF868**. Delivered to 18MU 5.44. Served with Metropolitan Com. Sqdn., Hendon 9.44 (1316 Flt. for use of the Netherlands Dept. of Naval Affairs and Ministry of War). To 18MU 4.45, Allied Flight, Hendon 5.46 and then to the Belgian Govt. 4.9.46. Serialled **D3** with the Belgian Air Force and taken on charge 4.9.46. Served with 367th Escadrille and later the 21st Smaldeel. Cat.5 21.8.52.

6740   Supplied to the Air Council with military serial **NF869**. Delivered to 18MU 5.44. Served with Metropolitan Com. Sqdn., Hendon 14.9.44 (1316 Flt. for use of the Netherlands Dept. of Naval Affairs and Ministry of War). To Dutch Government 17.11.45. Converted to Rapide by de Havilland at Witney. Reg'd **PH-RAE** to Netherlands Government 8.10.45. Operated by KLM under lease 19.9.45 to 1.4.46. Serialled **V-3** with the Royal Netherlands Air Force 15.5.46 and operated by 334Sqdn. Named *Gelderland*. Reg'd **PH-VNC** [CofR 640] with the Staat der Nederlanden 30.8.48. Used by the United Nations in Israel. Returned to Royal Netherlands Air Force as **V-3** on 8.10.48. Reg'd **PH-TGC** [CofR 312] to K.L.M. 20.11.52 (Note: K.L.M. give the date as 26.10.52). Reg'd **PH-OTA** to K.L.M. Aerocarto NV 3.5.54 and named *Gelderland* again. To Aero-Ypenburg NV 20.7.62 and then to General Aviation te Rotterdam NV 18.8.66. Cancelled 18.11.66 and presented to Avifauna childrens playground at Alphen. In late 1968, the aircraft was acquired for the Royal Netherlands Air Force Museum at Soesterberg and restored to its former military colours, marked as **V-3** and again named *Gelderland*. Completely refurbished in hangar 4 and on display since 1969.

6741   Supplied to the Air Council with military serial **NF870**. Delivered to 18MU 5.44. Served with Metropolitan Com. Sqdn. 9.44, 1316 Flt. 15.9.44, 18MU 4.45, 63Grp. Com. Flt. 4.48. To storage 5MU 6.49. SOC on sale to Air Enterprises Ltd., Croydon 13.1.50. Reg'd as **G-ALWY** [CofR 14906 18.1.50] and CofA no.10804 issued 24.3.50. Named *The Ventnor Flyer*. Undercarriage, propellers and engines damaged when pilot undershot at Port Ellen, Islay 19.4.52 or 19.5.52. Written off and reg'n cancelled 1.7.52.

6742   Supplied to the Air Council with military serial **NF871**. Delivered to 18MU 5.44. Taken on charge by Royal Navy at Middle Wallop 11.45. At Stretton 1.49, Donibristle 7.49 to at least 7.50. With 782Sqdn. at Donibristle 1950 coded 803/DO and at de Havilland 1.51 to 7.51. At Abbotsinch 1.52 and at Lee-on-Solent 7.52 to 7.54 at least. In store at Stretton in 1955. SOC at Lossiemouth in the late 1950s and noted in store inside there mid 1960. In store with the Aircraft Holding Unit at Lossiemouth 1.62.

6743   Supplied to the Air Council with military serial **NF872**. Delivered to 18MU 5.44. Taken on charge by Royal Navy at Evanton 17.10.345. At Stretton 1.49 to 7.50 at least and with 782Sqdn. at Donibristle 1.51 to 7.51 at least. With de Havilland (presumably at Witney for overhaul) 1.52. To Arbroath by 7.52 to 1.53 at least and then at Lossiemouth 7.53 and West Raynham 7.54. Coded 857/LP at Lee-on-Solent some time. SOC at Lossiemouth 10.9.54 and scrapped 9.54.

6744   Supplied to the Air Council with military serial **NF873**. Delivered to 18MU 5.44. Taken on charge by Royal Navy at

Evanton 7.9.45. At Stretton 1.49 to 1.50 at least, then Anthorn 7.50, Shorts 11.50 to 1.54 at least (used by Shorts Ferry Flight from 3.11.50 until 17.5.52) and with de Havilland 7.54. SOC at Lossiemouth in the late 1950s. Put up for tender as scrap at Lossiemouth and purchased by Hants and Sussex Aviation Ltd. for usable components. Due to bad state of the aircraft, reported cut up and burnt at Lossiemouth 8.60. However, fuselage reported in store with Hants and Sussex, Portsmouth 3.63.

6745   Supplied to the Air Council with military serial **NF874**. Delivered to 18MU 5.44. Served with Berlin Com. Sqdn. 6.45, 18MU 7.45 and Metropolitan Com. Sqdn. 1.46. To Belgian Government 4.9.46. Serialled **D2** with the Belgian Air Force and taken on charge 4.9.46. Later coded ZC-K. SOC 1957.

6746   Supplied to the Air Council with serial **NF875** but did not enter military service. Initially to 18MU 5.44, then to Airwork and General Trading Co. for modifications in 1945. Reg'd **G-AGTM** [CofR 9717 19.9.45] for Iraq Petroleum Transport Co. Ltd., Haifa and CofA no.7229 issued 6.12.45. Cancelled as sold abroad to Lebanon 24.4.53 and reg'd **OD-ABP** to Arab Contracting and Trading Co. Ltd. 23.9.55. Reg'n cancelled as sold in Jordan 23.4.62. Reg'd **JY-ACL** still with Arab Contracting and Trading 4.62. Restored as **G-AGTM** to Edward Arthur John Gardener, trustee of the assets of the Army Parachute Association 25.3.64. Aircraft was delivered via Gatwick 10.4.64 and later named *Valkyrie*. To Richard Charles John Brinton, trustee of the assets of the Parachute Regiment Free Fall Club 1.3.67. Extensively damaged at Netheravon 26.2.68 and removed from register 31.8.68. Ownership changed to Donald Hughes, trustee of the assets of the Army Parachute Association 4.11.68 however and the aircraft was and certainly flying again at Netheravon by 6.69. To Sealion Shipping Ltd. (a Martin Barraclough company), Redhill 8.3.78. By 5.78 had been painted up as a Navy Dominie with markings NF875 and coded 603/CH. Offered for sale 3.80 and to Mike Russell of Russavia Ltd. to as The Russavia Collection, Duxford. Used for joyriding at Duxford. Ground-looped on landing from a pleasure flying sortie, Duxford 21.6.87 ending up amongst parked cars and badly damaged. Russavia, by now renamed The Aviation & Heritage Collection, moved to Rush Green 10.90. To David Geddes t/a Aviation Heritage Ltd. 1.3.94 and restoration continued at Rush Green by Ben Borsberry. Moved to Farnborough 1.8.95 – a more convenient location, closer to Borsberry's home in Reading. Flew again by 4.97. Still owned by Aviation Heritage but with Air Atlantique Historic Flight and arrived Coventry 1.99. Aviation Heritage purchased by Air Atlantique 5.02.

6747   Supplied to the Air Council with serial **NF876** but did not enter military service. Initially to 18MU 5.44. To de Havilland Aircraft Co. Ltd. 19.3.46. SOC on transfer to Associated Airways Joint Committee 20.8.46. Converted to Rapide by de Havilland at Witney. Reg'd **G-AHXV** [CofR 10441 11.7.46] to The Ministry of Supply 11.7.46 for operation by the A.A.J.C. pool and CofA no.8059 issued 16.8.46. To British European Airways Corporation 14.8.46 as Mk3. Aircraft ran into a ditch at end of landing run on water-logged airstrip at North Ronaldsay, Orkney 15.1.49. Aircraft was engaged on an emergency ambulance flight. No injuries.

6748   Supplied to the Air Council with military serial **NF877**. Delivered to 18MU 6.44. Served with Metropolitan Com. Sqdn. 9.44 and to Allied Flt. and then to Royal Netherlands Air Force, taken on charge 23.9.44. Serialled **V-1** with the Royal Netherlands Air Force 15.5.46 and operated by 334Sqdn.. Reg'd **PH-VNA** for the United Nations for use in Israel 30.8.48. Transferred to the United Nations Organisation in Palestine 8.10.48. Returned to the Royal Netherlands Air Force as **V-1** and SOC 28.9.56 on sale to U.K. Reg'd **G-APBM** [CofR R5982 13.5.57] to Aerocontacts (Aircraft Distributors) Ltd., Gatwick. To Air Couriers (Transport) Ltd., Croydon 21.5.57. Converted to Mk6 and CofA issued 3.9.57. Based at Croydon, then Biggin Hill. Cancelled as sold in France 21.7.60. Reg'd **F-OBRU** to Ste Ardic Aviation, Dakar. Delivered ex Biggin Hill 30.7.60 and arrived at Dakar 9.8.60. CofA issued 1.8.60. Destroyed at Podor 8.6.62.

6749   Supplied to the Air Council with serial **NF878**. Delivered to 18MU 6.44 but no record of subsequent military service. To Airwork and General Trading Co., Gatwick 26.8.45. CofA application made by Airwork on behalf of Iraq Petroleum Co. Ltd. A CofA survey was carried out at Heston and aircraft was then flown to Loughborough for painting and weighing. This unusual requirement to position the aircraft back to Brush Coachworks was due to special fuel tankage of 38 gallons each side. Records comment, "Gatwick conversions were limited to 30 gallons each side due to de Havilland loading instructions which no longer applies"). Reg'd **G-AGTN** [CofR 9718 19.9.45] to Iraq Petroleum Transport Co Ltd, Haifa. CofA no.7230 issued 17.12.45. CofA renewed 14.2.51 when TTSN 4242.45 hrs. Survey carried out at Tripoli, Lebanon. Time since last CofA renewal 1949 - 252.15, 1950 - 557.50 and 1951 - nil. Reg'd **TJ-ABJ** to Air Jordan Co. Ltd. 2.52. Written off on take-off at Amman Airport at 7.45am on 1.5.53. Swung on take-off, struck lamp standard and destroyed.

6750   Supplied to the Air Council with military serial **NF879**. To Royal Navy at Donibristle 9.6.44. To de Havilland 12.10.45 and returned to Royal Navy. At Stretton 1.49 to 7.49 at least, 781 Sqdn., Lee-on-Solent 1.50 to 7.50 at least and with de Havilland 1.51 and 7.51. To 782Sqdn. at Donibristle coded 802/DO 7.52 to 7.53 at least. With Airwork Ltd. still at Donibristle 1.54 and at Lossiemouth by 7.54. SOC at Lossiemouth in the late 1950s. Reported parked at Lossiemouth without wheels early 1960. Put up for tender as scrap at Lossiemouth. Purchased with others (nine in all) by Hants and Sussex Aviation Ltd., Portsmouth. Few usable components due to bad state of aircraft. Cut up and burnt by Hants and Sussex at Lossiemouth 8.60.

6751   Supplied to the Air Council with military serial **NF880**. To Royal Navy at Donibristle 9.6.44. To 782Sqdn. Donibristle 4.1.46. Serving with AH 1.49, Donibristle 1.50, at de Havilland 7.50, AO 7.51, Yeovilton 7.53 and Lossiemouth 7.54. With Shorts Ferry Unit 8.58. Noted stored at Lossiemouth mid 1960.

6752   Supplied to the Air Council with military serial **NF881**. To Royal Navy at Donibristle 9.6.44. To 782Sqdn. Donisbristle 4.1.46 coded 804/DO in .49. Serving at Stretton 1.49, 782Sqdn. Donibristle 1.50, to de Havilland for attention 7.51, AO 1.52, Brawdy 1.53 and at Culdrose coded CU-999 in '60. Later at RNAS Lossiemouth and noted in store there with Aircraft Holding Unit 1.62. Broken up.

6753   Supplied to the Air Council with military serial **NF882**. Served with Flying Wing Yatesbury and used by No.2 Radio School 6.44, No.4 Radio School 3.45, 5MU 12.46. SOC on sale to Airwork Ltd., Croydon. Reg'd **G-AJVB**.[CofR 11615 29.5.47] but CofA no.9597 already issued 10.5.48! Sold to Iraq Petroleum Transport Co. Ltd., Haifa 30.6.47. Cancelled from register 13.12.51 on sale to Arab Wings Association Ltd. reg'd **TJ-AAZ** 12.51. To Arab Airways (Jerusalem) Ltd. 8.53. To Arab Contracting & Trading Co. Ltd. reg'd **JY-AAZ** 4.54. Sold to Companie Bretonne Aeronautique, Brest reg'd **F-BHDY** & French CofA issued at Toussus-le-Noble 19.7.55. To Aero Club de Limousin, Limoges 10.57 and in use for parachutist transport. Cancelled as destroyed 15.8.63 and noted lying in a heap at Limoges 6.65.

6754   Supplied to the Air Council with military serial **NF883**. Served with A.T.A. HQ White Waltham 6.44, 1680 Flt. Prestwick 1.46. Handed over to Ministry of Supply and passed to A.A.J.C. at Renfrew 16.4.46. Delivered Renfrew, via Connel Bridge to Inverness-Longman 26.4.46. Reg'd **G-AHLN** [CofR 10161 8.5.46] to Scottish Airways Ltd., Renfrew and CofA no.7781 issued 16.10.46. Operated first revenue service 22.11.46. Absorbed by B.E.A.C. on formation 1.2.47. To Ulster Aviation Ltd., Newtownards 23.4.48. To North West Airlines (IOM) Ltd., Ronaldsway 21.5.51. Sold abroad to France? (according to official paperwork) 1.12.52. Reg'd **F-BGOQ** and CofA issued to Ste. Jules-Richard, Toussus-le-Noble 2.4.53. Destroyed Toussus 6.7.53 and reg'n cancelled 10.12.53.

6755   Supplied to the Air Council with military serial **NF884**. Served with 13Grp. Com. Flt. 6.44, 18MU 3.46, 66Grp. Com. Flt. 4.48, 5MU 12.48. SOC to Wilks and Chandler 11.1.50 but reg'd to V. H. Bellamy t/a Flightways Ltd., Eastleigh as **G-ALWM** [CofR 14895 30.1.50]. Sold abroad to France 20.6.50 & export CofA issued 23.8.50. To Jean Lebreton t/a Companie l'Autrex reg'd as **F-OAGP** and operated by Maroc Air Service. Crashed Melilla, Spanish Morocco 17.5.53 before intended transfer to the Far East for Lebreton's operations in Indochina. Reg'n cancelled 2.4.54.

6756   Supplied to the Air Council with military serial **NF885**. Served with No.4 Delivery Flt., at Milfield .44?, 18MU 10.45, Metropolitan Com. Sqdn. 12.45, 18MU 9.46. SOC to Field Aircraft Services Ltd., Croydon and reg'd **G-AJFO** [CofR 11254 29.1.47]. Sold abroad to Belgium 29.4.47 and allocated **OO-CDF** but not

taken up. Restored as **G-AJFO** 15.7.47 for Franco-British Commercial & Industrial Co. Ltd., London W1 and CofA no.8983 issued 23.7.47. Destined for Air Madagascar but both this and its travelling companion, G-AJFN c/n 6520, were burnt out on engine start up at Kosti, Anglo-Egyptian Sudan 3.12.47! (Note: The official register incorrectly identifies **G-AJFO** as c/n 6725 ex NF855, but close scrutiny of Ministry of Defense and Royal Navy records would seem to indicate that c/n 6756 is the more likely identity for this aircraft).

6757   Supplied to the Air Council with military serial **NF886**. Served with A.T.A. HQ White Waltham 6.44, No.1PTS 1.46 (later renamed No.1P&GTS), 5MU 6.48. SOC on sale to Air Navigation & Trading Co. Ltd., Squires Gate 29.10.48 but reg'd to Lancashire Aircraft Corporation Ltd., Samlesbury as **G-ALPK** [CofR 12743 3.5.49]. CofA no.10573 issued 16.9.49. To Air Taxi (Cumberland) Ltd., Carlisle 22.10.57. To Tyne Tees Air Charter Ltd., Newcastle-upon-Tyne 18.4.61 and arrived Woolsington following day. Name changed to Tyne Tees Airways Ltd. 22.2.63. Sold 7.64 and eventually reg'd to Kenneth George Dobson, Blackbushe 31.3.65 and delivered ex Bicester 11.4.65. CofA expired 4.6.66. To Maj. Michael Ray Heeney, trustee of the assets of the Parachute Regiment Free Fall Club. Transported to Netheravon by road for spares use. Fuselage noted languishing in the open during 1968.

6758   Supplied to the Air Council with military serial **NF887**. Served with 1422 Flt. 2.45 until stored 5MU 6.47. SOC on sale to Southern Aircraft (Gatwick) Ltd. Reg'd **G-AKOM** [CofR 12100 8.12.47] but CofA no.9913 not issued until 12.7.50. To Chevalier Declercq, Le Zoute reg'd **OO-DCB** and CofR no.885 issued 14.12.51. Cancelled from Belgian register 3.11.54 and restored as **G-AKOM** to Avionics Ltd., Croydon 12.11.54. Sold abroad to France 12.4.55 and U.K. reg'n cancelled 10.6.55. To Department de la Guyane and operated by Soc. Aerienne des Transports Guyane-Antilles. Reg'd **F-OGAU** & French CofA issued 7.5.56. The CofA expired 6.60, but it was reported damaged at Inini 5.8.60 and we presume, caused by a storm when on the ground!

6759   Supplied to the Air Council with military serial **NF888**. Served with A.T.A. HQ White Waltham 6.44 and then stored 18MU 5.46. SOC on sale to Field Consolidated Aircraft Services Ltd., Croydon. Reg'd **G-AHPV** [CofR 10267 22.5.46]. Noted with Tollerton Aircraft Services Ltd. 19.6.46 and after civilianisation, CofA no.8013 issued 19.9.46. Sold abroad 12.8.46. To the Aircraft Operating Company of Afica and reg'd **ZS-AYG** 30.10.46. Crashed at El Adem, Libya whilst on delivery 31.10.46.

6760   Supplied to the Air Council with military serial **NF889**. Delivered to No.1 Radio School 6.44. Cancelled after a Cat.E flying accident 20.3.45. Whilst on a radio exercise and flying at a height of 5000', the Rapide was flown into by a Spitfire (AR395 from 1653CU) and crashed to the ground and caught fire at Witham-on-Hill, Rutland 20.3.45. Six fatalities. The Spitfire had just broken away from a simulated attack on a Lancaster. SOC 1.4.45.

6761   Supplied to the Air Council with military serial **NF890** and initially to 76MU 6.44. Shipped Glasgow to Capetown per *S.S. Lalan Chattor* 7.44. As **SAAF1365**, served with Signals School and 11OTU 'A' flight in '44. With 61Sqdn. 1.46 until placed into storage at 15AD. Briefly with 28Sqdn. from 17.3.46. For sale 12.4.46 and offer of £3522 offered by Southern Rhodesia Government. To Central African Airways Corporation 1.6.46 and reg'd **VP-YFA** 26.7.46. To Commercial Air Services Ltd. and reg'd **ZS-BZU** 14.7.49. To Drakensberg Air Services, Ladysmith in 1951. Overturned on landing in strong wind Mokhotlong, Basutoland 10.9.54 and written-off.

6762   Supplied to the Air Council with military serial **NF891** and initially to 76MU 24.6.44. Shipped to India per S.S. *City of Kimberley* 20.8.44, arriving Bombay 26.9.44. Reg'd **VT-ASC** 1.11.44 with the incorrect identity 'BCL89403' (see below) and operated by Government of India. Sold by Director-General of Aircraft Disposals 27.3.46. To Indian Air Survey & Transport Co. Ltd., Calcutta 22.7.47. Name changed to Air Survey Co. of India Ltd. 1948. Broke up in mid air over Somaranpet, 70 miles north-west of Nagpur, while en route Hyderabad to Nagpur and all three occupants were killed 22.1.60. (Note: de Havilland c/n 6762 should be Brush works number BCL89413. Does this entry shoot our theory down in flames or is there an error in the Indian records? Having had considerable experience with Indian administrators during his working life, Bernard King tends to think that the latter is more likely!).

6763 Supplied to the Air Council with military serial **NF892**. Served with ADGB Com. Sqdn. Northolt 6.44, Transport Command Northolt 3.45, 18MU 7.45, Metropolitan Com. Sqdn. 1.46 and then to storage at 18MU 5.46. SOC on sale to Airwork Ltd., Gatwick and reg'd **G-AJKH** [CofR 11372 19.3.47]. To Iraq Petroleum Transport Co. Ltd., Haifa 16.5.47. CofA no.9290 apparently not issued until 8.1.48. To Anglo-Iranian Oil Co. Ltd., Abadan 3.11.47. Seized by Iranian authorities at the time of oil nationalisation 10.51 and U.K. reg'n finally cancelled 29.10.54. Reg'd **EP-AAV** and continued in use as a transport by Iran National Oil Co. Fate not recorded.

6764 Supplied to the Air Council with military serial **NF893**. Served with No.1 Radio School 6.44, Com. Flt. Wyton 11.45, 18MU 4.47. SOC on sale to Darlington and District Aero Club Ltd. 26.8.47. Reg'd **G-AKLA** [CofR 12013 23.10.47]. To Lancashire Aircraft Corporation Ltd., Samlesbury 8.6.49. CofA no.9829 issued 18.1.50. Reg'n lapsed due to "long term storage" 9.11.50, but restored 3.2.51. To Aeroservices Ltd., Croydon 6.4.54 and operated by West London Air Charter Ltd. 4.54. During a ferry flight from the U.K. to Hanoi, the pilot became lost and forced landed 38 miles north-west of Jodhpur, India 15.6.54. The aircraft struck a ravine, was extensively damaged and declared a total loss. Reg'n cancelled 10.9.54.

6765 Supplied to the Air Council with military serial **NF894**. Served with No.1 Radio School 6.44, 18MU 4.46. SOC on sale to Birkett Air Services Ltd., Croydon 10.1.47. Reg'd **G-AJBJ** [CofR 11150 20.1.47] and CofA no.8928 issued 26.3.47 to Airwork General Trading Co. Ltd., on behalf of Birkett. Company ceased operations 21.4.53 due to lack of joy flight contracts. To Airwork Ltd., Scone 1.5.53. To Air Navigation and Trading Co. Ltd., Blackpool 19.7.55. Cancelled as WFU on CofA expiry at Squires Gate 10.10.57. Aircraft dismantled by 4.58 and wings taken to the owner of A.N. & T., R. L. Whyham's property at Kirkham. Re-erected and was flying again by 1959. Cancelled as WFU on CofA expiry 14.9.61 and dismantled at Squires Gate. Fuselage noted there 12.68. Sold to Sam Westwell 1969 who was unable to restore it. To Northern Aircraft Preservation Society 25.10.69 and moved to Peel Green, Manchester. To Midlands Aircraft Preservation Society around 1970 and stored at Husbands Bosworth. Fuselage moved to Coventry by 3.76. Moved to Chirk by road 16.6.78 and restored to John Pierce Aviation Ltd., Ley Farm, Chirk 15.8.78. Plans to re-engine with Gypsy Queen Mk. 30 engines did not come to fruition due to CofA problems. Noted partially restored at Chirk 6.87, with the floor from G-AKRN and the centre section from G-AHAG. Noted still in storage 10.01.

6766 Supplied to the Air Council with military serial **NF895**. Served with No.4 Radio School 6.44. Presumably after an accident, to de Havilland for major inspection 9.4.46 and declared Cat.E. Remains sold to D. J. Adis 29.5.47.

6767 Supplied to the Air Council with military serial **NF896**. Served with 16Grp. Com. Flt. 6.44 until placed into store 18MU 10.46. SOC on sale to Tyne Taxis Ltd. (Air Division), Newcastle-Woolsington. Reg'd **G-AKME** [CofR 12042 1.3.48] and CofA no.10106 issued 7.5.48. To Wolverhampton Aviation Ltd. 21.2.50. Burnt out on engine start up, Lympne 30.6.50.

6768 Supplied to the Air Council with military serial **NR669** and initially to 18MU. To Royal Navy at Evanton 7.9.45. Served with ST .48-.50, Shorts .51, DH in .52, AO in .53 and again with Shorts .54-.55. Noted parked outside Lossiemouth devoid of wheels early 1960! Purchased along with eight others by Hants & Sussex Aviation, but due to the bad state of the aircraft, few parts were found usable and they were burnt at Lossiemouth 8.60.

6769 Supplied to the Air Council with military serial **NR670**. Delivered to 18MU 7.44 and served at St. Mawgan 30.5.46. To French Air Force Comm. 236, 25.6.46, arrived Pau 8.46. Served with BE703 at Pau and ELA56 at Persan-Beaumont. SOC 11.5.56. To **F-BDJX** SFASA, later SFATAT at St. Yan and French CofA issued 29.10.57. Based Lille from 1961 and Strasbourg from 1964. CofA expired 1.68.

6770 Supplied to the Air Council with military serial **NR671**. Served with Halton No.1 School of Technical Training Stn. Flt. 6.45, 18MU 5.46. SOC to Brooklands Aviation Ltd. 27.2.47. Reg'd

G-AJHP [CofR 11305 14.2.47] and CofA no.9155 issued 16.5.47. Converted to Mk6 at some stage. To G.Q. Parachute Co. Ltd., Fairoaks 25.7.51 and used as the private aircraft of the Chairman & Managing Director since 1934, The Hon. (John) Raymond (Cuthbert) Quilter. Fitted with four executive seats plus radio operator's seat and 9 gallon long range tank fitted. Delivered ex Fairoaks to Hants and Sussex Aviation Ltd. at Portsmouth and cancelled as sold in Algeria 12.3.60. Reg'd **F-OBOI** to Compagnie Generale de Transports en Algerie – CGTA, Algiers. French CofA issued 6.5.60. Delivered via Lympe 27.4.60. To Societe Generale d'Affretements Aeriens – SGAA, Algiers 5.61. CofA suspended 4.62.

6771 Supplied to the Air Council with military serial **NR672**. Delivered to 18MU 7.44. Taken on charge by Royal Navy 30.10.45. At Evanton 12.46. Served with ST 1948-1954. SOC at Stretton 29.11.54 and broken up there 11.54.

6772 Supplied to the Air Council with serial **NR673** but did not enter military service. Delivered to 18MU 7.44. Converted to Rapide by de Havilland at Witney and CofA no.7093 issued 11.9.44. To British Ambassador, Montevideo. Shipped per Liberty Ship 1696 29.9.44 and arrived in Uruguay 20.10.44. Aircraft named *Condos de los Andes*. SOC 25.6.47. Believed sold to Peru. Eventual fate unknown.

6773 Supplied to the Air Council with serial **NR674** but did not enter military service. Delivered to 18MU 7.44. SOC on sale to Hunting Aviation 3.12.45. Converted to Rapide by de Havilland at Witney. Reg'd **G-AGZU** [CofR 9871 22.1.46] to Hunting Air Travel Ltd., Luton. CofA no.1359 issued 12.2.46. To Cecil Kay Aircraft (1945) Ltd., Elmdon 25.10.46. Nominal change to Cecil Kay Ltd. 18.11.47. To Herts & Essex Aviation Ltd., Broxbourne, Hertfordshire 1.4.48. Nominal change to Herts & Essex Aero Club (1946) Ltd., Broxbourne 22.4.48. Later moved to Stapleford, Essex. Sold to South Africa 28.4.55. To Alan Coutts Williams t/a Enterprise Clothing Manufacturers SA Ltd., Durban reg'd **ZS-DLS** 28.4.55. To Ladysmith Air Charter Services, Ladysmith. To J. L. Palframan, Pietermaritzburg, 12.57. To Arthur Mechin, Baragwanath, date unknown. Dismantled at Baragwanath and badly damaged by vandals by the early 1970's. Reg'n cancelled 19.4.71. Remains to the S.A.A.F. Museum 1976.

6774 Supplied to the Air Council with serial **NR675** but did not enter military service. Delivered to 5MU 7.44. To de Havilland 15.4.46 and converted to Rapide prior to sale by de Havilland at Witney. U.K. CofA no.8819 issued 6.12.46. Sold to Brazil and reg'd **PP-OMD** to Organicao Mineira de Transportes Aereos – O.M.T.A. However, somewhat mysteriously, never entered on the Brazilian register. Therefore, there is some doubt that the aeroplane ever went to South America and later history is unknown.

6775 Supplied to the Air Council with military serial **NR676** but did not enter military service. Delivered to 5MU 7.44. Flown to de Havilland at Witney 15.4.46 and civilianised to Rapide standard. Reg'd **G-AIWY** [CofR 11042 29.11.46] to de Havilland Aircraft Co. Ltd., Witney but CofA no.8740 issued 3 days earlier! Cancelled as sold abroad 7.1.47 and had arrived Denmark by 26.2.47. Reg'd **OY-AAO** to Falcks Redningkor AS 6.10.47 and CofA no.260 issued. First revenue service 13.10.47. To R. H. A. Peech, Frederikshavn 23.6.61 at which time the aircraft had flown 3813hr. and 40mins. To Danfly, Kalstred 13.2.63. Last flight Kastrup to Kalstred 19.10.63 and stored in the open for two years and obviously deteriorated badly. Following an approach by Dansk Flyvehistorisk Forening, Greve Lerchen-Lerchenborg, owner of Danfly, presented the Rapide to them. They dismantled the aircraft 3.66 and moved it by road initially for exhibition at their depot in Ole Romer's Street, Helsingor. After a few years moved for storage at Jernbjerg near Slagelse, then to a farm near Grundsomagle, to Rudbjerggard near Egeskov. By 1979 stored at Engagergard near Vaerlose, some 20km north-west of Copenhagen. Finally displayed at Danmarks Flyvemuseum, Helsingor in the colours of Falcks Redningkor 2.02.

6776 Supplied to the Air Council with military serial **NR677**. Delivered to 18MU 7.44. To Royal Navy at Donibristle 30.8.45. SOC at Lossiemouth late 1950's. With Shorts Ferry Division, coded 600/CH and named *Cliff's Cab*. Parked outside at Lossiemouth without wheels early 1960. Put up for tender as scrap and purchased by Hants & Sussex Aviation Ltd. A few

DH89 c/n 6782. Fairey Surveys operated G-AHXW latterly from their base at White Waltham when Heathrow operations compelled closure of their former Hayes base. Here seen at Denham.

DH89 c/n 6792. Early use of a corporate aeroplane, G-AHKV when with the brewers Ind Coope & Allsopp and flown from their private airfield at Tatenhill, near England's brewery capital, Burton-on-Trent.

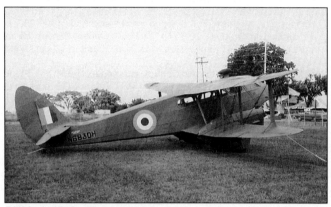

DH89 c/n 6782. After many years in the aerial survey role, offered for sale and somewhat unusually for the type, sold to an American buyer. Now exhibited by the E.A.A. at Oshkosh, Wisconsin.

DH89 c/n 6792. G-AHKV moved on to the Automobile Association and in their distinctive black and yellow livery, the Rapide was a frequent sight over major events, directing traffic flow from on high!

DH89 c/n 6784. G-AGLE was one of three purchased by International Airways in July 1948 and used them to operate services as a B.E.A. Associate, Croydon and Bournemouth to Cowes.

DH89 c/n 6794. With additional cockpit glazing, used for more than 30 years by the Air Survey Co. of India, Calcutta. To a private owner in the U.S.A. in 1978 but now displayed at Wright-Patterson.

DH89 c/n 6790. G-AKZB, whilst in B.E.A. service was very badly damaged when landing at St. Just December 1961, but thanks to the rugged structure, there were no serious injuries to those aboard.

DH89 c/n 6801. Languishing at Usworth in damaged condition in April 1974 after it nosed over in February 1969, we were surprised to hear of G-AJSL's sale to Australia in 1983! There, it slowly recovers.

usable components removed and aircraft cut up and burnt at Lossiemouth 8.60.

6777 Supplied to the Air Council with military serial **NR678**. To No.1 Radio School 7.44, coded TCR/U, later TCR/C. Reportedly sometime with Stn. Flt. Halton and coded THA/C. To storage at 18MU 10.47 but moved to 5MU for further storage10.48. Sold to Short Brothers & Harland Ltd., Rochester 11.1.50. Reg'd **G-ALWJ** [CofR 14892 21.1.50] and CofA no.10802 issued 20.4.50. Sold abroad to Kenya 12.10.53. Converted to Mk4 standard by Flightways Ltd., Eastleigh prior to delivery. Reg'd as **VP-KLL** to Noon and Pearce Air Charters and Agencies Ltd., Nairobi. Delivered ex Eastleigh 4.11.53. Sold to J. E. F. Wilkins (Caspair Ltd.), Mazinde by 1955. Considered beyond economical repair after a forced landing on the Magad Road, 40 miles from Nairobi 20.1.58 due to fuel starvation. However, salvaged and rebuilt. Re-reg'd **5Y-KLL** to Caspair Ltd. 1.65. Last check III 28.7.64. CofA renewed 31.7.65 but cancelled from register later in the year. Fate unknown.

6778 Supplied to the Air Council with military serial **NR679**. Delivered to 18MU 7.44. Served with Metropolitan Com. Sqdn. 10.45, 18MU 7.46, 25Grp. Com. Flt. 9.47, 18MU 2.48, 61Grp. Com. Flt. 4.48. Placed into storage 5MU 2.49. SOC on sale to Robert Alan Short and partner James Henry Tattersall, Croydon 28.4.49. Reg'd **G-ALNS** [CofR 12701 21.4.49] and CofA no.10603 issued 16.9.49. To Walter Hutchinson, Eastleigh 15.9.49. To Hampshire School of Flying Ltd., Eastleigh 2.12.50. To Sydney George Newport t/a Arab Contracting and Trading 11.12.51. Converted to Mk4 during 1955. To Aerocontacts (Aircraft Distributors) Ltd., Gatwick 3.4.64. Sold in the Congo 22.10.64. Arrived at Leopoldville-Ndolo 14.4.64. (Note: The construction numbers for Rapides 9Q-CPF/CQF/CQT/CYE are unknown and this is likely to be one of these).

6779 Supplied to the Air Council with serial **NR680** but did not enter military service. Delivered to 6MU 9.44. Reg'd **G-AGLO** [CofR 9545 27.10.44] for the Secretary of State for Air and believed intended for operation by Allied Airways. Not delivered and the reg'n not taken up; never subsequently used on any other aircraft. Converted to Mk.II during 1945. To Royal Aircraft Establishment 5.45 and then for storage at 18MU 8.46. Sold to Olley Air Service Ltd., Croydon. Reg'd to them as **G-AKSC** [CofR 12164 27.1.48]. To Sir Brograve Campbell Beauchamp Bt., t/a The Demolition and Construction Co. Ltd., London W1 28.2.48. CofA no.9970 issued 16.3.48. Reg'd in the name of The Demolition and Construction Co. Ltd. 8.7.49. To East Anglian Flying Services Ltd., Southend 4.5.53. To Aeroservices Ltd., Croydon 27.9.54. Converted to Mk4 12.1.55. Cancelled on sale abroad to French New Caledonia 3.8.55. To **F-OATC** Societe Caledonienne de Transportes Aeriens – TRANSPAC. To Aero Club Caledonian, Noumea Magenta 1965. CofA expired 8.66.

6780 Supplied to the Air Council with serial **NR681** but did not enter military service. Delivered to de Havilland at Witney for conversion to Rapide 11.8.44. SOC to A.A.J.C., Speke. Reg'd as **G-AGLP** [CofR 9546 28.10.44] to Railway Air Services Ltd., Speke and CofA no.7111 issued 2.2.45. Leased to Jersey Airways 5.45 and became their first aircraft to land back in the Channel Islands after liberation 26.5.45. Used to open service London (Croydon)-Guernsey-Jersey 21.6.45. Probably returned to R.A.S. in July with delivery of Jersey Airways own aircraft. Operated by Isle of Man Air Services during 1946. Absorbed by B.E.A.C. on formation 1.2.47. To Charles W. J. Allen t/a Allen Aircraft Services, Old Coulsdon 6.48. To Christopher Leslie Burton t/a International Airways Ltd., Croydon 1.7.48. Leased to Jersey Airlines 3.49 to 18.4.49. WFU at Croydon 1.4.52 but noted Portsmouth 12.4.52. Finally cancelled as permanently withdrawn from use 31.8.59.

6781 Supplied to the Air Council with serial **NR682** but did not enter military service. Delivered to de Havilland at Witney for conversion to Rapide 11.8.44. To A.A.J.C., Speke 23.1.45. Reg'd **G-AGLR** [CofR 9547 28.10.47] to Railway Air Services Ltd., Speke. CofA no.7112 issued 13.1.45 as Mk3. Reverted to civil colour scheme by 3.46. Absorbed by B.E.A.C. on formation 1.2.47. To Lees-Hill Aviation (Birmingham) Ltd. 24.6.48. Company acquired by D. & C. Everall 5.9.51. Company name changed to Don Everall (Aviation) Ltd. 29.1.52 and aircraft continued to be based at Elmdon. On 7.10.56, while inbound to Elmdon from Le Bourget, the port engine failed due to fuel starvation near Daventry. The Rapide was unable to maintain height and crashed in a field and caught fire at Four Oaks Cross

Roads, Berkeswell, near Coventry at 2027 hrs and was destroyed on impact and the ensuing fire. It is reported that the pilot and owners were fined £145 after the accident. Reg'n cancelled 30.5.57.

6782 Supplied to the Air Council with serial **NR683** but did not enter military service. Initially delivered to 5MU 7.44 and then to de Havilland at Witney for conversion to Rapide 19.3.46. SOC to the A.A.J.C. 20.8.46. Reg'd **G-AHXW** [CofR 10442 11.7.46] to The Ministry of Supply for operation by the A.A.J.C. pool and CofA issued 16.8.46. Handed over to B.E.A.C. on formation 1.2.47. Later named *John Nicholson*. To A. J. Whittemore (Aeradio) Ltd., Croydon 14.4.53. Converted to Mk4 during 1954. To Fairey Aviation Co.Ltd., Hayes 2.11.54. Nominal change to Fairey Aviation Ltd., Hayes 25.6.59. Further change to Fairey Air Surveys Ltd., White Waltham 30.8.60. "Air" dropped from the company title 30.12.63. To G.R.M. Airwork Ltd., Staverton 27.2.68. Renamed G.R.M. Developments Ltd. 14.8.69. In 4.69, the aircraft was valued at £3000. By 20.7.70, operated by P.S.L. (Precise Surveys Ltd.) Developments Ltd., Worcester (an associate company of G.R.M. Developments). Fitted with wide angle vision blisters on both sides of the fuselage aft of the cockpit bulkhead. Also a survey camera aperture and mounting in the floor by the door and an oblique camera port in the side of the fuselage aft of the door. Total time at 2.4.69 was 8239 hours. Re-reg'd **N683DH** to R. M. Puryean, Portola Valley, California 2.71 and cancelled to U.S.A. 16.3.71. . Painted in "military marks" and delivered via Lympe to Rotterdam for shipping to the U.S. Erected at Newark and flown to San Jose, California. Later reg'd to J. R. O'Brien & R. M. Puryean and based at Redding CA. Donated to the Experimental Aircraft Association Museum, Franklin, Wisconsin 27.3.74 for rebuilding at Burlington. Rebuild completed but aircraft remained dismantled at Burlington 4.80 pending completion of a purpose built museum building at Wittman Field, Oshkosh WI. Painted blue and silver and named *Sir George Hardie* [sic] after George Hardie, the E.A.A.'s historian!

6783 Supplied to the Air Council with serial **NR684** but did not enter military service. To 5MU 7.44. Converted to Rapide prior to sale by de Havilland, presumably at Witney, 3.5.46. U.K. CofA no.8834 issued 16.12.46. Became **OB-RAH-197** with Grupo de Transportes No.42. Fate unknown.

6784 Supplied to the Air Council with military serial **NR685**. Delivered to 5MU 7.44 but did not enter military service. Instead, to A.A.J.C., Speke and converted to Rapide by de Havilland at Witney. Reg'd **G-AGLE** [CofR 9535 14.12.44] and operated by Railway Air Services. CofA no.7152 issued 12.2.45. In use by Scottish Airways 14.5.45. On short term lease to Jersey Airlines, after liberation of the Channel Islands, pending delivery of their own aircraft, for London service which opened 21.6.45. Transferred to B.E.A.C. on formation 1.2.47. To Charles W. J. Allen t/a Allen Aircraft Services, Old Coulsdon 15.6.48. To Christopher Leslie Burton t/a International Airways Ltd., Croydon 1.7.48. Aircraft tipped on nose whilst landing in gusty conditions at Croydon 15.9.48, causing minor damage. En route Bovingdon to Croydon 27.3.49, both engines lost power, possibly due to fuel starvation. A forced landing was made at Rosehill recreation ground, Sutton. The aircraft was not damaged but had to be dismantled and transported to Croydon as there was insufficient room to take off. On hire to Jersey Airlines, summer 1949. Withdrawn from use at Croydon 1.11.51. Remains sent to Portsmouth and noted on the scrap heap there 1952. Finally cancelled as permanently withdrawn from use 31.8.59.

6785 Supplied to the Air Council with military serial **NR686**. To Metropolitan Com. Sqdn. Hendon 8.44. Used by Inspector General, Royal Belgian Air Force. SOC to Belgian Government under "Mutual Aid". To Royal Belgian Air Force, serialled **D4** and later coded ZC-M. SOC 1957. Re-reg'd **OO-ARN** to Cogea Nouvelle, Keerbergen 25.7.57. CofA no.1145. To Air Brousse SPRL, Leopoldville-Ndolo 8.59. Crashed and burned in an accident at Luozi, Congo 20.6.60. Reg'n cancelled 5.9.60.

6786 Supplied to the Air Council with military serial **NR687**. Served with 15Grp. Com. Flt. Liverpool-Speke 9.44, HQ Com. Flt. Leavesden 8.45, 18MU 11.46, Staff College, Andover 10.48. During service life, sometime coded QK/F and KEB. SOC "to spares" 22.5.52. To Hants and Sussex Aviation Ltd., Portsmouth reg'd **G-ANAH** [CofR R.4055 24.6.53]. CofA issued 3.3.54. To Vickers-Armstrong Ltd. 3.54. Sold to Uruguay 26.8.54 and reg'n cancelled 10.10.54. To Federico Oetzmann, Montevideo and reg'd

CX-API 9.54. Although still shown on August 1972 official register, believed to have succumbed during 1958. Actual fate unknown.

6787   Supplied to the Air Council with military serial **NR688**. Delivered to 24Sqdn. Hendon 18.8.44 then to Metropoliran Com. Sqdn. also at Hendon 8.9.44. Noted at Manchester-Ringway in 1946 coded CB-G. To Belgian Government 4.9.46 and taken on charge by the Royal Belgian Air Force serialled **D5**. Later coded ZC-N. To Cogea Nouvelle, Keerbergen reg'd **OO-ARI** and CofR no.1085 issued 11.7.56. Sold to U.K. 7.5.57 and reg'd **G-APBN** [CofR R5986 16.5.57] to Crewdson Aviation Ltd., Croydon. Marks not taken up however and they were cancelled again 29.9.57. Restored as **OO-ARI** 10.12.57. Arrived Croydon 24.4.58 but delivered on to an overseas owner a few days later. To Ste. Tunisienne de Reparation Aeronautique et de Construction, Tunis as **F-OBIA** and CofA issued 2.12.58. Operated as Aero-Sahara. CofA suspended 28.11.62 and possibly one of the aircraft noted as withdrawn from use at Tunis in 1970.

6788   Supplied to the Air Council with military serial **NR689**. Delivered to 76MU 8.44 where dismantled for shipment to South Africa. Shipped ex Birkenhead per *S.S. City of Calcutta* 22.9.44 and arrived Capetown 12.10.44. As **SAAF1366** 10.44. Saw service with 61Sqdn. 1.45 until stored 15AD 1.46. Brief service with 28Sqdn. 2.2.46 to 29.3.46. Disposed of to the Civil Aviation Council 19.7.46 and entered service with the Department of Transport reg'd **ZS-CAC** 10.9.46. Sold to an unknown owner and re-reg'd **ZS-BZC** 11.5.48. Confiscated in Trans-Jordan 19.11.51 and cancelled from the South African register on that date.

6789   Supplied to the Air Council with military serial **NR690**. Served with A.T.A. HQ White Waltham 9.44 until stored 18MU 6.46. SOC to Derek John Hayles, Portsmouth. Reg'd **G-AKYZ** [CofR 12335 18.5.48]. To W. A. Rollason Ltd., Croydon 24.6.48 and CofA issued 6.9.48. Sold abroad 15.9.48 via importer Sfreddo y Paolini Ltda., Zonda and reg'd **LV-AEO** 30.11.48. Somewhat confusingly, there are two reported accidents leading to the aircraft being written-off! Damaged at General Pacheco Airport, Buenos Airies 22.11.48 and deemed beyond economical repair prior to an Argentine CofA being issued. However, the aircraft was also reported to have overturned on take-off Pajas Blancos, Cordoba 24.1.49!

6790   Supplied to the Air Council with military serial **NR691**. Served with A.T.A. HQ White Waltham 9.44 until stored 18MU 8.46. SOC to Derek John Hayles, Southsea. Reg'd **G-AKZB** [CofR 12337 18.5.48] and CofA no.10187 issued 9.7.48. To Laurence Dudley Trappitt, Croydon 15.7.48. To Charles William John Allen t/a Allen Aircraft Services, Old Coulsdon 25.10.48. To British European Airways Corporation 11.2.49 and later named *Lord Baden Powell*. Converted to Mk6 8.60. Undershot in poor visibility on landing St. Just, Lands End 12.12.61. The aircraft struck the boundary fence and although severely damaged, there were no casualties. Written off, total time 8846 hours. Cancelled as destroyed 27.12.61.

6791   Supplied to the Air Council with military serial **NR692**. Served with headquarters A.T.A. 9.44 until stored 18MU 7.46. Sold to Butlins Ltd., London W1, the holiday camp operator. Reg'd **G-AKTD** [CofR 12190 19.2.48] and CofA no.10025 issued 14.4.48. To Air Couriers Ltd., Croydon 17.10.49. Sold abroad to France 4.5.51. To Ste. D'Exploitation Aeronautique l'Aero Club du Touquet, and reg'd **F-BFVM**. French CofA issued 8.5.51. Club moved to Eu during 1956. To Aero Club Colomb-Bechar c.1957. To C.G.T.A. 1.60. To S.G.A.A. 1.61. Destroyed at In- Amenas, Algeria 9.10.61.

6792   Supplied to the Air Council with military serial **NR693**. Delivered to 5MU 12.44 but no record of subsequent military service. To de Havilland for conversion at Witney 11.3.46. Reg'd **G-AHKV** [CofR 10143 23.4.46] to The Ministry of Supply. CofA no.7673 25.7.46. To the Associated Airways Joint Committee 26.7.46. Believed intended for operation by Isle of Man Air Services Ltd. but to B.O.A.C. (B.E.A. division) 25.7.46. Later named *Sir James Outram*. To A. J. Whittemore (Aeradio) Ltd. , Croydon 14.4.53. To Sky Neon Aviation Co. Ltd., London W1 4.2.54 and used for night time aerial advertising. Converted to Mk6 by Air Couriers by 1956. To Ind Coope and Allsopp Ltd., Tatenhill 3.1.56. To Automobile Association Ltd., Fairoaks 29.11.57. To Solair Flying Services Ltd., Birmingham 20.6.63. Last flight for Solair, Birmingham to Coventry 12.10.64. Solair failed and assets acquired by Midfly Ltd., Elmdon 5.1.65. To

Cartographical Services (Southampton) Ltd., Elmdon 23.8.66. CofA expired 3.12.68 and noted withdrawn from use at Elmdon. Cancelled from register 9.9.69 and eventually burnt.

6793   Supplied to the Air Council with military serial **NR694**. Delivered to 76MU 29.9.44 where dismantled for shipping to India. Delivered to Middlesborough 20.10.44 and shipped 30.10.44, arriving Bombay 8.12.44. SOC as "sold in India" 27.3.46. Sold by Director General of Disposals 4.46. Reg'd **VT-ASJ** 15.1.45 to Government of India. Reg'n cancelled 29.4.47.

6794   Supplied to the Air Council with military serial **NR695**. Delivered to 76MU 28.9.44 where dismantled for shipping to India. Delivered to Middlesborough 20.10.44 and shipped 30.10.44, arriving Bombay 8.12.44. SOC as "sold in India" 7.46. Reg'd **VT-ASQ** 3.45 to Indian National Airways Ltd., Calcutta. To Indian Survey and Transport Co. Ltd., Calcutta 21.5.46. Name changed to Air Survey Co. of India Ltd. in 1948. Still owned by them in 1977 and noted stored dismantled at Calcutta's Dum Dum airport 18.3.77. Re-reg'd **N2290F** to Elmer J. Gothard, Chehalis, WA 7.78. To John J. Schell, Graham, WA 7.79. To Wright-Patterson AFB for USAF Museum, arrived 13.11.89. Now displayed, painted to represent 'X7454' (c/n 6596), an aeroplane used briefly by the 8th Air Force at Abbots Ripton, Huntingdonshire.

6795   Supplied to the Air Council with serial **NR696** but did not enter military service. Converted to civilian standard by Airwork General Trading Co. 9.44. Reg'd **G-AGLN** [CofR 9544 2.10.44] to Anglo-Iranian Oil Co. Ltd., Abadan. CofA no.7106 issued 1.12.44. Shipped ex Birkenhead per *S.S. Registan* 27.12.44, arrived Basra 26.1.45. Crashed 20 miles from Abadan, Iran 15.12.46, 3 killed, whilst on flight from Masjid-i-Suleiman to Abadan. Reg'n cancelled 2.1.47.

6796   Supplied to the Air Council with military serial **NR697**. Served with 21Grp. Com. Flt. 10.44, coded FKO-A. Sold at Bircham Newton to Ciro's Aviation Ltd., Gatwick 9.3.47. Reg'd **G-AKGV** [CofR 11909 9.10.47] and CofA no.9796 issued 17.10.47. To William Dempster Ltd., Blackbushe 11.11.48. To John Anton Longmoor, t/a Vendair, Croydon 20.7.50. Sold abroad 25.7.50. Reg'd **F-BFPU** 8.50 to Ste. Air-Caen, named *Ville de Caen*. Arrived for J. P. Filhol, Baginton, c.1973. Still French reg'd, damaged when hangar collapsed at Cork, winter 1973. Further damaged by vandals whilst under repair 8.74. Aircraft repaired using parts from G-AGDP (c/n 6403) and flying by 10.74. For sale 11.74 for £4000. Restored as **G-AKGV** to Stuart Julian Filhol, Cork 7.11.75. Cancelled on sale to Canada 21.6.76. Sold to George LeMay, Acme ALB and flown to Canada via Prestwick 30.7.76. Reserved as **C-GXFJ** on arrival but there is no evidence that the reg'n was actually painted on the aircraft. Re-reg'd **C-FAYE** by 7.82 and named *Lady Faye*. Presented to the Ontario Bushplane Heritage Educational Centre by the LeMay family of Calgary ALB and arrived at the Canadian Bushplane Heritage Centre, Sault Ste. Marie ONT 20.10.99. Refurbished and placed on display early 2000.

6797   Supplied to the Air Council with military serial **NR698**. Delivered to 5MU 10.44. Served throughout with Telecommunications Flying Unit Defford from 9.45. To 5MU for storage 3.48. SOC on sale Robert Allan Short, Croydon 2.1.50. Reg'd **G-ALXU** [CofR 14927 24.1.50]. To W. A. Rollason Ltd., Croydon 16.4.50. Cancelled as sold to Transjordan 20.5.50. To Arab Airways Ltd. reg'd **TJ-AAV** 29.8.50. To Arab Airways (Jerusalem) Ltd. 8.53. Re-reg'd **JY-AAV** to Arab Contracting and Trading Co. Ltd. 4.54. Sold 1955 to Ste. Air Madagascar, reg'd **F-OASC** and CofA issued 22.4.55. Burnt out at Fort-Dauphin, Madagascar 20.5.57. Last owner also reported as T.A.I. and destroyed at Tien Yen 16.5.57. Reg'n cancelled 30.10.57.

6798   Supplied to the Air Council with serial **NR699** but did not enter military service. Initially delivered to 5MU 10.44. To de Havilland at Witney for civil conversion 3.5.46 and U.K. CofA no.8820 issued 6.12.46. Re-reg'd **OB-RAG-196** to Grupo de Transportes No.42. Fate unknown.

6799   Supplied to the Air Council with military serial **NR700**. Delivered to 76MU 10.44 where dismantled for shipping to Africa. Transported to Liverpool Docks 23.11.44 and shipped per S.S. *Silver Walnut* 2.12.44, arriving Takoradi, West Africa 20.12.44. SOC 1.1.47 in general clear up of records.

6800 Supplied to the Air Council with serial **NR701** but did not enter military service. Initially at 5MU 10.44. To the A.A.J.C. 13.8.46. Converted to Rapide by de Havilland at Witney. Reg'd **G-AHXX** [CofR 10443 11.7.46] to The Ministry of Supply for operation by the A.A.J.C. pool and CofA no.8061 issued 9.8.46. Handed over to B.E.A.C. 9.8.46. Sold to Malayan Airways Ltd. 4.6.52 and cancelled from U.K. register 1.8.52. Reg'd **VR-OAB** 9.52 to Malayan Airways Ltd. but operated by subsidiary Borneo Airways. Damaged at Lahaddutu 27.3.59. Cancelled as withdrawn from use 10.3.61 and scrapped.

6801 Supplied to the Air Council with military serial **NR713**. Delivered to 18MU 11.44. Issued to Technical Training Command Com. Flt. White Waltham 9.45 and later served with Com. Flt. Wyton 11.45, Com. Flt. Halton 8.46 and then stored 5MU 1.47. SOC on sale to Field Aircraft Services Ltd., Croydon 29.5.47. Reg'd **G-AJSL** [CofR 11550 8.5.47] & cancelled as sold abroad 16.6.47. Restored to Field Aircraft 17.1.48. To Trent Valley Aviation Ltd., Tollerton 29.9.49 and named *Friar Tuck*. Taken over by Eagle Aviation Ltd. 8.9.50. To Air Charter Ltd., Croydon 24.12.51. Returned to Eagle Aviation Ltd. 9.4.52. To Surrey Flying Services Ltd., Croydon 10.4.52. To Southern Flying Schools Ltd., Portsmouth 26.3.56. Name changed to Portsmouth Aero Club Ltd. 10.1.61. To Thomas Hutton Marshall, Christchurch 9.5.62. To P. E. Palmer Holdings Ltd., Bournemouth 28.8.62. To broker Shackleton Aviation Ltd., Cranfield 2.5.63. To Airgeneers Ltd., Staverton 5.10.64. To M. R. Heevey t/a The Parachute Regiment Free Fall Club, Netheravon 10.66 and named *Pegasus*. Nominal change the trustee to Lt. Richard Charles John Brinton 1.3.67. To Trent Valley Aviation Ltd., Castle Donington 30.5.68. While on charter to The Northern Parachute Centre, nosed over whilst taxiing Usworth 23.2.69 and reg'n cancelled as permanently withdrawn from use 17.12.70. Repairs, estimated at £1500, were beyond the resources of Trent Valley, who later went into liquidation. Still stored at Usworth in damaged condition 10.74. Moved to Baginton 2.77. Eventually to Australia and noted, Melbourne-Essendon 4.82 and Melbourne-Moorabbin 1.83. Work proceeding 3.97 to restore the aircraft to flying condition and reg'n **VH-UXZ (2)** allocated 1.95 for owner Maurice Howard Rolfe, Cheltenham VIC. (Also see c/n 6365 for first use of reg'n VH-UXZ).

6802 Supplied to the Air Council with military serial **NR714**. Delivered to 18MU 11.44. Served with Fighter Command Com. Flt. Northolt 12.44, Coastal Command Com. Flt., Leavesden 4.45 and returned to Coastal Command Com. Flt. 7.45. To 18MU for storage 4.46. Moved to 63MU for further storage 4.47. Sold to Russell Littledale Whyham of Air Navigation and Trading Co. Ltd., Squires Gate and reg'd as **G-AKMD** [CofR 12041 2.3.48]. To Butlins Ltd., London W1 18.5.48. CofA no.10143 issued 10.9.48. To Aviation Traders Ltd., Southend 9.8.49. To Aerocontacts Ltd., Gatwick 19.2.51. Cancelled as sold abroad 17.12.51. Reg'd **F-OAKD** to Ste. Air Madagascar 1.52. Destroyed by fire when starting engines at Bealanana, Madagascar 15.3.52. Registration cancelled 23.4.52.

6803 Supplied to the Air Council with serial **NR715** but did not enter military service. Delivered to 18MU 11.44. Converted to Rapide by de Havilland at Witney. Reg'd **G-AGNH** [CofR 9587 9.1.45] and CofA no.7158 issued 16.5.45. To British Overseas Airways Corporation, Whitchurch 17.5.45. Hired to East African Airways Corporation 10.8.45 and reg'd as **VP-KCT** from 2.8.46. Restored to U.K. register as **G-AGNH** [CofR R.656/2 13.8.49] to the Ministry of Transport & Civil Aviation for use by the Civil Air Attache, Baghdad. Cancelled when sold in Aden 6.7.56. Reg'd **VR-AAP** to Aden Airways Ltd. 2.57. Scrapped R.A.F. Salalah 11.59.

6804 Supplied to the Air Council with serial **NR716** but did not enter military service. Delivered to 5MU 11.44. To de Havilland at Witney for conversion to Rapide prior to onward sale by the manufacturer 3.5.46 and U.K. export CofA no.8811 issued 25.11.46. To **OB-RAF-195** Grupo de Transportes No.42. Fate unknown.

6805 Supplied to the Air Council with military serial **NR717**. Delivered to 5MU 11.44. Served with Metropolitan Com. Sqdn., Hendon 10.45 and Stn. Flt. Halton 7.46. SOC to Theodore William Morton (of Morton Air Services Ltd.). Reg'd **G-AKUS** [CofR 12228 11.3.48]. To Arther Westcar Weyman, London EC3 26.4.48. CofA no.10072 issued 19.8.48. To Mayfair Air Services Ltd., Croydon 20.8.48. Disappeared in Palestine (1948?) and listed as "written-

off" 16.5.50 and U.K. reg'n cancelled 29.5.50. Was with the Israeli Air Force, serialled S-77.

6806 Supplied to the Air Council with military serial **NR718**. Delivered to 5MU 11.44. Served with No.4 Radio School 8.45 and returned to 5MU for storage 3.46. To de Havilland at Witney for conversion to Rapide prior to onward sale by the manufacturer 9.5.46 and U.K. CofA no.9014 issued 18.2.47. Reg'd **VQ-PAR** to Aviron – The Palestine Aviation Co. Ltd. To Israeli Air Force 5.48. Re-reg'd **4X-ACU** to Arkia 13.11.49 (acquired from Mr. Milton Lang). Withdrawn from use as "too old" in 1954 and used to help with the rebuilding of 4X-AEI (c/n 6895) by Bedek Aircraft Corp. in 1955.

6807 Supplied to the Air Council with serial **NR719** but did not enter military service. Delivered to 5MU 11.44. To de Havilland at Witney for conversion to Rapide prior to onward sale by the manufacturer 9.5.46 and U.K. CofA no.8945 issued 15.1.47. Reg'd **PP-DPH** [CofR 2463] to Distribuidoro de Automoveis Studebaker Ltda. To Jose Lauvero Couto Melo. CofA expired 9.9.57.

6808 Supplied to the Air Council with **NR720** but did not enter military service. Delivered to 5MU 11.44. Converted to Rapide by de Havilland at Witney. Reg'd **G-AHXY** [CofR 10444 11.7.46] to The Ministry of Supply for operation by the A.A.J.C. pool and CofA no.8062 issued 13.9.46. Handed over to B.E.A.C. 11.9.46. Crashed while landing in darkness and fog at Renfrew 27.12.48, inbound from Benbecula and completely wrecked. Reg'n cancelled 17.2.49. Parts used to rebuild G-AFMF c/n 6432.

6809 Supplied to the Air Council with serial **NR721** but did not enter military service. Delivered to 5MU 11.44. Loaned to B.O.A.C., Whitchurch 9.3.46 and used for crew training until 9.46. Returned to 5MU 1.48. To Royal Aircraft Establishment 30.6.48. Still with R.A.E. in 1952 but ultimate fate unknown.

6810 Supplied to the Air Council with serial **NR722** but did not enter military service. Delivered to 5MU 11.44. Converted to Rapide by de Havilland at Witney. Reg'd **G-AHKU** [CofR 10142 23.4.46] to The Ministry of Supply and CofA no.7672 issued 14.6.46. Believed intended for operation by Isle of Man Air Services Ltd. but to B.O.A.C. (B.E.A. division) 14.6.46 and later, named *Cecil John Rhodes*. Converted to Mk6 prior to 9.60. To British Westpoint Airlines Ltd., Exeter 20.5.64 but already delivered to Exeter 3.5.64. To Frank Herbert Mann t/a British Westpoint 16.7.65. To Treffield Aviation Ltd., Castle Donington 26.7.66. Name changed to Treffield International Airways Ltd., 30.12.66. Carried "Dominie Airways" titles – a joy riding subsidary. To Mrs. Pamela Mary Scholefield, Exeter 8.11.67. To Kenneth Bryan Neely, St. Just 6.1.69. Operated by Scillonia Airways and named *Sir Richard Hawkins*. CofA expired 12.8.70. Reg'n cancelled as permanently withdrawn from use 16.5.72. Scrapped due to "glue failure".

6811 Supplied to the Air Council with serial **NR723** but did not enter military service. Delivered to 5MU 11.44. To de Havilland for conversion to Rapide at Witney 11.3.46. To the A.A.J.C. 27.6.46. Registered **G-AHKT** [CofR 10141 23.4.46] to The Ministry of Supply as a Mk3. May have been intended for operation by Isle of Man Air Services Ltd. but to B.O.A.C. (B.E.A. division) 20.6.46. CofA no.7671 issued 22.6.46. Later named *Lord Tennyson*. To A. J. Whittemore (Aeradio) Ltd., Croydon 14.4.53. To Whitely (Rishworth) Ltd. 22.6.54 and operated by Yeadon Aviation Ltd. Converted to Mk4 15.10.54. Nosed over while taxiing at Cherbourg 11.7.56 and damaged. To Hants and Sussex Aviation Ltd., Portsmouth 10.10.57 for repair. Sold abroad to "South America" 17.2.58 and left Portsmouth for London Docks by road 11.2.58. Reg'd as **F-OAUG** to Soc. Aerien de Transport Guyane-Antilles – S.A.T.G.A. CofA issued 10.9.58. Sustained material damage at Rochambeau 20.11.61. CofA suspended 11.62 and dismantled.

6812 Supplied to the Air Council with military serial **NR724**. To 5MU 11.44. To de Havilland for conversion to Rapide at Witney 19.3.46. SOC on transfer to the A.A.J.C. 28.4.46. Reg'd **G-AHKS** [CofR 10140 23.4.46] to Ministry of Supply 23.4.46, for operation by A.A.J.C. pool and used by Railway Air Services, Speke. Reg'd as a Mk3 to B.E.A.C. 23.8.46 and CofA no.7670 issued 26.8.46. Later named *Robert Louis Stevenson*. To Eagle Aircraft Services Ltd., Blackbushe 2.6.55. Converted to Mk4 by Hants and Sussex Aviation Ltd. and dismantled for overseas

DH89 c/n 6812. B.E.A. was by far, the largest civilian operator and G-AHKS served the Corporation from August 1946 to June 1955. Later in Malaya where it eventually succumbed in December 1960.

DH89 c/n 6838. LN-BEZ in Norway from October 1971, wears Rothmans livery; the cigarette maker was a major supporter of sporting aviation at the time. With Adrian Swire since June 1973.

DH89 c/n 6813. G-AIBB was one of four Rapides operated by Luton Airways extant from May 1958 to end 1959. Closely connected with McAlpine Aviation, a company still very much in existence.

DH89 c/n 6839. This three-quarters front view is for the modellers! Only an aficionado would detect that G-AHKA is the sole Mk5 version with manually operated variable pitch propellers.

DH89 c/n 6831. Registered 5H-AAN in August 1964, this aircraft was later operated in several East African countries and in the Seychelles, still wearing Tanzanian marks until sold to South Africa.

DH89 c/n 6843. The first aeroplane to be operated by the newly formed Middle East Airlines of Lebanon. In Argentina by March 1949, LV-AGW is seen here after certificate expiry 11th April 1965.

DH89 c/n 6837. Cumberland Aviation Services took delivery of the first of two Rapides in May 1959. Originally based at R.A.F. Silloth, G-AIUL moved with the company to Crosby Aerodrome in late 1960.

DH89 c/n 6850. No fewer than 8 L.A.C. aircraft lined up at Newcastle late 1950. They were participating in a defence exercise named "Emperor", the Rapides taking the unlikely role as hostile bombers!

shipment. Sold abroad to Singapore 2.6.55. Reg'd **VR-OAC** to Malayan Airways Ltd. 1955. To Borneo Airways Ltd. 1958. Damaged 14.5.58 when aircraft nosed over on landing at Brunei, due to tyre failure but repaired. Became a constructive total loss at Jesselton 21.12.60, but fuller details unknown.

6813   Supplied to the Air Council with serial **NR725**. but did not enter military service. Delivered to 5MU 11.44. Transferred to B.O.A.C. 1.7.46. Reg'd **G-AIBB** [CofR 10522 25.9.46] to Air Training Ltd., Aldermaston. Operated by the Central Training School but transferred with other assets of the school to Airways Training Ltd. on formation of that company 30.4.47. Ownership changed officially 20.10.47. CofA no.8470 issued 6.5.48. To Patrick Motors Ltd., Birmingham 6.12.48. Leased to Jersey Airlines 5.50. To Francis Henry Wilson t/a Starways Ltd., Speke 27.4.51. Leased to Wright Aviation Ltd., Speke 5.53. To Reginald James Gates t/a Federated Fruiterers Ltd., Speke (operated as Federated Air Transport) 2.12.53. Nominal change to RR. J. Gates t/a Federated Fruit Company 14.1.54. To Luton Airways Ltd. 1.5.58. Converted to Mk6 11.58. To Hants and Sussex Aviation Ltd., Portsmouth 23.3.60. Reg'n cancelled on sale to France 21.8.61. Delivered ex Portsmouth 31.8.61. Reg'd **F-OBVJ** to Ste. Ardic, Dakar, Senegal 9.61. Destroyed, but details unknown. CofA expired 8.62.

6814   Supplied to the Air Council with military serial **NR726**. Delivered to 5MU 11.44. Issued to 87Grp. Com. Flt. 10.45, serving continuously with them until storage 18MU 12.46. SOC on sale to Air Enterprises Ltd., Croydon. Reg'd **G-AKOC** [CofR 12090 11.12.47] and CofA no.10171 issued 20.7.48. To William Arthur Herbert t/a Cumberland Air Sevices Ltd. 18.3.48. Ownership changed 10.6.49 and sold abroad 21.7.49. Shipped to Australia and on arrival, assembled at Cairns for the Queensland Ambulance Transport Brigade reg'd **VH-CFA(1)**. Named *Gron Owens* 11.49. Inbound to Cairns after collecting a patient from Vanrook Station 26.11.51, the pilot was unable to find the airfield due to smoke from bush fires, drifted out to sea and after fuel starvation, crashed into the sea six miles off Simpson's Point near Double Island, some 15 miles north of Cairns. The pilot and attendant were rescued but the patient and aircraft were lost. (Note: also see c/n 6713 for second use of the Australian marks).

6815   Supplied to the Air Council with serial **NR727** but did not enter military service. Delivered to 5MU 1.12.44. Converted to Rapide by de Havilland at Witney 17.5.46. Reg'd **G-AIYE** [CofR 11073 12.12.46] to Olley Air Service Ltd., Croydon. CofA no.8823 issued 23.12.46. To British Transport Commission 16.2.53, then Cambrian Air Services Ltd., Cardiff three days later. Converted to Mk4 during 1954. To R. A. Peacock (Aviation) Ltd., Croydon 3.5.54. To Lawrence Saville Dawson, Sherburn-in-Elmet 22.9.54, operated by Yeadon Aviation. Cancelled on sale to France 20.3.57. Reg'd **F-OAYS** to Ste. Nord Africaine de Transports Aerienne, Bone, Algeria and delivered ex Croydon 20.3.57. CofA issued 5.4.57. Cancelled at Bone 18.5.62 and broken up.

6816   Supplied to the Air Council with military serial **NR728**. Delivered to 5MU 12.44 and stored until issued to Royal Aircraft Establishment 1.48. Reg'd **G-ANJR** [CofR R4321 12.12.53] to A. J. Whittemore (Aeradio) Ltd., Croydon. CofA issued 15.4.54. Operated by Continental Aircraft Services Ltd. for delivery flight to Madagascar. Slight damage sustained in forced landing near Gulu, Uganda, 27.4.54 whilst on delivery. Sold abroad to Madagascar 8.7.54 and reg'n cancelled 10.8.54. Reg'd **F-OAKX** to Air Madagascar 7.54 and French CofA issued 25.11.54. Destroyed 15.8.56 and reg'n cancelled 8.3.57.

6817   Supplied to the Air Council with military serial **NR729**. Served with No.4 Radio School 1.45. To 5MU for storage 2.47. SOC as Cat.E and sold 29.5.47 to D.J. Adis, presumably for spares use.

6818   Supplied to the Air Council with military serial **NR730**. Delivered to 5MU 12.44. Served with 64Grp. Com. Flt. 4.48. To 5MU for storage 3.50. SOC on sale to International Air Exports Ltd., London WC2 16.8.50 and reg'd to them as **G-AMDG** [CofR 15064 17.8.50]. To Autowork (Winchester) Ltd. 26.10.50. Sold abroad 8.3.51 and U.K. reg'n cancelled 1.9.51. Reg'd **F-OAIR** to COTECI and French CofA issued 3.4.51. To Maroc Air Service, Rabat 7.52. To Cie. D'Autrex (Lopez, Loreta et Cie.) 6.53. Crashed 2.4.54 and caught fire south of Phu Nhac, near Nam Dinh, Thai Binh province. All 9 occupants killed and aircraft totally destroyed. Reg'n cancelled 1.6.54.

6819   Supplied to the Air Council with military serial **NR731**. Taken on charge 23.9.44. Issued to 1316 Flt. and delivered 31.12.44. With Metropolitan Com. Sqdn. 1.45. Converted to Rapide by de Havilland at Witney. SOC on sale to Netherlands Government and reg'd **PH-RAF**. Leased to K.L.M. 19.9.45 to 1.4.46. To Royal Netherlands Air Force, 334Sqdn. with serial **V4** 1946. To **PH-VND** 4.9.48 and operated for United Nations in Israel. Returned to Royal Netherlands Air Force again as **V4**. SOC 23.1.52 and broken up 1957.

6820   Supplied to the Air Council with military serial **NR732**. Possibly to de Havilland for conversion 16.1.45. CofA no.7175 issued 14.4.45. To J. Parks & Son Ltd. for packing 26.4.45. Shipped to Callao, Peru per S.S. *Laguna* 24.5.45. Arrived 4.7.45 for the Air Attache in Lima. Sold to Linea Aerea del Pacifico Sur Ltda. 1.48. Fate unknown.

6821   Supplied to the Air Council with military serial **NR733** but did not enter military service. Delivered to 18MU. SOC on sale to Arthur Wesley Coombs t/a Aeroways, Croydon 21.5.48. Reg'd as **G-ALBA** [CofR 12386 27.5.48] and CofA no.10201 issued 21.7.48. To Autowork (Winchester) Ltd. 17.7.48 and wore Britannic Aviation titles. To Russell Alfred Gunton, Cowes 8.6.49. To Somerton Airways (Cowes) Ltd. 6.1.51. Ceased operations 4.51 and to Robert Alan Short, Croydon 8.8.51. To Skegness Airport Ltd. 3.10.51. Name changed to Skegness Air Taxi Services Ltd., Boston 19.3.53. Sold 12.54 and reg'd to Airviews Ltd., Manchester 11.7.55. To Ezra Desmond Kayton & Adrian Ross, Elstree 19.1.59. Used as a private aircraft at Elstree until 5.59 when flown to Swansea for start of commercial charter work with Trans-European. To Trans-European Aviation Ltd., Baginton 29.1.60. From 2.60 to 3.60, leased to Skycraft, an Irish charter company and used to carry goods on behalf of the Federated Fruit Company between 8.2.60 and 2.3.60. CofA expired 29.9.61. Noted withdrawn from use at Baginton 5.63 and broken up for spares there at the end of 1964. Cancelled as permanently withdrawn from use 28.8.64.

6822   Supplied to the Air Council with military serial **NR734**. Served with Coastal Command Com. Flt. Northolt 2.45, 41OTU 2.45, 58OTU 3.45, at Hawarden 8.45. To storage at 18MU 5.46. SOC on sale to Derek John Hayles, Portsmouth. Reg'd **G-AKYY** [CofR 12334 18.5.48]. Passed on to W. A. Rollason Ltd., Croydon 24.6.48 and CofA issued 8.11.48. Cancelled on sale abroad 23.11.48. Reg'd as **LV-AES** to Sfreddo y Paolini Ltda. 26.2.49. Served with Aero Express Barcella, named *Marmolin I*, probably from about 11.50. To Taxis Aereos Argentinios SA – TAASA 10.58. To Vilata Aria y Pizarro 5.62. CofA expired 1964.

6823   Supplied to the Air Council with military serial **NR735**. Delivered to 5MU 11.44. With Gloster Aircraft Co. Ltd., Hucclecote 10.45. SOC on sale to Gloster Aircraft Co. Ltd. and reg'd **G-AHRH** [CofR 10279 22.5.46]. CofA no.7793 issued 18.10.46. Converted to Mk6. To Hants and Sussex Aviation Ltd., Portsmouth 2.2.59. Cancelled as sold abroad to Algeria 12.2.60. Reg'd **F-OBOH** to Ste. Air Oasis, Laghouat 2.60. Delivered via Lympne 16.2.60 and French CofA issued 25.2.60. CofA suspended 20.5.60 and broken up.

6824   Supplied to the Air Council with serial **NR736** but did not enter military service. Delivered to 5MU 11.44. SOC on transfer to the A.A.J.C., Speke 12.7.46. Converted to civil Rapide standard by de Havilland at Witney 7.46. Reg'd **G-AHKR** [CofR 10139 23.4.46] for The Ministry of Supply 23.4.46. To B.O.A.C. (B.E.A. Division) 6.6.46. CofA no.7669 issued 9.7.46. To B.E.A.C. named *Robert Louis Stevenson*. Written off 15.4.47 when inbound to Ronaldsway from Speke. Aircraft diverged from track and flew into Slieau Ruy mountain, near Greeba, 4 miles NNE of Ronaldsway. Although the aircraft turned over, it did not catch fire but 2 crew and 5 passengers were injured. No fatalities. Reg'n cancelled 19.9.47.

6825   Supplied to the Air Council with serial **NR737** but did not enter military service. Delivered to 5MU 11.44. SOC on transfer to the A.A.J.C., Speke 9.9.46. Converted to Rapide by de Havilland at Witney. Reg'd **G-AHXZ** [CofR 10445 11.7.46] to The Ministry of Supply for operation by the A.A.J.C. pool and CofA no.8063 issued 5.9.46. Handed over to B.E.A.C. 5.9.46 as a Mk3. Named *Charles Dickens*. Aircraft was burnt out at Renfrew 28.8.51, when a fire, started by the starboard engine during routine maintenance, spread to the fabric and fuselage. Reg'n cancelled 1.3.52.

6826   Supplied to the Air Council with military serial **NR738** 13.12.44. To Halton 6.45. To 5MU 1.47. SOC on sale to Field Aircraft Services Ltd., Croydon 29.5.47. Reg'd **G-AJSJ** [CofR 11548 8.5.47] and CofA no.9375 issued 25.7.47. To Franco-British Commercial and Industrial Co. Ltd., London W1 14.7.47. Destined for Air Madagascar, forced landed en route in Tunisia due engine trouble 18.9.47. Badly damaged and reg'n cancelled 3.12.47.

6827   Supplied to the Air Council with military serial **NR739** 13.12.44. To Halton 6.45 coded THA/H. Converted to Mk.II 6.45. To No.4 Radio School, Swanton Morley 22.3.48, 5MU 8.4.49. To A.T.D.U. Fort Grange 31.12.50. Brakes locked while taxying at Weston-super-Mare, swung and nosed over. Remains brought from Weston at end of 1957. Reg'd **G-APKA** [CofR R6243 7.1.58] to Hants and Sussex Aviation Ltd., Portsmouth. Cancelled on sale to Sierra Leone 8.2.58. Reg'd **VR-LAE** to Sierra Leone Airways Ltd. 7.58. Named *Kassewe*. Delivered via Eastleigh 2.7.58. Reportedly all three Sierra Leone Airways Rapides (also see c/ns 6603 and 6963) were eventually burnt at Hastings Airfield, Freetown.

6828   Supplied to the Air Council with military serial **NR740**. Delivered to 5MU 1.45. Taken on charge by Royal Navy 17.10.45 and was in service at Evanton 12.46. SOC at Stretton 19.9.49. Scrapped 10.49.

6829   Supplied to the Air Council with serial **NR741** but did not enter military service. Delivered to 18MU 1.45. SOC on sale to Arthur Wesley Coombs t/a Aeroways, Croydon 27.5.48. Reg'd as **G-ALBB** [CofR 12387 27.5.48]. To Charles William John Allen, t/a Allen Aircraft Services, Old Coulsdon 24.8.48. To Ernest Arthur Taylor, Croydon 9.9.48 and CofA no.10271 issued on same day. Operated by I.A.S. (London) Ltd. on joy flights at London Airport, named *Pickles III*. When on approach to London Airport 1.8.52, caught in wake turbulence of a Stratocruiser which was one mile ahead in the landing sequence. The pilot lost control and the aircraft crashed 475 yards from the runway threshold. It had flown 554 hours since conversion. Reg'n cancelled 19.12..52.

6830   Supplied to the Air Council with military serial **NR742**. Served at Skeabrae (Orkneys) 1.45, Grimister (Shetlands) 8.45, Stn. Flt. Turnhouse 2.46, Res. Com. Turnhouse 10.46, 66Grp. Com. Flt. 3.48, with code RCI-H. To 18MU for storage 10.48. SOC on sale to Robert Alan Short, Croydon 2.2.49 but actually reg'd **G-ALGO** [CofR 12524 17.2.49] to Sqdn. Ldr. Kenneth James Nalson, Croydon. To Airwork Ltd., Croydon 14.9.49. To Anglo-Iranian Oil Co. Ltd., Abadan 25.10.49. CofA no.10710 issued 2.12.49. Struck a mast while flying low over oil refinery shortly after take off from Abadan 10.7.51. Crashed and burnt out, 2 killed. Reg'n cancelled as destroyed 11.7.51.

6831   Supplied to the Air Council with military serial **NR743**. To No.4 Radio School 1.45. To 5MU for storage 12.46. SOC on transfer to B.O.A.C. for operation by East African Airways Corpn. 1.7.47. Reg'd **VP-KEF** to E.A.A.C. 1947. To Seychelles-Kilimanjaro Air Transport Ltd. 1960. Re-reg'd **5H-AAN** still with Seychelles-Kilimanjaro 8.64. To Caspair Ltd., Mazinde. To A. D. Aviation Co. Ltd., Nairobi 1967. Aircraft damaged at Entebbe 3.3.69 when brakes seized whilst taxying. To W. J. Baker 1971. To Air Mahe 2.73 named *African Queen*, delivered ex Mombasa 21.2.73 and operated services between the Seychelles and Praslin Island. Allocated **VQ-SAG** 2.73 but not taken up. (Note: Even though based in other East African countries, flown throughout as 5H-AAN until sale to South Africa). Sold to John English and based at Progress airstrip, near Port Elizabeth, South Africa from delivery 12.74 and reg'd **ZS-JGV**. On rebuild, Port Alfred 11.02.

6832   Supplied to the Air Council with military serial **NR744**. Delivered 1.45. At 18MU 6.45 and later, maintained by Hurkus in Turkey for General Officer Commanding Eastern Command. To 61Grp. Com. Flt, Kenley 5.47 coded RCE/A. Returned to 18MU for storage 3.48. SOC on sale to Tyne Taxis Ltd., Newcastle-upon-Tyne 20.9.48. Reg'd as **G-ALET**. [CofR 12478 1.6.48]. To Capt. John Charles Higgins t/a Mannin Airways Ltd., Ronaldsway 15.10.48. CofA no.10403 issued 21.11.49. Transferred to Mannin subsidiary, North West Airlines (Isle of Man) Ltd., Ronaldsway 11.49. Sold abroad 10.9.51. Reg'd **F-OALD** to Ste. Des Caoutcholics d'Extreme-Orient, Saigon. Sold 5.60 and re-reg'd **XW-TAB** 9.60. However, according to Air Britain, it is believed these marks may not have been taken up, as a Boeing 307 Stratoliner wore them shortly after. Fate unknown.

6833   Supplied to the Air Council with serial **NR745** 12.44 but did not enter military service. To de Havilland at Witney 22.12.44 for civil conversion. U.K. CofA no.7166 issued 24.3.45. To No.2 Aircraft Packing Unit 27.3.45 for delivery to Southern Rhodesia. Arrived Cairo 13.4.45 and Salisbury 21.4.45. Reg'd **VP-YCO** to Southern Rhodesia Air Services 21.9.45. Became Central African Airways Corporation 1.6.46. To A.V. Airtransport. Reg'd **ZS-DDH** to Africair Ltd., 23.8.49. Reg'n cancelled as exported 29.1.60. To Southern Rhodesia but as no record of restoration, presumed acquired for spares use.

6834   Supplied to the Air Council with serial **NR746** 12.44 but did not enter military service. To de Havilland at Witney 22.12.44 for civil conversion. U.K. CofA no.7165 issued 24.3.45. To No.2 Aircraft Packing Unit 27.3.45 for delivery to Southern Rhodesia. Arrived Cairo 13.4.45 and reached Salisbury 21.4.45. Reg'd as **VP-YCP** to Southern Rhodesia Air Services 21.9.45. Became Central African Airways Corpn. 1.6.46. Reg'd **ZS-BYT** 9.4.48. Reg'n cancelled 29.6.48. Sold to Israeli Air Force 6.48.

6835   Supplied to the Air Council with serial **NR747** 12.44 but did not enter military service. Delivered to 18MU 5.45. SOC on sale to Brooklands Aviation Ltd., Sywell 10.3.47. Reg'd **G-AJHO** [CofR 11304 14.2.47] and CofA no.9380 issued 27.6.47. Presented by Rothmans of Pall Mall Ltd. to Maj. John Stafford Weeks, trustee of the assets of The Army Free Fall Parachute Association 27.6.63. Painted in the cigarette company's house colours at Sywell 13.7.63. To John Galbraith Clark, trustee of the assets of the Army Parachute Association, Netheravon 21.10.64. Painted in the colours of of their sponsor, Rothmans of Pall Mall Ltd. and named *Siegfried*. Converted to Mk4 during 1968. Offered for sale 11.74 but remained in service with the Parachute Association and substantially damaged at Netheravon 27.7.75 after loss of power on take-off and landing outside the airfield boundary. No injuries to the 8 persons on board. To East Anglian Aviation Society Ltd. 9.6.76 for rebuild to flying condition at Tadlow. First flown 20.5.87 wearing King's Flight colours and with special dispensation to wear **'G-ADDD'**. Reverted to **G-AJHO** shortly after. To Victor Gauntlett of Proteus Petroleum Aviation Ltd. Burnt out and destroyed 5.2.89 after an emergency landing near Oxford, following an inflight fire en route Kidlington to Shoreham. No injuries. Some remains subsequently noted lying at Rush Green.

6836   Supplied to the Air Council with military serial **NR748**. Converted to Mk.II. Delivered to 18MU 6.45 and then served with 1680 Flt. 8.45, 18MU 7.46, Fighter Command Com. Flt. 9.47, 5MU 2.49 and to ATDU, Fort Grange 12.50. Reg'd **G-ANEU** [CofR R4163/1 5.10.53] to C. E. Harper Aircraft Co. Ltd., Exeter and CofA issued 19.11.53. Sold abroad to France 26.8.54 and reg'd as **F-OAQU** to Ste. Des Transportes Aeriens du Gabon 9.54. CofA issued 10.9.54. Written off 18.1.55 when pilot lost control and crashed on approach to Ekouata airfield, French Equatorial Africa. Reg'n cancelled 11.10.55.

6837   Supplied to the Air Council with military serial **NR749**. Served briefly at Yatesbury 1.45 until placed into storage 5MU 8.45. Officially sold to Kenning Aviation Ltd., Burnaston 4.12.46 but had already been reg'd to them as **G-AIUL** [CofR 10980 8.11.46]. CofA no.8814 issued 8.5.47. To Air Transport (Charter) (C.I.) Ltd., Jersey 9.6.47, named *Saint Clement*. To Aerocontacts Ltd., Gatwick 21.1.52. To Charles Griffiths Bowers, Newcastle-under-Lyme 18.7.52. To Keale Street Pottery Co. Ltd., Stoke-on-Trent 7.8.52. To Wolverhampton Aviation Ltd. 9.6.54. To Anthony Strickland Hubbard, Croydon 22.3.57. Leased to Olley Air Service Ltd., at least during 1957. Reportedly re-engined with Gipsy Queen 3 engines in 1957. To the aircraft broker R. K. Dundas Ltd. 1.5.59. To Cumberland Aviation Services Ltd., Silloth 21.5.59 and moved to Crosby by 20.3.61. Converted to Mk6 prior to 1963. To Mayflower Air Services Ltd., Plymouth 2.4.63, the aircraft having been delivered to them on 28.3.63. To Albert John Collins, Jersey 15.10.64. Aircraft carried titles "Flower Air Services Ltd." at about this time – possibly a trading name of A. J. Collins. To Alfred Free Ward, Booker 30.5.67. Offered for sale by Aerial Enterprises, Booker 4.69 quoting a price of £500 as is, or £1500 with CofA. Cancelled as permanently withdrawn from use 6.4.73. Eventually arrived in a crate at Southend for the Museum where it stayed until at least 4.78. To Chirk 7.9.78 for rebuild and was still there 10.01, marked as 'G-AJCL'.

6838   Supplied to the Air Council with military serial **NR750**. To Stn. Flt. Halton 1.45, To 5MU 3.47. SOC on sale to A. Hamson and Son Ltd., Sywell 25.8.47. Reg'd **G-AKIF** [CofR 11943 24.9.47]. To Manx Air Charters Ltd., Ronaldsway named *Glen Wyllin*. CofA no.9807 issued 22.12.47. Owner name changed to Manx Airlines Ltd. 20.8.53. Aircraft operated by Skyflights for joy flights at Ramsgate – price 12/6, at least during the 1958 summer season! Delivered to Hants and Sussex Aviation Ltd., Portsmouth ex Ramsgate 6.9.58 and reg'd to them 16.10.58. To Thomas Hutton Marshall, Christchurch 5.2.59. To Southern Counties Aerial Contracts Ltd., Staverton 2.3.62. To Bardock Aviation Services Ltd., Staverton 5.3.63. To Kentair Charters (Biggin Hill) Ltd. 15.7.66. To Bernard Sydney Schofield, trustee of the assets of the Parachute Regiment Free Fall Club 2.5.68. Reg'n cancelled on sale to Norway 2.8.71 and delivered via Norwich two days later. Reg'd **LN-BEZ** to Petter F. Ringvold of Paralift and CofA issued 1.10.71. Returned to U.K. 2.73 and restored as **G-AKIF** to Adrian Christopher Swire, Booker 15.6.73. To Airborne Taxi Services Ltd., Booker (a Swire owned concern) 12.9.73. Painted, but not flown as **'G-ADAE'** for television programme "South Riding". Painted in U.S.A.A.F. markings at Booker 27.1.77 for a film about Glen Miller. Damaged 16.7.83 at Sparsholt when it ran into a fence during a crosswind landing, inbound from Booker. Two occupants uninjured and aircraft repaired. Engines shock loaded in heavy landing Duxford 1.8.95 but repaired. CofA expires 19.8.03 and still owned by Adrian Swire of Airborne Taxi Services.

6839 Supplied to the Air Council with serial **NR751** 12.44 but did not enter military service. Delivered to 18MU 1.45. To de Havilland at Witney for civil conversion 27.3.46. Reg'd **G-AHKA** [CofR 10123 16.4.46] to de Havilland Aircraft Co. Ltd. and CofA no.7726 issued 20.5.46. Officially sold to de Havilland 31.8.46. Converted to the sole Mk5 in early 1949. Sold abroad to French Guyana 7.12.53. Re-reg'd **F-OAQL** to Dept. de la Guyane. CofA issued 12.7.55 and operated by SATGA. Crashed 30.10.57 at Sophie Inini airfield, Cayenne, killing one person on the ground. Aircraft was badly damaged and cancelled from register 19.10.60.

6840 Supplied to the Air Council with military serial **NR752**. Converted to Mk.II. To 18MU 1.45. To Metropolitan Com. Sqdn. coded CB-D 9.45. Returned for storage at 18MU 11.46. Moved to 5MU 12.48. SOC on sale to Charles W. J. Allen, Old Coulsdon. Reg'd **G-ALWO** [CofR 14897 23.1.50] to Allen Aircraft Services Ltd., Croydon 23.1.50. To Wesley and Nash Ltd., Croydon 14.4.50. CofA no.10879 issued 10.5.50. Cancelled as sold abroad 1.6.51. Reg'd **VP-YHE** to Rhodesian Investment Trust Ltd., 1.7.51. Sold abroad 1952. Re-reg'd **CR-ADM** to Celestino de Armincao Neves, Quelihane 6.5.52. Crashed at Praia Zulala 15.3.55.

6841 Supplied to the Air Council with military serial **NR753**. Delivered to 18MU 1.45. Served with Royal Navy at Donibristle 20.8.45, with 753Sqdn. coded 601/LP at Lee-on-Solent 1947. Written off 31.5.48 when it collided with Anson NL248 whilst formating near Bulford, Wiltshire. The Dominie's tail plane was cut off and the aircraft crashed killing all three on board. The Anson landed safely. SOC at Old Sarum 31.5.48.

6842 Supplied to the Air Council with military serial **NR754**. To 18MU 1.45. SOC to Royal Navy 20.8.45. Burnt out 1.46, but further dewtails unknown.

6843 Supplied to the Air Council with military serial **NR755**. No record of military service and at 18MU 1.45. Converted to Rapide by de Havilland at Witney. U.K. CofA no.7237 issued 16.10.45. To B.O.A.C. 8.11.45 on behalf of Middle East Airlines and delivered to Beirut 22.11.45. Reg'd **LR-AAD** to Middle East Airlines 27.11.45, named *Sunneen*. Reg'n cancelled 19.12.47 and the aircraft left Beirut to return to U.K. same day. Stored at Ringway. Reg'd **G-AKZV** [CofR 12356 24.5.48] to W. A. Rollason Ltd., Croydon. Sold abroad to South America 30.12.48 and U.K. reg'n cancelled 24.1.49. Reg'd **LV-AGW** to importer Sfreddo y Paolina Ltda., Zonda 23.3.49. To Aerotransporte Rosario 31.1.64. CofA expired 11.4.65. (Note: Official Argentinian records show this aircraft incorrectly with c/n 6483!).

6844 Supplied to the Air Council with military serial **NR756**. To 18MU 1.45. To Royal Navy 24.10.45 at Evanton. SOC at Stretton 21.2.55. Flown to Speke for civil conversion but in the event, was not proceeded with. Reg'd **G-AOAO** [CofR R4928 22.3.55] to Reginald James Gates t/a Federated Fruit Company. To Hants and Sussex Aviation Ltd. 8.55 and ferried to Portsmouth on a special permit. CofA issued 4.1.56. Cancelled as sold in France 4.1.56. CofA issued 28.1.56. Reg'd **F-BHGR** to

S.F.A.S.A., Toussus-le-Noble 1.56. To S.F.A.T.A.T. To J. Noari, Toussus 1971. CofA expired 10.71. Stored at Etampes 1975-1977. Noted stored, dismantled at La Ferte Alais 6.79 and still there 2002.

6845 Supplied to the Air Council with military serial **NR769**. Delivered to 18MU 1.45. Served with No.4 Radio School, Swanton Morley 7.46, coded TSM-S. To 5MU for storage 4.49. SOC on sale to Wilkes and Chandler 12.1.50 but reg'd **G-ALWL** [CofR 14894 30.1.50] to V. H. Bellamy t/a Flightways Ltd., Eastleigh. CofA issued 25.1.51. To Southern Aerowork Ltd., Eastleigh 24.10.50. To Transair Ltd., Croydon 3.3.52. Cancelled as sold in France 5.3.52. Reg'd **F-BGPH** to Soc. Aigle Azur Indochine, Hanoi and French CofA issued 7.4.52. Damaged and reg'n cancelled 21.9.53. Re-reg'd **F-BEPE** to Cie. Laotienne de Commerce et de Transport, Hanoi 1.54. Re-reg'd **F-LAAE** to Cie. Veha-Akat, Vientiane 10.55 and CofA issued 20.10.55. Destroyed 1.61.

6846 Supplied to the Air Council with military serial **NR770** but did not enter military service. To de Havilland at Witney 16.2.45 for conversion to Rapide. No U.K. reg'n requested but export CofA no.7167 issued 19.6.45. Shipped ex Liverpool to Lisbon 1.8.45, per *SS Pandorian*, arriving in Portugal 4.8.45. To be delivered to Ministerio das Colonias Govenor General Luanda – for Angola. Re-reg'd **CR-LBH** 8.45 to Divisao Das Transportes Aereos Dos Servicos – D.D.T.A.S. Burnt out on ground at Ambriz, Portuguese West Africa 10.5.57 when starting engines.

6847 Supplied to the Air Council with military serial **NR771** 2.45. Converted to Rapide by de Havilland at Witney. No U.K. reg'n requested but export CofA no.7168 issued 19.6.45. Shipped ex Liverpool to Lisbon 1.8.45, per *SS Pandorian*, arriving in Portugal 4.8.45. To be delivered to Ministerio das Colonias for use by the Govenor General Luanda, Angola. Reg'd **CR-LBG** 8.45 to Divisao Das Transportes Aereos Dos Servicos – D.D.T.A.S. Sold to Transportes Aereos Sao Tome but the reg'n, issued in the CR-S series is unknown. Fate unknown.

6848 Supplied to the Air Council with serial **NR772** but did not enter military service. To de Havilland at Witney 22.2.45 for conversion to Rapide. Reg'd **G-AGOX** [CofR 9627 31.5.45] to B.O.A.C. CofA no.7184 issued 6.7.45. Hired to East African Airways Corporation and ferried to Nairobi ex U.K. 12.7.45. Operated in U.K. marks. U.K. reg'n eventually cancelled 2.8.46 and re-reg'd **VP-KCU** to East African Airways Corporation 5.9.46. Whilst operating a mail flight between Nairobi and Mombasa, the pilot was "unable to find the airfield" and forced landed near Garsen in the Tana River area, about 130 miles north of Mombasa 28.6.46. The aircraft was damaged beyond repair asnd abandoned.

6849 Supplied to the Air Council with serial **NR773** but did not enter military service. To de Havilland at Witney 22.2.45 for conversion to Rapide. Reg'd **G-AGOW** [CofR 9626 31.5.45] to B.O.A.C. and CofA no.7183 issued 6.7.45. Hired to East African Airways Corporation and ferried ex U.K. 11.7.45. Operated in U.K. marks. U.K. reg'n eventually cancelled 2.8.46 and reg'd **VP-KCV** 5.9.46. Returned to Ministry of Civil Aviation and stored in Kenya 11.8.49. To Airwork (East Africa) Ltd. 1951. Sold 10.51 and reg'd to J. E. F. Wilkins t/a Caspair, Mazinde 16.4.52. To Sudan Interior Mission, Khartoum/Malakal 26.7.54. Aircraft returned to Croydon as **VP-KCV** 9.56. Restored as **G-AGOW** to Stephen John Stevens, Kathleen Stevens & Herbert James Adams (Missionary Aviation Fellowship) 13.11.56. The U.K. marks were not taken up and the aircraft remained at Croydon and was gradually robbed of parts with some being used during the civilianisation of the Missionary Aviation Fellowship's other machine G-APJW. Reg'n cancelled 10.12.57 as withdrawn from use.

6850 Supplied to the Air Council with serial **NR774** but did not enter military service. Converted to civilian standard by de Havilland at Witney. Reg'd **G-AGOJ** [CofR 9614 27.4.45] to Isle of Man Air Services Ltd., Derbyhaven and CofA no.7177 issued 29.4.45. To Scottish Airways Ltd., Renfrew 10.9.45. Absorbed into B.E.A.C. on formation 1.2.47. To Lancashire Aviation Corporation Ltd., Samlesbury 8.7.48. To Skyways Ltd., Langley 28.2.55. Aircraft leased to Deutsche Luftwerbung (D.L.W.), Dusseldorf, from sometime prior to 7.55 and operated on services to the islands of Borkum and Norderney; remained on the U.K. register. Converted to Mk4 during 1957. Sustained damage to port undercarraige and part of fuselage while landing at Lympne

DH89 c/n 6858. Only two Rapides appeared on the Italian register and I-BOBJ is seen here, when operated by Aero Club Torino at Turin's Aeritalia Airfield until damaged beyond repair in 1965.

DH89 c/n 6900. The authors visited Brazil in February 1979 and after convincing VARIG of their bona fides, a senior official instructed a minion to crowbar off the end of the packing crate to reveal CR-LKR!

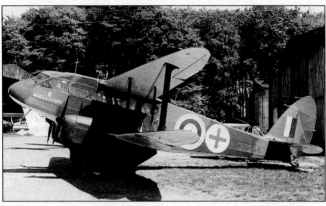

DH89 c/n 6862. G-AHGD appeared in camouflage and received special dispensation to wear serial Z7258. Unfortunately, the aircraft was destroyed in a fatal accident, June 1991.

DH89 c/n 6907. In use for pleasure flying and general charter work ex Newcastle as Mac Smith Air Charter from March 1960, G-ALGE had been delivered to Mac Smith Ltd. four months earlier.

DH89 c/n 6870. EI-AKH during its brief sojourn in Ireland with Skycraft Services of Dublin. Biggin Hill habitués in the 1960s may remember its return as G-AKSE with Air Couriers!

DH89 c/n 6907. N8053 seen on the Island of St. Maarten in the Nederland Antilles. Damage by strong winds in 1979 and prolonged open storage would not have aided a definite entry under "Survivors"!

DH89 c/n 6890. PH-RAA, with PH-RAB c/n 6891 behind, leased by the Nederland Government to K.L.M. and in this airline publicity photograph, perhaps the arrival reception on 19th September 1945?

DH89 c/n 6917. Eight Rapides were owned at various times by Croydon based Morton Air Services. Only three of the type remained with the company when they moved to Gatwick in 1959.

21.4.57 but repaired. Name changed to Skyways Coach Air Ltd. and operating from Lympne 5.59. When inbound from Rotterdam in bad weather, the aircraft bounced and swung on landing at Lympne and was damaged beyond repair 1.5.61. Accident attributed to pilot error. Reg'n cancelled 13.6.61.

6851 Supplied to the Air Council with military serial **NR775**. Delivered to 18MU 1.45. Served with Metropolitan Com. Sqdn. 9.45 until returned 18MU for storage 10.46. SOC on sale to William Alfred Webb, London SW14 27.5.48. Reg'd **G-ALAT** [CofR 12379 26.5.48]. To Elliot Trades Ltd., Cardiff 9.8.48 and CofA no.10211 issued 30.8.48. To John Hylton Watts, Stanley Kenneth Davies, Edward Keith-Davies & Care Lines Ltd., Cardiff To Cambrian Air Services Ltd. 13.4.49, named *Anglesey* and based Pengam Moors. To R. A. Peacock Aviation Ltd., Croydon 3.5.54. To A. J. Whittemore (Aeradio) Ltd. 18.11.54. Cancelled as sold abroad to France 24.1.55. Reg'd **F-BHCE** to SALS – Service de l'Aviation Legere et Sportive, Avignon 8.4.55. CofA issued 15.4.55. To Etat: C.R. de la 10eme Subdivision, Castelnaudary in 1958. CofA expired 3.69. Reg'n cancelled at the request of the owner Aero Club d'Alsace 8.11.69. Noted withdrawn from use at Strasbourg 1970.

6852 Supplied to the Air Council with military serial **NR776**. Delivered to Belgian Training School as new 23.2.45. To Belgian Government 1946. Re-reg'd **D6** Belgian Air Force 1946, coded OT-ZCJ. SOC 1954.

6853 Supplied to the Air Council with military serial **NR777** 2.45 and delivered to the Belgian Training School as new 23.2.45. Transferred to Belgian Government and taken on charge by Belgian Air Force 15th Wing with serial **D7**. Struck off charge 8.7.55. Rapide fuselage found in building near Antwerp airport during 1980s. Shipped to New Zealand and with Colin F. Smith, Mandeville, New Zealand and undergoing restoration in 1998 for a group of Swissair pilots. Reg'n **ZK-SWR** apparently reserved.

6854 Supplied to the Air Council with military serial **NR778**. To 18MU 2.45. To Ferry Unit 10.45. To 18MU 6.46. SOC on sale to Reid and Sigrist Ltd., Braunstone 5.12.46. Reg'd **G-AIYY** [CofR 11092 19.12.46] and CofA no.8848 issued 23.1.47. To Seear and Monford Ltd., London EC2 22.5.53. Nominal ownership change to J. K. Seear and Co. Ltd. 29.5.54. CofA expired 30.4.64 at Rochester, Kent and broken up during there 1965. Finally cancelled as permanently withdrawn from use 16.6.65.

6855 Supplied to the Air Council with serial **NR779** but did not enter military service. Delivered to 18MU 2.45. SOC on transfer to Ministry of Civil Aviation, Speke 17.10.45. Reg'd **G-AGUF** [CofR 9735 18.10.45] and CofA no.7235 issued 29.10.45. To Channel Islands Airways Ltd., Jersey and delivered 14.1.46. Handed over to B.E.A.C. 1.4.47. To John Arthur Ralph Helps, Amersham 2.6.48. Nominal change when Helps took on as joint owners Mrs. Monique Marie Rendall (nee Agazarian) and her husband Raymond Charles Rendall 7.10.48. Passenger seating increased to 9 (installation approved 3.4.52) by addition of a Rapide type seat on starboard side immediately forward of the rear bulkhead. To Mrs M. M. Rendall and C. C. Rendall 4.2.54. Aircraft was used by Island Air Services (London) Ltd. During take off at Ramsgate, wing struck ground and aircraft was written off 29.6.57. Reg'n cancelled as withdrawn from use 9.8.57.

6856 Supplied to the Air Council with military serial **NR780**. Used by de Havilland 2.45. To storage 18MU 6.47 but moved on to 5MU for further storage 7.48. SOC on sale to Bendix Home Appliances 12.1.50 but reg'd **G-ALWK** [CofR 14893 26.1.50] to Robert Charles Cox, Fairoaks. CofA no.10816 issued 4.4.50. To Wng. Cmdr. Hugh Charles Kennard c/o Air Kruise (Kent) Ltd., 21.8.51. Nominal change to Air Kruise (Kent) Ltd. 25.2.55. Further change to Wng. Cmdr. H. C. Kennard 8.8.55. Converted to Mk6 at some time. Cancelled as sold abroad to Algeria 15.4.57. Reg'd **F-OBAL** to Ste. d'Affretements Aeriens 7.57. and French CofA issued 31.7.57. To Air Fret. Arrived at Perpignan from Algiers 26.5.62. CofA suspended 7.62.

6857 Supplied to the Air Council with military serial **NR781**. To 18MU 2.45. To Royal Navy 24.10.45. Noted in store at R.N.A.S. Stretton 1955 and presumed broken up there.

6858 Supplied to the Air Council with military serial **NR782**. Delivered to 18MU 3.45. Served briefly with Berlin Com. Flt. 6.45 but placed into store 18MU 7.45. To Royal Navy 24.10.45 and at

Everton by 11.45. Still active at Lossiemouth 7.62 with code 999/CU. Reg'd **G-ASKI** [CofR R7965 12.7.63] to William Henry Wanstall Lucas, Plymouth and flown to Roborough on a permit. Sold to Hants and Sussex Aviation Ltd. 14.10.64, and flown to Portsmouth, again on a special permit. Converted to Rapide standard and CofA issued 28.1.65. Reg'n cancelled as sold in Italy 16.2.65. Reg'd **I-BOBJ** to Aero Club Torino 8.4.65. Italian certificate no.6925. Right wing damaged 18.9.65. Aircraft required a new main spar and was abandoned at Turin-Aeritalia airfield. CofA expired 28.4.67 and reg'n cancelled during 1972. Remains completely removed by 12.73.

6859 Supplied to the Air Council with military serial **NR783**. Inspected at Loughborough 19.2.45, total time since new 35 minutes. To 18MU 3.45. SOC to The Minister of Civil Aviation, Speke. Assumed to have been converted to Rapide prior to delivery. Reg'd **G-AGUG** [CofR 9736 18.10.45] and CofA no.7236 issued 8.11.45. Operated by Channel Island Airways Ltd., Jersey and delivered 15.1.46. Handed over to B.E.A.C. 1.4.47. Struck boundary marker at Guernsey 3.8.47 and damaged. To Lancashire Aircraft Corporation Ltd., Samlesbury 8.7.48. Cancelled as sold in Pakistan 11.4.53. Re-reg'd **AP-AGL** to Crescent Air Transport Ltd., Karachi 5.53. Returned crated to Croydon 19.7.56. Restored as **G-AGUG** to Morton Air Services 4.9.56. Based at Karachi and operated on behalf of Standard Vacuum Oil during 1957. Returned to Croydon during 1958. Damaged in India 28.6.59 when nosed over on take off. Temporary repairs completed on site and ferried back to Croydon. Repairs completed 22.6.60. Converted to Mk6 prior to 9.60. Both propellers and nose damaged 20.10.61 whilst taxying at Gatwick when wind lifted tail. Repairs completed at Gatwick 12.12.61. Sold abroad 10.1.63. Reg'd **F-OCAG** to Ste. Euralair, Dakar. CofA issued 22.12.62. Later with Cie. Senegaloise de Transports Aeriens – CSTA. CofA suspended 3.63. Damaged in accident at Ziguinchor, Senegal 27.3.63 and CofA suspended.

6860 Supplied to the Air Council with military serial **NR784**. To 57OTU 3.45. At Skeabrae 7.45, Grimister 8.45. To 13Grp. Com. Flt.. Dalcross 3.46, Turnhouse 5.46. To storage at 18MU 6.46. SOC on sale to Birkett Air Services Ltd., Croydon 20.1.47. To **G-AJDN** [CofR 11204 27.1.47] and CofA no.8967 issued 30.4.47. Company ceased operations 10.4.53 due to lack of joy riding contracts. To Airwork Ltd., Croydon 20.4.53. CofA expired 10.6.55 and did not fly during 1956 or 1957. To Hants and Sussex Aviation Ltd., Portsmouth 28.4.58 and delivered to Portsmouth 6.5.58 for conversion to Mk4 standard during overhaul. First flew as such 27.8.58 and CofA renewed 29.8.58. Cancelled on sale to Algeria 29.8.58. Reg'd as **F-OBIV** to Ste. Nord Africaine de Travaux Aeriens, Bone, Algeria. And delivered via Eastleigh 29.8.58. French CofA issued 8.9.58. CofA suspended 5.62.

6861 Supplied to the Air Council with military serial **NR785**. To 18MU 3.45. To Berlin Com. Flt. 6.45. To 18MU 7.45. Sold to Reid and Sigrist Ltd., Leicester 5.12.46. Reg'd **G-AIZI** [CofR 11102 30.12.46] and CofA no.8863 issued 25.3.47. To Rodney Reuben Carne, Elstree 31.3.52. Shortly after take off from Croydon bound for Le Touquet, power was lost on the starboard engine. Pilot lost control and the aircraft stalled and crashed near a church at Wallington, Surrey 14.9.52. Cancelled as destroyed on the same day.

6862 Supplied to the Air Council with military serial **NR786**. To 18MU 3.45. Then operated by Lancashire Aircraft Corporation Ltd., Samlesbury 7.45 and sold to them 28.3.46. Reg'd **G-AHGD** to Lancashire Aircraft Corporation Ltd., Samlesbury 1.4.46. CofA no.7646 issued 17.5.46. To Universal Flying Services Ltd., Kidlington 10.46. To North Sea Air Transport Ltd., Brough 31.10.49. To L. H. Riddell, Middleton St. George 6.4.51. To Lowe and Oliver Ltd., Booker 22.12.70. Painted in colours similar to B.E.A.'s for the anniversary of Channel Islands flights. To M. R. L. Astor, Booker 5.75 and later painted to represent Z7258 (also see c/n 6434). To Paul and Andrew Wood, Audley End 28.5.91. Stalled and crashed in a turn from 200ft at Audley End airfield 30.6.91 and destroyed. The pilot, the sole occupant, was killed. Insurance value £65,000. Ownership changed to R. Jones 27.11.91 and the mortal remains were placed into storage with Southern Sailplanes at Membury, Wiltshire.

6863 Supplied to the Air Council with military serial **NR787**. To 18MU 3.45. To 87Grp. Com. Flt. 6.45. To 18MU 11.46. Swanton Morley 2.48. To 5MU 4.49. SOC on sale to Air Navigation and Trading Co. Ltd., Squires Gate 26.1.50. Reg'd as

G-ALXJ [CofR 14917 31.1.50] to Mrs. Dorothy Whyham (of Air Navigation & Trading). CofA no.10831 issued 6.4.50. While on a flight carrying newspapers from Blackpool to Jurby, Isle of Man, the aircraft flew into cliffs at Skeirrip, near Laxey Head and fell back into deep water 10.7.51. The wreck was not recovered.

6864 Supplied to the Air Council with military serial **NR788**. Converted to Mk.II. To A.T.A. HQ White Waltham 3.45, 32MU 4.45 and to 18MU for storage 11.45. Reg'd **G-AKYX** [CofR 12333 18.5.48] to Derek John Hayles, Portsmouth 18.5.48. CofA no.10231 issued 29.7.48. Sold abroad 14.9.48. Reg'd **LV-AEN** to Sfreddo and Paolini Ltd. 9.48. To Compania Entrerriana Victoria de Aviacion 30.11.48. Named *Cuidad de Victoria*. Reg'd **LV-FFO** 19.1.53. To D. Avizaga and F. Escales 5.59. CofA expired during 1960 and noted in derelict condition Don Torcuato airfield, Buenos Aires 1966.

6865 Supplied to the Air Council with military serial **NR789**. Initially to 13Grp. Com. Flt. 16.3.45, then Grimister Stn. Flt. (Shetlands) 1.46, Dalcross 28.3.46, returned to 13Grp. Com. Flt. at Turnhouse 9.5.46, back to Dalcross 17.10.46, to Fighter Command Com. Sqdn. Bovingdon, 6.2.47. To 18MU for storage 27.10.47. Sold to Goodhew Aviation Co. Ltd., Kidlington 27.1.48. Reg'd as **G-AKSL** [CofR 12173 4.2.48] and CofA no.10075 issued 28.5.48. To Transair Ltd., Croydon 17.3.52. Sold abroad to France 1.4.52. Reg'd **F-BGPL** to Soc. Aigle Azur Indochine, Hanoi 4.52. CofA issued 30.4.52. Destroyed at Delhi, India 14.6.52, possibly en route to the Far East. Reg'n cancelled 8.8.52

6866 Supplied to the Air Council with military serial **NR790**. To 18MU 3.45. To Coastal Command HQ Com. Flt. 6.45. Written off 14.1.46 when starboard engine failed at low height after take off from Manorbier, Pembrokeshire. Hit bank during attempted subsequent forced landing. SOC 14.2.46, Cat.E.

6867 Supplied to the Air Council with military serial **NR791**. To 18MU 3.45. To unspecified Ferry Unit 10.45. To 18MU 6.46. SOC on sale to Blackburn Aircraft Ltd., 14.11.46. Reg'd **G-AIWZ** [CofR 11043 21.11.46] to Blackburn's subsidiary North Sea Air Transport Ltd., Hanworth and CofA no.8773 issued 13.1.47. Crashed at 0920 GMT 30.7.49 in a barley field adjacent to the NE corner of Brough airfield. Aircraft completely wrecked and pilot killed.

6868 Supplied to the Air Council with military serial **NR792**. Initially to 18MU 3.45 and served with 87Grp. Com. Flt. at Croydon 6.45. To storage 18MU 6.46. Reg'd **G-AJKI** [CofR 11373 19.3.47] but not officially sold to Airwork Ltd., Croydon until 3.10.47! CofA no.9291 issued 31.10.47. To Anglo-Iranian Oil Co. Ltd., Abadan 16.5.47. Seized by Iranian Authorities 10.51 but according to those in Britain, "sold abroad 10.51"! To Iran's National Oil Co. as **EP-AAY** 10.51 & British reg'n cancelled 12.51, though official records do not show cancellation to Iran until 29.10.54. Fate unknown.

6869 Supplied to the Air Council with military serial **NR793**. Initially at 76MU 20.3.45 for dismantling and packing. Shipped to Bombay ex South Shields 23.4.45 per *MV City of Florence* as a gift for the Nizam of Hyderabad. SOC 25.4.46 and reg'd **VT-CBY**. The Nizam controlled Deccan Airways and as this company was operating a Rapide aircraft in 1946, it is likely to have been this aircraft. To Air Services of India Ltd., Bombay 5.47. To Madras Presidency Airways Ltd. 8.48. With Vardaraja Airways Ltd., Madras 10.49, but returned to Madras Presidency Airways Ltd. 3.55. Damaged in a gale at Calcutta 4.8.61. Although still on the 1973 official register, as it had not been noted at Madras or elsewhere for many years, presumably the aircraft was no longer current. Actual fate unknown.

6870 Supplied to the Air Council with military serial **NR794**. Initially to Peterhead 3.45. With Church Fenton Stn. Flt. 9.45. To 18MU for storage 6.47. Sold to A. Hamson and Son Ltd., trading as Air Charter Experts 11.12.47. The aircraft was taken over by Manx Air Charters Ltd. via L.E.H. Airways prior to being entered on the civil register. Reg'd **G-AKSE** [CofR 12166 27.1.48] to L.E.H. Airways Ltd., London WC2. To Manx Air Charters Ltd., named *Glen Mona* and CofA no.9963 issued 10.3.48. Manx Air Charter became Manx Airlines Ltd. 2.53. Used by Silver City for a period, believed in 1957, in Libya for charter to oil companies. Delivered to Eastleigh 14.6.58 and reg'd to Vivian Hampson Bellamy 10.10.58.. Sold abroad to Eire 10.4.59. Reg'd **EI-AKH** to Skycraft Services Ltd., Dublin 14.5.59. The aircraft had already been

delivered from Eastleigh 8.4.59. Converted to Mk6 by 7.60. Returned to Biggin Hill 21.12.60 and restored to **G-AKSE** for Air Couriers (Transport) Ltd. 3.1.61. Sold abroad to France 7.4.63. and U.K. reg'n cancelled 15.6.63. Reg'd **F-BLHE** to Ets. Rousseau, Dinard and delivered via Gatwick 6.4.63. French CofA issued 11.4.63. Crashed and written off at Ile d'Ouessant 28.9.66, two killed. Aircraft was operating for Association des Aero Club de la Cote d'Emeraude at the time of the accident.

6871 Supplied to the Air Council with military serial **NR795**. To Stn. Flt. Skeabrae 3.45. Written off 1.6.45, Cat.E. The aircraft was seen flying over Millfield Camp, Orkney at an estimated height of between 40 and 60 feet. The aircraft then dived slightly and the under-carriage hit a Nissen hut and crashed 1.6.45. 4 killed. It was suggested that the aircraft either stalled or hit an air pocket, however evidence seems to indicate that the pilot was attempting a "beat-up" at the time. SOC 14.6.45.

6872 Supplied to the Air Council with military serial **NR796**. To 1316 Flt. and coded CB-L. To 18MU 3.45. To Metropolitan Com. Sqdn. Delivered 31.5.45 (for use of the Dutch Naval Service). To Allied Flt. 3.46. Sold to Royal Netherlands Air Force 15.5.46 and re-serialled **V-2**. Operated by 334Sqdn. and named *Zeeland*. Re-reg'd **PH-VNB** 3.9.48 and with K.L.M. from 8.9.48 to 27.9.48. Transferred to United Nations, Palestine 22.9.48. Returned to R.N.A.F. as **V-2**. SOC 28.9.56 and sold to the U.K., arriving Croydon as V-2. Reg'd **G-APBJ** [CofR R5985 14.5.57] to Aerocontacts (Aircraft Distributors) Ltd., Gatwick. CofA issued 3.6.57. Arrived at Croydon 6.6.57 as V-2. Sold abroad to Tunisia 6.9.57 and awaiting delivery flight ex Croydon 1.10.57. Re-reg'd **F-OBGE** to Ste. Tunisienne de Reparations Aeron et de Construction 4.58. CofA issued 20.3.58. Operated in the name Aero Sahara. CofA suspended 19.8.63. Noted derelict at Tunis airport 1970. Remains removed by 5.74.

6873 Supplied to the Air Council with serial **NR797** 4.45 but did not but did not enter military service. To de Havilland at Witney 10.4.45. Converted to Rapide. To Airwork General Trading Co. 31.4.45 for Iraq Petroleum. Reg'd **G-AGOP** [CofR 9620 25.5.45] to Iraq Petroleum Transport Co. Ltd., Haifa. CofA no.7178 issued 3.8.45. Crashed at mile post 100 on Syrian oil pipeline 25.6.48. Declared beyond repair 22.2.49 and cancelled as written-off 3.49.

6874 Supplied to the Air Council with serial **NR798** but did not enter military service. To de Havilland at Witney 10.4.45 for conversion to Rapide. Reg'd **G-AGOV** [CofR 9625 31.5.45] to B.O.A.C. CofA no.7182 issued 29.8.45. Hired to East African Airways Corporation and ferried to Nairobi ex Bournemouth 31.8.45. Operated in U.K. marks. Reg'n finally cancelled 3.8.46 and re-reg'd **VP-KCY** on ownership transfer to East African Airways 5.9.46. To Noon and Pearce Air Charters Ltd., Nairobi 10.8.51. To Caspair Air Charters & Agencies Ltd., Nairobi 27.11.51. Back to East African Airways 6.6.53. Returned to Caspair 15.8.60. Failed to take-off at Kaabong and destroyed 23.12.61.

6875 Supplied to the Air Council with serial **NR799** 4.45 but did not enter military service. To de Havilland at Witney 12.4.45 for civil conversion. Reg'd **G-AGOU** [CofR 9624 31.5.45] to B.O.A.C. CofA no.7181 issued 21.7.45. Hired to East African Airways Corporation and ferried to Nairobi ex U.K. 25.7.45. Operated in U.K. marks. Reg'n eventually cancelled 2.8.46 and officially re-reg'd **VP-KCW** on ownership transfer to East African Airways 5.9.46 but these marks were already being worn the previous month. Sold to Sir Alexander Gibb and Partners (Africa) Ltd., Salisbury 2.9.49 and re-reg'd **VP-YNN** 24.11.55. Reg'n cancelled 27.12.57 as withdrawn from use. Total time 6620.35 hours. Some parts used during rebuild of G-ADYL c/n 6895 at Untali, Southern Rhodesia after that aircraft's accident 30.7.57.

6876 Supplied to the Air Council with serial **NR800** but did not enter military service. To de Havilland at Witney 13.4.45 for conversion to Rapide. Reg'd **G-AGOT** [CofR 9623 31.5.45] to B.O.A.C. 31.5.45. CofA no.7180 issued 21.7.45. Hired to East African Airways Corporation and ferried to Nairobi ex U.K. 25.7.45. Operated in U.K. marks but reg'n finally cancelled 2.8.46 and re-reg'd **VP-KCX** on ownership transfer to East African Airways 5.9.46. To Jivraj's Air Services Ltd., Mombasa 18.10.48. Reg'n cancelled 31.10.50 and noted in dismantled state, Mombasa 7.51.

6877 Supplied to the Air Council with military serial **NR801** but did not enter military service. Converted to civilian Rapide. SOC on sale to Airwork General Trading Co. 31.4.45. Reg'd **G-AGOR** to Iraq Petroleum Transport Co. Ltd., Haifa [CofR 9621 25.5.48] and CofA no.7179 issued 3.8.45. Sold to Wiliam Henry Knights, trustee of The Missionary Aviation Fellowship, Khartoum [CofR R2105/1 10.4.53] Possibly the aircraft reserved as **VP-KJB** for Air Travel (Charters) Ltd. but not taken up (see notes after the reg'n to construction number cross-index). Cancelled from U.K. register 29.4.53 and reg'd **VP-KLB**. To Caspair Air Charters and Agencies Ltd., Mazinde 1954. Converted to Mk4. Nominal change to Caspair Ltd. 2.58. Re-reg'd **5Y-KLB** 8.65 by which time named *African Queen*. Ran off runway at Bukoba and written off 7.8.68. It is believed that the aircraft was conveyed to a monastery near the airfield and used for a time as a children's play thing.

6878   Supplied to the Air Council with military serial **NR802**. To 18MU 4.45. To 87Grp. Com. Flt. 6.45. To 18MU 4.46. SOC on sale to W. A. Rollason Ltd., Croydon 27.5.48. Reg'd **G-AKOG** [CofR 12094 4.12.47] and CofA issued 12.7.48. To Butlins Ltd., London W1 19.5.48. To Aviation Traders Ltd., Southend 9.8.49 although received by them a couple of months earlier. To Bond Air Services Ltd., Gatwick 7.11.50. Sold abroad to Northern Rhodesia 8.10.51 and reg'n cancelled 1.11.51. Arrived Croydon 17.10.51 incorrectly painted as **VP-KCH** but this was corrected to **VP-RCH** 27.10.51. To A. Mechin, Lusaka 11.51. To Lusaka Air Carriers 1952. To Fishair (Pvt) Ltd., Marandellas, 1954. Separate VP-R marks were discontinued 1953 and aircraft re-reg'd **VP-YLF** still with Fishair (Pvt) Ltd. 9.6.54. Cancelled 9.58 on sale to "French Territory". Reg'd **F-OBMQ** to Ste. L'Okoume de Libreville 5.59 and French CofA issued 5.5.59. To Aer. J. C. Brouillet et Cie. To TransGabon. CofA suspended 5.63. (Note: Also see c/n 6443 for initial, incorrect allocation of G-AKOG).

6879   Supplied to the Air Council with military serial **NR803**. At Talbenny (Pembrokeshire) 4.45, Dunkeswell 2.46. At Valley 4.46 and then to storage 18MU 10.46. To AGT Co. Ltd. on loan to Springs Ltd. 7.47 (operated by service crew in military marks for undisclosed test work). Possibly also used by Martin-Baker Aircraft Co. Ltd. for a time. To storage 5MU 1.50. SOC on sale to Field Aircraft Services Ltd., Croydon 31.3.50. Reg'd **G-AMAI** [CofR 14991 4.4.50] to William Joseph Nobbs, Elstead, Surrey. CofA no.10895 issued 4.7.50. To Alfred George Sheppard, Richmond, Surrey 12.12.51. Exported to Spain 10.7.52. Reg'd **EC-AGP** to Felipe Beltran y Guell, Barcelona, 6.5.52. To Comercial Exportadova de Articulos Percederos SA, CEAPSA, Madrid-Barajas 22.12.56 and CofA no.166 issued. To storage inside the Cuatro Vientos museum, Madrid until sold to a German collector in 1985. To Joseph M. Koch, Augsburg 1987. Later moved to Lahr. Reg'd **D-ILIT** and first flew after resoration at Lahr 21.7.95. German CofA issued 9.11.95. Restored to **G-AMAI** when Joseph Koch t/a Island Aeroplane Company moved to Sandown, Isle of Wight. Named *The Sandown Flyer*. The peripatetic Koch moved back to Germany and the U.K. reg'n was cancelled 19.4.99. Restored as **D-ILIT** to Joseph Koch.

6880   Supplied to the Air Council with military serial **NR804**. To No.4 Delivery Flt. 4.45. To 18MU 11.45. To Halton 5.46 but returned to 18MU 6.47. SOC on sale to to East Anglian Flying Services Ltd., Southend. Reg'd **G-AKJZ** [CofR 11997 17.12.47]. Collected from Dumfries 27.1.48 and air tested after conversion to civil Rapide 31.5.49. CofA no.10262 issued 3.6.49. Apparently passed to Air Navigation and Trading Co. Ltd., Squires Gate 15.12.49, but this change does not appear in official documentation. To Anthony Strickland Hubbard, London NW1 14.8.58. Withdrawn from use at Biggin Hill after CofA expiry 13.7.59. Reg'n finally cancelled 22.10.63.

6881   Supplied to the Air Council with military serial **NR805**. To 18MU 4.45. To Berlin Com. Flt. 5.45. SOC to Belgian Government 2.9.46. To Belgian Air Force **D1** and TOC 2.9.46. Later coded ZC-H. Cat.5 24.2.53 and scrapped.

6882   Supplied to the Air Council with military serial **NR806**. To 18MU 4.45, then Berlin Com. Flt. 6.45 and returned to 18MU for storage 1.46. SOC on sale to Geoffrey Cecil Harrison Last, Croydon 27.5.48. Reg'd **G-AKZP** [CofR 12351 20.5.48] and CofA no.10179 issued 8.10.48. To Edwin Holden, Manchester 2.6.49. Sometime converted to Mk4. Operated by Melba Airways Ltd. from 1950 until the company was placed into liquidation 2.52. Aircraft then borrowed from the liquidator by Stanley Spencer's Tours Ltd., and used by them for pleasure flying at Manchester summer 1952. To Frank Swift, Manchester 14.1.53 and, as Ringway Air Charter, operated pleasure flights at Manchester

summer 1953. To Ringway Aircharter Services Ltd. 1.4.54. To Gordon, Woodroffe and Co. Ltd., London W1 14.3.56. Operated by Oilfields Supply and Trading Co. Inc., Tripoli, Libya during 1956 (carried titles "Robert H. Ray, Houston, Texas"). To Bahamas Helicopters (U.K.) Ltd. 12.4.57. Overturned and caught fire whilst making an emergency landing after running out of fuel, at Nabuel Beach, Hammamet, situated approx 25 miles SE of Tunis 16.3.57. The aircraft was en route to the U.K. for overhaul at the time.

6883   Supplied to the Air Council with military serial **NR807**. To 18MU 4.45 and served with 87Grp. Com. Flt. 5.45. To 18MU for storage 4.46. SOC on sale to Airwork and General Trading Co., 20.12.46. Reg'd **G-AJGZ** [CofR 11289 12.2.47] to Anglo-Iranian Oil Co. Ltd., Abadan. CofA no.9030 issued 13.5.47. Caught fire when starting engines and burnt out at Agha-Javi, Iran 16.7.49. Reg'n cancelled 30.7.49.

6884   First flew 26.4.45. Supplied to the Air Council with serial **NR808** but did not enter military service. Sold to Channel Island Airways Ltd., Croydon 25.7.45. To de Havilland at Witney 28.5.45 for conversion to civil Rapide. First flew 22.8.45. Reg'd **G-AGSH** and CofA no.7205 issued 25.8.45. Transferred to A.A.J.C. but continued in operation ex Jersey 27.8.45. Further change to The Minister of Civil Aviation, Jersey 11.46. Absorbed by B.E.A.C. 1.4.47. Named *James Keir Hardie*. To Airviews, Manchester 4.5.56. Cancelled on sale to Ireland 17.4.57. Delivered via Ringway 18.4.57. Reg'd **EI-AJO** to Air Kruise (Ireland) Ltd., Killarney 26.4.57. Irish reg'n cancelled 1.7.57 on sale back to U.K. and restored as **G-AGSH** to W. S. Shackleton Ltd., Kidlington 18.7.57. To M. L. Thomas t/a Jersey Airlines 7.2.58 and delivered ex Kidlington 11.2.58. Aircraft carried Alderney Airlines titles during 1958. Converted to Mk6 during 1960. Owners name changed to Airlines (Jersey) Ltd. 12.2.59. To Alares Development Co. Ltd., Jersey 9.8.61. Aircraft was re-acquired by B.E.A.C. 12.1.62 and operated until sold to British Westpoint Airlines Ltd., Exeter 2.5.64, delivered 3.5.64. To Grp. Capt. L. G. P. Marton and Sqdn. Ldr. J. Grant as trustees of the assets of R.A.F. (Abingdon) Sport Parachuting Club) 8.65. Remained with the club, although with various nominal changes of owner. Still flying 7.74, named *Paranymph* during 1974. Total time as of 21.7.74 was 14918.30 hours. Offered for sale at £6000 11.74. Sold to A. V. Heath t/a Pioneer Aviation Trust (Jersey) 26.2.75 and delivered from Abingdon same day. Nosed over on landing at Dinard inbound from Jersey 22.3.75, sustaining damage to underside of nose and both propellers. Repaired. To Brian Haddican & Partners 16.3.77. To Pioneer Aviation Ltd. 10.4.81. To Exeair Travel Ltd., Exeter 21.3.83. Re-possessed by finance company at Exeter and offered for sale by auction at Duxford 8.84. No buyer found and ferried to Biggin Hill for overhaul. Departed to Carlisle 3.85 and reg'd to Specialist Flying Training Ltd. at Crosby-on-Eden Airfield 8.3.85. Noted at Alderney Air Rally 14.6.85 with "Alderney Airlines" colours. To Philip Meeson of Venom Jet Promotions Ltd., Bournemouth 15.6.89. Painted in British European Airways livery and named *Jemma Meeson* after his daughter. To Techair (London) Ltd. 29.3.00 but still operated by Philip Meeson. Now named *James Keir Hardie* as when serving with B.E.A.C. 1947-1956.

6885   Supplied to the Air Council with military serial **NR809**. To 8OOTU (French) 5.45. Sold as **G-AGPI** [CofR 9638 13.6.45] to Channel Islands Airways Ltd., Jersey. CofA no.7187 issued 30.6.45. Converted to Mk3. To The Minister of Civil Aviation, Jersey 22.11.46. Absorbed by B.E.A.C. 1.4.47. To Frederick Arnold Hill t/a Lees-Hill Aviation (Birmingham) Ltd. 19.4.48. To Somerton Airways Ltd., Cowes 17.5.49. While inbound to Cowes, Isle of Wight, from Eastleigh, the pilot attempted to overshoot but struck trees and the roof of a house and crashed into a field outside the boundary of Somerton Airport 16.6.49. Badly damaged and written off. Had flown 4280 hours since conversion 6.45. Some remains were still visible at Somerton 3.52.

6886   Supplied to the Air Council with serial **NR810** but did not enter military service. Instead, to de Havilland at Witney for conversion to civil Rapide standard 16.5.45. SOC to Associated Airways Ltd., Speke but reg'd to Olley Air Service Ltd., Croydon as **G-AGSI** [CofR 9688 25.7.45]. CofA no.7206 issued at Speke 15.8.45. To British Transport Commission [CofR R2265/2 16.2.53]. To Cambrian Air Services Ltd., Pengam Moors 19.2.53. To aircraft dealer W. S. Shackleton Ltd., Cranfield 21.4.54. Cancelled as sold abroad 26.10.54 but restored to Shackleton briefly and flown on a permit Cardiff to Cranfield for conversion to Mk4 standard. Test flown 4.10.54 and CofA renewed 5.11.54.

Delivered to Queensland Ambulance Transport Brigade, Cairns QLD with the U.K. reg'n still applied 12.54 but eventually re-reg'd **VH-BFS** 2.55. To New Hebrides Airways Ltd. reg'd **VQ-FAZ** named *Miti Vaku* 4.5.60. However, on inspection, found "unusable" and WFU at Vila 4.5.62.

6887   Supplied to the Air Council with serial **NR811** but did not enter military service. To de Havilland at Witney 19.5.45 for conversion to civil Rapide. SOC to A.A.J.C. for use based Jersey 23.10.45. Reg'd **G-AGSK** [CofR 9690 25.7.45] to Channel Island Airways Ltd., Jersey. Delivered to Jersey 25.8.45. CofA no.7208 issued 27.8.45. To The Minister of Civil Aviation, Jersey 29.11.46. Handed over to B.E.A.C. 1.4.47. Later named *Lord Kitchener*. Transferred to Gibraltar Airways Ltd. 15.12.52. Sold abroad 2.10.53. Reg'd **TJ-ABP** to Air Jordan Co. Ltd., 2.10.53. Re-reg'd **JY-ABP** to Air Jordan Co. Ltd., 4.54. Dismantled 2.2.56.

6888   Supplied to the Air Council with serial **NR812** but did not enter military service. First flown 10.5.45 and to de Havilland at Witney 18.5.45 for conversion to civilian Rapide standard. Reg'd to Isle of Man Air Services Ltd., Derbyhaven as **G-AGSJ** [CofR 9689 25.7.45] and test flown after conversion 27.7.45. CofA no.7207 issued 15.8.45. Absorbed by B.E.A.C. on formation 1.2.47. To William George Cornwallis Hills-Grove-Hills t/a Island Air Services 13.5.48, St. Mary's. Named *Isles of Scilly*. To The British Wagon Co. Ltd., Rotherham 7.10.48 and reportedly operated on their behalf by Trent Valley Aviation 9.48 to 12.49. Sold abroad 2.12.49. Reg'd **OY-ACZ** 12.5.50 to Zone Redningskovnset Flkyretjenesten (Danish Red Cross). Ran out of fuel en route Laeso to Copenhagen 3.3.54 and was damaged beyond repair after the attempted forced landing at Lillerod (or Lynge) near Frederikssund. Reg'n cancelled 7.8.57.

6889   Supplied to the Air Council with military serial **NR813** but did not enter military service. To de Havilland at Witney 29.5.45 for conversion to civil Rapide. Reg'd **G-AGPH** [CofR 9637 13.6.45] to Channel Island Airways Ltd., Jersey. CofA no.7186 issued 30.6.45 and delivered to Jersey 12.7.45. Confusingly, records show "sold to Jersey Airways Ltd. 20.8.45", as Jersey Airways was re-named Channel Island Airways Ltd. 1.9.45! To The Minister of Civil Aviation, Jersey 22.11.46. Absorbed by B.E.A.C. 1.4.47. Later named *Sir Henry Havelock*. Overturned on landing 6.12.51 and later submerged by the incoming tide, Isle of Barra, Outer Hebrides. Reg'n cancelled 1.2.52.

6890   Supplied to the Air Council with military serial **NR814** but did not enter military service. To de Havilland at Witney 1.6.45 for conversion to civil Rapide and CofA no.7223 issued 1.9.45. SOC on sale to the Nederland Government 7.9.45. Reg'd **PH-RAA** and leased to K.L.M. from 19.9.45 to 1.11.46. Sold abroad 1947 and reg'd **VP-KEA** to East African Airways Corporation. Crashed and burnt out 24.1.54, on take off from a disused airstrip at Butiaba, Murchisson Falls, Lake Albert after rescuing the occupants of a Cessna 180. No injuries.

6891   Supplied to the Air Council with military serial **NR815** but did not enter military service. To de Havilland at Witney 1.6.45 for conversion to civil Rapide and CofA no.7224 issued 6.9.45. SOC on sale to the Nederland Government 26.9.45. Reg'd **PH-RAB** and leased to K.L.M. from 19.9.45 until 1.11.46. Sold abroad 1947 and reg'd **VP-KEB** to East African Airways Corporation 1947. Written off 15.10.51 at Kasese, Uganda, when swung on landing, hit a bank and nosed over. Total loss.

6892   Supplied to the Air Council with military serial **NR828**. Delivered to 18MU 5.45. Served briefly with Metropolitan Com. Sqdn. Hendon from 3.46. Returned to 18MU for storage 8.46. SOC on sale to Derek John Hayles, Portsmouth. Reg'd **G-AKZA** [CofR 12336 18.5.48] and CofA no.10198 issued 2.7.48. Despite a frustrated sale to a South African buyer, who had reserved reg'n **ZS-BZC** for his acquisition, another deal was done and the aircraft passed to W. A. Rollason Ltd., Croydon 15.10.48. Reg'n cancelled 8.11.48 and reg'd **LV-AEP** to the Argentinian importer Sfreddo y Paolini Ltda. 31.12.48. To Aero Express Barcella, named *El Santo*. To Vilalta Aria y Pizarro 30.3.62. CofA expired 3.63.

6893   Supplied to the Air Council with serial **NR829** but did not enter military service. Delivered to de Havilland at Witney for conversion to Rapide 30.5.45. CofA no.7225 issued 19.9.45. SOC on sale to Nederland Government 22.9.45. Reg'd **PH-RAC** and leased to K.L.M. from 19.9.45 to 1.11.46. Sold abroad 1947 and reg'd **VP-KEC** to East African Airways Corporation. Damaged beyond repair at Mafia Island, Tanganyika , 12.5.50 when it ran into rough ground, braked heavily and nosed over while landing in heavy rain, inbound from Dar-es-Salaam.

6894   Supplied to the Air Council with serial **NR830** but did not enter military service. Delivered to de Havilland at Witney for conversion to Rapide 18.6.45. CofA no.7233 issued 1.10.45. To B.O.A.C. 1.11.45. Purchased by B.O.A.C. on behalf of Middle East Airlines and delivered to Beirut 22.11.45. Re-reg'd **LR-AAE** still with M.E.A. 27.11.45, named *A Shahbah*. Reg'n cancelled 19.12.47 and departed Beirut for return to U.K. same day. Reg'd **G-AKZT** [CofR 12354 28.5.48] to Russell Littledale Whyham t/a Air Navigation and Trading Co. Ltd., Squires Gate. To aircraft broker R. K. Dundas Ltd. 28.3.52. Sold abroad 28.3.52 and U.K. reg'n cancelled 1.5.52. To Director of Civil Aviation and reg'd **CY-AAK** 9.4.52. Operated by the Ceylon Air Academy. Re-reg'd **4R-AAK** still with the Director of Civil Aviation 12.53 and continued to be operated by the Air Academy. Reg'n cancelled prior to 1970.

6895   Supplied to the Air Council with serial **NR831** but did not enter military service. To de Havilland at Witney 15.6.45 for conversion to Rapide. U.K. CofA no.7226 issued 19.9.45. SOC on sale to Nederland Government. Reg'd **PH-RAD** and leased to K.L.M. from 19.9.45 until 1.11.46. Delivered to K.L.M. via Croydon 26.9.45. Sold abroad 1947 and reg'd **VP-KED** to East African Airways Corporation. 1947. Sold to Israel and became **1306** with Israeli Air Force. Re-reg'd as **4X-AEI** to Arkia Israeli Inland Airlines 27.11.53. Rebuilt 1955 by Bedek Aircraft Corp. using parts of 4X-ACH and 4X-ACU. Sold abroad 22.8.55. Returned to Croydon as **4X-AEI** with identity tag "X6311". Aircraft incorrectly assumed to be c/n 6311 and restored as **G-ADYL** in error but remained so and to Aero Services Ltd., Croydon 8.55. To Mitchell Aircraft Ltd., Portsmouth 2.56. To Maj. Frederick George Fox, Fairoaks 2.56, named *The Rover*. Had accident on landing at Grand Reef Aerodrome, Umtali, Southern Rhodesia 30.7.57. Repaired by Skywork (Pvt) Ltd., Salisbury, using parts from the dismantled the reg'n VP-YNN (c/n 6875) and signed off for flight 12.12.57. WFU after CofA expiry at Fairoaks 16.12.58. Application for CofA renewal cancelled 1960. Removed to Luton 31.1.62, where it was broken up and burnt in 1964. (See c/n 6311 for original use of G-ADYL).

6896   Supplied to the Air Council with serial **NR832** but did not enter military service. To de Havilland at Witney 18.6.45 for conversion to Rapide. U.K. CofA no.7234 issued 5.10.45. To B.O.A.C. 1.11.45 on behalf of Middle East Airlines and delivered to Beirut 22.11.45. Reg'd **LR-AAF** to Middle East Airlines 27.11.45, named *Al Carmel*. Reg'n cancelled 19.12.47 and left Beirut for U.K. same day. Stored at Ringway. Reg'd **G-AKZW** [CofR 12357 24.5.48] to W. A. Rollason Ltd., Croydon. New CofA issued 16.8.48. To Mayfair Air Services Ltd., Croydon 19.8.48. To Harold Alfred Edward Towle 3.5.49 but continued in service with Mayfair. To Adie Aviation Ltd., Croydon 21.6.49. To Morton Air Services Ltd., Croydon 16.6.50. Cancelled as sold abroad to Portugese Guinea 26.4.52. Reg'd **CR-GAI** to the Government of Portugese Guinea 24.5.52. To Transportes Aereos da Guinea Portuguese. Cancelled from register by 11.80.

6897   Supplied to the Air Council with serial **NR833** but did not enter military service. Delivered to de Havilland at Witney for conversion to civilian standard 18.6.45 and U.K. CofA no.7254 issued 23.10.45. SOC as sold 5.12.45 and nominally with the Ministry of Supply for hire to B.O.A.C. to be operated by the newly formed Iraqi Airways reg'd **YI-ABD**. Their first scheduled service Baghdad to Basra was operated 29.1.46 and this aircraft was most likely used. To B.E.A.C. reg'd **G-AKDW** [CofR 11835 25.8.47]. To Short Bros. & Harland Ltd., Rochester 30.5.49 and operated as Rochester Air Charters from delivery 14.6.49. To Avionics Ltd., Croydon 27.5.58. Sold abroad to Belgium 23.6.58 and cancelled from U.K. register 10.7.58. Noted at Ostend 6.58 incorrectly marked **'F-BCBD'**. Noted again at Toussus-le-Noble this time with corrected reg'n **F-BCDB** 6.8.58. To Aerosud, Bone, Algeria with French CofA issued 21.11.58. To Societe d'Affretement Aerien (S.G.A.A.) mid '59. Repurchased by Aerosud 1.61. Company transferred to the mainland and re-named Air Fret 5.63; noted at Avignon during that month. At Nimes-Garons the following month when the CofA was suspended. Still hangared at Nimes '74, but stored engineless outside '75. To Aviodome Museum, Amsterdam 4.84. To the de Havilland Museum Trust Ltd., (Mosquito Museum), Salisbury Hall, Hertfordshire in exchange for a Bleriot 3.5.94. Displayed by the de Havilland Aircraft Heritage Centre, named *City of Winchester* by 3.02.

6898 Supplied to the Air Council with serial **NR834** but did not enter military service. To de Havilland at Witney 18.6.45 for conversion to Rapide. U.K. CofA no.7255 issued 23.10.45. To B.O.A.C., Croydon 17.11.45 but returned to de Havilland at Witney 5.12.45. SOC on sale to B.O.A.C. 1.1.46 for operation by the newly formed Iraqi Airways. (Officially hired from the Ministry of Supply). Reg'd **YI-ABE** to Iraqi Airways and delivered 13.1.46. Passenger services commenced immediately on arrival of the carrier's first aircraft. Returned to the U.K. and reg'd as **G-AKDX** [CofR 11836 25.8.47] to B.E.A.C. To Adie Aviation Ltd., Croydon 25.7.49. To World Evangelisation Trust Ltd., London N1 11.2.50. Cancelled on transfer to the Kenyan register 5.2.51 and reg'd as **VP-KIO** to Missionary Aviation Fellowship 2.51. Broken up 10.52.

6899 Supplied to the Air Council with serial **NR835** but did not enter military service. To de Havilland at Witney 20.6.45 for conversion to Rapide. U.K. CofA no.7245 issued 1.11.45 and exported to Portugal via Croydon 8.11.45. Reg'd **CS-ADI** to Companhia de Transportes Aereos and operated scheduled services between Lisbon and Oporto. Ceased operations in 1949. To the Portugese Air Force as FAP2307 1950 and operated by Base Area No.1 at Granja do Marquez, Sintra. Used for aerial survey and photography. (Note: c/n 6430, painted to represent FAP2307, is currently stored at Sintra for the Museo do Ar).

6900 Supplied to the Air Council with serial **NR836** but did not enter military service. To de Havilland at Witney 21.6.45 for conversion to Rapide. U.K. CofA no.7246 issued 3.11.45. To Portugal via Croydon 8.11.45. Reg'd **CS-ADJ** to Companhia de Transportes Aereos and operated scheduled services Lisbon to Oporto. Ceased operations 1949. Cancelled prior to 11.54. Subsequently to Transportes Aereos Sao Tome reg'd **CR-SAD**. To Aero Club de Angola **CR-LKR** 1970. Sold to the Brazilian airline VARIG and intended for display in their planned company museum at Porto Alegre. Noted by the authors, still crated at Porto Alegre after shipment from Africa 29.1.79. Restored at their Porto Alegre base and painted **PP-VAN** to represent their first aircraft. More recently displayed at Museu Aerospacial da Forca Aerea Brasiliera, Avenue Mal Fontenelle, Compo dos Afonsos, Rio de Janeiro.

6901 Supplied to the Air Council with serial **NR837** but did not enter military service. To de Havilland at Witney 21.6.45 for conversion to Rapide. U.K. CofA no.7247 issued 6.11.45 and sold to Portugal passing through Croydon on delivery 8.11.45. Reg'd **CS-ADK** to Companhia de Transportes Aereos and operated scheduled services Lisbon to Oporto. Ceased operations 1949. Cancelled prior to 11.54. Subsequently to Transportes Aereos Sao Tome reg'd **CR-SAE**. To Aero Club de Angola reg'd **CR-LKS** 1970. Noted in open storage, Lourenco Marques 1975.

6902 Supplied to the Air Council with serial **NR838** but did not enter military service. To de Havilland at Witney for conversion to civilian Rapide standard 25.6.45. With the Ministry of Aircraft Production and CofA no.7277 issued 26.11.45. Transferred to A.A.J.C., reg'd **G-AHGG** [CofR 10030 2.5.46] and operated by Railway Air Services Ltd., Speke. To Air Commerce Ltd., Croydon 19.8.46. Absorbed by Olley Air Service Ltd., Croydon 27.12.46. Sold abroad 10.4.52. To Liberian National Airlines reg'd **EL-AAA**. To Air Brousse SPRL, Leopoldville-Ndolo reg'd **OO-CMS** [CofR C267 13.3.56]. Whilst en route Leopoldville to Port Francqui 8.7.56, made forced landing near Kikwit and was badly damaged. Reg'n cancelled 11.10.56 and parts used for OO-CRS (c/n 6559) and OO-CJS (c/n 6429).

6903 Supplied to the Air Council with serial **NR839** but did not enter military service. To de Havilland at Witney for conversion to civilian Rapide standard 29.6.45. CofA no.7268 issued 19.11.45. Transferred to A.A.J.C. 11.4.46 and reg'd **G-AHGF** [CofR 10029 2.5.46] and initially in service with Railway Air Services Ltd., Speke. To B.E.A.C. on formation 1.2.47. Absorbed by British European Airways Corp. on formation 1.2.47. To Lees-Hill Aviation (Birmingham) Ltd. 5.7.48 and operated for another Hill owned company, Solent Airways, Southampton. Nominal change to Frederick Arnold Hill t/a Lees-Hill Aviation (Birmingham) Ltd. 28.4.49. To aircraft broker W. S. Shackleton Ltd., Cranfield 20.6.52. To V. H. Bellamy t/a Hampshire Aeroplane Club, Southampton 23.2.53. First Rapide to be converted to Mk4 standard, carried out by Flightways Ltd. summer 1953. To K. G. R. Bloomfield 26.9.53 and flown U.K. to New Zealand, arriving Gisborne 17.4.54. Leased to Gisborne Aero Club reg'd **ZK-BFK** 30.4.54. To Airwork Co. Pty. Ltd. reg'd **VH-AWG** 4.11.57. To R.

G. Carswell t/a Carsair Air Services Pty. Ltd., Mount Pleasant QLD 15.5.59 and re-reg'd **VH-BIF**. To M. Ward, Brisbane QLD 11.60. Negotiations were in hand for sale to Northern Star School of Parachuting .63 but sale not completed. WFU Brisbane-Archerfield QLD late 1965 due deterioration of wood and fabric and cancelled from register 6.5.66. Burnt by Department of Civil Aviation fire crew 3.6.68.

6904 Supplied to the Air Council with serial **NR840** but did not enter military service. To de Havilland at Witney for conversion to civilian Rapide standard 25.7.45. U.K. CofA no.7269 issued 16.11.45 and sold to Divisao Transportes Aereos de Angola (D.T.A.) reg'd **CR-LBN**. Fate unknown.

6905 Supplied to the Air Council with serial **NR841** but did not enter military service. To de Havilland at Witney for conversion to civilian Rapide standard 30.7.45. U.K. CofA no.7271 issued 20.11.45 and sold to Divisao Transportes Aereos de Angola (D.T.A.) reg'd **CR-LBO**. To Transportes Aereos de Cabo Verde reg'd **CR-CAA** by 1959. Fate Unknown.

6906 Supplied to the Air Council with serial **NR842** but did not enter military service. To de Havilland at Witney for conversion to civilian Rapide standard 26.7.45. Hired from the Ministry of Supply to British Overseas Airways Corporation for operation by Iraqi Airways reg'd **YI-ABF**. U.K. CofA no.7299 issued 17.12.45 and delivered 13.1.46. To Arthur Robert Pilgrim reg'd **G-ALGC** [CofR 12512 3.1.49]. To Wilfred Henry Cornish Barton 22.6.49. To Melba Airways Ltd., Barton 8.9.49. To Wolverhampton Aviation Ltd. 17.7.52. To Helliwells Ltd., Walsall 11.2.53. To Tube Investments (Group Services) Ltd., Elmdon 4.9.58. To Luton Airways Ltd. 10.10.58 and converted to Mk6 prior 4.59. To Keens (Watford) Ltd., Elstree 9.2.60. De-converted from Mk6 prior to 5.61! To Derek Clifford Cole & Kenneth Bryan Neely, Blackbushe 21.5.63. Over-ran on landing Biggin 9.3.64, tipped onto nose and cracked a main spar, but repaired. Chartered to Booilushag Ltd., Ronaldsway 23.10.64. Was being operated by Neely's company Scillonia Airways Ltd. named *The Bishop* 7.65. Withdrawn from use 7.66 and noted at Shobdon without engines 9.67. Cancelled as permanently withdrawn from use 28.2.73.

6907 Supplied to the Air Council with serial **NR843** but did not enter military service. To de Havilland at Witney for conversion to civilian Rapide standard 26.7.45. Hired from the Ministry of Supply to British Overseas Airways Corporation for operation by Iraqi Airways reg'd **YI-ABG**. U.K. CofA no.7300 issued 17.12.45 and delivered 29.1.46. To W. A. Rollason Ltd., Croydon reg'd **G-ALGE** [CofR 12514 5.1.49]. To Melba Airways Ltd., Barton 8.9.49. To Wolverhampton Aviation Ltd. 6.5.52. To Kenning Aviation Ltd., Burnaston 3.6.54. To Lawrence Saville Dawson o/b Yeadon Aviation, Leeds-Bradford 1.6.56. To Mac Smith Ltd., Newcastle-Woolsington 8.12.59 and name subsequently changed to Mac Smith Air Charter Ltd. 7.3.60. Jointly owned with Cumberland Aviation Services Ltd., Carlisle 24.3.61. Cancelled on sale to Irish Republic 5.7.62. To J. Farrell, A. O'Hara & Partners, Weston reg'd **EI-AMN** 31.7.62. Reg'n cancelled 25.8.64 on sale to Aero Club Centre Alsace Marin la Meslee, Colmar reg'd **F-BLXX** & CofA issued 18.9.64. To Centre Parachutisme, Strasbourg 2.70 named *Desiree II*. To Aero Club Doncourt 8.70. Last operated by Moselle Parachutisme, Metz. Sold to Daniel S. Foley, Bloomfield Hills MI via dealer Geert E. Frank and shipped to U.S.A. ex Rotterdam 15.9.73. Reg'd **N8053** 7.73. Painted in c.1947 British European Airways colours and operated by Kingston Aircraft, Plum Island MA. Flown to St. Maarten, Netherland Antilles by William Crorey 1975 with the intention of operating cargo flights to and from the Dominican Republic carrying fruit and vegetables. Not operated and apparently abandoned, the aircraft was badly damaged by strong winds 9.79. Ownership was subsequently in dispute and one claimant was the noted aviation and travel author Richard Bach. Last sighted 12.81 in long grass in a very poor state.

6908 Supplied to the Air Council with serial **NR844** but did not enter military service. Converted to civilian Rapide standard by de Havilland at Witney 29.9.45. SOC on transfer to A.A.J.C. and reg'd to Railway Air Services Ltd., Liverpool as **G-AGUU** [CofR 9749 30.10.45]. CofA no.7262 issued 10.1.46. Handed over to B.E.A.C. on formation 1.2.47 and named *Sir Colin Campbell*. Sold to Malayan Airways 4.6.52 and U.K. reg'n cancelled 1.8.52. Reg'd **VR-OAA** 9.52. Believed still operated in 1957 but finally cancelled as withdrawn from use 10.3.61.

DH89 c/n 6926. Operated by Scenic Flights at Land's End in the late 1960s, G-AHAG provides an aerial view of the exposed shoreline to another load of visitors to the West Country.

DH89 c/n 6944. Following withdrawal from use March 1969, Hunting Surveys presented G-AHED to the R.A.F. Museum. Stored at a number of locations since, the current resting place is Cosford.

DH89 c/n 6930. For southern enthusiasts, Perth resident G-ALAX was always elusive. Photographed In happier times, this Rapide has lain in open storage in a Hampshire garden for more than 30 years.

DH89 c/n 6952. G-AKRS was one of eight Rapides operated on scheduled services to Cowes and Sandown, Isle of Wight from their base at Croydon and also from Gatwick and Southampton.

DH89 c/n 6931. Registered to various members of the Whyham family, large numbers of Rapides have passed through the hands of Air Navigation & Trading Co. G-AKSG was with them until 1954.

DH89 c/n 6953. One of many Dominies that were delivered as hostilities were drawing to a close and therefore, saw no military service. Sold to Air Services of India Ltd. at Bombay as VT-AVX.

DH89 c/n 6938. Shipped to de Havilland of Canada, probably in kit form, YV-B-BPE was the sole Venezuelan Rapide. Delivered November 1949, it was destroyed just two months later.

DH89 c/n 6963. VR-LAD was one of three Rapides supplied to Sierra Leone Airways in 1958. Replaced by larger capacity Heron aircraft from 1962, all three were eventually burnt at Freetown.

6909 Supplied to the Air Council with serial **NR845** but did not enter military service. To de Havilland at Witney for conversion to civilian Rapide standard 31.7.45. U.K. CofA no.7309 issued 18.12.45 and hired from the Ministry of Supply by British Overseas Airways Corporation for Iraqi Airways reg'd **YI-ABH**. Re-imported 12.48 believed by A. R. Pilgrim and stored Ringway. Eventually reg'd **G-ALGI** but details are unusually sketchy in the official records. To Walter Westoby t/a Westair Flying Services Ltd., Blackpool 13.1.49. To broker W. S. Shackleton Ltd. 13.3.52. To C. E. Harper Aircraft Co. Ltd., Exeter 7.4.52. Sold abroad to France 21.9.53. To Ste. des Transportes Aeriens du Gabon (T.A.G.) reg'd **F-OAND** and French CofA issued 25.9.53. Crashed 6.54 and reg'n cancelled 23.9.54.

6910 Supplied to the Air Council with serial **NR846** but did not enter military service. For conversion to civilian Rapide standard by de Havilland at Witney 31.7.45 but instead the necessary work was carried out by Brush at Loughborough 10.8.45. SOC to A.A.J.C. and reg'd to Scottish Airways Ltd., Renfrew as **G-AGUR** [CofR 9746 9.11.45]. CofA no.7257 issued 20.12.45. Handed over to B.E.A.C. on formation 1.2.47 and named *Lord Roberts*. To C. E. Harper Aircraft Co. Ltd., Exeter 30.11.53. To Ronald Myhill, Exeter o/b Autair 15.7.54. A tyre failed on landing Frankfurt and the pilot elected to try an overshoot and go around whilst reviewing the situation 2.8.54. Crashed and destroyed. Cancelled from register as destroyed 28.9.54.

6911 Supplied to the Air Council with serial **NR847** but did not enter military service. Converted to civilian Rapide standard by de Havilland at Witney 4.8.45. SOC on transfer to A.A.J.C. and reg'd to Isle of Man Air Services Ltd., Derbyhaven as **G-AGUP** [CofR 9745 24.10.45]. CofA no.7256 issued 20.12.45. Handed over to B.E.A.C. on formation 1.2.47 and named *Sir Robert Peel.* To Airlines (Jersey) Ltd. 18.8.52. To Hants & Sussex Aviation Ltd. Portsmouth 30.5.57. Cancelled as sold abroad 26.2.58. To Air Ivoire and delivered ex Portsmouth 19.2.59. Reg'd **F-OBGY** 6.5.58. To C. N. Para de Biscarosse reg'd **F-BJUZ** and CofA issued 22.3.62. Noted at La Ferte Gaucher .63. CofA expired 10.64 and withdrawn from use.

6912 Supplied to the Air Council with serial **NR848** but did not enter military service. Converted to civilian Rapide standard by de Havilland at Witney 9.8.45. SOC to A.A.J.C. and reg'd to Great Western and Southern Airlines Ltd., Speke as **G-AGUV** [CofR 9750 30.10.45]. CofA no.7263 issued 9.1.46. Handed over to B.E.A.C. on formation 1.2.47 and named *General Gordon*. Transferred to Gibraltar Airways Ltd. 13.1.53 and was operating scheduled services to Tangier later the same month. Sold to A. J. Whittemore (Aeradio) Ltd., Croydon 18.2.54 and converted to Mk4, test flown 31.3.54 To Iraq Petroleum Transport Co. Ltd., Haifa but operated by Airwork Ltd. 5.4.54. Burnt out in accident at Tarif, Bahrain 27.4.54 and cancelled from register 25.5.54.

6913 Supplied to the Air Council with military serial **NR849** but did not enter military service. Sold to Air Taxis Ltd., Barton. Reg'd **G-AGZO** [CofR 9866 26.1.46]. CofA no.7405 issued 11.2.46. Nominal ownership change to Air Taxis (Croydon) Ltd. 18.3.47. Another nominal change to Frederick Thomas Bingham t/a Air Taxis Ltd., Croydon 13.1.48. To Marshall's Flying School Ltd., Cambridge 31.7.48. Nominal change to Marshall Flying Services Ltd., Cambridge 9.4.52. Converted to Mk6 29.9.60 but subsequently listed as a Mk4 erroneously. In any event, de-converted 9.61. Sold abroad to France 24.5.62. To Ets. Rousseau Aviation as **F-BGZJ** with CofA issued 3.7.62. Visited Guernsey 12.7.62 but cancelled from French register 26.9.62. To R. van Risseghem, Antwerp reg'd **OO-ITI** [CofR 1436 5.10.62]. Destroyed Kolwezi, Congo by Saab J.23 fighters of the United Nations 29.12.62. Cancelled from register 28.7.64.

6914 Supplied to the Air Council with serial **NR850** but did not enter military service. Converted to civilian Rapide standard by de Havilland at Witney 16.8.45. Sold to The Aircraft Operating Co. of Africa Pty. 18.3.46 and reg'd **ZS-ATV** 12.4.46. U.K. CofA no.7540 issued 18.3.46. Forced landed Thysville Airfield, Leopoldville, Congo 5.6.51. On attempting to take-off again, the aircraft crashed and was destroyed by fire. Reg'n cancelled 26.10.51.

6915 Supplied to the Air Council with military serial **NR851** but did not enter military service. Converted to civilian Rapide standard by de Havilland at Witney 23.8.45. Sold to The Aircraft Operating Co. of Africa Pty. 23.3.46 and reg'd **ZS-ATW** 12.4.46.

U.K. CofA no.7539 issued 22.3.46. Caught fire during engine start up Beit Bridge landing ground, Southern Rhodesia 11.12.46.

6916 Supplied to the Air Council with serial **NR852** but did not enter military service. Converted to civilian Rapide standard by de Havilland at Witney 23.8.45. SOC to British American Air Services Ltd., Croydon reg'd **G-AGWC** [CofR 9780 13.12.45] and CofA no.7316 issued 21.1.46. To Air Transport Charter (C.I.) Ltd. and named *Saint Lawrence* 9.4.47. Taken over by the financial institution Lambert's Trust 27.10.50 and re-reg'd to them. To Aerocontacts Ltd., Gatwick 21.1.52. Sold abroad 9.7.52 and reg'n cancelled 1.9.52. To Crescent Air Transport Ltd., Karachi reg'd **AP-ADM**. Cancelled from register on CofA expiry 17.9.53.

6917 Supplied to the Air Council with serial **NR853** but did not enter military service. Converted to civilian Rapide standard by de Havilland at Witney 1.9.45. SOC on sale to Morton Air Services Ltd., Croydon reg'd **G-AGWR** [CofR 6794 8.12.45] and CofA no.7302 issued 25.1.46. Sold abroad 30.4.54. Reg'd **OY-DYA** to Zone Redningskorpset Flyvetjenesten (Danish Red Cross) 15.6.54. Sold abroad 21.4.56 and delivered to Europa Flyg, Stockholm-Brooma 25.4.56 reg'd **SE-CDI**. Whilst en route Malmo to Norrkoping 23.12.56, encountered a heavy snowstorm near Vimmerby and shortly after, the port engine began to run unevenly and eventually failed. Whilst trying to restart the engine, the starboard Gipsy Queen also faltered. The captain prepared for a forced landing but at the last moment, he noticed that the area for his intended landing was strewn with rocks and he therefore veered away and brought the stricken machine down in an area of birch trees! There were no casualties to the two crew and unusually in such circumstanes, the aircraft did not catch fire but was damaged beyond economical repair.

6918 Supplied to the Air Council with serial **RL936** but did not enter military service. Converted to civilian Rapide standard by de Havilland at Witney 1.9.45. SOC to Morton Air Services Ltd., Croydon reg'd **G-AGWP** [CofR 9793 8.12.45] and CofA no.7301 issued 18.1.46. Operated on behalf of Standard Vacuum Oil Co. in Karachi 1957 and damaged Talhal strip 16.12.57. To Aerocontacts (Aircraft Distributors) Ltd., Gatwick 22.6.60. Sold abroad 28.9.60 for operation in the Congo by The United Nations Organisation. Believed operated as **UN-71**. To Air Brousse SPRL, Leopoldville-Ndolo reg'd **OO-CJE** [CofR C324 15.11.60]. Re-reg'd **9O-CJE** when independence gained 1.1.60. To Cogeair .62? Later operated by A.M.A.Z., Kinshasa. Possibly re-reg'd **9Q-CJE** when prefix changed 8.9.62. Apparently nosed over Mweka in 1962, causing damage to nose and propellers. Fate unknown.

6919 Supplied to the Air Council with serial **RL937** but did not enter military service. Converted to civilian Rapide standard by de Havilland at Witney 6.9.45 and sold directly to Sweden. U.K. export CofA no.7358 issued 16.1.46 and reg'd to Svensk Flygtjanst AB (Swedish Air Services) at Stockholm-Bromma as **SE-APH** 25.2.46. To Fourschou AB, Vondeso 22.11.46. Destroyed in hangar fire at Bromma 9.4.47.

6920 Supplied to the Air Council with serial **RL938** but did not enter military service. Converted to civilian standard by de Havilland at Witney 4.10.45 and sold directly to Brazil. U.K. export CofA no.7396 issued 18.1.46. To Arco Iris Viacao Aerea and reg'd **PP-AIA** 1.46. To Adhemar de Barros Filho .51. To Erlindo Salzano 1.54. Written-off Coroata, Maranhao 10.5.56.

6921 Supplied to the Air Council with serial **RL939** but did not enter military service. Converted to civilian standard by de Havilland at Witney 4.10.45 and sold directly to Brazil. U.K. export CofA no.7410 issued 25.1.46. To Arco Iris Viacao Aerea and reg'd **PP-AID** 2.46. Believed to have crashed at Sao Paulo 11.12.46 and cancelled from the register 18.12.46.

6922 Supplied to the Air Council with serial **RL940** but did not enter military service. Converted to civilian Rapide standard by de Havilland at Witney 10.10.45 and sold directly to Brazil. U.K. export CofA no.7409 issued 25.1.46. To Arco Iris Viacao Aerea and reg'd **PP-AIB** 2.46. Written-off Fartura 24.12.46.

6923 Supplied to the Air Council with serial **RL941** but did not enter military service. Converted to civilian Rapide standard by de Havilland at Witney 4.10.45 and sold directly to Brazil. U.K. export CofA no.7411 issued 28.1.46. To Arco Iris Viacao Aerea and reg'd **PP-AIC** 2.46. To Adhemar de Barros Filho .51. Damaged beyond repair .52 and cancelled from register 11.5.53.

6924 Supplied to the Air Council with serial **RL942** but did not enter military service. Converted to civilian Rapide standard by de Havilland at Witney 25.10.45. U.K. export CofA no.7462 issued 14.2.46 and sold to de Havilland Aircraft of South Africa 17.3.46 for onward sale to Southern Rhodesia Air Services Ltd. Noted at Croydon early .46 as **VP-YDF**. Re-named Central African Airways Corporation 1.6.46. To Northern Rhodesia Aviation Services Ltd. reg'd **VP-RBU** .50. Restored as **VP-YDF** 10.50. To Fishair (Pvt.) Ltd. via Field Aircraft Services of Rhodesia Ltd. 1952. Broken up for spares use 1956.

6925 Supplied to the Air Council with serial **RL943** but did not enter military service. Converted to civilian Rapide standard by de Havilland at Witney 31.10.45. U.K. CofA no.7513 issued 20.2.46 and sold to de Havilland Aircraft of South Africa 17.3.46 for onward sale to Southern Rhodesia Air Services Ltd. Noted at Croydon early .46 as **VP-YDE**. Re-named Central African Airways Corporation 1.6.46. To Commercial Air Services Ltd., Johannesburg reg'd **ZS-BZV** 8.49. To Drakensberg Air Services (Pty) Ltd. .51. To Air Brousse SPRL, Brazzaville reg'd **OO-CJT** [CofR C268 27.10.56]. Crashed due to fuel starvation Kasa near Banzyville 5.10.60. (Note: 9Q-CJT appeared 6.63 but this is generally considered to be the former 9O-CJD c/n 6607. In any event, parts of c/n 6925 and VP-YOL c/n 6666 were used during the re-build of c/n 6607!).

6926 Supplied to the Air Council with serial **RL944** but did not enter military service. Converted to civilian Rapide standard by de Havilland at Witney 1.4.45, reportedly for Organizacao Mineira de Transportes Aereos, Brazil. However, SOC on sale to Lancashire Aircraft Corporation Ltd., Samlesbury. Reg'd **G-AHAG** [CofR 9882 31.1.46] and CofA no.7437 issued 18.2.46. To Universal Flying Services Ltd., Kidlington 17.10.46, but moved to Fairoaks 26.2.47. Merged into North Sea Aerial Transport Ltd. 31.10.49 and based Brough, East Yorkshire. To Hawker Aircraft Ltd., (Hawker Blackburn Division) Brough 6.12.63. Re-named Hawker Siddeley Aviation Leasing Ltd. 20.7.65. Later with Hawker at Dunsfold 5.7.65 as temporary replacement for Rapide G-AHGC, pending delivery of DH104 Dove G-ASMG. Intended to be burnt by Hawker Sports Club 5.11.65 but decision reversed. Instead, to Kenneth Bryan Neely, Blackbushe 5.4.66 and o/b by Scillonia Airways named *Bryher*. Neely apparently imprisoned in Kuwait and the assets of Scillonia/Scenic Flights were sold in his absence to pay off debts. Officially to Montague de Cartier, Compton Abbas 28.5.70 but reported as sold to D. Toms, Hayle for just £205! Noted Halfpenny Green inscribed "Thames Valley Airsports" 3.72. To Mike Ewart Revens Coghlan, Compton Abbas 1.2.73. CofA expired 15.7.73 and placed into storage near Ford Airfield from 11.74. Further storage at Mike Coghlan's home, Blandford Forum, Dorset by 7.77. To Ralph Jones t/a Southern Sailplanes, Membury 14.3.80. Nominal change to Pelham Ltd., Membury 2.3.00 and continues under slow rebuild.

6927 Supplied to the Air Council with serial **RL945** but did not enter military service. Converted to civilian Rapide standard by de Havilland at Witney 13.11.45 and sold directly to Brazil. U.K. export CofA no.7471 issued 18.2.46. To Organizacao Mineira de Transportes Aereos **PP-OMB** 2.46 but never actually entered on Brazilian register! Ultimate fate unknown.

6928 Supplied to the Air Council with serial **RL946** but did not enter military service. Converted to civilian Rapide standard by de Havilland at Witney 13.11.45. SOC on sale to de Havilland Canada 11.1.46 and probably shipped in kit form. To de Havilland Aircraft of Canada reg'd **CF-DIM** 9.8.46. Featured the extended fin. To G. H. Wheeler, Toronto ONT 4.51, though delivered earlier on 16.1.51. To Matane Air Services, Matane PQ 12.51. Caught fire whilst starting engines at Matane 19.6.53.

6929 First Mk.II variant and delivered to the Air Council with military serial **RL947**. Initially with 18MU 1.46. Issued to Com. Flt. Wyton 6.46. Returned to 18MU for storage 7.47. Sold to R. N. D. Miller, chief pilot for E. J. Connellan, Alice Springs NT 11.3.48 and export CofA issued 9.4.48. Reg'd **VH-BKR** 3.48 & delivered with c/n 6543. Nominal change to E. J. Connellan t/a Connellan Airways Ltd. 31.1.51. Re-reg'd **VH-CLH** 5.11.58. WFU 31.7.62 and broken up for spares use, Alice Springs.

6930 Supplied to the Air Council with military serial **RL948**. Delivered to 18MU 1.46. Served with 27Grp. Com. Flt. 6.46 coded TSO/C, Empire Radio School 9.47. Returned to 18MU for storage 2.48. SOC on sale to Arthur Wesley Coombs t/a Aeroways,

Croydon Airport. Reg'd **G-ALAX** [CofR 12383 27.5.48] and CofA no.10282 issued 16.10.48. To Autowork (Winchester) Ltd. 7.9.48. To Saunders-Roe Ltd., Cowes 10.6.49. To George Keith Tulloch, Perth 21.7.60. CofA expired 8.3.67 and rebuild being undertaken by McAlpine Aviation at Luton 9.67. Rebuild abandoned and cancelled as permanently withdrawn from use 7.12.67. Presented to The Shuttleworth Trust. Loaned to Midland Aircraft Preservation Society 1970/71. Acquired by the Durney Aeronautical Collection, Andover, Hampshire prior to 2.74 and has remained stored in the rear garden of a private house there ever since.

6931 Supplied to the Air Council with military serial **RL949**. Delivered to 18MU 1.46. Served with Com Flt Wyton 6.46 and returned to 18MU 9.47. SOC on sale to Russell Littledale Whyham t/a Air Navigation & Trading Co. Ltd., Squires Gate. Reg'd **G-AKSG** [CofR 12168 28.1.48] and CofA no.10146 issued 23.8.49. To Silver City Airways Ltd., Stansted 10.2.54. To V. H. Bellamy, Eastleigh 27.5.55. Converted to Mk4 and sold abroad 10.5.56. To Ste. Air-Ouest, Nantes reg'd **F-BHAF** and CofA issued 10.7.56. To S.G.A.A. 2.60. To Ste. Air Oasis .60. CofA suspended 3.62.

6932 Supplied to the Air Council with military serial **RL950**. Delivered to 18MU 1.46. Served with Handling Sqdn. Hullavington 7.46. At 18MU again 9.46 then to Staff College Booker 2.47 and returned 18MU 1.48. SOC on sale to Arthur Wesley Coombs t/a Aeroways, Croydon. Reg'd **G-ALAZ** [CofR 12386 21.5.48] but believed not taken up. U.K. export CofA no.10200 issued. To Autowork (Winchester) Ltd. 17.7.48 and sold abroad 27.7.48. To Air Congo reg'd **OO-CFI** [CofR C117 5.8.48]. Operated by SABENA 20.4.49 – 19.12.50. To Divisao de Exploracao dos Transportes Aereos do Angola (D.T.A.) reg'd **CR-LCK** 19.12.50 o/b Aero Club de Angola. Noted in open storage Luanda 1974/77.

6933 Supplied to the Air Council with military serial **RL951**. Initially at 18MU 2.46 and to King's Flight, R.A.F. Benson, Oxfordshire 7.46. Forced landed due fuel exhaustion "1 mile north of Mount Farm" 11.11.46. Deemed Cat.E and SOC 10.2.47.

6934 Supplied to the Air Council with serial **RL952** but did not enter military service. Converted to civilian Rapide standard by de Havilland at Witney 20.12.45. SOC on transfer to Ministry of Supply and Aircraft Production for British Overseas Airways Corporation 12.4.46. Reg'd **G-AHGH** [CofR 10031 2.5.46] and operated by Railway Air Services Ltd., Liverpool. CofA no.7525 issued 6.3.46. To British European Airways Corp. on formation 1.2.47. To Patrick-Duval Aviation Ltd., Birmingham 8.6.48. Name changed to Patrick Motors Ltd. 9.8.48. Sold abroad 10.6.53. To Svenska Aero AB, Stockholm-Bromma reg'd **SE-BXZ** 31.7.53. To Westlund Rosen & Gustavsson AB .55 (continued to be operated by Svenska Aero). Reg'n cancelled 13.12.65.

6935 Supplied to the Air Council with serial **RL953** but did not enter military service. Converted to civilian Rapide standard by de Havilland at Witney 1.1.46. SOC on transfer to Ministry of Supply and Aircraft Production for British Overseas Airways Corporation 12.4.46. Reg'd **G-AHGI** [CofR 10032 2.5.46] and operated by Railway Air Services Ltd., Liverpool. CofA no.7562 issued 18.3.46. To B.E.A.C. on formation 1.2.47. To Patrick-Duval Aviation Ltd., Birmingham 3.6.48. Name changed to Patrick Motors Ltd. 9.8.48. Sold abroad to French Indo-China 13.11.52. To Ste. Indochinoise des Plantations Reunies de Minot, Saigon reg'd **F-OANF** and CofA issued 30.5.53. To Cie Veha-Akat, Vientiane reg'd **F-LAAF** and CofA issued 27.9.56. Reported as destroyed 2.5.58 but actual details unknown.

6936 Supplied to the Air Council with serial **RL954** but did not enter military service. Converted to civilian Rapide standard by de Havilland at Witney 2.1.46. Reg'd **G-AGZJ** [CofR 9861 12.1.46] to British American Air Services Ltd., Croydon. CofA no.7463 issued 1.4.46. To Stanley Kenneth Davies c/o George Elliot & Co. Ltd but operated by Cambrian Air Services, Cardiff 23.6.47 and named *Carmarthen*. Nominal change to J. H. Watts, S. K. Davies, E. Keith-Davies & Care Lines Ltd. t/a Cambrian Air Services 13.4.49. CofA expired 30.6.50 and cancelled from register 3.9.50. Noted WFU at Cardiff 4.52.

6937 Supplied to the Air Council with serial **RL955** but did not enter military service. Converted to civilian Rapide standard by de Havilland at Witney 2.1.46. Reg'd **G-AGZK** [CofR 9862 12.1.46] to British American Air Services Ltd., Croydon. CofA no.7464 issued 21.3.46. To Iraq Petroleum Transport Co. Ltd., for operation in

Libya and Lebanon 30.10.47. Apparently withdrawn from use 13.12.51 and sold to Arab Airways, Amman for spares use. Reg'n cancelled 1.11.52. Destroyed in hangar fire Amman 9.5.53.

6938 Supplied to the Air Council with serial **RL956** but did not enter military service. Converted to civilian Rapide standard by de Havilland at Witney 2.1.46. Sold to de Havilland Canada and probably shipped in kit form. Marks **CF-DIN** allocated but not taken up. To Compania Anonima de Estudios y Construction Riego, Caracas reg'd **YV-P-BPE** and delivered 9.11.49. Forced landed and turned over in a swamp flooded to a depth of around 5 feet at Tucacas, approximately 100 miles west of Caracas 17.1.50.

6939 Supplied to the Air Council with military serial **RL957**. Initially at 18MU 1.46. To Wyton Com. Flt. 6.46. Engine faltered on take-off, swung, hit fence and nosed over Staverton, Gloucestershire 24.1.47. Deemed Cat.B 24.1.47 but re-categorised as Cat.E2 10.3.47.

6940 First flown 3.1.45 and supplied to the Air Council with military serial **RL958**. Initially to 18MU 2.46 and as subsequent service use is not documented, assumed stored until sale to Short Bros. & Harland Ltd., Rochester as **G-AKRP** [CofR 12152 27.1.48]. CofA no.9952 issued 14.2.48. Converted to Mk4 standard 1955. To Avionics Ltd., Croydon 20.6.57. Sold abroad to France 2.10.58 and reg'n cancelled 10.11.58. Allocated **F-DAFS** but not taken up. To Agricolavia, Rabat as **CN-TTO** 13.2.59. To Henri M. Carton, Tit-Mellil .63. To Para-Club du Maroc .69. WFU on CofA expiry 4.72 and noted hangared with wings detached Casablanca 11.75. Reportedly swapped by Frenchman Jean Salis for a Harvard engine 6.5.77. Then confused ownership by American nationals including Ray Jones until apparently abandoned Bremen docks .79. Rescued by Bob Wirth and stored. Purchased by Rex H. Ford t/a Fordaire Aviation .94 and restored to British register as **G-AKRP** 15.10.99. Protracted re-build initially at Little Gransden and latterly at Sywell making its post restoration first flight 6.4.00. Named *Northamptonshire Rose*.

6941 Supplied to the Air Council with military serial **RL959**. Initially to 18MU 2.46, then served with Staff College White Waltham 7.46, Reserves Command 10.46, Staff College Andover 3.48 and then to storage 5MU 10.48. SOC on sale to J. H. Watts & partners, Cardiff. Reg'd **G-ALRW** [CofR 12779 16.5.49] to Cambrian Air Services Ltd., Cardiff and CofA no.10624 issued 28.7.49. Aircraft named *Merionydd*. Nominal change to J. H. Watts & Partners t/a Cambrian Air Enterprises 7.7..50. Further nominal change back to Cambrian Air Services Ltd., Cardiff 25.1.52. To Patrick Motors Ltd., Birmingham 30.10.52. Cancelled on sale to France 25.9.53 via broker W. S. Shackleton Ltd. To Ste. Francaise de Radio-Electrique, Angers reg'd **F-BGXT** and French CofA issued at Le Bourget 3.10.53. To Air Ouest 5.56. To S.G.A.A. 2.60. To Air Saoura .61. To Rousseau Aviation, Dinard end .65. To Ste. Aeronautique de l'Est & operated for Mary & Cie, Strasbourg 1.67. To l'Aero Club de l'Aube, Troyes for para dropping early .68. To l'Aero Club Moselle Parachutisme, Doncourt-les-Conflans .69. CofA expired 10.70 and cancelled at the request of the club 6.3.72.

6942 Supplied to the Air Council with military serial **RL960**. Delivered to 18MU 2.46. Served with Staff College White Waltham 8.46 and Reserves Command 10.46 until returned to 18MU for storage 2.48. SOC on sale to Arthur Wesley Coombs t/a Aeroways, Croydon. Reg'd **G-ALAY** [CofR 12384 27.5.48] and CofA issued 29.7.48. To W. A. Rollason Ltd., Croydon 23.11.48. Sold abroad to South America 30.12.48 and reg'n cancelled 24.1.49. Imported to Argentina by Speddo & Paolini Ltda., Zonda, Reg'd **LV-AGX** and CofA issued 23.3.49. To Domingo Engaborde (or Erracaborde) reg'd **LV-FET** 5.10.51. Crashed 29.2.60 and reg'n cancelled 12.7.60.

6943 Supplied to the Air Council with military serial **RL961**. Initially to 18MU 2.46. To Technical Training Command Com. Flt. 3.47 coded "TWY/G" and believed operated by No.1 School of Photography, Wellesbourne Mountford. Returned to 18MU for storage 10.47. SOC on sale to Robert Alan, Croydon 2.2.49 but reg'd **G-ALGN** [CofR 12523 17.2.49] to Sqdn. Ldr. Kenneth James Nalson, Croydon. CofA no.A2705 issued 11.10.51. Sold to Aerocontacts Ltd., Gatwick 14.12.51. Sold abroad to Madagascar 28.1.52. To Air Madagascar & reg'd **F-OAKE** with CofA issued Ivato 5.2.52. Destroyed in landing accident Port Berge 17.2.53 and reg'n cancelled 10.12.53.

6944 Supplied to the Air Council with serial **RL962** but did not enter military service. To de Havilland at Witney for conversion to civilian standard 18.2.46. To Marshall's Flying School Ltd., Cambridge reg'd **G-AHED** [CofR 9977 27.2.46]. CoA no.7537 issued 25.4.46. Name changed to Marshall Flying Services Ltd. 4.52. Cvtd to Mk6 standard prior 21.7.60 but de-converted prior to 7.61! To Hunting Surveys Ltd., Leavesden 20.4.61. Nominal change to Hunting Surveys & Consultants Ltd., Leavesden 4.5.67. CofA expired 17.4.68 and cancelled as permanently withdrawn from use at Leavesden 3.3.69. Donated by Hunting to the R.A.F. Museum and roaded for storage at Henlow. Expected to move on to the R.A.F. Museum's Restoration and Storage Centre at Cardington, Bedfordshire for further storage around 8.75. Temporarily at the R.A.F. Museum's restoration centre at Wyton 7.00. More recently at the R.A.F. Museum's Michael Beetham Conservation Centre at Cosford and noted there 11.01.

6945 Supplied to the Air Council with serial **RL963** but did not enter military service. Civilianised to Rapide standard by de Havilland at Witney 18.2.46. Sold to Portsmouth Aviation Ltd. reg'd **G-AHEB** [CofR 9976 27.2.46] and CofA no.7535 issued 17.4.46. To Weston Air Services Ltd., reg'd **EI-ADP** 29.8.47. Irish CofA no.3D. Flown to Cambridge for overhaul by Marshall Flying Services 30.3.55 and restored as **G-AHEB** to John Bennett Peak & John Chapman, Cambridge 2.4.55. To Airlines (Jersey) Ltd. 25.11.55. Sold abroad to France 8.2.57 and reg'd **F-BHVQ** with CofA issued Toussus-le-Noble 16.2.57. To S.F.A.S.A. and initially operated by l'Aero Club Biscarosse for parachuting. To Centre Inter-Clubs, Avignon-Caumont, again for parachuting 2.7.59. Withdrawn from use at Avignon but permit issued for single flight to Castelnaudary 30.6.65 and subsequently broken up there.

6946 Supplied to the Air Council with military **RL964** but did not enter military service. Civilianised to Rapide standard by de Havilland at Witney 18.2.46. Sold to Lancashire Aircraft Corporation Ltd., Samlesbury and reg'd **G-AHEA** [CofR 9975 27.2.46]. CofA no.7536 issued 12.4.46. Official records state "aircraft in long term storage"; reg'n lapsed 9.11.50 but restored 3.2.51. To R. A. Peacock (Aviation) Ltd., Croydon 31.3.54. To A. J. Whittemore (Aeradio) Ltd., Croydon 18.11.2.54. Sold abroad 22.1.55. To Service de l'Aviation Legere et Sportive reg'd **F-BHCF** and CofA issued Toussus-le-Noble 1.3.55. Based nominally at St. Cyr, but actually operated for parachuting at Chalons-sur-Saone. CofA suspended at Castelnaudary 19.10.64 and broken up.

6947 Supplied to the Air Council with serial **RL965** but did not enter military service. Civilianised to Rapide standard by de Havilland at Witney 18.1.46. U.K. CofA no.7625 issued 12.4.46. To Air Services of India Ltd., Bombay, reg'd **VT-AVW** and named *Gagenratna* 9.3.46. Was awaiting delivery Hatfield 5.46. Fate unknown but not listed within the Air Services India fleet 10.'48.

6948 Supplied to the Air Council with serial **RL966** but did not enter military service. Civilianised to Rapide standard by de Havilland at Witney 18.1.46. Sold to Morton Air Services Ltd., Croydon reg'd **G-AHIA** [CofR 10074 8.4.46] and CofA no.7606 issued 8.4.46. To Skyways Ltd., Langley 27.2.50. Taxied into excavations and damaged beyond repair at Maritsa on the Island of Rhodes 5.3.51. Reg'n cancelled as destroyed 11.6.51.

6949 Supplied to the Air Council with military serial **RL967**. Delivered 18MU 3.46. Served briefly with 26Grp. Com. Flt. from 3.47 but returned to storage at 18MU 7.47. SOC on sale to Olley Air Service Ltd., Croydon. Reg'd **G-AKSD** [CofR 12165 27.1.48] and CofA no.9971 issued 26.11.48. To Windmill Theatre Transport Co. Ltd. 24.11.48 and named *Windmill Girl*. Severely damaged Malaga when blown into a tractor during a gale 21.12.58. Repairs carried out locally. To Hants & Sussex Aviation Ltd., Portsmouth 7.3.60. Leased to Hunting Surveys during summer 1961. Sold abroad to France 24.8.61 and departed Portsmouth on delivery 15.9.61. To Ste. Ardic, Dakar reg'd **F-OBVI**. Over-ran runway and hit trees Podor, Senegal 17.9.62. Damaged beyond repair and CofA subsequently cancelled.

6950 Supplied to the Air Council with military serial **RL968**. Delivered to 18MU 3.46. Was in service Sperry Gyroscope, Hanworth 3.47 but returned to 18MU 7.47. SOC to Short Brothers & Harland Ltd., Rochester. Reg'd as **G-AKRR** [CofR 12153 27.1.48] and CofA no.9953 issued 25.2.48. To George Charles Heighington, London SW13 9.4.52. Sold abroad to Sudan 8.11.52 for Varoujan Vanian and reg'n **SN-ABB** reserved 14.5.52. Sale not completed and restored to Heighington 16.9.52. Cancelled

DH89 c/n 6967. Purchased at a knock down price by Fairey Aviation in April 1946, G-AHJS remained in service with them for a further four years after the take-over by Westland Aircraft in June 1961.

The first DH89A c/n 6342. de Havilland flew the prototype DH89A in November 1936 using test marks E.4 which were also worn by the DH89 prototype c/n 6250 for its first flight in April 1934.

DH89 c/n W.1001. The penultimate DH89A, built up from parts by de Havilland at Witney, G-AJGS was registered October 1947, certified in March 1948 and then stored at Aberdeen just a year later.

DH89A c/ns 6348 and 6349. Delivered to the Lithuanian Air Force in April 1937. They wore serials 701 and 702 but painted in a dark colour on a dark ground, they are almost indiscernible.

DH89 c/n W.1001. After 17 years in store, G-AJGS was moved by road to Booker for restoration. With dispensation to wear G-ACZE, this low houred example is currently stored at Haverfordwest.

An unidentified Dominie fuselage displayed at an employee families' day at Loughborough during the war. Alongside are other exhibits showing the Brush concern's contribution to the war effort.

DH89 c/n W.1002. In the last quarter of 1947, de Havilland built up a second example at Witney. G-AKJS was broken up by a French company 1965 and parts used in replicas built for the Blue Max film.

The authors could never understand the sense of exiting a serviceable aeroplane! However, the sport appeals to many and at Netheravon, G-AIDL, G-AGTM and G-AJHO await their next jumpers.

again to Sudan 8.11.52 but instead to Kassa Manu of Export & Supply Co. Ltd., Diredawa reg'd **ET-P-16** 18.11.52. Destroyed by fire during refuelling at Diredawa 3.9.53.

6951 Supplied to the Air Council with serial **RL980** but did not enter military service. Delivered to 18MU 3.46 but apparently did not enter service. SOC on sale to Olley Air Service Ltd., Croydon. Reg'd **G-AKSB** [CofR 12163 27.1.48] and CofA no.9969 issued 14.2.48. To R. T. Briscoe Ltd., Sekondi, Gold Coast 14.10.49. Cancelled from British register 8.2.50 and entered on Gold Coast register as **VP-AAA** with the same owner 17.2.50. To J. J. Martins, Sekondi late .52. Eventual fate unknown.

6952 Supplied to the Air Council with serial **RL981**. At 18MU 3.46 but did not enter military service. To John Dade, Bickley, Kent & reg'd **G-AKRS** [CofR 12154 27.1.48]. CofA no.9972 issued 9.4.48. Apparently used by the founding father and first Prime minister of the State of Israel, David Ben-Gurion, during the formation of Israel during the summer of 1948. To Air Enterprises Ltd., Croydon 1.2.49. To Airwork Ltd., Croydon 13.4.53. To Walter Westoby t.a Westair flying Services, Squires Gate 13.5.60. Leased to Bournemouth Air Taxi Ltd. t/a Bournair 23.5.62 and purchased by them 26.9.63. To Piper Products (Poole) Ltd., Bournemouth 16.1.64. To Tippers Air Transport Ltd., Baginton 5.10.64. To broker Shackleton Aviation Ltd. 2.9.65. To Bernard Wilfred Homnan, Middleton St. George 23.5.66. To Trent Valley Aviation Ltd., Castle Donington 15.10.68. After failure of Trent Valley, flown to Swanton Morley, Norfolk 23.7.70 and then to Shipdham for overhaul. To Robert Vincent Snook & Nigel C. L. Wright t/a Toftwood Aviation for operation by Arrow Air Services, Shipdham 24.11.70. Still dismantled Shipdham 4.75 and in 5.77, reportedly owned by Rob Lamplough. Presented to Israel for their Air Force Museum with Lamplough receiving a P.51 in exchange as part of the deal. Air tested after re-build 28.4.78 and flown to Israel, arriving Tel Aviv 20.5.78 marked **4X-970**. Re-painted as **"002"** a few days later. Flown by the IDFAF's Historical Sqdn. Now exhibited in the Isrtaeli Air Force Museum

6953 Supplied to the Air Council with serial **RL982** but did not enter military service. Converted to civilian Rapide standard by de Havilland at Witney 21.2.46. U.K. CofA no.7724 issued 1.5.46. Sold to Air Services of India Ltd., Bombay reg'd **VT-AVX** and named *Gaganraj*. Badly damaged when hangar collapsed Bombay-Juhu during a cyclone 21.11.48. Reported as sold to France or French Colonies 1950. (This could possibly be the aircraft that became **F-52** with Compagnie Laotienne et de Transport of Hanoi, which suffered an engine failure, crashed and caught fire at Nghia Lo, 150 miles north-west of Hanoi on 15.8.51).

6954 Supplied to the Air Council with serial **RL983** but did not enter military service. Converted to civilian Rapide standard by de Havilland at Witney 21.2.46. U.K. CofA no.7723 issued 1.5.46. Sold to Arab Air Association 29.5.46 and operated for Arab Airways Ltd. reg'd **TJ-AAA**. Named *Yarmouk* and delivered ex Croydon 6.9.46. Withdrawn from use Amman and destroyed by fire inside a hangar 9.5.53.

6955 Supplied to the Air Council with serial **RL984** but did not enter military service. Converted to civilian Rapide standard by de Havilland at Witney 21.2.46. U.K. CofA no.7775 issued 8.5.46. Sold to Arab Air Association 30.5.46 and operated for Arab Airways Ltd. reg'd **TJ-AAB**. Named *El Ordan* and delivered ex Croydon 6.9.46. To Arab Legion Air Force and probably the Rapide serialled **R-300** 1950. Crashed Jerusalem 1956.

6956 Supplied to the Air Council with serial **RL985** but did not enter military service. Converted to civilian Rapide standard by de Havilland at Witney 14.3.46. U.K. CofA no.7799 issued 23.5.46. Sold to Zone Redningskorpset Flyvetjenesten (Danish Red Cross) 24.4.46 and used as an air ambulance, reg'd **OY-DZY** 28.6.46. Inscribed "Luftreisedienst Niedersachsen" in 1954. Stalled and crashed into Copenhagen Sound shortly after take-off from Copenhagen-Kastrup in torrential rain 16.7.60. All 8 occupants were killed.

6957 Supplied to the Air Council with serial **RL986** but did not enter military service. Converted to civilian Rapide standard by de Havilland at Witney 14.3.46. U.K. CofA no.7769 issued 8.5.46. Sold to Air Services of India Ltd., Bombay reg'd **VT-AXG** named *Gagenrup*. Badly damaged when hangar collapsed Bombay-Juhu during a cyclone 21.11.48. Sold to Compagnie de Transports Aeriens Autrex, Hanoi reg'd **F-OAHL** and named *Nam Dinh* 1950.

CofA issued 19.1.51. Badly damaged and declared a total loss at Quangtur 26.4.54 and reg'n cancelled 1.6.54.

6958 Supplied to the Air Council with serial **TX300** but did not enter military service. SOC to de Havilland and civilianised to Rapide standard at Witney. Export CofA no.7835 issued 15.5.46. To Arab Air Association, in an overall orange scheme and operated for Arab Airways Ltd. as **TJ-AAC**. Named *Balka* and delivered ex Croydon 6.9.46. To Arab Legion Air Force with serial **R301** around 1951. Understood to have been withdrawn from use 1956 due to condition and lack of spares.

6959 Supplied to the Air Council with military serial **TX301** but believed not to have entered service. SOC to de Havilland and civilianised to Rapide standard at Witney. Export CofA no.7836 issued 23.5.46. To Arab Air Association in overall orange scheme and operated for Arab Airways Ltd. as **TJ-AAD**. Named *Raghadan* and delivered ex Croydon 6.9.46 To Arab Contracting and Trading Co. Ltd. reg'd **TJ-ACE** 16.6.52. Re-reg'd **JY-ACE** 4.54. Still with Contracting and Trading, re-reg'd **JY-ACG** by 10.61 and reported on a visit to Nicosia, Cyprus 17.5.62. Reg'd **G-ASRJ** [CofR R7058 25.3.64] to Edward Arthur James Gardener, trustee of the assets of the Parachute Regiment Free Fall Club, Netheravon. Arrived Gatwick 10.4.64. Nominal change to Thomas Leask, trustee of the assets of the Army Parachute Association 19.11.64. Further nominal change when transferred to Ian Thomas Candelent Wilson, trustee of the assets of the Rhine Army Parachute Association and named *Rheingold* 4.65. Yet a further change of trustee when to Capt. David Charles Parker, 4.3.69. Wood rot was discovered and deemed beyond economical repair at Netheravon 2.70 and officially WFU 27.3.70. However, Air-Britain reported that a rebuild was intended by 655 Aviation Sqdn. Army Air Corps at Detmold, Germany, but the aircraft was noted still in stripped down condition at Netheravon 31.7.71. Some parts now with the Durney Aeronautical Collection at Andover.

6960 Supplied to the Air Council with serial **TX302** but did not enter military service. To de Havilland and civilianised to Rapide standard at Witney. No U.K. reg'n applied for but export CofA no.7837 issued 23.5.46. To O.M.T.A. reg'd **PP-OMC**. Written-off Araguari, Minas Gerais 4.2.47.

6961 Supplied to the Air Council with serial **TX303** but did not enter military service. Instead, SOC 22.3.46 to de Havilland and civilianised to Rapide standard at Witney. Export CofA no.8016 issued 14.6.46. To Arab Air Association, delivered via Croydon 6.9.46 in overall orange scheme and operated for Arab Airways Ltd. as **TJ-AAE**, named *Moab* and later *Yarmouk*. To Arab Contracting and Trading Co. Ltd. and re-reg'd **JY-AAE** 30.8.54. Returned to U.K. reg'd **G-ASRM** [CofR R4070 26.3.64] for Aerocontacts (Aircraft Distributors) Ltd., Gatwick. Cancelled on sale to Dr. Gorecki, Leopoldville, Congo 27.7.64. Operated by Soc. Colimpexe in the Belgian Congo, believed as **9Q-CPF** but see below. When being operated by Air Brousse SPRL, struck a building on take-off N'dolo 9.12.66 and damaged beyond repair. (Note: The construction numbers for Zaire reg'd Rapides 9Q-CPF/CQF/CQT/CYE are not confirmed).

6962 Supplied to the Air Council with serial **TX304** but did not enter military service. SOC 6.7.46 to Airwork Ltd., Croydon and civilianised to Rapide standard by de Havilland at Witney. Reg'd **G-AHTS** [CofR 10338 3.6.46] to Anglo-Iranian Oil Co. Ltd., Abadan. CofA no.7859 issued 22.6.46. Overshot runway at unknown location in the Middle East and written-off 29.4.47. Reg'n cancelled 29.1.48.

6963 Supplied to the Air Council with serial **TX305** but did not enter military service. To de Havilland and civilianised to Rapide standard at Witney. Reg'd **G-AHPU** [CofR 10266 25.6.46] to Hunting Air Travel Ltd., Luton and CofA no.7957 issued 29.6.46. To John Eric Steel t/a Steel and Co. Ltd., Sunderland 28.7.49. To Luton Flying Club Ltd. 3.4.57. To Vivian. H. Bellamy, Eastleigh 1.7.57. Converted to Mk4 standard during 1958. Sold abroad to "Nigeria" 5.3.58. To Sierra Leone Airways reg'd **VR-LAD** named *Loma* and delivered ex Eastleigh 26.5.58. Reportedly all three Sierra Leone Airways Rapides (also see c/ns 6603 and 6827) were eventually burnt at Hastings Airfield, Freetown.

6964 Supplied to the Air Council with serial **TX306** but did not enter military service. To de Havilland and civilianised to Rapide standard at Witney. Reg'd to Anglo-Iranian Oil Co. Ltd., Abadan as **G-AHTR** [CofR 10337 3.6.46] and CofA no.7858 issued 4.7.46. Burnt out at Abadan 10.7.50 and reg'n cancelled 31.7.50.

6965 Supplied to the Air Council with serial **TX307** but did not enter military service. To de Havilland and civilianised to Rapide standard at Witney. Reg'd **G-AHWF** [CofR 10401 25.6.46] to Hunting Air Travel Ltd., Luton. CofA no.7958 issued 4.7.46. To Iraq Petroleum Transport Co. Ltd. 7.3.49. To Anglo-Iranian Oil Co. Ltd., Abadan 10.11.50. Seized by the Iranian authorities and reg'd to National Oil Co. as **EP-AAW** 10.51. Eventual fate unknown.

6966 Supplied to the Air Council with serial **TX308** but did not enter military service. To de Havilland and civilianised to Rapide standard at Witney. Reg'd **G-AHTT** [CofR 10339 3.6.46] to Anglo-Iranian Oil Co. Ltd., Abadan. CofA no.7860 issued 18.7.46. Seized by the Iranian authorities and reg'd to National Oil Co. as **EP-AAX** 10.51. Somewhat belatedly, cancelled to Iran 29.10.54. Eventual fate unknown.

6967 Supplied to the Air Council with serial **TX309** but did not enter military service. To de Havilland and civilianised to Rapide standard at Witney. To Fairey Aviation Co. Ltd. reg'd **G-AHJS** [CofR 10115 16.4.46]. CofA no.7725 issued 18.7.46. Nominal change to Fairey Aviation Ltd., Hayes 25.6.59. Further change to Westland Aircraft Ltd. (Fairey Aviation Division) 20.6.61. To Hantsair Ltd., Eastleigh 11.1.65. To Robin Air Ltd., London WC1 22.6.65. To Three Counties Aero Club, Blackbushe and WFU there 5.66. Possibly to East Midlands by road for spares use and reg'n finally cancelled as permanently withdrawn from use 13.7.73.

6968 Supplied to the Air Council with serial **TX310** but did not enter military service. To de Havilland and civilianised to Rapide standard at Witney. To Eric Leslie Gandar Dower t/a Allied Airways (Gandar Dower) Ltd. reg'd **G-AIDL** 23.8.46 and CofA no.8252 issued 5.9.46. Used extensively by Gandar Dower as his personal aircraft and fitted with carpet, cabin heating and a toilet, named *The Wanderer*. Absorbed into British Europeran Airways Corp. fleet on formation 1.2.47 but placed into storage at Aberdeen. Purchased at auction after seizure via a court order, by Goodhew Aviation Co. Ltd., Kidlington 27.4.50. To W. S. Shackleton Ltd. 12.10.50. To E. S. Fox of Fox's Glacier Mints Ltd., Leicester as company transport 25.10.50. Converted to Mk6 1959. To A. J. Flatley, Ringway 11.12.61. To Midland Metal Spinning Co. Ltd., Wolverhampton 11.4.62. To G. C. Stacey of The Army Parachute Association 17.3.67. To Capt. Mike Hood t/a Southern Joyrides Ltd., Biggin Hill 13.6.77 and operated joy rides ex Biggin mid week and at Sandown, Isle of Wight at weekends. Struck on the ground by an Ercoupe aircraft, which went out of control 7.7.79 but repaired. To Snowdon Mountain Aviation Ltd., Caernarfon 11.3.87, operating as Air Caernarfon from 1.4.92. To Atlantic Air Transport Ltd., Coventry 26.5.95 and continues in operation with their Historic Flight.

6969 Supplied to the Air Council with serial **TX311** but did not enter military service. Instead, SOC to de Havilland 15.4.46 and converted to civilian Rapide standard at Witney. Export CofA no.8641 issued 24.10.46. To South West Air Transport (pty) Ltd. as **ZS-AXS**. To Suidair International Airways Ltd. 12.49. To A. Shaban, Germiston .51. Sold abroad 30.8.51. To Igusi (Rhodesia) Ltd. reg'd **VP-YIU**. To H. D. Hooper .53. To The Corner House (Pvt.) Ltd. .54. To Jorge Candido Guerva, Beira reg'd **CR-AEQ** 15.2.55. Operated by Taxi Aereo de Mocambique (TAM) and noted, possibly abandoned, at Beira 9.59.

6970 Supplied to the Air Council with military serial **TX312** but did not enter service. Instead, SOC 7.5.46 to de Havilland and civilianised to Rapide standard at Witney. Export CofA no.8588 issued 10.10.46. To Arco-Iris Viacao Aereo SA reg'd **PP-AIE**. Crashed Ararangua, Santa Catarina region 31.10.48 and cancelled from the register 11.2.49.

6971 Supplied to the Air Council with serial **TX313** but did not enter military service. Instead, SOC 7.5.46 to de Havilland and civilianised to Rapide standard at Witney. Export CofA no.8589 issued 10.10.46. To Arco-Iris Viacao Aereo SA reg'd **PP-AIF**. To Adhemar de Barros Filho .51. Dbr 13.6.52 and cancelled from register 13.6.52.

6972 Supplied to the Air Council with serial **TX314** but did not enter military service. Instead, SOC 20.5.46 to de Havilland and civilianised to Rapide standard at Witney. Export CofA no.8621

issued 15.10.46. To Arco-Iris Viacao Aereo SA reg'd **PP-AIG**. Brazilian CofA expired 20.3.49. Fate unknown.

6973 Supplied to the Air Council with serial **TX315** but did not enter military service. Instead, SOC 20.5.46 to de Havilland and civilianised to Rapide standard at Witney. Export CofA no.8590 issued 10.10.46. Sold abroad to Peru as **OB-RAA-156** and operated by Transportes Aereos Militares, Grupo de Transportes No.42. Fate unknown.

6974 Supplied to the Air Council with serial **TX316** but did not enter military service. Instead, SOC 28.5.46 to de Havilland and civilianised to Rapide standard at Witney. Export CofA no.8591 issued 10.10.46. Sold abroad to Peru as **OB-RAB-157** and operated by Transportes Aereos Militares, Grupo de Transportes No.42. Fate unknown.

6975 Supplied to the Air Council with serial **TX317** but did not enter military service. Instead, SOC 14.6.46 to de Havilland and civilianised to Rapide standard at Witney. Export CofA no.8656 issued 24.10.46. Sold abroad to Peru as **OB-RAC-158** and operated by Transportes Aereos Militares, Grupo de Transportes No.42. Fate unknown.

6976 Supplied to the Air Council with military serial **TX318** but did not enter service. Instead, SOC 19.6.46 to de Havilland and civilianised to Rapide standard at Witney. Export CofA no.8657 issued 29.10.46. Sold abroad to Peru as **OB-RAD-159** and operated by Transportes Aereos Militares, Grupo de Transportes No.42. Fate unknown.

6977 Supplied to the Air Council with serial **TX319** but did not enter military service. Instead, SOC 2.7.46 to de Havilland and civilianised to Rapide standard at Witney. Export CofA no.8716 issued 5.11.46. To Peru as **OB-RAE-160** and operated by Transportes Aereos Militares, Grupo de Transportes No.42. Fate unknown.

6978 Purchased by the Air Council and allocated R.A.F. serial **TX320**, but order cancelled. Not built.

6979 Purchased by the Air Council and allocated R.A.F. serial **TX326**, but order cancelled. Not built.

6980 Purchased by the Air Council and allocated R.A.F. serial **TX327**, but order cancelled. Not built.

6981 Purchased by the Air Council and allocated R.A.F. serial **TX328**, but order cancelled. Not built.

6982 Purchased by the Air Council and allocated R.A.F. serial **TX329**, but order cancelled. Not built.

6983 Purchased by the Air Council and allocated R.A.F. serial **TX330**, but order cancelled. Not built.

6984 Purchased by the Air Council and allocated R.A.F. serial **TX331**, but order cancelled. Not built.

6985 Purchased by the Air Council and allocated R.A.F. serial **TX337**, but order cancelled. Not built.

6986 Purchased by the Air Council and allocated R.A.F. serial **TX338**, but order cancelled. Not built.

6987 Purchased by the Air Council and allocated R.A.F. serial **TX339**, but order cancelled. Not built.

6988 Purchased by the Air Council and allocated R.A.F. serial **TX361**, but order cancelled. Not built.

As described in the Brush Coachworks chapter, the following Dragon Rapide fuselage, is believed to have been built as a trial run, prior to them being awarded substantial contracts for series production of the type.

89232   Brush Coachworks Ltd. build number as no de Havilland DH89 construction number issued. Fuselage only built 11.41 and supplied to Canada. To Maritime Central Airways reg'd **CF-BNJ** 2.6.42. To Spartan Air Services Ltd., Ottawa 30.4.52 and used for survey work. Withdrawn from use sometime prior to CofA expiry 20.8.55. To S. Banville, Quebec City PQ. Apparently abandoned, the wreck was destroyed by fire after a woman set light to it, to stop children using it as a plaything and possibly hurting themselves!

At what was the de Havilland Repair Unit at Witney in Oxfordshire, two new aircraft were built up in 1947 using some new parts held in stock to repair damaged aircraft during the war years. In the case of the first aircraft, parts of the damaged c/n 6264 were also used in its construction.

W.1001   Built by de Havilland from parts at their Witney airfield and included substantial portions of c/n 6264 (q.v.). To de Havilland Aircraft Co. Ltd., Hatfield reg'd **G-AJGS** [CofR 11282 24.10.47]. CofA no.10004 issued 12.3.48. To Mrs. Mary Louisa Wilson, Aberdeen 23.2.48. To Miss Caroline Brunning, Aberdeen 19.12.49. Operated by Allied Airways (Gandar Dower) Ltd., Aberdeen and named *The Vagabond*. Withdrawn from use after CofA expiry 3.49 and stored at Dyce. Conveyed to Booker by road 8.66 and re-assembled by Personal Plane Services Ltd. by 1.67. To Alfred Free Ward 30.5.67.

To Aerial Enterprises Ltd., Booker 25.3.68. To Fred Ludington, Delray Beach, Florida, U.S.A. and departed Halfpenny Green on its delivery flight 28.8.70. Cancelled from U.K. register as permanently withdrawn from use 15.11.73. Acquired by Bob Schulz and flown to Hamburg Airport, near Buffalo, New York late 1976/early 1977. He intended to re-cover the aircraft during the winter of 77/78, paint it in British European Airways colours and operate joy flights over Niagara Falls. The plan did not come to fruition and a United States was not issued. Eventually sold to Brian A. Woodford t/a Wessex Aviation & Transport Ltd., Chalmington 1984. Woodford had the aircraft painted in Edward, Prince of Wales colours and obtained special dispensation for the aircraft to wear the original reg'n of the parts aircraft c/n 6264. Reg'd **G-ACZE** [CofR dated 23.1.85]. Stored Henstridge, Somerset following CofA expiry 8.95 and subsequently moved to Haverfordwest, Pembrokeshire.

W.1002   Built by de Havilland from surplus parts at their Witney airfield and first flown using test reg'n **E.0228**. To Fairey Aviation Co. Ltd., Hayes reg'd **G-AKJS** [CofR 11990 3.11.47]. CofA no.9863 issued 2.12.47. Converted to Mk6 during 1959. To Airwork Services Ltd., Bournemouth 21.9.59. To Reginald James Gates t/a Federated Fruit Co., Speke 26.7.62. To Harold Best-Devereux 13.5.65 (Air Britain reported that Federated received an Aero Commander aircraft in part-exchange), although delivered to his base at Panshanger much earlier on 3.11.64. Sold to France 21.6.65. To Rousseau Aviation, Dinard 8.65 and parts used in the building of Fokker D.VII replica aircraft used in "The Blue Max" film. Some parts may also have been used during the rebuild of 6V-AAC c/n 6470.

Readers should note that civil registrations/military serials that cannot be definitely connected to a construction number, have been allocated a note number. Fuller details may be found in chapter 5.6. Registrations in parenthesis denote "not taken up". A few aircraft have a digit after the registration, denoting a subsequent use of the same marks for a different airframe.

ADEN

VR-AAL	6700
VR-AAP	6803

ANGOLA

CR-LAT	6453
CR-LAU	6452
CR-LAV	6451
CR-LAX	See 2
CR-LBG	6847
CR-LBH	6846
CR-LBN	6904
CR-LBO	6905
CR-LCK	6932
CR-LCO	6430
CR-LKR	6900
CR-LKS	6901

ARGENTINA

LV-AEN	6864
LV-AEO	6789
LV-AEP	6892
LV-AER	6609
LV-AES	6822
LV-AGR	6581
LV-AGV	6399
LV-AGW	6843
LV-AGX	6942
LV-AGY	6550
LV-FEP	6550
LV-FET	6942
LV-FFO	6864

AUSTRALIA - CIVILIAN

VH-AAG	6668
VH-ABN	6253
VH-ADE	6341
VH-AHI	6633
VH-AIK	6497
(VH-ATU)	6713
VH-AWG	6903
VH-BFS	6886
VH-BGP	6648
VH-BIF	6903
VH-BKM	6543
VH-BKR	6929
VH-CBU	6530
VH-CFA [1]	6814
VH-CFA [2]	6713
VH-CLH	6929
VH-ECW	6530
VH-IAN	6655
VH-UFF	6270
VH-UUO	6259
VH-UTV	6655
VH-UVG	6314
VH-UVI	6318
VH-UVS	6265
VH-UVT	6319
VH-UXT	6346
VH-UXZ(1)	6365
VH-UXZ(2)	6801
VH-UZY	6384

AUSTRALIA - MILITARY

A3-1	6270
A3-2	6314
A33-1	6259
A33-2	6318
A33-3	6270
A33-4	6346
A33-5	6253
A33-6	6384
A33-7	6341

AUSTRIA

OE-FAA	6690

BELGIUM - CIVILIAN

OO-AFG	6458
OO-APO	6273
OO-ARI	6787
OO-ARN	6785
OO-CNP	6458
OO-DCB	6758
OO-ITI	6913
OO-JFN	6273
OO-	6417

BELGIUM - MILITARY

D1	6881
D2	6745
D3	6739
D4	6785
D5	6787
D6	6852
D7	6853

BELGIAN CONGO

OO-CCD	6442
(OO-CDE)	6520
(OO-CDF)	6756
OO-CFI	6932
OO-CJD	6607
OO-CJE	6918
OO-CJS	6429
OO-CJT	6925
OO-CJU	6380
OO-CJW	6508
OO-CJX	6658
OO-CMS	6902
OO-CRS	6559

BRAZIL

PP-AIA	6920
PP-AIB	6922
PP-AIC	6923
PP-AID	6921
PP-AIE	6970
PP-AIF	6971
PP-AIG	6972
PP-DPH	6807
PP-LAA	6449
PP-OMA	6449
PP-OMB	6927
PP-OMC	6960
PP-OMD	6774
PP-VAN [1]	6449
PP-VAN [2]	6900

CAMEROONS

TJ-ABJ	6749
TJ-ABM	6600
TJ-ABP	6887
TJ-ACE	6959

CANADA

CF-AEO	6279
CF-AVJ	6295
CF-AYE	6304
CF-BBC	6307
CF-BBG	6354
CF-BBH	6370
CF-BFL	6373
CF-BFM	6371
CF-BFP	6374
CF-BND	6375
CF-BNE	6376
CF-BNG	6472
CF-BNJ	89232
CF-DIM	6928
(CF-DIN)	6938
CF-PTK	6254
C-FAYE	6796
C-GXFJ	6796

CAPE VERDE ISLANDS

CR-CAA	6905

CEYLON (Also see 4R-)

CY-AAI	6736
CY-AAK	6894

CHILE

CC-CIC-0034	See 1
CC-???	6468
CC-???	6820

CHINA (NATIONALIST)

?	6385
?	6388
?	6389
?	6390
?	6391
?	6392
38	6444
43	See 19

DENMARK

OY-AAO	6775
OY-ACV	6467
OY-ACZ	6888
OY-DAS	6347
OY-DIN	6272
OY-DYA	6917
OY-DZY	6956
(OY-...)	6401

EGYPT

SU-ABP	6298
SU-ABQ	6299
SU-ABR	6302
SU-ABS	6303
SU-ABU	6313
SU-ACS [1]	6641*
SU-ACS [2]	6544
SU-ACT [1]	6642*
SU-ACT [2]	6551

*Registration order uncertain

ETHIOPIA

ET-P-16	6950
ET-P-22	6700

FIJI

VQ-FAL	6707
VQ-FAM	6471
VQ-FAN	6577
VQ-FAZ	6886

FINLAND

OH-BLA	6347
OH-BLB	6401
OH-DHA	6347
OH-DHB	6401
OH-VKH	6347
OH-VKI	6401

FRANCE - CIVILIAN

(F-APES)	6309
F-AQIL	6382
F-AQIM	6383
F-AQIN	6393
F-AQJH	6395
F-AQJI	6396
F-AQOH	6403
F-AQOI	6407
F-ARII	6420
F-ARIJ	6424
F-ARIK	6425
F-ARIL	6427
F-ARIM	6428
F-AZCA	6541
F-BAHX	6547
F-BAHY	6276
F-BAHZ	6522
'F-BCBD'	6897
F-BCDB	6897
F-BDJX	6769
F-BEDI	6516
F-BEDX	6547
F-BEDY	6276
F-BEDZ	6522
F-BEFU	6555
F-BEKB	6596
F-BEPE	6845
F-BFEH	6723
F-BFPU	6796
F-BFVM	6791
F-BFVR	6563
F-BGIS	6608
F-BGOL	6559
F-BGON	6541
F-BGOQ	6754
F-BGPG	6729
F-BGPH	6845
F-BGPI	6635
F-BGPJ	6703
F-BGPK	6474
F-BGPL	6865
F-BGPM	6476
F-BGXH	6582
F-BGXT	6941
F-BGZJ	6913
F-BHAF	6931
F-BHCD	6706
F-BHCE	6851
F-BHCF	6946
F-BHDY	6753
F-BHFM	6575
F-BHGR	6844
F-BHOB	6578
F-BHTH	6714
F-BHVQ	6945
F-BJUY	6367
F-BJUZ	6911
F-BLHE	6870
F-BLHZ	6709
F-BLXX	6907
(F-BOHL)	6470

FRANCE - MILITARY

"6663"	6663
"6669"	6669
"6671"	6671
"6674"	6674
"6684"	6684
"6705"	6705
"6731"	6731

FRENCH OVERSEAS – AFRICA

F-OABH	6606
F-OADX	6547
F-OADY	6276
F-OADZ	6522
F-OAGP	6755
F-OAHL	6957
F-OAIH	6715
F-OAIL	6724
F-OAIR	6818
F-OAKD	6802
F-OAKE	6943
F-OAKF	6448
F-OAKX	6816
F-OALD	6832
F-OAME	6573
F-OAND	6909
F-OANF	6935
F-OANU	6671
F-OAOS	6620
F-OAOY	6480
F-OAPS	6638
F-OAPT	6447
F-OAQL	6839
F-OAQU	6836
F-OAQY	6566
F-OAQZ	6553
F-OARH	6580
F-OASC	6797
F-OATC	6779
F-OATD	6629
F-OATT	6367
F-OAUE	6325
F-OAUG	6811
F-OAUH	6611
F-OAVG	6270
F-OAVZ	6453
F-OAXK	6584
F-OAYN	6504
F-OAYS	6815
F-OAZT	6577
F-OBAL	6856
F-OBAQ	6424
F-OBDV	6591
F-OBGE	6872
F-OBGY	6911
F-OBHH	6487
F-OBHI	6408
F-OBIA	6787
F-OBIO	6507
F-OBIV	6860
F-OBKH	6477
F-OBMQ	6878
F-OBOD	6412
F-OBOH	6823
F-OBOI	6770
F-OBRU	6748
F-OBRV	6525
F-OBRX	6470
F-OBVI	6949
F-OBVJ	6813
F-OBVL	6657
F-OCAG	6859
F-OCBX	6563
F-OCHF	6735

FRENCH OVERSEAS – CARIBBEAN

F-OGAU	6758

FRENCH OVERSEAS – INDO-CHINA

F-LAAB	6724
F-LAAC	6729
F-LAAE	6845
F-LAAF	6935
F-LAAL	6408
F-52	See 24

FRENCH OVERSEAS – MOROCCO

F-DABY	6487
(F-DAFS)	6940

GABON

TR-LKQ	6715

GERMANY

D-IDAK	6467
D-IGEL	6347
D-IGUN	6437
D-ILIT	6879

GOLD COAST

VP-AAA	6951

GREAT BRITAIN - CIVILIAN

E.4 [1]	6250
E.4 [2]	6342
E.9	6421
E.0220	See 7
E.0228	W1002
G-ACPM	6251
G-ACPN	6262
G-ACPO	6253
G-ACPP	6254
G-ACPR	6255
G-ACTT	6257
G-ACTU	6258
G-ACYM	6269
G-ACYR	6261
G-ACZE [1]	6264
G-ACZE [2]	W.1001
G-ACZF	6268
G-ACZU	6274
G-ADAE	6272
'G-ADAE'	6838
G-ADAG	6266
G-ADAH	6278
G-ADAI	6287
G-ADAJ	6276
G-ADAK	6281
G-ADAL	6263
G-ADAO	6275
G-ADBU	6280
G-ADBV	6286
G-ADBW	6288
G-ADBX	6289
G-ADCL	6277
G-ADDD [1]	6283
'G-ADDD' [2]	6835
G-ADDE	6282
G-ADDF	6284
G-ADFX	6290
G-ADFY	6291
G-ADIM	6293
G-ADNG	6297
G-ADNH	6300
G-ADNI	6301
G-ADUM	6315
G-ADUN	6316
G-ADUO	6317
(G-ADUP)	6319
G-ADWZ	6309
G-ADYK	6310
G-ADYL [1]	6311

G-ADYL (2)	6895
G-ADYM	6312
G-AEAJ	6320
G-AEAK	6324
G-AEAL	6325
G-AEAM	6326
G-AEBW	6327
G-AEBX	6328
G-AEGS	6335
G-AEKF	6332
G-AEMH	6336
G-AEML	6337
G-AEMM	6339
G-AENN	6340
G-AENO	6341
G-AEOV	6342
G-AEPE	6344
G-AEPF	6353
G-AEPW	6350
G-AERE	6355
G-AERN	6345
G-AERZ	6356
G-AESR	6363
G-AEWL	6367
G-AEXO	6368
G-AEXP	6369
G-AFAH	6377
G-AFAO	6372
G-AFEN	6399
G-AFEO	6405
G-AFEP	6406
G-AFEY	6402
G-AFEZ	6408
G-AFFB	6409
G-AFFC	6410
G-AFFF	6386
G-AFHY	6417
G-AFHZ	6418
G-AFIA	6419
G-AFLY	6426
G-AFLZ	6429
G-AFMA	6430
G-AFME	6431
G-AFMF	6432
G-AFMG	6433
G-AFMH	6434
G-AFMI	6435
G-AFMJ	6436
G-AFNC	6442
G-AFND	6443
G-AFOI	6450
G-AFRK	6441
G-AFSO	6445
G-AGDG	6547
G-AGDH	6548
G-AGDM	6584
G-AGDP	6403
G-AGED	6621
G-AGEE	6622
G-AGFU	6463
G-AGHI	6455
G-AGIC	6522
G-AGIF	6509
G-AGJF	6499
G-AGJG	6517
G-AGLE	6784
G-AGLN	6795
(G-AGLO)	6779
G-AGLP	6780
G-AGLR	6781
G-AGNH	6803
G-AGOJ	6850
G-AGOP	6873
G-AGOR	6877
G-AGOT	6876
G-AGOU	6875
G-AGOV	6874
G-AGOW	6849
G-AGOX	6848
G-AGPH	6889
G-AGPI	6885
G-AGSH	6884

G-AGSI	6886
G-AGSJ	6888
G-AGSK	6887
G-AGTM	6746
G-AGTN	6749
G-AGUF	6855
G-AGUG	6859
G-AGUP	6911
G-AGUR	6910
G-AGUU	6908
G-AGUV	6912
G-AGWC	6916
G-AGWP	6918
G-AGWR	6917
G-AGZJ	6936
G-AGZK	6937
G-AGZO	6913
G-AGZU	6773
G-AHAG	6926
G-AHEA	6946
G-AHEB	6945
G-AHED	6944
G-AHFJ	6545
G-AHGC	6583
G-AHGD	6862
G-AHGF	6903
G-AHGG	6902
G-AHGH	6934
G-AHGI	6935
G-AHIA	6948
G-AHJA	6486
G-AHJS	6967
G-AHKA	6839
G-AHKB	6596
G-AHKR	6824
G-AHKS	6812
G-AHKT	6811
G-AHKU	6810
G-AHKV	6792
G-AHLF	6494
G-AHLL	6576
G-AHLM	6708
G-AHLN	6754
G-AHLU	6633
G-AHPT	6478
G-AHPU	6963
G-AHPV	6759
G-AHPW	6678
(G-AHPX)	6429
G-AHPY	6561
G-AHRH	6823
G-AHTR	6964
G-AHTS	6962
G-AHTT	6966
G-AHTY	6608
G-AHWF	6965
G-AHXV	6747
G-AHXW	6782
G-AHXX	6800
G-AHXY	6808
G-AHXZ	6825
G-AIBB	6813
G-AIDL	6968
G-AIHN	6498
G-AIUI	6675
G-AIUJ	6724
G-AIUK	6640
G-AIUL	6837
G-AIUM	6519
G-AIUN	6602
G-AIUO	6467
G-AIWG	6497
G-AIWY	6775
G-AIWZ	6867
G-AIYE	6815
G-AIYP	6456
G-AIYR	6676
G-AIYY	6854
G-AIZI	6861
G-AJBJ	6765
G-AJCL	6722
'G-AJCL'	6837

G-AJDN	6860	G-AKSD	6949	G-AOAO	6844	X7329	6502
G-AJFJ	6587	G-AKSE	6870	G-AOZG	6603	X7330	6503
G-AJFK	6552	G-AKSF	6490	G-APBJ	6872	X7331	6504
G-AJFL	6631	G-AKSG	6931	G-APBM	6748	X7332	6505
G-AJFM	6496	G-AKSH	6471	(G-APBN)	6787	X7333	6506
G-AJFN	6520	G-AKSL	6865	G-APJW	6578	X7334	6507
G-AJFO	6756	G-AKTD	6791	G-APKA	6827	X7335	6508
G-AJGS	W.1001	G-AKTX	6639	G-APSD	6556	X7336	6509
G-AJGV	6589	G-AKTY	6563	G-ASFC	6679	X7337	6510
G-AJGZ	6883	G-AKTZ	6482	G-ASIA	6718	X7338	6511
G-AJHO	6835	G-AKUB	6488	G-ASKI	6858	X7339	6512
G-AJHP	6770	G-AKUC	6565	G-ASKO	6735	X7340	6513
G-AJKE	6555	G-AKUS	6805	G-ASRJ	6959	X7341	6514
G-AJKH	6763	G-AKVU	6476	G-ASRM	6961	X7342	6515
G-AJKI	6868	G-AKYW	6581	'G-AZZZ'	6578	X7343	6516
G-AJKW	6539	G-AKYX	6864	'G-RCYR'	6437	X7344	6517
G-AJKX	6457	G-AKYY	6822			X7345	6518
G-AJKY	6553	G-AKYZ	6789	**GREAT BRITAIN - MILITARY**		X7346	6519
G-AJMY	6511	G-AKZA	6892			X7347	6520
G-AJNA	6516	G-AKZB	6790	K4772	6271	X7348	6521
G-AJSJ	6826	G-AKZH	6529	K5070	6267	X7349	6522
G-AJSK	6500	G-AKZI	6536	'N6424'	See 20	X7350	6523
G-AJSL	6801	G-AKZJ	6549	P1764	6421	X7351	6524
G-AJTU	6558	G-AKZO	6575	P1765	6422	X7352	6525
G-AJVA	6600	G-AKZP	6882	P9588	6455	X7353	6526
G-AJVB	6753	G-AKZT	6894	P9589	6456	X7354	6527
G-AJXB	6530	G-AKZV	6843	R2485	6446	X7368	6528
G-AKBW	6585	G-AKZW	6896	R2486	6447	X7369	6529
G-AKDW	6897	(G-ALAS)	6484	R2487	6448	X7370	6530
G-AKDX	6898	G-ALAT	6851	R5921	6457	X7371	6531
G-AKED	6487	G-ALAU	6609	R5922	6458	X7372	6532
G-AKEU	6672	G-ALAX	6930	R5923	6459	X7373	6533
G-AKFO	6460	G-ALAY	6942	R5924	6460	X7374	6534
G-AKGV	6796	(G-ALAZ)	6932	R5925	6461	X7375	6535
G-AKGY	6723	G-ALBA	6821	R5926	6463	X7376	6536
G-AKIF	6838	G-ALBB	6829	R5927	6464	X7377	6537
G-AKJS	W.1002	G-ALBC	6572	R5928	6465	X7378	6538
G-AKJY	6447	G-ALBH	6607	R5929	6466	X7379	6539
G-AKJZ	6880	G-ALBI	6525	R5930	6467	X7380	6540
G-AKLA	6764	G-ALEJ	6484	R5931	6468	X7381	6541
G-AKMD	6802	G-ALET	6832	R5932	6469	X7382	6542
G-AKME	6767	G-ALGB	6706	R5933	6470	X7383	6543
G-AKMF	6617	G-ALGC	6906	R5934	6471	X7384	6544
G-AKMG	6635	G-ALGE	6907	R9545	6473	X7385	6545
G-AKMH	6704	G-ALGI	6909	R9546	6474	X7386	6546
G-AKND	6515	G-ALGM	6559	R9547	6475	X7387	6547
G-AKNE	6591	G-ALGN	6943	R9548	6476	X7388	6548
G-AKNF	6518	G-ALGO	6830	R9549	6477	X7389	6549
G-AKNN	6598	G-ALNS	6778	R9550	6478	X7390	6550
G-AKNV	6458	G-ALNT	6713	R9551	6479	X7391	6551
G-AKNW	6469	G-ALOV	6638	R9552	6480	X7392	6552
G-AKNX	6629	G-ALPK	6757	R9553	6481	X7393	6553
G-AKNY	6470	G-ALRW	6941	R9554	6482	X7394	6554
G-AKNZ	6550	G-ALVU	6526	R9555	6483	X7395	6555
G-AKOA	6618	G-ALWI	6703	R9556	6484	X7396	6556
G-AKOB	6492	G-ALWJ	6777	R9557	6485	X7397	6557
G-AKOC	6814	G-ALWK	6856	R9558	6486	X7398	6558
G-AKOD	6566	G-ALWL	6845	R9559	6487	X7399	6559
G-AKOE	6601	G-ALWM	6755	R9560	6488	X7400	6560
G-AKOF	6538	G-ALWN	6729	R9561	6489	X7401	6561
(G-AKOG)	6443	G-ALWO	6840	R9562	6490	X7402	6562
G-AKOG	6878	G-ALWP	6707	R9563	6491	X7403	6563
G-AKOH	6582	G-ALWY	6741	R9564	6492	X7404	6564
G-AKOI	6546	G-ALXA	6727	V4724	6442	X7405	6565
G-AKOJ	6580	G-ALXI	6690	V4725	6443	X7406	6566
G-AKOK	6474	G-ALXJ	6863	W6423	6300	X7407	6567
G-AKOM	6758	G-ALXS	6715	W6424	6326	X7408	6568
G-AKON	6620	G-ALXT	6736	W6425	6320	X7409	6569
G-AKOO	6468	G-ALXU	6797	W6455	6340	X7410	6570
G-AKOP	6636	G-ALZF	6541	W6456	6342	X7411	6571
G-AKOR	6577	G-ALZH	6448	W6457	6445	X7412	6572
G-AKOV	6612	G-ALZJ	6573	W9365	6301	X7413	6573
G-AKOY	6504	G-AMAI	6879	X7320	6493	X7414	6574
G-AKPA	6709	G-AMAM	6571	X7321	6494	X7415	6575
G-AKRE	6606	G-AMCT	6714	X7322	6495	X7416	6576
G-AKRN	6513	G-AMDG	6818	X7323	6496	X7417	6577
G-AKRO	6480	G-AMJK	6657	X7324	6497	X7437	6578
G-AKRP	6940	G-ANAH	6786	X7325	6498	X7438	6579
G-AKRR	6950	G-ANET	6700	X7326	6499	X7439	6580
G-AKRS	6952	G-ANEU	6836	X7327	6500	X7440	6581
G-AKSB	6951	G-ANJR	6816	X7328	6501	X7441	6582
G-AKSC	6779	G-ANZP	6682			X7442	6583

X7443	6585	Z7259	6433	HG727	6712	NR690	6789
X7444	6586	Z7260	6435	HG728	6713	NR691	6790
X7445	6587	Z7261	6436	HG729	6714	NR692	6791
X7446	6588	(Z7262)	6287	HG730	6715	NR693	6792
X7447	6589	Z7263	6293	HG731	6716	NR694	6793
X7448	6590	Z7264	6266	HG732	6717	NR695	6794
X7449	6591	Z7265	6288	HK862	6410	NR696	6795
X7450	6592	Z7266	6264	HK864	6399	NR697	6796
X7451	6593	AW115	6258	HK915	6323	NR698	6797
X7452	6594	AW116	6283	HK916	6322	NR699	6798
X7453	6595	AW155	6281	HK917	6321	NR700	6799
X7454	6596	AX806	6378	NF847	6718	NR701	6800
X7455	6597	BD143	6344	NF848	6719	NR713	6801
X7456	6598	HG644	6643	NF849	6720	NR714	6802
X7482	6599	HG645	6644	NF850	6721	NR715	6803
X7483	6600	HG646	6645	NF851	6722	NR716	6804
X7484	6601	HG647	6646	NF852	6723	NR717	6805
X7485	6602	HG648	6647	NF853	6724	NR718	6806
X7486	6603	HG649	6648	NF854	6725	NR719	6807
X7487	6604	HG650	6649	NF855	6726	NR720	6808
X7488	6605	HG651	6650	NF856	6727	NR721	6809
X7489	6606	HG652	6651	NF857	6728	NR722	6810
X7490	6607	HG653	6652	NF858	6729	NR723	6811
X7491	6608	HG654	6653	NF859	6730	NR724	6812
X7492	6609	HG655	6654	NF860	6731	NR725	6813
X7493	6610	HG656	6655	NF861	6732	NR726	6814
X7494	6611	HG657	6656	NF862	6733	NR727	6815
X7495	6612	HG658	6657	NF863	6734	NR728	6816
X7496	6613	HG659	6658	NF864	6735	NR729	6817
X7497	6614	HG660	6659	NF865	6736	NR730	6818
X7498	6615	HG661	6660	NF866	6737	NR731	6819
X7499	6616	HG662	6661	NF867	6738	NR732	6820
X7500	6617	HG663	6662	NF868	6739	NR733	6821
X7501	6618	HG664	6663	NF869	6740	NR734	6822
X7502	6619	HG665	6664	NF870	6741	NR735	6823
X7503	6620	HG666	6665	NF871	6742	NR736	6824
X7504	6621	HG667	6666	NF872	6743	NR737	6825
X7505	6622	HG668	6667	NF873	6744	NR738	6826
X7506	6623	HG669	6668	NF874	6745	NR739	6827
X7507	6624	HG670	6669	NF875	6746	NR740	6828
X7508	6625	HG671	6670	NF876	6747	NR741	6829
X7509	6626	HG672	6671	NF877	6748	NR742	6830
X7510	6627	HG673	6672	NF878	6749	NR743	6831
X7511	6628	HG674	6673	NF879	6750	NR744	6832
X7512	6629	HG689	6674	NF880	6751	NR745	6833
X7513	6630	HG690	6675	NF881	6752	NR746	6834
X7514	6631	HG691	6676	NF882	6753	NR747	6835
X7515	6632	HG692	6677	NF883	6754	NR748	6836
X7516	6633	HG693	6678	NF884	6755	NR749	6837
X7517	6634	HG694	6679	NF885	6756	NR750	6838
X7518	6635	HG695	6680	NF886	6757	NR751	6839
X7519	6636	HG696	6681	NF887	6758	NR752	6840
X7520	6637	HG697	6682	NF888	6759	NR753	6841
X7521	6638	HG698	6683	NF889	6760	NR754	6842
X7522	6639	HG699	6684	NF890	6761	NR755	6843
X7523	6640	HG700	6685	NF891	6762	NR756	6844
X7524	6641	HG701	6686	NF892	6763	NR769	6845
X7525	6642	HG702	6687	NF893	6764	NR770	6846
X8505	6369	HG703	6688	NF894	6765	NR771	6847
X8506	6405	HG704	6689	NF895	6766	NR772	6848
X8507	6368	HG705	6690	NF896	6767	NR773	6849
X8508	6377	HG706	6691	NR669	6768	NR774	6850
X8509	6257	HG707	6692	NR670	6769	NR775	6851
X8510	6350	HG708	6693	NR671	6770	NR776	6852
X8511	6286	HG709	6694	NR672	6771	NR777	6853
X9320	6269	HG710	6695	NR673	6772	NR778	6854
X9386	6282	HG711	6696	NR674	6773	NR779	6855
X9387	6336	HG712	6697	NR675	6774	NR780	6856
X9388	6406	HG713	6698	NR676	6775	NR781	6857
X9448	6263	HG714	6699	NR677	6776	NR782	6858
(X9449)	6309	HG715	6700	NR678	6777	NR783	6859
X9450	6337	HG716	6701	NR679	6778	NR784	6860
X9451	6408	HG717	6702	NR680	6779	NR785	6861
X9457	6290	HG718	6703	NR681	6780	NR786	6862
(Z7188)	6399	HG719	6704	NR682	6781	NR787	6863
Z7253	6426	HG720	6705	NR683	6782	NR788	6864
Z7254	6429	HG721	6706	NR684	6783	NR789	6865
Z7255	6430	HG722	6707	NR685	6784	NR790	6866
Z7256	6432	HG723	6708	NR686	6785	NR791	6867
Z7257	6431	HG724	6709	NR687	6786	NR792	6868
Z7258 [1]	6434	HG725	6710	NR688	6787	NR793	6869
'Z7258' [2]	6862	HG726	6711	NR689	6788	NR794	6870

NR795	6871	RL982	6953
NR796	6872	RL983	6954
NR797	6873	RL984	6955
NR798	6874	RL985	6956
NR799	6875	RL986	6957
NR800	6876	TX300	6958
NR801	6877	TX301	6959
NR802	6878	TX302	6960
NR803	6879	TX303	6961
NR804	6880	TX304	6962
NR805	6881	TX305	6963
NR806	6882	TX306	6964
NR807	6883	TX307	6965
NR808	6884	TX308	6966
NR809	6885	TX309	6967
NR810	6886	TX310	6968
NR811	6887	TX311	6969
NR812	6888	TX312	6970
NR813	6889	TX313	6971
NR814	6890	TX314	6972
NR815	6891	TX315	6973
NR828	6892	TX316	6974
NR829	6893	TX317	6975
NR830	6894	TX318	6976
NR831	6895	TX319	6977
NR832	6896		
NR833	6897		
NR834	6898		
NR835	6899		
NR836	6900		
NR837	6901		
NR838	6902		
NR839	6903		
NR840	6904		
NR841	6905		
NR842	6906		
NR843	6907		
NR844	6908		
NR845	6909		
NR846	6910		
NR847	6911		
NR848	6912		
NR849	6913		
NR850	6914		
NR851	6915		
NR852	6916		
NR853	6917		
RL936	6918		
RL937	6919		
RL938	6920		
RL939	6921		
RL940	6922		
RL941	6923		
RL942	6924		
RL943	6925		
RL944	6926		
RL945	6927		
RL946	6928		
RL947	6929		
RL948	6930		
RL949	6931		
RL950	6932		
RL951	6933		
RL952	6934		
RL953	6935		
RL954	6936		
RL955	6937		
RL956	6938		
RL957	6939		
RL958	6940		
RL959	6941		
RL960	6942		
RL961	6943		
RL962	6944		
RL963	6945		
RL964	6946		
RL965	6947		
RL966	6948		
RL967	6949		
RL968	6950		
RL980	6951		
RL981	6952		

In addition, it is understood that the following serials were allotted for 92 Dominie aircraft ordered but subsequently cancelled:-

X7355	Total 1
X7526	Total 1
RL987 – RL999	Total 13
RM112 – RM158	Total 47
TX320 – TX339	Total 20
TX361 – TX370	Total 10

GUINEA BISSAU

CR-GAI	6896
CR-GAJ	6529
CR-GAK	6511

ICELAND

TF-ISM	6670
(TF-ISN)	See 13
TF-ISO	6730
TF-KAA	6622

INDIA

VT-AHB	6308
VT-AIZ	6378
VT-AJA	6379
VT-AJB	6381
VT-ALO	6454
VT-ARF	6569
VT-ARK	6649
VT-ARL	6650
VT-ARM	6651
VT-ARN	6652
VT-ARR	6503
VT-ART	6656
VT-ARV	6657
VT-ARW	6661
VT-ARY	6681
VT-ARZ	6717
VT-ASA	6588
VT-ASC	6762
VT-ASJ	6793
VT-ASQ	6794
VT-AVW	6947
VT-AVX	6953
VT-AXG	6957
VT-CBY	6869
VT-CHZ	6724

INDIA - MILITARY

HX790	6381
HX791	6454
MA961	See 21
MA963	6649
MA964	6650
MA965	6651
MA966	6652

INDONESIA

PK-AKU	6296
PK-AKV	6292
PK-AKW	6294

IRAQ

YI-ABD	6897
YI-ABE	6898
YI-ABF	6906
YI-ABG	6907
YI-ABH	6909
YI-FYA*	6416
YI-HAD*	6415
YI-ZWA*	6414

*Collected by Royal Iraqi Air Force pilots so may have been quasi-military aircraft.

IRELAND

EI-ABP	6341
EI-ADP	6945
EI-AEA	6433
EI-AGK	6458
EI-AJO	6884
EI-AKH	6870
EI-AML	6709
EI-AMN	6907

ISRAEL - CIVILIAN

4X-ACH	See 17
4X-ACN	See 18
4X-ACU	6806
4X-AEH	6496
4X-AEI	6895
4X-970	6952

ISRAEL-MILITARY

1301	6806
1302	6639
1303	6536*
1304	6617
1305	6602
1306	6895
1307	See 22
1308	6549*
1309	6834*
1310	6496
S-71	See 22
S-72	6639
S-73	See 23
S-74	6617
S-75	6602
S-76	6536
S-77	6805
"002"	6952

*It is thought that ten aircraft were operated by the Israeli Air Force as construction numbers are known for this quantity. However, there is some doubt whether both c/ns 6536 and 6636 ended up in Israel. Furthermore, the operation of c/n 6399 in Israel is doubtful as this aircraft was reported in Argentina as recently as April 1960.

ITALY

I-BOBJ	6858
I-DRAG	6260

JORDAN

JY-AAE	6961
JY-AAJ	6580
JY-AAV	6797
JY-AAZ	6753
JY-ABP	6887
JY-ACE	6959
JY-ACF	6961
JY-ACG	6959
JY-ACL	6746

KENYA - CIVILIAN

VP-KCG	6357
'VP-KCH'	6878
VP-KCJ	6366
VP-KCK	6267
VP-KCL	6394
VP-KCR	6413
VP-KCT	6803
VP-KCU	6848
VP-KCV	6849
VP-KCW	6875
VP-KCX	6876
VP-KCY	6874
VP-KEA	6890
VP-KEB	6891
VP-KEC	6893
VP-KED	6895
VP-KEE	6496
VP-KEF	6831
VP-KFH	6418
VP-KFI	6619
VP-KFV	6406
(VP-KFW)	6545
VP-KFX	6620
VP-KGE	6515
VP-KGS	6558
VP-KHF	6627
VP-KHJ	6387
VP-KIO	6898
(VP-KJB)	See 15
VP-KLB	6877
VP-KLL	6777
VP-KMD	6500
VP-KNC	6612
VP-KND	6640
VP-KNS	6492
5Y-KLB	6877
5Y-KLL	6777

KENYA - MILITARY

K-4	6366
K-8	6413
K-10	6394
K-11	6267*
K-16	6357*

*Serial to construction number order uncertain

LAOS

XW-TAB	6832
XW-TBI	See 16

LATVIA

YL-ABC	6351
YL-ABD	6352

LEBANON

LR-AAD	6843
LR-AAE	6894
LR-AAF	6896
LR-ABH	6469
OD-ABH	6469
OD-ABL	6672
OD-ABP	6746

LIBERIA

EL-AAA	6902

LITHUANIA - MILITARY

701	6348
6349	

LUXEMBOURG

LX-LAC	6607
LX-LAD	6525

MADAGASCAR

5R-MAM	6563
5R-MAN	6591
5R-MAO	6507
5R-MAP	6620

MOROCCO(Also see F-D)

CN-TTO	6940

MOZAMBIQUE

CR-AAD	6361
CR-AAE	6362
CR-AAM	6397
CR-AAN	6398
CR-AAT	6439
CR-AAU	6440
CR-ADH	6387
CR-ADM	6840
CR-ADT	6564
CR-AEQ	6969

NETHERLANDS - CIVILIAN

PH-AKU	6296
PH-AKV	6292
PH-AKW	6294
PH-RAA	6890
PH-RAB	6891
PH-RAC	6893
PH-RAD	6895
PH-RAE	6740
PH-RAF	6819
PH-OTA	6740
PH-TGC	6740
PH-VNA	6748
PH-VNB	6872
PH-VNC	6740
PH-VND	6819

NETHERLANDS-MILITARY

?X731	See 25
V1	6748
V2	6872
V3	6740
V4	6819

NEW ZEALAND - CIVILIAN

ZK-ACO	6259
ZK-AEC	6334
ZK-AED	6305
ZK-AEE	6306
ZK-AEW	6343
ZK-AGT	6423

ZK-AHS	6423
ZK-AKS	6647
ZK-AKT	6673
ZK-AKU	6662
ZK-AKY	6653
ZK-ALB	6655
ZK-ALC	6664
ZK-BAU	6654
ZK-BBP	6668
ZK-BCP	6648
ZK-BFK	6903
ZK-SWR?	6853

NEW ZEALAND - MILITARY

NZ523	6647
NZ524	6648
NZ525	6653
NZ526	6654
NZ527	6655
NZ528	6662
NZ529	6664
NZ530	6673
NZ531	6668
NZ555	6334
NZ556	6305
NZ557	6343
NZ558	6306
NZ559	6423

NORTHERN RHODESIA

VP-RBT	6665
VP-RBU	6924
VP-RCH	6878
VP-RCI	6660
VP-RCP	6659

NORWAY

LN-BEZ	6838
LN-BFB	6401

NYASALAND

VP-NAK	6659

PAKISTAN

AP-ADM	6916
AP-AFN	6552
AP-AGI	6457
AP-AGL	6859
AP-AGM	6504

PALESTINE

VQ-PAC	6399
VQ-PAR	6806
'VQ-PAR'	6952

PARAGUAY

ZP-TDH	6436
(ZP-???)	6589

PERSIA/IRAN

EP-AAA	6321
EP-AAB	6322
EP-AAC	6323
EP-AAD	6692
EP-AAE	6695
EP-AAN	See 5
EP-AAT	6696
EP-AAU	See 6
EP-AAV	6763
EP-AAW	6965
EP-AAX	6966
EP-AAY	6868
EP-ADM	6565
EP-ADN	6488

EP-ADO	6618
EP-ADP	6518

PERU - MILITARY

OB-RAA-156	6973
OB-RAB-157	6974
OB-RAC-158	6975
OB-RAD-159	6976
OB-RAE-160	6977
OB-RAF-195	6804
OB-RAG-196	6798
OB-RAH-197	6783
OB-	6772
434	See 26
438	See 27

PORTUGAL - CIVILIAN

CS-ADI	6899
CS-ADJ	6900
CS-ADK	6901
CS-AEB	6430

PORTUGAL - MILITARY

FAP2307	6899
'FAP2307'	6430

ROMANIA

YR-DNC	6338
YR-DRA	6329
YR-DRI	6330
YR-DRO	6331

SABAH (NORTH BORNEO)

VR-OAA	6908
VR-OAB	6800
VR-OAC	6812

SAO TOME

CR-SAD	6900
CR-SAE	6901
CR-S??	6847

SENEGAL

6V-AAC	6470

SEYCHELLES

(VQ-SAG)	6831

SIERRA LEONE

VR-LAC	6603
VR-LAD	6963
VR-LAE	6827

SOUTH AFRICA - CIVILIAN

ZS-AES	6256
ZS-AKT	6380
ZS-AME	6387
ZS-AOM	6411
ZS-ATV	6914
ZS-ATW	6915
ZS-AVY?	6362
ZS-AXS	6969
ZS-AYF	6429
ZS-AYG	6759
ZS-BCD	6477
ZS-BCI	6510
ZS-BCO	6678
ZS-BCP	6561
ZS-BCR	6564
ZS-BCS	6508
ZS-BCT	6627
ZS-BEA	6626

ZS-BEF	6507
ZS-BMV	6619
(ZS-BMW)	6637
ZS-BYT	6834
(ZS-BZC)	6892
ZS-BZC	6788
ZS-BZU	6761
ZS-BZV	6925
ZS-CAB	6411
ZS-CAC	6788
ZS-DDH	6833
ZS-DDI	6658
ZS-DDX	6411
ZS-DFG	6667
ZS-DFL	6387
ZS-DJT	6498
ZS-DLS	6773
ZS-JGV	6831

SOUTH AFRICA-MILITARY

1353	6507
1354	6508
1355	6512?
1356	6510
1357	6619
1358	6626
1359	6627
1360	6637
1361	6628
1362	6564
1363	6477
1364	6680?
1365	6761
1366	6788
1401	6411
1402	6387
6380	

SOUTHERN RHODESIA - CIVILIAN

VP-YAU	6285
VP-YBJ	6358
VP-YBK	6359
VP-YBT	6404
VP-YBU	6412
VP-YBZ	6256
VP-YCI	6658
VP-YCJ	6659
VP-YCK	6660
VP-YCL	6665
VP-YCM	6666
VP-YCN	6667
VP-YCO	6833
VP-YCP	6834
VP-YDE	6925
VP-YDF	6924
VP-YEZ	6680
VP-YFA	6761
VP-YHE	6840
VP-YIU	6969
VP-YKJ	6477
VP-YLF	6878
VP-YLV	6660
VP-YMW	6667
VP-YNJ	6412
VP-YNN	6875
VP-YNU	6508
VP-YOE	6500
VP-YOL	6666
VP-YOY	6678
VP-Y??	6833

SOUTHERN RHODESIA - MILITARY

SR8	6412
SR23	6412
SR24	6678
SR57	6666
?	6285
RRAF23	6412
RRAF57	6666
300	6412
301	6285
302	6256
303	6358
304	6359
305	6404

SPAIN – CIVIL 1st SERIES

EC-AGO	6262
EC-AZZ	6262
EC-W27	6262

SPAIN – CIVIL 2nd SERIES

EC-AAR	6420
EC-AAS	6424
EC-AAV	6425
EC-AAY	6277
EC-BAC	6420
EC-CAQ	See 4

SPAIN – CIVIL 3rd SERIES

EC-AAR	6420
EC-AAS	6424
EC-AAV	6425
EC-AAY	6277
EC-ABG	See 3
EC-AGP	6879
EC-AKO	6345
EC-BAZ?	6284

SPAIN - MILITARY

AVIACION MILITAR (later Republican

22-1	6310
22-2	6311
22-3	6312
?	6260
?	6262
?	6273
?	6274
?	6284
?	6291
?	6429

REPUBLICAN (several were captured and later served with the Nationalists)

LR-001	6382
LR-002	6383
LR-003	6393
LR-004	6395
LR-005	6396
LR-006	6424
LR-007	6425
LR-008	6420
LR-009	6427
LR-010	6428

NATIONALIST (includes some captured from the Republicans

1	6252
2	6277
3	?
5	6312
40-1	6252
40-2	6277
40-3	?
40-5	6312
6420	
40-?	6291
40-?	6424
40-?	6425

These serial to construction number tie-ups are compiled from contemporaneous reports but are not definitely confirmed.

SRI LANKA
(Also see CY-)

4R-AAI	6736
4R-AAK	6894

STRAITS SETTLEMENTS / SINGAPORE

VR-SAV	6360
VR-SAW	6364

SUDAN

(SN-ABB)	6950

SWEDEN

SE-APH	6919
SE-APS	See 8
SE-AYA	See 9
SE-AYB	See 10
(SE-BAL)	6325
SE-BTA	6519
SE-BTT	6467
SE-BXZ	6934
SE-CBU	6530
SE-CDI	6917

SWITZERLAND

CH-287	6250
HB-AME	6437
HB-AMU	6438

HB-APA	6250
HB-APE	6437
HB-APU	6438
HB-ARA	6250

SYRIA

SR-AA?	See 11
SR-AA?	See 11

TANZANIA

5H-AAM	6492
5H-AAN	6831

TRANSJORDAN - CIVILIAN

TJ-AAA	6954
TJ-AAB	6955
TJ-AAC	6958
TJ-AAD	6959
TJ-AAE	6961
(TJ-AAI)	6399
TJ-AAJ	6580
TJ-AAP	6443
TJ-AAQ	6546
(TJ-AAU)	6715
TJ-AAV	6797
TJ-AAZ	6753

TRANSJORDAN - MILITARY

R300	6958
R301	6443

TUNISIA

TS-BME	6573

TURKEY

TC-AGA	6686
TC-ARI	6315
TC-BAY	6316
TC-CAN	6317
TC-DAG	6372
TC-ERK	See 12
TC-HAD	6687
TC-LAV	6643
TC-MUT	6644
TC-NUR	6645
TC-PER	6688
TC-VAN?	6688
TC-VUR	6689
TC-ZOR	6646

UGANDA

VP-UAW	6631
VP-UAX	6418
VP-UBB	6619

UNITED NATIONS

'3'	6436

'9'	6819
UN-71	6918?
UN-72	See 14
UN-73	6430

UNITED STATES - CIVILIAN

N89DH	6709
N683DH	6782
N2290B	6588
N2290F	6794
N8053	6907
(N....)	W1001

UNITED STATES - MILITARY

'7522'	6639
X7346	6519
X7523	6640

URUGUAY

CX-ABI	6371
CX-ABL	6333
CX-API	6786

VENEZUELA

YV-P-BPE	6938

YEMEN - MILITARY

YEMEN 2	See 28
YEMEN 3	See 29

YUGOSLAVIA

YU-SAS	6332

ZAIRE (9O- commenced 1.1.61 and 9Q- 8.9.62)

9O-CJD	6607
9O-CJE	6918
9O-CJS	6429
9O-CJU	6380
9O-CJW	6508
9O-CJX	6658
9Q-CJD	6607
'9Q-CJD'	6666
9Q-CJE	6918
9Q-CJK	6704
9Q-CJU	6380
9Q-CJW	6508
9Q-CJX	6658
9Q-CPF	6961*
9Q-CQF	6667*
9Q-CQT	6704*
9Q-CYE	6778*

*The registration to construction number tie-ups for the last four Zaire Rapides are not confirmed.

5.6 de Havilland DH89 Dragon Rapide - Unidentified Aircraft

Despite our best efforts, a number of DH89s have defied identification. We would be delighted to hear from anyone able to positively identify these aeroplanes.

1. CC-CIC-0034, of the Club Aereo de Linares. Reported damaged at El Maizel airstrip, Linares 23.3.53. This is thought to be c/n 6468
2. CR-LAX, believed to have been allocated to a DH89 in 1940
3. EC-ABG, with Iberia and registered 9.7.51, the former EC-CAQ
4. EC-CAQ, with Iberia 11.1.43. Subsequently registered EC-ABG in the 3rd series
5. EP-AAN, an unknown aircraft believed operated by Iranian State Airlines (Govt. of Persia, Ministry of Posts and Telegraphs).
6. EP-AAU, an unknown aircraft believed operated by Iranian State Airlines (Govt. of Persia, Ministry of Posts and Telegraphs).
7. E.0220, a class B allocation to de Havilland was worn by an unknown Dominie in October 1943, fitted experimentally with constant speed propellers.
8. SE-APS, allocated to an unknown DH89 but not taken up
9. SE-AYA, allocated to an unknown DH89 but not taken up
10. SE-AYB, allocated to an unknown DH89 but not taken up
11. SR-AA?, Syrian Airways apparently had two Rapides in airline service 1953-55. Probably former Misr Airwork aircraft but further details unknown
12. 'TC-ERK', on display at Turk Hava Kuvvetleri Hava Muzesi (Turkish Air Force Air Museum) at Istanbul Airport. Carries spurious marks actually worn by DH86 c/n2355. Thought to be either c/n 6687 formerly TC-HAD or possibly c/n 6688 formerly TC-DER
13. TF-ISN, allocated to an unknown DH89 for Icelandair but not taken up
14. UN-72, operated on behalf of the United Nations in the Congo
15. VP-KJB, reservation for Air Travel (Charters) Ltd. but not taken up. Possibly c/n 6877 which later became VP-KLB
16. XW-TBI, said to be a Rapide of Veha Akat but no further information. Could this be the aircraft noted at Vientiane 25.11.69?
17. 4X-ACH, parts of which said to have been built into 4X-AEK by Bedek Aircraft Corp. in 1955
18. 4X-ACN, registered to Aviron 4.7.49 and cancelled 10.1.50 as scrapped. Thought to be the former Israel Air Force 1307
19. '43' named *Fuling*, reported as a DH89A aircraft delivered to the China National Aviation Corp. However, the type against this record, has been deleted by hand and the words "Beech Staggerwing" are substituted
20. 'N6424', an incorrect identity for a Dominie, appears on a R.A.F. record card as operated by 24Sqdn. Hendon and written-off after being shot up on landing 'Drum' (possibly Dreux), France 18.5.40
21. MA961, worn by an unknown impressed Indian aircraft – possibly c/n 6569
22. S-71, Israeli Air Force (IDFAF) and has also been quoted with serial 1307. In various places, the construction number is often given as 6399, but we consider that aircraft ended its days in Argentina. The problem is further compounded by the registration 4X-ACN also being quoted as c/n 6399 from time to time!
23. S-73, Israeli Air Force (IDFAF)
24. "F-52", operated by Compagnie Laotienne de Commerce et de Transport of Hanoi, suffered engine failure at Nghia Lo 150 miles north-west of Hanoi 15th August 1951. According to reports, the aircraft was damaged by fire, presumably following a forced landing. Possibly c/n 6953
25. ?X731, wearing Dutch national insignia – a photograph appears in this book
26. Peruvian Air Force coded 434, land plane
27. Peruvian Air Force coded 438, float equipped
28. YEMEN 2, a former Egyptian aircraft. Not delivered and instead, to Arab Legion Air Force
29. YEMEN 3, a former Egyptian aircraft. Not delivered and instead, to Arab Legion Air Force

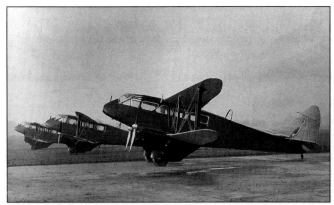

Thought to be c/ns 6310, 6311, and 6312, DH89Ms built for the Spanish military and collected from Hatfield in January 1936. All three were captured by the Nationalists but none survived the war.

DH91 Flamingo G-AFDM. Not a de Havilland Biplane Transport but illustrates a typical Croydon scene, immediately prior to the war, with 1 DH84, 2 DH89A and no less than 5 DH90s in view. (Brain Staner)

For the reasons outlined in Chapter 8.1, this de Havilland photograph of three ambulance aircraft assembled at Hong Kong for Nationalist China, is now known to show c/ns 6385, 6388 and 6389.

Supplied by the Dutch National Archives, we have been unable to discover the identity of, what looks like, ?X731. We include the image for those who like to utter, "why didn't you ask me"!

A poor quality photograph but an impressive line-up of Republican aircraft at their Escuela Polimotores (Multi Engine School) at Totana in the Murcia region of south-east Spain.

The actual aeroplane cannot be indentified, but this impressive three-quarters front shot is one of three operated by the Prestwick based company, Scottish Airlines.

Equally impressive is this view of eight of the fourteen aircraft that served the New Zealand Air Force during the war years. The majority survived military service and were snapped up by civilian operators.

Obviously a staged publicity photograph showing the sole DH89 and eight DH84s operated by Air Dispatch. The company later built up a large fleet of DH90s.

de Havilland
DH90 Dragonfly

DH90 c/n 7500. First flown with de Havilland test marks E.2 on 12th August 1935, the world's first purpose built business aircraft reposes at Hatfield, by then wearing the pukka registration G-ADNA.

DH90 c/n 7508. As G-AEDT with Brian Woodford. As an agent for Bell in the Far East, his fortune was made at the time of Vietnam and on return home, he amassed a unique set of de Havilland aircraft.

DH90 c/n 7502. Under British protection, the Kingdom of Iraq was founded 11th July 1921. Prince Ghazi, a car and aeroplane fanatic, became Sovereign in late 1933 and received YI-HMK in May 1936.

DH90 c/n 7510. Wearing the striking Western Airways colour scheme, G-AEDH was impressed March 1940 and did not survive the war, being struck off charge in January 1941.

DH90 c/n 7504. Delivered to the London Aeroplane Club and based on the west side of DH's Hatfield Airfield, G-AECW was a popular acquisition with the membership, flying extensively up until the war.

DH90 c/n 7512. A de Havilland photograph, shot near Hatfield prior to delivery to Rhodesia in August 1936. Written-off in December 1936, two other Rhodesian examples survived a little longer!

DH90 c/n 7508. VH-AAD, when with Griffith Aero Club in New South Wales from June 1956, until sale in the U.K. August 1963. Also in the U.S.A. for a time, but returned to Australasia in late 1997.

DH90 c/n 7515. Another example in executive use was the Thomas Guinness owned G-AEDJ and often flown in connection with the Guinness family's brewing interests.

6.1 de Havilland DH90 Dragonfly – Development

Soon after Dragon Rapide deliveries commenced, de Havilland receive a number of orders from large organisations requiring a private aircraft to transport their executives. These early users of corporate aircraft were mainly connected to the oil and chemical industries.

Geoffrey de Havilland and his design team at Hatfield were soon beevering away to produce a design that would cater for this totally new market and the DH90 Dragonfly flew for the first time on 12th August 1935.

With seating for five, two in the cockpit, provided with dual controls, one on the starboard side and a bench seat for a further two passengers at the rear of the cabin.

Unlike the previous members of the Dragon family which had a plywood box structure with external spruce stringers and with an outer fabric covering, the Dragonfly used the new form developed for the DH88 Comet racer. The fuselage consisted of a monocoque shell of pre-formed plywood, stiffened with spruce stringers along the top and sides. The wings were also quite different to its predecessors, with a slight backwood sweep and a high aspect ratio.

Fuel was carried in dual 30 gallon tanks situated in the centre section of the wing immediately aft of each engine. Located between the front and rear spars, the area was especially strengthened to carry the load. A supplementary 25 gallon tank was located in the rear fuselage.

An impressive array of instruments was standard and included a Sperry Artificial Horizon, P.3 type flight log, an eight day clock and a fuel guage for each of the three fuel tanks. As the DH84 and DH89 before, the aircraft was equipped with a wind driven generator. Two Gipsy Major engines were employed, each driving a wooden fixed pitch twin bladed propeller covered with the renowned Schwartz protective finish.

The first production aeroplane, registered G-AEBU, made its maiden flight on 15th February 1936. Powered by 142 h.p. Gipsy Major II engines and with provision for variable pitch aircrscrews, earning this derivative the nomenclature DH90A, G-AEBU was retained by de Havilland as the DH90A demonstrator until sold to a French buyer in May 1938.

At £2,650, the price was high, but purchasers received a well equipped aircraft which achieved maximum performance on low power due to the revolutionary new method of construction. Prominent owners of the day in the U.K. were Lord Beaverbrook (Canadian born newspaper baron) with G-AEHC c/n 7514, Charles J. Donada (a London based businessman) with G-AEDK c/n 7517, William Lindsay Everard (Unionist MP for Melton 1924-45, Chairman of Everards Brewery Ltd., Director of the vinegar maker John Sarson & Son Ltd. and also of Alliance Assurance Ltd.) with G-ADXM c/n 7509, Sir William John Firth (Chairman of the steel manufacturer Richard Thomas & Co.) with G-AEEK c/n 7518, Loel Guinness (of the brewing family) with G-AEDJ c/n 7515, Lt-Col. Edward Townley Peel M.C., D.S..O. (Chairman of merchants Peel & Co. Ltd., Alexandria, Egypt) with G-AEXI c/n 7554, The Rt. Hon. Sir Philip Albert Gustave David Sassoon (at the time of purchase was Under-Secretary of State for Air) with G-AEDT c/n 7508, Arthur H. Youngman as nominee for H. Gordon Selfridge (American born founder in 1909 of Selfridge Department store in London) with G-AECX c/n 7505 and The Hon. Charles John Frederic Winn (2nd son of 2nd Baron St. Oswald) with G-AEDV c/n 7524.

Notable overseas purchasers included two French Barons, the Maharajah of Indore, and His Majesty King Ghazi, who ruled Iraq ineffectually from 1993 until his death in a car accident in 1939. Construction number 7539, appropriately registered PH-KOK, was supplied for the use of J. E. F. de Kok, General Manager and Chief Executive of Royal Dutch Shell in the Netherlands.

Shell Oil was a major Dragonfly user with four other aircraft in addition to that noted above. These were used by affiliates around the world with two in Argentina and one each in Nigeria and Singapore.

However, the largest fleet was operated by the Croydon based company, Air Dispatch, controlled by The Honorable Mrs. Victor Bruce. This very interesting lady was born Mildred Mary Petre in 1895. She married the youngest son of 2nd Baron Aberdare, The Hon. Victor Bruce, in 1926. Her remarkable exploits on land, sea and air subsequently, deserve a complete chapter in this book! She held 17 world records for motoring, including the longest distance driven within a 24 hour period – an incredible 2164 miles! On the sea, she broke the record for a double crossing of the English Channel by motor boat and amongst many aviation records, she was the first to fly solo from England to Japan. Just for good measure, she was an outstanding horsewoman and in 1939, was first in the show jumping event at the Royal Windsor Horse Show! Equally unspectacular, was her husband who does not seem to warrant an entry in *Who's Who* and the couple were divorced in 1941. Returning to Air Dispatch, they were operating from Croydon in the latter half of the 1930s and operated a large fleet of de Havilland biplane transports as air taxis and were also the instigator of the scheduled service network linking many of the airfields that circled London.

A few airlines purchased new build Dragonfly aircraft including Wilson Airways of Nairobi with two, Linile Aeriene Romane Exploatate de Stat (L.A.R.E.S.) with three, Divisao de Exploracao dos Transportes Aereos – D.E.T.A. in Mozambique and Misr Airwork of Egypt each owned a single example and Primeras Lineas Uruguayas de Navigacion Area (P.L.U.N.A.) with two. Until its fairly recent destruction in a fire at the museum, the first of P.L.U.N.A.'s aircraft was displayed in Montevideo.

New aircraft for use by the military, were delivered to Denmark and Sweden but many others were taken over from civil operators during the second world war and served in Australia, Canada, India, Kenya, the Netherlands and South Africa. Sixteen were impressed for service use by the Royal Air Force. Few of these were returned to civil use after the war, as the Dragonfly suffered from a high write-off rate. The type had a reputation for being a handful during the take-off and landing phases of flight. A vicious swing could develop which often progressed into a complete gound loop, usually writing off the undercarriage and damaging the spars in the process. Pilots with little experience of the type were taken completely by surprise by this sudden and rapid state of affairs and were often unable to take remedial action in time, before major damage ensued. During wartime, priority to communications and general transport aircraft obviously took second place to fighting aircraft with accident and combat damage. Probably flown regularly by the owner/pilots in peacetime, these incidents would not have been so prevalent and if an accident did happen, such expensive flying machines would have been repaired.

As is shown within chapter 8.4, there are only two survivors, one each in the U.K. and New Zealand.

6.2 de Havilland DH90 Dragonfly – Specifications

Type:	Private touring and executive transport
Capacity:	2 crew and 3 passengers
Country of origin:	Great Britain
Production period:	1935-1938
Engines:	DH90: 2 X de Havilland Gipsy Major I, inverted 4 cylinder in-line air cooled piston engines each of 130.h.p.

DH90A: 2 X de Havilland Gipsy Major II, inverted 4 cylinder in-line air cooled piston engines each of 142 h.p.

First flight:	12th August 1935 (at Hatfield)
Total number built:	67
Production by:	de Havilland Aircraft Co. Ltd., Hatfield, Hertfordshire (first delivery March 1936 and the last in November 1938)

Dimensions (all variants)

Wing span:	43' 0" (m)
Wing area:	256 sq. ft. (sq m)
Length:	31' 8" (m)
Height:	9' 2" (m)

Weights:	Landplane	Seaplane
Empty:	2,487 lb (1130.5 kgs)	3,050 lb (1386.4 kgs)
Max take-off:	4,000 lb (1818.2 kgs)	4,300 lb (1954.5 kgs)

Performance:		
Initial rate of climb:	730' per minute	600' per minute
Max speed:	144 m.p.h.	130 m p.h.
Cruise speed:	125 m.p.h.	110 m.p.h.
Service ceiling:	18,000'	-
Range:	900 miles	-
Fuel capacity:	85 gallons	

6.3 de Havilland DH90 Dragonfly - Production

7500   First flown 12.8.35 at Hatfield using test marks **E.2**. Reg'd **G-ADNA** [CofR 6135 15.8.35] to The de Havilland Aircraft Co. Ltd., Hatfield. [Note: entered into King's Cup Air Race 9.35 but withdrawn]. CofA no.5305 issued 17.1.36. CofA lapsed 16.1.37, but visited Farnborough 9.37, so probably operated by de Havilland under manufacturer's permit. To Albert Batchelor, Ramsgate [CofR 8313 22.1.38], perhaps operated by Thanet Aero Club Ltd., Ramsgate. CofA renewed 14.3.38. To Southern Airways Ltd., Heston (part of the Straight Corporation) 27.1.39 and operated by another Straight company, Western Airways Ltd., Weston-super-Mare. Reg'n cancelled as "owner changed" 17.4.40. To 6AACU Ringway same day. Impressed as **X9452** 10.5.40. To 8AACU Cardiff 24.8.41. To Air Service Training Ltd. 8.6.42. To de Havilland at Witney 19.8.42 and SOC 30.8.42.

7501   Reg'd **G-AEBU** [CofR 6705 8.2.36] to de Havilland Aircraft Co. Ltd., Hatfield. Modified to DH90A standard with Gipsy Major II engines on the production line. CofA no.5322 issued 15.2.36 and retained by de Havilland as the DH90A demonstrator. Until sale abroad 5.38. U.K. CofA renewed 19.5.38 and delivered to Auguste A. Boyer, Paris as **F-AQEU** 31.5.38. To Societe Francaise de Transports Aeriens 6.38. To Spanish Republicans and flown to Barcelona by Boyer. Fate unknown.

7502   Export CofA no.5469 issued 28.4.36. To H. M. King Ghazi of Iraq, Akerkuf reg'd **YI-HMK** 27.5.36 and named *The Golden Eagle*. Probably later saw service with the Iraqi Air Force after King Ghazi was killed in a motoring accident 4.4.39. Fate unknown.

7503   CofA no.5388 issued 9.5.36. Reg'd **G-AEDW** [CofR 6784 10.3.36] to H. B. Legge & Sons Ltd., Hamsey Green, Surrey. Reg'n cancelled as sold 2.38 (and CofA renewed 11.3.38). To Rhodesia & Nyasaland Airways Ltd. and reg'd **VP-YBR** 3.38. Badly damaged in crash on take-off Gwelo 5.10.38. Presumably repaired as also reported as being the aircraft which crashed near Kasama 1.1.39.

7504   Reg'd **G-AECW** [CofR 6747 29.2.36] to The London Aeroplane Club Ltd., Hatfield. CofA no.5369 issued 28.7.36. To The de Havilland Aircraft Co. Ltd., Hatfield [CofR 8393 9.3.38]. Operated on special permit by de Havilland throughout the war for communications until CofA expiry 10.10.44. To spares and reg'n cancelled as permanently withdrawn from use at census 23.11.45.

7505   Reg'd **G-AECX** [CofR 6748 28.4.36] to Arthur H. Youngman as nominee for H. Gordon Selfridge, American born founder in 1909 of Selfridge Department store in London. CofA no.5462 issued 20.5.36. Operated by Selfridge ex Heston (piloted by his son-in-law Viscomte de Sibour) on clandestine flight to Spanish Nationalists late 7.36 on behalf of Socony-Vacuum Oil Co. to arrange oil supplies. Reg'n cancelled on sale abroad 3.38 (and CofA renewed 2.3.38). To Air Services of India Ltd., Bombay reg'd **VT-AKC** 4.38. Flown back to U.K. during period 17.7.39 to 24.7.39. Restored as **G-AECX** 9.8.39 to International Air Freight Ltd. but operated by Air Dispatch Ltd., Croydon. Reg'd 23.1.40 to The Hon. Mrs. Victor Bruce but still operated by Air Dispatch Ltd. Used for Army Co-operation night flying contract, initially at Croydon, but later at Cardiff's Splott airfield. Reg'n cancelled as "owner changed" 22.6.40. Impressed as **AX855** 2.6.40 and used as a hack by A.T.A. HQ White Waltham. To Hawker Aircraft 26.8.41. To Station Flight Northolt 16.12.41. To de Havilland at Witney 29.1.42 and SOC 22.2.42.

7506   Export CofA no.5461 issued 28.5.36. To de Havilland Canada; erected and test flown Downsview 26.6.36. Reg'd **CF-AYF** [CofR 1758 16.7.36] to W. M. Archibald, Creston BC. Reg'd [CofR 1849 3.11.36] to Consolidated Mining & Smelting Co. of Canada Ltd., Trail BC. Badly damaged in heavy landing Kimberley BC 12.10.46 and wreck donated to the Trail Flying Club.

7507   Reg'd **G-AEFN** [CofR 6876 28.4.36] to Walter G. Robson, Heston. CofA no.5460 issued 6.6.36. To Air Commerce Ltd., Heston 18.2.39. Reg'n cancelled as sold 28.3.40. Flown to 6AACU Ringway 28.3.40 and impressed as **X9390** 31.3.40. To 7AACU 3.5.40. To de Havilland at Witney for repair 20.9.40. To 7FPP 3.2.41. To 9MU for storage 4.4.41. Crashed following engine failure near Cosford Waterworks 10.9.41 and SOC 18.9.41.

7508   CofA no.5490 issued 19.6.36. Reg'n **G-AEDT** reserved 2.36 and issued [CofR 6777 9.5.36] to The Rt. Hon. Sir Philip Albert

Gustave David Sassoon, Hendon who at that time was Under-Secretary of State for Air. Reg'n cancelled as sold 7.38. Reg'd in Australia as **VH-AAD** 17.3.38 (or 25.3.38) to Adastra Airways Pty Ltd., Mascot. Forced landed Gerringong Beach NSW 20.1.39 - no injuries to the four occupants and little damage. Reg'd 14.6.51 to Bush Pilots Airways Pty. Ltd., Cairns QLD. Leased to Queensland Ambulance Transport Brigade, Cairns QLD for one year commencing 11.51 to replace their lost DH89 VH-CFA, and again 10.53-11.54 to replace the second VH-CFA which also crashed! To Kingsford-Smith Aviation Service Pty Ltd., Bankstown NSW 25.11.54. To Griffith Aero Club, Griffiths NSW 8.6.56. Sold to Charles Beech Gordon Masefield (knighted 1997) & Lord Trefgarne 8.63. Australian reg'n cancelled 2.9.63. Reg'd **G-AEDT** 3.10.63 to David, Lord Trefgarne; named *Endeavour*. Flown back to U.K. by Masefield & Trefgarne, departing Bankstown 1.12.63 and arriving Gatwick on the night of 23-24.12.63. To Shoreham for overhaul and CofA renewed 30.7.64. Flown to U.S.A. via Iceland departing the same day and to Tallmantz Museum, Santa Ana CA. Reg'n cancelled as sold in USA 2.5.66. Reg'd **N2034** early 1967 to Rosen Novak Auto Co., Omaha, NB and delivered 1.67. Sold to Joe L. Terteling, Boise ID and delivered 4.69. U.S. reg'n probably not used and to store. Auctioned 20.9.86 and bought by Brian Woodford for $41,000. Reg'n cancelled 23.4.87 and shipped to U.K. for rebuild by Ron Such of The Aeroplane Co., Sarisbury Green, Hampshire. Restored as **G-AEDT** 27.4.87 to Brian Woodford of Wessex Aviation & Transport Ltd., Henstridge, Somerset. Re-flown 15.7.88 and CofA renewed 19.7.88. CofA lapsed 18.7.91. Sold late .96 to Colin Smith, Mandeville, New Zealand and shipped out 8.97. Reg'd 12.9.97 to Barry K. Donovan, c/o Cathay Pacific Airways, Kai Tak, Hong Kong. Reg'n cancelled as sold in New Zealand 23.3.98 and to **ZK-AYR** 1.4.98 for Colin Smith of Croydon Aircraft Co. Ltd., Mandeville. Assembled and re-flown 7.4.98. Offered for sale in 2001.

7509   Reg'n **G-AEDU** originally reserved 11.35 but not taken up. Instead, reg'd **G-ADXM** [CofR 6480 9.5.36] to (William) Lindsay Everard, Unionist MP for Melton 1924-45, Chairman of Everards Brewery Ltd. & director of the vinegar maker John Sarson & Son Ltd. and Alliance Assurance Ltd. Delivered 27.6.36, named *The Leicestershire Vixen II* and based at Everard's private strip at Ratcliffe Hall, Leicestershire; CofA no.5488 issued 20.6.36. Everard was knighted 1939. Reg'n cancelled as "owner changed" 4.40, although other sources give the date as 29.2.40. To 110 (AAC) Wing, Ringway 3.40. Impressed as **X9327** 31.3.40. To 6AACU 21.5.40. To 8AACU 24.8.41 and later used by Cardiff Com. Flt. To Tactical Air Force Com. Flt. White Waltham 21.6.43. SOC as scrap 22.7.44.

7510   Reg'd **G-AEDH** [CofR 6766 7.36] to Samuel Harris, Redhill and operated by Croydon Airways Ltd., Croydon. CofA no.5489 issued 2.7.36. Receiver appointed to Croydon Airways Ltd. 16.3.37 and aircraft sold. Reg'd [CofR 8119 25.9.37] to Plymouth Airport Ltd., Roborough. Reg'd 15.2.39 to their associate company also owned by the Straight Corporation - Western Airways Ltd., Weston-super-Mare. Cancelled as "owner changed" 8.3.40. Impressed as **AV987** 12.5.40. Served with 110 (AAC) Wing, Ringway 10.5.40, 6AACU 16.5.40, Ringway Stn. Flt. 5.12.40 but SOC 1.1.41.

7511   Reg'd **G-AEDI** [CofR 6767 14.5.36 but had been reserved 2.36] to British Continental Airways Ltd., Croydon but not delivered. CofA no.5513 issued 13.10.36. Reg'n cld as sold abroad 10.36 and reg'd **VR-SAX** to the Shell Co. offshoot, Asiatic Petroleum Co., Singapore. Delivered by air, departing Croydon 27.12.36 but damaged an undercarriage compression leg when it swung on landing Ghemines (Qaminis), Libya. Repaired by Misr Airwork in Cairo and finally arrived Penang 26.1.37. Damaged on landing Tourane, Indo-China 20.11.37; rebuilt in situ over three months, departing 27.2.38 only to have undercarriage collapse on landing Vientiane. Rebuilt again and flown out 31.5.38 and returned to Singapore. Badly damaged, yet again on landing, at Alor Star 1.12.38 en route back to U.K. Shipped to Penang and sold for rebuild. Reg'd .39 to Wearne's Air Services Ltd., Singapore. Impressed into 'B' Flight Malayan Volunteer Air Force 1.12.41. Destroyed in air raid Kallang 20.1.42.

7512   To Rhodesia & Nyasaland Airways Ltd., Salisbury with export CofA no.5595 issued 21.7.36. Reg'd **VP-YAX** 8.36. Crashed near Gwelo 20.12.38; no casualties.

DH90 c/n 7524. Used as an executive aircraft by The Honourable Charles Winn from October 1936 and kept at Croydon. Impressed from Birkett Air Service in March 1940, it crashed in September 1941.

DH90A c/n 7532. One of two Dragonflies used by Uruguay's national airline, CX-AAR is seen here displayed in the centre of Montevideo on the occasion of a national anniversary.

DH90A c/n 7526. ZS-CTR was shipped back to the U.K. for Tony Haig-Thomas in 1979 and it then languished at Hatfield where this elicit shot was taken when bunking around the factory one Saturday!

DH90A c/n 7532. Located at the newly established Museo Aeronautical by the authors on a South American extravaganza in 1979, the rare survivor was destroyed by fire in December 1997.

DH90A c/n 7526. Rebuilt by the master, Cliff Lovell, at Hannington, this aircraft then spent time in the U.S.A. Purchased as a wreck by Torquil Norman 1988 and rebuilt by Cliff, G-AEDU flew again in 1992.

DH90A c/n 7538. Thought to have been photographed when with the unusually named Ginger Coote Airways in late 1941, CF-BPD was destroyed as a result of a ground-loop at Edmonton ALB in April 1943.

DH90A c/n 7529. Used by both the Republicans and Nationalists during the Civil War, G-ANYK arrived back in the U.K. aboard a Bristol Freighter July 1956. Destroyed in an accident La Baule June 1961.

DH90A c/n 7555. Somewhat 'twitchy' on the ground, G-AEWZ was one of the very few to survive military service, but was damaged beyond repair when ground-looped on take off at Elmdon, in March 1961.

7513 To QANTAS Empire Airways Ltd., Brisbane with export CofA no.5615 issued 6.8.36. Reg'd **VH-UXB** 26.10.36. Damaged on take-off Mount Isa, QLD 25.12.38; repaired. Damaged in forced landing Alexandra, QLD 19.6.41; repaired. Damaged in forced landing Daly Waters, QLD 8.5.43; repaired. Badly damaged when swung on take-off Brisbane-Archerfield 13.7.43 but repaired. Undercarriage collapsed on landing Cloncurry, QLD 28.1.46 and again at the same location on 16.1.47, but this time on take-off. Reg'd 25.2.47 to E. J. Connellan t/a Connellan Airways, Alice Springs, NT. Nominal change to to Connellan Airways Ltd. 14.3.51. Cancelled as permanently withdrawn from use 17.9.51.

7514 Reg'd **G-AEHC** [CofR 6919 5.36] to 1st Baron Beaverbrook of New Brunswick, Croydon (possibly reg'd in name of A. E. Millar?). CofA no.5516 issued 14.7.36. Nominal ownership change to London Express Newspapers Ltd. [CofR 7586 9.1.37]. Operated by Personal Airways Ltd., Croydon on behalf of the newspaper group on an internal route survey following the Maybury Committee Report. Crashed Darnaw, Minnigaff Parish, Kircudbrightshire 2.2.37 en route Renfrew to Speke; killing Leslie T. Jackson of Personal Airways, Major Harold Pemberton, aviation editor of Daily Express and two other Express staff members. Reg'n cancelled as permanently withdrawn from use 4.37.

7515 Reg'd **G-AEDJ** [CofR 6768 6.36] to Thomas Loel Evelyn Bulkeley Guinness (1906-88), Unionist MP for Bath 1931-45. Aircraft kept at Heston. CofA no.5514 issued 3.7.36. Reg'd [CofR 8227 17.11.37] to Algernon J. D. Jameson, Heston. To International Air Freight Ltd., Croydon and operated by Air Dispatch Ltd. 11.10.39. Used for Army Co-operation night flying contract, initially at Croydon, but later at Cardiff's Splott airfield. Reg'n cancelled as "owner changed" 22.6.40. Impressed as **AV992** 2.6.40 and to A.T.A. HQ White Waltham. To Vickers-Armstrong Ltd. for communication duties by 6.41. SOC as Cat.E1 12.2.45.

7516 Reg'd **G-AEDG** [CofR 6764 29.7.36 but had been reserved 2.36] to The Hon. James Valentine Fairbairn, MP for Flinders VIC in the Commonwealth of Australia. Named *Spirit of Flinders*. CofA no.5606 issued 13.8.36. Departed Lympne 14.9.36 and arrived Darwin 3.10.36, flown by the owner and Owen F. Y. Thomas. British reg'n cancelled as sold abroad 10.37. Still with Fairbairn of Derrinallum VIC reg'd **VH-ADG** 12.10.37. Fairbairn was Australian Minister for Air and Civil Aviation but this was his own aircraft, based on his private strip. Requisitioned by Government and delivered 10.39. Eventually to Airlines (WA) Ltd., Maylands to replace their impressed DH84 VH-URY. Reg'd 5.9.40 and named *Murchison*, later *RMA Port Hedland*. Overturned on take-off Guildford, WA 1.12.47. Reg'n cancelled 12.1.48.

7517 Reg'd **G-AEDK** [CofR 6769 3.7.36] to businessman Charles J. Donada, Heston. CofA no.5569 issued 5.9.36. Reg'd 30.1.39 to Mutual Finance Ltd., and operated by Air Dispatch Ltd., Croydon. Used for Army Co-operation night flying contract, initially at Croydon, but later at Cardiff's Splott airfield. Reg'd 12.3.40 to their associate, Anglo European Airways Ltd., Cardiff. Reg'n cancelled as sold 7.7.40. Operated by RAF Gosport 2.7.40. Impressed as **AW164** 7.7.40. To 15Grp. Com. Flt., Hooton Park (later Speke) 21.3.41. SOC by 2MPRD Eaglescliffe as scrap 17.12.43.

7518 Reg'd **G-AEEK** [CofR 6817 27.6.36] to Sir William (John) Firth, Heston/Brooklands. CofA no.5555 issued 11.9.36. Firth (1881-1957) was Chairman & Managing Director of steel sheet manufacturer Richard Thomas & Co. Ltd. Crashed Upper Beeding, near Shoreham, Sussex 17.8.37 when struck power lines; Sir William and the pilot were unhurt. Wreck taken to Hatfield 18.8.37 but reg'n cancelled as permanently withdrawn from use 12.37.

7519 To Baron Sternberg de Armella, Paris with export CofA no.5633 issued 27.8.36 and reg'd **F-AOZC** 23.9.36. To M. Bleustein 5.38. Returned to Air Dispatch Ltd., Croydon by 1.39 and reg'd as **G-AFRF** 9.3.39 to Mutual Finance Ltd. Nominally in E. R. Noddings 15.4.39 but operated by Air Dispatch Ltd., Croydon. CofA renewed 7.3.39. Used for Army Co-operation night flying contract, initially at Croydon, but later at Cardiff's Splott airfield. To their associate Anglo-European Airways Ltd., Cardiff 12.3.40. Reg'n cld as sold 22.6.40. Impressed as **AV993** 2.6.40 and operated by A.T.A. HQ White Waltham. To Vickers-Armstrong Ltd. 10.6.41. Damaged at Weybridge 24.6.41, but presumed repaired. To de Havilland at Witney 27.7.42 and SOC 11.8.42.

7520 Export CofA no.5575 issued 8.7.36. To London & Rhodesian Mining & Land Co. Ltd., Salisbury reg'd **VP-YBB** 7.36.

Crashed in fog Donga, 13 mls from Selukwe 20.10.38, whilst operated by Flights Ltd.; 5 killed including pilot Danby Gray & A. R. Metlerkamp, Chairman of Southern Rhodesia Electricity Supply Commission.

7521 Export CofA no.5655 issued 14.9.36. To Baron Jules de Koenigswinter, Paris with reg'n **F-AOYK** 23.9.36. To Roger Seligman 1.38. Sold to Airwork Ltd., Heston, reg'd **G-AFVJ** 12.6.39 and CofA renewed 11.7.39. Sold to Allflights Ltd., Heston 13.7.39, but not officially reg'd to them. Impressed as **X9337** 31.3.40. Served with 110 (AAC) Wing Ringway and 7AACU 3.5.40. Slightly damaged 24.9.40 when struck by a number of bullets whilst target towing. To 8AACU 11.12.40. Undercarriage collapsed on take-off Old Sarum 24.6.41. To de Havilland at Witney & SOC 2.7.41.

7522 No U.K. CofA issued and shipped to Canada. First flown October 1936 and reg'd **CF-BBD** [CofR 1836 24.10.36] to de Havilland Aircraft of Canada Ltd., Downsview ONT. In use as a demonstrator and later, for trainning Royal Canadian Mounted Police pilots at Toronto from 3.37. Damaged when in ground collision with Toronto Flying Club Puss Moth CF-CDM 19.4.37. Re-reg'd **CF-MPC** and delivered to the Royal Canadian Mounted Police 15.7.37, named *Crocus*. Transferred to Royal Canadian Air Force as **7628** and taken on charge 23.7.40 at RCAF Rockcliffe. SOC 12.6.41 on return to the police and presumed restored as **CF-MPC**. Cancelled on re-reg'n **CF-BXU** 30.5.45 to Johannesson Flying Service, Winnipeg. Reg'd 30.10.45 to A. J. Danes & F. B. Wilson, Yellowknife NWT. Badly damaged in forced landing following engine failure, Thorhild ALB 23.12.45.

7523 To Vacuum Oil Co. of South Africa Ltd., with CofA no.5653 issued 12.9.36. Flown out late 9.36 by Capt. Walters. Reg'd **ZS-AHV** 9.2.37. Impressed as **SAAF 1403** 3.40. Fate not recorded.

7524 Reg'd **G-AEDV** 10.36 to The Hon. Charles John Frederic Winn, Croydon (2nd son of 2nd Baron St. Oswald). CofA no.5580 issued 8.10.36. To Birkett Air Service Ltd., Heston 16.6.37. Reg'n cancelled as sold 27.3.40. To 110 (AAC) Wing, Ringway same day. Impressed as **X9389** 31.3.40. Served with 7AACU 3.5.40 and 8AACU 25.8.41. Crashed soon after take-off in fog from Weston Zoyland, in the Polden Hills at Chedzoy, Somerset 3.9.41; Flt. Lt. J. R. M. Sales & Sgt. H. W. Bellingham killed.

7525 To Director of Railways, Iraq with export CofA no.5663 issued 17.9.36. Reg'd **YI-OSD**. Possibly subsequently operated by the Iraqi Air Force. Fate unknown.

7526 Export CofA no.5689 issued 14.10.36. To The Railway Administration of Portuguese East Africa reg'd **CR-AAB** but operated by Divisao de Exploracao dos Transportes Aereos – D.E.T.A., Lourenco Marques. To South Africa and reg'd **ZS-CTR** 27.9.61 for A. G. Mechin, Johannesburg. Noted wfu Baragwanath 8.74. Sold to an American, Wayne Kerr c.1976-77 but remained stored in South Africa. Sold to U.K. 6.79 and reg'd **G-AEDU** (a reg'n originally reserved for c/n 7509 which instead became G-ADXM) 4.6.79 to Anthony Haig-Thomas & Martin C. Barraclough. Briefly stored Hatfield until rebuilt by Cliff Lovell at Walkeridge Farm, Hannington and reflown 1.7.81. CofA renewed 10.7.81 and based Duxford, later Old Warden. Sold at Christies auction, Duxford 14.4.83 for £35,000. Reg'n cld as sold 2.6.83 and flown to U.S.A., departing U.K. 13.6.83 and arriving Clark County Airport, Sellersburg IN 15.7.83. Reg'd **N190DH** 6.83 to Charles A. Osborne Jnr., Louisville KY. Badly damaged in take-off crash Clark County Airport, Sellersburg IN 22.9.87. Reg'n cancelled 8.4.88. Wreck purchased by T. P. A. Norman and returned to U.K. for rebuild by Cliff Lovell, then located at Coombe Bissett, Wiltshire .88, but later at Lower Upham, Hampshire. Reg'd **G-AEDU** 28.4.92 to Torquil P. A. Norman, Rendcomb, Gloucestershire. Rebuilt and eventually reflown 4.8.92. CofA renewed 2.12.92. Flown to U.S.A.; departing U.K. 11.7.95 and arrived Portland ME 16.7.95 for visit to the Experimental Aircraft Association's annual convention at Oshkosh, Wisconsin. Aircraft left in U.S.A. but collected the following year and returned U.K. 12.8.96. Reg'd to Alexander J. Norman, t/a Norman Aeroplane Trust, Rendcomb 8.7.97.

7527 To R. E. Grant-Govan, Delhi reg'd **VT-AHW** [CofR 290 15.7.36] and CofA no.5676 issued 29.9.36. Delivered 9.11.36. Reg'n cancelled 2.9.41. Impressed as **AX797** 1941. Operated by Ratmalana Stn. Flt. 7.43 until at least 26.11.43. SOC 31.12.43.

7528 To Wilson Airways Ltd., Nairobi with export CofA no.5646 issued 1.9.36. Reg'd **VP-KCA** 30.9.36 and used as an air ambulance. Impressed into Kenya Auxiliary Air Unit 9.39 as either **K-13** or **K-14**. (See note within registration/serial to construction number cross-index).

7529 Export CofA no.5674 issued 29.9.36. To Gustave Wolf, Constantine, Algeria, reg'd **F-APDE** 9.10.36. To G. Prieur, Algiers 3.38. To Societe Francaise de Transports Aeriens 10.38. To Spanish Republican Forces mid .38 (serial either "**706**" or "**756**"?). Captured by the Nationalists and serial **40-4** issued. To Iberia as **EC-BAA** 3.41. Re-reg'd **EC-AAQ** .45. Sold to Rodolfo Bay Wright, Tangier 7.48 and reg'n finally cancelled 12.3.49. To M Petermans, Brussels (acquired in exchange for an Argus OO-PET, which became EC-AEN in 1953) reg'd **OO-PET** 13.9.49. Cancelled on sale to France 24.2.53. Reg'd **F-OAMS** to I. Daunes, Tangier 16.7.53. Delivered from Toussus-le-Noble to Jersey 8.54 and reg'd **G-ANYK** 20.1.55 to British European Airways Corporation. Intended as an executive aircraft for the airline with contrived reg'n **G-ABEA**, but in the the event, neither plan was executed. Flown to Eastleigh aboard Silver City Airways Bristol 170 Freighter G-AMWC 1.7.56 and reg'd 25.7.56 to Owen Hill. Rebuilt over many months, flew again 27.3.59 and CofA renewed 27.5.59. To John R. T. G. Jarvie and Bryan H. M. Winslett 27.11.59. To Metropolitan Air Movements Ltd., Biggin Hill 20.12.60.. Undercarriage collapsed on landing La Baule 23.6.61. Reg'n cancelled as destroyed 2.10.61.

7530 To de Havilland Canada without CofA. To Royal Canadian Mounted Police, Ottawa; reg'd **CF-MPA** [CofR 1945 1.5.37] named *Anemone* and delivered 5.5.37. Transferred to Royal Canadian Air Force as **7626** 29.7.40. Operated by 3 Training Command. SOC 28.1.43.

7531 To de Havilland Canada without CofA. To Royal Canadian Mounted Police, Ottawa; reg'd **CF-MPB** [CofR 1974] 29.5.37 named *Buttercup* and delivered 29.5.37. Transferred to Royal Canadian Air Force as **7627** 23.7.40. Crashed Oshawa 19.6.42 but repaired. SOC 19.6.44 and reg'd **CF-BZA** 1.6.45 (or 11.6.45) to T. P. Fox, Verdun PQ. Reg'd 1.11.45 to Associated Airways Ltd., Edmonton ALB. Crashed Indian Lake, NWT 17.11.48. Reg'n cld 8.10.49 but the rear fuselage is said to be extant at Edmonton Museum.

7532 Export CofA no.5665 issued 18.9.36. To Alberto & Jorge Marquez Vaeza, founders of Cia. Primeras Lineas Uruguayas de Navegacion Aerea - P.L.U.N.A., Montevideo reg'd **CX-AAR** 10.36 and named *Churrinche*. Believed withdrawn from use 1949. To Uruguayan Air Force Museum (Museo Aeronautica), Montevideo (by .79). Destroyed by fire at the museum 4.12.97.

7533 To de Havilland Australia with export CofA no.5695 issued 21.10.36. Reg'd **VH-UXA** 24.1.37 to Fostars Shoes Air Transport Ltd., Sydney NSW. To Harry McEvoy of Fostars Air Transport Pty Ltd., Mascot and flown on a Hong Kong trip by Frank McEvoy & family; departing Mascot 27.5.37 and returned Darwin 7.7.37. Flown on Donald Mackay's Central Australian Expedition 19.7.37 to 21.8.37. Departed Mascot 23.2.39 for U.K. via China flown by Harry McEvoy. Australian reg'n cancelled 17.4.39 and reg'd **G-AFTF** 15.4.39 to Eric E. Noddings, a director of Air Dispatch Ltd, Croydon. CofA renewed 29.4.39. Used for Army Co-operation night flying contract at Croydon. Reg'n cancelled as "owner changed" 11.8.40 and impressed as **BD149** same day. Saw service with 8AACU at Weston Zoyland, at Old Sarum 10.40 and at Cardiff 11.40. Destroyed in an accident 16.5.42 but further details unknown. SOC as Cat.E1 21.5.42.

7534 Export CofA no.5668 issued 22.9.36. To Alberto & Jorge Marquez Vaeza, founders of Cia. Primeras Lineas Uruguayas de Navegacion Aerea – P.L.U.N.A., Montevideo reg'd **CX-AAS** 10.36 and named *San Alberto*. Reg'n cancelled as withdrawn from use 1946 but remained on the 1950 civil register!

7535 Export CofA no.5704 issued 4.11.36. To de Havilland South Africa reg'd **ZS-AIK** 18.12.36. To Witwatersrand Technical College. Impressed as **SAAF1408** .40. Restored as **ZS-AIK**. Crashed Rustenburg 31.5.51.

7536 Export CofA no.5729 issued 7.12.36. To Jacques Dupuy, Paris reg'd **F-APAX** [CofR 4974 31.12.36]. To Edouard Daubree, Tangier 7.37. Returned to UK and with Air Dispatch Ltd., Croydon by 1.39. To The Hon. Mrs. Victor Bruce, Croydon (operated by Air Dispatch Ltd.) reg'd **G-AFRI** 27.3.39. CofA renewed 4.4.39. Used for Army Co-operation night flying contract, initially at Croydon, but later at Cardiff's Splott airfield. To associate company Anglo-European Airways Ltd, Cardiff 24.1.40. Impressed as **AV994** 2.6.40 and operated by A.T.A. HQ White Waltham. When in use by 3FPP, struck by landing Tiger Moth BB687 when taxiing R.A.F. Westwood, Peterborough 4.5.41. To de Havilland at Witney 8.5.41 and SOC 24.5.41.

7537 Export CofA no.5691 issued 16.10.36. To Shell Mex Argentina Ltd. reg'd **R326** and named *Gavilan de la Selva*. Erected and flown Buenos Aires - San Fernando Aerodrome 6.1.37. Later re-reg'd **LV-RDA**. Destroyed in hangar fire at San Fernando 25.11.37. Replaced by c/n 7563.

7538 To de Havilland Canada without CofA. To Royal Canadian Mounted Police, Ottawa reg'd **CF-MPD** [CofR 2017] 26.6.37 named *Dandelion* and delivered 26.6.37. To Noorduyn Aircraft Ltd., Montreal PQ 2.9.38 and later re-reg'd **CF-BPD** 8.12.38. Reg'd 6.4.39 to Leavens Bros Air Services, Toronto ONT. To Ginger Coote Airways Ltd., Vancouver BC 1.9.41. Became Canadian Pacific Air Lines 1.42. Ground-looped on take off and badly damaged Edmonton ALB 13.4.43. Aircraft scrapped.

7539 Export CofA no.5705 issued 9.11.36. To Royal Dutch Shell, Ypenburg reg'd **PH-KOK** [CofR 236] 11.11.36. Used by J. E. F. de Kok, General Manager and Chief Executive of Royal Dutch Shell in the Netherlands. Re-reg'd **PH-ATK** 4.7.38 to same owner. Impressed into LVA 1.9.39 and serialled **962**. Destroyed Ypenburg 10.5.40 struck off records 4.7.41.

7540 Export CofA no.5715 issued 20.11.36. To Maharaja of Myurbhanj, Orissa reg'd **VT-AHY** [CofR 292] 15.1.37. Impressed 15.5.40 as **V4734** and used by AHQ India Com. Flt., New Delhi. Operated by Bengal Com. Flt. .43. Swung on take-off and crashed into ditch Barrackpore 28.5.43. Soc 1.2.44.

7541 Export CofA no.5712 issued 17.11.36. To Count Franco Mazzotti Biancinelli, Milan reg'd **I-DRAG** [CofR 1977] 19.1.37. Possibly operated by Ala Littoria. Damaged 2.37 and returned by road to W. A. Rollason at Croydon for repairs. Eventual fate unknown.

7542 Export CofA no.5735 issued 15.12.36. To Jean Raty, Neuilly-sur-Seine and reg'd **F-APFK** 31.12.36. Cancelled after 1939.

To de Havilland Canada without CofA; erected and first flown Downsview 19.7.37. Reg'd **CF-BFF** 20.7.37 to de Havilland Aircraft of Canada Ltd., Downsview ONT and fitted with Fairchild floats 21.7.37. To Consolidated Mining & Smelting, Trail BC 6.8.37. Sold back to de Havilland 9.37 and leased to Canadian Airways Ltd., Montreal PQ .37. To RCAF as **7623** and taken on charge 30.7.40 at RCAF Trenton ONT. Crashed Toronto Island Airport 23.9.41; repaired. Again crashed Toronto Island Airport 4.5.42 but repaired and into storage after test flying 3.8.42. Sold 15.11.42 to Clark Ruse Aircraft; sale cancelled. Sold 26.1.43 to de Havilland Aircraft of Canada Ltd. Reg'd **CF-BFF** 5.12.42 to Quebec Airways Ltd., Montreal PQ. Reg'd 14.12.45 to de Havilland Aircraft of Canada Ltd, Downsview ONT. To L. A. Seguin, Rouyn PQ 16.2.46. To Gold Belt Air Service Ltd, Rouyn PQ 16.7.48. Hit soft spot on ice while landing Ottawa River 20.12.49; partly submerged and damaged beyond repair.

7544 Reg'd **G-AESW** [CofR 7617 3.2.37] to William A. Rollason, Croydon. CofA no.5815 issued 4.3.37. To Nash Aircraft Sales & Hire Ltd., Croydon 12.7.39.. To Air Taxis Ltd., Croydon 24.7.39. Was being operated by A.T.A. HQ White Waltham on outbreak of war. Reg'n cancelled as sold 10.5.40 and impressed as **AV976** 12.5.40. Served with 110 (AAC) Wing, Ringway 13.5.40. Allotted to 7AACU at Castle Bromwich 16.5.40 but possibly not delivered. Used for spares at Ringway and SOC 11.11.40.

7545 To Maj-Gen. H. H. The Maharaja of Indore (Maharajadhiraj Raj Rajeshwar Sawai Shree Yeshwant Rao Holkar Bahadur) with export CofA no.5804 issued 27.2.37. Reg'd **VT-AIE** [CofR 298 3.10.36]. Impressed .41 as **HX792**. SOC 4.9.43. Possibly restored to **VT-AIE**, but reg'n cancelled 4.1.46.

7546 To de Havilland Australia with export CofA no.5764 issued 19.1.37. Reg'd **VH-UXS** 5.8.37 to Southern Airlines & Freighters Ltd., Melbourne VIC. Sold 21.7.39 & reg'd 2.10.39 to T. H. McDonald, Cairns QLD and operated by Guinea Airways Pty. Ltd.,

Port Moresby PNG. Reg'n cancelled on impressment 16.1.42 and allotted RAAF serial **A43-1**. Converted to air ambulance at Guinea Airways 6.2.42. Received 11.2.42 at 2CF. To 1AD 16.2.42. Damaged port mainplane on landing Archerfield QLD 10.8.42. Received at 3AD Archerfield 17.8.42 and passed to Aircrafts Pty Ltd. 21.8.42 for repair. Returned to 3 AD 23.4.43 but swung on take-off 24.4.43 and port undercarriage damaged beyond repair. After further repairs, to Parachute Training Unit, Laverton 9.11.43 to temporarily replace the accident damaged DH84A A34-79 (q.v.). To 3AD Amberley 6.12.44. Sold 9.3.45 to L. McDonald, Cairns QLD for £850 and collected by McDonald 14.3.45. Reg'd **VH-UXS** 8.8.45 to T. H. McDonald, Cairns QLD. Reg'd 12.11.45 to Brown & Dureau Pty Ltd., Melbourne VIC. Reg'n cld 28.9.49. Reg'd 28.12.50 to same owner. Reg'd 21.7.54 to R. N. Hunt, Conargo NSW. Reg'd 21.1.56 to Austral Motorcycles Pty Ltd, Newcastle NSW. Reg'd 9.4.56 to D. L. Hilder, Merewether NSW. Reg'd 20.5.65 to L. G. Randall, Shoal Bay, NSW. Withdrawn from use at Darwin and struck from register 17.7.68.

7547   To L'Aviation Civile Romaine with export CofA no.6051 issued 20.9.37. Reg'd **YR-FLY** 1.10.37 to Liniile Aeriene Romane Exploatate de Statul – L.A.R.E.S. Scrapped 10.45.

7548   To L'Aviation Civile Romaine with export CofA no.6066 issued 27.9.37. Reg'd **YR-FLO** 1.10.37 to Liniile Aeriene Romane Exploatate de Statul – L.A.R.E.S. Withdrawn from use 9.44.

7549   To L'Aviation Civile Romaine with export CofA no.6083 issued 14.10.37. Reg'd **YR-FLU** 23.10.37 to Liniile Aeriene Romane Exploatate de Statul – L.A.R.E.S. Withdrawn from use 1940.

7550   To Swedish Air Force with export CofA no.5940 issued 9.6.37. To **Fv906** (as type Trp3) and coded 6-3. Later codes included 8-99, 8-67, 8-57 and 8-68. Crashed 8.6.42 and SOC 5.43.

7551   To Haerens Flyvertropper (Danish Army Air Force) with serial **S-23**. U.K. export CofA no.5882 issued 24.4.37.

7552   To Haerens Flyvertropper (Danish Army Air Force) with serial **S-24**. U.K. export CofA no.5888 issued 27.4.37. Almost certainly seized when Denmark was over run and subsequently operated by the Germans.

7553   To Misr Airwork with export CofA no.5981 issued 22.7.37. Reg'd **SU-ABW** to Misr Airwork Ltd. Returned to the U.K. and reg'd **G-AIYJ** [CofR 5.12.46] for Cyril Geoffrey Alington, Birmingham. CofA renewed 18.2.47 but lapsed 17.2.48. To Southern Aircraft (Gatwick) Ltd., Gatwick 2.3.48. Sold 7.3.49 and reg'n cancelled as permanently withdrawn from use 14.3.49.

7554   Reg'd **G-AEXI** [CofR 7825 20.5.37] to Lt-Col. Edward Townley Peel M.C., D.S..O., chairman of merchants Peel & Co. Ltd., Alexandria, Egypt. CofA no.5929 issued 27.5.37. Reg'n cancelled as permanently withdrawn from use 11.38 but in fact to Kenya and reg'd **VP-KCS** .38 to Wilson Airways Ltd., Nairobi-Wilson aerodrome. To Kenya Auxiliary Air Unit 9.39. (Note: Two DH90s flew with the Unit, serialled K-13 and K-14 but the tie-up is uncertain).

7555   Reg'd **G-AEWZ** [CofR 7805 10.4.37] to Air Service Training Ltd., Hamble. CofA no.5971 issued 9.7.37. Operated by 3 ERFTS and (wef 11.39) 11 AONS Hamble (later Watchfield). Reg'n cancelled by Secretary of State 10.1.41. Impressed as **DJ716** 10.1.41 and remained operated by 11AONS. To 10MU 19.3.41. Crashed 8.7.41 but repaired and to 39 MU 29.8.41. Issued 30.11.41 to Short Brothers (Rochester & Bedford) Ltd. SOC on sale to 5.46 to Short Bros. Reg'd **G-AEWZ** 30.5.46 to Short Bros (Rochester & Bedford) Ltd. and operated by Rochester Air Charter Service, Rochester. CofA renewed 23.8.46. Reg'd 12.1.48 to Short Bros & Harland Ltd., Rochester. To Frederick T. Bingham, Lockerley 20.12.48 but operated on his behalf by Hampshire School of Flying, Eastleigh. Sold to Vivian H. Bellamy, t/a Flightways, Eastleigh 23.6.49. To Silver City Airways Ltd, Blackbushe 19.7.50. Again to Vivian H. Bellamy, Eastleigh 9.6.60. To Ronald M. Wilson of Devonair Ltd. but operated by Coventry Flying & Country Club, Baginton 7.10.60. Ground-looped on take-off Elmdon 3.3.61. Wreck to Baginton but repairs abandoned. Reg'n cld as pwfu 30.7.64. Forward fuselage last reported in use as a garden shed!

7556   Reg'd **G-AFAN** [CoR 8105 21.7.37] to The de Havilland Aircraft Co. Ltd., Hatfield. CofA no.6008 issued 5.8.37. Reg'n cld as

sold abroad 9.37. Reg'd in Turkey as **TC-IDE** 8.37 to Devlet Hava Yollari. Aircraft ended up in Spain and served with the Republican Forces during the Civil War, possibly as **LY-001**.

7557   To de Havilland Canada without CofA. Stored until RCAF Acceptance flight 27.7.40. Issued to RCAF as **7624** 1.8.40. Operated by 4 Training Command. Soc 8.1.45. Reg'd **CF-BXV** 22.2.45 to Johannesson Flying Service, Winnipeg MT. Ground-looped on landing Winnipeg 3.4.45 and written off.

7558   To de Havilland Canada without CofA. Stored until issued to Royal Canadian Air Force as **7625** 1.8.40. Crashed Claresholm 6.5.42. Soc 8.3.43.

7559   Reg'd **G-AEXN** [CofR 7838 5.37] to The de Havilland Aircraft Co. Ltd., Hatfield. CofA no.5892 issued 16.6.37. To Edward D. Spratt, Hatfield [CofR 8008 19.7.37]. To The Hon. Max Aitken (son and heir of 1st Baron Beaverbrook - see c/n 7514) & Brian S. Thynne, Hendon [CofR 8392 8.3.38]. To Mutual Finance Ltd. and operated by Air Dispatch Ltd., Croydon 30.1.39. Crashed Hampden, near High Wycombe 21.7.39. Reg'n cancelled 29.3.40.

7560   To Air Travel (NZ) Ltd. with export CofA no.5989 issued 22.7.37. Reg'd **ZK-AFB** 23.9.37 to Air Travel (NZ) Ltd, Hokitika. To Canterbury Aero Club, Christchurch [3.52]. To Aircraft Engineering of NZ Ltd and operated by Wairarapa & Ruahine Aero Club. To A. J. Bradshaw; named *Kiwi Rover*. Reg'd 13.5.61 to Air Charter [NZ] Ltd., Christchurch. Lost en route Christchurch-Milford Sound 12.2.62; 5 killed including pilot [and owner of Air Charter (NZ) Ltd.] Brian G. Chadwick.

7561   Export CofA no.6011 issued 6.8.37. To Louis J. Mahieu, Brussels reg'd **OO-JFN** [CofR 416] 25.9.37. Possibly operated by Banque Nationale de Belgique, where owner was director. To Estafette Escadrille, Aeronautique Militaire 10.9.39. To II Group, 2 Regiment 4.40 and retreated to Frejorques, France 5.40. Handed over to Vichy Government on Franco-German armistice 8.40. Marks unknown but Belgian reg'n cancelled 4.3.46.

7562   Export CofA no.6105 issued 28.10.37. To de Havilland Australia, erected at Sydney-Mascot and test flown 28.1.38. Reg'd **VH-UTJ** 23.2.38 (or 9.3.38) to North Western Airlines Ltd., Moree NSW. Undercarriage collapsed on take-off Narromine NSW 16.1.40; repaired. To QANTAS Empire Airways Ltd., Sydney 3.10.40. Damaged on landing Breddon QLD 6.5.43; but repaired. Crashed on landing Breddon QLD (again) 21.10.43; but repaired. Undercarriage collapsed on landing Cloncurry QLD 14.10.45 and repaired yet again. Reg'd 18.10.46 to E. J. Connellan t/a Connellan Airways Ltd., Alice Springs, NT. Nominal change to Connellan Airways Ltd. 14.3.51. Damaged by fire Ammaroo NT 8.1.48 (or 9.1.48). but repaired. Destroyed by fire refuelling Tennant Creek NT 9.8.55. Reg'n cancelled 28.9.55.

7563   To Eagle Oil, Argentina with CofA no.6218 issued 4.3.38. Reg'd **LV-KAB** to Shell Mex Argentina (Pty) Ltd. to replace the ill fated c/n 7537 and named *Gavilan de la Selva*. Erected and test flown Buenos Airies - San Fernando Aerodrome 21.5.38. Crashed on high ground following a collision with Ju52/3m PP-SPF over Botafogo Bay, Rio de Janeiro 8.11.40. Pilot Colin Abbott was killed in this rare fatal accident to an aircraft operated by the Shell Company.

7564   Export CofA no.6261 issued 29.4.38. To Miss M. Reynolds, South Africa reg'd **ZS-ANM** 28.6.38. Impressed as **SAAF1404** 1940. Restored as **ZS-ANM** 1946. Crashed Pietersburg 18.8.49.

7565   Export CofA no.6246 issued 7.4.38. Purchased for operation by the Shell Company of Nigeria Ltd. for £3400 and reg'd **VR-NAA**. Departed Croydon 16.6.38 but was destroyed when it hit an anthill on take-off Abecher 25.9.38. Abecher, in French territory, was an alternate landing ground for Imperial Airways and due to its isolated position, salvage was impossible. Serviceable components were therefore removed, packed for transport back to England and the wreck abandoned.

7566   Export CofA no.6390 issued 5.9.38. To Air Travel [NZ] Ltd., Hokitika reg'd **ZK-AGP** as Fleet No.5. Crashed into the sea off Westport after a propeller came off in flight 21.12.42; 4 passengers killed.

ARGENTINA

R326	7537
LV-KAB	7563
LV-RDA	7537

AUSTRALIA - CIVILIAN

VH-AAD	7508
VH-ADG	7516
VH-UTJ	7562
VH-UXA	7533
VH-UXB	7513
VH-UXS	7546

AUSTRALIA - MILITARY

A43-1	7546

BELGIUM

OO-JFN	7561
OO-PET	7529

CANADA - CIVILIAN

CF-AYF	7506
CF-BBD	7522
CF-BFF	7543
CF-BPD	7538
CF-BXU	7522
CF-BXV	7557
CF-BZA	7531
CF-MPA	7530
CF-MPB	7531
CF-MPC	7522
CF-MPD	7538

CANADA - MILITARY

RCAF7623	7543
RCAF7624	7557
RCAF7625	7558
RCAF7626	7530
RCAF7627	7531
RCAF7628	7522

DENMARK - MILITARY

S-23	7551
S-24	7552

EGYPT

SU-ABW	7553

FRANCE

F-AOYK	7521
F-AOZC	7519
F-APAX	7536
F-APDE	7529
F-APFK	7542
F-AQEU	7501
F-OAMS	7529

Note: OO-JFN (7561) was handed over to the Vichy Govt 8.40, no reg'n known.

GREAT BRITAIN - CIVILIAN

E.2	7500
(G-ABEA)	7529
G-ADNA	7500
G-ADXM	7509
G-AEBU	7501
G-AECW	7504
G-AECX	7505
G-AEDG	7516
G-AEDH	7510
G-AEDI	7511
G-AEDJ	7515
G-AEDK	7517
G-AEDT	7508
(G-AEDU)	7509
G-AEDU	7526
G-AEDV	7524
G-AEDW	7503
G-AEEK	7518
G-AEFN	7507
G-AEHC	7514
G-AESW	7544
G-AEWZ	7555
G-AEXI	7554
G-AEXN	7559
G-AFAN	7556
G-AFRF	7519
G-AFRI	7536
G-AFTF	7533
G-AFVJ	7521
G-AIYJ	7553
G-ANYK	7529

GREAT BRITAIN - MILITARY

V4734	7540
X9327	7509
X9337	7521
X9389	7524
X9390	7507
X9452	7500
AV976	7544
AV987	7510
AV992	7515
AV993	7519
AV994	7536
AW164	7517
AX797	7527
AX855	7505
BD149	7533
DJ716	7555

INDIA-CIVILIAN

VT-AHW	7527
VT-AHY	7540
VT-AIE	7545
VT-AKC	7505

INDIA-MILITARY

HX792	7545

IRAQ

YI-HMK	7502
YI-OSD	7525

ITALY

I-DRAG	7541

Note: A "new" Dragonfly was collected from Hatfield in Spring 1937 by Count Carlo Felice Trossi, a racing driver for the Alfa-Romeo team and President of Scuderia Ferrari. Whilst this might actually have been I-DRAG being re-delivered following repair, more likely it would have been a different aircraft borrowed temporarily when their own machine was undergoing repairs in England. If the latter is correct, it would surely have remained on the British register and G-AESW (7544) is a likely candidate, since the owner of this aircraft, W. A. Rollason, was commissioned to repair I-DRAG.

KENYA - CIVILIAN

VP-KCA	7528
VP-KCS	7554

KENYA - MILITARY

K-13	7528?
K-14	7554?

MOZAMBIQUE

CR-AAB	7526

NETHERLANDS - CIVILIAN

PH-ATK	7539
PH-KOK	7539

NETHERLANDS - MILITARY

LVA 961	7539

NEW ZEALAND

ZK-AFB	7560
ZK-AGP	7566
ZK-AYR	7508

NIGERIA

VR-NAA	7565

ROMANIA

YR-FLO	7548
YR-FLU	7549
YR-FLY	7547

Note: It has been suggested that a fourth Dragonfly was in use by LARES, but this is unconfirmed.

SPAIN

EC-AAQ (3rd series)
7529

EC-BAA (2nd series)
7529

EC-BAB (2nd series)
Note 1

Note 1: The reg'n EC-BAB is not confirmed but if correct, it would have been the second surviving aircraft handed over to Iberia after the Civil War.

SOUTH AFRICA - CIVILIAN

ZS-AHV	7523
ZS-AIK	7535
ZS-ANM	7564
ZS-CTR	7526

SOUTH AFRICA - MILITARY

SAAF1403	7523
SAAF1404	7564
SAAF1408	7535

SOUTHERN RHODESIA

VP-YAX	7512
VP-YBB	7520
VP-YBR	7503

STRAITS SETTLEMENTS/ SINGAPORE

VR-SAX	7511

SWEDEN - MILITARY

Fv.906	7550

TURKEY

TC-IDE	7556

UNITED STATES

N190DH	7526
N2034	7508

URUGUAY

CX-AAR	7532
CX-AAS	7534

Note: In addition, an unidentified Dragonfly seaplane was reportedly being operated by Empresa de Plata, Montevideo .38.

de Havilland
DH92 Dolphin

7.0 de Havilland DH92 DOLPHIN

A new design was assembled in the Hatfield experimental shop during the summer of 1936, to test suggested improvements in the light of operational experience with the Dragon Rapide. Of significance was the allocation of construction number 6400 to the prototype.

Selection of this c/n, suggests that de Havilland were already thinking that DH89 production would terminate before the 150th airframe (c/n 6399). Obviously, like nearly everybody else in the U.K. at the time, de Havilland were not anticipating the forthcoming conflict and the consequent need for large numbers of suitable transports, for the communications and training roles which would be admirably filled by the existing DH89.

Major differences to the Rapide, that it was probably intended to replace, included, a two crew cockpit with dual controls, similar to that fitted to the DH86A, a larger tail fin, an access door towards the rear on the starboard side allowing external access to the main luggage compartment, a hinged nose cone giving access to an extra luggage compartment – similar to that provided on the DH90 Dragonfly and an all important toilet. Another enhancement was the incorporation of a retractable step on the port side. Turn-around delays due to reliance on mobile steps provided by the airfield, has always been a problem and the on-board retractable arrangement was a novel advancement. On-board air stairs are now the order of the day, but it was not until 15 years after the Dolphin first flew, that later series Vickers Viscount aircraft were offered to the airlines with integral steps.

The new aeroplane, like the Dragonfly that preceded it, had mainplanes of unequal length and had ailerons on the upper wings only. Inboard of the engines on each side, additional strengthening allowed the installation of twin 40 gallon fuel tanks. Faired and unfaired fixed undercarriage legs were tried but both arrangements were eventually discarded in favour of one of a fully retractable type, similar in design to that fitted to DH88 Comet racing aircraft.

Variable pitch propellers were intended, but in the event, for the very few flights undertaken, fixed pitch wooden propellers were used.

All these new features contributed to the aircraft being found to be structurally overweight. de Havilland would surely have been able to sort this problem, given time, but their priorities leaned towards quantity production of earlier types such as the DH82A Tiger Moth and the development of the DH91 Albatross. Therefore, after only flying on a few occasions, the decision was taken to scrap the sole prototype late in 1936.

DH92 - Data

Type:	Utility transport
Capacity:	Pilot and up to 8 passengers
Country of origin:	Great Britain
Production period:	-
Engines:	2 X inverted de Havilland Gipsy Six series II, 6 cylinder in-line air cooled piston engines each of 204 h.p.
First flight:	9th September 1936 (at Hatfield)
Total number built: 1	
Production by:	de Havilland Aircraft Co. Ltd., Hatfield, Hertfordshire

DH92 - Specifications

Dimensions (all variants)	
Wing span:	Upper: 50'-6" (15.32m), Lower: 45' 0" (13.65m)
Wing area:	393 sq. ft. (42.3 sq m)
Length:	36'-0" (11.87m)
Height:	10'-3" (3.36m)
Weights:	
Empty:	Unknown
Max take-off:	6,600 lb (3000 kgs)
Performance:	
Initial rate of climb:	Unknown
Max speed:	Estimated 161 m.p.h. (259 kms per hour)
Cruise speed:	Unknown
Service ceiling:	Unknown
Range:	Unknown
Fuel capacity:	80 gallons

DH92 - Productionl

Reg'd **G-AEMX** [CofR 7292 27.8.36] to de Havilland Aircraft Co. Ltd., Hatfield. However, first flew wearing test marks **E.3** 9.9.36. Found to be structurally overweight and no CofA issued. Testing abandoned and believed scrapped soon after Geoffrey de Havilland Jr. flew the aircraft for a second time on 21.11.36. Reg'n cancelled as permanently withdrawn from use. (Note: Entered by de Havilland 8.36 in the Schlesinger African Air Race to Johannesburg ex Portsmouth on 29.9.36 and to be flown by Hugh Buckingham. Allocated the race no.9, but the entry was withdrawn early 9.36).

After the scrapping of its planned replacement, de Havilland built approximately 250 more Rapides at Hatfield before the production line was moved to Loughborough, where Brush completed a further 336 of the type.

8.1 Commercial Operations

It was originally intended to include complete lists of all operators, both civil and military, to show that de Havilland biplane transports of the 1930s were in use throughout the world for a wide variety of tasks and were often the mainstay of well known air transport concerns extant to the present day.

However, once the onerous task of producing a compendium was completed, we realised that we were going to end up with an unwieldy and, it must be said, an expensive book. Furthermore, particularly in the case of the Dragon Rapide, the list included the names of dozens of private individuals which, on reflection, was quite meaningless. Several hundred redundant Dominies were available at a bargain price from 1946 onwards and many demobilised air force pilots used up their severance pay to purchase a machine and attempt to enter the world of aircraft hire and reward. What better way of earning a crust, combining a flying career in civvy street, instant employment without having to obey orders from superiors and in an industry that would surely grow with even greater vigour than the years of rapid expansion leading up to the war?

As can be seen from the production listing, the best of the redundant Dominies, many straight from the factory and directly into store at maintenance units, were snapped up by the bigger players. Those with lesser funds, were often left with aircraft in poor condition and needing extensive work prior to certification. Unable to afford the additional expense, many unconverted Rapides languished at numerous sites around the country. Therefore, the dreams and aspirations of many came to nought and aircraft changed hands often, usually without moving an inch!

We therefore provide a sample of the countries and operators that used the various models featured in this volume. Perhaps in the future, a further publication will appear detailing the worldwide development of air transport. One thing is certain however, such a book would feature de Havilland biplane transports throughout!

ADEN

Aden Airways Ltd.
DH89   VR-AAL (6700), VR-AAP (6804)

ALGERIA

Aerotec(hnique), Algiers
Certainly in existence in 1946, this concern purchased a Rapide in April 1954 and it remained in service until sold in 1957.
DH89   F-OAPT (6447)

Aerosud, Bone
Founded in 1956 and three Rapides were purchased with the first two arriving in 1958 and the third in 1959. On independence, the company moved to France, variously reported, either to Nimes or Avignon. Charters were few and far between and the company stopped flying all together in 1965 and was liquidated in 1967.
DH89   F-BCDB (6897), F-BEFU (6555), F-BHTH (6714)

Air Oasis, Laghouat
This charter outfit commenced operations with a Nord 1203 Norecrin in 1957. Two Rapides were added in 1960 but all flying seems to have ceased during the winter of 1962.63.
DH89   F-BHAF (6931), F-OBOH (6823)

Air Saoura, Colomb-Bechar
Active from the end of 1960, Air Saoura operated a small number of light aircraft in addition to the two Rapides. F-BGXT survived and was flown home when the owner decided to move back to mainland France in 1965.
DH89   F-BGIS (6608), F-BGXT (6941)

Compagnie Generale de Transports en Algerie (C.G.T.A.)
From small beginnings in 1958, a fleet of 3 Boisavia aircraft were joined by a Jodel D.140 and two Avro 19s in 1959 and four Rapides followed in 1960. However, the company ceased trading in 1961.
DH89   F-BFVM (6791), F-OAPT (6447), F-OBHH (6487), F-OBOI (6770)

Societe Generale d'Affretements Aeriens (S.G.A.A.), Algiers
Founded in 1956 by Roger Colin, their first Rapide was received in mid 1957 and by the beginning of 1961, 11 more of the type had joined the fleet. In 1962, the company re-located to Nimes and renamed Air Fret, commenced cargo flying with a diverse fleet of piston engine airliners and had progressed to a Boeing 707 by the time of the company's demise. F-BCDB moved with the company to France and apparently in fair condition, is now with the de Havilland Aircraft Museum Trust at Salisbury Hall.
DH89   F-BCDB (6897), F-BFEH (6723), F-BFVM (6791), F-BGIS (6608), F-BGXT (6941), F-BHAF (6931), F-BHTH (6714), F-LAAL (6408),
         F-OAPT (6447), F-OAUE (6325), F-OBHH (6487), F-OBOI (6770)

Societe Nord-Africaine de Travaux Aeriens, Bone
This small concern was founded in 1956 and two Rapides were purchased in England, one each in 1957 and 1958. The certification of both aircraft expired in May 1962 and they were then broken up prior to the company founder joining the mass exodus to France on Algeria's independence.
DH89   F-OAYS (6815), F-OBIV (6860)

ANGOLA

Divisao de Exploracao dos Transportes Aereos de Angola – D.T.A.,
DH89   CR-LAV (6451), CR-LAU (6452), CR-LAT (6453), CR-LBH (6846), CR-LBG (6847), CR-LBN (6904), CR-LBO (6905), CR-LCK (6932)
         CR-LCO (6430)
DH90   CR-AAB (7526

ARGENTINA

Tuyavion SRL
DH89   LV-AER (6609)

AUSTRALIA

Adastra Airways Pty. Ltd., Mascot, New South Wales
Originally set up to provide aerial survey on contract to the Government and private mining companies. The DH90 was used in this role and also for their daily return flight from Sydney to Bega.
DH83   VH-UQU (4051)
DH90   VH-AAD (7508)

Adelaide Airways Ltd.
Commenced operations October 1935 as a subsidiary of the Adelaide Steamship Co. Initially operated exclusively within South Australia but a route to Broken Hill, New South Wales was commenced before the end of the year. Further expansion followed in July 1937, when the company took over the Adelaide to Perth service from the ailing West Australian Airlines. Merged with Holyman's Airways 1sy July 1936 to form Australian National Airways Pty. Ltd.
DH84   VH-URE (6029)
DH89   VH-UUO (6259), VH-UVI (6318), VH-UVT (6319)

Airlines of Australia Ltd., Mascot, New South Wales
DH84   VH-URG (6046)
DH89   VH-UUO (6259), VH-UVS (6265)

Air Travel and Survey Pty. Ltd.
Crashed in the U.K. prior to departure for Australia.
DH84   VH-UZX (6084)

Airlines (West Australia) Ltd., Maylands, Western Australia
DH84   VH-URY (6082), VH-UZZ (6097)
DH89   VH-UFF (6270)
DH90   VH-ADG (7516)

Australian National Airways Pty. Ltd., Melbourne, Victoria
Formed 1st July 1936 and incorporated the assets and routes of Adelaide Airways and Holyman's Airways. Airlines of Australia Ltd. taken over in 1942. Company purchased by Reg Ansett 1957 and the joint operation renamed Ansett – A.N.A.
DH84   VH-URD (6037), VH-URE 6029), VH-URG (6046)
DH86   VH-USW (2315), VH-UUB (2326)
DH89   VH-UFF (6270), VH-UUO (6259), VH-UXT (6346), VH-UXZ (6365)

Alpine Airways Pty. Ltd.
DH89   VH-AAG (6668)

Butler Air Transport Co., Perth, Western Australia
DH84   VH-AAO (6112), VH-AEF (2057), VH-AIA (2086), VH-URU (6088), VH-URV (6089)
DH89   VH-UUO (6259)

Carpenter & Co. Ltd., W. R., Sydney, New South Wales
Also see entry for their subsidiary Mandated Airlines under Papua New Guinea.
DH86   VH-ADN (2313), VH-UYU (2359), VH-UYV (2360), VH-UYW (2361), VH-UZX (2323)
DH89   VH-UZY (6384)

Carsair Air Services Pty. Ltd., Mount Pleasant, Queensland
Founded by R. G. Carswell around 1960.
DH89   VH-AAG (6668)

Connellan, E. J. (later Connellan Airways), Alice Springs, Northern Territory
Founded by Eddie J. Connellan in 1939. Expanded rapidly with survey flights, mail, cargo and an extensive network of passenger routes. Also contracted to the Flying Doctor Service to supply an ambulance aircraft on demand. One more Rapide VH-BKM (6543) was destroyed in Australia during its delivery flight from England. Company purchased by East West Airlines and the name changed to Northern Airlines.
DH84   VH-AXL (2071)
DH89   VH-AHI (6633), VH-AIK (6497), VH-BKR (6929), VH-UZY (6384)
DH90   VH-UXB (7513), VH-UTJ (7562)

Darwin Air Taxis Ltd., Darwin, Northern Territory
DH89   VH-AAG (6668), VH-ECW (6530)

Holyman's Airways Pty. Ltd., Launceston, Tasmania
Holyman Brothers Pty. Ltd. and Tasmanian Aerial Services Pty. Ltd., both based at Launceston, amalgamated 18th October 1932 and the joint company was named Holyman's Airways Pty. Ltd. In turn, merged with others to form Australian National Airways on 1st July 1936.
DH83   VH-UQM (4010)
DH84   VH-URD (6037), VH-URG (6046)
DH86   VH-URN (2301), VH-URT (2312), VH-USW (2315), VH-UUB (2326)
DH89   VH-UFF (6270)

James Air Charter, Wollongong, New South Wales
DH89   VH-UFF

James Taxiplane Ltd., Maylands, Western Australia
DH83   VH-ABU (4047)

MacRobertson-Miller Aviation Co. Ltd.
DH83   VH-UDD (4063), VH-USJ (4058), VH-UTP (4039), VH-UVL (4015),
DH84   VH-ABK (6062), VH-URF (6045), VH-URW (6080), VH-URX (6081), VH-URY (6082), VH-UVN (6106)
DH86   VH-USC (2307), VH-USD (2308), VH-USF (2310), VH-USW (2315)

Marshall Airways, Bankstown, New South Wales
DH84   VH-AOE (2058), VH-AQU (2048)

Muir Aviation, Darwin, Northern Territories
DH84   VH-DMA (6029), VH-DMB (2072)

North Australian Aviation Services, Darwin, Northern Territory
DH84   VH-AFH (2085), VH-BDS (2081)

Northern Queensland Airways, Cairns, Queensland
A single Dragon was purchased but did not enter service as it was written-off prior to delivery.
DH84   VH-UZG (6027)

North WesternAirlines Ltd., Moree, New South Wales
DH90   VH-UTJ (7562)

QANTAS Empire Airways Ltd., Longreach, Queensland (later at Sydney, New South Wales)
As may be expected, QANTAS operated the largest fleet of de Havilland biplane transports in Australia but somewhat surprisingly no Rapides.
The Fox Moths were mainly operated on behalf of air ambulance organisations in Queensland as were a number of the Dragons.
DH83   VH-URI (4084), VH-USL (4096), VH-UUS (4044), VH-UZC (4048), VH-UZD (4040)
DH84   VH-AEF (2057), VH-AIA (2086), VH-AMN (2059), VH-AOK (2056), VH-AOR (2042), VH-AOT (2050), VH-AQW (2068),
         VH-ASU (2079), VH-AXL (2071), VH-AYM (2031), VH-BAF (2027), VH-BAH (2055), VH-BDS (2081), VH-URD (6037),
         VH-URY (6082), VH-UZF (6065)
DH86   VH-USC (2307), VH-USD (2308), VH-USE (2309), VH-USF (2310), VH-USG (2311), VH-USW (2315), VH-UUA (2306)
DH90   VH-UTJ (7562), VH-UXB (7513)

Queensland Flying Services, Brisbane, Queensland
DH84   VH-AOK (2056), VH-UXG (6077)

Rockhampton Aerial Services, Rockhampton, Queensland
DH89   VH-ABN (6253)

South Queensland Airways Pty. Ltd.
DH84   VH-ABK (6062)
DH86   VH-ADN (2313)

Tasmanian Aerial Services Pty. Ltd., Launceston, Tasmania
This company and Holyman Brothers Pty. Ltd. amalgamated on 18th October 1932 and the joint company was named Holyman's Airways Pty.
Ltd. In turn, merged with others, to form Australian National Airways Pty. Ltd. 7th November 1936.
DH83   VH-UQM (4010)
DH84   VH-URD (6037)

Trans-Australia Airlines
Mainly operated on behalf of various air ambulance services.
DH84   VH-AEF (2057), VH-ALL (2022), VH-AMN (2059), VH-ASU (2079), VH-BAH (2055)

West Australian Airways Ltd., Perth, Western Australia
DH84   VH-URE (6029), VH-URO (6068)
DH89   VH-UUO (6259)

BAHRAIN

Gulf Aviation Ltd.
DH86   G-ADUF (2334), G-ADUH (2336), G-ADVJ (2338)

BELGIUM

Cogea Nouvelle, Keerbergen
DH89   OO-ARN (6785), OO-ARI (6797)

BELGIAN CONGO

Air Brousse SPRL
DH89   OO-ARN (6785), OO-CJU (6380), OO-CJS (6429), OO-CJW (6508), OO-CRS (6559), OO-CJD (6607), OO-CJX (6658),
         OO-CMS (6902), OO-CJE (6918)

Air Congo
DH89   OO-CFI (6932)

BRAZIL

Arco Iris Viacao Aerea SA
DH89   PP-AIA (6920), PP-AID (6921), PP-AIB (6922), PP-AIC (6923), PP-AIE (6970), PP-AIF (6971), PP-AIG (6972)

Organizacao Mineira de Transportes Aereos SA - O.M.T.A.
DH89   PP-OMA (6449), PP-OMB (6927), PP-OMC (6960), PP-OMD (6774)

Viacao Aerea Sao Paulo SA - V.A.S.P., Sao Paulo
DH84   PP-SPC (6085)

Viacao Aerea Rio-Gradense SA – VARIG, Porto Allegre
Despite legal difficulties which prevented them using the Rapide purchased in 1942, VARIG's management obviously believed that the acquisition of their first aeroplane was important enough, to import another example from Africa in the 1970s. This was totally reconditioned at their Porto Allegre base and is now exhibited, wearing contrived marks PP-VAN, in Rio de Janeiro.
DH89   PP-LAA (6449)

CANADA

Associated Airways Ltd., Edmonton, Alberta
DH90   CF-BZA (7531)

Austin Airways Ltd., Timmins, Ontario
Originally founded on 22nd May 1935 to serve settlements in the Hudson Bay area.
DH83   CF-ATX (4049)

British North American Airways
DH89   CF-AYE (6304)

Canadian Airways
Formed 5th May 1928 and one of ten small Canadian bush operators that merged on 30th January 1942 to form Canadian Pacific Airlines Ltd.
DH83   CF-API (4000)
DH84   CF-APJ (6024), CF-AVD (6086)
DH89   CF-AYE (6304), CF-BBH (6370), CF-BNG (6472)

Central British Columbia Airways
DH83   CF-DIQ (FM.17)

Central Northern Airways, Winnipeg, Manitoba
DH89   CF-BND (6375)

A. Fecteau Air Transport Aerien, Senneteere, Quebec
Utilising Fox Moth CF-ATX, Arthur Fecteau commenced operations in 1936 and went on to purchase the first Canadian built example. In later years, a major user of the various S.T.O.L. products of de Havilland of Canada. Since May 1968, a subsidiary of Quebecair Inc.
DH83   CF-ATX (4049), CF-BFI (FM.1)

Ginger Coote Airways
One of ten small Canadian bush operators that merged on 30th January 1942 to form Canadian Pacific Airlines Ltd.
DH89   CF-BNG (6472)

Gold Belt Air Service Ltd., Rouyn, Quebec
DH90   CF-BFF (7543)

Johannesson Flying Service, Winnipeg, Manitoba
DH90   CF-BXU (7522), CF-BXV (7557)

Maritime Central Airways
DH89   CF-BNJ (89232)

Newfoundland Airways
DH83   CF-BNM (FM.5)

North-Air Services Ltd., Lac l'Orange
A Rapide was purchased in the U.K. and it was intended to operate the aircraft on floats, but the plans came to nought.
DH89   CF-PTK (6254)

Ontario Provincial Air Service
DH83   CF-APG (4038)

Parson's Airways, Kenora, Ontario
DH83   CF-BNO (FM.7)

Polaris Charter Co. Ltd., Yellowknife, North West Territories
Founded by Maxwell C. Ward to provide passenger transport to the isolated communities in the Arctic regions of Northern Canada and also serving trappers, carrying their pelts to Yellowknife for onward shipping. Always a live wire in Canada's aviation world, in 1953 Wardair was formed and in 1962, as Wardair Canada Ltd., he entered the trans-Atlantic charter market
DH83   CF-DJC (FM.29)

Prospector Airways
DH83   CF-ATX (4049)

Quebec Airways Ltd., Montreal, Quebec
One of ten small Canadian bush operators that merged on 30th January 1942 to form Canadian Pacific Airlines Ltd.
DH84   CF-AVD (6086)
DH89   CF-AEO (6279), CF-AVJ (6295) CF-AYE (6304), CF-BBC (6307), CF-BBH (6370), CF-BFL (6373)
DH90   CF-BFF (7543)

Queen Charlotte Airlines
DH89   CF-AYE 6304), CF-BND (6375)

Spartan Air Services
DH89   CF-BNJ (89232)

CAPE VERDE ISLANDS

Transportes Aereos de Cabo Verde
CR-CAA (6905)

CHILE

Linea Area de Pacifico Sur Ltda.
This company operated at least one Rapide (c/n 6820) in early 1948 but further information and the registration are unknown.

CHINA

A total of seven aircraft were purchased by the Military Council of the Nationalist Government of China. We quote verbatim from the 11th May 1938 edition of the Hong Kong newspaper, South China Morning Post:-

"Hospital Planes – British Machines Being Assembled Locally. The second trio of six English planes brought to Hong Kong for assembly for the Chinese Government by the Far East Aviation Corporation are at present being unpacked. These planes, de Havilland DH89s are similar in most respects to the DH86 except that they have two engines instead of four. They were designed for use as hospital planes and were the first machines for which permission was granted for them to be assembled and flown from Hong Kong. The three original planes, delivered some weeks ago to Chinese pilots who flew them from Kai Tak, are all destroyed. Two of them crashed on landing in China, one completely breaking up, while the third was shot down by Chinese anti-aircraft fire when it appeared over a Chinese airport in its original colours, which were not the same as those on ambulance planes used by the Chinese Medical Corps. Each plane carries four stretchers and can carry a load of 2,000 pounds".

This article aids identification of the three unfortunate ambulance aircraft illustrated in this book. The original photograph shows a DH60GIII Moth Major aircraft VR-HCU lurking in the distance. This aircraft was cancelled from the Hong Kong register by 30th April 1938 and as the article appeared the following month, the picture can only show the first three! The second batch, c/ns 6390/6391/6392, are thought to have been fitted out as passenger transports for China National Aviation Corporation (an American owned company in which Pan American had a major interest). Amongst the de Havilland archive, there is a picture of a single DH89A in ambulance colour scheme shot at Kai Tak and we are tempted to surmise that the final machine, c/n 6444, is that aeroplane, perhaps purchased to cover the disastrous attrition!.

DJIBOUTI

Air Djibouti
DH89   F-OCBX (6563)

EGYPT

Misr Airwork, Cairo
DH83   SU-ABA (4022), SU-ABG (4024)
DH84   SU-ABH (6028), SU-ABI (6031), SU-ABJ (6051), SU-ABZ (6032)
DH86   SU-ABN (2320), SU-ABO (2329), SU-ACR (2334), SU-ABV (2342), SU-ACR (2334)
DH89   SU-ABP (6298), SU-ABQ (6299), SU-ABR (6302), SU-ABS (6303), SU-ABU (6313), SU-ACS (6544), SU-ACT (6551)
DH90   SU-ABW (7553)

Peacock Air Charter, Alexandria
DH86   G-AJNB (2342)

FIJI

Air Viti
DH83   VQ-FAT (4033)

Fiji Airways Ltd.
DH89   VQ-FAL (6707), VQ-FAM (6471), VQ-FAN (6577)

FINLAND

Aero Oy
Two Rapides were ordered "for experiments with internal services" according to an article that appeared in *The Aeroplane* magazine dated 23rd December 1936.
DH89   OH-BLA (6347), OH-BLB (6401)

Lentohuolto Oy
DH89   OH-VKH (6347), OH-VKI (6401)

Savon Lentolinjat Oy
DH89   OH-VKH (6347), OH-VKI (6401)

FRANCE

Air Caen, Carpiquet Airfield, Caen
Purchased in 1950, Air Caen's Rapide served them well for over 20 years until sale back to the country of origin. Although the aircraft flew little during the period, its more frequent short hops were to Jersey in the Channel Islands.
DH89   F-BFPU (6796)

Air France, Paris
Three Rapides were purchased from British European in November 1947 and they were delivered to Ivato in Madagascar, via Le Bourget April 1948. Use of the French registrations was fairly brief, for they were changed to the French overseas series F-OADX/DY/DZ respectively in May 1949.
DH89   F-BEDX (6547), F-BEDY (6276), F-BEDZ (6522)

Air Ouest, Nantes
DH89   F-BGIS (6608), F-BGXT (6941), F-BHAF (6931)

Rousseau Aviation, Dinard
The five Rapides listed below were purchased for onward resale, but in the event, were used By Rousseau for local services in Britanny. Two other aircraft were purchased for dismantling and some parts were built into Fokker replicas for the Blue Max film. Rousseau also provided another Rapide to the film maker which was used as a camera ship. The proprietor, Claude Rousseau, sold out to Soc. Auxiliarede Services et de Material Aeronautiques who also owned Touraine Air Transport and the two networks were integrated in 1973.
DH89   F-BEKB (6596), F-BGXT (6941), F-BGZJ (6913), F-BHOB (6578), F-BLHE (6870)

FRENCH GUYANA

Societe Aerienne de Transport Guyane Antilles
DH89   F-OAQL (6839), F-OAUG (6811), F-OAXK (6584), F-OBVL (6657), F-OCHF (6735), F-OGAU (6758)

GABON

Transportes Aeriens du Gabon, Libreville
DH89   F-OAIH (6715), F-OAND (6909), F-OAPS (6638), F-OAQU (6836), F-OATF (6629), F-OAVZ (6453)

Compagnie Aeronautique Jean-Claude Brouillet, Libreville
DH89   F-OAIH (6715), F-OBAQ (6424), F-OBMQ (6878), F-OBOD (6412)

GERMANY

Hamburg Aero-Lloyd
DH89   D-IDAK (6467)

Hanseatische Flugdienst gmbh
DH89   D-IDAK (6467)

GREAT BRITAIN

Aberdeen Airways Ltd. (later Allied Airways (Gandar Dower) Ltd.)
DH84   G-ACAN (6000), G-ACLE (6044), G-ACNJ (6072), G-ACRH (6078), G-ADFI (6100
DH86   G-AETM (2353)
DH89   G-ACZE (6264), G-ACZF (6268), G-ADAH (6278), G-ADDE (6282), G-ADDF (6284), G-AGDM (6584), G-AGHI (6455), G-AIDL (6968)

Adie Aviation Ltd., Croydon, Surrey
DH89   G-AFMF (6432), G-GJG (6517), G-AKZW (6896)

Aerial Enterprises Ltd., Booker Aerodrome, High Wycombe, Buckinghamshire
DH89   G-AGJG (6517), G-AJGS (W.1001)

Aikman Airways Ltd., Croydon, Surrey (also at Thame, Oxfordshire)
DH89   G-AKND (6515)

Air Charter Ltd., Croydon, Surrey (also at Bovingdon, Hertfordshire and later at Stansted and Southend, Essex)
DH84   G-ADDI (6096)
DH89   G-AFHY (6417), G-AGFU (6463)

Air Charter Experts Ltd., Ronaldsway, Isle of Man
DH89   G-ADAE (6272), G-AEMH (6336)

Air Commerce Ltd., Croydon, Surrey
DH89   G-AERZ (6356), G-AFEP 6406), G-AHGG (6902)
DH90   G-AEFN (7507)

Air Couriers (Transport) Ltd., Croydon, Surrey (later at Biggin Hill, Kent and finally at Gatwick, Sussex)
DH89   G-AKNN (6598), G-AKNY (6470), G-AKSE (6870), G-AKTD (6791), G-ALBI (6525), G-APBM (6748)

Aircraft and Engineering Services Ltd., Croydon, Surrey
DH89   G-ACPP (6254), G-AFHY (6417), G-AJMY (6511), G-AKVU (6476)

Air Dispatch Ltd., Croydon, Surrey
Formed 9.7.34 by the Honourable Mrs. Victor Bruce, with a nominal capital of £100. The company was the driving force behind "Inner Circle Airlines", connecting the many airfields surrounding London.
DH84   G-ACBW (6009), G-ACCZ (6015), G-ACET (6021), G-AEKZ (6028)
DH89   G-ADAK (6281), G-ADNH (6300)
DH90   G-AECX (7505), G-AEDJ (7515), G-AEDK (7517), G-AEXN (7559), G-AFRF (7519), G-AFRI (7536), G-AFTF (7533)

Air Enterprises Ltd., Croydon, Surrey and Glasgow-Renfrew Aerodromes
Founded by Messrs. Henry, Arthur & Francis Carr plus Thomas Hudson at Croydon April '47. Rapide G-AFMJ joined the fleet in December 1947 and scheduled passenger services commenced from Southampton to Cowes, Isle of Wight and from Croydon and Gatwick to Cowes with an extension to Sandown on the Croydon service in July 1948. These services, operated during the summer months only, continued each year until the company ceased to trade in 1953. In winter, aircraft were used extensively for ad hoc passenger and freight work and in addition, Air Enterprise enjoyed a lucrative contract with the United Nations Commission to operate air services in Israel from 1947-1949. Although Airspeed Consul aircraft were normally used, Rapide G-AKRS was chartered for the use of the forthcoming Prime Minister David Ben-Gurion in Spring 1948. This aircraft is now the major exhibit at the Israeli Air Force Museum, Tel Aviv Airport.
DH89   G-AFMJ, G-AKNX, G-AKNY, G-AKNZ, G-AKOA, G-AKOB, G-AKRS, G-ALWY

Air Kruise Ltd., Lympne, Kent (also at Ramsgate and Lydd in Kent and Blackbushe in Hampshire)
DH89   G-AESR (6363), G-AEWL (6367), G-ALWK (6856)

Airlines (Jersey) Ltd., Jersey, Channel Islands
DH89   G-AGHI (6455), G-AGLE (6784), G-AGLP (6780), G-AGSH (6884), G-AGUP (6911), G-AHEB (6945), G-AIBB (6813),
         G-AKED (6487), G-AKNE (6591), G-AKNF (6518), G-AKNX (6629), G-AKOA (6618)

Airmotive Company Ltd., Pwllheli, Caernarvonshire (also operated from Speke)
DH89   G-AFOI (6450)

Air Navigation & Trading Co. Ltd., Squires Gate, Lancashire
DH84   G-ACIT (6039), G-ADDI (6096)
DH86   G-ADUF (2334)
DH89   G-ACPP (6254), G-AHJA (6486), G-AJBJ (6765), G-AJKW (6539), G-AKOY (6504), G-AKSG (6931), G-AKZT (6894), G-ALXI (6690),
         G-ALXJ (6863), G-APSD (6556)

Air Taxi (Cumberland) Ltd., Carlisle, Cumberland
DH89   G-ALPK

Air Taxis (Croydon) Ltd.
DH84   G-ACHV (6035), G-ACNJ (6072), G-ACPX (6075), G-AECZ (6105)
DH86   G-AEJM (2351)
DH89   G-AGZO (6913)
DH90   G-AESW (7544)

Air Transport Charter (C.I.) Ltd., Jersey, Channel Islands
DH89   G-AFFB (6409), G-AGWC (6916), G-AIUL (6837)

Airviews Ltd., Manchester
DH89   G-AFRK (6441), G-AGDM (6584), G-AGSH (6884), G-ALBA (6821)

Airwork Ltd., Blackbushe, Hampshire (later at Gatwick, Sussex)
DH89   G-AESR (6363), G-AJDN (6860), G-AKJS (W.1002), G-AKRS (6952), G-AKTZ (6482)

Anglo-European Airways Ltd., Cardiff
DH84   G-ACBW (6009), G-ACEK (6019), G-ACKU (6066)

Arrow Air Services Ltd., Shipdham, Norfolk
DH89   G-AKRS (6952)

Astral Aviation Ltd., West Hartlepool (later at Newcastle-upon-Tyne)
DH89   G-AKNN (6598)

Atlantic Coast Air Service (founded by Robert T. Boyd)
DH84   G-ACCR (6011)

Barnstaple and North Devon Air Service, Barnstable, Devon
DH84   G-ACCR (6011)

Bees Flight Ltd., Sandown, Isle of Wight
DH89   G-AKMH (6704)

BCI (British Cellulose Industries) Airways Ltd., Barton Aerodrome, Manchester
DH89   G-AFMF (6432)

Birkett Air Services Ltd., Heston, Middlesex (later Croydon, Surrey)
Company registered 31st October 1932.
DH89   G-AJBJ (6765), G-AJDN (6860), G-AKTZ (6482)
DH90   G-AEDV (7524)

Blackpool and West Coast Air Services Ltd. (Renamed West Coast Air Services Ltd. 1937 and later still, to Isle of Man Air Services Ltd.)
Company registered 3rd April 1933. One of the airlines absorbed by B.E.A.C. on formation 1st February 1947.
DH83   G-ACFC (4053), G-ACFF (4060)
DH84   G-ACGU (6034), G-ACPY (6076), G-ADCP (6092), G-ADCR (6094)
DH86   G-ADVJ (2338), G-ADVK (2339), G-ADYH (2344), G-AENR (2352)
DH89   G-AENO (6341), G-AERN (6345)

Bond Air Sevices Ltd., Sywell, Northamptonshire (also at Southend, Essex and Gatwick, Sussex)
DH86   G-ADUH (2336), G-ADVJ (2338)
DH89   G-AKOG (6878)

Bournemouth Air Taxi Company Ltd., Hurn Airport (also traded as Bournair)
DH89   G-AKRS (6952)

British Air Transport Ltd., Redhill, Surrey (also at Croydon and Kenley, Surrey)
DH83   G-ACCF (4046)

British Airways Ltd., Eastleigh (later at Gatwick). Some aircraft were also reported as based at Abridge, Essex.
DH84   G-ACAP (6002), G-ACEU (6022), G-ACEV (6023), G-ACMC (6053), G-ACMJ (6058), G-ACNG (6069), G-ACNI (6071),
         G-ACOR (6073)
DH86   G-ADEA (2323), G-ADEB (2324), G-ADEC (2325), G-ADYC (2340), G-ADYD (2341), G-ADYE (2346), G-ADYG (2343),
         G-ADYH (2344), G-ADYI (2345), G-ADYJ (2348)
DH89   G-ACPN (6262), G-ACPO (6253), G-ADAE (6272), G-ADAG (6266), G-ADAH (6278), G-ADAI(6287), G-ADAJ (6276),
         G-ADAK (6281), G-ADAL (6262), G-ADBU (6280), G-ADBX (6289), G-ADDF (6284), G-ADIM (6293)

British American Air Services Ltd., Heston, Middlesex (also at White Waltham, Berkshire and later at Bovingdon, Hertfordshire)
DH84   G-ACGU (6034)
DH89   G-ADFX (6290), G-AGWC (6916), G-AGZJ (6936), G-AGZK (6937)

British Continental Airways Ltd., Croydon, Surrey
DH84   G-ACOR (6073)
DH86   G-ADEA (2323), G-ADEB (2324), G-ADEC (2325), G-ADMY (2327), G-ADYC (2340), G-ADYD (2341), G-ADYF (2347)

British European Airways Corporation, Northolt, Middlesex
The British Government announced that a new State owned airline would take over all domestic schedules with effect from 1st February 1947. Absorbed on that date were, Great Western and Southern Airlines, Isle of Man Air Services, Railway Air Services and Scottish Airways. This nationalisation was treated with great disdain by the majority of operators, who had struggled to build a network of scheduled airline services in the years leading up to the war. Most vociferous were E. L. Gandar Dower of Allied Airways in Aberdeen and Channel Island Airways, resident in Jersey and Guernsey. These two companies managed to hold on to their independence for a few weeks more but Channel Island Airways became part of the Corporation on 1st April 1947 and Allied Airways followed a few days later on the 12th April. No fewer than 39 Dragon Rapides were on the books of the various airlines absorbed in the spring of 1947 but it seems probable that some never actually flew with B.E.A. and were stored pending onward sale in 1947/1948.
DH84   G-ACIT (6039), G-ADDI (6096) – leased for a short time
DH89   G-ACPP (6254), G-ACZF (6268), G-ADAJ (6276), G-AERN (6345), G-AEWL (6367), G-AFEZ (6408), G-AFOI (6450),
         G-AFRK (6441), G-AGDG (6547), G-AGDM (6584), G-AGEE (6622), G-AGHI (6455), G-AGIC (6522), G-AGIF (6509),
         G-AGJF (6499), G-AGJG (6517), G-AGLE (6784), G-AGLP (6780), G-AGLR (6781), G-AGOJ (6850), G-AGPH (6889),
         G-AGPI (6885), G-AGSH (6884), G-AGSJ (6888), G-AGSK (6887), G-AGUF (6855), G-AGUG (6859), G-AGUP (6911),
         G-AGUR (6910), G-AGUU (6908), G-AGUV (6912), G-AHGF (6903), G-AHGH (6934), G-AHGI (6935), G-AHKR (6824),
         G-AHKS (6812), G-AHKT 6811), G-AHKU (6810), G-AHKV (6792), G-AHLL (6576), G-AHLM (6708), G-AHLN (6754),
         G-AHXV (6810), G-AHXW (6782), G-AHXX (6800), G-AHXY (6808), G-AHXZ (6825), G-AIHN (6498), G-AJCL (6722),
         G-AJSK (6500), G-AJXB (6530), G-AKDX (6898), G-AKZB (6790)

British Hospitals Air Pageants Ltd., Hanworth, Middlesex
DH83   G-ABUP (4001)

British Overseas Airways Corporation – B.O.A.C.
Formed 1st April 1940 to operate overseas services formerly undertaken by Imperial Airways. Inherited from Imperial, the backbone of their fleet was initially 6 DH86 aircraft. Although a total of 27 Rapides were nominally owned by B.O.A.C. at various times, only a handful were actually operated by the Corporation; HK917 (6321) was an Iranian aircraft impressed by the R.A.F. and flown on their behalf by civilian crews of B.O.A.C. and G-AFEN (6399) was similarly used in the Middle East, flown from Heliopolis. Though registered to B.O.A.C., G-AHGH (6934) and G-AHGI (6935) were flown by Railway Air Services crews. Two Dominies, X7485 (6602) and NR721 (6809), were loaned by the R.A.F. for training purposes at Whitchurch and in this role, Rapide G-AIBB (6813) was later pressed into service. Four aircraft, G-AHKR (6824), G-AHKT (6811), G-AHKU (6810) and G-AHKV (6792) were registered to the B.E.A.C. Division of B.O.A.C. but this incongruous situation was rectified soon after by the two new corporations going their independent ways. The airline aided a number of airlines setting up operations after the war and, without exception, all utilised the DH89 of which large stocks were then available surplus to R.A.F. requirements. Aircraft were transferred to B.O.A.C. after preparation to Rapide standard at Witney. Except in the case of East African Airways Corporation, British registrations were not allocated, the aircraft being delivered with their overseas marks already applied. Airlines involved were: Aden Airways with VR-AAL (6700), Iraqi Airways with YI-ABD (6897), YI-ABE (6898), YI-ABF (6906), YI-ABG (6907), YI-ABH (6909) and Middle East Airlines in the Lebanon with LR-AAD (6843), LR-AAE (6894), LR-AAF (6896). Arrangements for Nairobi based East African Airways Corporation were slightly different however. One aircraft appeared on the Kenyan register, VP-KEF (6831) but six others were initially flown by British based crews and flown for a time wearing British marks. These were G-AGNH (6803), G-AGOT (6876), G-AGOU (6875), G-AGOV (6874), G-AGOW (6849) and G-AGOX (6848) and the subsequent marks may be seen under the Kenya heading.
DH86   G-ACPL (2300), G-ACWC (2304), G-ACWD (2305), G-ADFF (2328), G-ADUF (2334), G-ADUI (2337)
DH89   See text.

British South American Air Services Ltd., Croydon, Surrey
DH86   G-ADMY (2327)

British Westpoint Airlines Ltd., Exeter, Devon
DH89   G-AGSH (6884), G-AHKU (6810), G-AIUL (6837), G-AJCL (6722), G-ASKO (6735)

Brooklands Aviation Ltd., Weybridge, Surrey (also Sywell, Northamptonshire and Shoreham, Sussex)
DH89   G-AJHO (6835), G-AJHP (6770), G-AKJY (6447), G-AKSH (6471)

Cambrian Airways Ltd., Pengam Moors Airfield, Cardiff (also at Pwllheli and later at Cardiff-Rhoose and Speke)
DH89   G-AGSI (6886), G-AGZJ (6936), G-AIYE (6815), G-AJCL (6722), G-AKUB (6488), G-AKUC (6565), G-ALAT (6851),
         G-ALRW (6941), G-ALZJ (6573)

Cecil Kay Aircraft (1945) Ltd., Birmingham-Elmdon
DH89   G-AGZU (6773)

Channel Island Air Services Ltd., Jersey, Channel Islands
DH89   G-AESR (6363)

Channel Islands Airways Ltd. (t/a both Guernsey Airways and Jersey Airways)
DH84   G-ACCE (6010), G-ACMC (6053), G-ACMJ (6058), G-ACMO (6062), G-ACMP (6063), G-ACNG (6069), G-ACNH (6070),
         G-ACNI (6071), G-ACNJ (6072)
DH86   G-ACYF (2313), G-ACYG (2314), G-ACZN (2316), G-ACZO (2318), G-ACZP (2321), G-ACZR (2322), G-ADVK (2339),
         G-AENR (2352)
DH89   G-ADBV (6286), G-ADBW (6288), G-AGLP (6780), G-AGPI (6885), G-AGSH (6884), G-AGSK (6887), G-AGUF (6855),
         G-AGUG (6859), G-AHXX (6800)

Chrisair Aviation Services Ltd., Ramsgate, Kent (later at Sywell, Northamptonshire)
DH84   G-ADDI (6096)

Ciro's Aviation Ltd., Gatwick, Sussex
DH89   G-AFMA (6430), G-AKGV (6796)

Commercial Air Hire Ltd., Croydon, Surrey
Company registered 7.8.34, capital £500. Commenced operations during the month with an early morning newspaper delivery service from Croydon to Paris. This service was usually operated by Dragon G-ACCR, Commercial's first aircraft.
DH84   G-ACAP (6002), G-ACBW (6009), G-ACCR (6011), G-ACDN (6018), G-ACEK (6019), G-ACKB (6055), G-ACKC (6056),
        G-ACKU (6066), G-AEMI (6110), G-AEMK (6112)

Crilly Airways Ltd., Braunstone, Leicestershire
DH83   G-ACEY (4057)
DH84   G-ACCZ (6015), G-ACDN (6018), G-ACLE (6044)

Cumberland Aviation Services Ltd., Carlisle, Cumberland (also traded as Casair)
DH89   G-AIUL (6837), G-ALGE (6907)

Darlington and District Aero Club Ltd.,
Registered 6th August 1947, and the two Rapides were added to their charter and air taxi fleet in 1948 and 1950. Charters were few and far between during the winter of 1951/52 and the decision was taken to discontinue that side of the business and instead, to concentrated on the flying training side.
DH89   G-AKOE (6601), G-ALXA (6727)

Denham Aero Services Ltd., Denham, Buckinghamshire
DH89   G-AKOP (6636), G-AKTX (6639)

Derby Aviation Ltd., Burnaston, Derbyshire
DH89   G-AEAL (6325), G-AIUK (6640), G-AIUL (6837), G-AKME (6767)

Don Everall (Aviation) Ltd., Wolverhampton
DH89   G-AGDP (6403), G-AGLR (6781), G-AHPT (6478), G-AKZO (6575)

Dragon Airways Ltd., Pwllheli (later moved to Speke and later still, to Newcastle)
DH89   G-AHPT (6478), G-AIYP (6456), G-AKOB (6492)

Eagle Aviation Ltd., Aldermaston, Berkshire (later moved to Luton, Bedfordshire and then Blackbushe, Hampshire)
DH89   G-HKS (6812), G-AJSL (6801), G-AJXB (6530), G-AKOB (6492)

East Anglian Flying Services Ltd., Southend, Essex (also at Ipswich, Suffolk)
DH89   G-AEMH (6336), G-AKJZ (6880), G-AKOV (6612), G-AKRN (6513), G-AKSC (6779)

Eastern Air Transport Ltd., Skegness, Lincolnshire
DH83   G-ABVJ (4006)

East Riding Flying Club (Speeton) Ltd., Speeton, Yorkshire
DH89   G-ALZF (6541)

Federated Air Transport Ltd., Speke
DH89   G-AIBB (6813), G-ANZP (6682), G-AOAO (6844). Also X7437 (6578) and X7498 (6615) for spares use.

Flight Charter Ltd./Flightways, Eastleigh, Hampshire
DH89   G-AHGF (6903), G-AHGH (6934), G-AIYP (6456), G-AKNE (6591), G-ALAX (6930)
DH90   G-AEWZ (7555)

Gandar Dower, E. L., Aberdeen
DH89   G-ADAH (6278), G-AIDL (6968), G-AJGS (W.1001)

Giro Aviation Co. Ltd., Hesketh Park, Southport, Lancashire
DH83   G-ACCB (4042), G-ACEJ (4069)

Goodhew Aviation Ltd., Kidlington, Oxfordshire
DH89   G-AIDL (6968), G-AKSL (6865), G-AKVU (6476)

Great Western & Southern Airlines Ltd., Shoreham, Sussex (later Speke and at Land's End)
Great Western Railway inaugurated Cardiff to Plymouth scheduled services 11.4.33, using a Westland Wessex aircraft chartered from Imperial Airways. Service extended to Birmingham (Castle Bromwich) 22.5.33.
DH84   G-ACPY (6076), G-ADDI (6096)
DH89   G-ACPP (6254), G-ACPR (6255), G-ACYM (6269), G-AGEE (6622), G-AGIF (6509), G-AGUV (6912)

Hampshire Aeroplane Club, Southampton, Hampshire
DH86   G-ACZP (2321)

Hargreaves Airways Ltd. (Wheels & Wings)
DH89   G-AIUI (6675)

Herts and Essex Aero Club Ltd./Thurston, Stapleford, Essex
DH89   G-AGZU (6773), G-AKTY (6563), G-AKZH (6529), G-ALXT (6736)

Highland Airways Ltd., Inverness-Longman Aerodrome
Company registered in Edinburgh 3.4.33 to operate air services in Northern Scotland from a base to be established at Inverness. Managing Director was Capt. E. E. Fresson, Chairman R. Donald – managing director of Macrae and Dick Ltd., foremost Inverness bus and coach opera-tor. Commenced scheduled services Inverness to Wick, continuing to Kirkwall and Thurso, initially with Monospar aircraft 8.5.33.
DH84   G-ACCE (6010), G-ACET (6021), G-ACGK (6033), G-ACIT (6039), G-ADCT (6095)
DH89   G-ADAJ (6276), G-AEWL (6367)

Hillman's Saloon Coaches & Airways Ltd., Brentwood (later based Romford-Maylands and renamed Hillman's Airways Ltd.)
Hillman took delivery of a DH80 Puss Moth G-ABSB from de Havilland dealer Brian Lewis Ltd. in November 1931 and commenced air taxi work from a Brentwood, Essex base. Using Puss and DH83 Fox Moths, scheduled services Romford (Maylands) to Clacton were commenced on 7th April 1932 and two months later, the service was operated every 3 hours during daylight hours. Less than a month after the model's first flight, Dragon G-ACAN was flown to Hillman's base at Romford where aviatrix Amy Mollison named the aeroplane *Maylands*. Commenced twice daily Romford to Paris scheduled service using DH84s 1st April 1933, substantially undercutting the fares charged by existing operators. Commenced Romford to Manston summer only service, serving the seaside resorts of Margate and Ramsgate.

DH83	G-ABVI (4004), G-ABVJ (4006), G-ABVK (4005)
DH84	G-ACAN (6000), G-ACAO (6001), G-ACAP (6002), G-ACBW (6009), G-ACET (6021), G-ACEU (6022), G-ACEV (6023)
DH86	G-ADEA (2323), G-ADEB (2324), G-ADEC (2326)
DH89	G-ACPM (6251), G-ACPN (6252), G-ACPO (6253), G-ADAG (6266), G-ADAH (6278), G-ADAJ (6276), G-ADAL (6263), G-ADDF (6284)

Hornton Airways Ltd., Gatwick, Sussex
DH89   G-AIUO (6467)

Hunting Air Travel Ltd., Luton, Bedfordshire (later at Gatwick, Sussex and Croydon, Surrey)
DH89   G-AGZU (6773), G-AHPU (6963), G-AHWF (6965)

Imperial Airways Ltd., Croydon, Surrey (absorbed on formation of British Overseas Airways Corporation)
DH83   VO-ABC (4093), VO-ADE (4094)
DH86   G-ACPL (2300), G-ACVZ (2303), G-ACWC (2304), G-ACWD (2305), G-ADCM (2317), G-ADCN (2319), G-ADFF (2328), G-ADUE (2333), G-ADUF (2334), G-ADUG (2335), G-ADUH (2336), G-ADUI (2337), G-AEAP (2349)

Independent Air Travel Ltd., Bournemouth, Hampshire
DH89   G-AJXB (6530), G-ALZJ (6573)

Inter-City Air Services Ltd., Hereford
DH89   G-AKOV (6612), G-AKRO (6480)

International Airways Ltd., Croydon, Surrey
DH89   G-AGHI (6455), G-AGLE (6784), G-AGLP (6780)

Island Air Charters Ltd., Jersey, Channel Islands
DH89   G-AHPT (6478), G-AJFK (6552)

Island Air Services Ltd., St. Mary's, Isles of Scilly (later at Heathrow and Gatwick Airports)
Formed in June 1945 and initially operated a frequent connecting service from Land's End to St. Mary's. Their first Rapide was acquired in April 1948 and it was immediately pressed into service, pleasure flying from the public enclosure on the north side of Heathrow Airport! Substantial revenue was earned from the "flips" costing £1 and very rare for an air taxi operator, I.A.S. (London) as they had now become, was able to close down for the quiet winter months. A second Rapide was added in September 1948 and a third was leased from Airwork for the 1949 season. Pleasure flights were additionally carried out that year at both Northolt and Croydon Airports. Several more Rapides were added, including one to replace the ill-fated G-ALBB that crashed at Heathrow on 1st August 1952, after being upset by the prop wash of a Boeing Stratocruiser which the Rapide was following to land after another pleasure flight. This lucrative business ended in 1956 however, when the authorities gave I.A.S. notice to quit, as they felt that there was no longer a place for pleasure flying activities at the rapidly expanding airport. In 1957, pleasure flying was undertaken at Ramsgate, but demand down in the wilds of Kent was only a tiny fraction of the heady days in the London area and the company closed at the end of the season.
DH89   G-AESR (6363), G-AFFB (6409), G-AGJG (6517), G-AGSJ (6888), G-AIYP (6456), G-ALBB (6829)

Isle of Man Air Services Ltd.
DH84   G-ADCP (6092)
DH89   G-ADBW (6288), G-AEAJ (6320), G-AEAK (6324), G-AEAL (6325), G-AEAM (6326), G-AEBW (6327), G-AFEZ (6408), G-AFRK (6441), G-AGLP (6780), G-AGSJ (6888), G-AGUP (6911)

Kenning Aviation Ltd., Burnaston, Derbyshire (later at Sherburn-in-Elmet, Yorkshire)
DH89   G-AIUI (6675), G-AIUJ (6724), G-AIUK (6640), G-AIUL (6837), G-AKZH (6529)

Kentair (Charters) Ltd., Biggin Hill, Kent
DH89   G-AKIF (6838)

Lancashire Aircraft Corporation Ltd., Samlesbury, Lancashire
DH86   G-ACZP (2321)
DH89   G-AGOJ (6850), G-AGUG (6859), G-AHAG (6926), G-AHGD (6862), G-AJKW (6539), G-AJKX (6457), G-AJKY (6553), G-AJMY (6511), G-AKLA (6764), G-AKNN (6598), G-AKNV (6458), G-AKNW (6469), G-AKOD (6566), G-AKOE (6601), G-AKOY (6504), G-AKRO (6480), G-ALEJ (6484), G-ALPK (6757)

Lees-Hill Aviation (Birmingham) Ltd., Elmdon
DH89   G-AGLR (6781), G-AGPI (6885), G-AHGF (6903)

Luton Airways Ltd., Luton, Bedfordshire
DH89   G-AHLF (6494), G-AIBB (6813), G-ALBC (6572), G-ALGC (6906)

Luxury Air Tours Ltd., Croydon, Surrey
DH84   G-ACDL (6016

MacSmith Air Charter Ltd., Newcastle
DH89   G-ALGE (6907)

Maddox Airways Ltd., Brooklands, Surrey
DH84   G-ACIU (6041)

Mannin Airways Ltd., Ronaldsway, Isle of Man
DH89   G-AKOF (6538), G-AKOH (6582), G-AKOK (6474), G-ALET (6832)

Manx Air Charters Ltd., Ronaldsway, Isle of Man
DH89   G-AEMH (6336), G-AJGV (6589), G-AKGY (6723), G-AKIF (6838), G-AKSE (6870)

Marshall's Flying Services Ltd., Cambridge
DH89   G-AGZO (6913), G-AHED (6944), G-AHLM (6708), G-AKNN (6598)

Mayfair Air Services Ltd., Croydon, Surrey (also at Thame, Oxfordshire)
DH89   G-AGJG (6517), G-AIUN (6602), G-AKMF (6617), G-AKTX (6639), G-AKUS (6805), G-AKZI (6536), G-AKZJ (6549), G-AKZW (6896)

Mayflower Air Services Ltd., Plymouth, Devon
DH89   G-AHLM (6708), G-AIUL (6837), G-ASKO (6735)

McAlpine Aviation Ltd., Fairoaks, Surrey (moved to Luton, Bedfordshire 1957)
DH89   G-ALBC (6572)

Melba Airways Ltd., Manchester-Barton
DH89   G-AEMH (6336), G-AJMY (6511), G-AKMG (6635), G-AKNX (6629), G-AKZP (6882), G-ALGC (6906), G-ALGE (6907)

Metropolitan Air Movements Ltd., Biggin Hill, Kent
DH90   G-ANYK (7529)

Mid-Fly Ltd., Elmdon
DH89   G-AHKV (6792), G-AJKW (6539)

Midland Airways Ltd., Sywell, Northamptonshire
DH83   G-ABVJ (4006)

Midland & Scottish Air Ferries Ltd., Renfrew
Company registered 10.3.33 by Scottish bus and coach operator, John Cuthill Sword. Commenced thrice weekly scheduled services Glasgow-Renfrew to Campbeltown, continuing to Islay 1.6.33.
DH83   G-ACBZ (4040), G-ACCT (4047), G-ACCU (4048)
DH84   G-ACCZ (6015), G-ACDL (6016), G-ACDN (6018), G-ACET (6021), G-ACJS (6042), G-ACNI (6071)

Morton Air Services Ltd., Croydon, Surrey (on closure, moved to Gatwick, Sussex)
DH89   G-AGUG (6859), G-AGWP (6918), G-AGWR (6917), G-AHIA (6948), G-AKOR (6577), G-AKUS (6805), G-AKZW (6896),
        G-ALBH (6607)

Murray Chown Aviation Ltd.,Staverton, Gloucestershire
DH89   G-AIYP (6456), G-AKOV (6612), G-AKRO (6480)

Newman Airways Ltd., Panshanger, Hertfordshire and Croydon, Surrey
DH89   G-AKPA (6709)

North Eastern Airways Ltd.
DH84   G-ACLE (6044)

North Sea Air Transport Ltd., Brough, Yorkshire
DH89   G-AHAG (6926), G-AHGD (6862), G-AHLU (6633), G-AIWG (6497), G-AIWZ (6867)

North-West Airlines (IOM) Ltd., Ronaldsway, Isle of Man (secondary base at Nutts Corner, Belfast)
DH89   G-AGIF (6509), G-AHLN (6754), G-AKOH (6582), G-AKOK (6474), G-ALET (6832)

Northern Airways, Cramlington Aerodrome, Newcastle-on-Tyne
Founded by George Nicholson. Renamed Northern & Scottish Airways Ltd. and later as Scottish Airways Ltd.
DH83   G-ACED (4064)
DH84   G-ACFG (6027), G-ACJS (6042), G-ACMO (6062), G-ACNG (6069), G-ACNH (6070), G-ACOR (6073)
DH89   G-ADAG (6266), G-ADAH (6278), G-ADBU (6280), G-ADDF (6284)

Oldstead Aircraft Ltd., Newcastle
DH89   G-AFMF (6432)

Olley Air Service Ltd., Croydon, Surrey
DH83   G-ACFC (4053)
DH84   G-ACEK (6019), G-ACNA (6067), G-ACPY (6076)
DH89   G-ACTT (6257), G-ACYM (6269), G-ACYR (6261), G-AENN (6340), G-AEPE (6344), G-AEPW (6350), G-AERN (6345),
        G-AFEP (6406), G-AGSI (6886), G-AHGG (6902), G-AIYE (6815), G-AKSB (6951), G-AKSC (6779), G-AKSD (6949)

Patrick-Duval Aviation Ltd., Elmdon
DH89   G-AHGH (6934), G-AHGI (6935), G-AIBB (6813), G-AKNX (6629), G-AKNY (6470), G-AKOA (6618), G-AKVU (6476),
        G-ALRW (6941)

Peterborough & Spalding Aviation Ltd., Spalding, Lincolnshire (later at Peterborough-Westwood Aerodrome)
DH89   G-AEMH (6336), G-ALBH (6607)

Pine's Airways, Porthcawl (at Squires Gate, Lancashire when company restarted after the war)
DH83   G-ACEX (4056)

Portsmouth Aviation Ltd.
DH89   G-AFMG (6433), G-AHEB (6945), G-AHED (6944)

Portsmouth, Southsea and Isle of Wight Aviation Ltd.
DH83   G-ACCA (4041), G-ACIG (4072)
DH84   G-ACRF (6077)

Private Air Hire Service Ltd., Croydon, Surrey
DH89   G-AJKE (6555)

Provincial Airways Ltd., Croydon, Surrey
Formed 12.10.33, taking over the assets of International Airlines. Capital £10,000.
DH83   G-ACCF (4046), G-ACEX (4056), G-ACEY (4057)
DH84   G-ACBW (6009), G-ACDL (6016)G-ACKD (6052)

Railway Air Services Ltd., Croydon, Surrey (moved to Renfrew during the war)
DH84   G-ACHV (6035), G-ACNG (6069), G-ACNI (6071) - possibly leased, G-ACPX (6075), G-ACPY (6076), G-ACVD (6084),
        G-ADDI (6096), G-ADDJ (6097), G-ADED (6098), G-ADEE (6099)
DH86   G-ACPL (2300), G-ACVY (2302), G-ACVZ (2303), G-ACZP (2321), G-ADYH (2344), G-AEFH (2350), G-AENR (2352),
        G-AEWR (2354)
DH89   G-ACPP (6254), G-ACPR (6255), G-AEAJ (6320), G-AEAK (6324), G-AEAL (6325), G-AEAM (6326), G-AEBW (6327),
        G-AEBX (6328), G-AERZ (6356), G-AFFF (6386), G-AGLE (6784), G-AGLP (6780), G-AGLR (6781), G-AGUF (6855),
        G-AGUG (6859), G-AGUU (6908), G-AHGF (6903), G-AHGG (6902), G-AHGH (6934), G-AHGI (6935), G-AHKS (6812),
        G-AIHN (6498

Ringway Air Charter Services Ltd., Manchester
Founded in spring 1953 to operate pleasure flying from Manchester's Rinway airport.
DH89   G-AKZP (6882), G-ALBA (6821)

Rochester Air Charter Service Ltd., Rochester, Kent
Charter flying subsidiary of the aircraft manufacturer Short Bros. and Harland, operated their first charter flight on 19th June 1947.
DH89   G-AGDP (6403), G-AKDW (6897), G-AKRP (6940), G-AKRR (6950), G-ALOV (6638), G-ALWI (6703), G-ALWJ (6777),
        G-AMCT (6714). Also NF862 (6733), acquired for spares use.

St. Christopher Travel-Ways Ltd., Croydon, Surrey
DH89   G-AIYP (6456)

Sandown and Shanklin Flying Services, Lea-on-Solent, Hampshire
DH83   G-ACEA (4055)

Scillonia Airways Ltd., Land's End, Cornwall
DH89   G-AHAG (6926), G-AHGC (6583), G-AHKU (6810), G-AJCL (6722), G-ALGC (6906)

Scottish Airlines Ltd., Prestwick
DH89   G-AKSF (6490), G-ALBH (6607), G-ALBI (6525)

Scottish Airways Ltd. Inverness and Renfrew
DH84   G-ACET (6021), G-ACIT (6039), G-ACMO (6062), G-ACNG (6069), G-ACOR (6073), G-ADCT (6095)
DH86   G-ACZP (2321)
DH89   G-ADAJ (6276), G-AEWL (6367), G-AFEY (6402), G-AFFF (6386), G-AFOI (6450), G-AFRK (6441), G-AGDG (6547),
        G-AGDH (6548), G-AGED (6621), G-AGIC (6522), G-AGIF (6509), G-AGJF (6499), G-AGJG (6517), G-AGLE (6784),
        G-AGOJ (6850), G-AGUR (6910), G-AHLL (6576), G-AHLM (6708), G-AHLN (6754)

Scottish Motor Traction Co. Ltd., Renfrew
DH83   G-ABWF (4008), G-ACDZ (4054), G-ACEA (4055), G-ACEB (4058), G-ACEC (4059), G-ACEE (4065), G-ACEI (4068),
        G-ACEJ (4069)
DH84   G-ACDM (6017), G-ACDN (6018), G-ACET (6021)

Silver City Airways Ltd., Langley, Buckinghamshire
DH86   G-ACZP (2321)
DH89   G-AJKW (6539), G-AKOE (6601)
DH90   G-AEWZ (7555)

Sivewright Airways Ltd., Manchester-Ringway (maintenance base at Barton Aerodrome)
DH89   G-AGDM (6584), G-AJMY (6511), G-AKMG (6635)

Skegness Air Taxi Services Ltd., Skegness, Lincolnshire
DH89   G-ALBA (6821)

Skyflights Ltd., Ramsgate, Kent
DH89   G-AKIF (6838)

Skytravel Ltd., Liverpool
DH86   G-ACVY (2302), G-ACZP (2321), G-ADYH (2344), G-AENR

Skyways Ltd., Langley, Buckinghamshire
DH89   G-AHFJ (6545), G-AHIA (6948), G-AKNW (6469), G-AKOR (6577)

Skyways Coach-Air Ltd., Lympne, Kent
DH89   G-AGOJ (6850)

Solair Flying Services Ltd., Coventry (also at Birmingham)
DH89   G-AHKV (6792), G-ALBC (6572)

Solent Airways Ltd., Eastleigh, Hampshire
DH89   G-AHGF (6903)

Somerton Airways Ltd., Somerton Aerodrome, Cowes, Isle of Wight
DH89   G-AGPI (6885), G-ALBA (6821)

Southampton Air Services Ltd., Eastleigh, Hampshire
DH89   G-ADAE (6272)

South Coast Air Services Ltd., Shoreham, Sussex
DH89   G-APSD (6556)

Southern Aircraft (Gatwick) Ltd.
DH89   G-AIUM (6519), G-AJTU (6558), G-AKFO (6460), G-AKOM (6758), G-AKON (6620), G-AKOO (6468)

Southern Airways Ltd., Ramsgate, Kent
DH84   G-AECZ (6105)

Southern Counties Aerial Contracts Ltd.
DH89   G-AKIF (6838)

Southern Flying Services Ltd.
DH83   G-ACEB (4058)

Spartan Air Lines Ltd., Cowes, Isle of Wight
Company registered 2.2.33 with J. de C. Ballardie, Capt. H. H. Balfour, W. D. L. Roberts and Lt-Col. L. A. Strange as directors. Commenced twice daily services Cowes, Isle of Wight to Heston using Spartan Cruiser aircraft 12.4.33.
DH84   G-ACNG (6069)

Stanley Spencer's Tours Ltd., Manchester-Ringway
DH89   G-AKZP (6882)

Starways Ltd., Liverpool
DH89   G-AIBB (6813)

Steiner's Air and Travel Services Ltd., Speke
DH86   G-ADUH (2336)
DH89   G-AFMF (6432), G-AIUN (6602)

Surrey Flying Services Ltd., Croydon, Surrey
DH83   G-ABUT (4002)
DH84   G-ACIU (6041)
DH89   G-AJSL (6801)

Tippers Air Transport Ltd., Coventry
DH89   G-AKRS (6952)

Transair Ltd., Croydon, Surrey (on closure, moved to Gatwick, sussex)
DH89   G-AKMG (6635), G-AKSL (6865), G-AKVU (6476), G-ALWI (6703), G-ALWL (6845), G-ALWN (6729)
Trans European Airways Ltd., Fairwood Common, Swansea, Glamorgan (later at Coventry)
DH89   G-AFFB (6409), G-ALBA (6821)

Treffield Aviation Ltd., Sywell, Northamptonshire (later at Castle Donington)
DH89   G-AHKU (6810)

Trent Valley Aviation Ltd., Tollerton Aerodrome, Nottinghamshire
DH89   G-AGSJ (6888), G-AJSL (6801)

Trent Valley Aviation Ltd., Castle Donington
DH89   G-AHJA (6486), G-AJSL (6801), G-AKRS (6952)

Tyne Taxis Ltd. (Air Division), Woolsington Airport, Newcastle
DH89   G-AKME (6767), G-ALEJ (6484)

Tyne Tees Air Charter Ltd., Woolsington Airport, Newcastle
DH89   G-ALPK (6757)

Ulster Aviation Ltd., Newtownards, Northern Ireland
DH89   G-AGIF (6509), G-AHLN (6754)

Union Air Services Ltd., Gatwick, Sussex
DH86   G-ADUH (2336), G-ADVJ (2338)

United Airways Ltd.
DH84   G-ACMC (6053), G-ACMJ (6058), G-ACNI (6071)
DH89   G-ADAE (6272), G-ADBU (6280), G-ADBX (6289)

Universal Flying Services Ltd.
DH89   G-AHAG (6926), G-AHGD (6862), G-AHTY (6608)

Utility Airways Ltd., Hooton Park
DH83   G-ACEC (4059), G-ACEY (4057)

Valley Motor Aero Services Ltd.
DH89   G-AGJG (6517)

Westair Flying Services Ltd., Squires Gate, Lancashire
DH89   G-AJKW (6539), G-AKMH (6704), G-AKRS (6952), G-ALGI (6909)

West Cumberland Air Services Ltd., Kingstown Airport, Carlisle, Cumberland
DH89   G-AKNN (6598)

Western Airways Ltd., Weston-super-Mare, Somerset
Norman Edgar, trading as Norman Edgar (Western Airways) Ltd., operated a Puss Moth on behalf of Bristol based chocolate manufacturer, J. S. Fry & Sons with a first flight from the Fry family home at Somerdale, Somerset to Heston. Commenced twice daily scheduled services Bristol to Cardiff using DH83 Fox Moth G-ABYO 7th September 1933. Renamed Western Airways Ltd. 18th October 1938 after the company was purchased by Whitney Straight's Straight Corporation.
DH83   G-ABYO (4012)
DH84   G-ACAO (6001), G-ACCZ (6015), G-ACJT (6043), G-ACLE (6044), G-ACMJ (6058), G-ACMP (6063), G-ACPX (6075),
            G-AECZ (6105)
DH86   G-AETM (2353)
DH89   G-ACTU (6258), G-ADBV (6286), G-ADDD (6283), G-AFSO (6445)
DH90   G-AEDH (7510)

West of Scotland Air Services Ltd., Renfrew
DH83   G-ACDZ (4054)

Westward Airways (Land's End) Ltd., Land's End, Cornwall
DH89   G-AIYR (6676)

William Dempster Ltd., Blackbushe, Hampshire
DH89   G-AFMA (6430), G-AKGV (6796)

Wrightson & Pearce Ltd., Heston (traded later as Wrightways Ltd., Croydon, Surrey)
DH84   G-ACHX (6036), G-ACKU (6066)
DH86   G-ADMY (2327), G-ADYI (2345), G-AEJM (2351)

Windmill Theatre Transport Co. Ltd., Croydon, Surrey
DH89   G-AKSD (6949)

Wrafton Flying Club Ltd., Chivenor, Devon (also traded as Devonair)
DH89   G-AKNY (6470)

Wright Aviation Ltd., Hooton Park
DH89   G-AHPT (6478), G-AIBB (6813)

Yeadon Aviation Ltd., Leeds, Yorkshire
DH89   G-AHKT (6811)

Yellow Air Taxi Company, Elmdom
DH89   G-ACPP (6254)

Yorkshire Aeroplane Club Ltd., Sherburn-in-Elmet, Yorkshire
DH89   G-ALGB (6706)

ICELAND

Flugfelag Islands h.f. (Icelandair), Reykjavik
DH89   TF-ISM (6670), TF-ISO (6730)

Flugskolinn Thytur HF (Flying School Thytur)
DH89   TF-KAA (6622)

INDIA

Air India, Bombay
DH89   VT-ARK (6649), VT-ARL (6650), VT-ARM (6651), VT-ARN (6652)

Air Services of India Ltd., Bombay
DH83   VT-AJW (4083)
DH89   VT-AHB (6308), VT-AJB (6381), VT-ALO (6454), VT-AVW (6947), VT-AVX (6953), VT-AXG (6957), VT-CHZ (6724)
DH90   VT-AKC (7505)

Himalaya Air Transport and Survey Co., Delhi
DH83   VT-AFT (4091), VT-AGI (4062)

Indian Air Survey and Transport Ltd., Calcutta
DH83   VT-AEN (4081)
DH89   VT-ARF (6569), VT-ARR (6503), VT-ARV (6657), VT-ARW (6661), VT-ARY (6681), VT-ASA (6588), VT-ASC (6762), VT-ASQ (6794)

Indian National Airways, Calcutta
DH83   VT-AEM (4078), VT-AFB (4086)
DH84   VT-AEK (6050), VT-AEL (6048), VT-AES (6065)
DH89   VT-AHB (6308), VT-ARF (6569), VT-ARY (6681), VT-ASA (6588), VT-ASJ (6793)

Irrawadda Flotilla and Airway Ltd., Rangoon, Burma
DH83   VT-AFZ (4092)

Madras Air Transport Service, Madras
DH83   VT-AEQ (4082)

Madras Presidency Airways, Madras
DH89   VT-ARK (6649), VT-ASJ (6793), VT-CBY (6869)

Nalanda Airways Ltd., Patna
DH83   VT-CLS (FM.18), VT-CLT (FM.39), VT-CLU (FM.51), VT-CLV (FM.52)

Tata and Sons Ltd., Bombay
DH83   VT-ADZ (4032), VT-AFI (4088)
DH86   VT-AKM (2306), VT-AKZ (2308)
DH89   VT-AIZ (6378), VT-AJA (6379), VT-AJB (6381)

INDO CHINA

Aigle Azur Indochine, Hanoi
To carry out scheduled flying in the region, previously undertaken by the French Air Force, seven Rapides were purchased in the U.K. in early 1952. After checks were carried out at either Le Bourget or Toussus, the fleet was flown out to Hanoi and were then immediately put into service. After just one year however, Aigle Azur's operations elsewhere were given priority and the six surviving aircraft were sold on to smaller local operators.
DH89   F-BGPG (6729), F-BGPH (6845), F-BGPI (6635), F-BGPJ (6703), F-BGPK (6474), F-BGPL (6865), F-BGPM (6476)

Compagnie de Transports Aeriens Autrex (Lopez-Loreta et Cie.), Hanoi
Founded by Jean Lebreton, who was already the agent for Auster Aircraft in Hanoi, the company was authorised to commence passenger transport flights in 1948 and thankfully, they operated using the abbreviated name Cie. D'Autrex! Operations ceased in 1954 and the surviving Rapides were passed to Laos Air Service.
DH89   F-BAHX (6547), F-BAHY (6276), F-BGPI (6635), F-BGPJ (6703), F-OABH (6606), F-OAGP (6755), F-OAHL (6957),
        F-OAIR (6818), F-OAQY (6566), F-OAQZ (6553)

Compagnie Laotienne de Commerce et Transport (C.L.C.T.), Hanoi
Though nominally based at Hanoi, much of this company's work was in Laos. Operating since at least 1949, two Rapides were purchased in India at the end of 1950 to supplement their small existing fleet of Norseman aircraft. A further three joined L.C.L.T. from Aigle Azur in late 1953 but it is possible that F-BGPK was not used. Operations ceased at the end of 1955 and the 3 survivors were transferred to Veha-Akat.
DH89   F-BEPE (6845), F-BGPG (6729), F-BGPK (6474), F-OAIL (6724), F-52 (6953?)

Laos Air Service, Vientiane
After the cease fire and independence, this company commenced internal services using two former d'Autrex Rapides. A third aircraft, c/n 6408, purchased in the U.K., did not reach Laos, instead ending up in Algeria.
DH89   F-BGPJ (6703), F-LAAL (6408), F-OAQY (6566)

Veha Akat, Vientiane
From October 1955, took-over the flights and most of the assets of C.L.C.T. Three Rapides came from that company and a fourth from a private owner in 1956. Two were destroyed in accidents during 1958, a third in 1960 and the sole survivor, c/n 6724, was broken up in 1961.
DH89   F-LAAB (6724), F-LAAC (6729), F-LAAE (6845), F-LAAF (6935)

IRAQ

Iraqi Airways
DH89   YI-ABD (6897), YI-ABE (6898), YI-ABF (6906), YI-ABG (6907), YI-ABH (6909)

IRELAND

Aer Lingus Teoranta
DH84   EI-ABI (6076), EI-ABI (6105)
DH86   EI-ABK (2338), EI-ABT (2336)
DH89   EI-ABP (6341)

Aer Turas Teoranta
DH89   EI-AML (6709)

Air Kruise (Ireland) Ltd.
DH89   EI-AJO (6884)

Iona National Airways Ltd.
DH83   EI-AAP (4003)

Republic Air Charters Ltd.
DH89   EI-AGK (6458)

Skycraft Services Ltd.
DH89   G-ALBA (leased), EI-AKH (6870)

Weston Air Services Ltd.
DH84   EI-AFK (6105)
DH89   EI-ADP (6945), EI-AEA (6433)

ITALY

ALA Littoria S.A.
DH89   I-DRAG (6260)
DH90   I-DRAG (7541)

IVORY COAST

Air Ivoire
DH89   F-OATT (6367), F-OAUE (6325), F-OBGY (6911)

JAPAN

Japan Aerial Transport Co.
DH83   4 aircraft, c/ns 4013, 4016, 4079 and 4080, one of which was registered J-BEIG.

JORDAN

Air Jordan Co. Ltd.
The survivor, TJ-ABP, was re-registered to JY-ABP in April 1954.
DH89   TJ-ABJ (6749), TJ-ABP (6887)

Arab Airways
In addition to those listed below, TJ-AAI (6399) and TJ-AAU (6715) were noted at Croydon but not delivered. The company was renamed Arab Airways (Jerusalem) Ltd. in August 1953.
DH89   TJ-AAA (6954), TJ-AAB (6955), TJ-AAC (6958), TJ-AAD (6959), TJ-AAE (6961), TJ-AAJ (6580), TJ-AAP, (6443), TJ-AAQ (6546),
            TJ-AAV (6797), TJ-AAZ (6753), TJ-ABM (6600)

KENYA

Caspair Air Charters, Nairobi-Wilson
Founded immediately after the war by J. E. F. Wilkins at Mazinde (now more usually written as Masindi) and is the longest established company operating third level services in East Africa. Now based at Wilson where aircraft maintenance is carried out for third parties, both charter and scheduled flights continue with a diverse fleet, mainly catering for visitors to Kenya for animal safaris.
DH89   VP-KCJ (6366), VP-KMD (6500), VP-KHF (6627), VP-KND (6640), VP-KLL (6777), VP-KEF (6831), VP-KCV (6849), VP-KCY (6874),
            VP-KLB (6877)
DH90   VP-KCA (7528), VP-KCS (7554)

East African Airways Corporation, Nairobi, Kenya
Incorporated on 1st January 1946 as the national airline of the four countries which comprised British East Africa, namely Kenya (with a 67.7% holding), Uganda (22.6%), Tanganyika (9%) and Zanzibar (0.7%). Six Rapides were initially crewed by B.O.A.C. and were flown for a time on the British register as G-AGNH (6803), G-AGOT (6876), G-AGOU (6875), G-AGOV (6874), G-AGOW (6849) and G-AGOX (6848).
DH89   VP-KCJ (6366), VP-KCT (6803), VP-KCU (6848), VP-KCV (6849), VP-KCW (6875), VP-KCX (6876), VP-KCY (6874),
            VP-KEA (6890), VP-KEB (6891), VP-KEC (6893), VP-KED (6895), VP-KEE (6496), VP-KEF (6831), VP-KNS (6492),

Noon and Pearce Air Charters Ltd., Nairobi-Wilson
DH83   VP-KDS (4035)
DH89   VP-KFV (6406), VP-KFX (6620), VP-KLL (6777), VP-KCY (6874)

Wilson Airways, Nairobi-Wilson
DH84   VP-KAW (6047), VP-KBA (6059), VP-KBG (6079)
DH89   VP-KCG (6357), VP-KCJ (6366), VP-KCK (6267), VP-KCL (6394), VP-KCR (6413)
DH90   VP-KCA (7528), VP-KCS (7554)

LATVIA

Valsts Gaisa Satiksme (Ministry of Commerce, Post and Telegraph Department)
DH89   YL-ABC (6351), YL-ABD (6352)

LEBANON

DH89   LR-AAD (6843), LR-AAE (6894), LR-AAF (6896).

LUXEMBOURG

Cie. Luxembourgosie de Navigation Aerienne, marketed as Luxembourg Airlines
DH89   LX-LAC (6607), LX-LAD (6525)

MADAGASCAR

Air Madagascar
Founded in February 1947 by Messrs. Gallois, Pain and Raynaud. The first Rapide to be imported arrived in October 1947 and the last in December 1958. Thirteen aircraft were actually operated although a total of sixteen were purchased. No less than 3 were destroyed whilst on delivery, with G-AJFN and G-AJFO both catching fire on start-up in the Sudan and a third, G-AJSJ, was lost when traversing the Sahara Desert.
DH89   F-BEDI (6516), F-BFVR (6563), F-OAKD (6802), F-OAKE (6943), F-OAKF (6448), F-OAKX (6816), F-OANU (6671), F-OAOS (6620),
            F-OARH (6580), F-OASC (6797), F-OAUH (6611), F-OBDV (6591), F-OBIO (6507)

MOROCCO

Maroc Air Service, Rabat
The company imported a Rapide in June 1950 and obtained a second in 1952. Both were sold on to d'Autrex in Indochina mid 1953.
DH89   F-OAGP (6755), F-OAIR (6818)

MOZAMBIQUE

Divisao de Exploracao dos Transportes Aereos – D.E.T.A., Lourenco Marques
DH89   CR-AAD (6361), CR-AAE (6362), CR-AAM (6397), CR-AAN (6398), CR-AAT (6439), CR-AAU (6430)
DH90   CR-AAB (7526)

Taxi Aereo de Mocambique – T.A.M.
DH89   CR-AEQ (6969)

NETHERLANDS

Koninklijke Luchtvaart Maatschappij NV - K.L.M.
Six aircraft leased from Nederland Government from September 1945 to November 1946 to enable services to recommence after the war.
DH89   PH-RAA (6890), PH-RAB (6891), PH-RAC (6893), PH-RAD (6895), PH-RAE (6740), PH-RAF (6819)

NEW CALEDONIA

Societe Caledonienne de Transports Aeriens (also traded as Transpac)
DH89   F-OATC (6779), F-OAVG (6270), F-OAZT (6577)

NEW ZEALAND

Air Charter (N.Z.) Ltd., Christchurch
DH90   ZK-AFB

Air Travel (N.Z.) Ltd., Hokitika
DH83   ZK-ADI (4097), ZK-AEK (4033), ZK-AGM (4085)
DH90   ZK-AGP (7566)

Airwork (N.Z.) Ltd., Christchurch
DH89   (6668)

Cook Strait Airways Ltd.
DH89   ZK-AED (6305), ZK-AEE (6306),

East Coast Airways Ltd.
DH84   ZK-ADR (6090), ZK-ADS (6091)

Mount Cook Airlines
DH89   ZK-AGT (6423), ZK-AKY, (6653), ZK-ALB (6655), ZK-BCP (6648)

New Zealand National Airways Corporation
DH83   ZK-AEK (4033), ZK-AGM (4085)
DH89   ZK-AGT (6423), ZK-AKS (6647), ZK-AKT (6673), ZK-AKU (6662), ZK-AKY (6653), ZK-ALB (6655)

Ritchie Air Services Ltd.
DH89   ZK-AKY (6653), ZK-ALB (6655)

Rolvin Airways, Palmerston North
DH84   ZK-AXI (2057)

Southern Scenic Airways, also traded as Southern Scenic Air Services and West Coast Airways Ltd.
DH89   ZK-AGT (6423), ZK-AKS (6647), ZK-AKT (6673), ZK-BAU (6654)

South Island Airways Ltd.
DH89   ZK-BBP (6668)

Southland Airways Ltd., Invercargill
DH83   ZK-ADC (4025)

Trans Island Airways
DH89   ZK-BCP (6648), ZK-ALB (6655)

Union Airways Ltd.
DH84   ZK-ADR (6090), ZK-ADS (6091)
DH86   ZK-AEF (2330), ZK-AEG (2331), ZK-AEH (2332)

NORTH BORNEO

Three Rapides were operated by the Malayan Airways Ltd. subsidiary, Borneo Airways.
DH89   VR-OAA (6908), VR-OAB (6800), VR-OAC (6812)

NORTHERN RHODESIA

Zambesi Airways
DH83   VP-RAY (FM.33

PAKISTAN

Crescent Air Transport
DH89   AP-AGI (6457), AP-AFN (6552), AP-AGL (6859)

PALESTINE/ISRAEL

Arkia – Israel Inland Airways
In addition to the three listed below, Arkia also had 4X-ACH and 4X-CAN, construction numbers unknown.
DH89   4X-ACU (6806), 4X-AEH (6496), 4X-AEI (6895)

Palestine Airways Ltd. (also traded as Aviron – The Palestine Aviation Co.)
DH89   VQ-PAC (6399)

PAPUA NEW GUINEA

Guinea Air Traders
DH84   VH-AAC (6025), VH-BMX (2049)

Guinea Airways Ltd., Lae (Head office and maintenance base Adelaide, South Australia)
DH83   VH-UQR (4017), VH-UQS (4019), VH-UTY (4041), VH-UZL (4064)
DH89   VH-ABN (6253), VH-UFF (6270)

Madang Aerial Transport, Madang
DH83   VH-UDD (4063)

Madang Air Charters, Madang
DH84   VH-AOE (2058), VH-AQW (2068)

Mandated Airlines Ltd., Salamaua
DH83   VH-UBB (4090), VH-UQO (4021), VH-UQP (4020), VH-UQS (4019), VH-UQU (4051), VH-UUS (4044)
DH84   VH-AAC (6025), VH-AKX (2061), VH-AOP (2010), VH-AOQ (2011), VH-AOS (2006), VH-APL (2051), VH-AQW (2068),
         VH-ARI (2029), VH-ARJ (2028), VH-AYB (2065), VH-BDB (2063), VH-URW (6080), VH-USA (6074), VH-UTX (6104), VH-UVB (6102)

Papuan Air Transport
DH83   VH-UTY (4041)

Parer Air Transport
Run by R. J. P. Parer.
DH83   VH-AAX (4059)

Taylor's Air Transport
DH84   VH-AAC (6025), VH-AFK (2024)

Territory Airlines Pty. Ltd., Goroka
Formed in 1951. As Talair, continues to operate an extensive network of scheduled services in New Guinea to the present day.
DH84   VH-AIA (2086), VH-APL (2051), VH-AQW (2068), VH-BDC (2083),

Wewak Air Transport, Wewak
Run by Kevin Parer.
DH84   VH-AAC (6025), VH-AEA (6073), VH-AON (2019), VH-ASX (2039), VH-BDC (2083)

PERSIA/IRAN

Iran State Airlines – Iranair
Operated as a department of the Ministry of Posts and Telegraphs, in addition to the six aircraft listed below, they are thought also to have used
EP-AAN and EP-AAU for which the construction numbers are unknown.
DH89   EP-AAA (6321), EP-AAB (6322), EP-AAC (6323), EP-AAD (6692), EP-AAE (6695), EP-AAT (6696)

PORTUGAL

Companhia de Transportes Aereos
DH89   CS-ADI (6899), CS-ADJ (6900), CS-ADK (6901)

PORTUGESE GUINEA (GUINEA BISSAU)

Transportes Aereos da Guine Portuguese – T.A.G.P.
DH89   CR-GAI (6896), CR-GAJ (6529)

ROMANIA

Liniile Aeriene Romane Exploatate de Statul – L.A.R.E.S.
DH89   YR-DNC (6338), YR-DRA (6329), YR-DRI (6330), YR-DRO 6331)
DH90   YR- FLO (7548), YR-FLU (7549), YR-FLY (7547)

SENEGAL

Air Senegal
DH89   F-OBRU (6748), F-OBRV (6525), F-OBRX (6470), F-OBVI (6949), F-OBVJ (6813), F-OCAG (6859)

SIERRA LEONE

Sierra Leone Airways
DH89   VR-LAC (6603), VR-LAD (6963), VR-LAE (6827)

SINGAPORE

Wearne's Air Services Ltd.
DH86   VR-SBC (2323), VR-SBD (2313)

SOUTH AFRICA

Aircraft Operating Co. of Africa Pty. Ltd.
DH84   ZS-AEF (6026), ZS-AEI (6017)
DH89   ZS-ATV (6914), ZS-ATW (6915), ZS-AYF (6429), ZS-BEA (6626)

Africair Ltd.
DH89   ZS-BCI (6510), ZS-DDH (6833), ZS-DFG (6667)

African Air Transport, Baragwanath
DH84   ZS-AEG (6030), ZS-AEH (6054)
DH89   ZS-AES (6256)

African Flying Services
DH89   ZS-AKT (6380)

Commercial Air Services Pty. Ltd., Johannesburg
Founded as a charter and maintenance organization in 1943. Scheduled services to Welkom commenced 1949 with later extensions to Bloemfontein, Durban and Kroonstad. Since 1967 has traded as Comair.
DH89   ZS-BCI (6510), ZS-BZU (6761), ZS-BZV (6925)

Drakensberg Air Services
DH89   ZS-AKT (6380), ZS-AOM (6411), ZS-BZU (6761), ZS-BZV (6925)

Ladysmith Air Charter Services
DH89   ZS-DLS (6773)

Maluti Air Services
DH89   ZS-BEA (6626)

Owenair Pty. Ltd., Wynberg (founded by Owen G. Davies)
DH89   ZS-BCP (6561)

South West Air Transport Pty. Ltd. (later South West African Airways Ltd.)
DH89   ZS-BCI (6510), ZS-BEF (6507)

Suidair International Airways Ltd.
DH89   ZS-DDH (6833)

Trans-Oranje Air Services Pty. Ltd., Zastron
DH89   ZS-AKT (6380), ZS-BEA (6626)

SOUTHERN RHODESIA

Central African Airways Corporation, Salisbury
Formed in 1946 to provide air service between Northern and Southern Rhodesia and Nyasaland, the company was dissolved when Air Rhodesia was established 1st September 1967.
DH89   VP-YBJ (6358), VP-YBK (6359), VP-YBU (6412), VP-YCI (6658), VP-YCJ (6659), VP-YCK (6660), VP-YCL (6665), VP-YCM (6666),
         VP-YCN (6667), VP-YEZ(6680), VP-YFA (6761), VP-YCP (6834), VP-YDE (6925), VP-YDF (6924)

Rhodesia and Nyasaland Airways
DH83   VP-YAD (4034)
DH89   VP-YAU (6285), VP-YBJ (6358), VP-YBK (6359), VP-YBT (6404), VP-YBU (6412), VP-YBZ (6256)
DH90   VP-YAX (7512), VP-YBR (7503)

Victoria Falls Airways
DH89   VP-YCM (6666), VP-YCN (6667), VP-YNU (6508), VP-YEZ(6680)

SPAIN

Automobiles Fernandez Aerotaxi, Barcelona
DH83   EC-TAT (6020)

Iberia SA
DH89   EC-AAS (6424, EC-AAV (6425), EC-AAY (6277), EC-ABG (?), EC-BAC (6420), EC-CAQ (?)
DH90   EC-BAA (7529), EC-BAB (?)

Lineas Aereas Postales Espanolas – L.A.P.E.
DH89   EC-AGO (6262)

SRI LANKA

Rapid Air
DH89   4R-AAI (6736)

STRAITS SETTLEMENTS - SINGAPORE

Wearne Brothers Ltd. trading as Wearne's Air Services Ltd., Singapore
DH89   VR-SAV (6360), VR-SAW (6364)

SWEDEN

Dragon Aviation AB
DH89   SE-CBU (6530)

Svensk Flygtjanst AB (Swedish Air Services), Bromma Airfield, Stockholm
Two Rapides were used with the second, SE-BXZ delivered in 1953, flown with Swedish Aero titling.
DH89   SE-APH (6919), SE-BXZ (6934)

SWITZERLAND

Alpar Schweizerische Luftverkehrs AG, Berne
Merged with other operators, including Aero St. Gallen who owned HB-ARA (6250), to form Swissair 26th March 1931.
DH89   HB-AME (6437), HB-AMU (6438)

SYRIA

Syrian Airways was formed on 21st December 1946 and in 1953-55 were operating two Rapides. Thought to be former Misr Airwork aircraft, their identities are unknown.

TUNISIA

Societe Tunisienne de Reparation Aeronautique et de Construction, Tunis
Operating as an aircraft repair organisation, the company also encompassed a charter arm trading as Aero Sahara. Four Rapides were purchased with the first arriving in June 1956. The key personnel left Tunisia for mainland France and the three surviving Rapides were abandoned at El Aouina, the main airport for Tunis. Standing in the open in very poor condition, they were last noted in March 1970.
DH89   F-OAME (6573), F-OAYN (6504), F-OBGE (6872), F-OBIA (6787)

TURKEY

Devlet Hava Yollari
DH86   TC-ERK (2355), TC-FER (2356), TC-GEN (2357), TC-HEP (2358)
DH89   TC-ARI (6315), TC-BAY (6316), TC-CAN (6317), TC-DAG (6372)
DH90   TC-IDE (7556)

Hurkus Airlines, Ankara
DH86   TC-ERK (2355), TC-FER (2356), TC-GEN (2357), TC-HEP (2358)
DH89   TC-ARI (6315)

URUGUAY

Cia. Aeronautica Expresso del Plata
DH89   CX-ABI (6371)

Cia. Primeras Lineas Uruguayas de Navegacion Aerea - P.L.U.N.A., Montevideo
DH86   CX-AAH (2325), CX-ABG (2346)
DH90   CX-AAR (7532), CX-AAS (7534)

ZAIRE

A.M.A.Z., Kinshasa
DH89   9Q-CJE (6918), 9Q-CJK (6704), 9Q-CJT (6607), 9Q-CJU (6380), 9Q-CJW (6508), 9Q-CJX (6658)

8.2 Military Operations/Units – Abbreviations/Location

AUSTRALIA

DH83   A41-1 (4047), A41-2 (4015), A41-3 (4044), A41-4 (4048)
DH84   A34-1 through to A34-11, impressed into military service. A34-12 through to A34-98, new build in Australia.
DH86   A31-1 (2360), A31-2 (2313), A31-3 2326), A31-4 (2315), A31-5 (2307), A31-6 (2310), A31-7 (2323) and A31-8 (2359)
DH89   A3-1 (6270), A3-2 (6314), A33-1 (6259), A33-2 (6318), A33-3 (6270), A33-4 (6346), A33-5 (6253), A33-6 (6384) and A33-7 (6341)

AAC   Anti Aircraft Command
AACU   Anti Aircraft Co-operation Unit
AAU   Air Ambulance Unit
              1AAU, Laverton 15.2.41, embarked on R.M.S. Queen Mary to Middle East 11.4.41, Sicily 20.7.43, Italy 13.9.43 & embarked for return to Australia 2.44.
              2AAU, Fairbairn ACT 1.3.42 - 26.2.42, Kingaroy QLD 26.2.43 - 7.9.44, Archerfield QLD 7.9.44 - 7.1.46
AD   Aircraft Depot
              1AD, Point Cook VIC 1.3.26 - 2.12.94
              2AD, Richmond NSW 1.1.36 - 1.7.92
              3AD, Amberley QLD 16.3.42 - 30.6.92
              5AD, Wagga Wagga NSW 23.3.42 - 22.2.46
              7AD, Cowra NSW 15.5.42 - 24.12.42
AOS   Air Observers School
              1AOS, Cootamundra NSW
              2AOS, Mount Gambier SA
AP   Aircraft Park
              2AP, Laverton VIC 1.5.40 - 19.12.40, relocated to Bankstown NSW 19.12.40 - 28.3.45 (with a detachment at Schofields NSW)
APU   Aircraft Performance Unit
ARD   Aircraft/Airframe Repair Depot
              13ARD, Tocumwal NSW 12.12.42, Breddan QLD 22.3.43 - 13.10.47 (with detachments at Macrossan, Garbutt & Cooktown QLD during 1943
              14ARD, Ascot Vale VIC 30.10.42 - 22.9.43, re-located to Gorrie NT 22.9.43 - 20.10.45, Pearce WA 20.10.45 - 31.7.46 (with detachments at Birdum NT during 1942 & Darwin NT during 1944 known as 14ARD Forward
              15ARD, Port Moresby PNG to 19.7.46 (with detachments to Ward's Strip PNG during 1943 and Cape Gloucester PNG during 1944)
ATS   Armament Training School
              1ATS, Laverton VIC, re-located to Cressy VIC 31.7.39.
AWC   Allied Works Council
CF   Communications Flight (later known as CU, Communications Unit)

1CF, Laverton VIC 2.12.40 - 6.4.42, re-located to Essendon VIC 6.4.42 but returned to Laverton 17.7.42.

2CF, Sydney-Mascot NSW 2.12.40 - 19.5.42, Wagga Wagga NSW 29.5.42 - 29.10.43. Name changed to 2CU

3CF, Sydney-Mascot NSW 20.6.42 - 29.10.43

4CF, Archerfield QLD 7.9.42 - 29.10.43. Name changed to 4CU

5CF, Townsville QLD 30.11.42 - 29.10.43. Name changed to 5CU

6CF, Manbullo NT 11.12.42 - 27.2.43, Batchelor NT 27.2.43 - 29.10.43. Name changed to 6CU

8CF, Pearce WA

CFS   Central Flying School
Point Cook VIC, re-located to Camden NSW 18.5.40.

CMU   Care & Maintenance Unit
Evans Head NSW

CRD   Central Recovery Depot
2CRD, Richmond NSW 15.1.44 - 30.6.46

CU   Communications Unit
1CU, Ex 1CF. Laverton VIC from 29.10.43

2CU, Ex 2CF. Wagga Wagga NSW 29.10.43 - 31.7.44

4CU, Ex 4CF. Archerfield QLD 29.10.43 - 16.4.46

5CU, Ex 5CF. Townsville QLD 29.10.43 - 24.5.46 (with detachments at Mareeba QLD during 1944 & 1945, Merauke in Dutch New Guinea during 1945 Higgins Field QLD in 1945

6CU, Ex 6CF. Batchelor NT 29.10.43 - 7.10.45, Darwin NT 7.10.45-19.3.46

7CU, Pearce WA 24.11.43 - 10.11.44, Guilford WA 10.11.44 - 2.7.45, Dunreath WA 2.7.45 - 31.5.46 (with detachments at Exmouth WA during 1943, Corunna Downs WA during 1944 and 1945, Nookanbah, Broome, Mucha, Cunderin all WA during 1944 and Port Hedland WA during 1945

8CU, Ex 1RCS. Goodenough Island PNG 4.11.43 - 14.11.43, Madang PNG 14.11.43-4.3.46 (with detachments at Amaru, Kiriwina, Kwaipomata all PNG during 1943, Momote & Port Moresby PNG plus Mios Woendi, Dutch New Guinea during 1944

9CU, Port Moresby PNG 4.11.43 - 7.9.44, Lae PNG 7.9.44 - 20.3.45 (with detachments at Amau & Kwaipomata PNG during 1944. Name changed to 9LASU

EFTS   Elementary Flying Training School.
1EFTS, Originally as 2FTS at Melbourne-Essendon VIC & Adelaide-Parafield SA. Re-named 1EFTS 2.1.40. To Tamworth NSW 28.5.44. Disbanded 12.12.44.

3EFTS, Melbourne-Essendon VIC. Disbanded 1.5.42.

5EFTS, Narromin NSW 24.5.40 - 14.8.44

ERFTS   Elementary & Reserve Flying Training School

FTS   Flying Training School
1FTS, Point Cook VIC

LAC   Leading Aircraftsman

LASU   Local Air Supply Unit

Ldr.   Leader

MPRD   Mediterranean Personnel Reception Depot

MU   Maintenance Unit

OTS   Operational Training Unit
5OTS, Forest Hill NSW, re-located to Tocumwal NSW 20.10.43.

PTU   Paratroop Training Unit
At Laverton VIC, re-located to Tocumwal NSW 16.11.42 and to Richmond

RCF   Rescue & Communications Flight
1RCF, Port Moresby PNG 1.10.42-3.11.43. (Name changed to 1RCS=Rescue & Communications Unit 1.11.42)

RCS   Rescue & Communications Squadron

RIMU   Radio Installation & Maintenance Unit

RSU   Recovery & Salvage Unit or Repair & Servicing Unit
1RSU, Ex 1SRU. Higgins Field QLD 1.1.45 - 4.1.45, Mount Druitt QLD 4.1.45 - 23.5.45, Morotai Island PNG 23.5.45 - 17.6.45, Labaun, British North Borneo 17.6.45 - 26.12.45

10RSU, Amberley QLD 15.5.42-1.9.42, Lowood QLD 1.9.42-26.11.42, Bredden QLD 26.11.42-25.12.43, Macrossan QLD 25.12.43-13.2.44, Milne Bay PNG 13.2.44-24.11.44, Nadzab PNG 24.11.44-1.8.45 (name changed to 10RSU=Repair & Servicing Unit 1.1.45), Lae PNG 1.8.45-24.11.45

12RSU, Townsville QLD 15.1.42-18.5.42, Charters Towers QLD 18.5.42-2.10.42, Bredden QLD 2.10.42-16.12.43, Kiriwina PNG 16.12.43-13.5.44, Tadji PNG 13.5.44-29.11.45 (name changed to 12RSU=Repair & Servicing Unit 1.1.45). With detachments at Noemfoor & Los Negros, both PNG during 1944.

15RSU, No unit history held by RAAF Histroical Section.

17RSU, Pearce WA 19.5.42, Cunderin WA 29.6.42, Pearce WA again 13.7.44 (name changed to 17RSU=Repair & Servicing Unit 1.1.45). Disbanded 12.2.46.

SFTS   Service Flying Training School
5SFTS, Uranquint NSW

7SFTS, Deniliquin NSW 30.6.41-16.12.44

Sqdn.   Squadron
32Sqdn., Jacksons, Port Moresby PNG 21.2.42, Horn Island QLD 26.4.42, Camden NSW 18.9.42, Lowodd QLD 5.44. Disbanded 30.11.45.

33Sqdn., Townsville QLD 16.2.42 - 25.12.42, Port Moresby PNG 25.12.42 - 1.1.44, Milne Bay PNG 1.1.44 - 15.1.45, Lae PNG 15.1.45 - 11.3.46, Townsville QLD 11.3.46 - 13.5.46

34Sqdn., Darwin NT 23.2.42 - 5.3.42, Daly Waters NT 5.3.42 - 13.5.42, Batchelor NT 13.5.42 - 15.7.42, Hughes NT 15.7.42 - 27.8.42, Manbullo NT 27.8.42 - 13.12.42. Reformed at Adelaide-Parafield SA 3.1.43 - 12.4.45, Pitu Island PNG 12.4.45 - ?.1.46, Richmond NSW ?.1.46 - 6.6.46 (with detachments at Batchelor NT, Archerfield, Higgins Field & Townsville, all QLD during 1944 & Tengah, Singapore for repatriation of prisoner of war flights

35Sqdn., Pearce WA ?.2.42 - 6.4.42, Maylands WA 6.4.42 - 5.8.43, Pearce WA again 5.8.43 - 11.8.44, Guilford WA 11.8.44 - 3.2.45, Townsville QLD 3.2.45 - 10.6.46 (with detachments at Archerfield & Higgins Field QLD during 1944 and Morotai Island PNG during 1945)

36Sqdn., Laverton VIC 11.3.43 - 17.7.42, Melbourne-Essendon VIC 17.7.42 - 11.12.42, Townsville QLD 11.12.42 - 19.8.46, Schofields NSW 19.8.46 - 8.3.53 (with detachments at Tadji, Morotai Island and Torokina, all PNG and Tengah, Singapore for repatriation of prisoner of war flights during 1945)

SRU   Salvage & Repair Unit

Stn. Flt.   Station Flight

TAF   Tactical Air Force

TU   Telecommunications Unit
50TU, Wagga Wagga NSW 26.10.42, Tocumwal NSW 20.10.43, Williamtown NSW 7.44. Disbanded 1.2.46.

60TU, Nowra NSW 5.6.43, Jervis Bay NSW 14.9.43, Nowra again 4.3.44. Disbanded 31.3.44.
WAGS   Wireless & Gunnery School (also known as Wireless Air Gunners School in some documentation)
      1WAGS, Ballarat VIC 22.4.40 - 23.1.46
      2WAGS, Parkes NSW 9.1.41 - 12.2.44
      3WAGS, Maryborough QLD 18.9.41 - 6.12.44

AUSTRIA

DH83   A129 (4061)
DH84   64 (6101

BELGIUM

DH89   D1 (6881), D2 (6745), D3 (6739), D4 (6785), D5 (6787), D6 (6852)and D7 (6853)

CANADA

DH83   A145 (4094)

DENMARK

Two each of Dragon and Dragonfly aircraft were purchased for operation by Haerens Flyvertropper (Danish Army Air Force). The second Dragonfly S-24, was almost certainly seized when Denmark was over run and subsequently operated by the Germans.
DH84   S-21 (6060) and S-22 (6061)
DH90   S-23 (7551) and S-24 (7552)

FINLAND

Henry McGrady Bell purchased a DH86 in February 1.2.40 and donated it to the Finnish Government for use as an ambulance aircraft. And it was modified by Airwork Ltd., Gatwick with positions for 12 stretchers and 2 attendants. Registered **OH-SLA** (although already in unofficial use on a Waco ZQC-6!). Allocated the Finnish Air Force serial **DH-1** but not taken up. Instead, Re-registered **OH-IPA** 2.40 and operated by the Finnish Naval Coastguard Service. Written-off Helsinki-Malmi 2.5.40 after ground collision with a Brewster aircraft serialled BW-394. Although damage to the DH86 was said not to be severe, the necessary replacement parts could not be obtained from de Havilland, due to more urgent commitments to the war effort.
DH86   DH-1 (2353)

FRANCE

DH89   At least seven aircraft were used by the French.
DH90   One (c/n 7561) was handed over to the Vichy Government, ex Belgium, in August 1940.

GERMANY

DH89   C/ns 6348/6349, formerly of the Lithuania Air Force, are likely to have been captured by German forces when the country was over run 4.42 and it is possible that both Rapides then saw service with Luftflotte 2. C/ns 6351 and 6352: both aircraft were seized by Russian forces in June 1940 and used for communications flights. One is reported to have been grounded very soon after this having sustained damage. The other is reported to have been collected from Riga in 5.42 and flown to Tallinn in a drab olive colour scheme with radio call sign SB+AH and used thereafter for courier flights to Konigsberg, dropping food and mail to the island of Tuttarsaare in the spring of 1943 when with NSGr11 unit.
DH90   It was reported in the book Luftwaffe Test Pilot by Hans-Werner Lerche's, published by Jane's in 1980, that at least one Dragonfly was operated by the Luftwaffe at the Rechlin test establishment coded and was coded **RP+MY**. Another one, or just possibly the same one, was based at Orio al Serio, Bergamo, Italy during the period 1943/45. These were probably captures, one possibly F-APFK (c/n 7542), another may have been ex Royal Danish Air Force S-24 (c/n 7552).

GREAT BRITAIN

DH83   A total of ten were impressed into military service, including one which served with the Royal Navy.
DH84   A total of seventeen were impressed into military service, including one deemed unsuitable and scrapped.
DH86   A total of twenty one were operated. A few former civilian machines were purchased before the war and were used by 24 Squadron at Hendon as transports. The rest were impressed, mainly in the Middle East and were pressed into service as ambulance aircraft locally.
DH89   Only four British registered Rapides were impressed in the U.K., but five further aircraft operating in the Middle East were taken over by the R.A.F. and allotted serials. Information on the the bulk orders as radio trainers and communications aircraft etc., is detailed within the production histories.
DH90   Total of seventeen impressed into military service.

A.A.C.U. Anti-Aircraft Co-operation Unit
      1AACU, Farnborough (Formed 1.12.40)
      2AACU, Gosport
      6AACU, Ringway
      7AACU, Castle Bromwich
      8AACU, Filton
ADF   Aircraft Delivery Flight
      1ADF, Formed at Hendon 25.3.41, transferred to Croydon 23.1.42
AGS   Air Gunners' School
      7AGS, Stormy Down
      10AGS, Barrow-in-Furness
AONS   Air Observers' Navigation School
      6AONS, Staverton, Gloucestershire (formerly at Shoreham as 6CANS)
      7AONS, Prestwick, Ayrshire (detachments to Perth on occasion)
AOS   Air Observers' School
      4AOS, West Freugh (became 4(O)AFU 5.42)
      10AOS, Dumfries (became 10(O)AFU 5.42)

A.T.A. Air Transport Auxiliary, headquartered at White Waltham
B&GS Bombing and Gunnery School
10B&GS, Dumfries
C.A.N.S. Civil Air Navigation School
No.6, Shoreham
CU Camouflage Unit
1CU, Baginton, transferred to Hendon 8.11.40 and to Stapleford 1.6.42
Flt. Flight
1680Flt., Abbotsinch
FPP Ferry Pilots Pool (A.T.A.)
2FPP, Whitchurch
3FPP, Hawarden
6FPP, Ratcliffe
7FPP, Sherburn-in-Elmet
FU Ferry Unit
12FU, Melton Mowbray
Grp. Group – mainly Communications Flights
13Grp, Woolsington
15Grp, Hooton Park, transferred to Speke 1943
43Grp, Hendon
83Grp, Redhill
MPRD Metal Produce and Recovery Depot
1MPRD, Cowley
2MPRD, Eaglescliffe
MU Maintenance Unit
5MU, Kemble, Gloucestershire
6MU, Brize Norton, Oxfordshire
8MU, Little Rissington, Oxfordshire
9MU, Cosford
10MU, Hullavington, Gloucestershire
12MU, Kirkbride
18MU, Dumfries
20MU, Aston Down
22MU, Silloth
27MU, Shawbury
29MU, High Ercall
44MU, Edzell
47MU, Sealand
48MU, Hawarden
76MU, Wroughton
(O)AFU (Observers') Advanced Flying Unit
1(O)AFU, Wigtown
2(O)AFU, Millom
6(O)AFU, Staverton
9(O)AFU, Penrhos
OTU Operational Training Unit
8OTU, Dyce (photo reconnaissance training), transferred to Haverfordwest 9.44
13OTU, Bicester, Oxfordshire, transferred to Harwell 11.10.44, Middleton St. George 22.7.45
41OTU, Old Sarum, Wiltshire, transferred to Hawarden 15.11.42
51OTU, Cranfield, Bedfordshire
52OTU, Debden, Essex, transferred to Aston Down 1.8.41
53OTU, Heston, Middlesex, Transferred to Llandow 7.41, Kirton-in-Lindsey 10.5.43
54OTU, Church Fenton, transferred to Charter Hall 5.43 (also operated from a satellite base at Winfield)
55OTU, Usworth, transferred to Annan 4.42 (became No.4 Tactical Exercise Unit at same location 26.1.44
SFF Service Ferry Flight
11SFF, Dumfries
Sqdn. Squadron
4Sqdn., Linton-upon-Ouse, transferred to Clifton Yorkshire 8.40
24Sqdn., Hendon, with detachment in France 1940
26Sqdn., Gatwick, moved to Detling Kent 1.43, returned to Gatwick 4.43, again to Detling 6.43. To Ballyhalbert 7.43 with a detachment at Church Fenton. Moved to Hutton Cranswick 7.43 and to Royal Naval Air Station Lee-on-Solent 5.44
225Sqdn., Odiham, Hampshire. Moved to Old Sarum 6.40 and to Tilshead 7.40 with numerous detachments. To Thruxton 7.41 with a detachment to Dumfries 31.7.42. To Macmerry 8.42. Moved overseas 1.11.42.
271Sqdn., Doncaster Yorkshire, formed from a detachment of 1680flt. The squadron itself with detachments at Donibristle and Hendon
418Sqdn., Debden Essex. Moved to Bradwell Bay 5.42 and flown by Canadian crews
510Sqdn., Hendon, formed from 'A' flt. of 24Sqdn.
526Sqdn., Longmans Inverness
527Sqdn., Castle Camps. Moved to Snailwell 2.44 and to Digby 4.44
614Sqdn., Odiham, Hampshire 1940, transferred to Grangemouth 6.40 and to Macmerry 3.41
SS Signals School
No.1, Cranwell
No.2, ?
TEU Tactical Exercise Unit
3TEU, Annan, transferred to Aston Down 14.7.44

INDIA

A total of eight Rapides and two Dragonfly aircraft were impressed into military service in India.
DH89 AX806 (6378), HX790 (6381), HX791 (6454), MA961 (6569?), MA963 (6649), MA964 (6650), MA965 (6651) and MA966 (6652)
DH90 V4734 (7540), HX792 (7545)

INDONESIA

A single DH86 was collected by an American National Frank Gregnare and flown from Darwin to Penang. Whether this gentleman was a sympathiser or purely a dealer is unknown but later, the aircraft was in use with Indonesian Republican forces marked as **RI-008**. Eventually captured by Dutch forces at the rebel base of Manguwo 12.12.48 and broken up at Bandoeng the following year.

DH86   RI-008 (2344)

IRAQ

DH84   16 (6003), 17 (6004), 18 (6005), 19 (6006), 20 (6007), 21 (6008), 22 (6012) and 23 (6013)

IRELAND

A single DH84 aircraft was modified by Airwork at Heston to Eire's military use specification and fitted with wireless, bomb racks, a camera and accommodation for a towed target. Delivered to the Irish Army Air Corps and eventually crashed at Baldonnel in December 1941.

DH84   DH18 (6071)

ISRAEL

Formed on 27th December 1947 at Sde Dov, the Tel Aviv squadron was initially responsible for all air operations in Palestine/Israel during the War of Independence. The squadron's tasks were listed as, liaison, transport, intelligence gathering, escorting vehicle convoys and pilot training but illicit use of arms certainly took place!. Sde Dov Airfield remained under the control of the British until May 1948 and guns, ammunition and bombs had to be smuggled on to the base past the British guards.

DH89   It is thought that ten aircraft were operated by the Israeli Air Force. Construction numbers are known for this quantity, but there is some doubt whether both, c/n 6536 and 6636 ended up in Israel. Furthermore, the operation of c/n 6399 in Israel is doubtful as this aircraft was reported in Argentina as recently as April 1960.

KENYA

Operated by the Kenyan Auxiliary Air Unit (K.A.A.U.)

DH89   K-4 (6366), K-8 (6413), K-10 (6394), K-11 (6267) and K-16 (6357). The serial to construction number tie-ups for the last two are thought to be correct.

DH90   K-13 and K-14, c/ns 7528 and 7554, but order unknown. One was allocated to Nairobi Communications Flight and the other to the Air Defence Unit, Tanganyika in September 1939. K-13 bent its port undercarriage leg on landing at Mogadishu in Somalia 14.4.42 but was presumably repaired. Both were allocated to Khartoum 6.5.42. K-13 spent time at both 117MU and 139MU. K-14 was loaned by the Communication Squadron to 117MU. One was still on charge with 139MU in 8.43.

LITHUANIA

DH89   701 (6348), 702 (6349)

NETHERLANDS

DH89   V1 (6748), V2 (6872), V3 (6740) and V4 (6819). Four operated. In addition, an unidentified Rapide wearing the serial ?X731 and Dutch insignia is illustrated on page 140.

NEW ZEALAND

DH83   NZ566 (4097). Impressed into military service.
DH84   NZ550 (6091) and NZ551 (6090)
DH89
DH86   NZ552 (2330), NZ553 (2331) and NZ554 (2332). All impressed into military service.

PERU

Five aircraft were purchased in October 1946 from surplus R.A.F. stocks and operated by Transportes Aereos Militares, Grupo de Transportes No.42. These were supplemented by further unused R.A.F. aircraft with OB-RAF-195 (6804) purchased November '46, OB-RAG-196 (6798) and OB-RAH-197 (6783) both in December 1946. The digits after the call-sign are the certificate numbers and were painted on the aircraft. Furthermore, it is thought that c/n 6772 operated for the British Ambassador's use in Uruguay since October 1944, might also have gone to Peru. Two unknown aircraft have been illustrated in recent years. One, coded 434 fitted with wheeled undercarriage and 438 on floats, are likely to be two of the above aircraft, but the call-sign to code tie-ups are unknown.

DH89   OB-RAA-156 (6973), OB-RAB-157 (6974), OB-RAC-158 (6975), OB-RAD-159 (6976), OB-RAE-160 (6977)

PORTUGAL

The only Rapide was used for aerial survey and photography by the Portugese Air Force and operated by Base Area No.1 at Granja do Marquez, Sintra. (Note: c/n 6430, painted to represent FAP2307, is currently stored at Sintra for the Museo do Ar).

DH84   FAP504 (6111), FAP505 (6113), FAP506 (6114)
DH89   FAP2307 (6899)

RUSSIA

DH89   C/ns 6351 and 6352, originally delivered to Latvia, were seized by Russian forces in June 1940 and used for communications flights.

SOUTH AFRICA

DH83   SAAF1413 (4035). Impressed into military service.
DH84   SAAF1414 (6054) and SAAF1570 (6017)
DH89   A total of seventeen were operated by the South African Air Force
DH90   Three aircraft

SOUTHERN RHODESIA

DH84   260 (6030)
DH89   Eight aircraft

SPAIN

DH83   30-147 (4087)

DH84   At least thirteen examples were purchased in the U.K.and elsewhere during the Civil War, joining the civilian EC-TAT (6020) pressed into service by the Republicans.

DH89   c/ns 6310 to 6312 were supplied to Spain as DH89M Military Rapides. They were equipped to carry four stretchers, and could also carry three machine-guns with one backward firing, one forward firing Vickers 'E' gun in the cockpit, and one in the floor of the cabin which was also modified for camera use. Up to twelve 27lb bombs could be carried under the belly. Performance improvements included cruising speeds of 130mph, climb rates of 900ft per min and 4hr 30min duration, but only with all hatches closed. (Pictured *The Aeroplane* 11.12.35 p710). All three were captured by Nationalist forces in July 1936 and used as bombers during that month in the fighting for the Somosierra Passes near Madrid. In July or early August they were incorporated into a new group known as Grupo 20. In the middle of August, two second hand aircraft arrived at Burgos from England to bring the number of aircraft in Nationalist service to five, and at this stage 'military' serials were issued, **1** through to **5**, later changed to **40-1** through to **40-5**, although which aircraft wore which serial is uncertain. What is known, is that **40-5** was shot down on the Madrid front near Segovia 26.8.36 by a Heinkel He.51 of the Condor Legion in mistake for a Republican aircraft, killing the two crew and another suffered exactly the same fate 19.10.36. A further Rapide crashed on take-off at Zaragoza during the first week of September 1936 and was burnt out. The two remaining aircraft were then named after the pilots of the aircraft shot down in error, **40-1** becoming *Capitan Pouso* and **40-2**, *Capitan Vela*. It is reported, that when the group disbanded, the two Rapides remained on strength. (Also see c/n 6277 reference 40-2, passed to Iberia as EC-AAY).

DH90   It is believed that 3 DH90s were used by the Republican forces during the Civil War. The first received, was the sole Turkish Dragonfly TC-IDE (c/n 7556) delivered in 1937 and F-APDE (c/n 7529) plus F-AQEU (c/n 7501) followed in 1938. They were based at Totana, Murcia and were allocated serials in the LY- range and photographs of LY-001, believed to be c/n 7556, are known. Two survived the conflict and were allotted serials in the 40- range by the winning Nationalists. One was 40-4 c/n 7529. They were both handed over to Iberia in the early 1940s as detailed in the production history.

Somewhat amusing is the story of purchasing agents travelling to the U.K. to purchase Dragons and Dragon Rapides. They would often turn up at the vendor's premises at the same time and, almost by agreement, decide which side the aircraft would join! More often than not, the purchases would change sides several times, even prior to their departure for the Iberian Peninsula!

SWEDEN

DH90   Fv906 (7550)

TRANSJORDAN

DH89   R300 (6958), R301 (6443)

TURKEY

DH84   The serials worn are unknown, but c/ns 6087, 6107, 6108 and 6109 were used

UNITED NATIONS

A small number of DH89 aircraft were flown by Dutch crews in Palestine

UNITED STATES

A few Rapides were loaned to the 8th Air Force in Summer 1944 and were used as hacks for general transport purposes and to transfer crews. Flown by American crews but the R.A.F. serial numbers were retained. In memory of the part they played, the example exhibited at Wright-Patterson is painted to represent X7454, based at Abbots Ripton for a three month priod from April 1944.

YEMEN

Two unidentified DH89 aircraft but known to have formerly been operated by Misr Airwork are to be found in Unknown Aircraft on page 138.

8.3 Fiery Ends

During the inputting stage of the material appertaining to Dragon Rapide production, we were struck by the number of aircraft destroyed on the ground by fire, either during refuelling or on engine start-up. Accidents, that take place during the take-off and landing phase of flight are the more usual reason resulting in an aircraft's demise, but this certainly does not apply in the case of de Havilland's most numerous biplane transport. Records indicate that between 7 and 10% of the 729 produced, were destroyed by fire on the ground when stationary.

The reasons why the type was so vulnerable, are explained by Ian Callier who has been involved with civil aviation throughout his working life and to him, we are indebted. His often amusing comments follow, describing the circumstances surrounding so many examples of this wonderful type, succumbing to a fiery end.

DURING REFUELLING

Most Rapide operations were by a single owner-operator who also acted as the pilot. Normally on landing, it was customary to send the passengers to use the Airport's facilities for refreshments and to use the American term, avail themselves of the rest room, whilst the pilot stayed with his aircraft to arrange refuelling. The object of this exercise was to reduce ground time as much as possible and allowed the pilot only to cross the apron once in order to pay the necessary landing fee, fuel charges and to consume a quick cup of tea.

Dragon Rapide fuel tanks are situated immediately aft of each engine. Their filler caps are just 15 inches aft of the hot engines which meant that any fuel vapour escaping during the refuelling process, could quiet easily meet hot fumes still rising from the engine cowlings with catastrophic results. On occasion, aircraft came to a stop on the apron, in a slightly down-wind position and this helped to waft the fumes towards the hot engine.

The pilot's seemingly efficient arrangements on the ground, could mean that, far from expediting the journey time, it could actually stop the journey dead!

ON START-UP

The exhaust outlet from the Gipsy Queen engine of the Rapide was approximately 15 inches below the fabric wing. If at start-up the engine was over-primed, it could lead to excess fuel being discharged through the exhaust in the form of an 18 inch long flame curling up towards the lower surface of the wing. If the engine had started, this was no problem, as the propeller wash would instantly direct the flame aft and away from the wing. If, on the other hand, the engine failed to start and the priming had been over-enthusiastic, difficulties could ensue.

In the days of regular Rapide operations, it was customary for the start-up to be overseen by a member of ground staff equipped with a fire extinguisher. It is traditional for fixed wing aircraft pilots to be seated on the left side but of course, in the case of the Rapide, there is only one place in the cockpit. To be in the pilot's eye, the marshaller would automatically position himself on the port side. Starting procedure is for the starboard engine first and it's exhaust is situated on the starboard side of the engine, somewhat shielded from the marshaller's vision. The primary indication he got of a problem was seeing passengers rapidly tumbling out of the door situated on the port side, as the starboard wing was swiftly consumed by fire! This problem was also known to seriously hamper the commencement of the journey!

Listed below are details of 28 aircraft known to have been destroyed by fire on start-up, but there were probably many more for which actual reason for destruction has been lost over the passage of time. Eagle eyed readers will notice that the earlier Rapides were not prone to such start-up fires and this is probably due to Ki-gass type engine primers not being fitted to them.

DATE	REGISTRATION	C/N	LOCATION
12.5.37	VH-UVS	6265	Mascot Airport, Sydney New South Wales
17.5.39	CF-AVJ	6295	St. John, New Brunswick
5.7.45	CF-BFP	6374	Walker Lake, Quebec
11.12.46	ZS-ATW	6915	Beit Bridge, Southern Rhodesia
21.9.47	VP-UAW	6631	On Island of Zanzibar
3.12.47	G-AJFN	6520	Kosti, Sudan
3.12.47	G-AJFO	6756	Kosti, Sudan
27.7.48	SU-ACS	6544	Zaafarene, Egypt
16.7.49	G-AJGZ	6883	Agha-Javi, Iran
23.7.49	R9562	6490	Prestwick, Ayrshire
29.11.49	VP-KFV	6406	Masindi, Uganda
30.6.50	G-AKME	6767	Lympne, Kent
28.8.51	G-AHXZ	6825	Renfrew
29.9.51	VH-AIK	6497	Turkey Creek, Northern Territory
15.3.52	F-OAKD	6802	Bealanana, Madagascar
6.9.52	ZS-BCI	6510	Welkom, South Africa
28.9.52	AP-AFN	6552	Karachi
13.2.53	F-BGPM	6476	Siem Reap, Cambodia
19.6.53	CF-DIM	6928	Matane, Quebec
16.3.54	F-OAOY	6480	Colomb-Bechar, Algeria
30.7.54	OD-ABH	6469	At oil pumping station H3 in Syria
22.2.55	ZS-BEA	6626	Otjimarongo, South West Africa
16.3.55	F-OAPS	6638	Ekouata, Sudan
18.3.55	VP-KND	6640	Kisumu, Kenya
14.11.56	F-OAHH	6612	In Madagascar
10.5.57	CR-LBH	6846	Ambriz, Angola
13.9.66	5H-AAM	6492	Dar-es-Salaam, Tanganyika
30.3.68	VH-ECW	6530	Bluckall, Queensland

Mercifully, there is no record of serious injury or fatality to the occupants as a result of these conflagrations and we therefore ask your forgiveness for the slightly light-hearted character of this chapter.

However, they did ensure quite a number of red faces over the years. None more so perhaps than at Kosti in the Sudan on 3rd December 1947. Rapides G-AJFN (c/n 6520) and G-AJFO (c/n 6756) were both en route from the U.K. for delivery to Air Madagascar. Got it in one, both aircraft were destroyed by fire, due directly to over-priming in separate incidents but on the same day! Air Madagascar did not have much luck with their Rapide fleet, for in addition to these two, a third crashed when on delivery, whilst one aircraft that did enter service with them, F-OAHH, was destroyed by fire on start-up in November 1956.

8.4 The Survivors

DH83

Sixteen known survivors, including two replicas (CF-BNI/ZK-ARQ) out of a total of 154 produced.

Reg	C/N	Notes
'CF-BNI' Heritage	-	A replica for display purposes only, using some original parts, may be seen at the Prince of Wales Northern Centre, Yellowknife, NWT. Loaned to the Western Canada Aviation Museum 1985-1987.
CF-BNO	FM.7	Undergoing restoration for display at the Canadian Bushplane Heritage Centre, Sault Ste. Marie ONT
CF-DIX	FM.24	In the ownership of Henry Boulanger, Winnipeg ALB since November 1961 but no recorded sightings for many years and therefore presumed in store
CF-DJB	FM.28	Displayed on floats and suspended from ceiling, National Aviation Museum, Rockcliffe, ONT
G-ACCB	4042	Undergoing restoration with a private vowner, Nuneaton, Warwickshire
G-ACEJ	4069	In flying condition, Hungerford – Denton Manor
G-AOJH	FM.42	In flying condition, Rendcomb, Gloucestershire
N12739	4026	Undergoing rebuild by Joel M. Hirtle, Westerville, Ohio
VH-USJ	4058	Currently undergoing rebuild with the Croydon Aircraft Co. at Mandeville, New Zealand
VH-UVL	4015	Was in flying condition with Ken Orrman, Blairgowrie VIC but recently sold to Dr. Robert Fox, Kellyville NSW and may well have moved on to a new home at Bankstown
ZK-ADI	4097	In flying condition with the Croydon Aircraft Co. at Mandeville, New Zealand
ZK-AEK	4033	In flying condition with Sir Timothy (William) Wallis, Wanaka, New Zealand
ZK-AGM	4085	Arrived U.K. early 2003 for rebuild at Hungerford – Denford Manor, Berkshire
ZK-APT	FM.48	Undergoing restoration to flying condition by S. & G. Smith at Tech Air, North Shore, New Zealand
ZK-AQB	FM.49	Undergoing restoration to flying condition by Croydon Aircraft Co., Mandeville, New Zealand
ZK-ARQ	FM.53	Some parts of this Canadian example, not completed at de Havilland, have found their way to New Zealand and are being built into a replica by Jim Lawson at Manurewa, N.Z.

DH84

Ten known survivors out of a total 202 (115 built in the U.K. and a further 87 in Australia).

Reg	C/N	Notes
EI-ABI [2]	6105	In flying condition and operated by former Aer Lingus aircrew from Dublin
G-ACET	6021	Nearing completion to flying condition by Michael Souch in Hampshire, using a fuselage constructed by Croydon Aircraft Co., Mandeville, New Zealand
G-ACIT	6039 Wiltshire.	Displayed since arrival 7.83 at Science Museum Air Transport Collection and Storage Facility, Wroughton, Noted 3.03 wearing Highland Airways colour scheme and named *Aberdeen*
G-ECAN	2048	Being prepared to flying condition by Cliff Lovell at Chilbolton for Torquil P. A. Norman, Rendcomb, Gloucestershire
N34DH	6096	In flying condition with airline captain Mike Kimbrel on his farm strip at Oakville, Washington
VH-AML	2081	In flying condition with Michael William Hockin, Castlecrag, NSW as A34-92. Normally kept at Point Cook VIC
VH-AON	2019	Owned by the Rural City of Wangaratta VIC and displayed at the now defunct Drage's Air World
VH-SNB	2002	Displayed Royal Museum of Scotland – Museum of Flight at East Fortune
VH-UXG	6077	Owned by D. R. Porter, Wynnum QLD and currently undergoing restoration by Greg Challinor of Mothcair at Murwillumbah NSW
ZK-AXI	2057	In flying condition with S. & G. Smith, North Shore, New Zealand

DH86

There are no known survivors of the 62 examples built. The last flying DH86, G-ACZP was damaged beyond repair at Madrid-Barajas 21st September 1958 and the hulk was noted dumped there in poor condition during the late 1960s. Reports in the 1970s of "substantial portions of a crashed DH86 located in Australia/Papua New Guinea", but nothing concrete on this discovery in recent years. The son of Viv Bellamy's plan to build a *new* DH86 in the U.K. during the mid 1990s, using substantial parts of a DH89, seem to have come to nought!

DH89

50 known survivors out of 729 produced.

Reg	C/N	Notes
C-FAYE	6796	Presented to the Ontario Bushplane Heritage Educational Centre by the LeMay family and displayed at the Canadian Bushplane Heritage Centre, Sault Ste. Marie ONT
CF-BND	6375	Displayed at Western Canada Aviation Museum, Winnipeg Airport MB
CF-PTK	6254	Displayed at Reynolds Heritage Preservation Foundation, Wetaskiwin ALB by 5.02
D-IGUN	6437	See "G-RCYR" below
D-ILIT	6879	In flying condition with J. M. Koch. (Formerly G-AMAI and displayed in the Koch Aircraft Collection, trading as the Island Aircraft Co., Sandown, Isle of Wight)
EC-AKO	6345	Undergoing restoration at Museo de Aeronautica y Astronautica, Cuatro Vientos, Madrid
F-AZCA	6541	In flying condition with Jean Salis, la Ferte Alais
F-BHCD	6706	Displayed Musee de l'Air, Paris - Le Bourget
F-BHGR	6844	Stored by Jean Salis at La Ferte Alais and last noted 12.02
G-ACYR	6261	Displayed Museo de Aeronautica y Astronautica, Cuatro Vientos, Madrid
G-ACZE	6264	Brian Woodford's Wessex Aviation & Transport Ltd. Was in flying condition Henstridge, Somerset wearing King's Flight colours until stored 8.97. Moved to Haverfordwest for further storage 9.00
G-ADAH	6278	The Aeroplane Collection, displayed in the Aviation Gallery of the Manchester Museum of Science and Industry
G-AEML	6337	In flying condition with Amanda Investments Ltd., Rendcomb, Gloucestershire.
G-AGJG	6517	M. J. & D. J. T. Miller. CofA expired March '86 and currently on long term rebuild at Duxford, Cambridgeshire
G-AGSH	6884	In flying condition with Philip Meeson's Venom Jet Promotions Ltd, based Bournemouth-Hurn Airport. Painted in British European Airways livery and named *Jemma Meeson*
G-AGTM	6746	In flying condition with Air Atlantique and operated by their Aviation Heritage division from Coventry for joy riding
G-AHAG	6926	In storage by Ralph Jones, trading as Southern Sailplanes at Membury, Berkshire
G-AHED	6944	At the R.A.F. Museum's Michael Beetham Conservation Centre at Cosford and noted there 11.01
G-AHGD	6862	Remains stored by Ralph Jones, trading as Southern Sailplanes at Membury, Berkshire
G-AIDL	6968	In flying condition with Atlantic Air Transport's Historic Flight. Normally located at Caernarfon, Gwynedd for joy riding
G-AIUL	6837	Stored by John E. Pierce at Ley Farm, Chirk, Clwyd. Marked as 'G-AJCL'
G-AIYR	6676	In flying condition with Fairmont Investments Ltd. and operated by Classic Wings/Clacton Aero Club, Essex
G-AJBJ	6765	Stored by John E. Pierce at Ley Farm, Chirk, Clwyd
G-AKDW	6897	Rebuild continuing by de Havilland Aircraft Museum Trust Ltd., Salisbury Hall, London Colney April '00
G-AKIF	6838	In flying condition with Airborne Taxi Services Ltd. (Sir Adrian Christopher Swire), Duxford, Cambridgeshire.

G-AKOE	6601	Stored in British Airways colour scheme by John E. Pierce at Ley Farm, Chirk, Clwyd.
G-AKRP	6940	In flying condition with Rex H. Ford of Fordaire Aviation, Sywell, Northamptonshire
G-ALAX	6930	Stored in the open at D. Johnson's home, Andover, Hampshire. (Durney Aeronautical Collection).
G-ALXT	6736	Displayed since arrival 7.81 at Science Museum Air Transport Collection and Storage Facility, Wroughton, . Wiltshire. Noted 3.03 wearing Railway Air Services colour scheme, named *Star of Scotia*
'G-RCYR'	6437	Was displayed within the terminal building adjacent to the roof gardens entrance, Frankfurt Airport by Air Classik. Last flown as D-IGUN but presumably painted to represent the famous G-ACYR preserved at the Museo del Aire at Cuatra Vientos, Madrid. Stored elsewhere by February 2003
N89DH	6709	Purchased at auction by Bob Hook, Joplin, Missouri and placed into long term storage October '87
N2290B	6588	To John Cournoyer and Albert Stix I of the Historic Aircraft Restoration Museum, St. Louis, Missouri 6.2.03. Last reported when flown by then owner Michael Kimbrel from his Washington State home to the E.A.A. Convention, Oshkosh, Wisconsin in 1981
N2290F	6794	Displayed U.S.A.F. Museum, Wright-Patterson Air Force Base, painted to represent X7454, flown for a three month period by U.S. personnel from Abbots Ripton, Huntingdonshire in support of the 8th Air Force.
N683DH	6782	Donated to the Experimental Aircraft Association and displayed in their museum at Wittman Field, Oshkosh WI
OO-CNP	6458	Displayed Musee Royal de l'Armee, Parc du Cinquantenaire/Jubelpark 3, B-1040 Brussels
OY-AAO	6775	Displayed Danmarks Flyvemuseum, Helsingor
'PP-VAN'	6900	Purchased in Mozambique by Brazil's national airline VARIG and restored by them at their Porto Alegre base to represent their first aircraft. More recently displayed at Museu Aerospacial da Forca Aerea Brasiliera, Avenue Mal Fontenelle, Compo dos Alonsos, Rio de Janeiro
'TC-ERK'	?	Displayed at Turk Hava Kuvvetleri Hava Muzesi (Turkish Air Force Air Museum) at Istanbul Airport. Carries spurious marks actually worn by DH86 c/n 2355. Unfortunately, the museum's records do not show the Rapide's origin. Thought to be either c/n 6687 formerly TC-HAD or possibly c/n 6688 formerly TC-DER as these two aircraft, were the last known survivors in Turkey
V3	6740	Displayed Luchtmacht (Royal Netherlands Air Force) Museum, Soesterberg, Netherlands
VH-BGP	6648	In flying condition with Rural City of Wangaratta VIC and kept at the defunct Drage's Air World
VH-UTV	6655	In flying condition with Dr. Robert Fox, Kellyville NSW and based Bankstown
VH-UXZ [2]	6801	Nearing flying condition with Maurice Howard Rolfe, Moorabbin VIC 9.01
ZK-AHS	6423	Displayed Museum of Transport (MOTAT) Auckland
ZK-AKS	6647	In flying condition with Colin F. Smith's Croydon Aircraft Co. at Mandeville
ZK-AKU	6662	In flying condition with D. W. Gray at Auckland's Ardmore airfield, painted in R.N.Z.A.F. markings and wears original serial NZ528
ZK-AKY	6653	In flying condition with the Croydon Aircraft Co. at Mandeville, painted in the colours of New Zealand National Airways Corporation and named *Tui* (a native bird)
ZK-???	6853	With Colin F. Smith's Croydon Aircraft Co., Mandeville, New Zealand on rebuild. Formerly Belgian Air Force D7 with Brush works number 89504. It is understood that the reg'n ZK-SWR has been reserved
ZS-DLS	6773	In very poor condition, transferred from Baragwanath to S.A.A.F. Museum 1976
ZS-JGV	6831	In flying condition with John English, Port Elizabeth and operated from Progress, Plettenburg Bay but last reported at Port Alfred on rebuild November 2002
"002"	6952	Displayed Israeli Air Force Museum, Hatzerim Air Force Base, Tel Aviv (marked as VQ-PAR)
FAP-2307	6430	Portugese Air Force, stored at Museo do Ar storage facility, Sintra

In addition, the full scale plastic replica displayed outside the Liverpool Marriott South Hotel at Liverpool-Speke Airport must be mentioned. Painted in Railway Air Services colours to represent their G-AEAJ *Star of Lancashire,* though it wears the name *Neptune* after Neptune Developments who have an 80% interest in the hotel now occupying the old terminal building.

Furthermore, as these words are written, we have received reports that a model of the Automobile Association's G-AHKV has recently been added to the Milestones Museum collection in Basingstoke, Hampshire. Said to be substantial in size, we have been unable to ascertain whether it is full scale and therefore worthy of an entry here!

DH90

Just two complete survivors out of 67 produced.

CF-BZA	7531	Rear fuselage only survives at Edmonton Museum, Alberta
CX-AAR	7532	Displayed for many years at the Museo Aeronautica, Montevideo but destroyed by fire there 4th December 1997. Some small parts thought to remain
G-AEDU	7526	In flying condition with Torquil P. A. Norman, Rendcomb, Gloucestershire
ZK-AYR	7508	In flying condition with Croydon Aircraft Co. at Mandeville, owned by a New Zealand national currently flying with Cathay Pacific Airways, Hong Kong

DH92

As is recorded elsewhere, the only Dolphin produced, suffered a severe weight problem with the result that performance left a lot to be desired! The sole example was withdrawn shortly after taking to the air and was hastily dismantled.

8.5 Abbreviations used in this volume

A&AEE	Aeroplane & Armament Experimental Establishment
A.A.J.C.	Associated Airways Joint Committee
A.T.A.	Air Transport Auxiliary
B.E.A.C.	British European Airways Corporation
B.O.A.C.	British Overseas Airways Corporation
B/u	Broken up
C.F.S.	Central Flying School
Cld	Cancelled
C/n	Construction number
CofA	Certificate of airworthiness
CofR	Certificate of registration
Com.	Communications
D/d	Delivery date
Dbf	Destroyed by fire
Dbr	Damaged beyond repair
Dest	Destroyed
E. & W.S.	Electrical and Wireless School
E.T.P.S.	Empire Test Pilots School
Flt.	Flight
Grp.	Group
HQ	Headquarters
M.P.R.D.	Metal Produce & Recovery Depot
MV	Motor Vessel
N.A.C.	National Air Communications
No.	Number
O/b	Operated by
Pwfu	Permanently withdrawn from use
Reg'd	Registered
Reg'n	Registration
R.M.A.	Royal Mail Airliner
SOC	Struck off charge
SS	Steam ship
T/a	Trading as
TOC	Taken on charge
Wef	With effect from
Wfu	Withdrawn from use

8.6 Royal Air Force Accident and Repair Categories

In 1941, the Royal Air Force introduced a system to categorise the extent of damage due to an accident or deterioration. This system was adopted by a number of overseas air forces shortly after.

Whilst not a complete list of the various categories used, the following list shows those that are used in this book.

Cat.A	Repairable on site by unit
Cat.B	Beyond repair on site
Cat.C	Ground instructional airframe
Cat.E	Write-off
Cat.E1	Components
Cat.E2	Scrap

8.7 Index to Photographs

DH89

China (c/n 6385)	140
China (c/n 6388)	140
China (c/n6389)	140
CF-BBG	74
CF-BNG	80
CH-287	58
CR-AAM	74
CR-AAN	74
CR-LKR	118
FAP2307	76
D-IGUN	80
Spain (c/n 6310)	140
Spain (c/n 6311)	140
Spain (c/n 6312)	140
EI-AKH	118
EI-AML	102
F-AZCA	88
F-BEDX	66
F-BEDY	66
F-BEDZ	66
F-BHCD	102
F-BHFM	88
E.4	128
G-ACPO	58
G-ACTT	58
G-ACTU	58
G-ACYR	58
G-ACZE (2)	128
G-ADAE	66
G-ADAL	58
G-ADDF	66
G-AEMH	66
G-AEPE	66
G-AERN	74
G-AESR	74
G-AFEN	74
G-AFEO	76
G-AFFB	76
G-AFMF	76
G-AFRK	80
G-AGDM	88
G-AGDP	74
G-AGHI	80
G-AGLE	110
G-AGOJ	114
G-AGSH	Front
G-AGTM	128
G-AGWR	118
G-AHAG	124
G-AHEA	114
G-AHED	124
G-AHGC	88
G-AHGD	118
G-AHJS	128
G-AHKA	114
G-AHKS	114
G-AHKV	110
G-AHLF	84
G-AHLM	102
G-AHLN	106
G-AHXW	110
G-AIBB	114
G-AIDL	128
G-AIUL	114
G-AIYR	100
G-AJGS	128
G-AJHO	128
G-AJKW	84, 114
G-AJKY	114
G-AJSL	110
G-AJXB	84
G-AKGY	102
G-AKJS	128
G-AKJY	80
G-AKLA	114
G-AKME	106
G-AKMG	94
G-AKMH	102
G-AKNV	114
G-AKNW	80
G-AKNX	94
G-AKOK	84
G-AKOY	114
G-AKRS	124
G-AKSC	106
G-AKSG	124
G-AKZB	110
G-ALAX	124
G-ALEJ	114
G-ALGE	118
G-ANZP	100
G-APBM	106
G-ASFC	100
G-ASKO	102
K4772	58
R9555	84
X7332	84
X7372	84
X7382	88
X7386	88
X7398	88
X7413	88
X7452	88
X7454	94
X7524	94
Z7258	76
Z7261	76
HG694	100
HG708	100
NF847	102
NF867	106
I-BOBJ	118
LN-BEZ	114
LV-AER	94
LV-AGW	114
Lithuania 701	128
Lithuania 702	128
N683DH	110
N2290F	110
N8053	118
OH-BLB	74
OO-CNP	80
D2	106
OY-AAO	106
PH-RAA	118
PH-RAB	118
V3	106
SU-ABS	66
TC-ARI	66
TC-BAY	66
TC-CAN	66
TF-ISM	100
TF-KAA	94
VP-KNS	84
VP-YBT	76
VR-LAD	124
VT-AJB	74
VT-AVX	124
YI-ZWA	76
YV-B-BPE	124
ZK-AEC	66
ZK-AGT	76
ZK-AKU	100
ZK-AKY	94
ZK-ALB	94
NZ531	100
ZS-AES	58
4R-AAI	102
5H-AAN	114
6V-AAC	80

9.0 Bibliography

Air Ambulance	Iain Hutchinson, Six Decades of the Scottish Air Ambulance Service, published by Kea Publishing 1996
Aircraft Camouflage & Markings 1907-54	Bruce Robertson, published by Harleyford Publication Ltd. 1956
Aircraft of the R.A.A.F. 1921-71	Geoffrey Pentland & Peter Malone, published by Kookaburra Technical Publications 1971
Annals of British & Commonwealth Air Transport 1919-1960	John Stroud, published by Putnam & Co. Ltd. 1962
Archive	Edited by David Partington, historical civil aviation magazine, published quarterly by Air-Britain (Historians) Ltd.
British Civil Aircraft 1919-1959	A. J. Jackson, published in two volumes by Putnam & Co. Ltd. 1959
British Civil Aircraft since 1919	A. J. Jackson, published in three volumes by Putnam & Co. Ltd. 1973
British European Airways, An Illustrated History of	Phil Lo Bao, published by Browcom Group PLC 1989
British Independent Airlines from 1946	Tony Merton Jones, published in four volumes by LAAS International 1976/77. A reprint, with correction of some typographical errors, casebound in one volume and with the title "British Independent Airlines 1946 – 1976", was published by The Aviation Hobby Shop 2000
Brush Aircraft Production at Loughborough	A. P. Jarram, published by Midland Counties Publications (Aerophile) Ltd. 1978
Bush Horizons	Squadron Leader N. V. Philips, published the Air Forces Association (Zimbabwe) 1998. The story of aviation in Southern Rhodesia 1896-1940
Cadet Corps Airframes	A booklet published by Midland Counties Aviation Society April 1975
Canadian Air Transport, Pioneering in	K. M. Molson, published by James Richardson & Sons Ltd., Winnipeg March 1974, 2nd edition February 1975
Civil Aircraft Registers of Great Britain 1919-1998	A. B. Eastwood, published in two volumes by The Aviation Hobby Shop 1999
de Havilland Aircraft since 1909	A. J. Jackson, published by Putnam & Co. Ltd. 1969 with revised editions in 1978 and 1987 (edited by the late A. J. Jackson's son R. T. Jackson)
de Havilland in Canada	Fred W. Hotson, published by CANAV Books 1999
de Havilland Rapide, The	Peter W. Moss, (no.144 in the Profile Publications Ltd. series)
DH84 Dragon	Graham M. Simons, published by International Friends of the DH89, undated
DH86 Express	Graham M. Simons, published by International Friends of the DH89, 1987
DH90 Dragonfly	Graham M. Simons, published by International Friends of the DH89, 1987
Flight of the Starling, The	Iain Hutchinson, the story of Scottish pioneer aviator Capt. Eric Starling, published by Kea Publishing 1992
Flying Against the Elements	Peter V. Clegg, reminiscences of Aberdeen Airways and its founder Eric Leslie Gandar Dower, privately published by the author 1987
Flypast	Roy Humphreys, in a two-part article October/November 1990 (issues numbered 111 & 112), eamined the role of the Malayan Volunteer Air Force as they faced the Japanese in an article entitled "Unarmed, Unescorted & Unwanted"
Forgotten Pilots, The	Lettice Curtis, a Story of the Air Transport Auxiliary 1939-45, privately published by Miss E. L. Curtis 1971, 2nd edition 1982
Impressment Logs	Peter W. Moss, published in four volumes plus index by Air-Britain 1962
Indian Air Force 1933-73, Aircraft of the	Pushpindar Singh, published by B. Chowdhri for The English Book Store, New Delhi 1974
Irish Civil Aircraft Register, 70 Years of the	Peter J. Hornfeck published by BN Historians 1999
Journal – Aviation Historical Society of	An article "The DH89 Rapide in Australia" Volume 18 Number 2, edition published Australia April/June 1977
Journal – Aviation Historical Society of Zealand	Graham C. Atkinson, an article "A Brief History of Cook Strait Airways" Volume 20 New New Number 4, edition published Summer 1977
Le Trait d'Union issue no.190	Jacques Chillon, an article "The French Dragon Rapide after the War" in the edition published March-April 2000
Pilot Magazine	In the October 1974 issue (Volume 8 Number 10) published by Lernhurst Publications Ltd., Gary Studd described the flight of Dragon Rapide 4R-AAI from Ceylon to England
Popeye Lucas – Queenstown	F. J. Lucas, published by A. H. & A. W. Reed. Wellington 1968
Railway Air Services	John Stroud, published by Ian Allan Ltd., 1987
Rivals in the North	Peter V. Clegg, the story of the Scottish aviation pioneering rivals, Captain Ernest Edmund Fresson O.B.E. and Eric Leslie Gandar Dower, privately published by the author 1988
Royal Flying Doctor Service, The	John Bilton in association with Joan Brunt & Professor J. MacDonald Holmes, published of Australia, on behalf of the Federal Council of the Royal Flying Doctor Service of Australia 1961
Shower of Spray & We're Away, A	Captain Fred Ladd with Ross Annabell, published by A. H. & A. W. Reed. Wellington 1971, reprinted 1972
Spanish Civil War 1936-1939, Aircraft of the	Gerald Howson, published by Putnam & Co. Ltd. ISBN 0851778429
Sword in the Sky	Peter V. Clegg, reminiscences of Midland & Scottish Air Ferries and its founder John Cuthill Sword, privately published by the author 1990
Vintage Aircraft	Graham M. Simons. Issue Number 28 in September 1983 under the title "Workshop Report", reported on the restoration of DH89A G-AJHO by the East Anglian Aviation Society Ltd.
Winged Shell	Hugh Scanlan, "Oil Company Aviators 1927-87" published by Alison Hodge 1987
Wings Over the Glens	Peter V. Clegg, published by GMS Enterprises 1995
Wingspan Magazine	In issue number 78 dated August 1991, six articles by different authors appeared under the title "Rapides Recalled"